CW01521254

Economic Security for a Better World

Economic Security for a Better World

ISBN 92–2–115611–7

ILO
Economic security for a better world
Geneva, International Labour Office, 2004

Living conditions, working conditions, economic conditions, income distribution, social security, employment security, developed country, developing country, 03.03.6

ISBN: 92-2-115611-7

ILO Cataloguing in Publication Data

Printed in Geneva, Switzerland

SCR / ATA

Preface

This study is about economic insecurity, what it means to people and their societies, and what can be done about it. Insecurity affects everybody at some time. But it affects many people throughout their lives, with serious consequences for their well-being and for that of their families and communities. Much economic insecurity is unnecessary. We could do so much more at international and national levels to reduce it.

Poverty and economic insecurity are not synonymous. However, as argued in a Director General's report entitled "Working out of Poverty",[1] those who are economically badly off or unemployed, or who face discrimination or oppression, have to struggle every day, worried about what lies ahead, and are thus unable to exercise or develop their capabilities. As the 21st century evolves, we will surely devote more attention to policies and institutions to strengthen economic security. For the ILO, that is a crucial part of our dedication to *decent work*, the dream of helping to ensure that more people across the world find opportunities to work in dignity, for the benefit of their families, communities and themselves.

This analysis does not commit the ILO to particular policies. Rather it provides new and sometimes disturbing information that national policymakers, employers, unions and others should examine as they reflect on what policies they would wish to advocate or implement.

Over the past five years, the ILO's Socio-Economic Security Programme has taken a fresh look at the most fundamental questions underlying how we organize work and how that connects to broad social goals. The work stems from a decision of our Governing Body to support the systematic compilation of information on socio-economic and labour security, thereby contributing to the measurement of decent work. The Programme was asked to collect data to quantify the forms of insecurity, for analysis and the development of responses.[2] The results shed light on the problems we face in a globalizing world and considers people's views on what should be done.

Coming shortly after the report of the World Commission on the Social Dimension of Globalization, this book should enrich the debate on how we can build a fair globalization.[3] It takes forward a commitment to make the ILO a *listening* Organization,

---

[1] International Labour Office (ILO): *Working Out of Poverty*, Report of the Director-General, 91st Session, International Labour Conference (Geneva 2003).

[2] ILO: *Strategic Policy Framework, 2002-05, and Preview of the Programme and Budget Proposals for 2002-03: Consolidating the Decent Work Agenda* (GB.279/PFA/6).

[3] World Commission on the Social Dimension of Globalization: *A Fair Globalization: Creating Opportunities for All* (Geneva, 2004).

devoted to developing a knowledge-based approach. The foundation of this study rests on going out to ask people across the world about their work, about their needs and about their aspirations. In doing so, besides creating a global databank on social policies, it has acquired detailed information by visiting thousands of factories and thousands of families in many countries.

It looks at poverty, for example, in its subjective and objective aspects, asking what people feel they lack and the reasons, as much as about the amount of money they earn, about the instability of their income as much as the level, and the deductions many experience. We see, for instance, that women are often impoverished by losing control of the income they earn.

It asks whether people who are income-poor are aware of policies intended to help them, and whether they are receiving assistance. It asks about the skills they possess, and whether they have the opportunity to use them. It asks about the discrimination they face and about what forms of discrimination they witness. In short, it seeks to present a picture of patterns of insecurity.

The World Commission's report reached several conclusions that have a bearing on this analysis. Thus, it concluded, *"Basic security is a recognized human right, and a global responsibility"*. This is confirmed by the opinions expressed by over 40,000 people interviewed in the course of the People's Security Surveys, summarized in chapter 12. Across the world, from China to Chile, from South Africa to the Russian Federation, people think basic economic security is desirable for their fellow citizens.

Another finding deserves attention. Economic security, as one might expect, leads to more *happiness*. The unalienable right set out so eloquently in the American Declaration of Independence to "...Life, Liberty and the pursuit of Happiness" is too rarely the subject of rigorous study. No doubt one reason is the difficulty of defining what exactly we mean by happiness, so there will be questions about the statistical basis for that finding. However, that economically more secure people tell us they feel happier makes common sense. And in a world full of anxiety and anger, we must find ways of improving the sum of human happiness. This report sheds light on how we might go about it.

Readers might also wish to note a link between conclusions of this report, which draws on so many new data (backed by many from other sources) and another key conclusion of the Commission: *"A global commitment to deal with insecurity is critical to provide legitimacy to globalization."* Those in positions of leadership should look at policies in terms of whether they contribute to the security of the least well off in their societies. This ethical principle is spelt out in the first chapter, and guides the analysis of succeeding chapters.

There are aspects of the following that will be contested; this is how it should be. We still know so little about the realities of the world of work and the impact of social policy that we need to explore new ways of portraying them. This leads to a final point. The ILO set up the Programme that did this work in order to look at the linkages between work, economic security and social protection policies. It has focused on seven forms of work-related security, all of which are important. It concludes that creating an environment in which all of these are improved is what decent work is all about.

Juan Somavia
Director-General ILO

Tables of contents

Part III.

Introduction and Acknowledgements

This report draws on a great deal of material collected over a four-year period. As such, we have been able to draw on over 250 technical papers, 15 household surveys, 14 enterprise surveys and a databank of statistics collected for over 100 countries. It is, in a sense, a stocktaking report, assessing the various forms of social and economic security, trying to present a coherent global picture from numerous contributions from around the world. As a result, it is impractical if not impossible to thank all the very large number of people who have made a contribution.

What has been so clear throughout the preparatory phase is that the topic of insecurity has a resonance all over the world and with people of all social and economic backgrounds, whether they be affluent or poor, employed, unemployed, educated or less so, man or woman. The challenge of making the world more economically secure, as part of a more general challenge, is something to which everybody can relate.

This is not a very conventional "report" and it is not a very conventional "book", in that it contains exploratory analysis and has been written by a team. It consists of three Parts. Part I paints the concept of economic security that the ILO's Socio-Economic Security Programme seeks to promote and that seems appropriate to give substance to the ILO's notion of "decent work". It also provides a contextual analysis of factors associated with "globalization" that appear to have implications for the extent and pattern of economic and social insecurity. Part II draws on the Programme's global database and from its two types of survey to provide a picture of trends in the seven forms of labour-related security around the world, in each case providing a national index of performance. This leads up to the presentation of a national **Economic Security Index**, as applied to 90 countries. Part III considers a range of innovative organizations and emerging policies that promise a future of improving economic and social security.

This analysis has been written by a team based mainly in the ILO's Socio-Economic Security Programme, consisting of the following, in alphabetical order: Pascal Annycke, Florence Bonnet, Sukti Dasgupta, Jose B. Figueiredo, Azfar Khan, Ellen Rosskam, Ajit Singh, Guy Standing and Laci Zsoldos. Excellent assistance was provided by Smita Barbattini, Christian Colussi, Mila Cueni, Liyuwok Dupuy, Kristian Kall, Julie Lim, Nona Iliukina, Sylvie Renault and Carol Rodríguez.

Contributions and comments have also been made by the following: Carl Afford, Richard Anker, Igor Chernyshev, Ian Gough, Renana Jhabvala, Naila Kabeer, Karin Kockum, Sriram Natrajan, Gabriel Palma, Rajendra Paratian, Uma Devi Sambasivam, John Sender, Miriam Abu Sharkh, Hilary Silver, Rosamund Stock, André Wagner, Frances Williams, Alan Wood, Geof Wood, Marc Wuyts and Ann Zammit.

A special expression of gratitude is due to the Programme's International Advisory Board, consisting of Tony Atkinson, Lourdes Beneria, Sam Bowles, Robert Boyer, Tatyana Chetvernina, Robert Deacon, Zsusza Ferge, Ian Gough, Dalmer Hoskins, Renana Jhabvala, Naila Kabeer, Katherine McFate, Claus Offe, Philippe van Parijs, Raymond Plant, Ashwani Saith, Juliet Schor, Ajit Singh and Eduardo

Suplicy. We are also grateful for the encouragement given by Assane Diop, Executive Director of the ILO's Social Protection Sector.

The work has been made possible by the generous financial support provided by the Government of The Netherlands, through the ILO-Netherlands Partnership, and by grants from the Ford Foundation and the Rockefeller Foundation. Fieldwork in several countries has also been facilitated by the UNDP. We are most grateful for all those who have supported the work.

Also thanks are due to all those who participated in the various People's Security Surveys and the Enterprise Labour Flexibility and Security Surveys around the world, including the dozens of social scientists and statisticians who have been involved. Many thousands of people have been interviewed, often at great length, including workers and managers in all regions of the world. Their cooperation has been much appreciated. And gratitude is due to our national correspondents in the many countries where data were collected for the global database. This is only one output from that work. For the list of external collaborators, please see Appendix. Although it is almost invidious to single out any of those, we do wish to acknowledge the pleasure of having collaborated with SEWA (the Self-Employed Women's Association of India). The joint fieldwork in and around Ahmedabad was significant at a forma-tive stage in the development of the People's Security Surveys.

None of the above, with the exception of the team, is necessarily in agreement with all the analysis or conclusions, and neither they nor their various institutions should be held responsible for opinions or recommendations made in the course of the work.

Indeed, much of the material is exploratory, raising questions without necessarily providing strong responses. Many of the data are novel or preliminary, reflecting in part the evolving nature of ideas around economic security. As far as possible, we have alluded to the tentative character of some of the data, and want to caution against the making of comparisons between the results of the two types of surveys as applied in the various countries. This is why findings reported in the text are deliberately not given to one decimal point. The sin of misplaced precision from micro-data is all too common, particularly with complex information gathered in difficult social and economic circumstances. This applies to many macro-economic and social data as well.

That stated, we believe the data and the information system developed in the course of the work are the most comprehensive available — and the most reliable — on the subject of economic security, and provide a solid base on which to build.

Executive summary

This review, based largely on work in the ILO's Socio-Economic Security (SES) Programme, aims to provide a picture of the emerging patterns of economic security across the world. It draws primarily on a Global Database of national statistical indicators on social and labour policies, coupled with information from People's Security Surveys covering over 48,000 people in 15 countries, and information from Enterprise Labour Flexibility and Security Surveys covering over 10,000 firms in 11 countries.

While it is the first attempt to give a global picture, it does not try to cover all aspects of economic security, or summarize all the work on related subjects by others, although due reference is made to much of that work. Rather, it highlights findings from the Programme over the past four years, and gives particular attention to some issues that have been neglected or given relatively little attention.

Underlying the empirical work is a perspective that reflects the ILO's long-standing values and principles, trying to position them in a 21st century context, in which social and economic rights are placed at the centre of policy thinking and in which social solidarity and voice are regarded as essential. The following very briefly summarizes the contents and highlights a few points that may be of particular interest.

PART I

Chapter 1

defines economic security, and the seven forms of labour-related security. It also considers the nature of risk and uncertainty, arguing that old forms of "social security" focus on contingency risks, whereas much of the economic insecurity experienced by people across the world are systemic risks that are not easily covered by "social insurance" or other selective measures. In that context, the chapter derives three conclusions that are effectively premises for much of the following:

- Basic economic security should be a human right, and this should be defined in terms of advancing real freedom. After identifying the seven forms of labour-related security, it argues that primacy should be given to income security and representation security.

- Policies and institutional changes should be assessed by whether or not they satisfy two tests or principles. The first is the Security Difference Principle, that to be socially just they should improve the position of the least secure groups in society. The second is the Paternalism Test Principle, that they should not impose controls on some groups that are not imposed on the most free groups in society.

- Globally, there has been a secular increase in the incidence and severity of natural, economic and social disasters, including civil conflicts, that involve mass insecurity.

Chapter 2

considers how the model of policies and institutions known as the Washington Consensus may have influenced the extent and incidence of economic insecurity in the era of so-called "globalization". It highlights a few features that are particularly relevant for labour market and social policy changes considered in subsequent chapters. Among the main points are:

- Globalization has not been associated with a dramatic increase in economic growth, as its advocates claimed it would, and indeed has been associated with a slowing of growth in many countries, with the major exceptions of China and India.

- More crucially, globalization has been associated with an increase in economic instability and a greater incidence of economic crises.

- There has been a rapid, and relatively unanalysed, growth in private regulation of economic activity and policy.

PART II

A central feature of the report is a series of national economic security indexes, covering each of seven forms of labour security and a composite Economic Security Index. Each of these is drawn from the SES Global Database, by combining various Input indicators (policy variables), Process indicators (institutional variables) and Outcome indicators (statistical reflections of the effectiveness of those policies and institutions). The indexes, calculated for over 100 countries, are presented in Chapters 4 to 11.

Each of these chapters devotes a section to relevant illustrative findings from the People's Security Surveys (PSS), household surveys that have been conducted by the Programme in Argentina, Bangladesh, Brazil, Chile, China, Ethiopia, Ghana, Hungary, India, Indonesia, Pakistan, the Russian Federation, South Africa, the United Republic of Tanzania (hereafter "Tanzania") and Ukraine. The PSS have collected detailed information on many aspects of social and economic security from about 48,000 individuals and households.

The chapters also present findings from the Programme's Enterprise Labour Flexibility and Security Surveys (ELFS), conducted in Azerbaijan, Brazil, Chile, China, Indonesia, the Republic of Moldova, Pakistan, the Philippines, the Russian Federation, Tanzania and Ukraine. These have provided detailed data on labour practices in over 10,000 firms, highlighting various forms of worker insecurities and securities.

Chapter 3

Income security is a reflection of payment systems, levels of wages, access to benefits and services, and the assurance of some kind of income support in times of need. In many respects, global trends have been unfavourable in the era of globalization. The extent of poverty has been understated, particularly in Africa. The number of "working poor" has grown in industrialized countries. Wealth inequality is greater than income inequality but income inequality has grown. One form of inequality that has worsened is the functional distribution of income, with the share of national income going to labour shrinking. But the biggest story is that there is income polarization, with a tiny elite receiving a very large and growing proportion of national incomes.

Increased wage flexibility has meant wider differentials and a loss of entitlement to enterprise benefits and services for many groups of workers, as well as diminished prospects for many millions of workers who could have expected those benefits and services to come with development.

While income flexibility has increased in labour markets, the general orientation of social protection systems has been changing quite dramatically. Probably the biggest source of increased income insecurity is the series of changes taking place in healthcare systems. In general, multi-tier systems are emerging, in which workers and their families bear an increasing share of the costs, while facing increased risks and uncertainty. Use of the price mechanism in health services is intensifying inequities and inequalities, often threatening the survival of households. This sphere of social policy must be given top priority over the next decade, and what changes occur there will be crucial for determining whether economic security will improve or not.

Over the past decade, it has been pension reform that has attracted most attention. Here too there is room for disquiet, given the increased differentiation between levels and entitlements, and the dim prospect of entitlement to a pension for many millions of people as they move towards old age. However, the good news is that more policymakers and social scientists are aware of the limitations and drawbacks of the reforms that were pushed with such zeal in the 1980s and 1990s.

Income insecurity for the unemployed has also intensified in many countries, with a growing majority not receiving support from their governments. Even in industrialized countries, only a minority receive unemployment benefits or adequate income support from their governments.

- Poverty is underestimated, particularly in African countries.

- Income inequality has grown within many countries, and functional income distribution has become more unequal. Standard measures, such as the Gini coefficient, do not adequately capture these trends, because it is the very rich who have become much richer, while the poor have often become poorer. Middle-income groups have retained roughly the same share of national income in all the regions of the world.

- Social security systems have become less universal, less solidaristic, less protective and more differentiated, contributing to the growth of inequality and economic insecurity. Conditionalities for entitlement to state benefits have been tightened.

- The average age of retirement and entitlement to full state pensions has risen by about a year for men and half a year for women.

- Unemployment insurance benefits are fading, with fewer of the unemployed obtaining entitlement; they are an inappropriate form of social protection in flexible labour markets.

Chapter 4

This chapter deals with monitoring income security and it reviews aspects of individual and household income security that rarely receive much empirical attention, including the non-retention of income by women, which has contributed to women's impoverishment in so many societies, access to non-monetary benefits, the incidence of instability of earned incomes, and the differential costs of personal crises. It also highlights a particular phenomenon that makes many statistics misleading – *wage arrears,* or the non-payment of contractual wages.

It then presents two national indexes, for old-age income security and for overall income security. These are estimated for 96 countries, showing that some countries have provided much greater income security than others, and that the pacesetters do not correspond well with countries as ranked on a per capita income basis. Key points:

- A major form of income insecurity and impoverishment is income instability, with large numbers of people receiving income irregularly, often after extensive delay.

- Income transfers between households, long regarded as a form of social protection in developing countries, are actually quite limited, notably in African countries.

- In developing and transition countries, the vast majority of people are anxious and pessimistic about their future income security, particularly in old age.

Chapter 5

Labour market security has been a casualty of the abandonment of a commitment to full employment by governments around the world, even though there was never a proper commitment in that women were long regarded to a secondary labour force. Globally, higher levels of unemployment have been accompanied by new or enlarged forms of "labour slack" (a measure of labour underutilization that takes account of involuntary part-time working, lay-offs and discouraged non-participation in the labour force).

- Unemployment is a poor measure of labour underutilization, and global estimates of unemployment should be regarded as unreliable. The unemployment rate is also not a good proxy for labour market security, as shown by a comparison of the ranking of countries by the two measures.

- The level of unemployment in China is much higher than conventional measures suggest.

- The extent of hidden unemployment, mainly in the form of "unpaid leave" and "partially paid leave", continues to be huge in 'transition' countries, as shown for Azerbaijan, China, Republic of Moldova, the Russian Federation and Ukraine, for example. Extended maternity leave is also used to disguise unemployment among women.

Chapter 6

Employment security has also declined around the world. The primary factor is that, contrary to the expectation that in the course of development a growing proportion of the labour force would move into regular, protected, full-time wage jobs, in fact economic informalization has grown almost everywhere.

In addition, governments in countries where there had been substantial improvements in employment security in the post-1945 era have introduced legislative and institutional changes designed to weaken it, notably by weakening employment protection.

- Informalization of labour relations has continued to characterize the world economy. This chapter shows that a better approach to measuring this is via a labour informality continuum, rather than a conventional dichotomy of informal-formal sectors or "economies".

- The more informal a person's labour, the lower the income, on average. However, gender-based income differentials grow with growth in formality.

- An Employment Security Index is presented for 99 countries for which the relevant data are available, showing that Scandinavian countries continue to provide a greater degree of this form of security than other countries.

Chapter 7

Work security is associated with occupational health and safety, and a low prospect of injuries or illness in the course of work. The global picture could be greatly improved. To assess this, better statistical information is needed than is available in most countries.

Beyond that, the drift to self-regulation and weaker forms of representation security have eroded work security in some countries. However, perhaps the most striking aspect of developments in this sphere is the emergence of new forms of work-related insecurity or their greatly increased incidence and severity.

- The risks of injuries and accidents remain very high, and have grown in many places because of the weakening of institutional safeguards. Weaker worker representation has contributed to this.

- Stress has become a major form of work insecurity, affecting millions of workers, many of whom are in affluent countries where labour intensity has increased, and where time squeeze has become a modern hazard for many more occupational groups.

- Harassment in and around the workplace remains a menacing form of work insecurity in very many countries.

- A workplace work security index is proposed, and in developing countries is shown to be typically higher in large-scale firms, in publicly owned enterprises and in foreign-owned firms.

- Western Europe is the only region where all countries score high on work security.

Chapter 8

Skills security is more than can be captured by the notion of "human capital". Indeed, the focus on human capital may have resulted in a deterioration of real security in the areas of education and skill enhancement, in that education unrelated to market activity is undervalued.

- Although many workers feel they lack the skills they need, many possess skills that are not used in their work.

- According to a national skill security index, some countries that do well overall fail to provide anything like equal skills development for males and females, whereas some countries that do less well overall have reasonably equal outcomes.

- In all countries covered, there is a positive link between level of schooling and access to training. But often the returns to training are less for women than for men.

Chapter 9

Job security must be differentiated from employment security. It implies the possession of a niche in the work process, and the opportunity to pursue a "career". The biggest problem for those wishing to monitor job security (and the richer concept of "occupation security") is that data are woefully lacking in almost every country of the world. This chapter focuses on barriers to mobility in employment, including discriminatory labour practices, and job "satisfaction".

- Job security has been distorted by job demarcation and other rigidities associated with Taylorism.
- Discriminatory barriers remain a main reason blocking women from obtaining job security, restricting their mobility within job structures.
- Many workers do not plan their working lives, merely living from day-to-day to survive.
- The probability of job security is positively related to schooling. Women not only have a lower probability of upward mobility once in jobs but have a higher probability of downward mobility.

Chapter 10

Voice representation security has long been associated with trade unions, which have done much to improve working conditions around the world. But de-unionization has been extensive. Part of this has reflected structural changes in labour markets; part has reflected legislative changes designed to curb unions' powers and lessen their appeal to workers; part has reflected wider social changes; and part has reflected the failure of unions to address the concerns of many groups in society.

- De-unionization is a global phenomenon.
- Women comprise a low percentage of senior union officials all over the world.
- The presence of unions in workplaces contributes to better wages, more benefits and narrower wage differentials.
- In many countries, most workers are unaware of the existence of unions, and many who are aware of them are sceptical about their appeal or effectiveness.
- A national representation security index shows that representation remains strongest in Scandinavian countries, but that some developing countries have stronger representation than many richer countries.

Chapter 11

Economic security is essential for any society committed to the promotion of dignified or decent work. To measure this, the indexes of the seven forms of labour-related security are combined into an Economic Security Index. This is estimated for 90 ILO member States. Countries fit into four clusters (groups with similar scores on the index).

The "Pacesetters" are those with high scores on policy commitment to economic security *(Input indicators)*, on the existence of mechanisms or institutions to give effect to those commitments *(Process indicators)* and on economic security outcomes. The "Pragmatists" are those that do well in terms of outcome, but seem to have a relatively modest (or less than exemplary) commitment or/and relatively modest mechanisms to achieve good outcomes. The "Conventionals" are those countries in which there has been relatively strong formal commitment to the goals of economic security and there appear to be institutions to give effect to them, but where outcomes have been less than impressive. Finally, the "Much-to-be-Done" cluster consists of countries where the commitment, institutions and outcomes are all relatively weak, where there is much that could be done by policymakers, domestic and foreign advisers, and donors.

The results show that countries at all levels of national development could do better. Of course, it is easier for a rich country with well-established institutional capacities to achieve strong economic security for its population. Not all rich countries do so. But many lower-income countries could do much better without impeding their economic growth and development. Indeed, promoting economic security for citizens would help boost growth and development.

- There is an inverse correlation between economic security and income inequality. In other words, countries with a highly unequal distribution of income do significantly worse in terms of providing their populations with adequate economic security. Security is more evenly distributed around the world than income.
- Economic security is only weakly correlated with economic growth, but is adversely affected by premature economic openness. Controlling for level of national income, economic openness can lead to more economic security, but countries can be held back in that respect by premature opening of their capital account. Opening up the economy hastily may lead to social instability and economic outcomes that imperil whatever level of economic security has been achieved.
- Economic security is positively associated with political freedom and democracy.
- Economic security is positively correlated with a national Happiness Index. But skills security is inversely related to happiness.
- Decent workplace practices are positively related to productivity and employment change.

PART III

Chapter 12

This reviews data from the People's Security Surveys on attitudes to economic justice and security. Over 48,000 people were asked for their opinions on a range of principles of income distribution and social policy. The data show that there is popular support for policies to enhance economic security in many regions of the world.

- There is widespread support for redistribution, notably for the principle of limiting upper incomes. People living in rural areas, and those who are economically insecure in various ways, are more likely to be egalitarian than those living in cities.

- There is extensive support for a minimum income below which nobody should have to fall. Support for this crosses all groups in society, rich and poor, men and women. There is widespread support for universalism — the belief that all people, regardless of social or labour status, should be provided with income security — and for policies to provide security for those doing all socially valuable forms of work, not just labour.

- Although people who are economically insecure themselves are more inclined to support the principle of basic security for all, they may also be more likely to be intolerant and support discriminatory labour practices.

Chapter 13

This discusses emerging forms of voice representation security. An underlying theme is that it is impossible to envisage societies having strong economic security unless there are strong representative bodies giving security to all legitimate interests. If unions are not as strong as many would wish, are there alternative or complementary bodies that could assist in giving representation to people, as citizens? This chapter considers some of the initiatives and the obstacles to their success. It concludes that there are grounds for cautious optimism, even though many so-called civil society organizations should be regarded with scepticism, and in particular 'faith-based' policy should be reconsidered.

Chapter 14

For economic security, as argued in Chapter 1, basic income security is a fundamental or primary form of security, along with representation security. If the future is to be one of informal economic activities, flexible labour markets and growing recognition of the rights of those performing many forms of work that are not labour, what policies offer the prospect of ensuring adequate income security? The chapter begins by considering the main policies that have been promoted or tried in recent years, focusing mainly on developing countries.

It argues that countries should reduce the extent of subsidies, which have grown to enormous proportions, go disproportionately to richer groups and are inefficient. They comprise a high proportion of GDP, and could be redirected to enhance the basic security of those most in need.

The chapter also highlights flaws in the emphasis on "targeting" and "selectivity", i.e., making benefits and social services available only for groups identified by means-tests and behavioural conditions. It draws on the People's Security Surveys to show that selective, means-tested schemes usually fail to reach the poorer groups in society. It shows that popular schemes such as micro-credit and social funds have limited potential as vehicles for giving income security. However, it highlights several types of policy that do offer the prospect of enhancing income security as a right, including social pensions in South Africa and the bolsa familia in Brazil. And it argues that capital-sharing schemes, along the lines of the Alaska Permanent Fund, should be considered as one means of securing redistribution of wealth generated by natural resources.

Above all, the challenge for all countries is to move forward with policies that respect the two policy decision principles spelt out at the outset — that they should be regarded as socially just only if they improve the economic security of the least secure groups in society (and globally) and only if they do not impose controls (or "unfreedoms") on some that are not imposed on the most free groups. By these principles, we can promote societies that foster economic rights and an environment in which a growing majority can pursue a rewarding life of dignified or decent work.

ACRONYMS

ANC	African National Congress
BASI	ILO Business And Social Initiatives database
BPD	Business Partners for Development
BIS	Bank for International Settlements
BITC	Business in the Community
BRAC	Bangladesh Rural Advancement Committee
BSA	Business Strengthening America
CEACR	ILO Committee of Experts on the Application of Conventions and Recommendations
CEO	Chief Executive Officer
CIPA	Council on International and Public Affairs
CMU	Couverture Maladie Universelle
COSATU	Confederation of South African Trade Unions
COWAD	Community, Women and Development
CRAs	Credit Rating Agencies
CSO	Civil Society Organization
CSR	Corporate Social Responsibility
DESA	Department of Economic and Social Affairs, United Nations
DFID	Department for International Development, U.K.
DWI	Decent Work Index
DWP	Decent Workplace Index
DWSI	Decent Work Status Index
ECJ	European Court of Justice
ECOSOC	Economic and Social Council
EFA	Education for All
ELFS	Enterprise Labour Flexibility and Security Survey
EIRIS	Ethical Investment Research Service
EM-DAT/CRED	Emergency Events Database/Centre for Research on the Epidemiology of Disasters, University of Louvain
EOP	Equal Employment Opportunity Policy
EPSI	Employment Protection Security Index
ESF	European Social Fund
ESI	Economic Security Index
ETI	Ethical Trading Initiative
EU	European Union
FDI	Foreign Direct Investment
FFSA	Fédération française des Sociétés d'Assurances

FTI	Fast Track Initiative
FTSE	Financial Times Stock Exchange
G6	Canada, France, Germany, Italy, Japan and United Kingdom
G7	Canada, France, Germany, Italy, Japan, United Kingdom, and United States
GASPP	Globalism and Social Policy Programmes
GATS	General Agreement on Trade in Services
GATT	General Agreement on Tariffs and Trade
GDP	Gross Domestic Product
GNP	Gross National Product
GRI	Global Reporting Initiative
HDI	Human Development Index
HIV/AIDS	Human Immunodeficiency Virus/Acquired Immune Deficiency Syndrome
IADB	Inter-American Development Bank
ICFTU	International Confederation of Free Trade Unions
ICLS	International Conference of Labour Statisticians
ICVS	International Crime Victim Survey
IDS	Institute of Development Studies
IFC	International Finance Corporation
IFI	Iraqi Freedom Investment Fund
IFRC	International Federation of Red Cross and Red Crescent Societies
IILS	International Institute for Labour Studies
ILO	International Labour Organization/Office
IMF	International Monetary Fund
IPEC	International Programme on the Elimination of Child Labour, ILO
IRS	Internal Revenue Service
ISI	Income Security Index
ISJP	International Social Justice Project
ISO	International Organisation for Standardisation
IT	Information Technology
IUF	International Union of Food, Agricultural, Hotel, Restaurant, Catering, Tobacco & Allied Workers' Association
JPS	Jaring Pengaman Sosial (Indonesian social safety net)
KILM	Key Indicators of the Labour Market, ILO
LDCs	Least Developed Countries
LFS	Labour Force Survey
LIFDCs	Low-Income Food Deficit Countries
LMSI	Labour Market Security Index
LO	Landsorganisationen (Danish Confederation of Trade Unions)
MBO	Membership-based organization
MEGS	Maharashtra Employment Guarantee Scheme
MIT	Massachusetts Institute of Technology
MKSS	Mazdoor Kisan Shakti Sangathan (Organization of Labourer and Peasant Power)
MSA	Mutualité sociale agricole
MSDs	Musculoskeletal Disorders
NAFTA	North American Free Trade Agreement
NCPs	National Contact Points
NEPAD	New Partnership for Africa's Development
NGO	Non-governmental organization
NIOSH	National Institute for Occupational Safety and Health
NNP	Net National Product
NOAPS	National Old Age Pension Scheme, India

NRE	Nouvelles régulations économiques
ODI	Overseas Development Institute
OECD	Organization for Economic Cooperation and Development
OPK	Operasi Pasar Khusus (Indonesian subsidized rice scheme)
OSH	Occupational Safety and Health
PATH	Programme for Advancement Through Health and Education
PEQ	Professional Qualification State Plan
PIRC	Pensions and Investment Research Consultants
PISA	Programme for International Student Assessment
PPP	Purchasing Power Parity
PRAF	Programa de Asignación Familiar
PROGRESA	Programa de Educación, Salud y Alimentación
PRSPs	Poverty Reduction Strategy Papers
PSS	People's Security Survey
RMI	Revenu minimum d'insertion
RPS	Red de Protección Social
SARS	Severe Acute Respiratory Syndrome
SAM	Sustainable Assets Management
SEED	InFocus Programme on Boosting Employment Through Small Enterprise Development, ILO
SEWA	Self-Employed Women's Association, India
SEWU	Self-Employed Women's Union, South Africa
SRI	Socially Responsible Investment
SSI	Skills Security Index
TRIPs	Trade-Related Aspects of Intellectual Property
TUC	Trade Unions Congress, United Kingdom
UNAIDS	Joint United Nations Programme on HIV/AIDS
UNDP	United Nations Development Programme
UNEP	United Nations Environment Programme
UNESCO	United Nations Educational, Scientific and Cultural Organization
UNICE	Union of Industrial and Employers' Confederations of Europe
UNRISD	United Nations Research Institute for Social Development
UNRWA	United Nations Relief and Works Agency
VRSI	Voice representation security Index
WCD	World Commission on Dams
WDI	World Development Indicators
WEF	World Economic Forum
WEO	World Economic Outlook
WER	World Employment Report
WHO	World Health Organization
WSI	Work Security Index
WTO	World Trade Organization

Concepts and Contexts

"Human happiness requires security –
know what to expect in given circumstances"[1]

Part I

[1]L.T. Hobhouse: The elements of Social Justice (London, George Allen and Unwin, 1922). p. 16

Chapter 1   Conceptualizing people's security

"Insecurity is worse than poverty." — Confucius

1.1 The idea of security

All human beings need a sense of security, to give a sense of belonging, a sense of stability and a sense of direction. People who lack basic security in themselves, in their families, in their workplaces and in their community tend to become socially irresponsible. They tend to behave opportunistically, and they tend to lose a sense of moderation. Moreover, periods and areas of mass insecurity have, historically, always bred intolerance, extremism and violence. Look around the world today.

This report is based on the premise that in recent years economic, social, political and technological developments have accentuated the insecurities experienced by people across the world. It will provide statistical support for the view that insecurity has indeed grown, and consider a broad range of policies and institutional changes that could ameliorate those insecurities. But in this initial chapter, we will spell out what is meant by insecurity and why it should be given much higher priority in policy reform in the early years of the 21st century.

A premise is that, while notions of *poverty* overlap with notions of *insecurity*, one could have one without the other. The same is true of the overlap between *inequality* and insecurity. Inequality is part of insecurity, particularly when that inequality is substantial. And the unequal distribution of insecurities is part of socio-economic inequality. These points should become clear in the course of the report.

Some people and communities are dreadfully insecure, but may not be poor by conventional definitions. Others may feel relatively secure in themselves, even if they are poor in an income or property sense. But it stands to reason that income poverty and inequality are major predictors of the incidence of insecurity.

Insecurity is *instrumentally* bad. It induces people to be less innovative than they otherwise would be, and less likely to take productive risk-taking options. It shortens people's time-horizons, makes them more opportunistic and narrows their choices. It heightens uncertainty and accentuates vulnerability.

This report is primarily about *economic insecurity*. Historically, capitalism was built on an uneasy trade-off in which the relatively affluent owners of assets, capital, bore the insecurity of entrepreneurial risk-taking, while taking much of the gains of the resultant economic growth. Some insecurity and uncertainty is necessary for growth, both for economic dynamism and for personal development. However, in recent decades, and apparently stretching into the future, it seems that ordinary workers and working communities — and societies on the edge of the capitalist economy — are being obliged to bear most of the worst forms of insecurity, whereas large-scale asset-holders are relatively well shielded from insecurity.

Indeed, the dominant model in the early part of the 21st century, which took shape in the late 20th century, is actually dependent on insecurity. Whereas for much of the 20th century, development was depicted as a march towards state-based social and economic security, portrayed as the welfare state and a complex array of protective regulations and institutions, now there is no future of security on offer, merely "the risk society".

It may well be that most groups are being exposed to more and greater risks. However, those at the top of the income and wealth spectrum have secured a high level of protection against those risks. There are many observers who believe that the economic system is throwing up more "winners-take-all" markets, where a tiny minority of talented or lucky individuals and firms receive a very high proportion of the economic rewards, while growing numbers face cumulative disadvantages.

This vision of a shifting pattern of risk and insecurity has a resonance even in low-income economies, since in recent years property rights have been increasingly entrenched there, legitimized by the spread of formal political democracy. It has been suggested that in some of those countries elites and the representatives of capital have accepted the introduction of formal political democracy in return for the preservation of considerable inequalities of income, wealth, status and power.

Insecurity is not just an individual phenomenon. One can have systemic insecurity — mass entitlement failure — as well as individual entitlement failure. In the course of structural transformations, systemic reorientations take place in relations of production and distribution, in support at times of need and in the normal reciprocities that make up notions of community. This may leave more people increasingly exposed to risks and uncertainty.

Economic insecurity is about risks <u>and</u> uncertainty. Insecurity cannot be reduced just to risk. Whereas with many risks, one could in principle estimate the probability of an adverse outcome, with uncertainty there is unpredictability. In practice, the vast majority of people everywhere do not know the risks they face or would see them as unpredictable. And, with a wider range of decision-making associated with modernization and globalization, and the shift from local to global influences, the risks and uncertainty both grow.

Economic insecurity is also about the *costs* of the adverse outcomes of risks, including psychological, financial and social status costs. And it is about the *capacity to cope* with the adverse consequences of those risks and the *capacity to recover* from adverse outcomes. It seems that there is a greater perception of risk, a greater incidence of people exposed to a wider range of risks, and a reduced capacity to cope with and to recover from the adverse consequences, in part because of the cumulative nature of "winning" and "losing" in a market society, in part because

of the whittling away of informal support networks (familial or other) and of formal state networks of support in case of need.

Insecurity realizes itself in numerous ways. Think of just a few of them: the stress that leads to alcoholism or drug addiction, mass hysteria ("running amok", as such behaviour is called in Malaysia), a morbid fascination with *fear studies* (or "sociophobics"), the fear economy, and endless talk of the "new risk society". We seem to be living in an era of fear. Consider the fact that in the United States, by 2002 there were over one million workers employed as security guards, and it is projected that this number could rise by 50% by 2010.

The spread of *gated communities* is another symptom of a profound societal disquiet even in affluent countries. In the most affluent country in the world, one in ten of its population now chooses to live in gated communities, enjoying relative affluence but fearful that some of their comforts may be taken by their less-prosperous fellow citizens. The very notion of "community" is dubious, since the gating process often seems to isolate people rather than bring them together. Segregated gated communities are spreading in Europe and elsewhere.

In all of this, there seems to be a refusal to recognize the role of inequalities. Yet insecurities threaten the rich as well as the poor. The film *American Beauty* encapsulated the radical insecurity that comes from wanting total security as the goal of being middle class; the film *Bowling for Columbine* shows the psychosis that comes from chronic insecurity.

It would thus be a gross oversimplification to equate economic and social insecurity with poverty, and even worse to treat it as almost synonymous with *underdevelopment*, located overwhelmingly in low-income developing countries.

One also cannot consider social and economic security without recognizing the renewed concerns over *terrorism*. The events of 11 September 2001 triggered the first new US government agency for many decades, aptly named the Department of Homeland Security, and was followed by wars in Afghanistan and Iraq. While this report is not about state security and the insecurities of war and terrorism, any global report on economic security must take note of their enormous implications and consider what policies are best suited to post-conflict societies.

1.2 Economic security as a human right

"Necessitous men are not free men."

— Franklyn Roosevelt, 1941

Basic security matters. Without it, incentives to work, learn and develop shrivel, and confidence wanes. Without it, people lose all sense of having control over their lives.[1] At the same time, lives become dependent on the largesse of others, and on (rare) good luck.

Economic security matters because human freedom and dignity matter to every human being. Equally, it should matter to every state in the world, as the broad range of international instruments to which such states are signatory attests. For these reasons, and particularly in the light of recent economic and social developments that imperil security in new and pervasive ways, security should become a high priority policy matter everywhere.

Security matters, also, because freedom and dignity matter. To be clear, *real* freedom cannot exist unless a certain level of economic security — *basic* security — exists. One only needs to have clear pictures of freedom and dignity, and of basic security, to see that this is so. In this chapter, we detail those pictures; freedom first, because the contours of basic security are shaped by the nature of freedom.

Our position starts from the assertion that every person everywhere has a right to basic security. This is more than "limiting the downside risks". It means limiting the uncertainties people face in their daily lives. It also means providing a social environment in which people — you, me and them — feel they belong to a range of communities, and have a fair and good *opportunity* to live a decent life and to develop through what the ILO is calling *decent* work.

So, is basic economic security a human *right*? We believe that it should be, and that it should be seen as a claim right, an ideal to which all policies and institutions should try to move. One must recognize that some insecurity is essential for dynamic societies and economies and for personal development. However, without basic security one cannot make rational decisions. Basic security must encompass:

- **Freedom from morbidity.** People cannot be expected to act freely and responsibly if they are on the margins of survival. They need a distance from catastrophe. A basically free and secure society may be defined in part as one in which all groups have an equal freedom from morbidity (or an equal risk of illness, injury and life-threatening events).

- **Freedom from fear.** The same equality must apply here, if basic security is to prevail.

- **Control of own development.** This must include the capacity to acquire education, and make decisions in real freedom.

- **Sustainable self-respect.** There is a "poverty of dignity", as well as a poverty of food or income. The person who is deprived of food may rob or may fall prey to social illness. The person who is deprived of dignity may take more violent action.

This last aspect is easily taken for granted or ignored altogether, but is of increasing significance given the growing sophistication of information manipulation, the growing concentration of the mass media, and the global pressures to "consume". People in all parts of the world are being encouraged to consume more and to act more opportunistically. It has been said that the pressure to be constantly "active" is a form of "infantilism" — individualism mixed with instantaneity — which undermines the processes by which we gain respect and social responsibility.[2]

More generally, the above elements comprise a set of commitments to what the philosopher Isaiah Berlin described as "negative liberty" and "positive liberty", the former concerning the absence of illegitimate constraints, the latter the opportunity for making real choices about substantial matters of personal development. "Negative liberty" — the absence or negation of controls — is not sufficient for real basic security. Indeed, freedom purely in its negative sense is a form or expression of insecurity. The autonomous individual is *in extremis* in chronic insecurity, without networks of reciprocity that provide security.

---

[1] R. Stock: *Psychological Approaches to Work Security*, SES Paper (Geneva, ILO, 2002).

[2] See, for examples of this direction of reasoning, P. Bobitt: *The Schield of Achilles, War, Peace and the Course of History* (New York, Knopf, 2002); R. Sennet: *Respect: The Formation of Character in an Age of Inequality* (London, Penguin, 2004).

Thus, some advances in freedom may intensify insecurity. One should not presume that there is a direct, simple relationship between "freedom" and "security". This is why we insist on the term "real freedom", as the combination of negative and positive liberty, the ability to make meaningful and desirable choices based on basic security.

1.3 Freedom and dignity

A principle on which surely all can agree is that coercion and freedom do not mix. A person who is forced to act or to refrain from acting by another is, to the extent of that coercion, not free. Thus, a person in prison is not free to go about as she pleases, to pursue her chosen occupation, to participate in the raising of her children. A worker subject to controls of every description, from detailed and rigid directions on exactly how to carry out every minute aspect of his employment duties to rules about how and when to interact with others in the workplace, lives a life of unfreedom at work. A person living in a regime that criminalizes anti-government speech is not free to express her political convictions in a public setting.

What is wrong with coercion, from the perspective of freedom, is that, when a person is coerced, she acts for a purpose or goal that is not her own, or she acts in a manner that she has not herself selected. A young person who has adopted as a life goal the pursuit of a certain occupational path is subject to coercion when her parents stand in the way of her pursuing the occupation, even if they do so "for her own good"; and in complying with her parents' directives — in effectively pursuing their goals rather than her own — she is not free.

Equally, coercion is inimical to freedom when the coerced person is forced to employ means to ends that he might embrace that are not means he would adopt on his own. For example, a pacifist may well have as a fundamental goal participating in efforts to change a foreign government's policies. But in being conscripted into his nation's armed services and being sent to fight against that foreign government, he is subject to coercion, regardless of the possible securing of a goal he shares with his government. His pursuit of a goal he shares, by those means, is not free.

Thus, "coercion" is inimical to freedom. Human beings can flourish only by establishing their own personal goals, or ends; by determining, in their own way, the means that are best suited to achieve those ends; and by pursuing those means. Freedom lies in that: the unimpeded capacity to establish one's own ends; the capacity, time and space to determine the way in which one will pursue those ends; and the capacity to engage in the pursuit.

If we accept that coercion is inimical to security, then we are led to reflect on the place of "controls" over choices and behaviour. These are, rather obviously, important in the sphere of economic security, and in particular in relation to the ILO's concept of decent work. There are legitimate controls, notably those connected with legally proper contracts or those concerned to protect the interests and safety of all. But many forms of control exercised over millions of people working around the world are anything but legitimate. For many, insecurity is a factor in the grudging acceptance of unjust controls and is thus a disciplinary device. Insecurity is instrumental in their unfreedom.

Underlying the value of freedom is human dignity. It is implicated both in the establishment of personal goals, and in the pursuit of the means for achieving them. Take the establishment of goals first. Human beings, we believe, must be able to choose for themselves who they are, and who they will be. This is self-definition; it is the basis of a person's sense of self, of self-worth. If the "dignity" of a person is measured, as it most surely is, by her sense of self-worth, then her power freely to choose what she will be by choosing her own goals and purposes is a basic source of her dignity.

This is not to say that persons are to be left alone to make this most important of choices, the choice of who to be. On the contrary, the more input the better: from parents, friends, colleagues, teachers and the like, who can provide information about what others have thought valuable, have cherished, have struggled for; about what is possible and what is not; about what goals have proved chimerical; and about what lives have proved happiest, fullest, richest. All these inputs are invaluable, and we count the person lucky who has been shown the widest range of choices, because the more he has considered in this way, the richer his ultimate choices are. But that they must simply serve as inputs for his ultimate *free* choice is beyond doubt; any other way of arriving at goals derogates from dignity.

The free selection of goals is necessary to lead a life of dignity. But it is obviously not enough. Positing goals and ends sets a person's agenda. Then the person, again employing whatever information she has access to, and her own practical and intellectual resources (developed and fortified by education, and aided by those within the social and familial ambit), attempts to figure out how to achieve the goals she has set for herself. She considers alternatives, makes plans, sometimes sacrifices some things for others, experiments, and learns from successes and from failures.

In short, she determines the means by which she believes she will achieve her ends, and pursues the means. And here too, dignity requires that she be the final arbiter of which means she will pursue. Here too, imposition by others derogates from her sense of self-worth. A person who has not been given the means, or who has been forced to obtain, by means not of her choosing, a goal that she herself has chosen will feel that the goal has been falsely achieved, that the attainment is not "her own", and will feel little sense of accomplishment in having achieved it. Means, as well as ends, are freely chosen in a life of dignity.

1.4 Security versus paternalism

This is why *paternalism* should be seen as a form of insecurity and a mechanism for inducing a sense of insecurity.[3] One form of paternalism is *clientelism*. It has often been said that the modern movement for human rights represents the painful evolution from clientelism to citizenship, where "the citizen" is someone with individual and collective rights, rather than merely someone who relies on charity, welfare or paternalistic gestures.

Some observers refer to the existence of patterns of *dependent security*, which is close to paternalism.[4] This is not real security, and is really a misuse of language. It is particularly important in the early years of the 21st century, when the state, with all its expanding electronic reach, can indulge in increasingly sophisticated forms of social engineering. Paternalism as a guide to state policy should be regarded with more than suspicion, and if allowed should be justified explicitly and monitored, as with the protection of children. Paternalism of any kind — familial, community, corporate or state-based — compromises freedom and imposes its own brand of insecurity. And yet it has a powerful hold on policymakers.

Paternalism is often well-meaning. For example, the language of "rights with responsibilities" is commonly used to justify imposing conditions on the poor for receiving state support. The trouble is that the directive nature of the imposed "responsibility" effectively removes the recipient from the realm of responsibility or freedom to a realm of *obligation*. Well-meaning paternalism easily blurs into discretionary and arbitrary coercion.

When national leaders and elites try to impose their view of "virtue", those who see the world differently and want to live by their own code of virtue are made more insecure and even marginalized or isolated. The imposition of a societal norm — however good and noble — is a means of making humanity fearful. Paternalism is no solution to insecurity.

A political project that preaches economic liberalization combined with moralistic virtue is certain to create a climate of insecurity. There is an inherent tension between what some have described as "middle-class" virtue — prudence, abstinence, thrift, frugality, fidelity and self-discipline — and the *praxis* of economic liberalism — risk-taking, opportunism, selfishness and egotism. The result is organized hypocrisy, with the poor and the near-poor being urged to behave "responsibly", while entrepreneurs and those around them are urged to behave as risk-takers, able to hire and fire according to their risk-taking skills and "brute luck", insured personally against "downside risks".

In the end, basic security should provide dignity and real freedom, while those who wish to become or remain relatively affluent should bear the greater risks of pursuing such a goal.

1.5 Security and identity

Security comes from possessing a sense of identity, a sense of belonging to a community and a sense of personal control. Modernization has meant the dissolution of intimate forms of identity, as Max Weber predicted. But the bureaucratic, procedurally predictable order that he thought would replace all that has not materialized.

---

[3]G. Standing: *Beyond the New Paternalism: Basic Security as Equality* (London, Verso, 2002).

[4]G. Wood: "Staying secure, staying poor: The 'Faustian Bargain'", *World Development*, Vol. 31, No. 3, 2003, pp. 455–471.

Ironically, when globalization is supposedly creating a "global village", in fact there is an almost desperate search to find ways of asserting a sense of identity, whether cultural, religious, national or local. Anthropologists have shown how states are looking for ways to do the same, to create loyal citizen.[5] In all of this, there is a worry that the "radical uncertainty about identity" is leading to cultural exclusiveness, and intolerance of — and violence against — "the other".[6]

There seems to be an existential insecurity associated with globalization. There is an anxiety, a stressful sense of pressure. Globalization has made people more inclined to measure their status and achievement by outside symbols and criteria, often quite unattainable. Thus, in Africa, globalization has seemed to mean that the poor are "licking at the shop window" (*lécher la vitrine*).[7] For the "salaryman" in places like Japan and other affluent countries, there is all the stress of losing status, "not measuring up". Some observers have even referred to a tendency of globalization to create "new markets for loyalty".[8]

As discussed in the next chapter, globalization is associated with privatization and individualization, which are in part superficially about giving individuals greater opportunity for making choices. But the shrinkage of the public sphere also induces "privatism", the tendency for people to be isolated by their lack of active involvement in social activities and social networks. This apparently goes with stultifying jobs and with low levels of education, which lead people to a lifestyle of passivity, the less educated being the most likely to become dependent on television.

The insecurity of "bowling alone" is channelled through passivity. For instance, in Italy, between 1988 and 1995 alone, the average daily time spent watching television increased by over 40 minutes to over 3.5 hours a day, every day of the year. Modern consumption is conducive to individualistic hedonism that creates an illusion of "absolute freedom" in an atmosphere of conformity.

The global crisis over the numerous threats to identity goes beyond the immediate subject of this report. But it is a part of the insecurity that all policymakers will have to address in the early decades of the 21st century.

1.6 Security as agency and "empowerment"

Security is often linked to three overlapping ideas — participation, agency and empowerment. Participation is seen as the opposite of passivity and social exclusion, agency is seen as the opportunity to make choices on life events, including participation, and empowerment is seen in much the same way.

Participation is a much-used term, but too rarely defined. It is multifaceted. One may be free to participate but not do so, due to apathy, indifference, or lack of capability. There is, for example, considerable concern about the future of democracy in the light of declining and low turn-outs at elections. Some see this as reflecting a perceived lack of capacity to influence policymaking, others see it as a rejection of the superficiality and cynical manoeuvring of politicians. But in any case, participation in social or economic activity does not necessarily mean engagement in it.

Empowerment, while often seen as the ability to make choices, is problematic, because it conjures up images of winners and losers, of power and of powerful interests. Sustainable security comes not from triumphs of one interest over another; it comes from disempowering the powerful, by creating circumstances in which no group or individual can abuse power to control others.

The notion of empowerment has several components. For example, one defence of micro-credit is that it is a means of providing a "pre-condition" for choice — i.e., a resource base for those provided with loans. It is also a means of providing "agency" — i.e., an

[5]P. Geschiere and B. Meyer: "Globalization and identity: Dialectics of flow and closure", Development and Change, Vol. 29, No. 4, 1998, p. 605; H. Vermeulen and C. Govers (eds.): *The Anthropology of Ethnicity: Beyond Ethnic Groups and Boundaries* (Amsterdam, Het Spinhuis, 1994).

[6]A. Appadurai: "Dead certainty: Ethnic violence in the era of globalization", Development and Change, Vol. 29, No. 4, 1998, pp. 905–925.

[7]A. Mbembe: *Notes on the Postcolony* (Berkeley, University of California Press, 1999).

[8]M.E. Price: "The market for loyalties: Electronic media and the global competition for allegiances", Yale Law Journal, Vol. 104, No. 3, 1994, pp. 667–705.

opportunity to make choices, and it is a means of achieving better security and welfare — i.e., realizing the consequences of exercising choice.[9]

According to another conceptual approach, micro-credit may increase women's "material" empowerment, their "cognitive" empowerment (through encouraging them to recognize their skills or their capacity to acquire skills), their "perceptual" empowerment (how others see them and treat them) and their "relational" empowerment (through altering gender relations within the family and society).[10] An individual's important cognitive breakthrough comes with recognition of constraints for what they are and recognition that they need not be accepted as inevitable.

As far as *agency* is concerned, there can be individual and collective agency. A highly individualistic society may be rather brutish and opportunistic, resulting in stressful competitiveness and chronic existential insecurity. At the other extreme, one based on overwhelming collective agency would stifle initiative and freeze relationships. For real security, one needs a balance.

It has been suggested that the transition from passivity to agency involves cognitive and relational empowerment. But how does the reverse occur? How does a loss of cognitive security occur, and what are the consequences, socially and individually? Some observers believe that the whirlwind of information and numerous conflicting signals associated with open societies, globalization and the ethos of individualism lead to cognitive insecurity, a sense of powerlessness and isolation, which in turn leads to social passivity and mindless consumerism.

1.7 Idiosyncratic versus systemic risk

Most low-income individuals, households, families and communities face what might be called systemic insecurity, or chronic, rather than stochastic (or what is sometimes called "idiosyncratic") insecurity. In other words, one or more "shocks" can easily jeopardize their capacity to function effectively. This has two important implications.

First, standard insurance schemes, suitable for the contingency risks typically addressed by social insurance, are likely to be absent, denied, too expensive or available only at a cost of loss of control over vital

assets (land, means of production, time, freedom, etc.).

Second, it means that people who are insecure, particularly if they have incomes, assets, or skills that put them below the "modal citizen" level, will be inclined to opt for a lifestyle of dependent security, placing themselves reluctantly or pathetically under the protective benevolence of someone, like a landlord, middleman, moneylender, chief, state bureaucrat, husband or gangster. This tendency, elegantly portrayed by James Scott as the "moral economy of the peasant", compromises long-term developmental freedom, because it typically forces the insecure person to devote time to activities that he or she would not wish to undertake, thereby blocking him or her from investing in more constructive activities. Some would say that the insecurity reduces their "agency".

The World Bank's Social Protection Division, among others, has presented a picture of the world as a giant risk society.[11] Yet it seems that the policies and institutional changes encouraged through the rhetoric of globalization, and the other changes considered in Chapter 2, are increasing exposure to risks and the incidence and depth of systemic shocks. Risk is increased if, for example, the incidence of disease increases, or if technological change accelerates, threatening the security that comes from the possession of certain skills. One could go further and say that each time the risk environment is increased, the modal citizen has to devote proportionately more of his or her time to risk control (or moderation) activity and proportionately less to developmental or freedom-enhancing activity.

Some have criticized the World Bank for failing to appreciate the nature of chronic risk due to inequality and concentrations of unaccountable power.[12] The distinction between idiosyncratic and covariant risk,

---

[9]N. Kabeer: *The Conditions and Consequences of Choice: Reflections on the Measurement of Empowerment*, UNRISD Discussion Paper DP108 (Geneva, UNRISD, 1999).

[10]M. Chen and S. Mahmud: *Assessing change in women's lives: A conceptual framework*, Working Paper No. 2, BRAC–ICDDRB Joint Research Project, Matlab, Dhaka, 1995.

[11]For the World Bank's view, see *World Development Report 2000* (Washington, DC, World Bank, 2000), Chapter 8, in particular.

[12]See, for instance, Wood, 2003, op. cit., p. 457.

besides being scientistic, does not capture this form of chronic insecurity. Even less attention has been given to what might be called reciprocity insecurity. The modal citizen can hope to rely on inter-generational networks of support and to a lesser extent on intra-community sharing of risks and rewards. To be strong, this reciprocal support system requires two conditions — there must be communities and there must be balanced reciprocities.

Both are weakened by the forces underpinning globalization and commodification in the early 21st century. The modal citizen supports his or her children for altruistic reasons but also in the hope that support in times of need will be forthcoming later. In a peasant society, where inter-generational linkages are part of life, and in a stable industrial society, where the lifecycle is neatly divided into a short pre-labour period, a long labour period and a short post-labour period, the reciprocity model might work reasonably well. But when both the pre-labour and post-labour periods are lengthened, and when the middle period is shortened or made more insecure, the reciprocity bargains are put under intolerable strain.

A similar fissure may take place in communal reciprocities. If elites feel that they can insure against all risks, they will feel less inclined to support supplicant community members, especially if the latter are chronically insecure. But the problem does not stop there, since the losers will inevitably be resentful of the good fortune of the elite and other "winners". They may indulge in acts of retributive justice. If the threatened winners are thereby induced to provide coping assistance to the insecure, that might modify the resentment. But it might not, because on both sides action is taken in a spirit of aggression or bitterness.

How can the modal citizen and the chronically insecure respond to risks? The standard set of mechanisms is (i) risk reduction, (ii) mitigation, and (iii) coping. To this, we should add (iv) reviving or recuperating. To cope is not to recover. "Getting by" is not "getting on".

Risk reduction is obviously easier when the risk is low, small and predictable. If the probability of an adverse event — for example, crop failure — is close to one, and the potential cost is catastrophe — loss of livelihood — both the modal citizen and the chron-

ically insecure will find risk reduction almost prohibitive. It is naïve to picture the chronically insecure as in a position to limit risk in such circumstances.[13] Only if an external institution (the state, the community, or a dominant interest) reduces the risk to manageable proportions can the chronically insecure take risk-reducing actions. This is why it is so important for the state to provide basic security, because only then can the modal citizen take additional steps to handle the risks.

As for mitigation, one may mitigate the potentially adverse effects by diversifying production or sources of income. But this is hard to do for most people, or if done usually has a negative effect, in that it means deliberately opting for low-productivity options. As for "coping", for most of the poor in most parts of the world the mix of options consists largely of appealing to informal support networks, through reliance on moneylenders, debt bondage, micro-finance and so on, and to a lesser extent to the formal state-based "social security", with civil society non-governmental organizations playing a role in the middle. Few of these mechanisms are reliable or costless, and are unlikely to be available for systemic shocks. They are unlikely to be liberating (or, as some would say, de-commodifying).

Recovery requires acquiring a sense of autonomy, of control. Ultimately, the more liberating risk-reducing policies and institutional mechanisms are those that do not offer "relief" from shocks but offer "preparation" for shocks as hazards. Put differently, the ideal policy mix is one that puts emphasis on *ex ante* protection rather than on *ex post* support.

---

[13] The peasant analogy made famous by Michael Lipton comes to mind here.

The management of risk

It is a truism that every action is a risk, as everything is in flux. Making decisions is to take risks. So what? In life, people seek to lessen risks and to ensure that the adverse consequences of adverse outcomes are minimized.

Among the questions that this train of thinking prompts are:

• What risks merit taking out an insurance policy?

• What role should governments be expected to play with respect to various types of risk?

• What responsibilities should individuals be expected to take?

• Who should pay and on what basis?

Among the issues are moral hazards and the less discussed immoral hazards. Moral hazards arise from a tendency for those receiving compensation for an adverse outcome to an insured risk — e.g., unemployment — to remain in that state, often because it would appear that they would be worse off if they moved out of it. Immoral hazards arise from situations in which because it would be too costly to make a desirable decision a person lies or acts illegally or illegitimately. If a person is caught in a *poverty trap,* where taking a low-income job would result in a loss of benefits that might be greater in value than the income earned from the job, there is an "incentive" not to declare the job. In such cases, a rational individual would weigh the risks and potential benefits of several possible courses of action.

The architects of the welfare states of the 20th century essentially decided that standard contingency risks should be covered by the state — ill-health, disability, unemployment, maternity, old age and poverty. The coverage for all these was linked to the performance of labour, or the willingness to perform labour. But as with all forms of insurance, questions of cause and responsibility cloud the picture. For instance, if a person is "careless" and becomes sick or is injured, should he or she be provided with compensation? Or should that person be provided with the same level of compensation as someone who took care but who still became sick? Some rich country governments are, for example, considering a policy of penalizing people who smoke or are obese by requiring them to pay more towards healthcare.

Governments in the era of globalization and market principles have tended to tighten the conditions for state benefits, just as insurance companies and commercial corporations have tightened conditions for entitlement to insurance benefits and even for acceptance in schemes of entitlement. As they have done so, individual insecurity has been intensified. In general, a poor person cannot insure to anything like the extent that a rich person can, and yet is almost certainly exposed to more risks, more uncertainty and more adverse outcomes. It is this perverse set of distributional outcomes that makes critics feel that individualizing risks and pursuing an individualized "account" system of risk management is profoundly unjust.

1.8 Social solidarity and community

The ideas of security, social solidarity and community commonly go together. The French Revolution's idea of *fraternité* is closely involved, as is the notion of reciprocity. In rethinking security for the 21st century, each of these ideas requires fresh consideration. It is particularly important because too many reject the need for, or desirability of, *social solidarity,* while too many abuse the notion of community.

Social solidarity is often regarded as the underlying principle of most variants of the "welfare state", implying a sense of sharing and compensatory redistribution. But in any society, a mix of altruism and self-interest prompts the modal citizen to devote time and resources to actions of social solidarity and structured reciprocity. The modal citizen will realize that social solidarity is a public good, from which he or she may gain, from which those he or she loves could be expected to gain, most notably children, and from which fellow citizens could be expected to gain. Social solidarity may involve more self-interest than most might wish to admit, in that by giving to the losers one may be securing one's future welfare from the threat of "retributive justice". However, the thinking behind social solidarity is that it is *ex ante* social protection. If that is abandoned, one is left with predominantly *ex post* measures. This distinction will concern us later.

The propensity to share in the interest of social solidarity is a sensitive variable rather than something fixed. The modal citizen will give some income, time and other assets if there is a prospect of preserving, creating or enhancing social solidarity. But if the underlying structure of society and the underlying economic system are such that social solidarity is made impossible, irrelevant to the winners, or too fragile, the modal citizen will be forced (or be induced) to be opportunistic and selfish. This will be a sub-optimal way of adapting, which will bring its own insecurity. Ultimately, *in extremis,* it will lead to a society in which "winners" will live a life of costly protective self-imprisonment (which characterized the lives of middle-class whites in South Africa under apartheid, and subsequently). Already, in several highly unequal societies, alongside a community of incarcerated "losers", a growing number of "winners" are seeking a scarcely secure existence in gated communities, sometimes given the ironic name of *privatopia.*[14]

Security comes, in part, from belonging to a community. This should not lead to an idealization of the notion of community, since one can be unwillingly incorporated into a community (imprisoned, long-term contract, "golden cage", etc.). These may require deference from ordinary members to patrons, elders, prison guards, chiefs, moneylenders and so on. However, without belonging to one or more communities, insecurity is very likely. Rules of thumb here should be that (i) people should have choices of community, (ii) entering and leaving chosen communities should be easy and not too costly, (iii) security comes from belonging to more than one community, and (iv) membership of a community should involve rights.

Modernization, and globalization, severs individuals from some communities — kinship, clans, etc. — through migration, urbanization, lower fertility, consumerist individualism, and — less often appreciated — the erosion of occupational identity and community. The last, which is linked to what we later call *job security,* is associated with more rapid technological change and technical divisions of labour, and with more varied relocations of production.

In any case, the reciprocities that characterize communities tend to become more fragile, and relations of moral ties and loyalty are weakened or are replaced by notions of contract, or what can better be described as contractual opportunism. "Imagined" ties of reciprocity and loyalty are no longer credible. Look after yourself! That seems to be a principle for a life of insecurity.

Communities, in short, are part of a secure society, to the extent that they foster balanced reciprocities and capability development. Ironically, the dominant ethos of policy debate in the 1980s and 1990s was anti-collective, even though the rhetoric was pro-community. The trouble is that most economic communities are rent-seeking devices vis-à-vis other interests. What the policymakers would like are income-sharing or security-sharing communities. But if regulating the rent-seeking is done too heavily, the other functions of community may be destroyed as well.[15]

Community can be a cover for an institutional arrangement of control — "plural clientelism" — in which the modal members are, in effect, offered dependent security if they adhere to freedom-curbing rules of patronage. It would be a mistake to think that this applies only in poor rural communities. It permeates corporations, bureaucracies and professional associations, wherever hierarchies exist.

By contrast, solidaristic communities challenge hierarchies. They tend to be disruptive, and thus are curbed by governments and bypassed by international donors and agencies, which want efficiency, stability and other conditions conducive to international "confidence" (rationalized as desirable to encourage foreign direct investment). Governments and donors may go further than this, and promote (financially, institutionally, legislatively and rhetorically) the type of community that is oriented to service, charity, "mitigating and coping" with crises, rather than the type that can mould structures so as to reduce the probability of shocks.

Take an obvious example. A highly inegalitarian society probably means that a large proportion of the population is living on the margins of chronic insecurity (losing the capacity to function). A government that encouraged coping communities alone would not be preventing the problem from arising, whereas solidaristic communities would focus on reducing the inequalities giving rise to the problem. Modern "governance" practitioners tend to favour mitigating-and-coping over risk-reducing bodies. This

---

[14] E. Mackenzie: *Privatopia: Homeowner Associations and the Rise of Residential Private Government* (New Haven and London, Yale University Press, 1994).

[15] Note that the rent-seeking communities that represent the interests of powerful elites have been treated differently from the rent-seeking communities that represent the insecure and workers.

is a further reason for being careful about idealising community as a panacea. Even calling some groups "pro-poor organizations" may miss the point.

1.9 Development as security

The notion of economic development should not be conflated with that of human development. In practice, spurts of economic development in various parts of the world have not resulted in corresponding spurts of real freedom or basic security. Indeed, in the short term at least, they have often been accompanied by human suffering, as large numbers of people have been pushed out of a system that had at least provided them with a set of entitlements. A peasant on an estate, for instance, might be able to look to the landlord as a patron in times of need. Turning the peasant off the land as commercial development proceeds might accelerate economic development, but the peasant's freedom will be accompanied by worse insecurity.

Throughout history, periods of rapid spurts of economic development have been associated with mass entitlement "failures". These are in the nature of "shocks" rather than individual contingency risks. The most significant of these as causes of insecurity are mass displacements.

Development involves an increase in risks and insecurities, including various forms of displacement, spatial, economic and social. The question is whether or not those affected should be protected or compensated. Consider the building of dams. According to the World Commission on Dams (WCD), physical displacement from large dams has affected between 40 and 80 million people in recent years.[16] This excludes those displaced by canals, power houses, and so on. And it excludes those affected upstream and downstream of dams. The Commission recognized that there is a systematic underestimation of the number affected, and drew attention to the lack of adequate compensation and resettlement assistance.

Displacements are major causes of mass insecurity in developing countries, and can rarely be covered by realistic insurance schemes. They suggest that a rights-based approach to social protection would be more appropriate than any other, an issue considered in Chapter 12.

1.10 Security in conflict

One cannot consider the promotion of security without reflecting on the events of 11 September 2001 and the global aftermath, including the wars in Afghanistan and Iraq. It would be inappropriate to dwell on those events here. Let us just acknowledge that insecurities breed hopelessness, and hopelessness breeds irresponsibility. In the context of generations of deprivation and humiliation, a sense of moral rage is understandable in places in the world characterized by poverty, underdevelopment and oppression.

This report is about economic security and work, not about security in the sense of military or national security, or about cultural or very broad notions of "human security". Yet economic insecurity contributes to civil and international conflict, and this in turn induces insecurities of all kinds, before, during and afterwards.[17] The world has been afflicted by a spate of wars in recent years, resulting in the death of several million people and the displacement of many, many millions — human insecurity on a vast scale (Figure 1.1).[18] "Post-conflict" is a new powerful image for strategic policymaking at the international level. A key point to bear in mind is that morbidity and mortality rates among non-combatants rise after a conflict has ended. This is well brought out in a recent report. The reasons include disease, epidemics, infrastructural breakdowns, post-war traumas, life-shortening disabilities, war-induced poverty and the collapse of informal and formal systems of social support.

---

[16] World Commission on Dams: *Dams and Development: A New Framework for Decision-Making*, Report of the World Commission on Dams (London and Sterling, VA, Earthscan Publications, 2000). Of all World Bank-funded development-induced displacement globally, large dams account for about 60%. Others have suggested that dams account for about 40% of the 10 million people displaced each year. Infrastructural projects may account for more than one million each year. For a review article, see R. Dwivedi: "Models and methods in development-induced displacement", *Development and Change*, Vol. 33, No. 4, Sep. 2002, pp. 709–732.

[17] F. Stewart and V. Fitzgerald: *War and Underdevelopment* (Oxford, Oxford University Press, 2001). On the vexed issue of "grievance" versus "greed" as an explanation for civil strife, and implicitly the role of insecurity, see J. Goodhand: "Enduring disorder and persistent poverty: A review of the linkages between war and chronic poverty", *World Development*, Vol. 31, No. 3, Mar. 2003, pp. 629–646.

[18] EM-DAT, CRED, University of Louvain, Belgium

[19] *The World Bank, Breaking the Conflict Trap: Civil War and Development Policy* (Washington, DC, 2003).

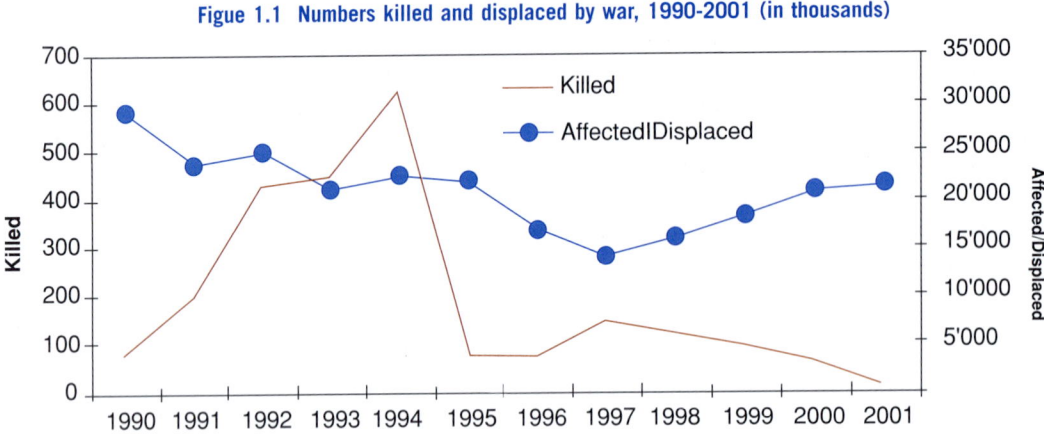

Figue 1.1 Numbers killed and displaced by war, 1990-2001 (in thousands)

Source: EM-DAT, CRED, University of Louvain, Belgium.

While we will steer round issues of insecurity associated with civil conflict and violence, some reference is made to desirable policies in "post-conflict" situations in the final chapter. For the most part, the analysis concentrates on the seven forms of work-related security and the pursuit of decent work.

1.11 Work-related security

Economic security is linked to a rich concept of work. Human beings, men and women equally, live and develop through their working lives, variously combining income-earning activities with reproductive activity, ideally caring for family, neighbours and reaching out to the broader community and society. We extend production through work, we help each other to survive, revive and develop. Work seen in this rich sense is much more than conveyed by the narrow notion of *labour*, associated with wages and a position of subordination in the productive system.

The ILO's Socio-Economic Security Programme has identified seven forms of security associated with work, which are or could be pursued by governments, employers, unions and others. For most of the past century, these have focused on labour, that is, wage-work, rather than on all forms of *work*. Briefly, the seven forms of work security are defined as follows:

- *labour market security.* Adequate employment opportunities, through state-guaranteed full employment;

- *employment security.* Protection against arbitrary dismissal, regulations on hiring and firing, imposition of costs on employers for failing to adhere to rules, etc.;

- *job security.* A niche designated as an occupation or "career", plus tolerance of demarcation practices, barriers to skill dilution, craft boundaries, job qualifications, restrictive practices, craft unions, etc.;

- *Work security.* Protection against accidents and illness at work, through safety and health regulations, and limits on working time, unsociable hours, night work for women, etc.;

- *skill reproduction security.* Widespread opportunities to gain and retain skills, through apprenticeships, employment training, etc.;

- *income security.* Protection of income through minimum wage machinery, wage indexation, comprehensive social security, progressive taxation to reduce inequality and to supplement those with low incomes, etc.;

- *representation security.* Protection of collective voice in the labour market, through independent trade unions and employer associations incorporated economically and politically into the state, with the right to strike, etc.

Looking at these forms of work-related security prompts the questions: Which, if any, should have priority, and what are the trade-offs? Are some negotiable? Our fundamental position is that basic security underpins real freedom; basic security is desirable, it is feasible and should be equalized in the Good Society of the 21st century. But certain forms of *labour*-based security may be neither essential nor even desirable; they may, at least, be tradable. For instance, strong employment security may act as a psychological barrier to sensible risk-taking by an individual worker; strong job security may impede technological innovation and "career development".

It appears that there is a need to explain why representation security is a form of security, rather than a means of pursuing security. One may wish to argue that it is an *instrumental freedom*. However, one could say the same for other aspects of security. We would rather take the view that representation security is the right to participation, which is the way to realize other rights and forms of security.[20] Representation covers both individual and collective forms. And it relates to the notion of "empowerment". The underlying purpose of Voice is to "disempower the powerful", in the sense that it creates "countervailing" bargaining capacity, negating the opportunistic inclinations of special interests.

We may reflect in this context on the well-known view that development represents the advance of freedom. "Development as Freedom" raises difficulties of interpretation. Moving from a feudal society to a market-based economy may be (and is) an advance for freedom. But it brings with it its own unfreedoms. Does it provide a licence for opportunism? Freedom to develop is not the same as freedom to take advantage of others' insecurities.

For people to be able to pursue the Good Life, defined for our purposes as a creative working life, they must have basic security. This involves both objective and subjective elements. Most fundamentally, it requires a social environment giving freedom from the threat of premature morbidity (illnesses, enfeeblement), relative to global and regional norms of decency. It means freedom from fear, from random or systematic violence, and access to housing, clothing and food. These fundamental basic needs are the crux of life. Beyond them we move to the ILO's mandate for the 21st century, the promotion of decent work.

Basic security requires a declining probability of impoverishment, it requires tolerable and declining inequality in all aspects of socio-economic security,

and it requires growing opportunity to pursue a sense of occupation through a working life. By occupation, we mean the personal ability to develop one's capacities through time, and the ability and good opportunity to combine a portfolio of statuses and sets of tasks at different periods of life.

This leads us to a fundamental claim. The security espoused in this report is for work, all forms of work, not just labour, or even just all forms of income-earning activity, including so-called informal economy activity. In other words, all legitimate productive and reproductive work should be given equal basic security, including such work as caring for children and the elderly, voluntary work and community work, as well as service activities that may not have the moral approval of a majority, as long as they do no harm to others and are chosen in real freedom.

1.12 Policy decision rules

Distributive justice requires policies and institutions that promote the attainment of basic needs and real freedom, which together constitute basic security. Priority should be given to the attainment and maintenance of basic security, with negotiable entitlement to other forms of security. In particular, basic economic security depends on:

- *Basic income security.* This requires a universal floor, as a human right. It may be regarded as a "constitutional right" or as a "republican right", that is, it should be seen as a fundamental objective of social, economic and political policy.
- *Voice representation security.* This requires the assurance that one's interests can be represented in social and individual bargaining, and should combine both collective representation and individual representation.

These two complement each other, and together are essential for equal good opportunity to pursue occupation. Unless representation security is ensured, the vulnerable will always remain vulnerable to loss of other forms of security.

---

[20] As a recent report noted, "Understanding participation as a right, rather than an instrument for greater aid effectiveness, has been one of the biggest shifts in agency thinking in recent years. It means switching from a technical to a political understanding of development." Institute of Development Studies: *The Rise of Rights*, University of Sussex Policy Briefing (Brighton, 17 May 2003).

In the light of these twin security needs, one can establish two principles by which policies and institutional changes should be assessed. These policy decision rules can be stated as follows:

- **The Security Difference Principle.** A policy or institutional change is just only if it reduces (or at least does not worsen) the insecurity of the least secure groups in society.
- **The Paternalism Test Principle.** A policy or institutional change is just only if it does not impose controls on some groups that are not imposed on the most free groups in society.

These principles may not seem very demanding. However, numerous policy proposals and policy decisions contradict them. One point that should be kept in mind about the first principle is that the "most insecure" are those who might be described as in chronic insecurity, analogous to the idea of chronic poverty. They have become so insecure that they are unable to recover and function effectively. Whatever assets were possessed have been forfeited; whatever technical skills they had have been rendered obsolete or ineffectual; whatever social skills they had have been lost in anomic despair; whatever rights they had have been lost by default.

A point in considering the Security Difference Principle, which draws on John Rawls, is how to define and position the most insecure.[21] In some cases, they will be simply the poorest, in others those with least assets (physical, financial and intangible). But in many cases where a policy decision is being contemplated, the most insecure will be those who would bear the greatest risk of loss of rights and/or entitlements, and who would do so involuntarily.

To give an example: the WCD, mentioned earlier, advocated a "rights and risks approach" for decision-making on dam building — a "recognition of rights and an assessment of risks". Security requires that this consideration should guide policymaking and implementation. Only if all interests have a Voice can one expect all the risks to be identified, and only if they are identified will there be a chance that those risks will be articulated and addressed, even if there is difficulty in ensuring that they are addressed. It is always important to recognize that the risk-takers are not necessarily — or indeed often — the risk-bearers. Usually, moreover, it is a matter of voluntary risk-takers and involuntary risk-bearers. The key idea of a rights-and-risks approach is that negotiation between the two groups should allow for more equitable sharing of risks and benefits. The approach also allows the interests of those bearing the greatest risks of loss of rights to be taken into account. These interests are often ignored, as was the case in the Enron debacle.

Some planners and managers have dismissed the WCD approach as impractical. And, citing the reservations of several governments in borrowing countries, notably China and India, the World Bank has refused to endorse it, supporting a managerial approach of internal-rate-of-return cost-benefit analysis. The other side, "movementists", is also sceptical, believing there would be "window dressing", in which power relations would prevail. Nevertheless, recognition of rights should be part of any policy decision.

Policy decisions in relation to poverty have had a tendency to differentiate between the so-called "deserving " and "undeserving" poor — an unedifying moralistic distinction. Another tendency should be equally avoided — that of targeting the "easy to assist", which may be a danger of policymaking and evaluations based on target indicators or quantitative "goals" (even Millennium Development Goals).

As for the Paternalism Test Principle, policies or conventional practices that constrain choice, however well intentioned, should be regarded as *prima facie* inappropriate unless demonstrated to be otherwise, and even then only if carefully monitored so that policymakers and policy implementers are held accountable. Policies that are made conditional on "normal" behaviour do not qualify. In assessing conventional relations of production and distribution, dependent security clearly fails the test. If a person or family has to rely on a patron to give them basic security, that is scarcely real security. The same is the case with all forms of bonded labour. Within families, patriarchal structures may provide women with apparent security, but if they have no sense of control over their lives such structures would not pass the Paternalism Test Principle.

---

[21]J. Rawls: *Theory of Justice* (Cambridge, Cambridge University Press, 1973).

1.13 Reflections

It is our underlying proposal that basic economic security requires basic income security coupled with sustainable Voice representation security. The one without the other would be inadequate. Representation security requires both individual rights — strongly advanced in some affluent countries, such as the United States — and collective rights in the form of solidaristic representation. In very few if any countries are both individual and collective representation security rights strong. Ensuring that there are equally strong individual and collective rights for all legitimate interests is a central challenge of the 21st century.

Before continuing, let us acknowledge several caveats.

First, like poverty, development and freedom, the notion of security has a vagueness that is both an attractive feature and a potential drawback. A danger is that it could lead to a policy agenda equivalent to an à la carte approach to human rights. The powerful may claim that they are doing whatever they can "to promote security" when in reality all they might be doing is promoting their own interests. This is why it is essential to have a clear definition of economic security and to formulate clear principles of policy for security.

Second, one can have too much security. It can be excessive instrumentally, for the stable functioning of society, for economic growth, and for freedom itself. And it can be excessive intrinsically. A totally secure person may easily become complacent, indolent and drift into a self-destructive lifestyle. Moreover, it is part of the human condition to have what might be called existential insecurity, a worry about our children, our spouses and others close to us.

Firms and societies could suffer analogous fates from excessive security. The basic security espoused by this report is of a type that should encourage legitimate risk-taking and innovations, and that can encourage each person to internalize and educate others to extend the social reciprocities that promote society (civil discourse and civil friendship) and social solidarity.

Chapter 2   The liberalization context of insecurity

"Globalization creates unprecedented new opportunities for sustainable development and poverty reduction."
Making Globalization Work for the Poor, United Kingdom Government White Paper, December 2000.

"The most profound danger to world peace in the coming years will stem not from the irrational acts of states or individuals but from the legitimate demands of the world's dispossessed."

Nobel Peace Prize Laureates, December 2001

2.1 Introduction

After the Second World War, world leaders made an unprecedented commitment to the promotion of social and economic security. The world was expected to move steadily to situations in which most citizens of the industrialized world were protected by social services, transfers and institutions that provided a dense network of security "from cradle to grave". In most of the developing world — even if there was an awareness that it was not possible quickly to provide this type of security — there was commitment to achieve it. Economic growth and development were built on security, and were expected to strengthen security — the means and the ends were twins.

Compare the situation nearly 60 years on. A feature of the currently orthodox model of growth is that labour insecurity, in the guise of "flexibility", is portrayed as a desirable (if not essential) engine of growth. Now it seems that not only is social and economic security a "barrier" to growth, but also that there is no reason to believe it should be a major development goal at all. People are expected to adapt to a world of insecurity.

This chapter is not intended to be a tour of "globalization and its discontents". Others have done that.[1] It simply aims to indicate some of the main contextual factors that seem to lead in the direction of increased economic insecurity, including slower and more volatile economic growth rates, unstable trade

and financial flows, loss of policy control by national governments, and the shift in many countries to policies consciously aimed at reducing security and increasing "flexibility" and individual responsibility for risk.

2.2 The Washington Consensus

The process now known as globalization began in the 1970s and 1980s with a number of coincidental changes. These included a switch of dominant technological paradigms (from "mass production" to microelectronics), major institutional shake-ups in international financial markets, and the construction of global supply chains by transnational corporations (TNCs) — in particular by transferring labour-intensive assembly operations to low-wage developing countries.

"Globalization" can be dated from the severing of the gold-dollar link in 1971. The process was reinforced by the abolition in 1974 of exchange controls on capital movements to and from the United States, and by the removal in 1975 of most barriers to entry to the New York Stock Exchange (followed by the London Stock Exchange). These events boosted international capital mobility and "competitive deregulation" in the 1980s.

_____

[1] See, for example, J. Stiglitz: *Globalization and its Discontents* (London, Allen Lane, 2002).

In the minds of many, globalization has become equated with global application of the so-called "Washington Consensus", which can be taken as implying 11 key policy commitments:

1. international financial market liberalization;
2. domestic capital market liberalization;
3. trade liberalization (particularly in developing countries);
4. labour market "flexibility";
5. secure individual property rights over physical and financial assets;
6. weak property rights over human assets (particularly skills);
7. a reduction in the size and role of the public sector, including privatization of publicly-owned productive assets, and an end to managed trade and industrial policies;
8. a system of taxation that is not only less progressive but also shifts taxes from capital to labour, and subsidies from labour to capital;
9. independent central banks (as part of a more general move towards the "technocratization" of economic policymaking);
10. a "social safety net" type of approach to social protection: i.e., more targeting, selectivity and conditionality;
11. privatization and liberalization of social policy.

Underlying this policy package is the belief that national governments must accept less "discretionary" power over national policymaking and adapt to the dictates of a global model, identified and promoted by the Washington-based international financial institutions. These institutions can in a sense be described as the midwives of globalization, and of economic liberalization in particular.

The International Monetary Fund (IMF), the World Bank and their regional associates have played an increasingly powerful role in shaping domestic policies, by ratcheting up the conditions attached to their discretionary provision of loans, grants and "technical assistance". In the past decade or so, these conditions have extended to the privatization and liberalization of social policy. Conditionality accentuates social and economic insecurity. It means not just that governments of poor countries lose control over their policymaking, but that they ultimately become less responsible for it too.

Moreover, the international financial agencies are undemocratic and unaccountable.[2] They are dominated by the G8 nations, which hold 49% of the votes. All major decisions require an 85% majority. So, as the United States has 17%, it can veto any resolution, even if every other country supports it. In practice, United States' voting strength ensures that IMF and World Bank support is given on terms acceptable to Washington.

The rules of the World Trade Organization (WTO), created in 1995, also constrain domestic policy to a far greater degree than before, when the WTO's predecessor, the General Agreement on Tariffs and Trade (GATT), concerned itself mainly with tariffs and trade in manufactures. WTO rules now cover many issues once considered the sovereign territory of governments, including industrial policy, farm subsidies, regulation of services, and intellectual property protection.

While the WTO is in principle more "democratic" than the international financial agencies — decisions are made by consensus, which gives each country, however small, the theoretical right of veto — in practice the big trading powers have a predominant say in setting the trade agenda and determining the outcome of negotiations. This has led to what many developing countries claim is a persistent bias in WTO rules against their interests, including constraints on use of industrial policy and failure to tackle the huge subsidies rich nations pay to their farmers and industrial corporations (see section 2.5).

In general, there has been a steady move away from what has been known as the Westphalian system, which granted states jurisdiction over their own territories, to what has been called "the new liberal cosmopolitanism", whereby national sovereignty is limited by institutions of a global order, set up to uphold liberal internationalism based on common legal norms and free trade.[3] This idea underlies the notion of *global governance*.

---

[2]The need to make them more democratic has been made by various bodies. See, for instance, World Commission on the Social Dimension of Globalization: *A Fair Globalization: Creating Opportunities for All* (Geneva, ILO, 2004).

[3]P. Taylor: "The United Nations in the 1990s: Proactive cosmopolitanism and the issue of sovereignty", *Political Studies*, No. 47, 1999, pp. 538–565.

Three trends are altering the governance of social, economic and labour market policy. One is the strengthening of the architecture of global governance through international agencies, many of which are seeking an enlarged role, largely to enhance the extent of market forces. Second is a strengthening of *regional blocs*, which may be interpreted as stepping stones on the route to full globalization, or as a means of offering regional economies a partial shield against global insecurities and instability.

Third, working in the opposite direction, there are pressures within states to decentralize responsibilities, reflecting a desire by central governments to cut back on their financial and administrative commitments. There is concern in many countries that, unless properly handled, this can accentuate inequalities and governance failure, including ineffective regulation of economic activities (see section 2.9).

The policy package of the Washington Consensus has also increased a tendency to discredit "politicians" at the expense of "entrepreneurs" and "technocrats", and shrinking the role of the state. It has thereby enhanced the independent power of supposedly neutral technical institutions, such as central banks, over "biased political" structures. It has led to the concentration of a globalized mass media, such that a small, seemingly shrinking number of individuals and corporations dominate the distribution of "information" and "news". And it has tended to replace collective entitlements by individual contributions. All of these — and there are others — have accentuated a widespread sense of powerlessness and insecurity.

2.3 Globalization — a paradigm for instability?

The world's economy has become both more "integrated" and more unstable, as we show in the next section. Thus, for example, the year 2002 started with the biggest ever default of a national economy — the economic and political implosion in Argentina — and the world's biggest corporate collapse of all time, with the bankruptcy of Enron, followed by WorldCom and a series of others. Before that, there was the Brazilian financial crisis of 1999, the Russian debt default and economic plunge in 1998, the East Asian financial crisis in 1997, the economic implosion of central and eastern Europe in the mid-

1990s, and the Mexican "Tequila" crisis in 1994. These disasters have thrown millions of people into devastating economic insecurity.

The outstanding economic features of the era of globalization are several. First, trade has doubled its share of global income since 1970 and now accounts for about a quarter of world GDP. Intra-firm trade has increased from about a fifth to over one-third of total trade over the same period.[4]

While trade has for many countries become an important engine of economic growth, it also amplifies the impact of economic shocks elsewhere in the world. To take just one example, the bursting of the telecom "bubble" in 2001, and the huge cutback in information technology (IT) investment that followed, had severe knock-on effects for East Asian economies such as Singapore and Taiwan (China), which recorded their worst trade and output performance for 30 years. According to the World Trade Organization, the slump in demand for IT products accounted for most of the slowdown in world trade seen in 2001. Increasing global interdependence brings with it increasing vulnerability for economies, while growing economic specialization induced by trade (on the "comparative advantage" principle) implies sometimes wrenching adjustments by workers and communities that inevitably produces insecurity (see also section 2.5).

Second, there has been a large increase in *foreign capital flows*, which have also become more volatile (section 2.6). Official aid in real terms has declined (section 2.7), so the growth has come in private capital flows that tend to be both unstable and pro-cyclical.[5] In 1990 private flows made up less than half of total resource flows to developing countries of about USD100 billion. In 2002 private flows

[4] United Nations Conference on Trade and Development (UNCTAD): *World Investment Report 2003* (Geneva, 2003).

[5] S. Griffith-Jones and J.A. Ocampo: "Facing the Volatility and Concentration of Capital Flows", in J.J. Teunissen (ed.): *Reforming the International Financial System: Crisis Prevention and Response*, The Hague, FONDAD, 2001; A. Singh and A. Zammit: "International capital flows: Identifying the gender dimension", *World Development*, Vol. 28, No. 7, 2000, pp. 1249–1268; J.E. Stiglitz: "Capital market liberalization, economic growth, and instability", *World Development*, Vol. 28, No. 6, 2000, pp.1075–1086.

accounted for three-quarters of total resource flows of just under USD200 billion. At the same time, short-term capital flows (portfolio investment and bank loans) surged from USD20 billion in 1990 to nearly USD150 billion in 1996, only to turn negative in 2001 and 2002.[6] Foreign direct investment (FDI), while less mobile than portfolio investment or bank credits, can also be fickle — increasing insecurity for many countries. Despite the recent downturn, FDI inflows are now by far the biggest component of net resource flows to the developing world. For some countries, foreign-owned enterprises account for over half total investment and trade. Half the exports by China, the world's biggest FDI recipient and its fourth largest exporter, are generated by transnational corporations.

At the same time as developing nations are facing larger and more volatile capital flows, their ability to cope with these through controls and restrictions has been consistently eroded. Until very recently, capital account liberalization was a condition of IMF lending to countries in difficulty and it is still insisted upon by the United States in its bilateral dealings. The United States bilateral trade pact with Chile signed in 2003, for instance, obliges Chile to renounce its right to use (previously successful) capital controls on inflows and outflows, and almost any trade and industrial policy measures. Commenting on this aspect of United States trade policy, Joseph Stiglitz said: *"One of the main dissatisfactions with globalization is precisely that it tends to deprive LDCs of the freedom to apply policies that can protect their economies and their citizens. It seems that special interests in industrialized countries have precedence over broader interests"*.[7]

Third, there has been considerable *financial market integration*, which almost definitionally impinges on the autonomy of national policymakers. Global foreign exchange transactions and short-term financial flows have soared, while financial markets increasingly move together in response to the same events and shocks. In the past, investment diversification internationally was a way of reducing risk; as some markets went down, others went up. Now, movements in the United States stock market, for instance, have an 80% correlation with movement of European stocks, whereas 20 years ago this statistic was only 40%. Financial globalization has also led to more intense competition between international banks for lending, and between fund managers

"to beat the market". The increase in short-termism and "herd" behaviour has amplified market volatility and raised risks for most investors, including the many individuals encouraged to put their faith — and pension investments — in stocks and bonds (see section 2.10).

Fourth, all over the world policymakers have been racing to make their markets more *competitive*, and in particular to increase incentives to invest and to reduce what are perceived as regulatory rigidities (see section 2.9). Labour markets have been subject to a whole series of changes intended to increase flexibility and lower labour costs. This contrasts with the prevailing wisdom in the preceding "Keynesian" era, when high or rising wages were seen as a means not only of boosting aggregate demand, and thus employment, but of raising productivity.[8] The emphasis on "competitiveness" has led to various ways of lowering wages and weakening the means of securing wage growth, issues considered in Chapter 3.

> **Lest we forget**
>
> "A plentiful subsistence increases the bodily strength of the labourer; and the comfortable hope of bettering his conditions and ending his days perhaps in ease and plenty animates him to exert that strength to the outmost."
>
> — Adam Smith, 1776.
>
> "A low wage business is always insecure."
>
> — Henry Ford, 1922.

A fifth trend is the re-orientation of *fiscal policy*. Traditionally, taxation was used to raise revenue to pay for public services and administration, and to reduce inequality by redistributing from the rich to the poor. But elites have successfully diverted taxation away from being an arm of progressive social policy.

---

[6] UNCTAD, 2003, op. cit., p. 4.

[7] Interview published in the *Journal Valor Econômico*, Brazil, 5 Feb. 2003.

[8] It may be recalled that, in the early 1960s, United States' wage-productivity guidelines stipulated that wages should rise proportionately to productivity growth.

Mexico — Ironies of globalization

In Mexico, after liberalization and the establishment of the North American Free Trade Agreement (NAFTA) in 1994, manufacturing exports and employment rose sharply for some years. However, real wages were lower at the end of the last century than 20 years previously despite a steady rise in productivity. The peso crisis of 1994-95 led to a drastic cut in wages that has not been recouped, enabling the owners of capital to make the major gains.

China's entry to the WTO in 2001 has had severe repercussions for Mexico, which sends more than 85% of its exports to the United States. Half its exports come from *maquiladoras*, in-bond assembly plants along the United States border employing low-wage low-skilled labour. Many of these jobs have shifted elsewhere, perhaps to China, which has much lower wages and almost equal access to the United States market. According to Mexican Central Bank data, 160,000 workers lost their jobs as a result of this exodus between June 2001 and February 2002 alone, i.e., one in eight *maquiladora* workers, mainly in electronics and textiles.

What is historically unique, but probably a sign of things to come, is that according to official data these 160,000 workers were blamed for having "priced themselves out of a job" because they had used their bargaining power to restrict their real-wage cut to "only" one-third in the 20-year period between April 1982 and April 2002.

There are several relevant aspects of the evolution of fiscal policy. First, tax on capital has been whittled away globally. Second, there has been a shift of tax incidence from capital to labour, in part because of import liberalization that has reduced the tax take. Third, the world has witnessed the growth of what might be called the subsidizing state, with over USD1 trillion paid out in subsidies in the mid-1990s or about 4% of global GDP.[9] Subsidies provided by developing countries equalled about 6.3% of their GDP — about a third of total government expenditure.

Fourth, in developed countries, in particular, there has been a *fiscalization of social policy*, by which fiscal sticks and carrots have been used to shape and condition individual behaviour, an inherently paternalistic policy.[10] This includes a rising incidence of labour subsidies, including so-called tax credits, which are in effect subsidies on low-wage labour. We will come back to this in considering global regulation.

2.4 Economic growth and volatility

Globalization has been defined as a regime of open markets based on free trade and free capital markets. Theoretically it should also include free labour markets involving free movement of labour between countries, which presumably should increase global economic efficiency in much the same way that free trade and free capital movements are expected to

do. But such migration is ruled out by political factors, mostly in rich countries.

Proponents of globalization, and the Washington Consensus in general, have long contended that a system of open integrated economies promotes higher rates of economic growth and reduces economic instability. What is the evidence?

Let us start with the growth record. Probably the best data-set to investigate what has happened to economic growth is the World Bank's WDI (World Development Indicators) databank; presented at constant 1995 USD, this gives information for the G7 and for 59 developing countries for 1960–2000.

Figure 2.1 shows that there was a downward trend in the rate of economic growth of developing countries after 1980 and an increase in the volatility of growth. Statistics refer to individual country growth rates and, unless otherwise stated, coefficients of variation are multiplied by 10. Although the great majority of countries had lower growth in 1980–2000 than in 1960-80, China and India (with Bangladesh) are notable exceptions (Figure 2.2).

---

[9]C. Van Beers and A. de Moor: *Public Subsidies and Policy Failures* (Northampton, Edward Elgar, 2001). See also W. Ascher: *Why Governments Waste Natural Resources: Policy Failures in Developing Countries* (Baltimore, Johns Hopkins University Press, 1999); N. Myers and J. Kent: *Perverse Subsidies: How Tax Dollars can Undercut the Environment and the Economy* (London, Island Press, 2001).

[10]This is analysed elsewhere. G. Standing, *Beyond the New Paternalism* (London, Verso, 2002).

Figue 2.1 Developing countries (59): Annual GDP growth (%) and variability, 1960-80 and 1980-2000

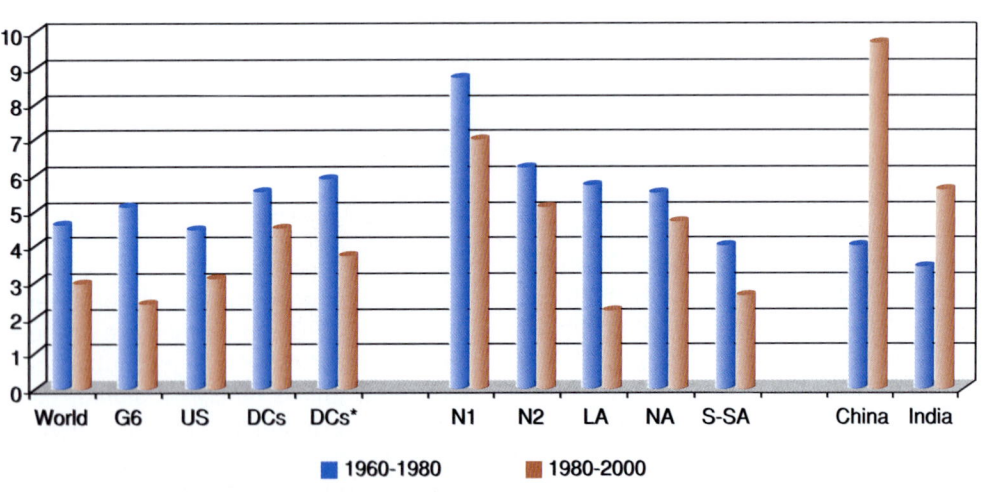

Source: World Bank: *World Development Indicators 2003*.

Figure 2.2 Regional diversity: Annual GDP growth (%), 1960–80 and 1980–2000

G6 = Canada, France, Germany, Italy, Japan and United Kingdom. US = United States. DCs = aggregate output of 59 developing countries. DCs* = DCs, excluding China and India. N1 = first-tier NICs (Hong Kong, China; Republic of Korea; Singapore and Taiwan, China). N2 = second-tier NICs (In donesia, Malaysia, Philippines and Thailand). LA = Latin American countries. NA = North Africa (Algeria, Egypt, Mo-rocco and Tunisia). S-SA = sub-Saharan countries, excluding South Africa.

Source: World Bank: *World Development Indicators 2003*.

The average annual growth rate of world output declined from 4.6% to 2.8% in these two periods. In the first, world output grew 2.5-fold, in the second only 1.7-fold. For G7 countries the slowdown was marked, from 5.1% to 2.4% a year. Even in the United States — in spite of the prosperity of the Clinton years — the average growth rate in the second period (3.2%) was below that of the first (3.5%). And despite China's and India's size and remarkable growth, the overall rate of growth in the 59 developing countries fell from 5.5% to 4.5% annually. If China and India are excluded the decline was even more pronounced, from 5.8% to 3.7%.

Of the five developing regions, Latin America experienced the largest drop in growth, from 5.6% to 2.2% annually. Whereas in the first period output trebled, in the second growth was only half that. In only 12 of the 59 developing countries did growth increase in the second period — one in Latin America (Chile), three in Asia (China, India and Bangladesh) and eight in sub-Saharan Africa (Benin, Burkina Faso, Chad, Ghana, Guinea Bissau, Mauritius, Senegal and Sudan). Finally, although only one in every five countries managed higher growth in the second period, these included three of the five largest (China, India and Bangladesh) with 40% of the world's population; however, the other nine with faster growth in the second period are relatively small, representing less than 7% of the remaining developing-country population.

The average annual rate of growth of world GDP per capita fell by half between these two periods, from 2.4% to 1.1% (Figure 2.3). As a result, while in the first 20-year period this indicator expanded by 67%, in the second it increased by less than 30%. In the G6, the slowdown was greater than the average, falling from 4.3% to 2% (Figure 2.4). Even in the United States there was a decline in growth of GDP per capita. And in spite of the remarkable performance of China and India, and a slowdown in population growth, the per capita growth rate in developing countries fell from 3.1% to 2.7%.

Figure 2.3 Developing countries (59): Annual GDP per capita growth (%) and variability, 1960–80 and 1980–2000

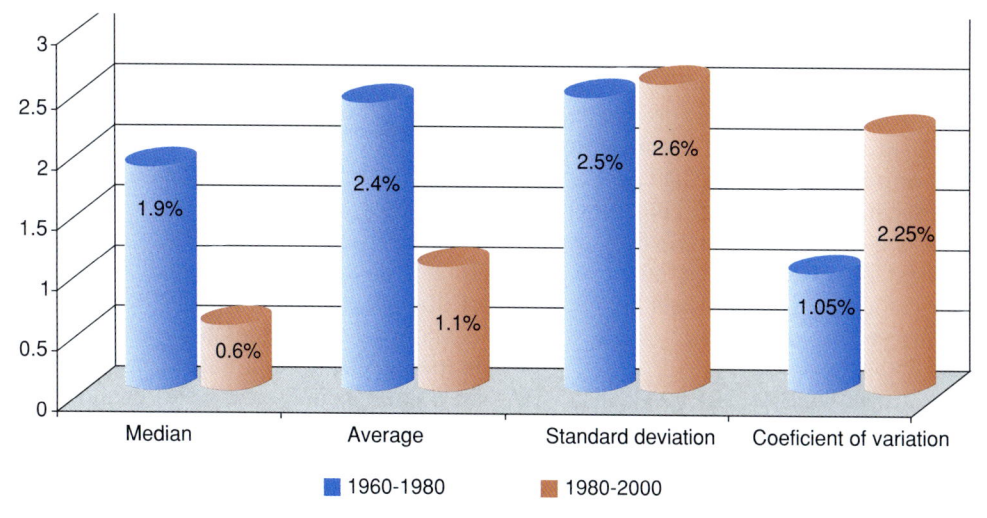

Source: World Bank: *World Development Indicators 2003*.

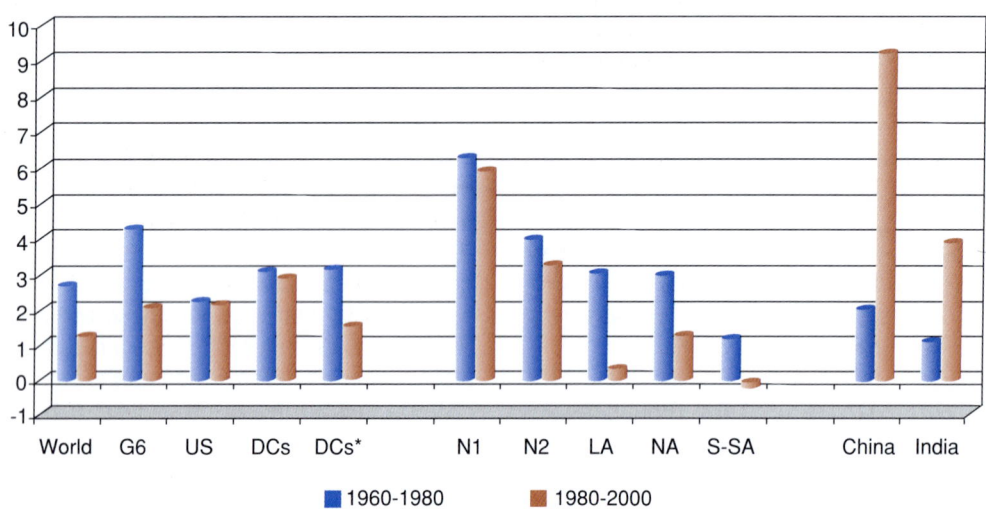

Figure 2.4. Regional diversity: Annual GDP per capita growth (%), 1960–80 and 1980–2000

■ 1960-1980   ■ 1980-2000

G6 = Canada, France, Germany, Italy, Japan and United Kingdom. US=United States DCs = aggregate output of 59 developing countries. DCs* = Developing countries, excluding China and India. N1 = first-tier NICs. N2 = second-tier NICs. LA = Latin American countries. NA = North Africa. S-SA = sub-Saharan countries, excluding South Africa.

Source: World Bank: *World Development Indicators 2003*.

Excluding China and India, the annual per capita growth rate for the other 57 developing countries fell by more than half, from 3.2% to 1.5%. Of all regions, Latin America had the largest decline, from 3% to just 0.4%. In the first period it almost managed to keep up with the increase in GDP per capita of the G7; in the second, "globalizing" Latin America had a growth rate one-fifth that of the G7. Even some large dynamic East Asian economies, such as Indonesia and the Philippines, posted lower per capita GDP growth in the second period.

With an average growth rate of GDP per capita of respectively 8.3%, 3.6% and 2.6% between 1980 and 2000 China, India and Bangladesh, with a combined population of 2.4 billion, were among a small number of countries with a better performance in the later period.

Thus globalization appears to have been associated with lower overall growth, a conclusion that does not change significantly if the periodization is altered. If the later period is divided into two sub-periods, 1980–90 and 1990–2000, economic growth was greater in the latter in most regions (and in the United States). Nevertheless, world GDP grew more slowly in both sub-periods than between 1960 and 1980.

It is also worth noting that India, while it grew faster in the second period than the first, did not grow significantly faster in the 1990s than in the 1980s. Thus it cannot be argued convincingly that the set of liberalizing policies of 1991 known as the New Economic Policy generated extra growth. Moreover, in the 1990s, agricultural and manufacturing output grew more slowly than previously. India's recent growth appears to be the result of rapid expansion of the financial services and communications sectors, which have delivered well-paid jobs to a minority of the Indian labour force. It has also led to a doubling of trade as a share of GDP, leaving the Indian economy more vulnerable to external shocks. Moreover, there are signs that some multinational companies are already shifting jobs and investment out of India, to lower-cost countries and, in the case of services involving direct contact with customers, back home.

There is a further way of looking at relative performance in the globalization era. After all, the orthodox view is that increased competition and extensive privatization should have resulted in much greater economic dynamism. The information technology revolution should also have boosted growth. Yet global economic performance was unimpressive.

What then of the claim that globalization has reduced economic instability? It seems if anything that the global economy has become more prone to economic crises, involving deep sudden downturns that spread from one country or region of the world to others. Even the IMF has accepted this. Perhaps reflecting its failure to predict the Asian crisis, the IMF stated in 1999 that crises have become "more severe and even less predictable and to come in waves".[11]

Figure 2.5 shows increased volatility of growth rates in 1980–2000 compared with 1960–80 in the G6, in the first-tier and second-tier Newly Industrializing Countries, in sub-Saharan Africa and above all in Latin America. The major exceptions are China and India. Figure 2.5 shows actual values for coefficients of variation (in other graphs they are multiplied by 10). If all developing countries were included (particularly the missing 15, mostly troubled, sub-Saharan countries), median per capita GDP growth in the second period would be close to zero.

Figure 2.5 G6, United States and DCs (59): Average coefficient of variation of annual GDP growth (%), 1960–80 and 1980–2000

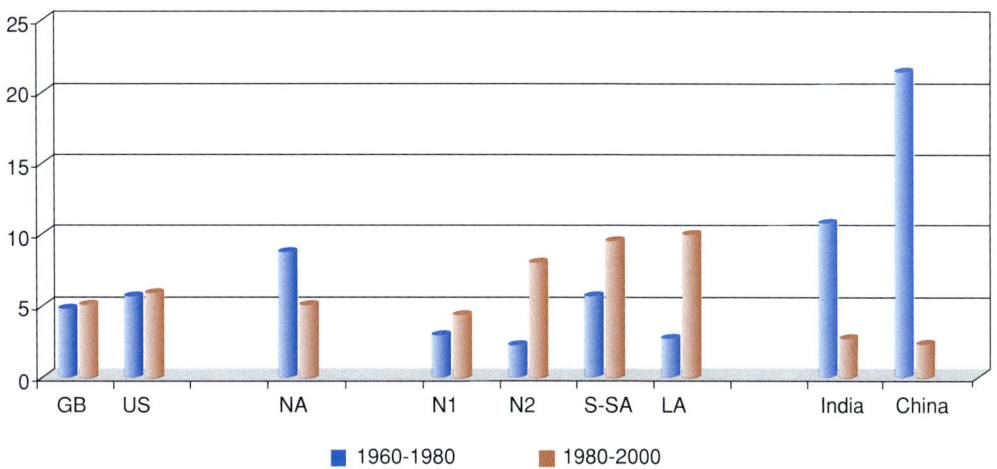

G6 = Canada, France, Germany, Italy, Japan and United Kingdom. US=United States. N1 = first-tier NICs. N2 = second-tier NICs. LA = Latin America. NA = North Africa. S-SA = sub-Saharan Africa (including South Africa).

Source: World Bank: *World Development Indicators 2003.*

[11] IMF: *World Economic Outlook 1999* (Washington, DC, Oct. 1999), p. 68. This may prove to be more of a *mea culpa* than correct, since the capacity to predict may improve in the light of increased knowledge of factors that precede each crisis.

The same phenomena, notably the asymmetries between China, India and Bangladesh and almost every other country, are found in the growth rates of GDP per capita in these two periods (Figure 2.6).

Figure 2.6 G6, United States and DCs (59): Average coefficient of variation of annual GDP per capita growth (%), 1960–80 and 1980–2000

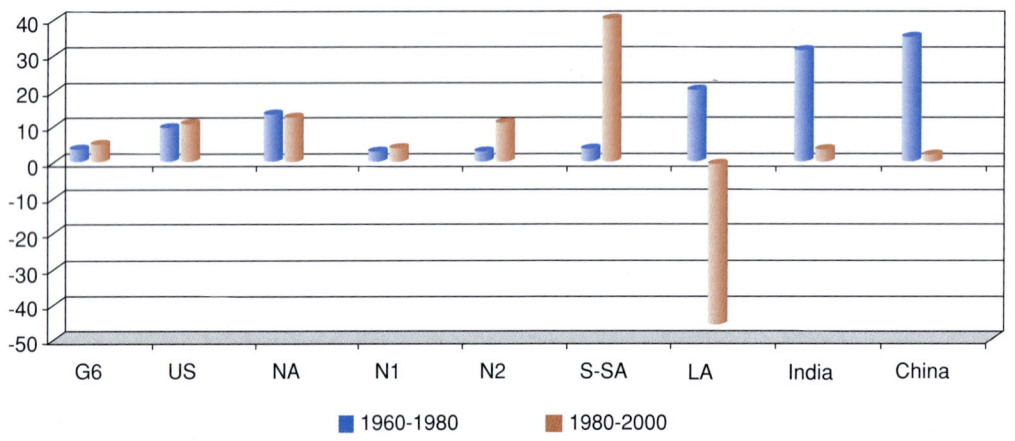

C6 = Canada, France, Germany, Italy, Japan and United Kingdom. US=United States. N1 = first-tier NICs. N2 = second-tier NICs. LA = Latin American countries. NA = North Africa. S-SA = Sub-Saharan countries, excluding South Africa.

Source: World Bank: *World Development Indicators 2003*.

Thus the evidence suggests that for many countries globalization generates instability. This seems to have been conceded by its proponents.[12] They now argue that this is the price countries pay for increased growth, and that instability can be coped with through a social security "safety net". But the growth record is at best unclear, while according to the orthodox theory, financial liberalization should engender economic stability. In fact, liberalization has been associated with currency and banking crises, which have created economic turbulence with drastic social consequences.[13]

The orthodox views have been challenged from several perspectives. In particular, critics make a distinction between trade liberalization (free trade) and financial liberalization (free capital mobility).[14] They argue that the former promotes economic growth, while the latter leads to lower growth and more economic instability and insecurity. Countries that have grown fast and industrialized have managed their trade opening, promoting export sectors while maintaining selective controls on imports, thus enabling them to achieve balance of payments equi-librium at high rates of economic growth. This learning-to-trade paradigm requires strong state co-ordination.

---

[12] See, e.g., K. Rogoff, et al.: *The Effects of Financial Globalization on Developing Countries: Some Empirical Evidence*, Occasional Paper 220 (Washington, DC, IMF, 2003); G. Kaminsky and S. Schmukler: *Short-Run Pain, Long-Run Gain: The Effects of Financial Liberalization*. IMF Working Paper 03/34 (Washington, DC, IMF, 2003). Note that volatility could be assessed in terms of standard deviation or by means of deviation from the regression line. The coefficient of variation seems to be the most appropriate, given the wide differences in average GDP growth rates of countries.

[13] A. Singh: "Asian capitalism and the financial crisis", in J. Eatwell and L. Taylor (eds.): *International Capital Markets: Systems in Transition* (Oxford, Oxford University Press, 2002).

[14] See, for example, D. Rodrik: *The New Global Economy and Developing Countries: Making Openness Work*. Policy Essay No. 24 (Washington, DC, Overseas Development Council, 1999); J. Bhagwati: *Why Free Capital Mobility may be Hazardous to your Health: Lessons from the Latest Financial Crisis*, remarks prepared for the NBER Conference on Capital Controls (Cambridge, MA, 7 Nov. 1998); Stiglitz, 2002, op. cit.

By contrast, financial opening is fraught with risks that cannot easily be overcome by governments of developing countries. And even the IMF has concluded:

"There is little evidence that financial integration has helped developing countries to better stabilize fluctuations in consumption growth, notwithstanding the theoretically large benefits that could accrue to developing countries in this respect. In fact, new evidence... suggests that low to moderate levels of financial integration may have made some countries subject to even greater volatility of consumption relative to that of output. Thus, while there is no proof in the data that financial globalization has benefited growth, there is evidence that some countries may have experienced greater consumption volatility as a result".[15]

Other reasons for doubting whether financial liberalization stabilizes growth include the view that liberalization increases competition between banks (and other financial institutions), leading them to take on more risky business and customers, and induces corporations and financial institutions to take a short-term approach to their activities.[16]

Finally, what has happened to the differences between countries in the era of globalization? In the middle-income group, only the six East Asian countries seem to be "catching up" with the G7 (Figure 2.7). In the low-income group, China was the only country with a relative income per capita much above what it was in 1960 (Figure 2.8). Indonesia and the Philippines (with a combined population of 286 million) were roughly back at 1960 levels, while India (as well as Bangladesh), in spite of rapid growth in the second part of the period, had still not recovered lost ground.

In sum, in the era of globalization, many countries experienced lower growth, while the volatility of growth of GDP and GDP per capita increased. The lower rates and the greater volatility of growth in most developing countries are two phenomena that could be expected to have a negative effect on economic security. And while rapid recent growth in China and India has undoubtedly pulled large numbers of people out of desperate poverty it may have increased insecurity as traditional ways of life and support systems have been disrupted (see box on China in the following section).

Figure 2.7 Middle income DCs: GDP per capita as a share of G7 GDP per capita

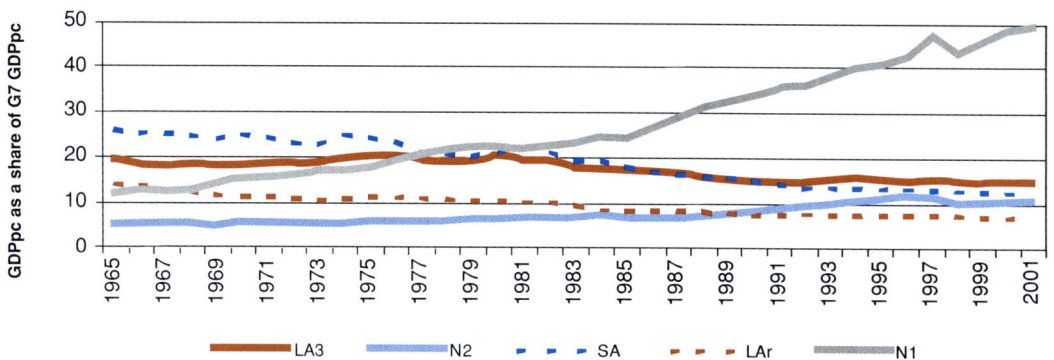

SA = South Africa. LA3 = Brazil, Mexico and Argentina. LAr = rest of Latin America. N1 = first-tier NICs. N2 = Malaysia and Thailand.

Source: World Bank: *World Development Indicators 2003.*

[15] IMF, 2003, op. cit.

[16] J. Furman and J.E. Stiglitz: *Economic Crises: Evidence and Insights from East Asia.* Brookings Papers on Economic Activity No.2 (Washington, DC, Brookings Institution, 1999); H. Kaufman: *On Money and Markets: A Wall Street Memoir* (New York, McGraw Hill, 2000); J. Williamson: *Prospects for Curbing the Boom-Bust Cycle in the Supply of Capital to Emerging Markets*, Discussion Paper No.2002/3 (Helsinki, WIDER, United Nations University, 2002).

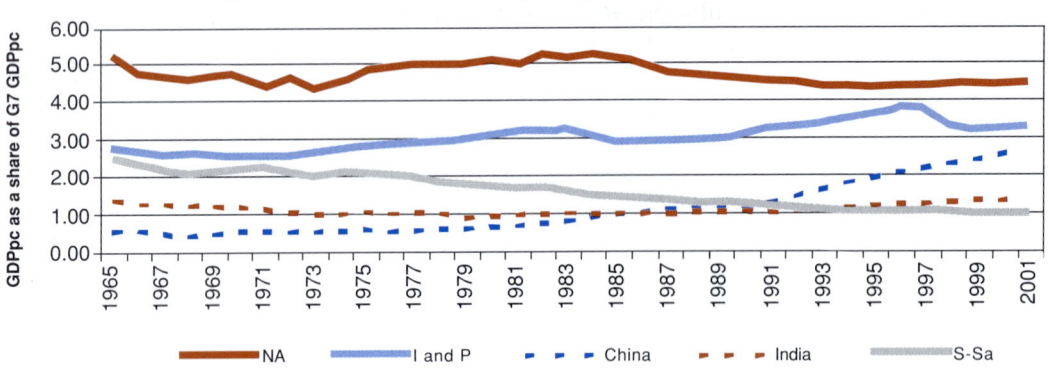

Figure 2.8 Low income DCs: GDP per capita as a share of G7 GDP per capita

NA = North Africa; I and P = Indonesia and the Philippines; S-SA = sub-Saharan Africa (excluding South Africa).

Source: World Bank: *World Development Indicators 2003.*

What of the future? Here, we would just note that one factor for instability in the global economy is its heavy dependence on the performance of the United States economy to generate growth. Yet many commentators, including the IMF, believe that the huge United States current account and public sector deficits are unsustainable and risk precipitating a dollar crisis, rising interest rates and a deep world recession. A related worry is growing political pressure to raise United States trade barriers, particularly to protect labour-intensive sectors such as textiles.

According to the United States Treasury Department, debt owed to foreign governments, central banks, private banks and other investors reached USD6.4 trillion in late 2003; by comparison, total taxes and other public revenue taken by the United States Government is about USD2 trillion a year. The budget deficit for 2002–03 approached USD400 billion and is predicted to exceed USD500 billion in 2003–04.

By the end of 2002, United States net external debt was 25% of GDP, and the IMF predicts that it could grow to 40% of GDP within a few years. Meanwhile, the trade deficit has been growing steadily, and is now running at half a trillion dollars annually. To finance the resulting current account deficit, now 5% of GDP, the United States needs to attract USD1.5 billion in overseas capital every day of the year.[17]

Thus American prosperity seems to depend on the rest of the world continuing to hold a large and rising proportion of United States assets. By 2000, this share was equivalent to 67% of United States GDP, up from 46% in 1995.[18] Much of that consists of bonds and equities that can be quickly sold — an inherently unstable situation.

2.5 Trade and the World Trade Organization

The World Trade Organization (WTO) has emerged as a primary global rule-setting agency, a role enhanced by its dispute adjudication process. Though each of the WTO's 146 members in theory has an equal voice, the "Quad" (United States, European Union, Canada and Japan) and a fairly small number of the larger developing countries have a preponderant influence.

Current international trade rules raise three main concerns. The first is the extent to which they continue to legitimate a pattern of economic disadvantage for many of the world's poorest and most insecure nations and people. For instance, rich countries have been allowed to continue to subsidize their farmers to the tune of over USD300 billion a year, shutting out imports from developing countries and undercutting their goods at home and in third markets. In effect, subsidized food is

---

[17] P. Kammerer: "Big-spending United States could fuel global crisis, says IMF", *South China Morning Post*, 9 Jan. 2004.

[18] Board of Governors of the Federal Reserve System: *Flow of Funds Accounts of the United States* (Washington, DC, 2001).

strengthening the security of rich-country producers and worsening the insecurity of poor-country farmers. Most of those subsidies, moreover, go to agri-business companies and large-scale farms rather than to impoverished or economically insecure small-scale farmers.

Requiring developing countries to subscribe to strict rules on intellectual property protection has also exacerbated insecurity. Simulations by the World Bank suggest that the WTO's agreement on Trade-Related Aspects of Intellectual Property (TRIPs) could almost quadruple the USD15 billion a year that developing countries paid industrialized nations in technology licence fees in 1998.[19] The high prices charged for patented AIDS drugs have also been a contributory factor in denying most African sufferers access to treatment (though more recently there have been moves to bring prices down dramatically). Lack of treatment has amplified the terrible insecurity in much of Africa caused by the AIDS pandemic, which is killing more than 6,000 people every day and has already left millions of orphans to fend for themselves.

The present trade round, known as the "Doha Development Agenda", has been billed as a development round aimed at redressing the balance of trade rules, especially in agriculture. But negotiations have stalled in the wake of the failed WTO meeting in Cancun in September 2003, and the European Union and the United States have shown themselves reluctant to make the big cuts in farm subsidies demanded by developing countries.

A second concern relates to WTO rules prohibiting the use of various industrial policy measures, including subsidies and local content requirements for foreign investment. Critics point out that some of the currently industrialized countries used such measures when they were industrializing.[20] Why should they have had that privilege and not currently industrializing countries? The effect of these international trade rules, pushed through by richer nations during the 1986-94 Uruguay round, is to further constrain policy choices by poor WTO members.

A third and important feature of the WTO for social and economic security of ordinary people around the world is the General Agreement on Trade in Services (GATS). Though the GATS does not require privatization and liberalization of public and social services, there are fears that countries will come under pressure to do so as part of the Doha round negotiations. Thus the European Union has asked trading partners to admit European companies into their water and energy sectors, while the United States has sought to increase access for its private education suppliers. Once foreign companies have entered the market, the GATS protects them from eviction and requires them to be treated on the same basis as domestic firms.

This said, a trading system based on multilateral rules gives countries more predictability and security than a free-for-all in which the most powerful can dictate terms at will. Though the WTO is dominated by the major traders, smaller countries can still influence trade policy by banding together to secure common interests — as they did in achieving an agreement at Doha in 2001 that puts public health concerns above patent protection for drugs. The failure of the WTO's Cancun meeting has raised the spectre of a proliferation of bilateral trade agreements, of which there are already over 300. Jagdish Bhagwati and other critics fear that these agreements, negotiated between highly unequal partners, could establish "templates" to be used subsequently to shape the multilateral system. The United States, for example, insists on conditions in bilateral accords relating to investment and intellectual property protection that go well beyond internationally agreed standards.

It should be noted that more open trade makes countries more dependent on developments in major export markets. There are continuing worries that trade barriers will go up in recession-hit industrialized countries, particularly to protect labour-intensive sectors subject to import penetration or other foreign competition. This is not a fear that is confined to manufacturing production. Already politicians in the United States are urging measures to prevent foreign outsourcing ("offshoring") of call centres and other service activities.

---

[19] World Bank: *Global Economic Prospects and the Developing Countries* (Washington, DC, 2002).

[20] See, for example, H.-J. Chang: *Kicking Away the Ladder* (London, Anthem Press, 2002).

In sum, the WTO has been instrumental in levering economic openness and liberalization of economic activities. However, the rules appear to have more effect in constraining policy choices by poor countries than those by richer WTO members. In particular, there has been little reduction in the

USD1 billion a day paid out to farmers in industrialized nations. The latest development is the potential consolidation of liberalization of social services in the GATS, which could restrict national policymaking to provide economic security through social services and social protection.

The WTO and China

The influence of China's integration into the global economic system is at an early stage. Accounting for about a quarter of the world's population and with an economy growing at about 8% a year, China's accession to the WTO and its deliberate process of pro-market reform will shape international developments for many decades.

Within China, the dislocation taking place dwarfs the adjustment process experienced in the rest of the world. One guesstimate by the United Nations Development Programme (UNDP) is that joining the WTO will lead to a loss of 40 million jobs due to the required abolition of employment-retaining subsidies.[21] The expectation is that more jobs will be generated in export-oriented sectors. But in the interim there will be a shift from false employment security (workers still on the payrolls of loss-making firms) to unprecedentedly by severe labour market and employment insecurity. China has introduced unemployment insurance and state pensions to cushion the adjustment costs. But the backlog of workers on extended lay-off coupled with the number displaced by structural changes will confront the authorities with an unprecedented challenge.

---

[21] Cited in *The Observer* (London), 27 Jan. 2002.

2.6 Foreign capital flows

Globalization has been associated with a massive increase in foreign capital flows, an increase in their volatility and some variations in their composition. For developing countries, a sense of the extent of variation can be gleaned from figure 2.9. The two

cycles reflect a fairly similar level of inflow in constant values, peak to peak. But there have been several compositional shifts; in particular, private capital flows have risen as a share of the total, and a greater share has come in (more footloose) portfolio and financial capital as opposed to foreign direct investment (FDI).

Figure 2.9 Africa, Asia and Latin America: Total net capital inflows in constant USD, 1970–2002

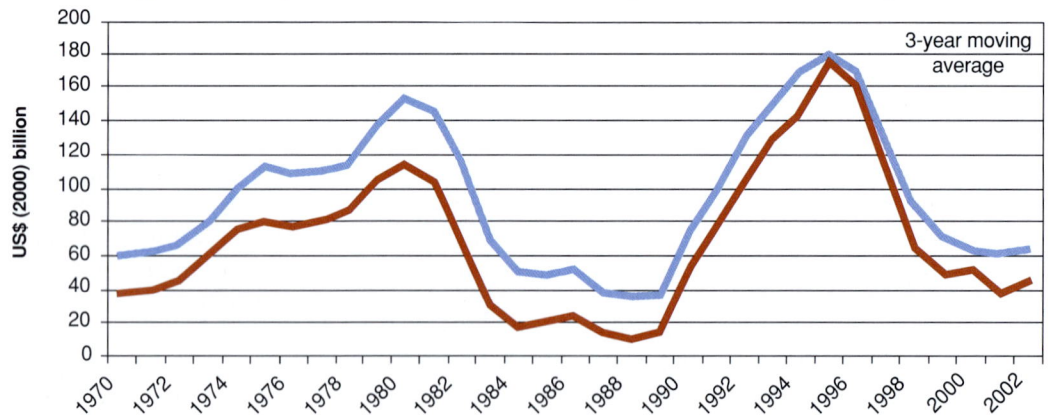

[T] = total net capital inflows; and [P] = net private inflows.

Note: Due to restrictions with the WEO data set, developing countries only include sub-Saharan Africa, Developing Asia and Latin America. However, in order to have an estimate for the whole African continent (and despite the problems of mixing data from IMF and World Bank sources), North Africa (Algeria, Morocco, Tunisia and Egypt) was added to sub-Saharan Africa using World Bank (Global Development Finance) data. All figures are in constant 2000 USD.

Source: IMF: *World Economic Outlook* (Washington, DC, IMF, 2003).

In addition, China has absorbed a growing share. Indeed, if China is excluded, in 2002 net private inflows into developing countries were negative, and in 2003 this trend continued. Of net FDI to developing countries between 1994 and 2002, three quarters went to just four developing countries: China, Brazil, Mexico and Argentina. The main "pull" factor in Mexico was the almost unrestricted access to the United States market after the North American Free Trade Agreement (NAFTA), while in Brazil and Argentina it was the privatization process, particularly of utilities.[22]

Large surges of capital to developing countries can be problematic. The flows are volatile, with outflows as much as 50% of inflows. The type and composition of the flows may not be what countries want or need. And where they account for a large proportion of GDP, as in small developing countries, changes can

have an impact that is hard to absorb. They also create a substantial increase in "factor payments" abroad (profit repatriation, interest and dividends). These have contributed to large negative transfers, notably from Latin America (Figure 2.10). Net outflows are also underestimated to the extent that multinationals use "transfer pricing" to reduce their size.

Figure 2.10 also indicates that, while FDI is conventionally regarded as more stable than bank loans or portfolio investment, it can have similar effects in making a country's finances more fragile by creating a stream of foreign exchange liabilities (in the form of dividend payments or profits repatriation). A short-term liquidity crisis can degenerate into a solvency crisis if other unfavourable factors intervene, as the experience of the Asian crisis countries also demonstrates.[23]

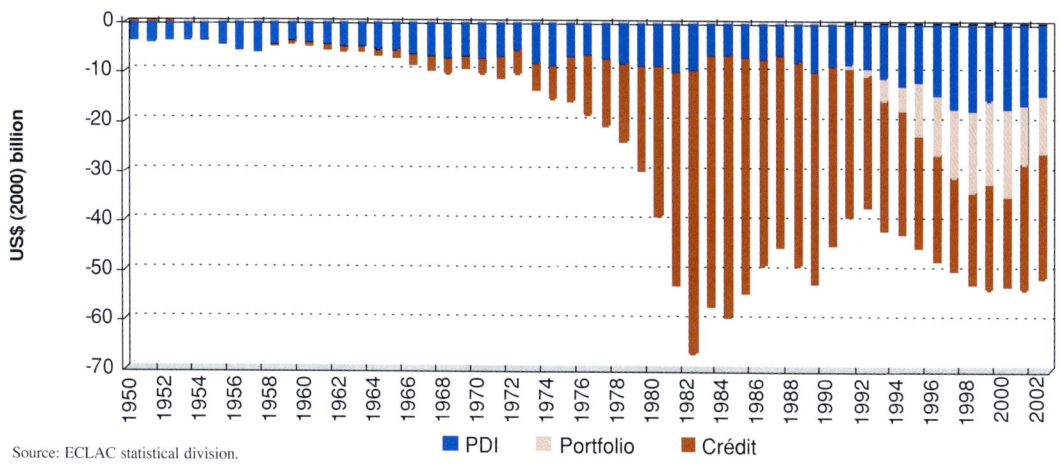

Figure 2.10 Latin America: Net factor payments abroad, 1950–2002

Source: ECLAC statistical division.

■ PDI   Portfolio   ■ Crédit

Further, for FDI to make a valuable contribution to economic development through promotion of technology and other spillovers, governments need to be able to monitor and regulate investment flows. However, industrialized countries are pushing, in the WTO and in bilateral investment agreements, for rules that restrict governments' ability to do this. The North American Free Trade Agreement, for example, has rules that allow multinationals to challenge new government regulations (such as environmental controls) that may affect them adversely.

Another feature of recent FDI is the multinationalization of production.[24] This means that more firms

are not only "multinational" in ownership and in location of production, but are also more amenable to switching their locus of production, particularly the assembly-end part of the value chain.

---

[22] Another feature, less often noticed, is that if China is excluded, most FDI (perhaps 90%) consists of take-overs (mergers and acquisitions). This puts a burden on weak stock markets.

[23] A. Singh: "Capital account liberalization, free long-term capital flows, financial crises and economic development", *Eastern Economic Journal*, Vol. 29, No. 2, Spring 2003, pp. 191–216.

[24] Between 1986 and 2000 global outflows of FDI increased at an annualized rate of over 26%, whereas exports of goods and services rose by 15.4%. UNCTAD: *World Investment Report 2001* (Geneva, UNCTAD, 2001).

This potential mobility has given their representatives enhanced power in their dealings with national and local governments. Often, that power works without it having to be exercised. Insecure policy-makers look anxiously at what foreign firms and investors want. One consequence is intense competition among countries to attract FDI, often at a high economic cost by way of subsidies or tax breaks.

The growth of FDI has also increased the elasticity of demand for labour.[25] In other words, in response to price and income variations, investment and employment vary to a greater extent and more rapidly than when there is little FDI.[26] This increased volatility of earnings and employment has increased the extent of economic insecurity among workers, as several studies have shown.[27] Indeed, some economists have argued that multinationals pay higher wages in part to compensate workers for the greater labour market volatility they anticipate.[28]

In sum, FDI has become an increasingly important source of investment for developing countries. But it is more volatile than domestic investment and depends on decisions taken in far-away boardrooms, with little if any local control or influence. These trends in themselves could be expected to increase economic insecurity.

2.7 Aid and debt

Most rich countries give a very small share of GDP in aid, and the total has fallen in real terms over the past two decades, as has the share of the United States (see Figure 2.11). In addition, more funds are being spent on immediate humanitarian needs rather than long-term development, and it is more than likely that the situation in Iraq and the so-called "war on terrorism" will affect the character and direction as well as the levels of aid provided for development purposes.

Figure 2.11 Aid to developing countries in USD billion (2002 prices), 1980-2002

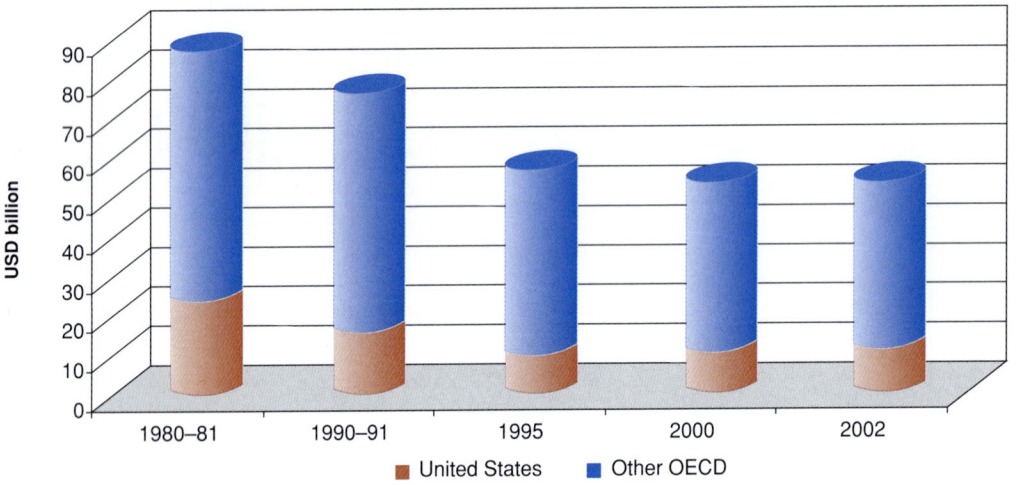

Source: J. Audley et al.: *Decoding Cancun: Hard Decisions for a Development Round,* Policy Brief No. 26, (Washington, DC, Carnegie Endowment, August 2003).

---

[25] M.J. Slaughter: "International trade and labour-demand elasticities", *Journal of International Economics*, Vol. 54, No. 1, 2001, pp. 27–56; F. Fabbri, J.E. Haskel and M.J. Slaughter: *Do Multinational Firms have More Elastic Labour Demands?* NBER Working Paper (Cambridge, MA, National Bureau of Economic Research, 2002). One suggestion is that it is driven by the greater substitutability of production labour and materials.

[26] Several studies have shown that multinational plants are more likely to close in response to economic downturns. See, e.g., Fabbri, Haskel and Slaughter, 2002, op. cit.; H. Gorg and E. Strobl: "Footloose multinationals?", *Manchester School*, 2002; A.B. Bernard and

J.B. Jensen: *The Death of Manufacturing Plants*, NBER Working Paper 9026 (Cambridge, MA, National Bureau of Economic Research, 2002).

[27] Rodrik showed a correlation between trade openness and growth volatility and government expenditure, deducing that globalization increased economic insecurity. D. Rodrik: *Has Globalization Gone Too Far?* (Washington, DC, Institute of International Economics, 1997).

[28] K.F. Scheve and M.J. Slaughter: *Economic Insecurity and the Globalization of Production*, NBER Working Paper 9339 (Cambridge, MA, National Bureau of Economic Research, 2002).

In recent years, donor countries have introduced a new instrument designed to influence government policymaking in low-income developing countries — Poverty Reduction Strategy Papers (PRSPs). The stated rationale of PRSPs is to increase aid-giving efficiency and foster improved *governance and accountability* of governments by drawing up a strategic plan to guide the coordinated disbursement of foreign aid and technical assistance.

A difficulty is that the process itself may fail simple tests of accountability, transparency and governance. Some observers argue that the claim that PRSPs strengthen national "ownership" of the policymaking process is moot, because donors have a coordinated single position and can thereby impose stronger conditionality. Others argue that the main outcome of PRSPs is to give the World Bank and IMF a greater coordinating role in the provision of aid and that, despite the rhetoric of poverty reduction, there is no emphasis given to redistribution, without which there is little prospect of substantial improvements in income security.

Reflecting *inter alia* the degree of integration and the resort to stabilization and adjustment policies, an alarming aspect of globalization is the scale of indebtedness of both the United States (see section 2.4) and developing countries. By the end of the 20th century, debt owed by developing countries to the IMF, World Bank, regional development banks, commercial banks and other financial institutions had risen to about USD2.5 trillion, more than the combined reserves of all the world's central banks. Many cannot repay the debt, and debt reduction plans have pushed numerous countries into the indignity and insecurity of losing control over national policy.

While more countries have become absorbed into the global economy, others, especially in Africa, have been cut off from global growth processes. There is a sense of *disconnectedness*, with no effective state to implement economic policies. Paradoxically, these countries are becoming more import dependent, but less export-competitive and investment attractive; this leads them to be cut off from capital flows, in particular from FDI.[29]

The situation of the African continent is the most alarming of all. Three-quarters of the world's poorest countries are in Africa, and economic growth overall was negative in the 1990s, leaving the average African living on less than USD2 a day.[30] Many countries are afflicted by chronic debt, rampant HIV/AIDS, drought and civil wars, while famine periodically hits the continent. Yet African countries have been forced to open up their economies, even though trade restrictions and subsidies in most OECD members impede their exports. Others are simply unable to take advantage of trade opportunities because they lack the physical and institutional infrastructure for exports.

2.8 Privatization and liberalization of social policy

The 1990s was the decade of economic privatization.[31] In that decade, 130 low-income and middle-income countries introduced private participation in infrastructure sectors, concentrated mainly in telecommunications and electricity. During those years, sales of state-owned companies worldwide amounted to more than USD600 billion, and the price paid by those acquiring them was often much less than their market value.

In Mexico, for example, the state-owned telecommunications company was sold in stages in the early 1990s for about USD9 billion; 18 months later, its market capitalization reached USD27 billion. In many other countries, similar rushed sales were orchestrated, benefiting those able to obtain the assets.

Although it had started in the 1980s and 1990s, the first decade of the 21st century may come to be regarded as *the decade of social policy privatization*. This has been led by pension reforms, initiated in Chile. But it has also affected healthcare and almost all other aspects of social benefits and services, including employment services, social care, prison services,[32] and education and training, as well as infrastructural public services such as water, sanitation, transport and energy.

---

[29] UNCTAD: *World Investment Report 2000* (Geneva, 2001).

[30] This is less than the subsidy of USD2.5 a day paid for each cow in the European Union!

[31] It took many forms, ranging from gentle partial liberalization measures to the predatory privatization of the ex-Soviet Union — *prikhvatizatsia*, in which the old *nomenklatura* turned de facto possession into de jure property rights, converting themselves into billionaires at the expense of society.

[32] See Chapter 5, section 5.9 on "The incarceration syndrome".

It is ironic that, at the same time as privatization is being extended to social policy on a large scale around the world, there is growing evidence of its high costs and deficiencies in providing adequate social protection. The switch to a private pension system has cost the Chilean government about 5% of GDP during the last 20 years (much more than it would have cost to eradicate poverty altogether); and there is little sign that this cost will fall in the near future. Less known is that in Argentina much of the public sector deficit, often blamed as the main cause of the December 2001 crisis, was due to the public expenditure needed to finance the switch of the pension fund from a public to a Chilean-style private system. Other countries have faced a similar drain on their national incomes.

Individuals too have faced higher costs, and often lower benefits as well, by the shift to individual pension accounts that obliges ordinary people themselves to bear — through their income in old age — the risks of the market. Privatized pension schemes have proved more expensive to governments than a basic state scheme would have been, while providing inferior benefits at greater risk and insecurity for contributors.

Privatization cannot sensibly be separated from *liberalization*. Essentially, the conventional wisdom is that public enterprises, especially monopolies, are both inefficient and contrary to "free markets". So governments have moved to mixed provision, allowing an increasing element of private competition where the public sector was once the sole provider, or indulging in some variant of "public—private" partnerships. Once that step is taken, external pressure builds up to allow foreign as well as national firms to enter the market and the WTO's GATS may then be used to make the presence of foreign firms a permanent feature.

There are several reasons for believing that privatization and liberalization are intensifying insecurity. Most worrying is when the state withdraws from a commitment to provide a social service or protection, leaving people to make their own arrangements. Such *de facto* privatization — withdrawal of a meals service, for example — is likely to leave unfilled gaps that intensify people's insecurity.

However, partial or complete privatization where a private provider does take over a service may also increase insecurity. For example, when public systems contract out part of their functions, concerns have been raised about the conditions of work of those providing the service, which often seem to deteriorate along with the services. One factor is that public sectors tend to be more unionized than the private substitutes.

Another worry is that private providers are likely to be more selective in the markets they wish to serve. They may wish to concentrate on those groups with the capacity to pay and those markets where the rates of return are high and relatively assured. Private providers are increasingly sophisticated in being able to calculate uninsurable risks, and are thus likely to wish to avoid coverage of people, communities and needs that could be costly. Governments can try to overcome this tendency, but doing so can be costly and inefficient. Regulations and subsidies are rather blunt policy instruments, particularly in developing countries where administrative machinery is weak.

A primary reason for citizens to be worried about privatization of services is that they are public goods that supply essential needs. Water, for example, is being privatized, accelerated by World Bank encouragement. In its latest *World Development Report*, the Bank states: "*There are few advantages to government's providing the service itself. That is why the past decade has seen many privatizations, concessions, and the like in water and energy.*"[33]

However, privatization inevitably prompts concerns (and insecurity) over such issues as discretionary supply, quality control and price. To some extent, these can be managed by establishment of effective *regulators* — separate from the providers, accountable, transparent, adequately funded and technically qualified. In many countries, these qualities are hard to ensure.

The combination of privatization and liberalization of social protection is likely to pose one of the major dilemmas of the early part of the 21st century. Will it lead, as some contend, to a social protection failure? Will social solidarity be undermined?

---

[33]World Bank: *World Development Report 2004: Making Services Work for Poor People* (Washington, DC, Sep. 2003), p. 28, para. 73.

Will democratic and cultural traditions be undermined by agendas determined by international financial agencies and elites? Will privatization lead to increased selectivity and conditionality in social protection provision? Will it lead to excessive "targeting"? Will a more virulent form of *dualism* be encouraged, of "public, poor — private, rich"? The image of "torn safety nets" is there, associated with systemic disentitlement.

It is too early to be sure about all this. However, there is ample evidence to justify a sense of unease, both for workers in the services and for the "clients" or "consumers". Unless carefully monitored and regulated, privatization can intensify problems of moral and immoral hazards, adverse selection and inequalities, affecting security services, pensions, healthcare, social care and employment services.

2.9 Regulations and regulation

Under the influence of the Washington Consensus, a global restructuring of the role of regulation and regulations has been taking place. Briefly, this began with the determined strategy of eroding the legitimacy of neo-corporatist governance, characterized by tripartism and various "boards" setting prices, wages, incomes, standards and procedures.

More recently, statutory forms of regulation have been weakened — including auditing rules and supervision — while policymakers have been lured into backing "voluntary codes of conduct", including "corporate social responsibility" initiatives, which have been promoted as alternatives to statutory regulation.

This trend has affected almost all areas of policy. For instance, many industrialized countries relaxed protective regulations in agriculture. In the most infamous case, the rollback in regulatory monitoring in the United Kingdom culminated in bovine spongiform encephalopathy ("mad cow disease") and the foot-and-mouth epidemic.

In many developing countries the capacity to implement regulations is limited, and has been eroded by abandoning old mechanisms. In India, deregulation has led to large price fluctuations and "wipe outs", in which farmers who could previously have

balanced poor and good harvests lose everything in the wake of a poor season. The orthodox answer is that these problems could be rectified by insurance markets. But even if these existed, their price would be prohibitive for poor and small-scale producers; there is thus a strong need for a government role, through such bodies as crop insurance boards that were abolished in the name of free trade.

Meanwhile, there has been extensive labour market re-regulation. It is a misnomer to call this *deregulation*. One might claim that the general direction of change has been towards protection of individual rights and a weakening in the protection of collective rights. Or one might claim that there has been a strengthening of the bargaining position of firms relative to workers. But one point is clear. Around the world, collective bargaining rights have been more restricted, or placed within legal confines to a greater extent than was the case before. The pursuit of labour market flexibility was led by the Thatcher Government in the United Kingdom and the Reagan administration in the United States, and then copied to varying extent by almost all other rich countries, with Germany being a reluctant follower early in the 21st century.

Among developing countries Chile, was in the vanguard during the Pinochet regime and others have followed suit. Reform of the Factory Acts, for instance, has weakened the position of regular wage workers in India. But it was in the industrialized countries that labour market re-regulation went furthest. As will be shown in later chapters, the pursuit of labour flexibility has had a profound effect on various forms of worker security.

Besides the changing character of statutory labour regulations, there has been a drift to what might be called *fiscal regulation*. Governments are using taxes, subsidies and benefits to guide behaviour, penalize certain activities and raise the rewards to some types of activity relative to others. Individual tax credits have been the most striking case of this.

A question is whether or not fiscal regulation is turning into something close to "social engineering"? Increasingly, fiscal policy is being used to alter people's behaviour, to encourage certain types of behaviour and activity and discourage others. In this respect, there is likely to be a "democratic deficit", and a lack of transparency and accountability, as well as a tendency to push people to conform to a single way of behaving, rather than allow for behavioural diversity.

Finally, *process standards* are becoming increasingly important in global trade, though they are "voluntary" and not part of the WTO system. Countries and firms face penalties in terms of market access unless they comply with certain labour or environmental standards. This may sound laudable. But those in a position to standardize and codify the rules will take the spoils. Often the rules are self-monitored and audited by non-transparent means. Often supposedly independent bodies, including NGOs, are co-opted by business or public bodies to formulate, monitor or revise standards and rules. Firms are supposed to comply, but compliance can be managed.

A relatively little noticed form of private regulation has been delegated to *credit rating agencies* (CRAs). In practice, this means the public rating and thus legitimation of corporations (and countries) by three United States-based firms — Moody's, Standard and Poor, and Fitch — all of which have expanded dramatically since the 1980s. Their role in globalization should not be underestimated. In effect, they determine the worth of corporations and countries by passing judgment (from a United States perspective) on practices and policies via their ratings. Thus, in 2003 Standard and Poor downgraded the shares of several major German corporations to "junk status" by applying United States standards to their pension fund provisions. This caused disquiet in Germany. Similarly, when Moody's put Japanese debt on a level with Botswana and Chile in the 1980s, the value of the yen promptly fell by 10% as investors moved funds out of the country.

The CRAs have become key players in assessing risk in the global economy. But they are powers in themselves, able to determine the security of companies, and thus workers in them. Many observers are worried that the CRAs are being given stronger quasi-regulatory powers.[34] They are creating "adaptation pressure" on non-United States firms and governments, and they are selling "rating evaluation services" to help the latter improve their ratings. They are quietly becoming an international institution shaping countries' macroeconomic policy. There is private authority without public accountability. Who will regulate the global private regulators, which are firmly embedded in the United States?

2.10 Pension fund capitalism

The pension fund industry is an enormous "actor" in the globalization drama. It represents the biggest consolidated body of funds in the world, and pension fund managers have become powerful financial entities. What has been their influence? Are they out of control? Do they lessen people's insecurity or intensify it?

While it is impossible to give definitive answers to these questions, they must be asked. Globally, in 1999, the total assets of pension funds, mostly private, comprised 46% of the world's total income, up from 30% merely seven years earlier; 56% of pension fund assets were held by United States funds, 9% by United Kingdom-based funds. This concentration represents enormous economic power.

Pension funds have become more volatile as they have grown. Between 1999 and 2002, they "lost" USD2,700 billion in value — equivalent to almost two years of the United Kingdom's total national income. By 2002, their assets were back to about a third of the world's income, or nearly twice the combined GDP of all low and middle-income countries. Almost certainly, they resumed their growth in 2003.

One issue is the size of pension funds in industrialized countries relative to the size of developing countries' stock markets. For example, the largest pension fund in the United States (Calpers) and the largest in Europe (ABP) each have financial assets of USD150 billion; this is similar to or larger than the total stock market capitalization of Argentina, Mexico or the Republic of Korea, or the combined value of Malaysia and Thailand. Both pension funds together have financial assets 20% larger than the capitalization of Brazil's stock market.

As major investors, pension funds can influence how companies behave or punish them for "bad" behaviour by selling their shares. Pension funds can be expected to push companies to maximize "shareholder value", if necessary at the expense of other goals, including security for employees. (One of the ways in which the managers of Enron ramped up

---

[34] An example is the proposed use of external credit ratings by bank regulators. Bank for International Settlements: *Overview of the New Basel Capital Accord*, Basel Committee on Banking Supervision Consultative Document (Basel, BIS, Apr. 2003).

its share price — and hence their own remuneration — was to oblige employees to invest pension contributions in the company's shares. When Enron collapsed, many workers lost both job and pension.)

At the same time, the volatility of pension funds — and the steady shift from defined benefit to defined contribution schemes — has increased the insecurity of millions of workers for whom the funds are now the primary pensions vehicle and who have seen billions of dollars wiped off future pension payments in the most recent stock market collapse.

A related aspect is the *financialization* of corporations. A large number of major corporations, including household-name manufacturers, have devoted a large and increasing proportion of their financial resources to speculative investments. Many ran into difficulties following the stock market plunge in 2001-02, leading to retrenchment, divestments and redundancies. Mergers and demergers, designed to enhance short-term profits and shareholder value, have often been to the detriment of long-term productive strategy or the employment and income security of workers.

It is possible that the extraordinary collapse of Enron in late 2001 may prove a defining moment in the evolution of the global economic system. For many, it epitomized the folly of leaving too much to "the market". It was also a stark demonstration of the enormous *security gap* between privileged elite "insiders", who were able to shield their income and wealth, and "outsiders", including the corporation's long-term workers, hitherto perceived as among the most secure workers in the United States economy, who overnight lost their pensions.

Remarkably, just before its disgrace and collapse, Enron had been identified by the American public as one of the ten best firms in which to work, and had been regarded by prominent monitoring — private regulatory — institutions as exemplary in terms of its "reporting on corporate social responsibility". Now Enron has become a metaphor for a brand of short-term financial opportunism that has characterized much economic activity in the era of globalization.

The affair has also demonstrated the inadequacy of relying on market forces and private or self-regulation to prevent abuses and ensure proper behaviour. Not only Enron managers but also outside legal and accounting professionals were compromised. There was

no alarm raised by bank analysts, ratings agencies, Enron's board of directors or the company's auditors, which received lucrative consultancy contracts from Enron as well as auditing fees. There was no responsible monitoring or self-monitoring by the professionals involved. There were no protective regulations in place to protect the company's workers from the consequences of wrongdoing by its managers or advisers.

Since Enron imploded, some other United States and European corporations have been caught in similar circumstances, including Worldcom in the United States, Ahold in the Netherlands and Parmalat in Italy. In the last case, the Italian Government promptly sought to provide a huge subsidy to keep the company going. Underwriting the risks of capital continues. But the costs for workers, and their communities, are huge.

2.11 Of shocks, terrorisms, wars, natural disasters and pandemics

Economic liberalization has been accompanied by a rise in systemic shocks, which imply systemic insecurity of a type that is hard to cover by standard forms of insurance. With globalization, economic crises in one country or region are more likely to transmit reverberations to others. The world has become fearful of "contagion" — so that, for example, following the Russian debt default in August 1998, two of the most affected countries in the world were Brazil and Argentina, even though they had practically no economic relationships with Russia.

In addition, both the frequency of such crises and their severity seems to have been increasing.[35] For example, in 1980-98, in Latin America and the Caribbean alone, there were over 40 crises in which per capita GDP fell by more than 4%.[36] The following box lists the countries hit by economic crises since 1990.

---

[35] J. Von Braun, P. L. Vlek and A.Wimmer: *Disasters, Conflicts and Natural Resource Degradations: Multidisciplinary Perspectives on Complex Emergencies*, Centre for Development Research, Annual Report 2001–02 (Bonn, ZEF, 2002).

[36] E. Skoufias: "Economic crises and natural disasters: Coping strategies and policy implications", *World Development*, Vol. 31, No. 7, 2003, pp. 1087–1102.

Economic / financial crises (1990–2003)[37]

Albania, Algeria*, Angola*, Argentina, Armenia, Azerbaijan, Bahamas, Barbados, Belarus, Benin*, Bolivia, Bosnia and Herzegovina, Brazil, Bulgaria, Burkina Faso*, Cameroon*, Chad*, Central African Republic*, Congo*, Chile, China*, Colombia, Costa Rica, Côte d'Ivoire*, Croatia, Czech Republic, Democratic Republic of the Congo*, Dominican Republic, Ecuador, Egypt*, Estonia, El Salvador*, Ethiopia*, Finland, Georgia, Guatemala*, Guyana*, Haiti, Hong Kong (China), Honduras, Hungary, Indonesia, Japan, Islamic Republic of Iran, Jamaica*, Kazakhstan, Republic of Korea, Kyrgyzstan, Lao People's Democratic Republic*, Latvia, Lebanon*, Lithuania, the former Yugoslav Republic of Macedonia, Madagascar*, Mali*, Malawi*, Malaysia, Mauritania*, Mexico, Republic of Moldova, Mozambique*, Nicaragua*, Niger*, Nigeria*, Norway, Pakistan, Peru*, Philippines, Poland, Romania*, Russian Federation, Rwanda*, Senegal*, Serbia and Montenegro, Singapore, Slovakia, Slovenia, Somalia*, Sri Lanka, Sudan*, Suriname, Sweden, Taiwan (China), Tajikistan, Thailand, Togo*, Turkey, Turkmenistan, Ukraine, Uruguay, Uzbekistan, Venezuela, Zambia*, Zimbabwe.

*Countries and territories that suffered at least one severe currency crash (1990–2001). Such a crash "refers to a 25% or higher monthly depreciation which is at least 10% higher than the previous month's depreciation".

In addition, partly due to the ecological neglect associated with looser regulation, the same could be said of natural disasters. In Latin America and the Caribbean alone, during 1980-99 there were 38 major droughts, floods, hurricanes, tropical storms, landslides, earthquakes, volcano eruptions and El Niño episodes.[38] Overcrowded cities with inadequate public infrastructure scarcely help. Even western Europe is feeling the effect of global warming, with a prolonged heat wave in 2003 that was responsible for the deaths of many thousands of people. In East Asia, it is moot whether the shock effects of the El Niño on the Philippines and Indonesia were greater or less than the effects of the Asian crisis of 1997-98. Over 180 countries were affected by natural disasters in the decade to 2002. One cannot expect ordinary people to be adequately insured against losses from devastating natural disasters — which is why rich nations normally pay compensation to their own citizens affected.

Natural disasters play a huge role in undermining economic security around the world. Over the past decade there seems to have been a pronounced upward trend in both weather-related and technological disasters, as well as in the total number of people directly affected by them (Figure 2.12).[39] Weather-related disasters are running close to twice their level in the mid-1990s, owing partly to the effects of global warming. The number of people affected by disasters in 2002, at over 600 million, was more than triple the annual average in the previous decade, mainly because of drought in India that affected 300 million people.

[37] Sources include: K. Rogoff and C. Reinhart: *FDI to Africa: The role of price stability and currency instability*, IMF Working Paper (Washington, DC, IMF, 2002); World Bank: *World Development Report 2000–2001: Attacking Poverty* (Washington, DC, 2001); Inter-American Development Bank: *Social Protection for Equity and Growth* (Washington, DC, 2000); IMF: *World Economic Outlook: Financial Crises: Causes and Indicators* (Washington, DC, 1998).

[38] Inter-American Development Bank (IADB): *Social Protection for Equity and Growth* (Washington, DC, 2000).

[39] International Federation of Red Cross and Red Crescent Societies (IFRC): *World Disasters Report: Focus on Ethics in Aid* (Geneva, 2003). See also United Nations Environment Programme (UNEP): *The Global Environment Outlook* (Nairobi, 2001); S.G. Cornford: *Socio-Economic Impacts of Weather Events in 2002* (Geneva, World Meteorological Organization, 2003).

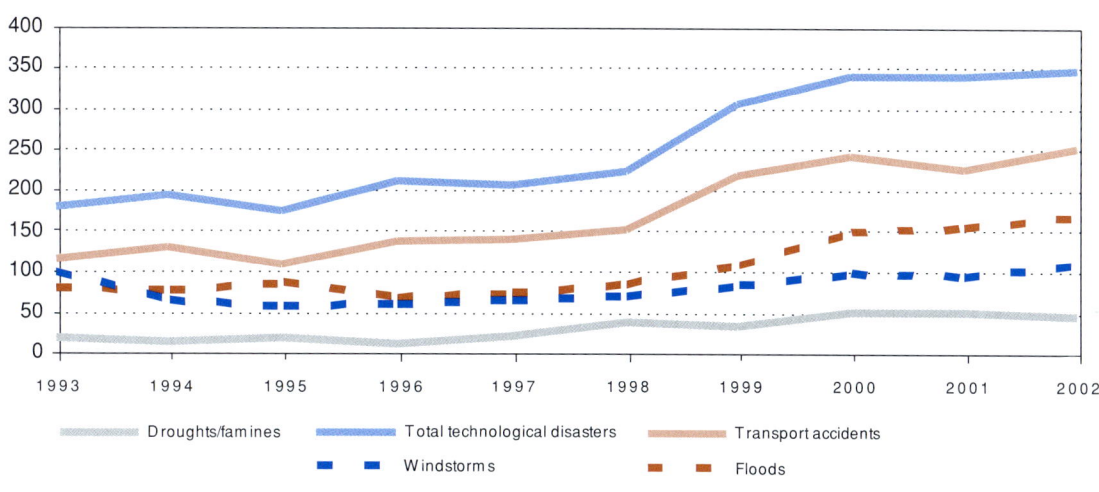

Figure 2.12 Total number of reported disasters, by type of phenomenon, 1993–2002

Source: EM-DAT, CRED, University of Louvain, Belgium.

The era of globalization has also coincided with numerous wars, including civil wars, as noted in Chapter 1. It has been estimated that as of late 2003 one in five of the world's nations was at war, leaving aside the rather vague notion of the global "war on terrorism". These, of course, create systemic insecurities for all those affected directly or indirectly, and cannot be dealt with adequately by conventional systems of social protection.

Finally, but certainly not least, globalization has coincided with the greatest health catastrophe in history, the *HIV/AIDS* pandemic. Besides lowering life expectancy in many countries, it has led to a decline in the proportion of "prime-age" adults, leaving many more orphans and elderly people without income-earners to support them in their old age. The ILO estimates that at least 26 million workers aged 15-49 are infected worldwide, and in Africa 11 million children have lost one or both parents to AIDS. In some African countries, the situation is threatening national survival. For example, in Uganda, the Ministry of Gender, Labour and Social Services reported in early 2002 that one in every four households in the country contained at least one child orphaned by AIDS or war.

Nobody sensibly attributes AIDS to globalization. However, cuts in public spending on health services, and lack of income support for victims and their families and communities, surely made the situa-

tion worse. Moreover, AIDS is not the only public health challenge. In 2003, a new global scare emerged, Severe Acute Respiratory Syndrome (SARS). Though the numbers affected may be relatively small, SARS epitomized something more eerie. New diseases are more easily transmitted to other parts of the world because of international mobility. And they may be harder to curb because of shrunken public health care services. The World Health Organization attributed the difficulties faced by China in containing SARS to the rundown public health system, especially in rural areas. Global health inequalities are also widening, with a growing gap in life expectancy between the richest and poorest nations.[40] Global health insecurity is certainly not disappearing.

2.12 A migratory world?

The era of globalization has undoubtedly been characterized by a greater increase in *capital mobility* than in labour mobility, or population mobility. Economic policy and institutional and regulatory changes have made capital mobility easier, while many

_____

[40] World Health Organization (WHO): *World Health Report 2003 — Shaping the Future* (Geneva, 2003).

barriers to labour mobility have been left intact or even strengthened. Some economists have argued that *the rights of capital have been strengthened relative to the rights of labour.*

Even so, an estimated 175 million people — 3% of the world's population — are living and working outside their country of citizenship, double the number 25 years ago. With migratory pressures growing as a result of both "pull" factors (the need for workers in ageing rich nations) and "push" factors (unemployment and poverty in poor countries), the International Organization for Migration says migrant numbers could rise to 230 million by 2050.

Some countries have become dependent on remittances from migrant labour, which globally amount to at least USD88 billion and probably much more. It has been said, for example, that the Philippines' most successful export is migrant labour, and that 25 million families are dependent on it. India receives six times as much in remittances from its emigrant workers as it receives in foreign aid. Remittances account for most of Pakistan's foreign exchange sources.

Many migrants, hoping to escape insecurity at home, endure high levels of economic insecurity in the destination country. They are often discriminated against and exploited (a problem exacerbated if they enter a country illegally), often taking low-paid unskilled work with poor working conditions and little employment or income security.

Perhaps the worst form of international migratory movement is the *trafficking* in human beings for prostitution and illegal highly exploitable labour. Though no one knows for sure, the United States government believes up to 900,000 people are trafficked across international borders each year, a trade that the ILO has estimated to be worth USD12 billion annually.

In addition, at the end of 2002 over 10 million people were classified as refugees, having fled their countries of origin because of violence or persecution. This figure excludes more than 4 million Palestinian refugees cared for by the United Nations Relief and Works Agency (UNRWA). Another 20–25 million internally displaced — half of them in Africa — have been forced to leave their homes by conflict or disaster. Nearly half a million asylum applications were lodged in industrialized countries in 2003, though the so-called "war on terrorism" and xenophobic pressures have led to a tightening-up of procedures and a reduced acceptance of refugees. As Ruud Lubbers, the United Nations High Commissioner for Refugees, has stated, "*No corner of the globe has been immune [...] Increasingly, governments exclude [refugees] from protection and detain them*".

Another reflection, and generator, of insecurity is the *global care chain* — most conspicuously represented by the flood of young women who take overseas jobs as nannies and maids, sending back a part of their earnings to pay for a carer for their own children. These migrant women live to go home, but rarely do so. Often, they develop a "hypothetical self" — an idea of the person they would be if only they were able to go home.[41]

More generally, migration can increase insecurity in sending communities, which lose their younger, more dynamic and often more educated people, as well as in host communities which may see migrants as disturbing settled ways of life and patterns of behaviour. However, barriers to mobility can be equally destabilising, within countries as well as between them.

In China, lack of a land ownership system holds back potential migrants, who fear losing land they cultivate if they leave to look for work elsewhere. This impedes efficient land consolidation, and accentuates the insecurity of rural workers. Nobody knows how many constitute China's "floating population", but estimates range from 40 million to 100 million.[42] The Chinese authorities have limited rural-urban movement by curbing migrants' job opportunities and access to housing.[43] But this has accentuated rural-urban income inequality as well as rural poverty.

---

[41] A. R. Hochschild: "Global care chains and emotional surplus value", in W. Hutton and A. Giddens (eds.): *On The Edge: Living with Global Capitalism* (London, Jonathan Cape, 2001), p. 133.

[42] Kam Wing, Chan: *Internal Migration in China: Trends, Determinants and Scenarios* (Washington, DC, World Bank, Mar. 2000).

[43] Cai Fang: *Migration and Socio-Economic Insecurity: Patterns, Processes and Policies*, SES Paper No. 36 (Geneva, ILO, Aug. 2003).

People on the move have been powerful agents of development throughout human history. But for many millions of people, moving reflects insecurity and too often accentuates it. Within developing countries, the recent past has been one of accelerating urbanization, which requires more public intervention and investment than has been prescribed in the globalization era.

The image of a large rural population surrounding cities and towns is giving way to one of an increasingly urbanized world. By 2007, for the first time in history, the world's urban population will exceed the rural population. Urbanization brings with it more economic insecurities, since networks of support that characterize rural society tend to be much more fragile or non-existent in urban areas. One should never romanticize the realities of rural living, as it is experienced in most parts of the world. However, though people in rural society may be poor, they often survive by means of the security provided by a complex set of networks giving balanced or structured reciprocities. These typically break down in urban areas, where personal relationships are often more transient and opportunistic. The 21st century will be the urban century. It will bring with it a host of insecurities, which we are only beginning to understand.

Migration and urbanization are creating new challenges for social and economic policy. Networks of social protection are weakened by the slow demise of *extended families*, due to migration, changing marriage and fertility patterns and economic factors. There is also a growth of *single-person and single-adult households* in affluent societies and in many urbanizing developing countries, the number of conventional *nuclear family households* has been shrinking due to single parenthood, divorce and remarriage, and other behaviour changes such as people in long-term monogamous relationships who do not marry or even live together. As a consequence, the distinction between married and single persons, on which much of social policy is based, has become increasingly arbitrary.

World economic growth in the globalization era has been erratic. There have been spectacular performances, most notably China's sustained growth. But in many parts of the world, sluggish would be the best word to describe what has happened. Large parts of the world have actually experienced much lower rates of economic growth than before. This includes many industrialized countries and some major developing countries, such as Brazil, where growth in per capita income averaged 4.4% per annum between 1948 and 1980 and only 0.2% between 1980 and 2003. As noted earlier, African countries performed even worse.

If the policies of the era have not had universal success in raising growth, it cannot be said that there has been a loss of faith. The dominant ethos has even involved a spread by "package deals" — the Washington Consensus, "structural adjustment", "shock therapy", "good governance", and so on. But these have all been geared to promote market economies, typically in the mould of the United States, with a residual "welfare state" and with extensive privatization of production and social policy. It has been extended to "corporate governance", in which maximizing shareholder value is the overriding objective, which inevitably has implications for the distribution of income and the incidence of risks and uncertainty.

The more liberalized economies and societies that have been encouraged to come into existence in the past few decades have brought with them new or more intense challenges, many associated with their increased exposure to capital mobility and diminished control over monetary and fiscal policy. This chapter has summarized the main factors justifying an expectation of greater social and economic insecurity for the majority of people around the world. There is no need for gloom in recognizing this. But it does mean that, if true, new policies and institutions will be needed to reduce it.

2.13 Conclusions

"We have always known that heedless self-interest is bad morals; we know now that it is bad economics."

— Franklyn D. Roosevelt,
Second Inaugural Address, 20 January 1937

---

[44]Even someone as critical of the Washington Consensus as Joseph Stiglitz has advocated that foreign assistance should aim to achieve "the transformation of societies", a highly paternalistic objective.

Mapping Economic Security

"There are districts in which the position of the rural population is that of a man standing permanently up to the neck in water, so that even a ripple is sufficient to drown him."[1]

Today, globally, it seems that more and more people are close to the margin of crisis.

For many, a tidal wave seems imminent.

[1] R.H. Tawney: *Land and Labour in China* (Boston, Beacon Press, 1966 edition; orig. 1931), p. 77.

PART II

Monitoring socio-economic security

Although there are ample reasons for being concerned about global trends influencing economic security, and thus about the general direction with respect to what the ILO has dubbed *decent work*, there has been relatively little information on actual patterns and trends. Part II — covering Chapters 3 to 11 — considers national statistical indicators of various forms of security, and explores how these can be used to monitor national levels and trends. Chapters 4 through 10 present indexes of each of the seven forms of social and economic security as identified in Chapter 1 and give estimated values for all those countries for which data have been obtained.

No statistical measure of a complex phenomenon can be fully satisfactory, either conceptually or empirically. What is important is that there should be an *underlying model or theory* to justify it. In this case, the framework is based on the view that the seven forms

of work-related securities comprise the full array of forms of *economic security*, and that high values of security in all seven respects would constitute *decent work*.

One of the criticisms of the UNDP's widely used Human Development Index (HDI) is that it leaves out structures and laws. In this regard, the procedure adopted in the following is a three-layered approach that tries to identify measures of political commitment to a particular form of security (input indicators), to identify measures of mechanisms or processes that are created to give effect to the commitment (process indicators) and to identify measures of the situation with respect to that form of security (outcome indicators). Thus, a good outcome in a particular period may be unstable if the country has not ratified international conventions or adopted principles in its constitution or if there are no institutions to maintain or promote that outcome.

The following draws on a specially created Global Socio-Economic Security Database, which has been created in the ILO, based in part on the SES Indica-

Data availability and quality

Globally, the state of data on security issues is lamentable. One reason is that issues of economic security have been given relatively low priority by governments; another is that most countries have weak statistical systems in general.

National data come from a wide variety of sources, some official, some from non-governmental organizations, such as employer organizations and trade union confederations, some from *ad hoc* surveys conducted by research institutes or international agencies. Often the data sources are unclear or "unscientific" in some way. Rarely are state-of-the-art statistical principles followed. In some cases, there are several equally valid approaches that could be adopted (or approaches of equally limited validity).

The SES Database makes some allowance for these deficiencies and national differences. These are noted in the software developed for users of the database.

Another well-known difficulty concerns variable dates or reference periods for any statistic. Censuses and surveys are conducted periodically, and although the United Nations and others have encouraged moves in the direction of standardization there is no global standard. Big numbers for the world cited in international reports — including reports by the ILO — are very unreliable guides to reality because most countries will not have collected data for that specific year, and may not have done so for five or even ten years. This report suffers from a similar drawback. We can only alert readers to this problem, stating that the principle followed is to take 1999 as the reference year for national or macro variables, and where data for 1999 are not available to take information for the nearest year available (1998 or 2000).

To deal with "missing data", one of two approaches is adopted, depending on feasibility. Either the country is omitted from the analysis, if data for two or more variables are missing, or an estimated value is *imputed*.

In spite of the limitations, we believe that the variables and indexes calculated from our data represent a "best shot" for monitoring economic security, and hope that the exercise in itself will prompt the collection and reporting of improved statistics on economic security and decent work.

tors Questionnaire completed by national and regional correspondents in many ILO member countries. A brief description of that follows here; more detailed information can be obtained from the sources mentioned in various footnotes.

1. A social and economic security database

To monitor security, the SES Programme needed to create a database on socio-economic security, and thus the elements constituting decent work. The scope and complexity of the notion of security meant very detailed data were needed: this has involved a complex data collection operation, including primary data, at three levels: society as a whole (the macro level), the firm or workplaces (the meso level) and the individual worker (the micro level). The resultant database can be described as follows.

- At the **macro level**, three databases covering over 100 countries, for 1990 and 1999:

- SES *Primary Database*, resulting from a specially designed questionnaire on the seven forms of socio-economic security, regrouping over 700 textual and quantitative variables disaggregated by sex and sector when appropriate. The data refer to the years 1990 and 1999 and have been screened to enter an on-line database utility for internal and external consultations, data export and updates. The questionnaires have been filled in by local specialists in over 100 countries.

- SES *Secondary Database*, complementing the primary data with relevant statistical information from existing regional and global sources, including primarily the ILO (KILM, LABORSTA, NATLEX) but also Eurostat, OECD, World Bank, etc.

- SES *Social Security Database*, a statistical file covering the eight "classical" branches of social security, each being described by more than 20 variables such as expenditure, eligibility rules, legal

arrangements and benefit rates. It was designed to allow for quantitative analysis and resulted therefore from a process of conversion of textual into statistically usable data. Information was derived from the ILO's Cost of Social Security Inquiry — generated by the Social Security Financial, Actuarial and Statistical Services - and the International Social Security Association database: Social Security Worldwide.

- At the **meso level**, the Enterprise Labour Flexibility and Security Survey (ELFS) is an instrument for collecting primary data from enterprises on labour, employment and income security of workers and managers.[1] The ELFS basically examines the implications of enterprise restructuring, in light of global developments, on the security of workers. It is fundamentally a workplace survey. The analysis of the data generated provides the ILO with information to formulate and promote policies to provide optimal levels of security at work, by focussing on firms as places where profitability, dynamic efficiency, flexibility and work-related security can be combined and fostered.

The ELFS Survey questionnaire is structured in such a way that it can easily be modified and adapted in accordance with the survey objectives and priorities. This is achieved because of its flexible construction built out of different modules or sets of questions, which can either be attached or detached from the core list of questions. Logically, these modules are correlated with the survey's objectives and uses. These modules include information on recruitment practices, discrimination (gender, ethnic, etc., both direct and indirect), industrial segregation, occupational segregation, training practices, employment restructuring, occupational mobility, working conditions, earnings and benefits, labour surplus and redundancy, and worker representation.

---

[1]Details on this series of surveys are given in *ELFS: A Manual for Training and Implementation* (Geneva, ILO, forthcoming).

Enterprise Labour Flexibility and Security Surveys (ELFS), 1998–2002

Country	Reference period	Number of firms	Sectors	Coverage
Azerbaijan	1999–2001	300	Manufacturing	National
Brazil	1998–2000	500	Manufacturing	3 regions
Chile	1998–2000	300	Manufacturing	3 regions
China	1999–2001	1 000	Manufacturing	3 cities
Indonesia	1998–2000	2 000	Manufacturing + services	5 regions
Moldova	1999–2001	300	Manufacturing	National
Pakistan	1998–2000	650	Manufacturing	3 regions
Philippines	1998–2000	1 300	Manufacturing + services	3 regions
Russia	1998–2000	400	Manufacturing	3 regions
Russia	1999–2001	300	Manufacturing	3 regions
Russia	2001–2002	300	Manufacturing	3 regions
Tanzania	1999–2001	380	Manufacturing + services	National
Ukraine	1998–2000	1 684	Manufacturing	26 regions
Ukraine	2001–2002	1 800	Manufacturing	26 regions

- At the **micro level**, the *People's Security Survey* (PSS), is a household survey that seeks to track the seven forms of work-related security comprising decent work, as well as highlighting people's aspirations and sense of social justice.[2] This survey instrument is the most experimental of the three major sources of information used in the following chapters.

Between 2000 and 2003, 15 surveys were conducted, data for the first 14 of which are presented in the following chapters and in many technical papers. Because of the fact that the instrument was being developed, and for budgetary reasons, the samples and survey design varied. In some countries, a national representative survey was conducted; in others, representative samples were drawn only from selected regions or from urban areas only. In Gujarat, India, a disproportionately large sample of women workers was chosen. And in Pakistan the sample was very specific, focusing only on workers in the transport sector in Karachi City.

The following table summarizes the various samples. The summary highlights an important point, which is that inter-country comparisons of results should be made with caution. In the text, this is indicated at various points, but the reader is urged to bear that in mind with regard to all comparisons of PSS results. What should be most useful is comparisons within particular countries or regions.

---

[2] Details on this series of surveys are given in: PSS: *A Manual for Training and Implementation* (Geneva, ILO, forthcoming). On methodology, see also R. Anker: *People's Security Survey*, paper presented at SES Technical Seminar, Geneva, Nov. 2001.

People's Security Surveys (PSS), 2000–2002

Country	Reference period	Rural (R) Urban (U)	Areas covered	Age groups	Number of households
Argentina	2001	U	3 metropolitan areas	15–64	2 800
Bangladesh	2001	R and U	Dhaka city	15–59	3 200
Brazil	2001	U	3 metropolitan areas	15–64	4 000
Chile	2001	U	3 metropolitan areas	15–64	1 180
China	2001	R and U	3 regions	18+	3 000
Ethiopía	2001	R and U	2 regions	16+	1 520
Ghana	2002	R and U	3 regions	15–64	3 000
Hungary	2000	R and U	National	18–59	1 000
India	2000	R + U	Gujarat	15–60	1 236
Indonesia	2001	R and U	4 provinces	15+	3 000
Pakistan	2001	U	Karachi city	15–64	750
Russia	2002	R and U	3 regions	15–72	2 316
South Africa	2001	U	2 metropolitan areas	15–64	1 600
Tanzania	2001	R and U	3 regions	14–65	1 950
Ukraine	2000	R and U	National	18+	8 200
Ukraine	2002	R and U	National	18+	9 400
Ukraine	2003	R and U	National	18+	9 400

Although both the ELFS and PSS are utilized to show micro-level patterns, and raise policy questions, the main part of the analysis concentrates on the data and indexes derived from the SES Global Database, recognizing that the state of global data in this respect leaves much to be desired.

2. A methodology for measuring security

If conceptualizing socio-economic security (or "human security") is hard, measuring is harder still. The objective is to devise measures of national levels of security, so as to (i) to assess and compare levels of security, (ii) to monitor the changing patterns, and (iii) to monitor and evaluate the impact of social and economic policies.

To achieve this, it is necessary to rely on proxy measures of performance. In this regard, a distinction must be made between an *index* and an *indicator*.

For any complex phenomenon, one can choose individual indicators of commitment and/or achievement. Empirical analysis depends on indicators. But they have limitations. Indicators can be *ad hoc*, and almost definitionally they capture only part of the situation.

An index is a composite measure of the targeted phenomenon, consisting of a combination of a selected group of indicators. The following chapters set out several Security Indexes, in the belief that they can reflect the multifaceted nature of the notion of security. The nature of an index is bound to make the results controversial. Because they combine several related phenomena, a challenge is achieving the appropriate balance of indicators.

The following, very briefly, describes the basic procedures and principles adopted for compiling national or macro indexes of the various forms of security:

(i) Categorizing Indicators:

To capture the various dimensions of any form of security, three types of indicator are developed:

- **Input indicators** are the national and international instruments and rules necessary to protect workers. These are identified, for instance, as the existence of basic laws or ratified ILO Conventions on work-related hazards, unfair dismissal, the right to organize, etc.

- **Process indicators** are the mechanisms or resources through which such "input" principles and rules are realized. Examples are the level of public expenditure on a particular form of security, the existence of labour inspectors, and the existence of labour-related tripartite boards.

- **Outcome indicators** are the elements that provide a measure of whether the Input and Process indicators appear to be effective, notably in ensuring protection to workers. For example, outcome indicators would assess the proportion of workers effectively protected, participating in collective agreements, or receiving benefits or pensions.

(ii) Indicator selection principles

- One key principle is the availability and reliability of data. Any indicator should be a reasonable, transparent proxy for a well-defined phenomenon, and have a correspondingly clear meaning. It should be robust, capable of statistical validation, measurable and comparable across countries or communities.

- The heterogeneity of national situations led us to develop two indexes, one for industrialized countries (ICs) and one for "less-developed countries" (LDCs). One reason is the difference in data availability in the two groups of countries. The indexes for the former tend to be the more complete because a wider range and more refined set of indicators are available. In some cases, the index for LDCs, because of data limitations, include imputed values for particular variables derived from the application of missing values techniques. However, final results presented in this report concern only a unique index covering both ICs and LDCs.

(iii) Data processing

- In this sort of exercise there is a great virtue in transparency and simplicity. *The more complex the way an index is constructed, the greater the suspicion that the data and reasoning have been "massaged".* Therefore, a simple additive model of analysis generating an ordinal scale has been applied.

- Any index raises difficulties of "scaling" and "weighting". On weighting, in general an equal weight approach is adopted. In other words, each indicator is given the same weight in the calculation of the sub-index (input, process or outcome indicators). However, the composite indexes presented in this report give outcome indicators double the weight of input and process indicators, based on the view that countries providing higher security, irrespective of the quality of their institutions and laws, should be regarded more favourably. Different sensitivity tests show that the results from double weighting better describe reality than results from an analysis that gives each sub-index equal weight. As a rule, since we did not wish to give disproportionate weight to the most formal and international component of the input indicators such as ILO Conventions, it has been allocated only half the weight of national components, such as national laws and regulations.[3]

- On scaling, the report follows the standard normalization procedure developed for the UNDP's Human Development Index (HDI), which can be defined as follows:

Normalized value X = [Actual–Minimum Value]/[Maximum — Minimum Value]

where X is the Security score (or value), Actual is the score attained by the country on a particular indicator, Minimum is the lowest value attained by any country on that particular variable, and Maximum is the maximum value attained by any country for that variable.

---

[3]For an alternative or complementary approach to a measure of freedom of association and collective bargaining, which relies on coding information from ICFTU reports, US State Department reports and reports from the ILO's Committee on Freedom of Association, see D. Kucera: *The Effects of Core Workers' Rights on Labour Costs and Foreign Direct Investment: Evaluating the Conventional Wisdom*, International Institute for Labour Studies Discussion Paper (Geneva, ILO, 2001).

- Where appropriate and statistically feasible, indicators and indexes should reflect gender differentiation. This is most commonly done by using the female/male ratio; if greater than one, it suggests a positive contribution against gender discrimination or for the level of security of women.

3. A diversity of indexes

In proposing indexes of various forms of security, and a composite **Economic Security Index**, this report ventures on well-trod ground. There are many related indexes. Perhaps the most celebrated is the UNDP's **Human Development Index** (HDI), which was originally presented as an alternative to an income-based measure of development. There are dozens of others, including such intriguing measures as a national **Water Poverty Index.** One that has been particularly useful for this report is the Civil Liberties Index, which includes indicators of "association and organization rights", "freedom of expression and belief", "rule of law and human rights", and "personal autonomy and economic rights".[4] Another is from the World Database of Happiness where happiness is measured by means of surveys on responses to a question on the level of life-satisfaction in general public samples. The dispersion of responses is also calculated to divide the mean of happiness in a nation and obtaining an **Equality-Adjusted Happiness index**. As such, this index focuses not only on the level of happiness but also on the inequality in happiness among citizens.[5]

Among other relevant exercises, the European Union in 2001 drew up a list of **Indicators for Social Inclusion.** The main objective is to provide EU member countries with comparable measures to monitor progress towards social inclusion and their National Action Plans on Social Inclusion. Seven indicators were initially proposed: distribution of income (quintiles), the share of the population below the poverty line (before and after transfers), the persistence of poverty, the proportion of jobless households, regional disparities, the extent of low education levels, and long-term unemployment. Others were added later, including indicators of health, housing and social participation.

There is also a **Social Protection Index** relating to working conditions that includes the percentage of GDP spent on pensions, coverage rates for male and female workers in the informal and formal economies, and the total number of hours worked, similarly disaggregated.

A Commitment to Development Index has been created by the United States Centre for Global Development. This measures the extent to which the policies of the world's richest countries reflect their stated goal of advancing the development of the world's poor countries. It is aimed at fostering debate about the role of rich country policies in development and at holding rich countries accountable for their decisions. Scores show that the "best" countries are not necessarily those with greatest aid-giving capacity. Thus Norway loses rank because of its agricultural import tariffs, and the United States emerges as one of the -meanest countries, even though it gives the largest absolute amount. The CDI ranks 21 countries.

Social scientists at the University of Antwerp have created a **Social Development Index**. This is a composite index measuring the degree to which countries respect the ILO's core standards — freedom of association, elimination of child labour, and elimination of discrimination and forced labour. For each of these, a "rights" index was built from a combination of indicators assessing the country's capability, together with the political will, to implement these standards. Two indicators are used for each, one "formal" referring to the ratification of the Convention, the other "real" reporting violations of the ILO provisions in question. Capability is defined by measures of income, education, health and political stability in the country. The SDI is calculated as a weighted average of the "rights" indexes.

The World Health Organization has begun to develop a means of measuring **Health System Performance**.[6] The WHO produces yearly a series of indicators that include life expectancy, probability of dying, deaths by cause, private and public health expenditure, etc. It also has composite indexes that come closer to policy concerns and help monitor the functioning and quality of health systems. One index is the

---

[4] Freedom House: *Freedom in the World: The Annual Survey of Political Rights and Civil Liberties* (New York, Freedom House, various years).

[5] World Data Base on Happiness: *Happiness in Nations (Rank Report* 2001-2003), (Rotterdam, Erasmus University, 2003), <http://www.eur.nl/fsw/research/happiness/hap

[6] World Health Organization: *World Health Report 2000* (Geneva, WHO, 2000).–nat/nat–fp.ht>.

Overall Health System Attainment. This covers level and distributional aspects of health system performance, and is based on the weighted contribution of 3 major components: level and distribution of health, responsiveness to health needs, and fairness of financial contribution.

Within the ILO there has also been significant work to identify **Indicators of Decent Work**. Readers are recommended to consult the technical papers emanating from that work.[7] We will however refer briefly to some of them.

The ILO office in Santiago produces **The Panorama Laboral**, in which a **Decent Work Development Index** (DWDI) is presented. The aim is to assess progress and cutbacks in the areas of employment and social protection in 21 countries in Latin America and the Caribbean. It covers the four pillars of the ILO strategy for achieving Decent Work, namely indicators on the implementation of labour standards, employment quality, social protection and social dialogue.

The ILO's Declaration Programme has created an **ILO Norms Index**. This has two components. The first takes account of a country's intentions, based on the number of Fundamental ILO Conventions ratified by the countries divided by total number of Fundamental ILO Conventions. The second is an assessment of the extent to which the country applies the principles and recommendations of the Conventions. This is based on the number of complaints the ILO Freedom of Association Commission has received, which can concern cases such as forced labour, discrimination practices, and restrictions on collective bargaining. The Index is the percentage distribution of the number of complaints among countries, and also measures the change in such distribution, indicating whether a particular country is doing better or worse than in the past.

The ILO's Employment Sector has created an **Employment Quality Index**, derived from a series of conventional indicators of employment, taking gender differences into consideration. These are: labour force participation rates; employment rates; the proportion of workers and wage-workers in the informal economy who contribute to social security; total and youth unemployment rates; male/ female differentials on wages and preceding indicators; and industrial and minimum wage rates, adjusted for productivity gains.

The ILO's Declaration Programme has created a measure of **Gaps in International Basic Workers' Rights**.[8] Gaps exists (i) when a government has less than full adherence to Fundamental ILO Conventions, principles and rights or related obligations; and (ii) when ILO supervisory or complaints mechanisms reveal legislative or other implementation problems in respect of basic workers' rights. Lack of adherence gives rise to an adherence gap. Revealed implementation problems give rise to an implementation gap. Adherence and implementation gaps add up to what is called the basic workers rights' gap, on a scale from 0 (no gap) to 100 (maximum gap). This gap can be calculated annually to track a country's progress and identify which factor — international adherence or revealed implementation — is responsible. Depending on the answer, different responses may be called for.

The ILO's Bureau of Statistics has proposed an approach based on seven indicators expressed in the form of rates, each of which covers a component of decent work.[9] They are: low pay, school non-enrolment, excessive hours of work, unemployment (total and youth), male/female labour force participation rate gap, and old-age without pension. The authors, while noting reservations such as international comparability and statistical bias, have exclusively used data from national labour force surveys to make some international comparisons of decent work deficits for 40 industrialized and industrializing countries. These results have been compared to country performance in terms of GDP and HDI.[10] Another approach defines ten characteristics of work that make a job decent, and proposes a preliminary evaluation of decent work on the basis of 30 readily usable indicators.[11]

[7]See, for example, the Special Issue of the *International Labour Review*, 2003.

[8]R. Böhning, 2003, op. cit. Among the difficulties with any "gap" index is the essentially arbitrary nature of the levels used to assess gaps.

[9]D. Bescond, A. Chataignier and F. Mehran: "Seven indicators to measure decent work: An international comparison", *International Labour Review*, Vol. 142, No. 2 (Geneva, ILO, 2003).

[10]I. Ahmed: "Decent work and human development", *International Labour Review*, Special Issue, Vol. 142, No. 2, 2003, pp. 263–271.

[11]G.S. Fields, "Decent work and development policies", *International Labour Review*, Special Issue, Vol. 142, No. 2, 2003, pp. 239–62. This paper considers how to develop an integrated approach to economic and social policy in the context of decent work and how it relates to economic growth.

The ILO's International Institute for Labour Studies and the In-Focus Programme on Social Dialogue have also developed measures of decent work or major aspects of it. One measure takes the four major components of decent work, employment, social protection, workers' rights and social dialogue, applied to 22 industrialized countries.[12] Another is based on indicators of core workers' rights by tradeables and manufacturing sectors, using 37 evaluation criteria of freedom of association and collective bargaining, five measures of child labour, six forms of forced labour and five gender inequality measures. In addition to country results, the analysis looks at the relationship to labour cost and foreign direct investment. A third project has focused on unionization rates and collective bargaining coverage by sector. It foresees the use of indicators on the formal and implementation dimensions of workers' rights, industrial relations processes and negotiated policy-making.[13]

4. A family of SES indexes

The SES Programme has built indexes for each of the seven forms of work-related security, concluding with a composite **Economic Security Index**. For presentation purposes, for each index, countries are classified in four *clusters*, designated **Pacesetters, Pragmatists, Conventionals** and **Much-to-be-done**.

The **Pacesetters** are those countries that have high scores on the index in question, with a score for that index above (or equal to) the sixth decile level.[14] Countries in this cluster must also have a score above the sixth decile for all three *input*, *process* and *outcome* sub-indexes. **The Pragmatists** are those countries that have high scores for the outcome sub-index (i.e., above the sixth decile value) but a lower value for either the input or process sub-index or both. **The Conventionals** are those countries with high values for the *input* and *process* sub-indexes but with unsatisfactory levels of the *outcome* sub-index. And the **Much-to-be-done** cluster consists of countries with low values for all three sub-indexes.

Countries in any one cluster do not necessarily have the same scores. It is therefore possible to differentiate between countries in the same cluster. It is also possible that a country classified, for example, as "Pragmatist" has a higher overall score than one classified as "Pacesetter". In this example, it would mean that the "Pragmatist" country is providing more security, but contrary to the "Pacesetter", does not have satisfactory scores in all dimensions, perhaps having poorly developed *input* or *process* dimensions, or both.

---

[12] D. Ghai: *Decent Work Indicators: Concepts, Models and Indicators*, ILO/IILS Discussion Papers Series No. 139 (Geneva, ILO, 2002).

[13] D. Kucera: The effects of core workers rights on labour costs and FDI: Evaluating the "conventional wisdom", IILS discussion Papers Series No. 130 (Geneva, ILO, 2001).

[14] The sixth decile was selected because it reflects a concern of "rigour", in that it avoids having countries with scores just above the median being classified as "exemplary".

Chapter 3   Income security: The deepening divide

"It is the absence of the threat of individual starvation which makes primitive society, in a sense, more human than the market economy, and at the same time less economic."

— Karl Polanyi[1]

3.1 The crux of economic security

Let us start with the most contentious and fundamental aspect of economic security, namely, income security. This is more than can be conveyed by standard notions of *poverty*, although that is obviously a part of it. Income security consists of an adequate level of income, a reasonable assurance that such an income will continue, a sense that the income is fair, relative to actual and perceived "needs" and relative to the income of others, and the assurance of compensation or support in the eventuality of a shock or crisis affecting income.

This chapter asks whether globalization has intensified income insecurity. It may have done so by altering the nature of the income "returns" to labour and production, while inducing the restructuring of systems of social transfers that complement money incomes. This could mean that more people have more unstable incomes and have less confidence that their income will continue.

A crucial argument is that, because of the economic, structural and regulatory changes reviewed in Chapter 2, more people are affected by *covariant risk* than by *idiosyncratic* risk, i.e., by structural or systemic shocks for which standard forms of insurance and support systems are ill-equipped.

This chapter will focus on developments in the globalization era, considering the evidence on the deepening divide between those with security and those without it, and the role of social policy. The next chapter will consider aspects of individual income security, mostly in developing countries, drawing in particular from the ILO's People's Security Surveys (PSS). It will conclude by presenting results for a na-

tional Income Security Index calculated for 96 industrialized and developing countries.

3.2 Enriching a concept

Income comes in many forms, which is why economists refer to "money income" as contrasted with "full income" or "social income".[2] Money income comes from wages, profits, rents or the proceeds of market sales. In addition, some workers receive *enterprise* (or *employer* or so-called *occupational*) *benefits* — non-wage entitlements that have a monetary value, such as free or subsidized food at work, paid leave, medical insurance benefits, subsidized housing and subsidized transport to and from the workplace. There are also *state benefits*, which may be disaggregated into *universalistic* rights-based benefits, *categorical* benefits for specified groups with definable characteristics deemed to merit compensation, *means-tested* benefits, and so on.

Then there are *community benefits*, which is a broad term to describe those transfers or valuable services provided by local authorities, or formal or informal associations, including charitable organizations and NGOs. And there are *family transfers*, the availability of which determines the income security of the vast majority of people in developing countries. For the more affluent everywhere, income may also come from *private benefits*, resulting from investments or wealth transfers.

---

[1] K. Polanyi: *The Great Transformation* (Boston, Beacon Press, 1957), pp. 163–164.

[2] For a more elaborated assessment of social income, see G. Standing, *Beyond the New Paternalism* (London, Verso, 2002).

> **A person's income security depends on**
>
> - what income he or she retains, not what he or she "earns";
> - the assurance of that income lasting beyond today;
> - the prospect of receiving adequate income in the future.
>
> Most poverty statistics measure what a person "earns" or nominally "receives".

Income does not come only in direct payments. A very important form of income consists of *public goods*, which are often provided for the whole community and are seen as one means of reducing the inequalities that arise in market economies. In practice, while some public goods reduce social inequality, many may generate further inequality since they may be used more or even exclusively by richer groups.

There are also negative incomes — the "private bads" and the "public bads" that are usually ignored, even though income-expenditure analysis is replete with references to "private goods" and "public goods". Again, "bads" may be shared equally or may be disproportionately borne by poorer or disadvantaged groups in society, as in the case of workers who live in environmentally degraded areas affected by pollution.

In sum, it is inappropriate to assess poverty and income security simply on the basis of earned *money* incomes. For most people, security arises from having a broad range of actual and potential incomes on which to be able to rely.

3.3 Poverty

Poverty is not the same as economic insecurity. But those suffering from impoverishment are likely to be among the most insecure. The stylized facts about global poverty have been well rehearsed, although in truth the quality of the data does not merit the exactitude with which they are presented and repeated. Poverty is both an absolute and a relative concept. A person with no shoes would be considered as poor in Peru, as would a person with no bicycle in China, and a person with no car in the United States.

For the record, in absolute terms, according to standard statistics, poverty has become increasingly concentrated in sub-Saharan Africa. No fewer than 40 African countries have average per capita incomes of less than USD500 per year. Between 1987 and 1998, the number of people in sub-Saharan Africa living on less than USD1 a day increased from 217 million to 291 million, which was about half the total population of the region. Sub-Saharan Africa accounts for about a quarter of the world's poor, so defined. In the 1970s, Africa accounted for about 15% of the world's poor and Asia accounted for about 83%. By the 1990s, Africa accounted for nearly 28%, while Asia accounted for 67%.[3]

This is not the place to go into the debates on the measurement of poverty in detail.[4] However, several points deserve emphasis. First, national poverty lines cannot adequately take into account differences in "basic needs baskets" that are determined in part by ecology, climate, social norms, and so on.[5] Second, the "purchasing power parity" formula used in many cross-country calculations is questionable.[6] Third, there are considerable differences between estimates of poverty derived from national accounts and those derived from household surveys.[7] The problem is compounded because the differences vary from country to country, so that in some cases national accounts data give higher poverty estimates than survey data, while in others it is the other way round. Some observers believe that survey data underestimate the income of the rich, making income inequality measures questionable, but not necessarily poverty estimates. Others suggest that there is a tendency to under-enumerate the poor, because of sampling

---

[3]N. Majid: *Globalization and Poverty*, Employment Paper 2003/54 (Geneva, ILO, 2003), p. 7.

[4]See, e.g., J. Boltvinik: *Poverty Measurement Methods — An Overview* (New York, UNDP, 2002).

[5]For a critique of the purchasing power parity approach, see S.G. Reddy and T.W. Pogge: *How Not To Count the Poor* (mimeo, Mar. 2003). <http://www.socialanalysis.org>.

[6]A. Deaton: *Counting the World's Poor: Problems and Possible Solutions*, Research Programme in Development Studies (Princeton, NJ, Princeton University, 2000).

[7]M. Karshenas: "Global poverty: National accounts-based versus survey-based estimates", *Development and Change*, Vol. 34, No. 4, Sep. 2003, pp. 683–712. Karshenas' estimates imply that the World Bank has underestimated the extent of poverty in African countries, and overestimated it in several other parts of the world, most strikingly in China, as well as in Indonesia and India.

procedures.[8] If so, both poverty and inequality would be underestimated.

In any case, the extent of poverty around the world has remained stubbornly high, in spite of a period of relatively rapid global economic growth. The slowdown of growth cannot have helped. There may have been a reduction in income poverty (although this is contested), but if so it is mainly associated with economic growth and with reductions in income inequality.[9] Lower growth and greater inequality lead to more poverty.

The target endorsed by the United Nations Millennium Summit in 2000 is to reduce income poverty in developing countries from 30% to 15% between 1990 and 2015. At the end of the 20th century about one-fifth of the world's population was impoverished, over 1.1 billion people. In the developing countries and transition countries excluding China, the poverty rate declined by 0.18 percentage points a year between 1987 and 1998. At that rate, it would take almost 60 years to reach the 15% poverty target.[10]

A key point to consider is the following paradox: *there can be a rise in money incomes that masks a rise in income poverty*. Thus, declining headcount figures based on measures of USD1 or USD2 per day may be misleading. To give a single realistic example, if a person, in becoming a wage-worker, loses access to non-monetary forms of income support, such as a food subsidy or an informal transfer mechanism, a rise in money income may actually mask an increase in poverty in terms of income insecurity.

Much has been written about the levels and trends in poverty in the two most populous countries of the world, China and India. In China, use of a national poverty line to measure the extent of poverty has been criticized, in part because coastal provinces have higher poverty lines than the national one, while interior provinces have lower lines. Small changes in the national measure would result in huge increases in recorded poverty. And if the poor were identified by expenditure per head rather than income, the number of people in poverty would increase from 14.7 million to 37.1 million.[11]

Whatever the numbers, some analysts believe distinctions should be made between *chronic poverty* and *transient poverty*.[12] Others would argue that it is mainly a matter of degree. Chronic poverty is when a person

is so poor that he or she cannot recover, in the way used to characterize *chronic insecurity*. But those subject to occasional poverty may be in jeopardy of moving into a chronic state.

Moreover, if there are more factors likely to induce greater income insecurity, a growing proportion of the population could fall into a band around any defined "poverty line". Then, although x% might be classified as poor at any moment, (x + y)% could be subject to poverty during the course of, say, a year. There is surely a strategic difference between a situation in which 20% are subject to poverty and one in which 40% are subject to it.

While conceptual and measurement quandaries abound, the analysis of poverty seems to be stuck in a rut. As several development economists, such as Ravi Kanbur, have pointed out, echoing earlier sceptical authors, the approach taken to the measurement of poverty over the past two decades of increasingly sophisticated empirical examination has implicitly or explicitly taken a *rational choice* perspective, the standard approach of neo-classical economists. Well-being or living standards are measured by a sum of expenditures on consumption goods and services, perhaps with a nod in the direction of giving value to "public goods" (goods and services to regulate and/or provide social protection).

This ignores the negative value of "public bads" and "private bads" as mentioned earlier. Consider a couple of basic and easily understood examples. If a woman goes out to work in a low-wage job, and this results in neglect of a child who becomes ill, the impression given by conventional statistics is that the family's living standard has gone up. The reality, obviously, is livelihood deterioration. More generally, if the poor

---

[8] See, for example, J. Sender: "Rural poverty and gender: Analytical frameworks and policy proposals", in H.J. Chang (ed.): *Rethinking Development Economics* (London, Anthem Press, 2003), pp. 407–423.

[9] Majid, 2003, op. cit., p. 23.

[10] G.A. Cornia and J. Court: *Inequality, Growth and Poverty in the Era of Liberalization and Globalization* (Helsinki, World Institute for Development Economics Research, Nov. 2001), p. 5.

[11] A. Hussain: *Urban Poverty in China: Measurements, Patterns and Policies*, SES Paper No. 34 (Geneva, ILO, 2003).

[12] D. Hulme and A. Shepherd: "Conceptualizing chronic poverty", *World Development*, Vol. 31, No. 3, Mar. 2003, pp. 403–423.

are induced or obliged to work excessive hours to obtain a modest increase in money income, fatigue may eventually lead to illness and loss of the capacity to labour.

The relationship with health is an ignored issue in most discussions of poverty trends. For example, the incidence of HIV/AIDS is much higher among the poor than among more affluent groups, and is much higher in poor African countries than in most of the rest of the world. This contributes directly to poverty and economic insecurity, because the cost of treatment, the cost of caring for orphans, and the cost of lost output represent a heavy burden on many low-income countries. The WHO Commission on Macroeconomics and Health estimated that AIDS has already cost countries of sub-Saharan Africa some 12% of annual national income.[13] It is an impoverishing pandemic.

Most HIV-positive persons are of working age, 37 million of the 40 million being aged between 15 and 49, of whom about 26 million are in sub-Saharan African countries.[14] Not only are poor adults dying, but they are leaving behind a generation of orphans and elderly relatives needing regular support, without either formal or informal transfer systems to provide it.

However, an indirect effect is less often appreciated. Over 22 million people have already died from AIDS.[15] But the incidence of death is much higher for the poor, particularly the rural poor, than for others.[16] The poor are less able to afford the medicines that can extend the life expectancy of AIDS sufferers. A consequence is that the extent of poverty is being disguised by the pattern of premature deaths concentrated among the absolutely poor. Dead souls do not count in the poverty statistics. In sum, poverty as an inadequacy of income is pervasive. But conceptual, measurement and analytical difficulties make it unwise to hinge too much on "poverty" per se.

3.4 Inequality as income insecurity

Income security is weakened by high levels of income inequality, and inequality is part of economic insecurity. Those living in a highly unequal society feel more vulnerable, anxious and resentful. Globalization has been associated with greater income inequality. This has been contested. But, as James Wolfensohn, World Bank President, succinctly put it: *"We live in a world scarred by inequality"*.[17] The issue is fundamental to our concern with insecurity. It is often said that we must learn to live with greater inequality. We should reject this pessimistic claim. It has been the refrain of the privileged throughout history. In that context, we may reflect on four forms of inequality.

(i) Inter-regional and international income inequality

Probably the least discussed aspect is the growth in inter-regional inequality across the world. Thus, in 1960 sub-Saharan Africa had a per capita income that was 19% of the world's average GNP per capita. By the end of the century, that had fallen to 10%. Meanwhile, North America had gone from 443% to 489% of the world's average level.

Global inequality is reflected in the inequality between nations. There are obviously big differences between countries. The United States is "richer" than Germany, which is "richer" than India, which is "richer" than Burundi. But inter-country comparisons of incomes may not be strictly correct, and even when adjusted on a "purchasing power parity" basis leave doubts, notably about the valuation of public goods and public and private "bads". To give a topical example: west Europeans are inclined to believe they do not need to spend much on personal security, whereas in the United States pervasive fears lead to many millions of dollars being spent on handguns, "safe rooms" and other physical security measures. Net incomes of US citizens should be adjusted downward to take account of that.[18]

---

[13] Commission on Macroeconomics and Health: *Macroeconomics and Health: Investing in Health for Economic Development* (Geneva, WHO, Dec. 2001).

[14] UNAIDS: *Report on the Global HIV/AIDS Epidemic 2002* (New York, 2002).

[15] United Nations Population Division, Department of Economic and Social Affairs: *The Impact of AIDS* (New York, UN Population Division/DESA, 2003).

[16] Among the numerous studies, see N. Nattrass: *The Moral Economy of AIDS in South Africa* (Cape Town, University of Cape Town, May 2003); J. Skordis and N. Nattrass: "Paying to waste lives: The affordability of reducing mother to child transmission of HIV in South Africa", *Journal of Health Economics*, Vol. 21, 2002, pp. 405–421.

[17] J. Wolfensohn: *Building an Equitable World*, Address to the Board of Governors of the World Bank, Prague, Sep. 2000, p. 7.

[18] R. Gordon: *Three Centuries of Economic Growth: Europe Chasing the American Frontier*, available at <http://facultyweb.at.northwestern.edu>.

In any event, the stylized facts about global incomes are stark enough, even though all statistics have to be treated as debatable. According to the World Bank, in 1999, world average income per head (at purchasing power parity) was about USD7,000. Countries designated as "high-income", with a total population of 900 million, had an average income of USD26,000 per capita. By contrast, the 5.1 billion people in developing countries had an average income of USD3,500, and about 2.4 billion lived in countries with an average per capita income of USD1,900. There is no sign that this gulf is closing. Indeed, between-country differences explain most of world inequality.[19]

Between 1965 and 1999, real incomes per head rose by 2.4% in the affluent countries, compared with 1.6% for the world as a whole. Average real incomes in sub-Saharan Africa fell, while those in the Middle East and North Africa stagnated. Only countries in East Asia did better than those in the affluent industrialized countries. Intriguingly, the proportion of the world's population in rich countries has been declining rapidly. In 1950, today's rich countries had 32% of the world's population; now they have 19%.

Another form of international inequality that does not show up in conventional presentations is *national indebtedness*. Many poor and middle-income countries (and several rich ones) have become highly indebted, which means that sooner or later their governments are going to have to hold down living standards in order to reduce debt levels. It is misleading to measure their per capita incomes without taking account of the threat of looming debt repayments, which, as vividly demonstrated in Argentina in 2002, could bring those incomes crashing downward at very short notice.

(ii) Functional income inequality

Income distribution has shifted in favour of owners of financial wealth, with the share of GDP going to capital rising and the share going to labour falling. Correspondingly, the incidence of taxation on capital has been falling, in many countries very sharply indeed, while the tax on labour has been rising. The share of tax revenue from capital in the United States (the model in the globalizing economy) fell from 27% in 1965 to 15% in 1999. In the European Union, the rate of fall was even faster, although the share remained higher.

The growth of functional income inequality — the distribution between "capital" and "labour" — is associated with globalization and with the impact of the policies of the Washington Consensus. In many countries, the change has been dramatic. For instance, in India, between the mid-1980s and the late 1990s, the share of value-added going to wages in the private corporate sector fell from 35% to 20%, while the share going to profits (before tax and after depreciation) rose by 15 percentage points.[20] In Mexico, the secular redistribution has been even more extraordinary (Figure 3.1).

Figure 3.1 Mexico: Wages and salaries as a share of GDP, 1950–2000

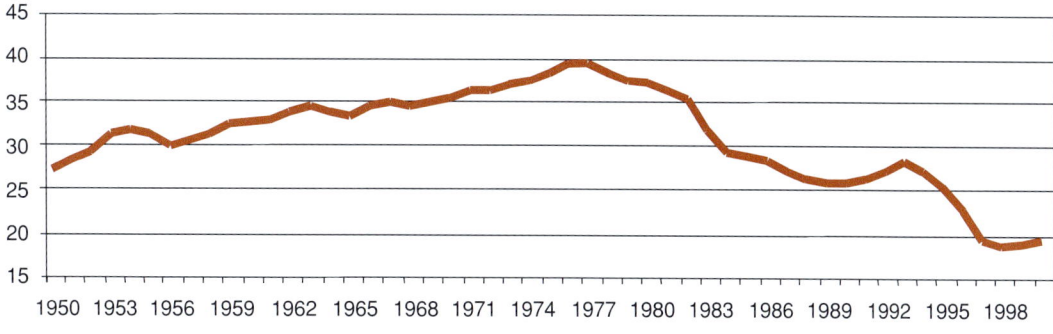

Note: "Wages and salaries" includes social security contributions and other payments made by employers.

Source: J.G. Palma: *The Mexican Economy since Trade Liberalization and NAFTA* (Geneva, ILO, 2003), p. 66.

[19] R.P. Korzeniewick and T. Moran: "World economic trends in the distribution of income, 1965–1992", *American Journal of Sociology*, Vol. 102, 1997, pp. 1000–1039.

[20] R. Nagaraj: "Indian economy since the 1980s: Virtuous growth or polarization?", *Economic and Political Weekly*, 5 Aug. 2000, pp. 2831–2839.

In some countries, the big shrinkage in the wage share occurred in the 1980s and stabilized in the 1990s. In others, the change has come later. But the key point is that the functional income distribution has become more skewed. This raises questions about how more income can be shifted to lower-income groups, especially since it appears to be increasingly hard to tax the more mobile factors of production.[21] Capital seems to be able to benefit from globalization, while labour is less capable of doing so.

(iii) Personal income distribution

In terms of personal incomes, over the past quarter of a century inequality has grown in many parts of the world. The exact changes are the subject of controversy among economists. Although there has been debate on the extent of global inequality and on international trends, the concern here is with intra-country inequality.[22]

One problem in attempting to assess the extent of inequality is that for many countries data are not available. They include oil-rich Middle East countries, where inequality is believed to be extreme. And in assessing inequality it is important to remember that in many countries *wealth* is more unevenly distributed than income. In the United States, the wealthiest 1% of households holds about 40% of all financial wealth, and the top 20% holds 94%.[23] The distribution of wealth widened in the 1990s, when the top 1% increased its net worth by 11.3% while the bottom 90% lost 4.4%.[24] The pattern may not be quite as dramatic in other countries, but it is generally true that if policy-makers wish to reduce inequality, more attention should be given to ways of redistributing wealth.

As far as incomes are concerned, the UNDP's *Human Development Report 1999* highlighted long-term developments in global income distribution. According to the sketchy data available, the income gap between the richest fifth of the world's population and the poorest fifth was about 3 to 1 in 1820; it was 11:1 in 1913, 30:1 in 1970, 60:1 in 1990 and 86:1 by the end of the 20th century. The richest 20% of the world's population living in the high-income countries earned 86% of world GDP, while the bottom 20% received 1%.

The region of the world with the most unequal income distribution is Latin America, where inequality has been growing. The World Bank has recently testified to this, finding that the top decile of income earners receives 48% of total income while the bottom decile receives 1.6%, compared to 29% and 2.5% respectively in industrialized countries.[25]

Can the economy grow while becoming more egalitarian?

The orthodox view is that economic growth and income inequality go together. As countries become richer everybody benefits from growth but differences between people's income widen, or at best remain constant.

A study on income distribution worldwide shows that this need not be the case.[26] It is possible to grow and reduce inequalities. Between 1980 and 1998, Indonesia not only reduced poverty rapidly — both at the USD1 and USD2 per day level — but compressed income distribution at the same time as it shifted to the right, reflecting higher average incomes. According to the Asian Recovery Information Centre of the Asian Development Bank, from 1996 to 2002 the Gini coefficient fell from 36.5% to 31.0% and the ratio of the income share of the highest to the lowest quintile fell from 8.4 to 6.6 (1999).

---

[21] H. Wachtel: "Tax distortion in the global economy", in L. Beneria and S. Bisneth (eds.): *Global Tensions: Challenges and Opportunities in the World Economy* (New York and London, Routledge, 2003), pp. 27–43.

[22] For one attempt to measure world income inequality based on household survey data, see B. Milanovic: *True World Income Distribution, 1988 and 1993: First Calculation Based on Household Surveys Alone* (Washington, DC, World Bank Development Research Group, Oct. 1999).

[23] E.N. Woolff and R.C. Leone: *Top Heavy: The Increasing Inequality of Wealth in America and What Can Be Done About It* (New York, New Press, 2002).

[24] Bank for International Settlements: *70th Annual Report 1 April 1999 - 31 March 2000* (Basel, 2000), p. 14.

[25] D. Ferranti et al.: *Inequality in Latin America and the Caribbean: Breaking with History?* (Washington, DC, World Bank, 2004). The "most equal" country, Uruguay, was more unequal than any country in Europe.

[26] M. Marti-i-Sala: *The World Distribution of Income*, NBER Working Paper Series No. 8933 (Cambridge, MA, National Bureau of Economic Research, 2002).

Growing income and wealth inequality implies at the very least that those at or near the bottom are doing relatively less well, and this in itself is a source of *relative deprivation*. However, growing inequality almost certainly also means that the situation of the poor is worsened in absolute terms, even though theoretically a widening of inequality could occur with a growth of incomes of all groups. Indeed, it was long assumed that growing inequality was necessary to promote economic growth in developing countries.

Nowadays, the more widely accepted thesis is that a reduction in inequality fosters economic growth, partly because of the effects on aggregate demand and investment. Highly inegalitarian societies do not have good records of ensuring income security for their poorer citizens, and sooner or later suffer adverse social developments that impinge on long-term development, or the sustainability of growth.

Moreover, some analysts argue that inequality is underestimated by available statistics, perhaps increasingly. This claim, based on cogent but anecdotal evidence, demands more systematic research and better data. Many of the factors that result in an underestimate of poverty noted earlier are also relevant for estimating the extent of inequality, including the effect of HIV/AIDS.

One factor is that higher-income earners receive a high and growing share of their income from perks and benefits that are either unmeasured or only partially taken into account. For instance, senior executives of many US corporations are provided with retirement funds guaranteed a high rate of return or with pension schemes that do not have the risks inherent in the so-called 401(k) pension plans provided to the workers in those companies. As it happened in the Enron case, 401(k) contributors may lose heavily if the company goes bankrupt.

Indeed, like some other countries, over the past quarter of a century the United States has witnessed the growth of an income-differentiating *multi-tier pension system*, with much more secure and higher pension entitlements for executives and senior professionals, with much lower retirement benefits for ordinary workers, and with those on the fringe left to depend on "social security". It has been estimated that in the United States the value of retirement money held by the median household fell by 11% between 1983 and 1998.[27] While executives were gaining from stock options and elaborate pension arrangements, companies were cutting pension contributions for ordinary workers.

Similar tendencies have been occurring in other countries. In effect, the distribution of risks has been changing to the disadvantage of poorer workers. By lowering risk for those earning high salaries, the full value of their income is raised. This is not measured in conventional income distribution statistics. Nor is the fact that a pension tied to one's own firm provides a less secure future income than one that is diversified through pension funds or through a public pension scheme.

Another example is *life insurance*. Many companies pay the premia on executives' life insurance, allowing them to cash in endowments years after they have retired or left the company. For ordinary workers, there is no such treatment. Many such perks widen inequality, and give the richer groups more income security than others.

Inequality also takes *categorical forms*, as defined by a characteristic such as race, nationality, creed or religion. This is mirrored by ugly realities. Even within countries, certain so-defined groups receive much lower incomes, are exposed to greater economic vulnerability, and experience correspondingly greater social and economic insecurity. All societies suffer from these structural inequalities and there must be concern that, if there is any overall growth of inequality, the most vulnerable groups will be most adversely affected. Thus, to give an example, in the United Kingdom, about 60% of the Pakistani and Bangladeshi communities live in poverty, compared with 16% of white families. This is typical of many countries at all levels of economic development.

---

[27] Research by Edward Wolff, reported in *International Herald Tribune*, 1 Mar. 2002, p. 15.

Inequality and poverty: Chile enters the 21st century

In Chile, in 2000, the average income of the top 10% of the population was among the highest in the world in absolute terms.

Meanwhile, the average family (four persons) needed to earn at least 2.5 times the minimum wage to afford the "basic" basket of goods and services used to define the poverty line. On average, only 1.04 people per family actually earned anything (if we take account of the fact that in some families nobody did so).

The following table gives the distribution of wage earners in Chile in 2000 according to whether they earned (i) the same or less than the minimum wage; (ii) 1 to 1.25 times the minimum wage; (iii) 1.25 to 1.5 times the minimum wage; and (iv) 1.5 to 2.4 times the minimum wage (i.e., just under what they needed to afford the "basket"). The figures imply that 60% of workers (1.9 million out of 3.1 million) would not be able to buy the "basket" if they were the only earner in the average family, which is close to reality as the average.

Of course, there are other incomes, subsidies and transfers, but the point is that 60% of the workforce did not earn enough to support the average family.

Multiple of minimum wage	<= 1	1–1.25	1.25–1.5	1.5–2.4	Sum
Zone					
Urban	11.6	14.9	11.5	22.3	60.4
Rural	32.9	31.6	14.0	12.7	91.1
Total	**14.0**	**16.8**	**11.7**	**21.3**	**63.8**
Activity					
Agrarian	31.9	30.4	15.3	12.6	90.2
Non-agrarian	11.1	14.6	11.2	22.6	59.5
Total	**14.0**	**16.8**	**11.7**	**21.3**	**63.8**
No. of employees in enterprise					
2–5	28.2	26.7	12.7	18.4	86.0
6–9	18.9	23.7	14.0	20.9	77.6
10–49	13.4	17.1	12.7	22.7	57.5
50–199	9.6	15.2	11.3	21.3	66.0
200 or more	7.5	9.2	9.3	20.8	46.8
Total	**14.0**	**16.8**	**11.7**	**21.3**	**63.8**

(iv) Polarization and middle-class stability

> "What do you call someone who was president of a dot.com company last year? … Waiter!"
>
> — Kenneth McGee,
> a vice-president of Gartner Group [28]

There is growing evidence of a changing character of income distribution, with a tiny minority receiving absurdly large amounts. For instance, the US Internal Revenue Service reported that the top 400 highest-income earners received 1.1% of all US income in 2002, up from 0.5% in 1992 — and that to be in that top 400 one had to earn a gross annual income of USD86.83 million.[29] Most of that income came from net capital gains, and the average tax rate was merely 22.3%. Moreover, it did not include tax-exempt interest income from government bonds, and represents income after deducting various items, such as self-employed health insurance. The picture is one of complete detachment from the mainstream of American society, let alone from the rest of the world.

There is much anecdotal evidence of this sort, but the standard way of measuring income inequality is not designed to pick up such a phenomenon.

The Gini and its discontents

The changing character of economic transactions and labour markets means an increasing probability of "winner-takes-all" and "losers-lose-all" situations, in which income polarization occurs. Unfortunately, the standard Gini coefficient may not detect this since it gives insufficient attention to extreme values in the distribution.

Accordingly, we made an attempt to measure income polarization, in terms of an adjusted Wolfson Index and other indexes of income polarization. It was finally decided to focus on the ratio of the income of the top decile (Decile 10) of the income distribution divided by the income of the bottom four deciles (Deciles 1–4). This has the virtue of being simple to understand. Some results are given later.

The insecurity of the non-poor should be considered at the same time as the insecurity of the poor. Of course, the latter deserves top priority. But insecurities cut across the income spectrum. At the bottom are the sad dejected people who live in the streets and who die there, detached from all society's institutions. Their insecurity is pitiful. Just above them are the "informalized", millions of people struggling to survive, unable to plan, confronted by forces that are increasingly distant. Just above them are workers fearful that at any time their jobs may disappear, their skills may become obsolescent and their anchors of stable support may prove illusory.

Then there is the global middle class, consumed by consumerism. Even the famous "white collar" professionals feel the insecurities of over-stretched budgets, stressful work schedules and irrelevance. We are also seeing the first MBSE (must-be-somewhere-else) generation, a growing body of people calling themselves consultants scurrying about their necessarily insecure business. And at the top of the pile is an elite detached from all national regulatory systems, earning vast fortunes, pursuing their nth billion on the edge of legality and decency.

Globally, the number of dollar millionaires has grown steadily, and even rose by over 2% in 2002, when the world economy was experiencing a downturn. According to the *World Wealth Report,* by 2003 there were 7.3 million dollar millionaires and some 58,000 "ultra high net worth individuals" with assets of more than USD30 million each.[30]

---

[28] Speech at World Economic Forum, Washington, DC, reported in *International Herald Tribune*, 9 Apr. 2001, p. 16.

[29] The report is posted on the IRS website: <http://www.irs.gov>.

[30] Merrill Lynch and Cap Gemini Ernst and Young: *World Wealth Report 2003.*

They are not our primary concern. But where is the economic security if the majority of the world is languishing in or near poverty while that elite steadily strengthen their relative and absolute position?

While income distribution has been widening, there is evidence that the middle classes (the middle-income groups) have retained a stable share of total income, with the gainers being at the top and the losers at the bottom. Is this a phenomenon found mainly in middle-income developing countries?

Comparing countries, there seem to be four "layers" of inequality (Figure 3.2). First, there are countries with relatively little inequality, consisting mostly of the ex-communist countries of central Europe and the non-English-speaking OECD countries; a second layer contains countries from several regions, comprising about three-quarters of the world's population, where inequality is greater but where the Gini coefficient is less than 0.4; third, inequality is greater in sub-Saharan Africa and the second-tier East Asian NICs; and fourth, there is Latin America, which has much greater inequality than any other region (even those with similar per capita incomes, such as North Africa).

The four layers correspond very closely to the share of total income obtained by the richest decile. In Latin America, this is nearly 45% of total income, whereas it is less than 25% in central and western Europe.[31]

Figure 3.2 Gini indices and log of income per capita

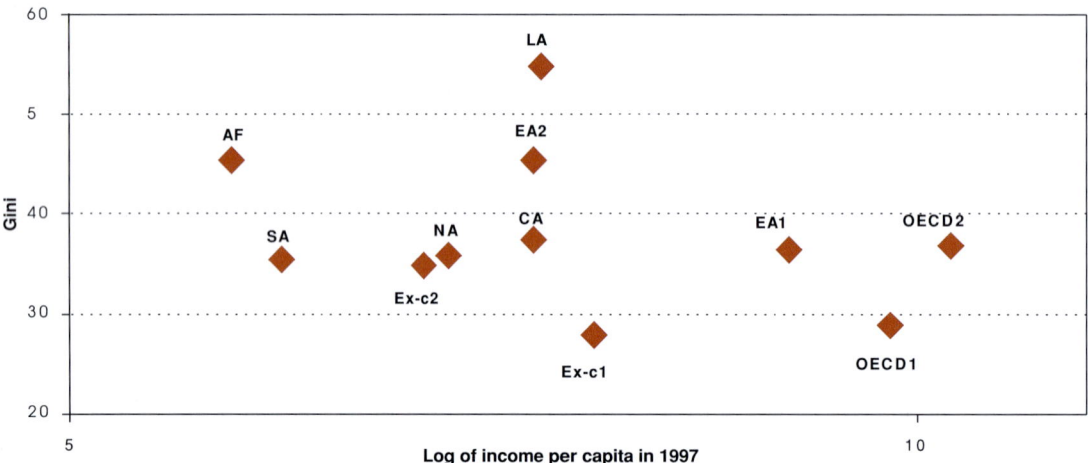

Note: Regional figures are median values.

Code: AF = sub-Saharan Africa; SA = South Asia and low-income East Asia; EA 1 = first-tier NICs; EA 2 = second-tier NICs; LA = Latin America; CA = Caribbean; NA = North Africa; ex-c1 = ex-communist countries of central Europe; Ex-c2 = ex-communist countries of the former Soviet Union; OECD1 = non-English-speaking OECD; OECD2 = English-speaking OECD.

Source: World Bank: *World Development Indicators 2003*.

[31]The similarity is due to the way the Gini index is calculated and this disparity across the world is reflected in the income share of the bottom four deciles.

However, when looking at the other 50% of the world's population, those within deciles 5 and 9 — the "middle classes" — the regional picture changes from one of disparity to one of remarkable similarity, as shown in Figure 3.3.

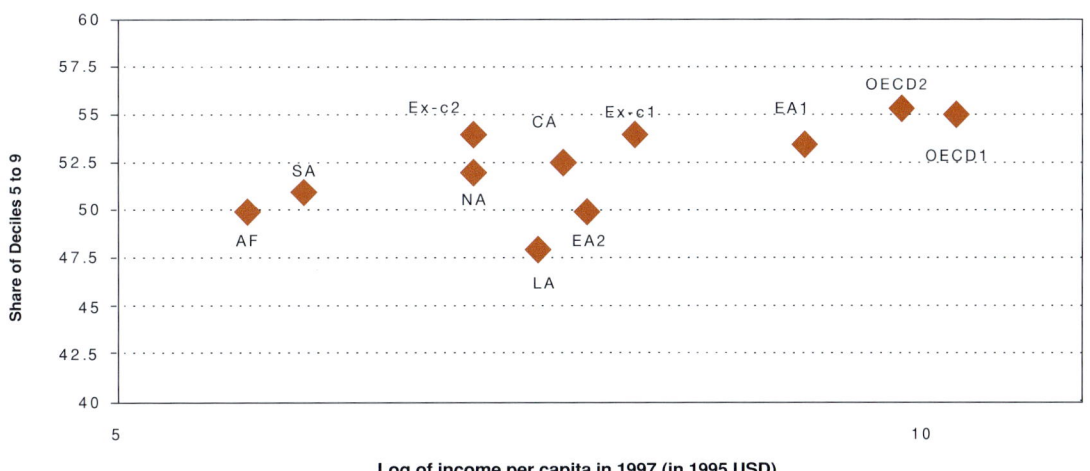

Figure 3.3 Middle-class income shares by regional income levels
(income shares of deciles 5 to 9 and log of income per capita)

Note: Regional figures are median values. Regions as in Figure 3.2.

Source: World Bank: *World Development Indicators 2003*.

The coefficient of variation also shows the regional contrast — the coefficients for Decile 10 and Deciles 1 to 4 are nearly four times greater than that of Deciles 5 to 9, and are nearly seven times larger than that of Deciles 7 to 9. Thus the "middle class" across the world benefits from a distributional "safety net". Regardless of national income per capita, type of political regime, economic policies, structure of property rights, or whether or not they belong to countries that managed to get their prices "right" or their institutions "right", the 50% of the population located between Deciles 5 to 9 seem able to count on about half the national income.

By contrast, the bottom 40% of the population may receive as much as one quarter of national income (as in the non-English speaking OECD and countries of Central Europe), or as little as 10% (as in Latin America). The regional distributional structure shown by the Gini coefficient reflects only the income disparities of those at the top and at the bottom of the distribution. This is peculiar, not just from a statistical viewpoint (the usefulness of the Gini coefficient

as an indicator of inequality), but also from an analytical one. In effect, political and economic developments (including globalization) have been associated with two distributional tendencies across regions in the world: a (better known) "centrifugal" movement in terms of income shares of the top and bottom deciles and a (less known) "centripetal" one in terms of the income share of Deciles 5 to 9.

More generally, the issues of most concern to our analysis are the detachment of groups at the top and bottom of the income distribution, leaving a global elite likely to be uninterested in the income security and welfare of most people in their own society, and leaving the poorest detached from the mainstream of their own society as well.

(v) The impact of fiscal and social policy

One factor behind greater income inequality has been the reduced progressivity of direct taxation. Starting with the 1986 Tax Reform Act in the United States, every industrialized country, except Switzerland and Turkey, lowered its top marginal income tax rate between 1986 and 1991 alone.[32] Income tax has ceased to be a redistributive instrument. Meanwhile, the tax on labour through social security contributions and other payroll taxes rose steeply relative to corporate profits tax, which may be interpreted as a shift from market-regulating to market-conforming fiscal policy.[33]

Throughout the world, taxes on capital have been coming down, while taxes on labour have risen in absolute and relative terms, compounded by the effect of a shift in social security contributions from employers to workers. Perversely, while fiscal policy has become more regressive, social policy may be moving in the same direction. Some of the reasons are considered later.

Inequality and redistribution: Robin Hood or Winners-Take-All?

The interrelationship between inequality and the extent to which social policy is redistributive is highly contested.

On one side is the evidence for the "Robin Hood paradox".[34] This argues that redistribution tends to be least when needed most and when best justified on economic efficiency grounds, while "more equal societies redistribute more".[35] The counter-attack, currently including some World Bank work, argues that the greater the primary inequality, the greater the redistribution.[36]

The jury is out.

Income security and property rights

The relationship between property rights as enshrined in law and the extent of inequality and income insecurity is poorly understood.

Property rights are often regarded as essential for economic growth, and much effort has been devoted to inducing developing countries to install models developed in today's rich countries. This can have perverse effects. For example, in the United States property rights were not established by wise leadership but emerged from informal practices among the poor, who operated their own systems that were subsequently ratified by laws.[37] To some extent they emerged as a means of protecting relatively disadvantaged groups. Had they been installed "from above", they may have given the interests and needs of the poor little attention. This is relevant for assessing the appropriateness of efforts to install property rights as part of the Washington Consensus.

With formal property rights, is there always more income security? Do formal property rights reduce the income security of the poor by reducing their access to the public "commons"?

---

[32] M. Hallerberg and S. Basinger: "Internationalization and changes in taxation policy in OECD countries: The importance of domestic veto players", *Comparative Political Studies*, Vol. 31, No. 3, 1998, pp. 321–352.

[33] D. Swank: "Funding the welfare state: Globalization and the taxation of business in advanced market economies", *Political Studies*, Vol. 46, 1998, pp. 671–692.

[34] P. Lindert: "When did inequality rise in Britain and America?", *Journal of Income Distribution*, No. 9, July 2000, pp. 15–25; "Three centuries of inequality in Britain and America", in A.B. Atkinson and F. Bourguignon (eds.): *Handbook on Income Distribution* (Amsterdam, North-Holland, 2000).

[35] B. Boadway and M. Keen: "Redistribution", in A.B. Atkinson and F. Bourguignon (eds.), 2000, op. cit., pp. 677–789.

[36] B. Milanovic: *A New Polarization Measure and Some Applications* (Washington, DC, World Bank, June 2000).

[37] H. de Soto: *The Mystery of Capital: Why Capitalism Triumphs in the West and Fails Everywhere Else* (New York, Perseus Book Group, 2000).

3.5 National economic crises and income insecurity

As noted in Chapter 2, the global economy has become more prone to economic crises, which involve deep sudden downturns, often spreading from one country or region of the world to others. Ordinary people cannot possibly foresee such shocks and the scope for insuring against them is limited.

The volatility of GDP levels and growth is greater in developing countries and the consequences of fluctuations are more severe there, as has been recognized by the IMF among others.[38] It is less clear which groups in society are most severely affected.

The standard answer is that the poor, women and those in the "informal sector" are most vulnerable.[39] To the extent the poor are more vulnerable definitionally, this is obviously true. However, in terms of income insecurity, there may be several paradoxes of crisis. In particular, those in the "informal economy" may not be as vulnerable as those in formal wage jobs, and a society in which there is a large informal economy may not be as vulnerable as one in which there is little or no informal economy.

The Asian crisis, while creating tremendous hardships, did not result in huge open unemployment, except in the most industrialized economy, the Republic of Korea. Nor did it lead to a sharp decline in life expectancy. To some extent, the rural informal economy acted as a shock absorber, and both rural and urban informal economies responded as a sponge, providing social protection of a sort. These images can be exaggerated, and one should not belittle the longer-term adverse effects. However, a contrast can be drawn with what happened in countries of the former Soviet Union after they were hit by the economic meltdown in the early 1990s. Millions of people died prematurely, concentrated among middle-aged men (although life expectancy declined for both men and women).[40]

Another example was what happened in Uzbekistan in the same period. Remarkably, Russians living there, who had been the relatively high-income group concentrated in "formal economy" activities, died in much greater numbers and suffered from a much higher incidence of morbidity than Uzbeks. The latter were able to tap informal networks of social protection, while in the Russian Federation itself and among the Russians in former Soviet satellites, there was no informal economy or support system on which to rely.

This is not to minimize the hardships of informal workers or women or other disadvantaged groups in the wake of economic crises. The point is that the system of production and the relations of distribution and social protection must be considered in their entirety before strong generalizations can be made.

National income volatility translates into individual and community income volatility. Among the implications is that a large and possibly growing proportion of the population in many countries move in and out of poverty and even destitution. This sort of experience can have devastating consequences, because the adverse effects of falling into poverty may be more durable than any beneficial effect from temporarily rising above water.

---

[38] International Monetary Fund: *World Economic Outlook 2002* (Washington, DC, Oct. 2002), Box 3.4, p. 125.

[39] IMF, 2002, ibid., p. 14. The Commission on Human Security, without giving any evidence, subscribed to this view. Commission on Human Security, 2003, op. cit., p. 83.

[40] For a summary of evidence, see G. Standing: *Russian Unemployment and Enterprise Restructuring: Reviving Dead Souls* (Basingstoke and New York, Macmillan, 1996).

Income variability and the 1990s "Bubble Economy"

There is evidence that people indulge in what has been called consumption smoothing, so that year-to-year variation in incomes is greater than year-to-year variation in consumption expenditure. If savings ratios are low, this may result in a proneness to personal indebtedness. Panel data, such as those generated by the Luxembourg Income Survey, can be used to determine whether there has been growing variability of incomes.

In the 1990s, for core workers and salariats in rich countries, there was a tendency to shift remuneration from money wages to "financial property" payments, in the form of shares and company pension and health funds. These gave the impression of sudden wealth as share prices rocketed. In addition, interest rates fell to almost zero, making consumer debt seem "cheap". Workers had an illusion of wealth, which led to a splurge of debt-funded consumerism.

When the bubble burst in 2000, some bitter lessons were learnt.

In the Netherlands, throughout the 1990s, the government encouraged all groups to invest in equity, so that by 1999 27% of households held shares. When combined with their stock market exposure through pension funds, which were investing in stock markets as well, 38% of households' net wealth was invested in the relatively risky stock market. Low interest rates and a widespread temptation to invest in the high-return stock market led many to take a "top up" loan on their homes, leading to a dramatic increase in household debt, which rose during the 1990s to an average of 188% of household disposable income.

When the US bubble burst in April 2000 the Amsterdam stock exchange plunged, leaving many people in financial crisis. Meanwhile, pension funds were hit by solvency problems, which in turn led them to increase contribution rates. It is widely thought that the extensive anxiety and insecurity generated by the stock market downturn led to increased support for right-wing xenophobic politicians in the subsequent general election.

3.6 State benefits: From de-commodifying to re-commodifying?

For much of the second half of the 20th century, the social wage of workers in industrialized countries, including the communist bloc, was bolstered by a widening array of state benefits. Globalization and changing labour relations have curbed these. In developing countries, the expected spread of state benefits, in terms of public health care provision, paid sick leave, maternity benefits, pension coverage, disability benefits and much else, simply has not occurred and in many countries has gone into reverse.

Income security is derived from having a wide range of sources of income and being able to rely on support in times of need. In this regard, the various forms of *welfare state* that crystallized after the Second World War in industrialized countries created a *labour citizenship*, in which the performance of labour, or the willingness to do so, entitled citizens to many social benefits and social services. These were based on contributions by employers and employees to cover contingency risks.

Since the 1970s such systems have been gradually whittled away and fragmented, in that groups have had access to a differentiated range and level of state benefits. There has been a shift of costs from employers to workers, and a shift from insurance benefits to means-tested social assistance.

From the 1970s onwards, the rising need for social transfers in the many countries afflicted by high unemployment, poverty and other adverse labour market trends led to a fiscal crisis — more money needed for transfers coupled with declining social security contributions. A short-term response was to raise social security and payroll "taxes", which rose sharply as a share of the wage bill. General or earmarked tax revenue came to be used to a greater extent. Then there were attempts to narrow the fiscal gap by cutting benefit levels by various devices and by increasing the number of conditions and the difficulty of meeting them for benefit entitlement.[41]

In industrialized countries, there has been a drift away from state social security based on contributions to tax-based relief (or nothing), and among the public there has been a loss of confidence in the future of insurance-based social security. In the United States,

---

[41]For an extended discussion of these trends, see Standing, 2002, op. cit.

only 10% of workers expect "social security" to be the most important source of income in their retirement. In Japan, a growing proportion of young people are opting out of the contributory pension scheme.

As income inequality grows, *social policy* is likely to become regressive, not more progressive. Increased stratification results in a shrinkage in social solidarity, so that voters tend to elect politicians who favour "middle class" interests. The reality is that in the early years of the 21st century powerful interests are pressing governments all over the world to cut public social spending, and in doing so reduce the income security provided by the State.

Private regulation of public spending

The private commercial "credit rating agencies" have been telling European governments they will be relegated to the second rank of borrowers unless they cut social spending.[42] They warn of rising pension and health care spending, due to population ageing and advances in medical technology. Globally, these are pushing up public spending, further raised by a growing incidence of "extreme weather events" (because governments act as "insurers of last resort") and by pressure to increase spending on "defence" (military goods and services). While spending rises, globalization has reduced the perceived ability of governments to raise revenue from taxes, particularly those levied on "footloose" capital.

The message coming from those private credit rating agencies is that governments must take a very long-term budgeting perspective and take pre-emptive action by cutting pension and health care "generosity", a view echoed by the IMF and the World Bank.[43]

One could make this a democratic issue. There is no iron rule that pensions or health care should be cut. Other spending could be reduced; other sources of revenue could be tapped. The debate should be open, transparent and comprehensive.

Social or state transfers can be central to income security. But it is clear that in most countries of the world even old-style labourist social security schemes are sketchy or non-operational. In some countries, particularly those designated as "transition" economies, the formal commitment to provide state benefits to workers has not been honoured. In countries of the former Soviet Union, this has been blightening people's lives in the past decade and a half. Thus, in Ukraine in 2002, although nearly one in every five industrial workers was entitled to a housing benefit or subsidy, less than half actually received it. For workers in the public sector, non-payment was even worse. A similar pattern existed in the case of transport allowances.

The failure in transition countries has been more than matched in the developing world. In most African countries, there is some government commitment to universal provision of social protection. In Tanzania, for instance, the right to social security is set out in the 1977 constitution (as amended in 1984, 1995 and 1998). This is really a commitment to achieve full coverage in the long term, which has not been met due to a lack of resources.[44] But the low coverage is also a reflection of priorities and a failure to ensure rights are respected. Only about 6% of the total population is covered by "formal social security schemes".[45] Benefits provided are few and involve amounts insufficient to avert poverty.[46]

---

[42] "In the long run we are all broke", *The Economist*, 22 Nov. 2003, p. 80.

[43] P. Heller: *Who Will Pay? Coping With Ageing Societies, Climate Change and Other Long-term Fiscal Challenges* (Washington, DC, IMF, 2003). <http://www.imf.org/external/pubs/nft/2003/wwp/index.htm>.

[44] F.S.K. Tungaraza and G. Mapunda: *The National Social Security Policy* (Dar-es-Salaam, Government Policy Paper, 2000).

[45] These are the National Social Security Fund, the National Health Insurance Scheme and the Community Health Fund. Some observers have given even lower estimates of national coverage. See, e.g., L. Steinwachs: *Extending Health Protection in Tanzania: Networking Between Health Financing Mechanisms*, Extension of Social Security Paper No. 7 (Geneva, ILO, 2002).

[46] S.M. Wangwe and P. Tibandebage: *Towards Social Security Policy and Reform in Tanzania*, paper presented at the National Social Security Fund Symposium, Dar-es-Salaam, 1999.

One difficulty in assessing social security coverage is the dearth of statistical information on social security systems. Most of the available data is largely textual, descriptive of laws and formal systems rather than of their operational effectiveness, and is thus inadequate for quantitative analysis. To overcome this limitation, we have established a global Social Security Database, in which legislative information has been converted into numerical data, allowing a statistical assessment of patterns of social security provision throughout the world.[47]

Of the 102 countries included in the database, only one in three has state (public) schemes of some sort covering all the eight conventional social risks paying out cash benefits (sickness, maternity, old age, invalidity, survivors, family allowances, work injury and unemployment). One in six covers half or fewer of these risks. Just over one in three countries has a statutory scheme for compensating workers for loss of earnings due to illness. Only one in two pays unemployment benefits.

Social security schemes can also be classified by type of programme. The *social insurance* type of programme was still widespread at the end of the 20th century. But the incidence varied substantially across countries. Countries with high values of the UNDP's Human Development Index (HDI) all have a social insurance programme of some kind and over half have some sort of *universal programme*. Among low-HDI countries, of which over 80% are in Africa, three in four have no social insurance scheme and none has any universal scheme, except Mauritius. In all African countries, the less effective types of scheme predominate, such as *employer liability* and *provident funds*.

An attempt was made to see if clusters of countries providing social protection in similar ways could be detected. Although indicators on effectiveness of social security schemes could not be measured because of lack of data, countries are classified according to number of social risks covered by national legislation, as well as by the level of expenditure on social security as a percentage of GDP and the quality of the programmes as measured by eligibility conditions for benefits. It turns out that only 17 of the 102 countries meet all those criteria satisfactorily. At the other extreme, 34 countries do not meet *any* of the criteria. In this latter group, ten are African, 12 Latin American and eight Asian. In the "pace-setter" group, there are no countries outside Europe; three in four are from western Europe, the rest being from eastern Europe.

Social security expenditure, as a percentage of GDP, is positively and significantly correlated with the HDI (R=51%) but only weakly correlated with the Gini measure of income distribution (R=31%). This suggests that, while social security may have a positive effect on human development, it does not have a strong redistributive role, which has been widely noted.[48] Social security has not been used to compensate for income inequality.

(i) Pensions and old-age income security

Ageing

The world is growing older. Globally the median age is expected to continue to rise, reaching 37 by 2050. Although developing countries have a low median age, they are already home to most people over the age of 60 in the world, even though the share of that age group is highest in affluent industrialized countries. In India, whereas the population is projected to grow by 49% between 1991 and 2015, the population aged 60 or over will grow by 107%.[49]

Population ageing poses growing challenges of perceived "dependency", strains on pension systems and challenges for labour market policy, notably in the sphere of training and retraining. It will also strengthen pressure to review the role of "care work" in all parts of the world.

[47] Main sources are International Social Security Association: *Social Security Programs Throughout the World* (Geneva, ISSA, 1999); *ILO Cost of Social Security Inquiry* (Geneva, ILO, 1998) <www.ilo.org/protection/socfas>; and F. Bonnet: *Whither Social Security? A Response Through Indicators*, SES Paper (Geneva, ILO, forthcoming).

[48] E.g., G. Esping-Andersen: *The Three Worlds of Welfare Capitalism* (Cambridge, Polity Press, 1990).

[49] Government of India, Ministry of Sound Justice and Empowerment: *First Report of Expert Committee for Devising a Pension System for India* (New Delhi, 1999).

For more than a century it has been a great hope of civilization that everybody could look forward to old age with a decent pension on which to live in reasonable comfort. Starting with the Bismarckian scheme, intended to supplement declining income as selected groups of workers grew older (and to deter core workers from joining labour movements), earnings-related social insurance was seen as the way forward for industrialized countries and, in time, for developing countries as they modernized their economies.

Table 3.1 Sources of income of elderly, selected industrialized countries, 2001

	Percentage of total average income among retired				
	Sweden	Germany	Japan	United States	Korea, Rep. of
Public pensions	80.1	75.8	67.5	56.6	5.9
Private pensions	1.9	9.1	1.6	16.4	0.6
Income from work	11.8	7.1	20.8	13.9	28.1
Savings	0.6	1.3	1.6	0.9	9.6
Earnings from investments	0.2	1.9	2.3	7.0	5.6
Child allowances	0.0	0.2	3.4	0.1	43.2
Other benefits	2.9	1.5	0.9	0.5	5.0
Other	2.5	3.1	1.9	4.6	2.0

Source: The International Study on Living and Consciousness of Senior Citizens, Policy Office for the Aged, Cabinet Office (Tokyo, Government of Japan, 2001), Table 28.

The variants of the Bismarckian and Beveridge schemes have been the subject of a vast literature. All we need to do here is highlight the trends in national pension systems that have a bearing on old-age income security. First, it is instructive to recall some of the recommendations of the World Bank's influential and enormously expensive report, *Averting the Old Age Crisis*, published in 1994. This stated bluntly: *"The first step is to reform the public pillar by raising the retirement age, eliminating rewards for early retirement ... downsizing benefit levels ... and making the benefit structure flatter. The second step is to launch the private pillar"*.[50]

The report was part of a strategy to promote the privatization of pension schemes and a shift from defined-benefit to defined-contribution schemes, preferably along the lines of the Chilean individual accounts pension system introduced in 1981.

Symbolism of Chile's pension reform

The Chilean pension reform, designed by Jose Pinera, a Harvard-educated economist who became Chile's Minister of Labour and Social Affairs, was intended to appeal to "formal sector" workers. The idea was to make them feel they had an interest in the market economy, as individual proprietors, as stakeholders, but without social ties to any collective interest group, not even to their employers.

Symbolism was part of the legitimation process, as Pinera himself emphasized. The scheme was carefully set to begin on May Day in 1981. And all members of the pension scheme receive their own account book (*libreta*), conveying a sense of individual social status.

---

[50]World Bank: *Averting the Old Age Crisis* (Washington, DC, 1994), p. 261.

In the globalization era, pension systems have been undergoing a twofold process of "reform", one in which governments have been transforming systems explicitly and one in which piecemeal adjustments have been changing the character of systems that have retained their old name. Recall that the main objective in the post-1945 period was to construct a universal pension system in which security in old age and social solidarity would be strengthened, through reliance on pay-as-you-go risk-sharing social security.

Since the 1980s, and particularly since the World Bank became involved in promoting pension reform in the 1990s, *multi-tier* pension systems have proliferated in which individual accounts have become the primary focus. The typical model has consisted of three or four tiers, including a basic means-tested state pension, an occupational (enterprise-level) second tier, a social insurance or mandatory individual savings account tier, and a private voluntary savings tier.

Reforms are dismantling social solidarity. In France, for instance, between the 1950s and 1970s corporatism slowly extended social rights from the public sector to the private. In 1993, the Balladur Government tightened eligibility conditions for full-rate old-age pensions and extended the contribution period from 37.5 to 40 years for private sector employees. This avoided social conflict as the changes did not apply to the public service, in which there were powerful unions. Then in 2003, the Fillon law phased in the extension of the contribution period to the public sector, presenting the reform as necessary for equity and universalism! So, although usually regarded as a rationalization for extending income security, an appeal to equity can be an instrument for weakening it.

The sum of the changes has scarcely conformed to an image of advancing income security. They can be summarized as follows:

- Employee and employer contributions to pension schemes have tended to rise. According to the Social Security Database, in the 90 countries for which there are reliable data, the mean contribution rate for workers rose from 3.7% to 4.8% of average income, and the employer contribution rate rose from 8.7% to 11.6% between 1989 and 1999. So, the cost for workers rose while the incentive for employers to avoid or evade pension contributions and obligations also rose.

- Nearly half the countries increased their employee contribution rates, with many of the others maintaining the same level. The intra-country variation in contribution rates has scarcely changed and has remained large.

- The legal retirement age increased on average by more than half a year for men and by more than one year for women. As one person noted, in many countries "the age of retirement is determined by circumstances rather than by law".[51] Many workers reach retirement age after being out of the labour market for years.

- Women's old-age income security may have improved relative to men's. Although there was some convergence, women's retirement age for entitlement to a pension has remained lower than men's and, as women on average live longer, they have more years of entitlement. This will have a positive redistributive effect in favour of women. However, because on average women have fewer years of contributions, and because working-age women face discrimination and other labour market disadvantages, they tend to receive lower pensions. In some countries, fewer women qualify for the full state pension. For instance, in the United Kingdom it was found that whereas 92% of men qualified for the full basic state pension, only 49% of women did.[52]

- The number of years of contributions to gain entitlement to a state pension increased during the 1990s. The number of years of contributions required to secure entitlement to a full state pension has increased even more.[53] Thus, there has been *implicit disentitlement* to state-based income security in old age.

- Defined-benefit pension schemes have declined, displaced by defined-contribution schemes that provide less security since they do not guarantee any pension level.

- Social insurance remains the main basis for state pensions, but there has been a decline in the number of countries in which social insurance

[51]M. Rocard: *Livre blanc sur les retraites* (Paris, Rapport officiel, La documentation française, 1991).

[52]N. MacErlean: "The devil is in the detail", *The Observer* (London), 8 Sep. 2002.

[53]For instance, in late 2003 the Italian government said that from 2008 it would increase from 35 to 40 the number of years of contributions for a full state pension.

schemes are the principal pension providers. Mandatory private insurance schemes have increased substantially, both as a main and as a supplementary "pillar".

- There has been a sharp decline in the number of countries operating an earnings-related defined-benefit system, as one would expect given the decline in social insurance-based systems.

- A few countries have a universal, tax-based pension scheme, in Scandinavia and in Oceania. But Australia has phased out its universal scheme, replacing it with a private occupational scheme and a means-tested assistance scheme.

- There has been an increase in the number of countries with a social assistance scheme, usually as a secondary pillar of the system.

- While there has been extensive *privatization* of pension schemes, the term should be used carefully. There have been degrees of privatization, from the substitution of administrative tasks in the public sector by private providers to a full replacement of public pensions by private provision. Various countries have introduced incentives to encourage individuals to shift to private pensions, as is planned in Italy.

- Countries that have introduced a mandatory private insurance scheme, beginning with Chile, have exacerbated workers' income insecurity. In part, this has reflected a rise in their contribution rates.

A claim made in favour of private individual accounts is that competition between pension providers would improve efficiency and bid up pensions to entice workers to change schemes. But there can be only a limited number of providers (e.g., only two in Bolivia), while for workers it is costly and cumbersome to switch schemes. Costs are also increased by high administrative, marketing and advertising costs. Inequities can multiply. Two workers of the same age, with the same number of years of service and the same number of contributions, may have different pensions simply because they belong to different pension fund administrations.

- The cost of pensions may be reduced with a switch to private individual accounts, but this may merely reflect the tightening of entitlement conditions, not the effect of competition between pension providers.

- Reforms in Latin America, being copied elsewhere, have phased in private mandatory insurance schemes, shifting from defined-benefit schemes to which employers and workers contributed, to defined-contribution schemes to which only workers contribute. Workers face a cut in their incomes because they now bear all the costs themselves. In Peru, for instance, wages were not raised after the shift from employer to employee contributions.

- Private pension funds have become enormously powerful, potentially in a position to alter their

Worker contributions and ILO Convention No. 102

According to Article 71 of ILO Convention No. 102 on Social Security (Minimum Standards), 1952, "the total of the insurance contributions borne by the employees protected shall not exceed 50% of the total of the financial resources allocated to the protection of employees and their spouses and their children".

In 1999, for the seven countries operating a mandatory private insurance pension schemes as a main programme, the average employer contribution rate was 5.8%, while the average worker contribution rate was 7.4%.[54] In the extreme cases, Bolivia, Chile and Peru cut employer contributions to zero, on the grounds that employers need not be involved in individual pensions.

Chile has never ratified ILO Convention No.102, although it did ratify an older Convention No. 35 on Old-Age Insurance (Industry, etc.), 1933, which states, "The insured persons and their employers shall contribute to the financial resources of the insurance scheme." The ILO Committee of Experts on the Application of Conventions and Recommendations has repeatedly stated that the Chilean old-age pension reform is not in conformity with Convention No. 35.[35] The Chilean government has argued that employer contributions are part of the worker's remuneration, which is negotiated either individually or collectively. Collective bargaining is not very strong in Chile.

---

[54]The countries were Australia, Bolivia, Chile, Hungary, Mexico, Peru and Poland. It is the first three that have not respected the ILO Convention article.

[55]See <http://webfusion.ilo.org/public/db/standards/normes/appl/index.cfm?lang=EN>.

commitments with impunity and bargain for privileges and rental income from governments. As noted in Chapter 2, the extraordinary concentration of financial wealth in pension funds and the extraordinary instability in their value represent a form of old-age income insecurity that cannot be overstated.

- Above all, the monetary value of state pensions has been under pressure from governments in an increasing number of countries where it is believed that ageing is "a time bomb".[56] Whether or not this is correct (and there is reason for some scepticism), there is a sense of panic among the

political leaders of western Europe. In 2003, the Prime Minister of Italy was lobbying for a *Maastricht del welfare*, an agreement among European Union members to oversee a general lowering of public pensions.

An outcome of the pension reforms of the past two decades is that poverty among the elderly population in developed countries has remained serious or even deteriorated, notably in those countries that have gone furthest in the private pension direction, such as Australia, Mexico, the United Kingdom and the United States (Table 3.2).

Table 3.2 Poverty rates among the elderly, industrialized countries

Country	Year	% Very poor	% Poor
Australia	1994	12.1 +	29.4 +
Austria	1997	3.4 -	10.5 +
Belgium	1997	3.7 -	11.7 -
Canada	1998	1.7 +	7.8 +
Czech Republic	1996	1.3 +	7.4 +
Denmark	1997	1.7 +	6.6 +
Estonia	2000	4.0	11.0
Finland	2000	1.1 +	8.5 +
France	1994	3.4 -	9.8 -
Germany	2000	5.2 +	11.6 +
Hungary	1999	1.3 -	3.7 -
Ireland	1996	2.8 +	24.3 +
Israel	1997	20.3 +	26.4 +
Italy	2000	5.6 +	13.7 +
Luxembourg	2000	1.1 +	3.7 -
Mexico	1998	23.2 +	29.9 +
Netherlands	1994	3.3 +	6.4 +
Norway	2000	1.2 +	11.9 -
Poland	1999	1.1 -	3.6 -
Romania	1997	12.7+	21.7 +
Russian Federation	2000	4.5 -	10.4 -
Slovakia	1992	7.8 -	13.8 -
Slovenia	1999	0.4	2.2
Spain	1990	9.7 +	17.9 +
Sweden	2000	3.9 +	11.3 +
Switzerland	1992	2.1 +	7.7 +
Taiwan, China	1995	4.7 -	8.4 -
United Kingdom	1999	10.2 +	20.9 +
United States	2000	15.0 +	24.7 +

Notes: Poverty rates are calculated as disposable income, after taxes and transfers, among 64-year-olds, as less than 40% ("very poor") and less than 50% ("poor") of the median per capita income of the national population, adjusted for household size. +/- after figures indicates increase/decrease compared with earlier years (if available).

Source: Luxembourg Income Survey, December 2003, latest year for each country. Available at <http://www.lisproject.org/keyfigures/povertytable>.

[56]For an assessment, see G. Standing: *Globalization and Flexibility: Dancing Around Pensions,* SES Paper No. 2 (Geneva, ILO, 2002).

Another outcome is that only a tiny minority in developing countries receive pensions, with a few exceptions, notably Brazil, Namibia and South Africa. But while the majority has seen a receding mirage of old-age income security, the middle classes and the rich have seen a rosier picture, of subsidized individual savings accounts looking after their lifetime needs. This scarcely points to old-age income security for the vast majority of the world's elderly.

(ii) Health care systems

The most important impediment to basic economic security is the absence of a reliable public health care service, or at least a health care service that is accessible, affordable and reliable. Even where one exists, many of the poor are unable to use it for one reason or another. Obviously the situation is worst in developing countries, particularly in rural areas. Thus, in Gujarat (India) the PSS found that 25% of rural households did not have access to public health care facilities, compared with 7% of urban households.[57] Cost and distance were the main factors, especially as eight out of every ten workers had to pay for all their health care costs.

The absence of a universal health care system is probably the main source of insecurity in developing countries, and the relative position of such countries has apparently deteriorated, since the latest data point to a widening of life expectancies between rich and poor countries.[58] But in practically every country of the world, there is dissatisfaction with the national health care system. Even in rich industrialized countries, opinion polls show that only small minorities are satisfied.[59]

In the United States, over 80% of people believe there is a need for "fundamental change" or "complete rebuilding". In many countries costs have risen sharply (doubling health care spending as a share of GDP in less than 50 years), waiting lists for operations and medical treatment have grown, and rationed access to treatment has become more explicit.[60] The situation is a far cry from a generation ago when the ethos of social solidarity dictated that there should be no rationing by price.

Health care reforms became a major sphere of social reform in the late 1990s, following the global focus on pension system reform. The trends have been similar. In both cases, an orthodox reform strategy was articulated by the World Bank, oriented to the construction of multi-tier systems. Essentially, the State is expected to provide a "safety net" primary health care system, often with a limited range of treatable illnesses and injuries, while voluntary or mandatory health insurance covers much of the remainder, with a "top up" private voluntary scheme for superior treatment.

Health systems have been squeezed between attempts by governments to curb public spending and rising demands for health care. The determination to cut spending has introduced new forms of income insecurity and intensified old forms, especially by making access to and cost of health care a means of increasing income inequality.

The rich country that has attracted most attention is the United States, where over 42 million people lack health insurance and thus affordable health care. The numbers in that situation have been rising. In one year alone, 2001, 1.4 million more people were added to those without insurance. Unemployment has been one factor, but more important have been low wages and the steep rise in insurance premiums. Health care reform in the United States has been a political battleground. Reforms agreed in Congress in December 2003 resulted in several million workers losing entitlement to medicine/drug benefits from their firms, even though subsidies were provided to employers.[61]

Similar trends have emerged in Europe. In France, still regarded by many, including the WHO, as having one of the best health care performances, patient costs have been rising, the number of public hospital beds has been cut sharply, small local hospitals have been shut in large numbers, and about one in every eight citizens has given up health care insurance for financial reasons. Even though for low-income earners

---

[57] Unni and Rani, 2002, op.cit.

[58] World Health Organization: *World Health Report* 2003 (Geneva, 2003).

[59] K. Donelan, R.J. Blendon, C. Schoen, K. David and K. Binns: "The cost of health system change: Public discontent in five nations", *Health Affairs*, Vol. 18, No. 3, 1999, pp. 205–216.

[60] D.M. Cutler: "Equality, efficiency and market fundamentals: The dynamics of international medical-care reform", *Journal of Economic Literature*, Vol. 40, No. 3, Sep. 2002, pp. 881–906.

[61] "Critics attack Medicare deal as move toward privatization", *Financial Times*, 18 Nov. 2003.

there is universal health insurance (CMU), more than a quarter of those entitled to it do not receive it. Ironically, as costs of treatment have risen, poorer households have been paying more. By spending less on consultations, often postponing treatment, and by seeking care later than the more affluent, they predictably suffer more later through higher morbidity, more premature deaths and, before that, higher costs.[62] Reforms being discussed entail yet more privatization.

The premise underlying these health care reforms is that health is a *private good* to be bought and sold in the market (i.e., "commodified"). The favoured approach is a *dual* or *multi-tier system*, in which those who can pay insure themselves for private care while those who cannot rely on a public sub-system that is mainly for the poor and uninsured.[63] This model has led to the promotion of mandatory medical insurance provided by private companies alongside private medical providers. Countries that have relied on the public sector for health care have been encouraged to privatize, most recently by the WTO's General Agreement on Trade in Services (GATS).[64] Pushed to cut spending, governments are enabling private companies to provide (or compete with) public services.[65]

Health system changes have also mirrored those in other spheres of social policy, including anti-poverty schemes. The principles are cost-efficiency, decentralization and targeting (or selectivity). Central governments have decentralized responsibility to local or regional bodies, reducing their political exposure while retaining budgetary control, often merely transferring funds for an "essential health package" of 10–15 interventions or services, as recommended by the World Bank.[66] The resultant system creates inequalities in access, disparities in citizens' costs, and chronic health-related income insecurity for the poor and near-poor.

In short, in many countries, a multi-tier system is emerging, in which a majority of the population suffer income insecurity due to a fear of impending health care costs. For the poor, means-tested basic health care brings its own uncertainties. For those just above poverty, ill health or an accident could be impoverishing or worse. They could be "too wealthy" to qualify for means-tested basic care but be unable to pay for insurance.

At the same time, the costs of health care for users have tended to rise. For example, governments have turned increasingly to user fees, which have restricted use of medical care. This has led to a drop in the number of outpatients in various African hospitals, notably by AIDS sufferers.[67] User fees may reduce moral hazards, but could lead to worse illhealth and thus higher costs for individuals and communities.

(iii) Unemployment benefits

Unemployment benefit schemes have been under strain. This is true even though more countries have a scheme of some sort than was the case in the 1980s, mainly because all countries of eastern Europe introduced them after the fall of communism when open unemployment emerged.

Unemployment is the least covered of the standard forms of contingency risk. It is not necessarily covered in the countries where unemployment rates are the highest but rather in those that are economically more affluent. Among the latter, variations in unemployment benefits and coverage are large: as much as one to four, if the measure is the cost of the programme relative to GDP.

Unemployment benefits have been one of the main pillars of the social insurance systems of industrialized countries. But they have been withering almost everywhere, and have scarcely spread to developing countries, even though they were proposed for a number of East Asian countries in the wake of the 1997–98 Asian crisis, and were introduced in the Republic of Korea.

---

[62]See the article by Martine Bulard in *Le Monde diplomatique*, 13 Dec. 2003. <http://mondediplo.com/2003/12/13socialsecurity>.

[63]World Bank: *Investing in Health* (Washington, DC, 1993).

[64]J. Lethbridge: *Liberalization of Health Care*, SES Paper (Geneva, ILO, forthcoming).

[65]J.D.R. Ensignia: *La seguridad social en América Latina: Reforma o liquidación?* (Caracas, Venezuela Nueva Sociedad, 1997).

[66]The Mexican Government has a package of 14. A.C. Laurell: "What does Latin American social medicine do when it governs? The case of the Mexico City government", *American Journal of Public Health*, Vol. 93, No. 12, Dec. 2003, p. 2029.

[67]C. Baylies: "The impact of AIDS on rural households in Africa: A shock like any other?", *Development and Change*, Vol. 33, No. 4, 2002, p. 617.

Since the 1980s, and particularly during the 1990s, income insecurity associated with unemployment has unquestionably increased, for the following reasons:

- the qualifying period of contributions to become eligible for unemployment benefits has increased;

- the calculation rate for benefit levels has been cut;

- employee and employer contribution levels have tended to rise, with the burden of costs shifting from employers to workers;

- in many countries the duration of benefit entitlement has been cut;

- conditions for initial entitlement have increased, and conditions for continued entitlement have been tightened;

- income replacement rates have tended to fall, in terms of average income if not in terms of the individual's past income;

- there has been a shift from contributory finance to tax-based funding, very strongly so in countries such as Germany.

In Germany, these changes have continued into the current decade. The Government's 2003 reforms have included quiet efforts to ease older unemployed off the unemployment register, allowed to keep unemployment benefits but not assisted to find jobs. This has apparently induced fears among some older workers that the Government will lower their subsequent pension.[68] So far, however, rich-country governments have not adopted plans to privatize unemployment insurance, as proposed by some ultra-liberal commentators.[69]

In developing countries, not only are unemployment benefit schemes rare, but even where they do exist few unemployed are covered by them. In Latin America, some countries have some sort of scheme but coverage is very low.[70] In Argentina, unemployment benefits reached just 6% of the unemployed in 1999, which was less than in previous years. And the situation there is better than in the vast majority of developing countries included in the Social Security Database.

Most of the unemployed in the world receive little or no support from their governments, particularly in developing and transition countries. This is illustrated in Ukraine, where most people have to rely on themselves or relatives when they lose a job or fail to receive their wages or fall ill (Table 3.3). Only a minority receive unemployment benefits for all or most of the time they are unemployed (Figure 3.4). And the amount they receive if they do obtain benefits is woefully inadequate.

Table 3.3 Ukraine: Main source of financial support in case of job loss (percentage of respondents)

Alternative source of financial support	In case of job loss	In case of non-payment of wages	In case of illness in the family
Relatives	51.9	48.6	53.6
Self-reliance	45.1	42.5	41.4
Friends and neighbours	19.5	22.2	21.4
Other household members work more	11.6	10.6	8.1
Government	10.3	5.9	12.6
Loans	8.8	13.7	13.5
Savings	7.4	9.0	9.1
Other household members take a job	6.6	3.8	3.1
Sale of assets	5.5	4.9	7.9
Non-governmental organizations	1.8	1.5	3.4

Note: Some respondents mentioned more than one source of support.

Source: Ukraine PSS 2002.

---

[68]"Older German unemployed cite pressure to leave jobless lists", *International Herald Tribune*, 22 Dec. 2003.

[69]J.M. Orszag and D.J. Snower: *From Unemployment Benefits to Unemployment Accounts*, Discussion Paper 532 (Bonn, Institute for the Study of Labour, 2002).

[70]ILO: *2001 Labour Overview: Latin America and the Caribbean* (Lima, 2001), p. 50.

Figure 3.4 Ukraine: Unemployed receiving unemployment benefit, by age and gender

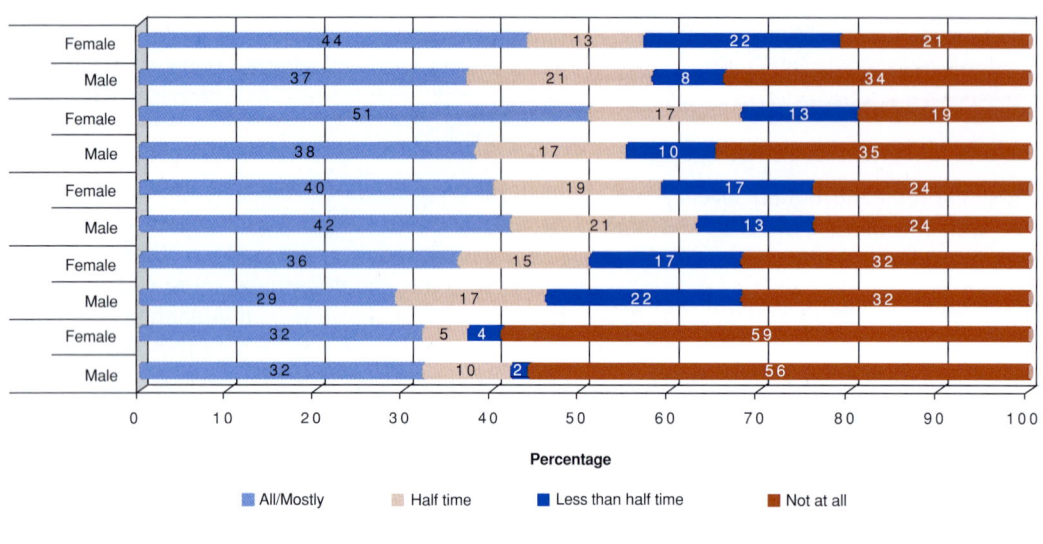

Source: Ukraine PSS 2002

The basic facts are daunting. The income insecurity of the unemployed is greater than it used to be and prospects of improvement are bleaker. While only a minority of countries operate unemployment benefit schemes, even in countries with such schemes only a minority of the unemployed actually receive benefits. Only a third do so in the United States. The amount received has dropped in many countries and the duration of entitlement has tended to shrink.

Country after country seems intent on lowering benefits, tightening conditionality, increasing contribution rates and shortening duration. The future of unemployment benefit systems looks bleak.

(iv) The rise of in-work tax credits

Scarcely noticed by commentators around the world, income transfers to low-income workers in jobs have become a major feature of labour markets and social protection systems in several industrialized countries, and have been evolving in others.

The United States Earned Income Tax Credit has become the biggest single transfer mechanism in the world, disbursing some USD40 billion a year. It is essentially a negative income tax, albeit paid on a family basis and paid only to those actually earning an

income. A growing number of other countries, mostly in Europe, have been introducing or extending similar schemes.

Tax credits may seem irrelevant for developing countries but, with the advance in technology and the spread of various sorts of voucher cards, they may not be far off in many middle-income countries.

A point to bear in mind is that earned-income tax credits are in effect a *labour subsidy*, paid to supplement low wages (and increasingly being extended to give some income security for those performing approved types of work).

3.7 The challenge

The immediate future appears to be an era of pervasive income insecurity for the vast majority of people. This prospect is obviously greater in the low-income countries of the world. Even if the Millennium Development Goal dream of halving poverty by 2015 were realized, the changing character of labour markets, the changing character of remuneration systems and the changing character of social protection systems do not promise a trend towards greater income security. This is surely not an acceptable prospect.

Why should wealthy countries have mass insecurity?

Alan Greenspan, Chairman of the US Federal Reserve Board, in a moment of candour, attributed the lack of inflation in the United States in the late 1990s, despite near-full employment in the conventional sense, to the prevalence of insecurity among workers and working families. Wealth does not seem to be associated with mass contentment.

By the late 1990s over 50% of all households in the United States had investments in the stock market, up from 25% in 1987. In spite of a subsequent fall in share prices, this has continued. The associated rise in an "investment culture" has put many more people at risk and has strengthened the role of financial capital.

In Japan, the world's second biggest economy, mass insecurity has been evidenced by high levels of suicide and *karoshi*, death from overwork. Although economic stagnation has played its part, wealth generated from a prolonged prior period of rapid economic growth has not been associated with mass security there either.

In western Europe, youthful discontent and a withering of the variants of the welfare state scarcely suggest that wealth there has removed mass insecurity.

Wealth, it seems, does not beget security.

One striking development of the globalization era is that income insecurity has increased in affluent countries as well. Policy-makers and powerful interests pressurizing them do not appear to give the same degree of attention to income security as their predecessors. Nor does wealth appear to lead to income security. The questions are whether or not this is necessary and whether or not it is desirable.

Poverty and inequality are the flip sides of income insecurity. There is ample reason for believing that redistributing income from the rich to the poor would improve income security, and ample reason for believing it would not slow economic growth. Indeed, the conventional wisdom has shifted to thinking that in many countries reduced inequality would in fact stimulate growth. However, raising people's income may not produce real security if *consumerism* is unchecked. Higher incomes lead to more "wants" — or *positional goods* — a striving for what others possess and for more. Wants become needs, and unmet needs are the source of discontent and insecurity. Many positional goods, such as unspoilt beaches, have a finite supply. The middle-income groups pursue those goods and services, and as they do so, drive up prices or fail to find them or to afford them when they do, leaving themselves frustrated and relatively deprived. They never have enough. This is the nature of the consumer society. It is one reason for the stronger public opposition to taxes; they are seen as encroaching on income needed for those positional goods.

Although it may not seem directly related to the primary concern over absolute poverty and dire need, limiting the pressure to consume is possibly among the most important long-term income security challenges. Meeting that should be seen as part of the struggle to defeat global poverty and inequality.

Chapter 4

Monitoring income security

4.1 Introduction

Seen globally and structurally, income insecurity seems to be pervasive. In this chapter, we will consider some relatively neglected aspects of income insecurity in developing and transition economies, hoping to encourage greater emphasis on these aspects, and will then present micro, meso and macro indexes of income security. The macro-level Income Security Index is estimated for 96 countries.

4.2. Experience of income insecurity

It may be useful to highlight the nature of income insecurity by means of an examination of data from the People's Security Surveys (PSS), which have attempted to identify objective and subjective aspects of the various forms of economic security. In doing so, the objective is not to present a complete picture, but rather to highlight aspects of income insecurity that are often overlooked.

Recall that income security is about the *level* of income (absolute and relative to needs), *assurance* of receipt, expectation of income adequacy now and improvement or deterioration in the future, both during a person's working life and in old age or disability retirement. Income security is about actual, perceived and expected income.

(i) Perceived income adequacy

Most people worry about not having enough money or resources with which to survive or live decently, and they worry about not having enough to meet likely contingencies.

In developing countries, insecurity of this kind is pervasive. The PSS ask questions about individuals' perceptions of the adequacy of their household's income for basic needs, and the results indicate a widespread sense of income inadequacy in many of the countries covered by the PSS (Table 4.1).

In Tanzania, for instance, about one in five said their household income was insufficient for their food needs, while about half said it was "just enough". So, a majority of households was in discomfort. Although many said housing was not a financial difficulty, more worried about not having enough for their clothing needs.

However, the main concern was not having enough income for health care - 40% of men and 36% of women thought they were "mostly not able to pay for treatment of common health problems", and a further 43% of men and 48% of women thought their income was merely just sufficient. Not surprisingly, in this respect at least, perceived income inadequacy was greatest for older age groups.

In Ghana, nearly half said their household income was insufficient for their food needs. More said it was insufficient for their clothing, and even more said it was insufficient for health care needs. Among households with children of school age, a majority (59%) said their income was inadequate for schooling needs.

In South Africa, bearing in mind that the PSS was conducted in the relatively affluent areas of Western

Cape and Durban, about one-third said their household income was insufficient for their food needs, and even more said that about their clothing, housing and health care needs. Unlike other countries, health care was not the most pressing concern, even though for many it was a major preoccupation.

In Ethiopia, a general question was asked about the adequacy of household income for basic needs. Although the PSS was concentrated in relatively affluent parts of the country, it is remarkable that 78% of men and 83% of women said their household income was inadequate, and scarcely anybody said it was more than adequate.

Most revealingly, when asked if the household had been forced by economic circumstances to adopt var-

ious coping mechanisms, about 12% of Ethiopian households said one or more young members had left school due to financial difficulties, about 8% had been obliged to sell some livestock and 7% had sold jewellery in distress sales. These actions are significant indicators of income insecurity.

In the Indian state of Gujarat, 82% of all workers in the PSS perceived their household income as less than adequate for their basic needs.[1] More women than men saw their households as poor, a pattern replicated in other countries, such as Indonesia.

In sum, in most countries a very large proportion of households feel economically insecure in terms of being able to obtain their most basic needs. Having insufficient income to ensure access to health care is

Table 4.1 Households with insufficient income for basic needs, by country
(percentage reporting their household income insufficient)

Country	Food Urban	Rural	Housing Urban	Rural	Clothing Urban	Rural	Health care Urban	Rural	Education Urban	Rural
Argentina	29.0	n.a.	39.2	n.a.	45.1	n.a.	41.9	n.a.	34.1	n.a.
Bangladesh	2.4	8.4	27.4	14.9	12.0	16.8	19.7	30.2	n.a.	n.a.
Brazil	20.2	n.a.	27.4	n.a.	35.2	n.a.	50.9	n.a.	24.2	n.a.
Chile	7.2	n.a.	9.4	n.a.	16.3	n.a.	16.8	n.a.	15.1	n.a.
China	7. 0		29.3		13.5		44.1		n.a	
Ethiopia	51.5	51.9	45.4	36.1	54.4	62.8	55.1	60.7	n.a.	n.a.
Ghana	44.1	48.5	45.8	54.0	46.3	55.2	51.2	61.7	55.2	62. 6
Indonesia	30.4	45.3	48.7	56.2	37.1	48.0	35.6	48.9	n.a.	n.a
Russian Federation	35.5	44.0	25.0	27.2	66.4	75.2	47.3	58.2	n.a.	n.a.
South Africa	33.4	n.a	40.8	n.a	42.4	n.a	38.9	n.a	n.a	n.a
Tanzania	18.1	23.9	13.5	12.0	20.7	30.2	32.0	45.5	n.a	n.a
Ukraine	65.1	64.6	69.2	58.1	84.0	83.4	81.7	84.3	59.5	61.7

Source: People's Security Surveys (PPS).
n.a. = not available.

---

[1] J. Unni and U. Rani: *Insecurities of Informal Workers in Gujarat, India*, SES Paper No. 30 (Geneva, ILO, 2002).

the number one concern almost everywhere. This reinforces the view that universal access to health care should be given the highest priority in social protection reform.

(ii) Access to services

The poor everywhere have worse access to social services than the more affluent and the distribution and costs of social services are generally regressive, worsening income inequality. Thus, it is well-established that the availability of good medical services varies inversely with the need for medical care.[2]

What do the PSS data tell us in this respect? They show that almost everywhere the most common stressful condition faced by low-income people is inadequate access to health care. This covers distance to facilities, cost of reaching them, obtaining access to them, being able to pay for them, and being able to rely on them. In Pakistan, 81% of urban transport workers expressed dissatisfaction with local health services. In Ukraine, 61% of all adults said the same and, as elsewhere, more of the lower-income groups were adversely affected. The pattern is well known, but it reinforces the view that the inequality of access to medical services actually worsens the underlying inequality of incomes.

Ironically, in many parts of the world, out-of-pocket spending to obtain health care is greater for the poor than for others, and it seems this part of private service has been growing. In most countries, a majority of the population simply cannot afford to obtain the health care they feel they need. In Tanzania, over three-quarters of respondents felt that way.

A related aspect is differential access to health care within the family unit. In Ethiopia, for instance, particularly in low-income families, allocation of scarce funds typically means that women are more often denied health care.[3] In Bangladesh, the pro-male bias in receiving medical treatment is greater in poor households.[4] This sort of reality is a hidden form of gender inequality.

As for access to health care for those in jobs, this is a rarity in developing countries and is also a form of international inequality. Even among those with "formal" jobs, most do not have such access. And in most countries women workers are less likely to be entitled to health care services through their jobs. This is shown in countries as dissimilar as Bangladesh and Chile. And most women in jobs do not have entitlement to paid maternity leave. In many countries, gender inequality extends to the probability of paid holidays - women in wage jobs are less likely to be granted them than men.

In sum, although the PSS provide more data than we have summarized here, differential access to basic social services vital to a functional existence is a feature of income insecurity, and a large proportion of the poor and non-poor do not have access to the most crucial of all services. The role of social security will be considered later at various stages of the analysis.

(iii) Informal transfer mechanisms for income security

Throughout the world, the main form of income support still consists of inter-personal transfers, and in particular of inter-household transfers in times of need. Africa is famous for its systems of "informal" social support, from tribal to domestic to the cooperative traditions implanted in Tanzania long ago. But do the social support networks survive? Have the structural adjustment and "modernization" trends eroded that capacity?

The PSS data shed light on some of these issues. Thus, in Ghana, 9% of men and 10% of women said they or their households provided assistance regularly to another household or to persons not in their household (Table 4.2). A further 27% of men and 26% of women said such support was provided occasionally. This is evidence of the lingering spirit of *ubuntu*, of social solidarity across households. Those with more schooling were more likely to provide assistance.

[2]D. Filmer: *Fever and its Treatment Among the More and Less Poor in Sub-Saharan Africa*, World Bank Policy Research Working Paper No. 2798 (Washington, DC, World Bank, 2002). This is further documented in the World Bank's *World Development Report 2004*.

[3]D. Rahmato and A. Kidanu: *Vulnerable Livelihoods: People's Security Survey of Urban Households in Ethiopia*, paper presented at ILO Workshop on Economic Security and Decent Work in Africa, Dar-es-Salaam, May 2003.

[4]S. Mahmud: "Actually how empowering is microcredit?", *Development and Change*, Vol. 34, No. 4, Sep. 2003, p. 600.

Table 4.2 Ghana: Households providing financial assistance to others (%)

		Yes, regularly	Yes, occasionally	No	Don't know
Education level	No schooling	6.1	27.3	61.3	5.4
	Primary	3.2	24.1	65.6	7.1
	Secondary	10.9	25.8	58.4	4.9
	Tertiary	20.7	32.6	45.2	1.5
Sex	Male	9.0	26.7	58.9	5.3
	Female	9.9	25.9	59.4	4.9
Region	Urban	12.5	27.5	55.9	4.2
	Rural	7.1	25.2	62.0	5.8
Household income level (in cedis monthly)	0–50 000	5.7	21.8	69.4	3.1
	51 000–100 000	5.1	25.0	64.2	5.7
	101 000–200 000	5.4	23.2	67.2	4.2
	201 000–400 000	9.6	26.2	57.5	6.8
	401 000+	17.1	33.5	44.9	4.5
Income adequacy for health care	More than sufficient	12.0	28.0	54.0	6.0
	About adequate	10.6	27.7	56.7	5.1
	Insufficient	8.5	24.4	62.0	5.1
	Don't know	8.0	40.0	48.0	4.0
Income adequacy for food	More than sufficient	13.4	33.3	48.4	4.8
	About adequate	9.6	26.0	59.1	5.3
	Insufficient	8.6	24.6	61.8	5.0
	Don't know	0.0	33.3	60.0	6.7
Total		**9.5**	**26.2**	**59.2**	**5.1**

Source: Ghana PSS 2002.

Table 4.3 Ethiopia: Households providing financial assistance to others (%)

		Yes, regularly	Yes, occasionally	No	Don't know
Education level	No schooling	2.1	7.9	90.1	2.1
	Primary	5.6	15.3	79.0	5.6
	Secondary and above	8.5	24.5	67.0	8.5
Sex	Male	5.9	17.5	76.6	5.9
	Female	4.2	12.5	83.2	4.2
Household income level (in birrs monthly)	1–150	2.7	12.5	84.8	2.7
	151–250	8.0	17.2	74.8	8.0
	251–500	7.7	24.6	67.6	7.7
	501+	15.9	29.3	54.8	15.9
Income adequacy for health care	Sufficient	5.1	10.2	84.7	5.1
	Adequate	8.1	23.3	68.7	8.1
	Insufficient	4.1	13.7	82.2	4.1
Income adequacy for food	Sufficient	8.2	37.7	54.1	8.2
	Adequate	6.9	18.3	74.7	6.9
	Insufficient	4.0	12.6	83.5	4.0
Total		**5.3**	**15.9**	**78.7**	**5.3**

Source: Ethiopia PSS 2001.

In both South Africa and Ethiopia, or at least in the areas covered by the PSS, inter-household financial support was more limited. Only one in five households in Ethiopia and South Africa gave financial assistance to other households, compared with two in five in Ghana. In South Africa, a large majority of richer households did not provide any income support to others, and the rich were less likely to support other households than lower-income groups. Unlike in Ghana and Ethiopia, the less educated were more likely to provide income support than the more educated.

These are important findings because they show that inter-household support is actually weak. While commercialization and the impact of societal shocks may have reduced the capacity of households to support others, it is also likely that in a stratified society households with the means to support others mainly mix with households that do not need support, while those that cannot support others mix with those in need.

Lack of inter-household transfers is one reason for recognizing that, in Africa as elsewhere, the State is needed to ensure that supportive transfers take place. Some have claimed that state transfers may merely substitute for inter-household and other informal transfers.[5] But other research accords with the PSS findings that in fact State transfers are modest and limited, at times of covariant risk in particular.[6]

---

[5] D. Cox and E. Jimenez: "Private transfers and the effectiveness of public income redistribution in the Philippines", in D. Van de Walle and K. Nead (eds.): *Public Spending and the Poor: Theory and Evidence* (Baltimore, Johns Hopkins University and World Bank, 1995).

[6] M. Rosenzweig: "Risk, implicit contracts and the family in rural areas of low-income countries", *Economic Journal*, Vol. 98, No. 393, 1988, pp. 1148–1170.

(iv) Women's control over their income

Throughout history, women's income insecurity has been worsened by the fact they have not been able to retain the income they have managed to earn and receive. This remains one of the main forms of gender inequality across the world, and one of the least to receive policy attention.

For example, in Tanzania, as in many other countries, women suffer from income insecurity in part because they do not retain their earned income. Not only do they work long workweeks, they find that much of their income is taken from them. According to Usu Mallya, of the Tanzania Gender Networking Programme, "In most rural areas, women do a lot of work to earn a living for their families. But all the income generated goes to men. Once it has landed in men's hands, women do not have access or right to it".[7]

The Tanzanian PSS data indicate that only one in every four women earning wage income keeps all that income. Another one in every four gives up all or most of her wage income, and one in every eight gives up about half of it. Taking all income into account, even more give up most of their income - over one in four gives up all or most of her income, and one in five gives up about half of it.

Although the situation is better in some other African countries, as shown in Table 4.4, non-retention is a means by which African women experience income insecurity. Overcoming this would do much to reduce their poverty and almost certainly the poverty of their children.

Outside Africa, women's capacity to retain their earned income varies considerably. In rural Bangladesh, for instance, women in poor households, irrespective of their own participation status, were found to be more likely to keep household income from all sources than women in non-poor households.[8] In most countries, the reverse pattern is the norm. Be that as it may, a large proportion of women are not able to retain their earned income - over 40% in Bangladesh, over 40% in Gujarat and over 75% in Indonesia.

A related aspect is control over the way their income is actually spent. This varies considerably. In Ghana, about three-quarters of the women said they alone determined how to spend their money, and most of the others said they decided jointly, usually with their husbands. But in China only 53% of women said they alone decided. In Bangladesh and India, far fewer could make their own decisions.

To measure income by how much a person earns is not enough to determine whether the person is suffering from income poverty. This point is systematically neglected in income statistics and social policy.

---

[7]Quoted in H. Mandari: "Women appeal for employers' consideration", *The Guardian* (Tanzania), 2 May 2003.

[8]Mahmud, 2003, op. cit., p. 595.

Table 4.4 Africa: Women's retention of earned income, by area and schooling (%)

| | Area | | Education | | |
	Urban	Rural	No schooling	Primary	Secondary+
Ethiopia					
Keep all	n.a.	n.a.	72.6	70.7	65.3
Give some	n.a.	n.a.	19.2	21.4	29.8
Give all	n.a.	n.a.	8.2	7.9	4.8
Ghana					
Keep all	47.6	58.7	55.6	58.5	51.9
Give some	44.1	32.2	36.5	30.7	39.5
Give all	2.1	1.4	1.4	0.3	2.2
Do not get money	6.2	7.7	6.5	10.4	6.4
Tanzania					
Keep all	21. 8	31.3	32.8	4.4	3.3
Mostly keep	27. 6	29.6	26.2	5.6	6.1
Keep about half	22. 2	13.1	13.2	2.5	1.7
Mostly give	16. 6	15.9	25.6	1.3	2.2
Give (taken) all	11. 8	10.1	3.3	1.3	1.7
South Africa					
Keep all	51.2	51.5	52.2	53.2	62.5
Give some	13.7	8.8	11.2	17.1	15.0
Give all	1.6	1.0	1.6	1.6	5.0
Do not get money	33.6	38.7	35.0	28.1	17.5

n.a. = not available.   Source: PSS.

(v) Shocks of living: Personal financial crises and coping mechanisms

The most dramatic insecurity comes with sudden major events in our lives — the loss of a parent or spouse, loss of a major source of income, a flood, a fire, or whatever. It is the capacity to be able to cope in the wake of such events that enables us to adjust and restore momentum to our lives.

To develop policies to respond to personal financial crises, we need to know which are the groups most affected, what are the main causes of a sudden debilitating financial crisis, and how people cope in adversity. All households in the PSS were asked whether they had experienced one or more financial crises in the past three years and, if so, how they had reacted.

In Tanzania, 50% of men and 46% of women respondents stated that they had experienced a financial crisis in the past three years (Table 4.5). The more schooling the person had received, the less likely he or she was to have experienced a financial crisis. In Ghana, 53% of men and 56% of women said they had experienced at least one financial crisis in the past three years.

In Gujarat, where the PSS was carried out just before the terrible earthquake that hit the region, about

Table 4.5 Households having experienced a financial crisis in past three years, by area (%)

Country	Urban	Both	Rural
Bangladesh	46.9		65.1
Ethiopia	34.2		48.1
Indonesia	37.4		38.1
Ghana	51.1		57.5
Tanzania	47.7		50.3
China		31.9	
Hungary	39.8		42.5
India	92.1		92.3
South Africa	34.2		33.3

Source: PSS.

half the households had experienced at least one financial crisis in the past year.[9]

What are the most serious *main crises?* In Tanzania, of those experiencing a crisis in the previous three years, 21% cited crop failure, 19% medical bills, 16% a natural disaster such as a flood, 11% business failure, 7% death of an income-earning household member, 6% loss of a job, 4% birth cost, and 3% loss of work due to illness.

In South Africa, crime and violence have also figured prominently in people's lives in recent decades. In the PSS, among those who had experienced a financial crisis in the previous three years, being a victim of theft was a common cause.

In all countries, in Africa, Asia, eastern Europe and Latin America, ill health or disability were among the most common causes of a household financial crisis. This further testifies to the universal need for health security.

By way of *coping mechanisms*, some people have support networks on which they can rely, some have institutions that give them assurance, many have neither. In many places networks break down or are eroded by structural changes that leave communities vulnerable to shocks. As noted in Chapter 3, the premature death of millions of people in the Russian Federation in the 1990s was fundamentally due to the lack of effective coping mechanisms, in the absence of any substantial informal economy or social protection system.[10]

In Africa, as in other parts of the world, many people have access to neither networks of support nor mechanisms of social protection. But can we discern how people respond to crises in the countries covered by the PSS?

[9]Unni and Rani, 2002, op. cit.

[10]S. Clarke: *Do Russian Households Have Survival Strategies?* (Coventry, University of Warwick, 2001, mimeo).

Table 4.6 Three most serious crises as percentage share of all main crises
(percentage of individuals having experienced a financial crisis in past three years)

Country	Urban Crises	%	Rural Crises	%
Bangladesh	1. Medical cost	26.4	1. Medical cost	29.6
	2. Business failure	25.5	2. Crop failure	17.8
	3. Loss of job	17.9	3. Marriage cost	12.6
Ethiopia	1. Commodity prices	24.0	1. Crop failure	28.8
	2. Cost of medicine	9.1	2. Commodity prices	16.3
	3. Loss of work — illness	8.6	3. Cost of medicine	10.0
Indonesia	1. Cost of medicine	32.7	1. Cost of medicine	33.2
	2. Loss of job	13.3	2. Crop failure	18.3
	3. Crop failure	11.1	3. Commodity prices	6.5
Ghana	1. Medical cost	38.3	1. Medical cost	41.5
	2. Funeral cost	16.9	2. Funeral cost	23.7
	3. Children's education	7.9	3. Children's education	4.8
Tanzania	1. Medical cost	22.1	1. Crop failure	32.3
	2. Business failure	15.1	2. Natural disaster (flood/cyclone)	17.2
	3. Natural disaster (flood/cyclone)	11.6	3. Medical cost	14.0
India	1. Loss of job/employment opportunities	31.8	1. Expenditure on social functions/Illness	45.9
	2. Expenditure on social functions/Illness	30.2	2. Rise in price of essential commodities or inputs	29.5
	3. Loss of work due to illness	16.5	3. Loss of job	14.9
South Africa	1. Death of a household member	9.3	n.a.	n.a.
	2. Loss of job/employment	6.5	n.a.	n.a.
	3. Death of wage-earning household member	3.6	n.a.	n.a.

Source: PSS.
n.a. = not available

In Gujarat, those hit by a sudden financial crisis usually go to relatives or neighbours for help, being unable to obtain loans from banks or other formal institutions.[11] Women have been able to benefit to some extent from SEWA (Self-Employed Women's Association), but for the most part they rely on relatives and neighbours.

Indeed, this remains the main means of coping across the world, as suggested in Table 4.7. Most people in times of crisis turn to relatives, then to their neighbours — and very rarely find succour from the State. While this has always been the case in low-income countries, in the early 21st century it is still the overwhelming reality against which progress should be measured.

There is one coping mechanism that has attracted a great deal of attention in recent years. Millions of families across the world, in distress or otherwise, send their children out to work for some petty income or oblige them to help out rather than go to school. Child labour is a sensitive issue in assessing poverty and income insecurity. Much of it is onerous and hazardous, and is properly a target for prevention schemes, such as those aided by the ILO's International Programme on the Elimination of Child Labour (IPEC). However, in many circumstances, families may have little or no choice, and children's contribution to production or to family income may be seen as regrettably essential.

[11] Unni and Rani, 2002, op. cit.

Table 4.7 On whom did the respondent mainly rely during the most serious crisis?
(percentage of those having experienced a crisis in past three years)

Country	Urban Whom	%	Rural Whom	%
Bangladesh	1. Relatives	66.9	1. Family/siblings/relatives	53.4
	2. Friends/neighbours	18.6	2. Moneylender	20.8
	3. Moneylender	4.6	3. Bank/other financial institution	13.1
Ethiopia	1. Friends/neighbours	25.7	1. Family/siblings/relatives	21.7
	2. Relatives	19.2	2. Friends /neighbours	20.8
	3. Officials/government	5.2	3. Officials/government	11.3
Russian Federation	1. Support from relatives	34.0	1. Support from relatives	33.2
	2. Other household members	18.8	2. Social payment from State	20.8
	3. Social payment from state	14.8	3. Other household members	15.6
Indonesia	1. Relatives	61.9	1. Relatives	61.2
	2. Friends/neighbours	21.0	2. Friends/neighbours	27.0
	3. Employer	4.3	3. Bank/financial institutions	2.1
Ghana	1. Friends/neighbours	35.3	1. Friends/neighbours	41.8
	2. Land or asset sales	25.9	2. Land or asset sales	25.7
	3. Money lenders	2.9	3. Money lenders	2.5
Tanzania	1. Relatives	50.3	1. Relatives	44.1
	2. Friends/neighbours	30.9	2. Friends/neighbours	33.5
	3. Employer	3.4	3. n.a.	n.a.
India	1. Relatives	66.1	1. Relatives	72.5
	2. Friends/neighbours/mayor	12.8	2. Bank/financial institution/cooperative	16.0
	3. Bank/financial institution/ cooperative	6.2	3. Friends/neighbours/mayor	4.8
South Africa	1. Friends/neighbours	21.2	n.a.	n.a.
	2. Bank	20.9	n.a.	n.a.
	3. Employer	3.8	n.a.	n.a.

Source: PSS.
n.a. = not available

In some places, parents and grandparents have opposed government efforts to stop their children doing income-earning work.[12] It is also not always clear whether attending a run-down, overcrowded local school is more valuable for the child or family. Ways need to be found to reduce child labour that ensure children have access to a proper education and compensate families for the loss of their children's earnings.[13]

In Bangladesh, Ghana and Tanzania, all countries where child labour is widespread, the PSS asked adults who were working on their own account whether any of their children aged between 6 and 13 were helping on their farm, in a business or in some other work. In the two African countries, the incidence of child work was high in both rural and urban areas, and in Bangladesh it was high in rural areas. However, a large proportion of the parents, particularly in Tanzania, claimed that the work in question did not interfere

_____

[12] See, for example, D. Mbulumi: "Parents cause of children's exploitation", *The Guardian* (Dar-es-Salaam), 12 Oct. 2002. The ILO is operating a project in Tanzania entitled "Promoting the linkages between women's employment and the reduction of child labour".

[13] International Programme on the Elimination of Child Labour: *Investing in Every Child: An Economic Study of the Costs and Benefits of Eliminating Child Labour* (Geneva, ILO, 2004).

with the schooling of the children. Moreover, child "labour" does not occur only in the poorest households (Table 4.8).

Nevertheless, one can suppose that the extent of child labour is increased by financial crises. Children who are not brought up by their own parents are more likely to be working. And in these coun-

tries, much of the child labour could be explained by a financial crisis in the household caused by the cost of medical treatment, crop failure or some other mishap. Child labour is in part a way of diversifying sources of income in the face of calamity and seasonality, and it has often been girls who have suffered from this more than boys.[14]

Table 4.8 Percentage of households with children doing economic work, by household characteristics

	Bangladesh	Ghana	Tanzania
Area			
Urban	12.6	37.5	25.9
Rural	40.7	37.9	37.6
Income adequacy for food			
Sufficient	34.9	33.6	32.8
Just enough	35.0	35.7	28.3
Insufficient	37.2	39.9	40.6
Income adequacy for health care			
Sufficient	28.6	38.2	37.9
Just enough	37.0	38.2	22.2
Insufficient	37.2	37.8	41.5

Source: PSS.

These results indicate that overcoming economic insecurity is likely to be the best way of reducing the incidence of deleterious forms of child labour. In most low-income environments, children may work to help the family survive and in some they may work because schools are inaccessible or unattractive. The best way of dealing with this complex set of circumstances is a combined set of remedial policies, along the lines considered in the final chapter.

Child labour is only one of the coping mechanisms that the poor have to consider. Most such mechanisms may bring short-term relief at the cost of long-term deprivation and chronic insecurity. Those having to make the decisions rarely have the luxury of being able to make sophisticated inter-temporal choices.

(vi) Personal income stability and regularity

The stability of income is clearly an aspect of income security. If income fluctuates erratically, it is

likely to affect the propensity to consume and to save. It may also induce passivity or a conservative state of mind, stifling initiative and, in extreme cases, inducing social illnesses (alcoholism, drug-taking, depression, and so on) that have long-term adverse effects on individuals, their families and the wider society and economy. Income stability is obviously particularly important for anybody earning a modest amount even at the best of times.

The PSS asked: "Over the past 12 months, has your monthly income been fairly regular, fluctuating or very irregular?" In Indonesia, only 19% of those who

---

[14]On coping strategies in general, see B. Agarwal: "Social security and the family: Coping with seasonality and calamity in rural India", in E. Ahmad, J. Dreze, J. Hills and A. Sen (eds.): *Social Security in Developing Countries* (Oxford, Clarendon Press, 1991). Seasonal variation in nutrition has been more marked among girls in low-income environments. J. Behrman: "Intra-household allocation of nutrients in rural India: Are boys favoured? Do parents exhibit inequality aversion?", *Oxford Economic Papers*, Vol. 40, No. 1, 1988, pp. 32–54.

received any income said that they received it fairly regularly, while over two-thirds said it fluctuated. There was no difference between men and women in this respect. But those working in urban areas and the more educated were more likely to have a regular income.

Table 4.9   (a) Stability of earned income payments, by gender (percentage of those with earned income)

Country	Male		Female	
	Regular	Irregular	Regular	Irregular
Urban areas				
Latin America				
Argentina	36.4	63.6	49.9	50.1
Brazil	45.6	54.3	57.9	42.1
Chile	33.4	66.6	21.9	78.1
Africa				
Ghana	22.2	77.8	24.9	75.1
Asia				
Bangladesh	31.7	68.3	49.3	50.7
Indonesia	31.9	68.0	32.5	67.5
Eastern Europe				
Hungary	66.8	33.2	69.1	30.8
Rural areas				
Africa				
Ghana	15.1	84.9	24.9	75.1
Asia				
Bangladesh	11.1	88.9	5.6	94.4
Indonesia	15.8	84.3	13.2	86.8
Eastern Europe				
Hungary	60.5	39.5	64.9	35.1

Source: PSS.

(b) China: Stability of earned income payments, by gender
(percentage of those with earned income)

	Male		Female	
	Regular	Irregular	Regular	Irregular
Employment status				
Wage and salaried	68.8	31.2	70.0	30.0
Self-employed	34.2	65.9	40.5	59.4
Education				
No schooling	47.0	53.0	54.5	45.5
Primary school	52.4	47.6	41.9	58.1
Lower secondary	54.6	45.4	59.1	41.0
Higher secondary	57.8	42.2	62.5	37.6
Vocational/technical	65.3	34.7	64.3	35.7
University	69.2	31.8	77.1	23.0
Ag				
Under 25 years	68.2	31.8	77.1	23.0
25–44 years	58.5	41.4	59.8	40.2
Over 45 years	63.4	36.6	68.1	31.9
Perception of income				
Well-off	82.6	17.4	94.4	5.6
Average	72.1	27.9	72.2	27.9
Low-income	48.1	51.9	49.3	50.7
Income adequacy for food				
Sufficient	69.3	30.7	72.1	27.9
Just enough	52.6	47.3	53.9	46.1
Insufficient	41.0	59.0	44.3	55.6
Income adequacy for health care				
Sufficient	70.1	29.9	77.6	22.4
Just enough	64.4	35.6	66.9	33.2
Insufficient	53.6	46.4	52.9	47.0

Source: China PSS 2001.

In Tanzania, most people said their household income fluctuated from month to month, particularly for those who relied largely or exclusively on non-wage income. Most of those with wage earnings said they were usually paid regularly each month. In Ghana, the vast majority of both men and women reported that their incomes varied very considerably from month to month — 81% of men and 78% of women. Particularly among women, the more educated were more likely to have a regular income. This is yet another source of inequality.

In Ethiopia, in spite of severe poverty, about half the households said that the income they received varied little from month to month; about a third said it fluctuated, and just over 12% said it was very irregular.

In China, about seven out of every ten salaried men and women receive regular income, while less than four in ten self-employed have regular incomes. The higher the level of education, the more chance a person has of receiving a regular income, and older workers are more likely to do so than younger ones, as are the

well-off compared with others. Those with regular income usually consider that their income is adequate for their health care and food expenses, while a majority of men and women with irregular incomes find it difficult to meet those basic needs. In short, it is not just the level of income at any one moment that matters.

The interval between receipt of income also makes a difference. This varies a great deal. For example, in Tanzania, less than two-thirds of those in wage labour are paid on a monthly basis while about a quarter are paid on a daily or piece-rate basis. A majority of labourers are paid on a daily or piece-rate basis, whereas over 90% of professionals and managerial workers are paid on a monthly basis — another aspect of income security inequality. And while over 90% of labourers had no employment contracts or had only verbal daily or weekly agreements, over 60% of professionals and managerial workers had written "permanent" contracts and 18% had written contracts of more than one year.

In Tanzania, although women are less likely than men to be in wage labour, more of the women tend to be paid on a monthly basis. In terms of the regularity of wage payment, a worrying feature is that 80% of labourers said that they were paid irregularly or very irregularly, whereas about 69% of white-collar workers said they were paid regularly. Overall, 52% of those in wage employment said they were paid regularly.

In Bangladesh, most workers said their income fluctuated, and the great majority of labourers said this was the case. In effect, unstable and irregular income is a form of inequality — the poor experience it much more.

(vii) Income security expectations: Short-term

In part, income security is a function of the expected situation in the near future and in the more distant future. To a large extent, expectations reflect current income and the nature of the economic system, but they also reflect the system of social policy and the prevalence and forms of networks of social solidarity.

Short-term income security expectations are easier for people to perceive than long-term ones. In Tanzania, for example, among all those in some sort of wage or salaried employment, 14% expected their

wage income to be higher in real terms 12 months hence, while only 8% expected it to be lower. Once again, there is an inequality in prospective income security — only 4% of labourers expected their income to be higher, whereas 16% of professional and managerial workers had that expectation; and 23% of labourers expected income to be lower, compared with only 1% of professionals and managers.

In all the PSS, people were asked about their income expectations — and in no country did a majority expect income to be higher in a year's time. Is that global pessimism or simple caution? The most optimistic were the Brazilians, among whom 48% expected their income to be higher, with the more educated slightly more likely to be optimistic, and optimism declining with age. In Argentina and Chile, just 17% and 25% respectively were optimistic, again more so among the more educated and the young. About 41% of South Africans in the PSS thought their income would be higher, and 39% of Bangladeshis, where men were more optimistic than women. Russians and Ukrainians were overwhelmingly pessimistic. Only 6% of Ukrainians and 17% of Russians expected their incomes to be higher.

Expectations condition behaviour and attitudes. While the macroeconomic and political climate will shape those expectations, it is apparent that age, education and social status do so as well.

(viii) Income security expectations: Old age

What then of longer-term expectations? Old age is rarely happy, goes a Russian saying. For the vast majority of people in all parts of the world, it is a time of dwindling happiness as pain and incapacity take over. But a modest degree of income security helps make much else bearable. Old-age income security is the dream of people everywhere; aspiring to it is part of the human condition. Achieving it is a rarity.

In developing countries, where the growing majority of elderly people live, most have continued to rely on their adult children and other relatives to support them. But with urbanization, increasing long-distance mobility and the shrinking size of families, support systems are becoming more fragile. Pensions are needed, yet for most people they are unknown.

Security as old age approaches is about expectations and realities. The PSS asks respondents what they expect their financial situation to be in old age. The resultant picture for developing countries is what might be expected — pervasive anxiety.

In Tanzania most people were uncertain about income security in their old age. Only 4% of men and women thought their financial situation would be good, about 8% thought it would be "adequate", and 34% of men and 36% of women thought it would be inadequate; the rest were unsure what to expect. So, pessimism was rife, with no significant difference between men and women.

In Ghana, the situation was different, with over two in every five adults thinking their situation would be satisfactory or good, and less than one-third thinking it would be inadequate. If anything, men were slightly more likely to be worried than women. Not surprisingly, the more educated the person, the more optimistic they were likely to be about their long-term future. The most likely of all to be worried were those whose income was insufficient for their food and other basic needs now.

In South Africa, only 19% of women and 21% of men thought their financial situation in old age would be good, while 37% of both women and men thought it would be inadequate. About one in five adults was uncertain. So, in spite of their country's greater wealth and per capita income, South Africans perceive greater long-term insecurity than Ghanaians.

In Ethiopia, 63% of men and 67% of women said they were worried about their likely financial situation in old age. Although the more educated were less likely to be pessimistic, a majority of those with secondary or tertiary schooling were also expecting old-age income insecurity.

In Africa, fear of old-age income insecurity is the reality for a majority of people, although it seems less common in Ghana than in the other countries covered by the PSS so far.

People in many other parts of the world are also desperately worried about their prospective income security in old age, perhaps nowhere more so than in eastern Europe. In Ukraine, a huge country of nearly 50 million people, about four in every five adults expect their income in old age to be inadequate.

People in most parts of the world still have to rely on their children to support them in old age. Thus, in Ghana, for example, over half of all the elderly respondents in the PSS said that their main source of financial support was their children.[15] But the traditional family-solidarity model of protection only works if successive generations are there and able to earn enough to provide for children and the elderly.

One of the scourges of AIDS in Africa is that, because the illness has hit prime age groups, orphans are being looked after by elderly relatives, who cannot look to their own children to provide them with income security in old age.

The PSS show that expected old-age income security varies and does not necessarily correspond to the income level of the country. Obviously, it depends in part on people's perceptions of adequacy, which is determined by current or prior living standards and their "class" position. However, in most developing countries a large number of people are uncertain what to expect. Of those with an expectation of the future, only small minorities look forward to an old age of good income security — about 3% in Ukraine, 4% in Tanzania, 6% in China and a little higher in other countries. In this respect at least there is no significant difference between men and women, or between those living in rural or urban areas. The reality in the countries covered is that substantial proportions of the population everywhere are anxious about the financial implications of growing old.

(ix) Relative incomes

Another aspect of income security is the sense of relative deprivation compared with self-determined peer groups, be it neighbours or people doing similar work or people with a similar level of education or vocational qualifications. The comparison that people make is often arbitrary, but for those concerned it is a personalized reality likely to influence social and economic behaviour.

This section is not intended to be a tour of the evidence on the complex subject of *relative deprivation*, on which there is a large and sophisticated literature.

---

[15]Apt and Amankrah, 2003, op. cit.

It is intended rather to highlight the need to incorporate this dimension in analysis and policy-making.

Let us focus on some African examples. Perhaps surprisingly, in Tanzania the number of people who felt that they were worse off than their neighbours was much greater than the number who thought they were better off. Thus, only 11% of men and 6% of women felt their income was greater than that of other local people, whereas 23% of men and 31% of women felt worse off than others. The more educated the person, the more likely he or she was to think their income was better than average.

Since the sample was random, this result needs some explanation. Does the sense of relative deprivation reflect reality or a false impression? Are people comparing themselves with the whole community around them, or are they comparing themselves with the group to which they think they belong or to which they aspire to belong, even though the question referred to all people living in their local area?

In Ethiopia under 2% said they felt better off than the average and about two thirds said they felt worse off than those around them. What this reveals and conceals is something that deserves to be assessed by Ethiopian researchers.

(x) Income satisfaction

The degree of satisfaction or dissatisfaction with one's current situation is a fundamental aspect of human security. It is also a vital aspect of life to be able to look forward with reasonable confidence in the expectation that what one is doing today will be the least one can expect for the future. But satisfaction and confidence are not necessarily simple positive functions of the level of income being received.

In poor countries, one might expect greatest dissatisfaction. In Tanzania, for example, most people expressed dissatisfaction with the income from their main economic activity. Even so, 26% of men and 32% of women expressed satisfaction, while 61% of men and 59% of women expressed dissatisfaction. The more educated were slightly more likely to express satisfaction.

In Ghana, by contrast, about 38% of men and women expressed satisfaction with the amount of income they earned from their work, while about a third were dissatisfied. Among men, but not among women, the more educated were more likely to be dissatisfied with the level of their income.

In Ethiopia, merely 25% of men expressed themselves satisfied with their employment income; 18% of men and 22% of women were "quite dissatisfied", and no less than 56% of men and 53% of women were "very dissatisfied". In other words, the pattern of dissatisfaction among Ethiopians is similar to that displayed in Tanzania.

In Tanzania, in terms of *benefits* other than wages, 19% of men and 21% of women in employment expressed satisfaction, with about 50% of both men and women being dissatisfied. Again, the more educated were more likely to be satisfied. In Ghana, about a third of men and women were satisfied and a third dissatisfied with their non-wage benefits. Among men, there was no difference between the more or less educated but women with less schooling were more likely to express satisfaction than those with more.

(xi) An individual income security index

By way of concluding this brief review of dimensions of income security, can we devise a micro-level income security index? Recall that, fundamentally, income security for an individual can be defined in terms of having an adequate income, a reasonably good relative income, a regular assured income, and access to non-wage benefits and income-supplementing (or income-replacing) entitlements.

Although income adequacy is tracked in the PSS in several ways, for this purpose it can be measured by giving a value of 1 if the respondent regards his/her income as adequate or more than adequate for his/her basic living needs, and 0 otherwise.

Income assurance is measured by two components: actual receipt of the income to which the person is entitled through work, and regularity of the income. Income assurance is given a value of 0.5 if *all* the income owed is received (measured by the experience of the previous three months), and a value of 0 otherwise. This gives this factor a lower weight in the overall index than other dimensions of income, but takes account of its significance. Income arrears are an important phenomenon in some transition economies.

Income regularity, or variability, is measured by giving a value of 1 if the respondent's monthly income from work was "regular" over the previous 12 months, a value of 0.5 if it "fluctuated", and a value of 0 if it was "very irregular".

Relative income is measured by a subjective variable, giving a value of 2 if the respondent regards the income as making him/her "well-off" in comparison with other people living and working locally, a value of 1 if the income is regarded as "average" by such comparison, and a value of 0 if it is regarded as "low".

Finally, a measure of access to non-wage enterprise benefits should be included, because these are often an important means of providing income security in and through work. There is no ideal measure of benefits because their value is hard to estimate, combining actual services with contingency entitlements to com-

pensate for the standard risks of life and work, such as illness. The measure adopted is crude but transparent. The PSS identifies 12 benefits that in principle someone could receive through work (e.g. subsidized food, sick leave, medical insurance, paid leave and subsidized transport). In Indonesia, most working people do not receive any of them. However, we have added to the other income security indicators a benefit indicator, defined as the number of benefits actually received (or to which the person was entitled) divided by three.

This set of measures gives a micro-level Income Security Index that can be normalized in the standard way to give a value of between 0 and 1. We evaluate the index for Indonesia, by way of an example. As Figure 4.1 shows, most men and women in Indonesia have very low income security and the vast majority of women have extremely low income security. We suggest that this is a valid way of analysing patterns of deprivation and insecurity, and will combine it with complementary indexes in later chapters.

Figure 4.1 Indonesia: Micro-level income security index, by gender

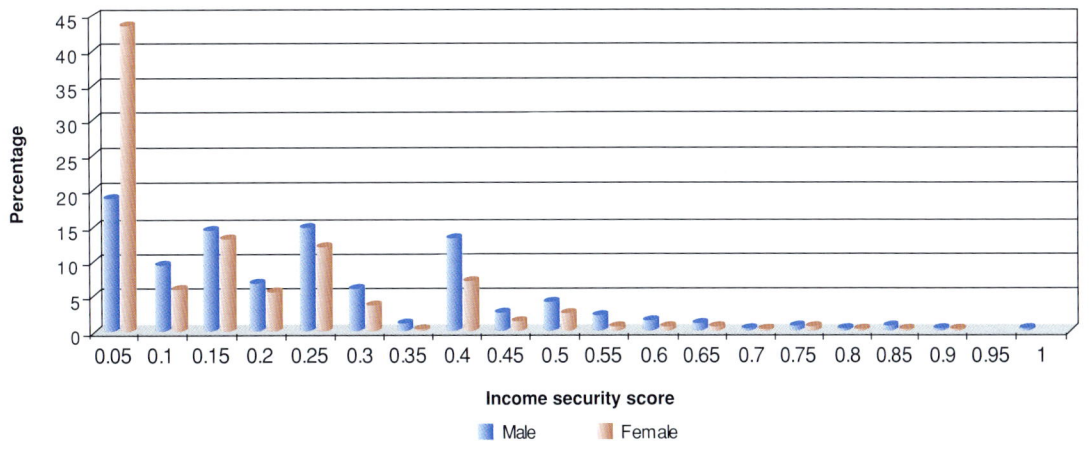

Source: Indonesia PSS 2001.

4.3 Income security in work

So far, we have considered aspects of income security in general. This section considers issues that relate to income earned through work, and changes in remuneration systems that have a bearing on income insecurity.

(i) Minimum wage

"The absence of a decent minimum wage only subsidises inefficient producers."

— Winston Churchill

The traditional way of providing basic income security for those in jobs has been a statutory minimum wage, set nationally, sectorally or occupationally. For several decades in the 20th century this seemed to be a primary route to income security for workers, and indeed in countries such as France it was raised to boost aggregate demand when needed.[16] However, the reality is that minimum wages have been eroded all over the world in the era of globalization, dropping in value absolutely and relative to average wages and becoming more varied.[17] Often, young workers or part-time workers are excluded from coverage or have lower minimum wages than others. Moreover, a minimum wage is much less likely to be effective in labour systems characterized by extensive informalization, flexible and precarious labour markets and high unemployment.

Although there are some exceptions, most notably the United Kingdom, the essential story is that the proportion of workers protected by minimum wages has declined, the level of minimum wages has fallen relative to average wages, differential minima have been introduced, meaning that the most vulnerable groups such as youth and women are often least protected, and governments have become less committed to the effective implementation of minimum wages.

In those developing countries where there is a minimum wage, workers are commonly unaware of its existence and are unlikely to have the capacity to demand it. In Tanzania in 2002 only 35% of men and women said they knew about it; most young people did not know. This should concern the unions, especially as the Trades Union Congress of Tanzania has been campaigning for a substantial increase in the minimum wage and for sectoral differentiation in the minimum wage. If workers do not know of its existence they are unlikely to pressurize employers to honour it, while certain employers are more likely to ignore it.

In Ethiopia, workers were asked if they were earning less than the official minimum income level: no less than 35% of men and 42% of women said they were, with a further 11% of men and 20% of women being unsure. This scarcely suggests that the statutory policy is an effective form of social protection. The fact is that statutory minimum wages or income limits rarely work very well.

(ii) Wage and income differentials

Across the world wage differentials have widened, in some cases sharply, as noted in Chapter 3. However, this stylized fact needs careful interpretation. The widening does not explain most of the growth in inequality or poverty. Nevertheless, an enormous gap has opened up between the earnings of executives and ordinary wage workers, with less striking growth in differentials between wages of salaried and manual workers.

In both developing and industrialized countries, there are wide earnings differentials based on worker status. By shifting more workers into lower-paying statuses, overall wages can be lowered. Thus, casual and piece-rate workers in Gujarat are earning much lower incomes than either regular workers with employment contracts or those nominally self-employed.[18]

One encouraging aspect is that in many countries gender-based earnings differentials have narrowed, although disparities remain large in many developing countries, in particular.[19] Unfortunately, there are many ways by which women may experience more income insecurity than men, rarely captured in official

---

[16]R. Boyer: *Is There a Welfare State Crisis? A Comparative Study of French Social Policy*, SES Paper No. 26 (Geneva, ILO, 2002).

[17]For review of the evidence of these changes, see Standing, 2002, op. cit.

[18]Unni and Rani, 2002, op. cit.

[19]See, e.g., ILO: 2001 *Labour Review: Latin America and the Caribbean* (Lima, 2001), pp. 22–44.

statistics. Among these is the tendency for women to face deductions from their income to a greater extent than men, and a tendency for women to find that their "costs of working" are less covered.

Thus, in Gujarat the PSS found that on average employers were shouldering three times as much of the

treatment costs for work-related accidents for men as they did for women.[20] This may indicate that women report fewer injuries, or that the jobs performed by women in that area are not notably hazardous, or that there is discrimination towards women and the work they perform.

The scandal of wage arrears

Ask a worker what wage he is earning, and then ask the firm what wage is being paid. Answers will be given and recorded. Too rarely have the collectors or recorders of wage statistics asked whether the amount stated was received or paid. In many industrialized countries that might not be a major source of inaccuracy or distortion. Elsewhere the picture is rather more opaque.

There is much anecdotal evidence that in low-income countries characterized by "informal" casual labour relations, wages are often not paid or are not paid in full, or are arbitrarily reduced by "informal" deductions. These are probably most serious where informal small-scale units escape weak or non-existent regulatory scrutiny and are not subject to the corrective demands of trade unions or other bodies that can exert pressure on employers and contractors to honour their commitments.

However, perhaps the major source of income insecurity in so-called transition countries over the past few years has been the non-receipt of wages. In Ukraine, for example, the ILO has tracked the incidence of wage arrears over the past decade and, while there has been an improvement in the past two or three years, the situation remains serious. **In 2002, over a three-month period, 27.5% of the employed had not received all the wages to which they were entitled.** Agriculture was the worst hit. Some 60% of rural workers had not received all their wages in the previous three months, and most of those had not received any wages at all for over two of those months. Probably because of the sectoral distribution of employment, men were more likely to be suffering from wage arrears.

The situation in the Russian Federation for some years was as bad as in Ukraine, but has now improved. In the Republic of Moldova, Azerbaijan and Georgia, where the ILO has carried out enterprise surveys, wage arrears remain common. China has also experienced wage arrears, although the main form it seems to have taken is through lay-offs, usually in preparation for eventual unemployment.

Wage arrears are a clear sign of income insecurity and deserve much more attention than they have received, in labour statistics and in policy design and policy monitoring. Governments should not let enterprises practise this with impunity.

(iv) Enterprise benefits

An important part of "social income" in any society is that provided by employers to workers in non-wage form, as "enterprise" or "occupational" benefits. Their value tends to be underestimated and they are a source of income inequality, since in many countries it is the relatively highly paid who also receive the most non-wage benefits, with the highest value.

In many countries, occupational benefits are determined through collective bargaining, either at industry level (as in the Netherlands, for example) or at national level (as is still common in the Nordic countries and in France), although individualized employment contracts are spreading almost everywhere. Often by

design, occupational benefits either complement or substitute for social security benefits, and may be used as a tactic to moderate wage growth on which contributions to social security and taxes are based. In any case, they contribute to intra-enterprise inequalities and to wider inequalities.

Most workers in developing countries receive little or nothing in such benefits, beyond subsidized food or transport. But a minority do receive some, and these tend to provide a modicum of income security that

---

[20] J. Unni and U. Rani: *Social Protection for Informal Workers: Insecurities, Instruments and Institutional Mechanism,* SES Paper No. 18 (Geneva, ILO, 2003).

their fellow workers and neighbours would envy. Table 4.10 gives the patterns of benefits revealed by the PSS in four African countries. While not much should be made of the actual percentages, it is worth noting that in general women are much less likely to have such income security and this applies to all benefits in all four countries.

Though non-wage benefits are often thought of in the context of large commercial enterprises, for most working people they consist of the informal support that landlords, middlemen or local employers may offer, which constitutes their social protection.

Table 4.10 Wage workers receiving specific non-wage benefits, by gender
(percentage of respondents entitled to and receiving specified benefit)

| | Entitled | | Received | |
	Male	Female	Male	Female
Ethiopia				
Paid holidays	20.8	10.6	n.a.	n.a.
Health benefits	14.5	7.1	n.a.	n.a.
Paid medical leave	21.4	9.4	n.a.	n.a.
Paid maternity leave	n.a.	10.4	n.a.	n.a.
Maternity benefits	n.a.	5.2	n.a.	n.a.
Unemployment benefit	2.4	0.8	n.a.	n.a.
Pension	22.3	9.4	n.a.	n.a.
Disability benefits	11.4	4.8	n.a.	n.a.
Free food	2.4	1.7	n.a.	n.a.
Free education	1.8	0.6	n.a.	n.a.
Other benefits	1.5	n.a.	n.a.	n.a.
Ghana				
Free/subsidized food	4.3	3.3	3.8	2.8
Free/subsidized transport	2.9	1.9	2.6	1.9
Paid leave	4.3	4.5	3.3	2.7
Paid maternity leave	n.a.	2.9	2.2	1.5
Paid medical care	6.4	5.3	3.7	3.4
Paid medical leave	5.3	4.6	2.1	2.5
Pension	5.0	4.4	1.5	0.6
Severance pay	2.3	2.8	0.9	0.7
Scholarship for children	2.2	2.1	0.6	0.3
South Africa				
Disability benefits	8.6	3.5	0.7	0.4
Free/subsidized food	2.1	1.8	1.8	1.3
Free/subsidized transport	2.1	0.9	1.6	0.5
Paid holidays	15.2	11.0	11.2	7.1
Paid maternity leave	n.a.	8.4	n.a.	2.2
Paid medical care	9.5	6.0	6.3	3.1
Paid medical leave	13.6	9.3	8.6	4.3
Pension	14.3	8.8	4.2	2.1
Severance pay	7.8	5.1	0.6	0.9
Scholarship for children	2.2	1.4	0.5	0.2
Tanzania				
Paid holidays	8.8	5.7	n.a.	n.a.
Paid medical care	8.2	3.9	n.a.	n.a.
Free/subsidized food	4.5	3.7	n.a.	n.a.
Paid medical leave	6.6	3.2	n.a.	n.a.
Paid maternity leave	n.a.	4.5	n.a.	n.a.
Severance pay	6.9	4.5	n.a.	n.a.

Source: PSS.
n.a. = Not available.

Perhaps the most important benefit of this type is the availability of loans or credit in times of need.[21] We can give some examples from the PSS. In Tanzania, for instance, 28% of those in wage employment said they were provided with loans or wage advances in times of personal crisis. This is an important form of income security.

However, informal credit is also often a hidden source of income inequality. Thus, white-collar and managerial workers are more likely to have access to such loans than labourers, only 12% of whom have access to such help. There is no apparent difference in this respect between men and women, but workers in rural areas seem more likely to have access to such loans (31% compared with 22% of those in urban areas).

As far as non-wage benefits are concerned, in Tanzania entitlement to a reasonably broad range of such benefits is widespread for the minority in wage jobs. That of course is the point: only a minority of the labour force has any prospect of receiving them. Of those in wage jobs, 53% said they were entitled to paid sick leave, with men being more likely to receive it. Here is a major form of socio-economic inequality. While over 61% of professionals and other white-collar workers receive paid sick leave, none of those working as labourers are so fortunate.

The pattern is similar for entitlement to redundancy (or retrenchment) compensation. While about 64% of all those in wage employment thought they would receive something, and while over 78% of those in white-collar jobs did so, none of those doing labouring jobs had any known entitlement. Much the same pattern was found for entitlement to a pension or provident fund benefits.

A majority of wage workers thought there was entitlement to maternity leave in their firm or establishment, but again this was concentrated among workers in higher-paying jobs. More interesting is that over 30% of wage workers thought it likely that in their firm a woman would lose her job if she became pregnant, and a further 32% said they did not know if this would happen or not. This is an area that needs more policy attention, since it must be a source of income insecurity for families dependent on women's wage earnings.

In India, most workers bear themselves the costs of ill health and work-related injuries and disease. The Gujarat PSS found that 70% of all casual labourers and wage workers were obliged to pay medical treatment costs for work-related accidents. And 93% of workers did not have life or accident insurance, indicating that medical treatment costs (for work-related injuries/illnesses) are paid entirely out of their own pockets.[22]

More generally, the era of workers' *industrial citizenship* through extensive enterprise-based benefits and services is past. But the era of salaried privileges through such benefits and services is definitely not past.

The picture gleaned from analytical work and anecdotal comment around the world is that payment systems in firms are becoming more flexible. There has been a shift from fixed to flexible wages, from collectively determined wages to individually determined ones, and a shift from enterprise benefits and services to monetary payments, at least for some groups of workers.

In general, albeit in some cases compensated by an increase in money wages, the reduction in enterprise benefits is one of the main ways by which workers' incomes have been made more flexible and insecure. This has been occurring on a major scale in China. Part of the erosion of traditional enterprise benefits has been attributed to the impact of foreign direct investment and privatization.[23] But nowhere has there been such a quick and widespread erosion in the extent of enterprise benefits as in the countries of eastern Europe.

One feature of the changing character of enterprise benefits is that "core" groups of relatively privileged workers and employees, typically those receiving higher salaries, have been gaining or retaining such benefits, while the lower-earning workers, and particularly those on precarious contracts, temporary and part-time workers and those on "probationary" contracts, are losing them.

[21]Loans and credit are also used in parts of the world as means of control over workers. For an interpretation of this phenomenon and for an argument for incorporating "control mechanisms" in analysis of economic security, see G. Standing: *Modes of Control: A Labour-Status Approach to Decent Work*, SES Paper No. 4 (Geneva, ILO, 2000).

[22]Unni and Rani, 2003, op. cit.

[23]X. Guan: "China's social policy: Reform and development in the context of marketization and globalization", *Social Policy and Administration*, Vol. 34, No. 1, 2000, pp. 115–130.

This dualistic tendency is pronounced in the case of health care benefits and is the main reason why over 40 million Americans are not covered by health care insurance. In eastern Europe the trend to dualism in this respect is also strong. Thus, the enterprise surveys in Ukraine show that temporary workers are rarely covered for medical services, and have to bear the cost including the time lost for work-related illnesses or accidents. Since 1993 the range and value of benefits provided by firms have shrunk in general, but non-regular workers have suffered most.[24]

Moreover, formal entitlement is often not backed up by actual entitlement. In countries of the former Soviet Union this has been a feature for the past decade and a half. Thus, in 2002 in Ukraine, whereas nearly one in every five industrial workers had entitlement to a housing benefit or subsidy, less than half of those received it. The same was true of transport allowances. The public sector was even worse in meeting its obligations. Moreover, the emerging distribution of enterprise benefits and entitlements is accentuating the growing income inequality. Those earning higher money incomes are also more likely to be entitled to a broad range of benefits.

In sum, enterprise benefits are potentially a means by which workers obtain income security. But they have become an important means of accentuating income inequality. For many workers in industrialized, transition and industrializing countries, there is no prospect of these benefits of "industrial citizenship".

4.4 Income security in the workplace

What would one expect to be the pattern of wages and benefits in a workplace providing decent income security for those working for it?

Little of the vast literature on economic equity relates to the microeconomics of the firm. An economically equitable firm is surely one in which differences in earnings and benefits between its members are no more than is required to ensure dynamic efficiency. This might be called the *Principle of Efficient Inequality*.

It is most unlikely this has been respected. It is extraordinary that acceptable wage differentials have widened dramatically in recent years. Plato would be disappointed by the modern world. His view was that,

in the interest of fairness, the highest paid should never receive more than five times the lowest paid. In the United States, chief executives now receive something like 600 times as much as the average worker. Gaps are widening elsewhere too.

Besides fairness, there are dynamic efficiency reasons to disapprove. Labour productivity depends on cooperation as well as individual effort. If differences between groups are wide, the more disadvantaged — or those who feel inequitably treated — will withhold "tacit knowledge" and not commit themselves to the exchange of knowledge that contributes to dynamic efficiency.[25] They may also tend to indulge in implicit or explicit sabotage. Equity induces loyalty, which boosts productivity. Narrow pay differentials strengthen group cohesion and trust of management, as well as productivity.[26] And narrow differentials induce commitment to management goals.[27]

This set of issues has caused mainstream reporting systems some difficulty. For example, the Global Reporting Initiative, admits that "employee remuneration" requires "further attention".[28] And the IFC as part of its Corporate Citizenship facility has urged firms to pay *"somewhat higher wages than average"*. This is more vague than it sounds.

We propose a workplace income security index that respects principles of economic equity, which can be adjusted to the structures and concerns of specific countries, types of firm and sector. Slightly different approaches can be taken in the countries covered by the ELFS. In the transition countries, three indicators were selected, giving greatest weight to the first, since it relates to treatment of the "worst off" in the workplace.

---

[24]L. Zsoldos and G. Standing: *Coping with Insecurity: The Ukrainian People's Security Survey 2002*, SES Paper No. 17 (Geneva, ILO, 2002).

[25]G. Hodgson: *Economics and Institutions: A Manifesto for a Modern Institutional Economics* (Oxford, Polity Press, 1988), p. 259.

[26]D. Levine: "Public policy implications of worker participation", *Economic and Industrial Democracy*, Vol. 13, 1992, pp. 183–206.

[27]D.M. Cowherd and D. Levine: "Product quality and pay equity between lower-level employees and top management: An investigation of distributive justice theory", *Administrative Science Quarterly*, Vol. 37, No. 2, 1992, pp. 302–320.

[28]See, for instance, Global Reporting Initiative: *Sustainability Reporting Guidelines* (Boston, 2002), p. 52.

As shown in Chapter 5, a disturbing phenomenon in eastern European enterprises in the 1990s was that some groups were paid little or nothing while being kept on the books. An equitable firm should have few workers, if any, in that situation. To take account of this, if more than 5% of the workers received the minimum amount paid, the firm was regarded as low on income equity. It was regarded as high on it if the minimum payment was equal to or greater than 50% of the average wage. These indicators are only proxies for what is desired, yet seem reasonable.

A second indicator is whether or not the average wage is good relative to that paid in other firms. Here, a sectoral measure is taken, to reflect technological and market factors. The proxy is whether the firm's average wage is greater than the industry's average.

Third, income security is regarded as better if the workplace provides benefits and entitlements that give security against contingencies and that improve workers' living standards. Since wages and incomes are only part of remuneration, the indicator is whether or not the firm provided workers with more than eight types of non-wage benefits. Thus, for eastern European countries, the income security index is:

$$EE = Min/Emp + M + AW/Ws + FB$$

where EE is the Economic Equity Index, and where

$Min./Emp$ = 1 if the percentage of the workforce paid the minimum payment is below 5%, 0 otherwise;

M = 1 if the minimum wage exceeded 50% of the average in firm, 0 otherwise;

AW/Ws = 1 if the average wage is above sector's average wage, 0 otherwise;

FB = 1 if the firm paid more than eight types of non-wage benefits, 0 otherwise.

In other countries (Brazil, Chile, China, Indonesia, the Philippines, Pakistan, South Africa and Tanzania), the following index was applied, with an adjustment in the case of South Africa to take account of the racial factor:

$$EE = Min/EMP + M + AW/Ws + Wnw/W + FB$$

where other variables are defined as above, but where

Min/EMP = 1 if less than 5% of the workforce is paid less than half of the average wage in the firm, 0 otherwise;

Wnw/W = 1 if average wage of non-whites is more than 80% of the average of all workers, 0 otherwise.

By way of example, note that over two-thirds of Indonesian firms performed poorly in terms of providing income security and economic equity (Figure 4.2). What is important is that this is a relative measure within the country, and that it can be shown that firms that provide workers with income security actually do better in other respects, a point to which we will return in later chapters.

Figure 4.2 Indonesia: Micro-level income security index

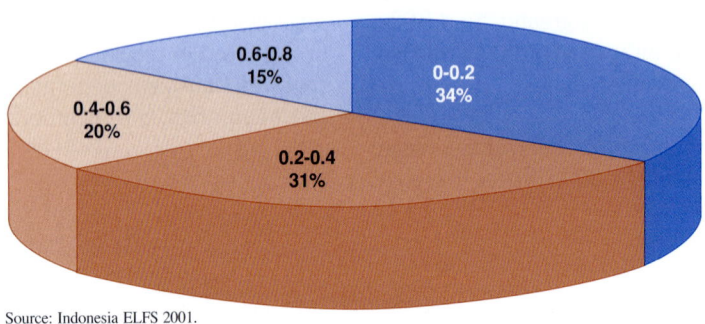

Source: Indonesia ELFS 2001.

4.5 An Income Security Index: A global assessment

Can we assess a country's performance in terms of providing an environment of income security? The following is an attempt to do so by means of a composite index of income security, based on the methodology outlined earlier, in which sets of input, process and outcome indicators are identified, combined and normalized as an index with a value between 0 and 1.

Before turning to the overall income security index and estimating it for ILO member States, a separate component index specifically for old-age income security is discussed.

(i) An Index of Old-age Income Security

The goal here is to measure the impact on old-age income security of social security programmes provided by the State or controlled by public policy. However, within the framework of public policy there is a wide variety of pension schemes with different institutional structures, coverage and modes of operation. Because of the lack of information on the multiplicity of private occupational pension schemes, we have opted to focus mainly on state-based old-age social security programmes in terms of coverage, benefits and sustainability. Our old-age income security index is constructed using the standard methodology for the various security indexes outlined earlier.

There are three *input* indicators. The first is a qualitative measure of the population covered by old-age pension schemes, which varies considerably between countries. In some, only a few groups such as civil servants are covered, leaving the majority of the population without protection. In others coverage may be extended, in principle, to all those in regular wage labour.

The second indicator examines whether or not the country has ratified Part V of ILO Convention No. 102 on "Social Security (Minimum Standards)", which was adopted in 1952 and deals with old-age benefits (specifically in Part V) and other social security branches[29] and Part III of Convention No. 128 on "Invalidity, Old-Age and Survivors' Benefits, 1967". In ratifying it, a member State must accept the stipulations for at least three of the nine social security branches specified. ILO Convention No. 128 is more specific and lays down benefit levels.

___
[29]The others are medical care, sickness, unemployment, old age, employment injury, family, maternity, invalidity and survivor's benefits.

States ratifying at least one of these two parts of the above Conventions can be considered as complying with international standards on pensions. The ILO also has procedures to assess how countries apply provisions of a Convention once ratified.[30]

For measuring old-age income security, we have examined ILO observations on compliance with these two Conventions since 1995, enabling us to distinguish between countries that have conformed to internationally agreed standards.

The third input indicator is a variable measuring the main types of pension schemes. Each type is characterized by extent of coverage and an implied pension adequacy. Although national old-age pension schemes vary enormously, shared features enable us to classify them into six types, based on the level of income security provided. Universal schemes are ranked highest, followed by social insurance schemes:

- *Universal* schemes, which are widely regarded as optimal for income security. They have the double advantage of being based on a needs-test principle (old age) and guaranteeing a decent pension for all.

- *Social insurance* schemes, usually employment-related, which generally pay earnings-related benefits.

- *Mandatory private insurance* schemes, which typically pay out lump sums, have low coverage and high levels of contribution evasion.[31]

- *Social assistance* schemes, which supposedly guarantee a means-tested minimum income safety net to all pensioners on condition of residence.

- *Provident funds* provide lump sums only and have similarities with savings accounts.

- *Employers' liability* schemes, which have the most limited coverage.

There are five *process* indicators. The first measures the overall employment rate for the age group five years younger than the statutory or standard retirement age. This is an indicator of the share of the economically active population contributing to old-age pension schemes. Focusing on that group not only discriminates between countries that have high activity rates but indicates whether older workers are among social security contributors and not beneficiaries of early retirement schemes or unemployment

benefits. In an ageing society, a high employment rate among older workers is a key to maintaining the financial sustainability of a pay-as-you-go pension system.

A second process indicator is life expectancy at retirement age.[32] Life expectancy at birth, at 60 or 65, is commonly used as a measure of the economic and social development level of a country, as in the UNDP's Human Development Index (HDI). However, a more appropriate measure is life expectancy at retirement age, which combines an exogenous element, (life expectancy), and an endogenous one, (pensionable age).

This indicator also gives information about the average length of time during which the pensioner will receive old-age benefits and as such can be considered as an indicator of "generosity". The longer life expectancy is at retirement age, the longer benefits will be paid out.

The third process indicator is old-age pension expenditure as a percentage of GDP.[33] This ratio measures the proportion of old-age public pension expenditure in national income and the effort undertaken to provide income security for the elderly.

The fourth process indicator is old-age dependency ratio, defined as the total population over legal retirement age divided by the economically active population aged between 15 and retirement age minus the number of unemployed. This ratio is a demographic measure of how many workers contribute per person over retirement age. Usually this ratio falls between 0 and 1, which means there are more people

---

[30]In cases of non-conformity, the ILO Committee of Experts on the Application of Conventions and Recommendations (CEACR) uses the "individual observation" procedure, a process that occurs when a State that has ratified a Convention does not comply with some of its provisions. The CEACR also applies a procedure called "Direct Request". This usually concerns minor cases or the beginning of an exchange of information between the State and the ILO, and accordingly has not been taken into account in distinguishing between countries.

[31]W. McGillivray: "Contribution evasion: implications for social security pension schemes", *International Social Security Review*, Oct.–Dec. 2001.

[32]Data from United Nations: *World Population Prospects* (New York, United Nations, 2001).

[33]Old-age pension expenditure data from ILO *World Labour Report* 2000, Table 14; R. Palacios and M. Pallarès-Miralles: *International Patterns of Pension Provision* (Washington, DC, The World Bank, Apr. 2000).

in employment than in retirement. So, the lower the old-age dependency ratio the lower the cost of pensions, and the more sustainable the old-age pension system.

To differentiate countries according to their level of affluence, GDP per capita is considered as a significant measure of income security and is used as our fifth process indicator for the old-age income security index. GDP per capita at purchasing power parity (PPP) provides internationally comparable information on levels of income and old-age pensions.[34]

Finally, there are three *outcome* indicators. The first consists of the average income replacement rate of old-age pensions, multiplied by PPP-adjusted GDP per capita. Although there are conceptual and statistical difficulties with the notion of replacement rate, it is defined here as average monthly benefits as a percentage of previous average monthly earnings.[35] It relates the level of old-age pensions to earnings in the same period, thereby adjusting for inflation. The higher the replacement rate, the better the income security for pensioners. The combination of a replacement rate with GDP per capita at PPP refines the international comparison by taking into account differences in living standards between countries.

The second indicator is the ratio of pensioners to the population over 59/64 years. This measures the effective coverage of the old-age pension system. In the ILO's *World Labour Report* 2000, values of this ratio are reported for ages 59 and 64. Although the actual retirement age may differ from these, the retained value for a country was the ratio for the age (59 or 64) closer to the domestic legal retirement age.

The third outcome indicator is the activity rate during the five years after retirement age.[36] A high activity rate may reflect the inefficiency of a pension system, due to an inappropriately low retirement age, low coverage of the population who have to continue to work for a living, a low pension level, etc. So it is assumed that the higher the activity rate during the five years after retirement age, the lower the effectiveness of an old-age pension scheme.

The results of the **Old-age Income Security Index** can be summarized quite briefly. Industrialized European countries perform better than the rest of the world, having a long tradition of social policy and collective bargaining. They are also the countries with the oldest demographic structure and the longest experience of developing old-age pension schemes for several generations of retired people.

Within Europe, the Nordic countries exhibit the best results. They have a universal basic flat-rate pension, paid on condition of residence to all the elderly over retirement age. On top of this, some have added a state earnings-related social insurance tier, which started in Sweden in 1960, later taken up by Norway and Finland. This social security "architecture" mixes high coverage with a high replacement rate.

Old corporatist and "Bismarckian" countries, such as France, Italy and Germany, are in the group with the next best results. Their pension architecture is not based on a universal flat-rate scheme, but started with earnings-related corporatist schemes that were extended to the majority of the working population through collective bargaining. Although earnings-related schemes usually provide high benefits, they do not provide full coverage of the population as they are employment-related. Means-tested assistance is supposed to guarantee a minimum coverage for the remainder.

The next group consists of other OECD countries, confirming the correlation between old-age pension expenditure and GDP per capita. It should however be noted that North American countries have a lower ranking relative to their economic resources.

Next are the eastern European countries and the former Soviet republics. The latter inherited the Soviet old-age pension system and reforms have been slow to produce much improvement.

---

[34] Comparisons based on PPP look at what a given income level will buy using a common consumer basket of goods and services, so abstracting from exchange rate movements.

[35] Data from ILO, *World Labour Report 2000*, op. cit., Table 13; Palacios and Pallarès-Miralles, 2000, op. cit.

[36] Data from the ILO's *LABORSTA 2001* and retirement age from SES Social Security Database.

After them come Latin American countries, while the last group is mainly composed of Asian and African countries with very limited old-age pensions. The scores would be even lower if countries such as Bangladesh, the Democratic Republic of Congo, Tanzania, Nepal, Sierra Leone and Somalia had been included. They were not included, either because there were no old-age pension schemes or because of a lack of information on existing schemes.

As Figure 4.3 shows, countries of western Europe have particularly strong input and outcome performances.

Figure 4.3   Average scores of input process and outcome for old-age income security, by region

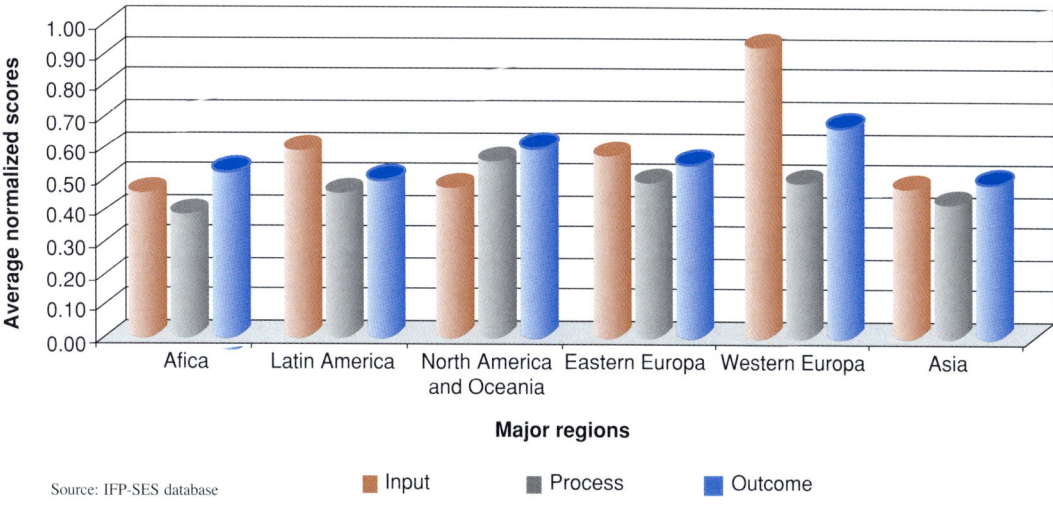

Source: IFP-SES database
■ Input   ■ Process   ■ Outcome

As presented, the Old-age Income Security Index considers the "main type of programme" as the relevant indicator. However, social security pension systems are usually a combination of several types of programme. If the two main types of programme were included in a measure of performance, would that make a difference?

Basing the old-age income security index on two main types of scheme rather than one may indicate what combination of types of scheme promise the best results. The revised index shows once again that the Nordic countries do best, the top scores coming from a combination of a universal and a social insurance programme. This supports a popular hypothesis that countries combining social insurance and universal programmes provide not only the best chance of covering the whole population, but also redistribute earnings-related benefits.[37] The combination provides security to the elderly and is effective in combating old-age poverty. However, such a combination has a cost. Nordic countries are among those with the highest expenditure per capita on social security. That is one reason for the benefit erosion and reforms that have taken place in recent years.

It is also apparent that only countries with high social security expenditure achieved high rankings in the two-scheme index, which confirms our initial index. Countries such as Japan and Canada also combine social insurance and universal schemes, but old-age pensions are low, averaging 24.9% of an average wage in Japan and 31.9% in Canada. By contrast, high social security expenditure in Nordic countries provides higher income security for the elderly, in terms of both coverage and a decent replacement rate.

Many OECD countries combine social insurance and social assistance. This means that in principle all the population is covered. Those with incomes below a given ceiling are eligible for means-tested social assistance benefits paid from general revenue. Social insurance usually provides higher benefits than that ceiling and is often earnings-related, which ensures income during working life and in retirement.

[37] J. Palme: Foundations and Guarantees of *Social Security Rights at the Beginning of the 21ˢᵗ Century*, paper presented at ISSA Conference, Vancouver, Canada, 10–12 Sep. 2002. <http://www.issa.int/engl/homef.htm>.

Pensioners should receive either social insurance benefits, or social assistance if they are poor. But this combination is less inclusive than the Nordic one, since the better-off are excluded from some benefits while many poor fail to receive the means-tested benefit, due to poverty traps, stigma and other reasons for low take-up.

Western European countries like France and Germany have achieved good results in combining social assistance and social insurance programmes, according to our indicators. But other countries combining similar types of programmes have not, notably Ireland and the United States. While combinations of social assistance and social insurance programmes have some common characteristics, they do not guarantee any pension level. The targeted security has a cost that not all countries are inclined to pay.

Other combinations seem even less satisfactory, either because of a gap in coverage or low level of pension. Lack of information for many developing countries prevents us from analysing their combination of old-age pension schemes. But other evidence tells us that they have the least old-age income security of all.

(ii) A national Income Security Index

What should go into an index of income security? Clearly, one must have measures for those actually earning income from work, for those on the margins of the labour market and for those outside the labour force depending on, or needing, income transfers on which to survive or exist in decency and security. It is particularly important to take into account the system of social protection, and in that regard an assessment of the prevailing system of *social security* is required.

The selected *input* indicators represent governments' formal commitment to income security. Thus, a positive value is given if the country has ratified ILO Conventions No. 102 on Social Security (Minimum Standards), 1952, Convention No. 26 on Minimum Wage-Fixing Machinery, 1928 and Convention No. 131 on Minimum Wage Fixing, 1970 and Convention No. 95 on Protection of Wages, 1949. Also included are two dummy variables for the commitment at national level to the income security of the employed, with a positive value for the existence of a minimum

wage law and a positive value for the existence of laws promoting or legitimizing collective bargaining.

The *process* indicators need to reflect the degree of comprehensiveness of the social protection system. The selected indicators, while not ideal, are the social security expenditure share of GDP and two dummies having a positive value for the existence of an unemployment benefits scheme and a positive value for the existence of a state pension.

The *outcome* indicators are of two types. The first type covers the whole population in each country. Its indicators are:

- the national poverty rate, as a measure of the size of the population economically at risk;

- GDP per capita expressed on a PPP basis and the Gini coefficient measuring income distribution (see Chapter 3 for reservations) to evaluate wealth and its distribution, assuming greater insecurity the lower the level and the more unequal the distribution;

- a measure of foreign indebtedness (external debt relative to gross national product) to reflect a country's vulnerability to a sudden loss of whatever level of national income security it has achieved (relevant for the sort of experience Argentinians endured in 2001–02);

- life expectancy at birth, as a proxy for overall public and individual health status. Several health indicators were reviewed, including the infant mortality rate. While highly correlated with GDP per capita, health indicators vary considerably across developing countries.

The second type refers to the income security of workers and the elderly retired. The corresponding indicators are:[38]

- the wage share in total value-added, representing the extent of a relatively secure form of income earning;

- the old-age income security index generated from the SES Social Security Database, reflecting the security of non-work income for mainly retired workers;

---

[38] Ideally an indicator representing the income security of the unemployed should be added, but information is not available for most countries on the share of the unemployed receiving a benefit. Unemployment is represented by a process indicator.

- the ratio of average female to male income, as a proxy for wage differentials, gender discrimination and disadvantage of female workers.

The overall Income Security Index (ISI) is estimated by normalizing each indicator and then adding the three categories of indicators, thereby giving the Outcome sub-index twice the weight of each of the other two.

There are 96 countries for which there are data for estimating this Index. Table 4.11 places the countries in four clusters — "Pacesetters", "Pragmatists", "Conventionals" and "Much-to-be-done". Only a few non-European countries are "Pacesetters" and none of them is from Africa, North or South. Countries from this continent, together with most countries from Asia and eastern Europe, do not provide adequate income security, and are either in the "Much-to-be-done" or the "Conventionals" clusters. Latin American countries are mainly "Conventionals".

Comparing individual country scores on income security shows that the 13 most secure, the "Pacesetters", are western European countries, headed by Norway. Next are non-European OECD countries, such as Japan, Canada, Australia and New Zealand, and the more economically advanced eastern European countries, such as the Czech Republic, Slovakia, Latvia, Poland and Hungary.

Countries in Latin America, North Africa and the Middle East constitute the bulk of those providing "middle range" income security. As most are "Conventionals" they have some formal policies and institutions that should promote income security, but have economic realities that make the outcomes less than satisfactory.

The least secure countries are concentrated in South and East Asia — including the highly populated countries of China, India, Indonesia and Bangladesh, in Central Asia and the Caucasus, and in sub-Saharan Africa. However, Mauritius and to a lesser extent South Africa, although classified in the "Conventionals" cluster, have achieved relatively high levels of income security compared to their neighbours, as indicated by their index scores.

Table 4.11 The income security index

High score on Outcome

Regions	High score on Input / Process — Pacesetters Countries		Low score on Input / Process — Pragmatists Countries	
Africa and Middle East			Israel	
Americas	Barbados Canada		Saint Kitts and Nevis United States	
Asia	Australia Japan	New Zealand	Korea, Republic of	
Eastern Europe and Central Asia	Czech Republic Latvia	Poland Slovakia	Belarus Estonia Hungary	Lithuania Slovenia
Western Europe	Austria Belgium Denmark France Germany Ireland Luxembourg	Netherlands Norway Portugal Spain Sweden Switzerland United Kingdom	Finland Greece	Iceland Italy

Low score on Outcome

Regions	High score on Input / Process — Conventionals Countries		Low score on Input / Process — Much-to-be-done Countries	
Africa and Middle East	Mauritius Tunisia Turkey Lebanon Algeria South Africa Burkina Faso Ghana	Senegal Benin Madagascar Nigeria Côte d'Ivoire Congo Congo, Dem. Rep. of Sierra Leone	Burundi Egypt Ethiopia Morocco	Mauritania Rwanda Zimbabwe
Americas	Argentina Brazil Costa Rica Chile Ecuador	Honduras Mexico Panama Venezuela	Colombia Dominican Republic	Peru Saint Vincent and the Grenadines
Asia	Philippines Sri Lanka		Bangladesh China India Indonesia	Nepal Pakistan Thailand
Eastern Europe and Central Asia	Bulgaria Croatia Moldova, Republic of	Romania Tajikistan Ukraine	Albania Georgia Russian Federation Azerbaijan Armenia	Uzbekistan Kazakhstan Turkmenistan Kyrgyzstan
Western Europe				

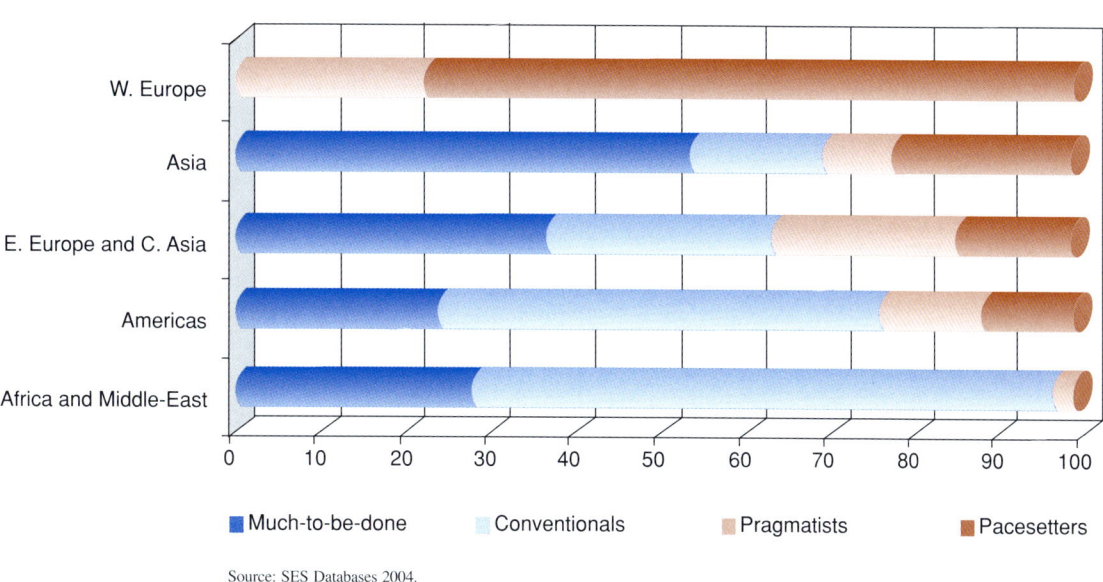

Figure 4.4 Income security index — Clusters by region

■ Much-to-be-done   □ Conventionals   □ Pragmatists   ■ Pacesetters

Source: SES Databases 2004.

4.6 Concluding remarks

At this point, we merely report the national scores on the income security index, reserving assessment until the other forms of security have been considered. Clearly, it is anticipated that there are links between the extent of income security and those other forms. In the final chapter, attention is focused on policies that seem to have most relevance to those countries that are in the "Much-to-be-done" cluster.

As far as the micro-level findings are concerned, we wish to highlight a key point. Income instability deserves much more attention in analysis of poverty and economic insecurity than it has received. Often that instability is inherent to the system of production and distribution and cannot be neatly portrayed in terms of specific contingency risks. More policy attention should be given to finding ways of stabilizing or "smoothing" income, which may not necessarily involve insurance-type schemes. Measures are needed to prevent the instability from arising and to limit its extent if it does. Such *ex ante* policies are the essence of *rights*. By contrast, *ex post* remedial policies are more subject to what might be called *discretionary* failure, in that receipt of income and benefits or otherwise will always be far from assured.

Chapter 5

Labour market security

5.1 Introduction

Labour market security arises from an environment in which there are ample opportunities for adequate income-earning activities, or where "supply" approximates "demand". As such, it is about the structure of opportunities as much as about the overall level. It is also about expectations, in that security arises from expecting that opportunities will improve or, if already good, will stay that way. Alan Greenspan, Chairman of the United States Federal Reserve Board, in the midst of the boom of the mid-1990s, when past economic models would have predicted that a tight labour market could have been expected to create strong inflationary pressure, made the point that American workers were not pushing for much higher wages because they feared losing their jobs.

In a market economy, the standard indicators of labour market security are the labour force participation rate (the share of the adult population in the labour force), the open unemployment rate, the average duration of open unemployment and the share of the unemployed in "long-term" unemployment. None is ideal as a reliable indicator.

One difficulty is that all measures focus on "labour". It is too often simply presumed that it is desirable to have a very high "employment rate" or to maximize the number of "jobs". Labour market insecurity can arise because people are obliged to look for jobs when they wish to do other forms of work such as caring for relatives or doing community work. There

is a danger in fostering a mass "jobholder" society — by no means all jobs should be regarded as promoting dignity, development, security or autonomy.

This chapter will summarize the global picture, focusing on aspects of unemployment and the specific features of a selected group of countries, and will then present a national Labour Market Security Index, estimated for 94 countries. Before that, let us reflect on three global trends that relate to the changing character of labour market security — the slow demise of agricultural livelihoods in developing countries, the "informalization" of economic activity, and global de-industrialization.

5.2 Agricultural disemployment in developing countries

Globally, about 1.3 billion people work in agriculture, which represents 45% of the world's labour force. In developing countries, 55% of the labour force is in agriculture. While the Latin American and Caribbean region has undergone steady urbanization, so that the rural workforce is only one-fifth of the total labour force, in the developing countries of Asia and Africa almost two-thirds of the labour force remains in rural areas (Table 5.1). Of course, not all of them eke out a living in agriculture, but a large proportion relies on it to survive.

Although agriculture and its associated activities are a chief source of employment for rural dwellers, being part of the working-age rural population does not imply having a job. Rural employment is conditioned by many factors, including the ecological niche in which production is carried out, the land tenure system, the social organization of production, size structure of landholdings, and the "technology" in use. The level of employment depends on labour utilization patterns, which vary over socio-cultural settings, between regions of a country and across national boundaries.

Table 5.1 Regional estimates of agricultural labour force

World	Total labour force		Agricultural labour force			
	Number (millions)	Average annual growth rate (%)	Number (millions)	Average annual growth rate (%)	Share in total labour force (%)	
	2000	1990–2000	2000	1990–2000	1990	2000
World	2948	1.8	1319	0.8	49	45
Developed countries	655	0.7	48	-2.3	10	7
Developing countries	2292	2.1	1271	1.0	61	55
Africa	324	3.1	195	1.9	66	60
— of which sub-Saharan Africa	270	3.0	179	2.0	71	66
Asia	1741	1.9	1029	0.8	65	59
Latin America and Caribbean	223	2.7	44	-0.1	25	20
Oceania	3	2.8	2	1.8	68	63
Low-income food-deficit countries (LIFDCs)*	1889	2.3	1138	1.1	67	60
Low-income countries	1107	3.3	644	1.8	66	58

* LIFDCs are defined by the FAO as those countries that meet two basic criteria. First, they have a per capita income below the ceiling used to determine eligibility for International Development Assistance (IDA), and second, they are net importers of a basket of basic foodstuffs whose volumes are aggregated by the calorie content of individual commodities. As of 2004, there are 83 countries classified as such: 44 in Africa; 23 in the Asia and the Pacific region; 6 in eastern Europe; 5 in Central Asia (former Soviet Union countries); and 5 in Latin America and the Caribbean.

Source: Food and Agricultural Organization (FAO): FAOSTAT Database

Over the last two decades the share of agricultural employment has declined all over the world. The fall has been driven by policy, often reflecting structural adjustment packages that have pushed countries to "modernize" agricultural production to make it more export-oriented. This has entailed more labour-saving technology and more chemical inputs. The expectation was that such technology would lead to higher incomes and so benefit all farmers, small and large. But modernization and commercialization have benefited mainly large-scale farmers and undermined small-scale producers, for whom the process has been impoverishing. This has been the experience of small farmers in Central America, Asia and Africa.[1]

Small-scale farmers make up a large share of the rural population in developing countries. Their position has been undermined by food production subsidies in rich countries, and liberalization and other structural adjustment policies in their own. Both have facilitated the sale of lower-cost competing crops from industrialized countries and have led to a fall in prices of locally grown staples that smallholders mainly produce. Small-scale farmers have also suffered because they have not been able to bear the costs associated with the new technology.[2]

[1]A. Kwa: *Agriculture in Developing Countries: Which Way Forward?* Occasional Paper No. 4 (Geneva, South Centre, June 2001).

[2]This is not new. In their examination of changes in South-East Asian agriculture and the Green Revolution in South Asia respectively, Scott and Gotsch noted that inputs associated with modern technology were sufficiently "lumpy" to create income and land thresholds below which innovation was unlikely. J. Scott: *The Moral Economy of the Peasant* (New Haven, Yale University Press, 1976); C. Gotsch: "Technological change and the distribution of income in rural areas", *American Journal of Agricultural Economics*, Vol. 54, No. 2, May 1972.

As a result, many have been pushed out of farming or into chronic "underemployment", or into rural out-migration and labour circulation.

Policies have encouraged the consolidation of land-holdings, which has also contributed to the decline in agricultural employment. Access has been denied to many (e.g., sharecroppers, tenant farmers), with rented-out lands being taken back by newly commercialized landowners or acquired in distress sales. This has fed the pool of landless and dispossessed with their famous "double freedom" — free of ownership and free to sell their labour as "a commodity". Even land-augmenting technology has not helped, since it has been mainly labour-saving. The low elasticity of labour demand in response to output growth has also meant that labour absorption in agriculture in most developing countries is either stagnant or declining. The movement of people out of the rural areas into urban areas reflects shrinking rural opportunities and growing unemployment.

This is development. This is freedom, in some sense of the term. But the insecurities for the generation that experiences the structural changes are well known and well chronicled from the historical experiences of today's industrialized countries. Those insecurities scarcely constitute real freedom.

5.3 Informalization as labour market insecurity

Throughout the world, as summarized in the next chapter, labour relations are being informalized. In developing countries, "formal" jobs have not expanded to keep up with the growth of labour supply, and as a result a majority have continued to enter "the informal economy", characterized by a lack of social protection, lack of regulatory safeguards and general precariousness. To some extent, this nebulous mix of activities has cushioned the insecurities and suffering among the poor. Often it has not.

The majority of working-age people in developing countries are working in informal activities. Some ILO estimates suggest that 50% to 70% of the developing countries' labour force is in informal work.[3] The figure for some countries, such as India and Bangladesh, is even higher. Most do not have full-time employment and the majority of these workers are "self-employed". A fairly high proportion performs casual work, i.e. they work only when they have jobs and remain unpaid for the rest of the time. Even so, there are obvious difficulties in establishing a clear picture on the number of workers in the informal economy, though many estimation exercises have been undertaken.[4]

The informal economy also acts as a sponge, absorbing a vast number of people who are without the means to earn and sustain a living and have been plunged into situations of distress. About 40% of people in the developing world live in absolute poverty. They are obliged to take on the most rudimentary forms of work or labour to ensure a basic subsistence. The poor cannot stay idle for long and therefore engage in any activity that can make a contribution to household income.

The PSS are revealing in this respect. In 13 of 15 surveys undertaken, at least a third of all households said that household income was not sufficient for food, and a higher proportion indicated that they did not have enough for basic health care needs. In India, Pakistan, Indonesia, Ethiopia, Tanzania, Ghana, South Africa, Ukraine and the Russian Federation, almost two-thirds of the respondents expressed dissatisfaction with their income-earning activity in terms of income. It may not be far-fetched to presume that they would also find informal work appealing to the extent that it would supplement their earnings.

Employment per se is not the problem. Indeed, workers in the informal economy often put in more time daily than other workers. The insecurity is revealed in excessive work, eroding health, welfare and the capacity to function. Failure to generate sufficient income is indicative of "inadequate" employment and has led many poorer households to restructure their labour allocation patterns to involve the elderly, care-providing women and children in income-earning activities. Many people in many jobs does not necessarily indicate a successful economy or society.

---

[3] ILO: *Women and Men in the Informal Economy: A Statistical Picture* (Geneva, 2002).

[4] See, for example, ILO: *ILO Compendium of Official Statistics on Employment in the Informal Sector* (Geneva, 2002). J. Unni and J. Charmes: *Measurement of Work*, paper presented at an informal consultation on Reconceptualizing Work, Geneva, ILO, 11-12 Dec. 2002.

In countries where cultural norms hinder women's employment the recent increase in women's participation is welcome, as long as their rights and civil liberties are protected. Often this is not the case, particularly for poorer women. Given the constraints in access to formal jobs, these women usually end up in informal employment where their exploitation and oppression are considerable.

The employment of children is a further reflection of the inability of working-age members of households to generate subsistence. Children's labour in many countries fills the income gap. For instance, a recent survey found that on average children were contributing as much as one-third to the household's income.[5]

Informal activities have been a survival mechanism, a means of diversifying risk and a means of informal social protection in the absence of something better. In the proper context, informal can be laudable — it is freedom to work in ways chosen by those performing it. But for most of those involved in the realities of urban slums and rural backwaters, it is a life of rugged reciprocities built on shared insecurities. The policies of recent years have not helped improve their lot.

5.4 Global de-industrialization:

Does globalization mean fewer manufacturing jobs? A clear trend of the globalization era is that manufacturing jobs have been shrinking in much of the industrialized world. However, the picture in developing countries has been mixed. While there have been increases in manufacturing employment in some countries, among the countries losing proportionately manufacturing jobs one finds so-called industrializing countries.

Old-style manufacturing jobs, while still plentiful in some parts of the world, are very unlikely to contribute a majority of the jobs in the 21st century. The old typical will become the new atypical.

In industrialized countries, manufacturing jobs have been disappearing for many years, ever since the 1970s. In all the major industrialized countries there have been huge drops in employment in the 1990s and early 2000s, which have not been offset by the slow growth of manufacturing employment in coun-

tries like the Netherlands and Australia.[6] Between 1990 and 2001 employment in manufacturing fell by 9% in OECD countries. The main factors contributing to this were improvements in productivity, the reorientation of production towards higher value high-technology products and the steady shift to services.

However, the interesting point is that de-industrialization is taking place around the world, with huge job cuts in manufacturing in some surprising places.[7] Contrary to what one might expect, job losses have been greatest in some of the more economically dynamic East Asian countries like China, Japan and the Republic of Korea. In some others, such as India, growth in manufacturing employment in the 1990s has hardly been noteworthy.

Between 1995 and 2002, big employment losses occurred in Japan and China. In the Japanese case this partly reflects the impact of prolonged recession, which led to a rise in unemployment, but it presents a puzzle in the case of China, the world's fastest-growing economy for some time. The figures for employment change in Chinese manufacturing vary by data sources, but there is a consensus that in this period employment in manufacturing went down by at least 15%. This was mainly due to the shedding of excess capacity associated with state-owned enterprises.

In the same period, in the Republic of Korea there was a cutback in manufacturing jobs of almost 12%. Needless to say, this represents a substantial loss in a country displaying one of the highest GDP growth rates globally. The impact of the economic crisis of the late 1990s appears to have lingered, and the chosen course towards bringing about increases in productivity has not led to a stabilization of jobs in manufacturing, let alone their creation.

---

[5] Pakistan Institute of Labour Education and Research: *Child Labour in Hazardous Industries: A Case Study of Urban Karachi* (Karachi, PILER, 2001).

[6] The two countries that buck the trend are Spain and Canada, where employment in manufacturing grew quite significantly in the 1990s and the first two years of the present decade.

[7] J.E. Hilsenrath and R. Buckman: "Factory layoffs are a global issue, research shows", *Wall Street Journal*, 20 Oct. 2003, reporting research by Alliance Capital Management, a brokerage firm in New York.

The story in the Russian Federation and Ukraine is similar. The teething problems of transition have acquired a sort of permanence. The ILO LABORSTA data indicate that employment in manufacturing fell by almost 42% in the Russian Federation between 1990 and 1995, and in Ukraine by 40% between 1995 and 2001. Looking at the present unstable economic situation in these countries, the declines look unlikely to be reversed, certainly not in the near future.

The situation in China has attracted most comment and the most misplaced polemic. The popular image is that it is absorbing jobs from the rest of the world. But the picture is not that simple. Whereas China is losing manufacturing jobs in net terms because of its internal dynamics, it is also gaining relative to others. For example, it is often claimed that China has gained at the expense of Mexico.

Loss of manufacturing jobs may be expected for the affluent OECD countries, where de-industrialization began in the 1970s, but the loss of such jobs in Mexico, an industrializing economy, particularly in the labour-intensive *maquiladora* sector (assembly-type operations for export), was not widely predicted (Figure 5.1). Some observers suggest that Mexico

has become uncompetitive by not lowering real wages and that, in the more open trading environment, jobs have migrated to other countries particularly China, because of favourable wage differentials.[8] But Mexican wages are low; the share of wages in total production costs is a single-digit figure. This has led one researcher to conclude ruefully that, in order for *maquiladora* operations to become competitive with China's equivalent, Mexico "will have to reduce wages not just to the level of China, but even lower".[9] Ironically, however, in Mexico manufacturing employment grew in the 1990s, while in China it was falling.

In short, the international redivision of labour will surely continue, perhaps at an accelerated pace in the next decade or so. But that should be no grounds for restrictive "protectionist" measures by those countries "losing" manufacturing jobs. The structural shifts are part of globalization, and will require adaptive social measures to facilitate them and enable them to occur in a calm, socially protected way. A risk-based international labour regime requires a different set of social policies than one based on stable national labour regimes, a point to which we will return in the final chapter.

Figure 5.1 Mexico: Decline in the number of employees and establishments in the *maquiladora* sector, January 2001–October 2002 (% fall)

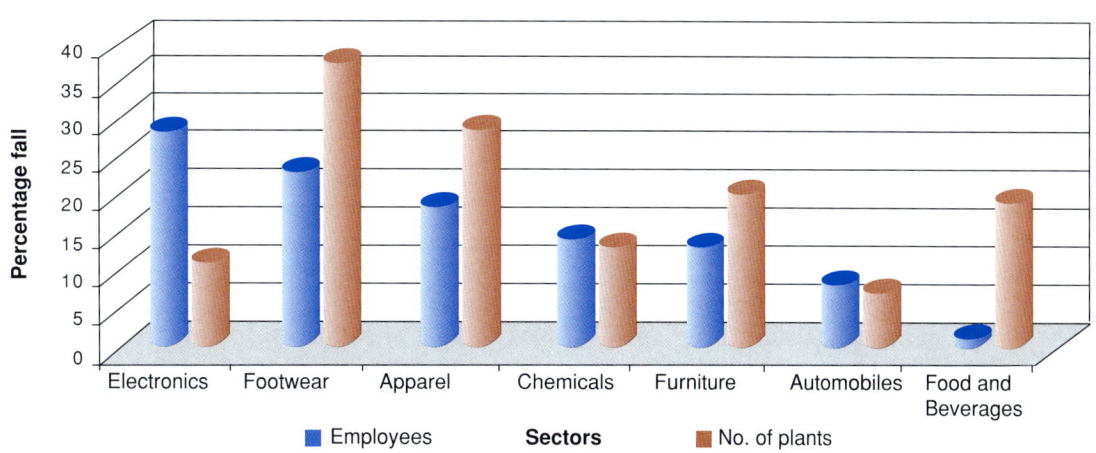

Source: Economic Commission for Latin America and the Caribbean (ECLAC): *Foreign Investment in Latin America and the Caribbean* (Santiago, 2002).

[8]"Does Mexico really want to move up the development ladder?", *The Economist*, 24 July 2003.

[9]G. Palma: *The Mexican Economy Since Trade Liberalization and NAFTA*, SES Paper (Geneva, ILO, forthcoming).

5.5 Global unemployment

If labour market security can be defined as access to reasonable income-earning activities, the unemployment rate is the most well-known indicator, even though we believe this is a poor index in highly industrialized countries, in transition countries, and in agrarian low-income countries. Quite simply, the unemployment rate is only reasonably reliable as an overall and cyclical indicator in an industrial country where the vast majority of workers are in full-time regular employment.

Although open unemployment is affected by definitional, structural and institutional factors, the global pattern can be discerned roughly. Without going into details, covered elsewhere, we may trace the main developments of recent years.

It is widely claimed that global unemployment has been on the rise since the 1980s. The quality of data makes any claim a matter of best guess. However, for countries where the ILO's Employment Sector has data, estimates suggest that total unemployment levels are now in the vicinity of 186 million (6.2% of the global labour force of about three billion).[10] The aftermath of 11 September 2001 included intensification of a global economic slowdown, leading to the loss of millions of jobs around the world and resulting perhaps in unemployment rising by over 20 million. Not too much should be made of these statistics, particularly as the official numbers in major countries such as China and the Russian Federation are very approximate, and those in Africa and some other parts of the world even more so.

(i) Unemployment in industrialized countries

After rising from historically very low levels in the 1950s and 1960s to historically high levels in the late 1970s through to the mid-1990s, open unemployment in industrialized countries tended to fall in the few years leading up to the end of the century.

Many commentators attributed that decline to the stream of measures introduced around the world designed to promote "labour market flexibility". Whether or not this was the case (and it is highly contentious), at the end of the 20th century the global recession associated with the economic slowdown in the United States, Japan and elsewhere led to a renewed rise in unemployment.

Europe has a mixed pattern, in which a few countries have lowered unemployment from the very high levels of a few years ago and others have experienced persistently high levels. Across the European Union, about 8% of the official workforce was unemployed in 2003. The situation in eastern Europe is still deeply distorted by statistical and institutional practices, meaning that a regional rate would be misleading, for reasons mentioned later. In North America, Canada has a slightly higher rate than the United States, which in 2003 had an unemployment rate of about 5.6%.

The situation in the United States is puzzling. A fairly severe recession hit the United States economy in 2000, but a recovery began in 2002 that continued through 2003. However, productivity rose by much more than output, resulting in a "jobless recovery", or a continuation of job-shedding. Indeed, in mid-2003 there were two million fewer jobs than in early 2001. Between 2000 and 2003, there were significant job losses in the private sector. There were over 9 million unemployed, including "discouraged workers", and a further 4.8 million were working part time because they could not find full-time jobs.

Job-destroying economic growth: The United States

"Before the 1991 recession, most people got their old jobs back ... After 1991, most people didn't get their old jobs back. Those jobs went abroad, or they were automated out of existence."

— Robert Reich, former US Secretary of Labor[11]

The unemployment rate statistic is also questionable. The official rate was around 5.5% in the late 1990s, but many observers claim that this omitted the millions of people who had given up looking for work, as well as those who were working fewer than 20 hours a week but would have liked to hold full-time jobs. According to the New York-based Council on International and Public Affairs (CIPA), the real unemployment rate, if properly calculated, would have been nearly twice the official rate at over 11%.[12]

---

[10] These estimates are taken from ILO: *Global Employment Trends 2003* (Geneva, 2004).

[11] Quoted in *Wall Street Journal*, 30 May 2003.

[12] The CIPA listed changes in the definitions of "employed"" and "unemployed" that had the combined effect of substantially reducing the number of people officially listed as being jobless.

No doubt others would vigorously contest that figure, but in a flexible labour market, with lots of people moving in and out of jobs, and many taking casual or part-time jobs, the unemployment rate can be moved up and down quite easily by refining the way labour underutilization is measured.

The CIPA study further claimed that the low official rate concealed the real employment crisis, which it called "the pauperization of work", i.e. the replacement of higher-paid jobs by those at or close to the minimum wage, usually temporary or part time, and often below the poverty line. It is true that by the mid-1990s poverty had risen to high levels by recent standards, with one in four Americans — about 64 million people — living in poverty or threatened by it.

Since 2000, the US economy has again gone through a protracted period of job losses. Most of these jobs may be permanently lost because of the structural changes the economy is undergoing.[13] It may also reflect the change in the nature of labour relations. In previous recessions, a widespread tendency was to lay off workers and to rehire them when the economy rebounded. That is no longer the case. Firms saw the downturn in demand as an opportunity to make permanent changes that would put them into a more competitive position for the anticipated upturn.

If this is an effect of globalization, we might expect to see a secular (long-term) upward shift in US unemployment. If so, this should not necessarily be interpreted as economic failure; it should however be seen as a potential opportunity to rethink social policy.

The labour market security situation in Japan has become alarming. While the official figure for unemployment has remained modest by international standards, hovering around 5% (3.5 million people), estimates made by the Japanese Government's Cabinet Office have put the real figure at well over 10%, or more than seven million people, counting those who have no jobs but who want them, even if not seeking them.

If the available estimated number of "surplus employed" (i.e. who are employed but surplus to the needs of production) were added to that, the figure would rise much further, bearing in mind that the

surplus may be over 8% of total employment. The dramatic rise in unemployment and in labour market insecurity in its various guises has been associated with the most shocking index of social distress — a rise in the number of suicides to over 30,000 a year, three times as many as killed in traffic accidents.[14]

In short, the situation in Japan is disturbing, in part because it has lasted for so long, without evident signs of improvement, and because of the significance of Japan in the world economy.

(ii) Labour market slack in western Europe

Unemployment is only one indicator of labour market security, and often not a very good one. Definitions change — numerous times in the case of the United Kingdom over the past 25 years. The unemployed may be put on "special schemes" that conveniently remove them from the unemployment statistics. For example, even in the relatively prosperous Netherlands, it is well known that the open unemployment rate has been kept in check by the device of putting large numbers of people on the WAO (*Wet Arbeidsongeschiktheid*), an invalidity scheme. But in many countries, the biggest single reason to be sceptical about the unemployment measure is that a large number of workers are in involuntary part-time work.

To provide a better picture of labour market insecurity in the European Union, an *index of labour market slack* has been calculated. The procedure for calculating the index is presented elsewhere;[15] essentially, it corrects the unemployment rate by adjusting unemployment and employment so that both are expressed in terms of full-time equivalents. It also includes discouraged jobseekers who are available for employment but have dropped out of the active labour force. One would wish to reproduce a labour slack index for all countries, but the desired information for most countries is simply not available.

---

[13] E. Groshen and S. Potter: "Has structural change contributed to a jobless recovery?", *Current Issues in Economics and Finance*, Vol. 9, No. 8, Aug. 2003.

[14] H. Motoyasu: "The reality of an age of 'ten million' unemployed", *Ekonomisuto*, 25 Dec. 2001.

[15] G. Standing: *Global Labour Flexibility* (Basingstoke, Macmillan Press, 1999), pp. 140–142.

Drawing on data from the annual Labour Force Survey conducted in European Union Member States, the figures for the standard unemployment rate and an estimate of labour slack for the period 1985–95 are shown in Figure 5.2. Although not all countries are covered for all years, because several were not EU members until recently, the unemployment figures show persistently high levels. Moreover, the levels of labour slack have been consistently higher than unemployment, often substantially so.

Figure 5.2 **Indicators of labour market insecurity (unemployment and labour slack), European Union*, 1983–2001**

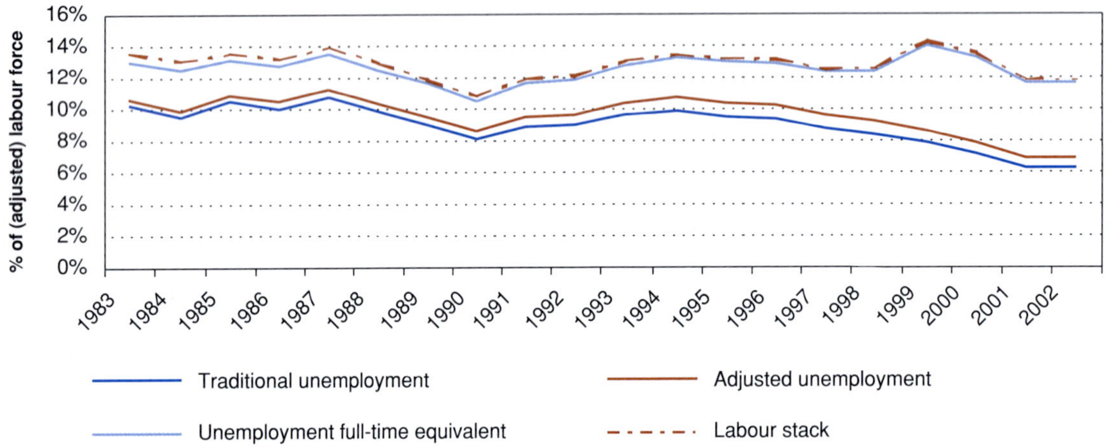

Note: * EU-12: Belgium, Denmark, Federal Republic of Germany, France, Greece, Ireland, Italy, Luxembourg, Netherlands, Portugal, Spain and United Kingdom.

Source: EUROSTAT Labour Force Survey (LFS) data.

(iii) Unemployment in China

Labour market insecurity in the world's most populous country, China, is very widespread, and will stay that way for some time in spite of the country's extraordinarily high rate of economic growth.

In recent years, government authorities have been preparing the population for a big rise in open unemployment. Although national statistics are limited, and in several respects misleading, there is ample reason for believing that the actual level is already very high. Certainly, independent studies show that the official statistics grossly underestimate the extent of unemployment.[16] Many millions of workers have been on extended lay-off or unpaid leave, which excludes them from being counted among the officially unemployed. They only started to show up as openly unemployed in late 2001. The ELFS findings show that firms using unpaid leave had on average 35% of their workers on leave in 2001.

In terms of labour market security, conventional statistics are misleading.[17] The unemployment rate typically mentioned is around 3.6%.[18] But this is actually a residual, which should not be used as a proxy for unemployment or for time-series analysis, let alone for international comparisons. Since China is the most populous country in the world, this is an important point, especially for those producing global reports. The low official rate does not reflect political concealment or even poor statistics. Rather, it reflects the institutional structure of the emerging labour market and social protection system. Our Chinese ELFS and the complementary PSS shed light on this process. But available official statistics also show that the extent of labour surplus is vast, dwarfing what is found in most of the rest of the world. This pattern of labour slack was also documented in an earlier ELFS, carried out in 1994–95.

---

[16] E. Gu: *The Institutionalization of Unemployment in China*, SES Paper No. 33 (Geneva, ILO, 2003).

[17] This is one reason for being very careful about global statistical information systems that rely on key indicators of the conventional type.

[18] This figure is only for the registered unemployed in urban areas. Rural unemployment is assumed to be zero. Some Chinese government statistics estimate rural unemployment to be more than a third of the total rural workforce. This does seem a lot, but even so the authorities admit that rural unemployment is at least a quarter of the rural workforce (see Chapter 2 in ILO *Global Unemployment Trends 2003* (Geneva, ILO, 2003).

Trying to obtain a picture of unemployment is difficult. However, it is important to try to do so because mass unemployment is arriving. In rural areas, where about 70% of the population still live, conventional statistics on unemployment per se are inappropriate. There are ample reports of extensive labour fluctuations, with seasonal and structural underemployment. One official report referred to 100 million of the 500 million rural workers being seasonally unemployed. Furthermore, privatization and related rural reforms are exacerbating rural underemployment and raising unemployment.[19]

At present, the openly unemployed are concentrated in urban areas, and seem to come mainly from the downsizing or bankruptcy of state, collective or co-operative enterprises. Because many of the marginalized migrate to the towns in an unregistered way, they are likely to disappear from any official count of unemployment. Yet because China has been urbanizing more rapidly than had been anticipated — the urban share of the population rising by ten percentage points between 1990 and 2000 — the rise in *open* unemployment can be expected to continue for this reason alone.

In urban areas, the residual unemployment is essentially very *long-term unemployment*.[20] The reason is that when enterprises have labour surplus, the practice has been to put workers on *lay-off*. Before 1998 most were described as something like "worker without post", so that formally they remained in the employed category. In 1998, the standard practice changed to put surplus workers on prolonged lay-off. In this status, they were entitled to receive a basic allowance from the enterprise *for up to three years*. Only if they were not re-employed or did not resign in that period did they then become classified as *unemployed*.

The existing national numbers are intriguing. Official statistics indicate that 706 million people were "employed" at the end of 1999, out of an "economically active" population aged 16 and above of 20 million. The employed represented 56% of the total Chinese population. Women comprised 46.5% of total employment, which is high by international standards, especially bearing in mind that the Chinese Population Census of 2000 indicated that there were something like 117 males for every 100 females in the country.

There were about 5.75 million *registered urban un-*

employed, up from 5.71 million at the end of 1998. But there were no registered unemployed in rural areas, which is where most people live. The number gives a registered urban unemployment rate of 2.6% if the registered number is divided by the economically active, or 2.7% if it is divided by the sum of the employed and registered unemployed. But since the economically active is meant to comprise the sum of the employed and unemployed, meaning that the difference between the economically active and the employed are the unemployed, the figures imply that actual urban unemployment was 11.64 million, which converts to an urban unemployment rate of 5.2%. Bear in mind that the draft Five-Year Plan submitted to lawmakers in March 2001 set a goal of keeping urban unemployment to under 5%.[21]

This would not be an alarming figure in a period of restructuring. However, it is still a distortion if one wishes to measure urban unemployment by the methodology used in most countries. Officially, at the end of 1999 there were nearly 9.4 million workers laid off. Though counted as employed, they were effectively unemployed, without jobs and merely waiting to be classified as unemployed or vaguely hoping for "re-employment". If they were deducted from the employment count, the registered unemployment rate would be 2.7%. But if they were also added to the registered unemployed, the unemployment rate would rise to 5.9%, while the urban unemployment rate would increase to 8.2%.

These figures come closer to measuring labour market insecurity, but to calculate accurately we would need estimates of the extent of labour underutilization among those nominally holding jobs.

---

[19] U. Patnaik and S. Natrajan: "Output and employment in rural China: Some post-reform problems", *Economic and Political Weekly*, 16 Sep. 2000, pp. 3420–3427.

[20] If one were to take the average share of very long-term unemployment in total unemployment characteristic of other countries as a guide to the level of unemployment in China, one would have to multiply the measured rate by something like six times to have an estimate of actual unemployment. We are not suggesting that this is what should be done, merely highlighting the limitation of the conventional unemployment rate as a "key indicator" of the labour market.

[21] The Ministry of Labour and Social Security issued an informative report in 2000 stating that: "the urban unemployment rate will be contained below 4%". Ministry of Labour and Social Security: *Vocational Training and Employment in China* (Beijing, 2000), p. 9.

According to anecdotal evidence, numerous workers are not formally laid off but are doing little or nothing in jobs — being "workers without posts" — while receiving no wage beyond a basic living allowance. They are suffering from a combination of labour market insecurity and income insecurity.

There is also strong evidence of labour surplus in Chinese enterprises. In the ELFS conducted by the Socio-Economic Security Programme and a government-backed research institute in 2001, managements were asked if their establishments had experienced one or more periods of more than two weeks in which they had inadequate work for their workforce. More than half said they had, but it was particularly pronounced for state-owned enterprises (74%) and collective enterprises (67%).

Furthermore, surplus labour was especially large in manufacturing, long seen as the key sector of employment growth, where two-thirds of the enterprises indicated that they had inadequate work for their workers. The average capacity utilization rate was also fairly low, an average of 69%, with a slightly lower than average rate being noted for manufacturing.

In sum, Chinese unemployment is high, rising and understated, and poses a huge challenge for the authorities as they continue with their ambitious strategy of modernization.

(iv) Unemployment in the Russian Federation, Ukraine and the CIS

Whereas employment and unemployment in central Europe gradually stabilized in the late 1990s, the situation in the Russian Federation, its neighbour, Ukraine, and most of the smaller satellite states in eastern Europe and central Asia, has been wretched for more than a decade, even though informal and unrecorded activity has greatly expanded.

Throughout the 1990s, open unemployment went unrecorded as did hidden unemployment, mostly in the form of unpaid administrative leave and so-called "wage arrears". Worst of all, some "unemployment" disappeared as a result of premature deaths among men (and to a lesser extent women), as well as growing criminalization, social illnesses and extensive concealed unemployment. Many of the unemployed have been incarcerated, having drifted into crime.

The employment situation deteriorated drastically with the introduction of economic reforms in the transition countries in the early 1990s. When the "command economy" prevailed, full employment was said to exist by definition. Even though underemployment was present, people's insecurities were mitigated by social benefits. However, in the 1990s labour market insecurity became extensive. Employment plunged, while state benefits dwindled.

The situation in the European transition economies, particularly the Russian Federation and Ukraine, has mirrored developments in China. The so-called "transformational recession" in the region deserved a better name.[22] In most countries, the downturn lasted for more than a decade. One can quibble with the exact numbers but, for example, in the Russian Federation total employment fell by more than a quarter in the 1990s, officially declining from 80 million in 1992 to 65.7 million in 1998.[23] Unemployment was long concealed by practices noted here, but rose sharply in reality.

Rising unemployment was fed by the restructuring of state-owned enterprises, which were facing budget constraints and either stopped hiring or started laying off workers. Though the private sector generated some jobs this was not enough to stem the rise in unemployment. The liquidity crunch led enterprises to resort to labour shedding and more flexible labour practices. One tactic was to put workers on long-term unpaid or partially paid administrative leave. The Russian ELFS monitored this from the early 1990s, and the latest round suggests that even now nearly a third of the workforce of enterprises surveyed in three *oblasts* (regions) is in those categories. They are essentially unemployed.

The extent of unpaid leave and the number of workers in wage arrears (i.e. not paid their wages for months) led to a degeneration of working conditions and

---

[22]J. Kornai: "Transformational recession: The main causes", *Journal of Comparative Economics*, Vol. 19, No. 1, Aug. 1994.

[23]GOSKOMSTAT (State Statistics Committee of the Russian Federation), quoted in V. Gimpelson and D. Lippoldt: *The Russian Labour Market* (Lanham Maryland, Rowman and Littlefield, 2001), Table 1.1, p. 14. For reasons for believing the decline was greater, see G. Standing: *Enterprise Restructuring and Russian Unemployment: Reviving Dead Souls* (London, Macmillan, 1996).

induced many older workers and those near retirement to drop out of the labour force altogether. Lacking employment and income support, many ran down their meagre assets and drifted into destitution and despair. Most appallingly, male life expectancy at birth declined by eight years between 1987 and 1995 to just 58 years — similar to many poor developing countries. The huge rise in mortality rates, particularly of men aged 40 to 49, also diminished labour supply.

In Ukraine the ELFS showed that, on average, enterprises are operating at less than half their capacity. And the managements of many firms admitted that further cutting employment would not lessen production. In other words, they could produce the same

with fewer workers. Managements have reacted to the labour surplus in various ways, the most common being to put workers on partially paid or unpaid administrative leave. If this were taken into account when calculating the unemployment rate, the latter be much higher than the official figure of 11%.

Ukraine and the Russian Federation are not alone. In nearly all the countries that were part of the former Soviet Union, extensive concealed unemployment, mostly in the form of unpaid administrative leave, continued through the 1990s. The ELFS conducted in the Republic of Moldova and in Azerbaijan revealed that the situation was nearly as bad there as in the Russian Federation and Ukraine, and the effects were also similar (Table 5.2).

Table 5.2   Share of workers on administrative leave, Azerbaijan and the Republic of Moldova

Country	Number of workers on fully paid administrative leave (%)	Number of workers on unpaid administrative leave (%)	Number of workers on partially paid administrative leave (%)
Azerbaijan	0.09	22.9	0.7
Moldova, Republic of	0.22	16.7	1.1

Source: Azerbaijan ELFS 2001; Republic of Moldova ELFS 2001.

This then is a region where labour market insecurity consists of a mix of open unemployment, inflated employment, concealed unemployment and marginalization. No doubt the situation is improving in some places, particularly where modern services have developed, typically concentrated in capital cities. The challenge remains to spread those opportunities.

(v) Unemployment in developing countries

Unemployment is chronic in developing countries. But it is very difficult to measure its extent, partly because of undeveloped statistical systems in many countries and partly because a large proportion of the population lives in rural areas, which are often not included in mainstream statistical exercises. Much of the urban workforce is in the informal economy and they too are often left out of the unemployment calculations.

To give an example, in Indonesia, while the official open unemployment rate was in the vicinity of 6% in 2000, it was estimated that almost 40% of workers

were underemployed.[24] Further, the open unemployment rate was more than twice as high in urban as in rural areas. Since there was a significant migration to the cities from the rural areas throughout the 1990s, this would suggest a serious lack of viable earning opportunities, or at least extensive underemployment that is not captured by conventional statistics.

Even conventional measures show a serious unemployment problem, exacerbated by slow employment growth. For example, figures released by the government of India, which relate only to the formal part of the economy, suggest that the unemployment rate was 10.9% in 1999. The government also estimated that between 1987 and 1993 employment grew at about 2.4% a year, but in the period since then employment growth had slowed to less than 1% per annum.[25] Job losses had occurred in both the public and private sectors.

---

[24] S. Dhanani: *Unemployment and Underemployment in Indonesia, 1976–2000: Paradoxes and Issues*, SES Paper No. 41 (Geneva, ILO, 2004).

[25] Planning Commission of India: *Economic Survey of India 2000–2001* (New Delhi, Government of India, 2002).

Statistics collated by the ILO's Employment Sector suggest that open unemployment rates in many parts of the developing world were high throughout the 1990s and the early years of the present decade; in 2003 estimates ranged from 12% in the Middle East and North Africa to 3% in East Asia.[26] Since figures for the East Asian region are heavily weighted by China, with a quarter of the world's labour force, the relatively low unemployment rate is certainly an underestimate. Similar qualifications apply to estimates for South Asia (including India, Pakistan and Bangladesh) where the unemployment rate in 2003 was put at 5%, and for South-East Asia (including Indonesia, Philippines and Thailand) where unemployment was estimated at just over 6%. Latin America averaged an 8% open unemployment rate in 2003 according to these data, and in sub-Saharan Africa unemployment was estimated at about 11%. However, it is very difficult to put precise numbers on the situation in Africa since many countries have no data, or have data that are outdated or disputed.

The problem in many developing countries is accentuated because labour force growth rate exceeds employment growth, even if the latter is positive. Even if strong employment-generation measures were taken, it is most unlikely these would be sufficient to absorb the increasing labour supply. In many countries, to clear the backlog would require double-digit annual growth rates of GDP. Such growth seems rather unlikely.

In developing countries the informal economy has acted as a buffer, providing a modicum of social protection and a labour-spreading survival mechanism. But it rarely exists separate from the rest of the economy. As the income of most informal economic activities depends on the circulation of money, reductions in the size of the formal economy (including the public sector) adversely affect informal activity. Policy-makers cannot count on the informal economy to promote vast new employment opportunities.

It may plausibly be concluded that the slowdown in output growth in the era of globalization has led to rising unemployment and underemployment, in both the formal and informal economy.

5.6 The demographics of unemployment

The patterns of labour market insecurity and unemployment are strongly affected by the demographic structure of the population. The illusion of "full employment" in the industrialized countries of the 1950s and 1960s largely reflected the low participation of women in the measured labour force, and women's perceived status as "secondary workers". Since then much has changed.

(i) The feminization of labour

Women used to be regarded as the bulk of the "secondary labour force", their unemployment disguised by withdrawal from the labour market in recessions. While the sexist image still persists, it is much weaker nowadays. What is relatively encouraging is that women's share of employment has grown, and with it female labour force participation rates have risen globally. Women also tend to stay in the labour market if they lose their jobs and are thus increasingly included in the unemployment count.

There is still a long way to go to achieve equality in labour market security but there has undoubtedly been a process of global feminization, in the double sense of more women being in income-earning activities and more jobs being of the type traditionally relegated to women. As such, it has been a very mixed blessing. We will return to this in the next section.

(ii) ... and masculinization of unemployment?

The time has come to give more attention to the specific problems that men face in evolving labour markets. In many countries their unemployment rate has risen relative to women's. And many more men seem to fall into "unemployment traps" due to a tendency for more entry-level job opportunities to be part-time or low-paid. This means that if they are receiving unemployment benefits or insurance-based transfers they would receive little more, or perhaps even less, if they took the available job.

---

[26]ILO: *Global Employment Trends* (Geneva, 2004), Table 1.

(iii) The elderly: Taking the baton from youth?

The world is ageing. For many years the main group of unemployed targeted for policy assistance has been youth. Young people still experience the highest unemployment rates around the world, and still receive the most attention. But it is workers in their 50s and 60s who constitute a rapidly growing number of the unemployed, even if they do not show up in the statistics to the extent that they might, due to early retirement schemes and a tendency not to record older workers in unemployment statistics.

In 2003, copying others, reforms introduced by the German government included efforts to ease elderly unemployed off the unemployment register, allowing them to keep unemployment benefits but not assisting them to find jobs.[27]

In many countries efforts have been made to lower the "headline" figure on unemployment, which have weakened the labour market security of various groups. Older workers have been severely marginalized — a trend that will surely be reversed in the next few years in ageing societies faced with the need for more workers to support the very old.

The verandah debate

One common claim about unemployment in developing countries is that actually those who are unemployed are not among the poorest in society, because the very poor cannot afford to be unemployed. Instead, they may die, or become so socially marginalized that they are not counted as available for work, or they may simply be obliged to do something to earn an income. Some observers have taken this line one stage further, saying that those recorded as unemployed in such societies are essentially "voluntarily" unemployed and that many come from more affluent households or are relatively educated.

As a generalization, this is a caricature and unfair. However, consideration of these issues should leave policy-makers and commentators sufficiently convinced that the unemployment number is not necessarily a good guide to the state of labour market security in developing countries.

The PSS data can shed some light on patterns of such security. If one takes as a measure of deprivation the adequacy of household income for health care needs, in countries as different as the Russian Federation, Ukraine and Indonesia almost as many non-poor as poor households have suffered from unemployment (Table 5.3). In Ghana, if anything, more affluent households were more likely to have someone who had been unemployed. However, in most of the countries, poor households were more likely to have experienced unemployment.

Table 5.3 Experience of unemployment in past 12 months by income adequacy for health care, by country (percentage responding "Yes")

Coubtry	Income for health care	
	Adequate	Inadequate
Russian Federation	20.2	23.6
Ukraine	51.7	53.7
Bangladesh	11.9	27.3
China	5.8	10.7
India	7.0	16.7
Indonesia	19.2	24.1
Ethiopia	23.9	30.5
Ghana	5.7	4.6
South Africa	41.6	63.1
United Republic of Tanzania	12.0	18.2

Source:PSS.

---

[27]"Older German unemployed cite pressure to leave jobless lists", *International Herald Tribune*, 22 Dec. 2003.

(iv) HIV/AIDS and disappearing prime-age workers in Africa

A key feature of labour market insecurity in Africa, in particular, is the loss of large numbers of prime-age men and women due to illness and death associated with HIV/AIDS. Disappearing skilled workers can be difficult to replace in African labour markets and their loss can threaten the survival of many industrial companies.[28] The situation has been compounded by the high incidence of civil wars, which has decimated the adult male population of some areas.

These scourges have led to a systematic erosion of the productive capacity of whole communities. AIDS is by no means a phenomenon solely affecting individuals and those immediately around them. The death or incapacity of adult income earners has forced some older and younger people into labour force activities, and blocked others from them.

(v) Migrating into insecurity?

Labour mobility occurs on a huge global scale, ranging from local forms of labour circulation to international transfers of executives and professionals. Much of the movement is motivated by desperation, with people forced to leave their homes by conflict, calamity or grinding poverty. Other movements are generated by demands for more workers from countries, mostly in the West, with ageing populations and a shrinking work force. With globalization, labour mobility can be expected to grow.

Labour mobility per se is to be welcomed; moving to escape oppression or to improve life's prospects is part of the human condition. But labour migration has two fundamental effects relating to overall labour market security. Research shows that typically migrants have lower unemployment rates than others, due in part to their willingness to take almost any type of job at lower wages. This tends to put downward pressure on wages in general, though migrants have often taken jobs that local residents might not be prepared to do. As such, there should be resistance to the common presumption that migration raises overall unemployment.

5.7 Barriers to women's labour market entry and job retention

There is one aspect of global labour market security that defies easy generalization. As with most forms of insecurity, traditionally women have suffered from labour market insecurity to a greater extent than men. Discrimination against women is probably universal, although much worse in some societies than in others.

Women in some cultures and countries face oppressive barriers to labour force entry. Cultural restrictions can be undermined by societal and economic pressures and tend to fade when education and economic incentives shape decisions. Nevertheless, at the individual level they do matter. Thus, in Bangladesh in the PSS more than one in four women (28%) said they were stopped from taking up employment, and this tendency was found just as much among the more educated as among those with little schooling. This was not simply a religious barrier. Far fewer women in Indonesia, also a Muslim country, said they were stopped from taking a job, only one in every 12. And there, the more educated the woman, the less likely she was to report any restriction. In both Ethiopia and South Africa, just 2% of women said they faced any restriction on labour force entry.

In Bangladesh the main justification mentioned was that the family felt that labour force work would result in "neglect of household chores" (35%). However, mentioned nearly as often was the belief that such work would lower "family prestige" (29%) — recalling what Thorstein Veblen famously described as American middle-class wives' propensity to be "vicarious consumers". A further 18% said their non-participation was due to "social/cultural reasons" and only 14% said "neglect of childcare" was the reason. In other words, all these factors were amenable to adjustments, to make labour force work a matter of prestige, to facilitate group-based childcare, to obtain household help, and so on.

Beyond the barriers to entry, there are barriers to employment retention and to labour force re-entry. In many developing countries, one still relatively

---

[28]P. Annycke: *The Impact of HIV/AIDS on Security for the Elderly in Africa*, paper presented at ILO Workshop on Economic Security and Decent Work in Africa, Dar-es-Salaam, May 2003.

under-appreciated factor is the impact of pregnancy and of expected pregnancies. In rural Ashanti (Ghana), for example, the PSS found that no less than one in six unemployed women cited it as a main cause of their unemployment.[29] In some cases, they had lost jobs due to a pregnancy and could not find their way back into employment; in others it was the anticipation that they would become pregnant that had prevented them from obtaining a job in the first place.

There are also barriers to mobility that threaten women's labour market security. In Bangladesh, for example, only about one in five women doing some labour force work thought it would be easy to find an alternative "socially acceptable" type of work if they had to stop what they were doing. It was much the same elsewhere (Table 5.4).

Table 5.4 Women's prospect of finding socially acceptable work if losing current main work
(percentage distribution of women's responses)

Country	Easy	Mixed	Difficult	Trend
Bangladesh	21.6	22.6	56.0	More difficult with increasing age, easier with more education
South Africa	20.5	22.9	56.6	More difficult with increasing age, easier with more education
United Republic of Tanzania	19.6	29.0	51.4	No pattern

Source: PSS.

Finally, in the former Soviet Union, women's labour market insecurity is underestimated as a result of institutional practices that should be prevented. In successive enterprise surveys in the Russian Federation and Ukraine, it has been observed that firms record a very high number of women on extended maternity leave. This has continued for more than a decade and should be seen in the context of the extremely low and still declining fertility rate in those countries.

Maternity leave as disguised unemployment

In the Russian Federation and Ukraine, it seems women have been encouraged to extend maternity leave for two or three years, as a result of overt encouragement by managements, or by the prospect of very low incomes if they returned to work, or because they were under no pressure from managements to return.

For example, in 2000, expressed as a weighted average share of employment, over 8% of all women workers in Ukraine were supposedly on maternity leave, amounting to 4% of the total male and female workforce. In official statistics, they were classified as employed, but we may surmise that most should not have been counted as such in line with international definitions or national practices in western European countries.

Firms that had cut employment had higher proportions of women on maternity leave than others (Figure 5.3). Unless one believes that employment cuts were associated with rising fertility, maternity leave was being used as a mechanism for limiting disemployment, or for concealing unemployment. This was accentuated by the regulation blocking firms from discharging women when they were on maternity leave. This could be regarded as *regulation failure*.

---

[29] N. Apt and J.Y Amankrah: *Assessing Insecurities at the Household Level in Ghana*, paper presented at ILO Workshop on Economic Security and Decent Work in Africa, Dar-es-Salaam, May 2003.

**igure 5.3 Ukraine: Percentage of employed women on maternity leave in 2000,
by enterprise employment change, 1999–2000**

Source: Ukraine ELFS 2000.

5.8 Perceptions of labour market insecurity

Most people fear unemployment, whether they have jobs or are contemplating entering the labour market in search of jobs. One finding in several countries is that people tend to think that the level of unemployment facing them is much higher than the statisticians estimate it to be. This is not necessarily due to any manipulation of those statistics. Rather it seems to suggest that what many people regard as unemployment is not the same as the conventional measures.

In developing countries, many of those with wage jobs fear losing them and having to drift into the informal economy. Thus, a large number of respondents in the PSS in Ghana said they were anxious about the prospect of finding another job if they lost their current one.[30] Over a third of all those with jobs considered it would be difficult to obtain another.

Ukraine deserves special mention because the SES Programme conducted the largest PSS with a nationally representative sample. In any country, labour market security could be said to be strong if there are ample opportunities for all adults to obtain income-earning activity, and if people think there are such opportunities and that they will continue in the medium-term future. Traditionally, in the Soviet system, workers in the main had strong labour market security as part of the commitment to labour *de-commodification*.

In the Ukraine PSS questions were asked about ac-

tual and perceived labour market security. First, people were asked what they thought about actual and expected trends in *unemployment*. Although estimates of current unemployment varied widely and showed little knowledge (the modal estimated rate was 40%), over half of all respondents from across the country thought unemployment would rise over the next 12 months, while only 5% thought it would fall. Middle-aged workers were relatively pessimistic about this.

Most of those in employment worked in establishments where at least some workers had been made redundant in the past 12 months, although nearly a third of them did not know how many had been made redundant. At least, the proximity to redundancy was the norm.

Some 14% of all Ukrainians in the sample had been unemployed at some time during the previous five years; for those in their 20s the figure was 31%. Men and women were equally likely to have been unemployed. Of those who had experienced some unemployment in the past five years, 53% had been unemployed during the previous year. Over 90% had searched for work during their unemployment.

---

[30] Apt and Amankrah, 2003, ibid.

Another aspect of labour market security is the perceived probability of finding alternative employment in the event of job loss. Confidence was not high. Only 3% of the employed thought it would be very easy to find another job and only 14% that it would be easy. By contrast, 32% thought it would be difficult and 28% very difficult. A majority of all age groups thought it would be difficult, with higher proportions among older workers. But most people, except among the young, would not be prepared to move to another area to take a job — only one in every four being willing to do so. The main reasons people gave for not being prepared to move were the difficulty of obtaining housing, family and the belief that they would lose social and economic networks of support.

Finally, there is the impact of entry to the global economy to consider. Much debate in the media across the world has alerted ordinary people to the notion of globalization. Do most people take any notice? Do they fear impending or actual economic forces? Or do they see entry to a global economy as opening up uncharted but exciting opportunities? These questions are particularly pertinent in a country such as Ukraine after its prolonged period as a closed economy. Accordingly, we asked the following question:

"Ukraine is entering the international market economy. Do you feel that globalization has a positive effect, a negative effect, or no effect on the chances of workers such as yourself of keeping their job/work?"

The question is complex; perhaps there are alternative formulations that would be a better gauge of underlying fears or hopes. Nevertheless, about half the respondents — the question was addressed only to those in employment — said that they "did not know". Of the remainder, the net balance was one of *fear* of globalization.

Whereas 13% thought it would have a positive effect, 19% saw it as negative and 17% believed it would have no effect. If one ignores the oldest group, simply because those employed in their 60s are likely to be rather selective of all those in that age group, then the replies indicate that hope scores over fear for the younger generation, while fear scores over hope for older age groups. However, except for those in their 20s, fear predominates, and in no age group did more than one in five have a positive expectation. There has not been a lot of hope in recent times.

Figure 5.4 Ukraine: Perceived effect of globalization on employment opportunities, by age (%)

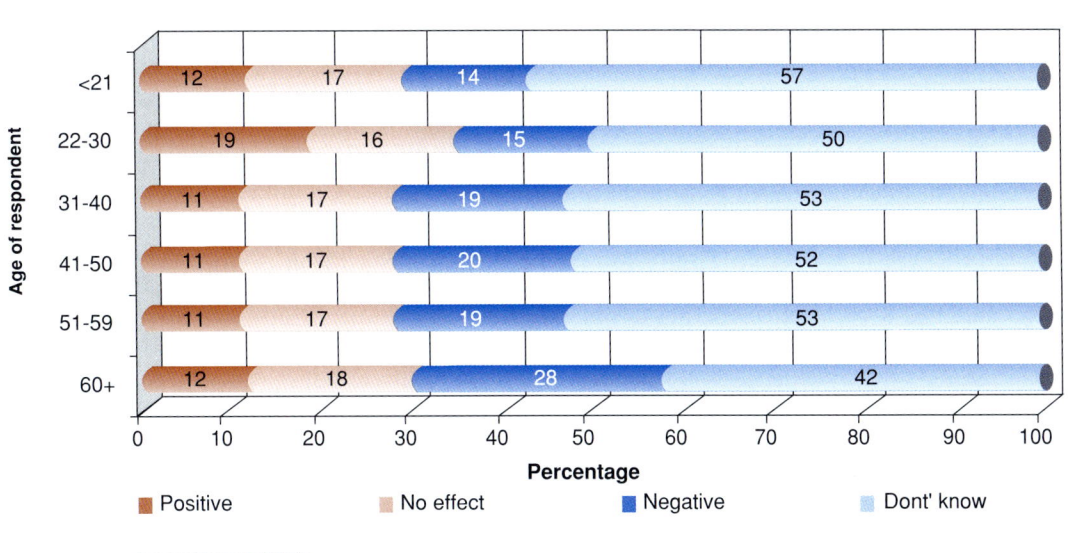

Source: Ukraine PSS 2002.

5.9 The incarceration syndrome

It may seem strange to place a section on putting people into prison in a chapter on labour market security. However, throughout modern history use of the prison has been a means of responding to social and economic crises, including periods of high unemployment. Almost invariably, the unemployed have a relatively high probability of being criminalized and a high probability of being sent to prison. Once there they do not show up in the unemployment statistics.

It is a sad indictment of humanity that the 21st century began with more people incarcerated than at any time in human history. Criminality has been globalized, and criminalization has become an outcome of dysfunctional and misguided social policy. These are strong claims.

The causes of high levels of crime and criminality are more in the nature of hypotheses than proven. But it surely cannot be coincidence that the ethos of the era of "marketization" is the encouragement of opportunistic behaviour and, paradoxically, a tendency of state policy to become more moralistic and judgmental of the losers in such a society.

In some societies, prison has come to shoulder extra-penological functions, with questionable success. Reintegration by incarceration is not appealing. Nor is "carceral affirmative action".[31] Incarceration has been implicitly racist — imprisonment rates have been much higher for disadvantaged groups. Arrest rates are similar for blacks and whites in the United States, but a black arrested is *eight* times more likely to be sent to prison than a white. On average a black person in the United States has a 29% probability of being sent to prison at some time during his or her life.[32]

The United States has a far larger proportion of its population in prison than any other country. At the turn of the 21st century that number passed two million, up from 1.4 million in 1992, when it was proportionately six times the number imprisoned in Canada, France and the United Kingdom.[33] The biggest cause of the difference is that the United States puts more of its convicted criminals in prison. The incarceration rate rose through the 1980s and 1990s.

The United States is not alone in having a rising number of people in prisons. But one factor behind the increased incarceration there and elsewhere is the liberalization of prison services, which is creating a self-serving "prison industrial complex" that is a threat to the security of many losers in the market society. Private prison companies have built prisons in places where unemployment is high or where local authorities have wanted to attract job-generating projects. The world's biggest prison service company is the Corrections Corporation of America, which now accounts for over 50% of all privatized prison places in the United States.[34]

The story does not stop with lobbying for increased prison capacity, which in itself encourages the propensity to jail offenders. Jail labour has increased but is not counted as employment. In the United States the number of prisoners employed in prison labour has nearly quadrupled in the past decade or so, much of the output being sold to the government and to major household-name corporations.

The insecurity of those who transgress is an under-told story. Tougher sentencing and more judgmental social policy may contribute. But extensive anecdotal evidence suggests that it also reflects commercial pressures to increase incarceration and to keep people in prison for longer. Once someone is incarcerated, the insecurities of later life are multiplied.

Putting a large number of one's citizens in prison cannot be a sign of a healthy society. There are also indications that the nature of the economic and social system is contributing to criminal behaviour at all levels of society. Opinion surveys in the United Kingdom and other European countries, where crime rates are much lower than in the United States, have shown that very high proportions of the middle class everywhere confess to having indulged in petty crime.

---

[31]L. Wacquant: *Les Prisons de la Misère* (Paris, Éditions Raisons d'Agir, 1999), pp. 71–94.

[32]T. Bonczar and A. Beck: *Lifetime Likelihood of Going to State or Federal Prison* (Washington, DC, Bureau of Justice Statistics Special Report, Mar. 1997).

[33]P. Mayhem and J. van Dijk: *Criminal Victimization in 11 Industrialized Countries* (The Hague, Netherlands Ministry of Justice, 1997).

[34]Characteristic of the diversification culture of global commerce, it is owned by Kentucky Fried Chicken.

We live in an opportunistic age, when people try to enrich themselves by doing what they think they can get away with. The example set by the ultra-wealthy trickles down through the middle class, and sadly it is mostly those at the bottom who are singled out for criminalization, and thenceforward to a life of scarred insecurity.

In the context of this chapter, the large number of the poor and unemployed in prison serve to disguise the full extent of the lack of income-earning opportunities, the essence of labour market security. We cannot deal with that further here, but incarceration is a labour issue.

5.10 A national Labour Market Security Index

To reiterate, labour market security may be defined as existing when there is a high level of access to reasonable income-earning activities. To monitor patterns and international differences, we have constructed a Labour Market Security Index (LMSI), intended to take account of policy commitments, instruments for providing opportunities for labour market security, and outcomes.

The *input* indicators are primarily selected on the basis of an institutional embedding of a commitment towards provision of labour market security. These are:

- whether or not the country has ratified ILO Convention No.122 on Employment Policy, 1964;

- whether or not the government or constitution of the country has a formal commitment to "full employment"; and

- the existence of an unemployment social security scheme and of legislation banning gender discrimination in recruitment.

The *process* indicators are selected to determine the commitment of governments, in practice. The identification of such indicators is problematic, but the idea here is to capture "commitment" through some measures such as:

- the existence or otherwise of a public employment service to help labour demand meet supply of jobs, both quantitatively through information dissemination and qualitatively through retraining and other skills-based initiatives;

- the public consumption per head of the working age population as a proxy for the importance of the public sector as an employer;

- as a measure of economic opportunity, the average annual growth rate of GDP during the previous decade and the coefficient of variation of annual GDP growth, to indicate how potentially favourable the market is for additional employment opportunities. It is assumed here that the more intensive the economic activity, the higher the probability of getting a job and securing an income; and

- gross capital formation as a percentage of GDP.[35] Investment is an important engine for growth and the component of final demand that is most likely to generate new jobs. The indicator has therefore been included to separate countries that devote a larger share of their income to the expansion of their productive capacity, from those whose commitment is low.

The *outcome* indicators were selected to capture the results of national economic policy and performance with respect to the labour market. Attempts have been made in spite of data limitations to include measures of success and failure of the different labour markets, notably in the formal and informal economies.

The basic *outcome* indicator of labour market security is the unemployment rate, but this is relatively unsatisfactory in transition economies and in agrarian countries with extensive "informal" activities. Accordingly, the unemployment rate is coupled with a set of indicators that together portray a pattern of opportunities, taking special account of gender inequalities. The variables include the unemployment rate, the ratio of male to female unemployment, employment as a percent of the working-age population, the ratio of female to male employment, the wage employment share of all those in income-earning activities, the female share of wage employment, and the average annual growth of employment between 1990 and 1999.

Finally, a "dummy" variable is added, to take account of the phenomenon of unpaid or partially paid administrative leave. The "dummy" corrects for the underestimation of the unemployment rate, by a factor of two, in transition countries of eastern Europe and China, where millions of workers appear to have labour market and employment security but are actually on extended lay-off.

---

[35] A more elaborate approach also included government expenditure on labour market policies as a share of GDP, but data for this exist for industrialized countries only.

The LMSI was calculated for 94 countries, and the results are presented in Table 5.4. The developed countries of western Europe, along with Canada and Japan, dominate the list of "Pacesetters". These are countries that have a strong constitutional and policy commitment to social welfare, even though the welfare state has been under strain.

Among the "Pragmatists" are some developed countries such as the United States, Australia, New Zealand, Luxembourg and Switzerland, which one might have expected to qualify as "Pacesetters". Being "Pragmatist" indicates a lack of policy commitment to labour market security. Admittedly, the reasonably high scores on outcome may indicate that all is well, but under the circumstance this is puzzling. In some of the transition countries, such as the Republic of Moldova, Tajikistan and Kyrgyzstan, there is reason to believe that there is a large amount of hoarded labour and extensive underemployment. Another notable country among the "Pragmatists" is Brazil, which has lost a large number of manufacturing jobs in recent years.

As expected, the poorer developing economies of Asia and Africa head the list of countries with low levels of labour market security. The sheer scale of numbers or the lack of capacity militates against better outcomes. However, any policy aimed at promoting labour market security must, as a first step, endeavour to develop an institutional infrastructure.

The "Conventionals" are true to form, although the inclusion of southern European countries seems confusing as they are economies where unemployment levels have fallen a lot, notably in Spain. The transition economies of eastern Europe and China owe a lot to the past where a commitment to full employment was enshrined in the constitution. Although many seem to have kept that commitment, transformational problems have multiplied. The positions occupied by countries of eastern Europe and Central Asia might be unexpected, but reflect realities. For example, some qualify as "Conventionals" because many laws from the Soviet period, although not strictly applied, are still in effect. But in practice most laws and codes on employment have been dismantled, reflecting the drift to a market economy.

Table 5.4 Labour Market Security Index (LMSI)

	High score on Outcome			
	High score on Input / Process		**Low** score on Input / Process	
Regions	Pacesetters Countries		Pragmatists Countries	
Africa and Middle East			Mauritius Israel	
Americas	Canada		Barbados Brazil Costa Rica	Honduras United States
Asia	Japan		Australia Korea, Republic of	New Zealand Philippines Thailand
Eastern Europe and Central Asia			Belarus Estonia Hungary Kyrgyzstan Latvia	Lithuania Moldova, Republic of Slovenia Tajikistan
Western Europe	Austria Belgium Denmark Finland France Germany Iceland	Ireland Netherlands Norway Portugal Sweden United Kingdom	Luxembourg Switzerland	

Low score on Outcome				
	High score on Input / Process		**Low** score on Input / Process	
Regions	**Conventionals Countries**		**Much-to-be-done Countries**	
Africa and Middle East	Algeria Egypt Ghana	Tunisia	Benin Burkina Faso Burundi Congo Congo, Dem. Rep. of Côte d'Ivoire Ethiopia Lebanon	Madagascar Mauritania Morocco Nigeria Rwanda Sierra Leone South Africa Turkey Zimbabwe
Americas	Colombia Chile	Panama	Argentina Dominica Ecuador Mexico	Peru Saint Vincent and the Grenadines Venezuela
Asia	China		Bangladesh Fiji India Indonesia	Nepal Pakistan Sri Lanka
Eastern Europe and Central Asia	Armenia Azerbaijan Croatia Czech Republic Georgia	Poland Romania Slovakia Uzbekistan	Albania Bulgaria Kazakhstan	Russian Federation Ukraine
Western Europe	Greece Italy	Spain		

Figure 5.5 Labour market security index: Clusters by region

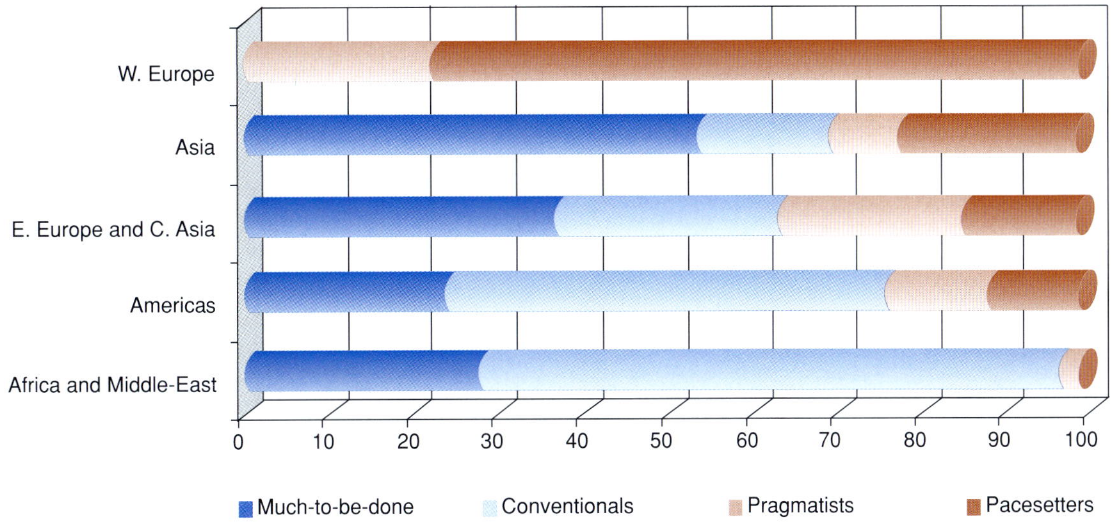
W. Europe
Asia
E. Europe and C. Asia
Americas
Africa and Middle-East
0
10
20
30
40
50
60
70
80
90
100
Much-to-be-done
Conventionals
Pragmatists
Pacesetters

Source: SES databases 2004.

Labour Market Security Index versus Unemployment Rate

For many years, the unemployment rate has been used as the proxy for aggregate demand and implicitly for measuring the extent of labour market security. We have indicated its failings, as have many others over the years.

Would moving to a labour market security index make any difference? Or is it simply a more complex measure of the same, in which case one might as well continue to use the unemployment rate?

Although there is no conclusive evidence that the LMSI would be "better", it is instructive to note that, while the two measures have a statistically significant correlation ($R^2 = -0.53$ significant at 0.01, 2-tailed), the ranking of countries by recorded unemployment rate does not correspond very closely to the ranking by the LMSI. This can be illustrated by comparing the top 25 countries ranked on the LMSI with their relative positions when ranked in terms of unemployment rate.

Ranking of countries by Labour Market Security Index (LMSI) — 1999	Ranking of countries by ascending order of Unemployment Rate - 1999	Ranking difference for LMSI	
A	**B**	**(B-A)**	
Norway	Iceland	Norway	+ 3
Sweden	Luxembourg	Sweden	+10
Ireland	Switzerland	Ireland	+ 6
Iceland	Norway	Iceland	- 3
United Kingdom	Netherlands	United Kingdom	+ 8
Canada	Portugal	Canada	+12
Netherlands	United States	Netherlands	- 2
Denmark	Republic of Korea	Denmark	+ 6
Finland	Ireland	Finland	+15
Austria	Austria	Austria	0
Israel	Japan	Israel	+11
Australia	Sweden	Australia	+ 4
Japan	United Kingdom	Japan	- 2
Germany	Denmark	Germany	+ 7
New Zealand	New Zealand	New Zealand	0
United States	Australia	United States	- 9
Portugal	Hungary	Portugal	-11
France	Canada	France	+ 7
Belgium	Belgium	Belgium	0
Luxembourg	Germany	Luxembourg	-18
Republic of Korea	Israel	Republic of Korea	-13
Switzerland	Barbados	Switzerland	-19
Barbados	Finland	Barbados	0
Hungary	France	Hungary	- 7
Slovenia	Slovakia	Slovakia	- 5

5.11 The future of labour market security

Globally, labour market insecurity is a feature of the era of globalization, even if the very high levels of unemployment experienced in western Europe in the 1980s and 1990s have been brought down moderately. The most dramatic aspect is the looming crisis in China, even though the economic dynamism in the world's most populous country is remarkable.

In developing countries, population growth is expected to continue at a rate faster than can be accommodated by employment growth, especially as many people will be entering the labour force in the next decade. Between 1995 and 2010, the number of new labour force entrants will be about 700 million. This is equivalent to the entire labour force of the industrialized world as of 1990. It has been further estimated that worldwide more than a billion jobs would need to be created within the next ten years to absorb those entering the labour force. To achieve anything like that would require much faster economic growth rates than have been the norm in the globalization era.

In industrialized countries, the priority issues differ. In the United States, it seems that a jobless recovery has added to the problem of a large number of low-productivity and precarious jobs. Correcting the budget and trade deficits will surely raise unemployment. In the European Union, the perceived problem has shifted from long-term unemployment to finding ways to raise the employment rate and the overall labour force participation rate to cope with an ageing population and demands on pensions and health care.

The outstanding general questions are: first, what are the prospects, in the early decades of the 21st century, of improving labour market security and making it fairly equal for all groups in society; and second, whether labour market security is as important as policymakers have regarded it, or at least as important as other forms of security. The answer to the first question is surely one of pessimism. The answer to the second is perhaps that it is "tradable", something that can be regarded as a lower priority as long as income security and the opportunity to pursue meaningful alternatives exist.

Chapter 6

Employment security

6.1 The idea of employment security

Employment security is protection against loss of income-earning work. For wage and salary workers, employment security exists when there is strong protection against unfair and arbitrary dismissal from employment, and where workers can obtain redress if they are subject to unfair dismissal.[1] To the extent that employment security is relevant for the "self-employed", it means protection against sudden loss of independent work and/or business failure. However, it is probably sensible to think that employment security is mainly something gained, to a greater or lesser extent, by those employed directly by a firm or organization or indirectly via some contractual arrangement.

Employment security is about risks and uncertainty, and can be assessed in terms of the *probability* of retaining a job or main work activity, and the protection given to those in work. One can assess this by reference to aspects of work that typically imply employment insecurity, such as size or ownership (property form) of a firm, or to means of *protection* provided by regulations, collective agreement or other institutional safeguards. It may also be assumed that if a worker has wage labour and his or her employment status is "casual", as opposed to "regular", then he or she may be regarded as suffering from employment insecurity.

Employment security is a function of the type of economy and structure of employment, so that it tends to be stronger where large-scale firms predominate and where the public sector is large. In reality, the vast majority of workers in most countries of the world have never had strong employment security.

A vast amount of political energy and related empirical research has been expended in recent years on the supposed links between employment security and unemployment. A standard refrain — voiced by the IMF and OECD, among others — is that strong security through employment protection legislation leads to high unemployment. An almost equally large literature exists on whether or not employment security has declined due to changes in the nature of employment relations.

This chapter will not review that literature, which is done elsewhere. Rather, it will highlight some of the main trends before presenting a national Employment Security Index, which is applied to 99 countries.

6.2 Subjective employment security

Numerous surveys in industrialized countries have found that people's perceptions of their degree of employment security have declined in recent years. Part of this could reflect actual changes in contracts and coverage by laws and institutions, part merely a feeling that economic and social arrangements are simply more uncertain. Let us consider this latter part. To some extent, all forms of insecurity at work are based on what people perceive and how these perceptions map onto behavioural and attitudinal responses.

---

[1] S. Dasgupta: *Employment Security: Conceptual and Statistical Issues*, SES Paper No. 10 (Geneva, ILO, 2001).

Perceived employment insecurity is the product of threat multiplied by powerlessness. It is the negative connotation that goes with threat or severity of threat, modified by coping mechanisms (or lack thereof) for dealing with these threats. Since this is a multiplicative model, if threat is zero then even if coping mechanisms do not exist the experienced insecurity will be zero. Similarly, if threat is high but coping mechanisms exist so that powerlessness is zero, then experienced insecurity will again be zero.

Essential elements of this Expectancy-Value Model are subjective perceptions of threats to continuity of a valued employment situation and perceptions of threat and powerlessness resulting from interpretations of information on available coping mechanisms. To this may be added another dimension — that of concern over employment loss — which compounds the "threat" and may give rise to demoralization, anger, sadness and stress.

Psychological studies of workers, in countries such as Israel, the Netherlands and the United Kingdom, reveal that subjective employment security is a positive function of trust in management, the existence of organizational safeguards, participatory controls inside enterprises, the financial status of the firm and the state of the external labour market.[2] Other studies have concluded that, although a minority of workers believe that they may lose their job within the next 12 months (not more than 20-30%), in numerous industrialized countries that proportion has been growing.

Studies have also shown that perceptions of insecurity are sensitive to people's own past experiences and their local information. And in both objective and subjective senses, jobs previously seen as "secure" have now become "insecure", which has fuelled people's beliefs about their own employment insecurity.

Other studies have shown that employment insecurity has an effect on psychological health. Employment insecurity has effects on several mental health indicators, cardiovascular symptoms, mental health outcomes, self-evaluation and self-esteem.[3]

The key point here is that, whether or not there have been trends in objective factors connected with employment security, there is widespread evidence that a very large percentage of workers in industrialized countries feel insecure about their employment.

6.3 Trends in employment security

There can be little doubt that, in large parts of the world, objective employment security has weakened in recent years, while in many developing countries hopes that traditionally weak or non-existent employment security would strengthen have almost evaporated.

Some analysts contest the claim that employment insecurity has increased, on the grounds that average job tenure has shown little change in industrialized countries studied.[4] However, average tenure is affected by ageing and employment growth. Youth tend to have very short employment tenure, so if there are more youthful labour force participants that in itself will pull down the average tenure, and vice versa. If employment is stagnant, average employment tenure will tend to rise, unless labour turnover behaviour changes dramatically.

One reason for believing that employment security has diminished is legislative. Since the 1980s, pressed by international agencies such as the IMF, OECD and the World Bank, governments have introduced many changes in laws and regulations to erode employment protection in the name of reducing labour market *rigidities*.[5] Legislative changes have also encouraged more "contingent" working, via temporary labour, agency labour, part-time working, and so on.[6]

Another reason for expecting employment security to have weakened in industrialized countries is *structural*. Traditionally, public sectors provided workers with a greater and more formalized sense of employment security than private firms. The tendency for

---

[2] J. Hartley et al.: Job Insecurity: *Copings with Jobs at Risk* (London, Sage, 1991).

[3] R. Stock: S*ocio-Economic Security, Justice, and the Psychology of Social Relationships*, SES Paper No. 8 (Geneva, ILO, 2000).

[4] For a sceptical view, see P. Auer et al.: *Stable or Unstable Jobs: Has Job Stability Decreased in Industrialized Countries?* Employment paper No. 26 (Geneva, ILO, 2001).

[5] The OECD played a role in creating this trend, arguing that strict employment protection reduced labour turnover. See, for example, OECD: *Employment Outlook* (Paris, various years).

[6] For a review of evidence, see, inter alia, W. Onubogu: *Employment Security in Europe and Canada: A Review of Recent Legislation in Three Countries*, SES Paper No. 20 (Geneva, ILO, 2002); Standing, 2002, op. cit.

public sectors to shrink and to contract out more public services to private providers has weakened employment security where it was strongest. Another factor has been the informalization and casualization that has been the outcome of the pursuit of more flexible labour relations.

Similarly, workers in services tend to have less employment security than workers in manufacturing. There has been a steady shift in the structure of employment towards services. That in itself could be expected to reduce employment security generally.

A third reason for believing that employment insecurity has spread in industrialized countries is the trend towards greater reliance on casual and temporary labour, with more work being contracted out, greater use of distance work, agency labour and so on. There is considerable evidence that this tendency has been widespread.[7]

The global trend seems to be towards *flexibilizing* the employment function, which is associated with weaker employment security. Also, to the extent that there is a relative growth in small-scale firms, characterized by high (labour) turnover, employment insecurity would be intensified by that trend as well.

Whatever the sector, within all types of firm, the Taylorist traditions that predominated for most of the 20th century have been modified in recent years. In some highly industrialized countries, such as Japan and the United States, even large corporations no longer offer their employees implicit contracts for lifetime employment.[8] More labour has become contingent, not only in the sense that much more labour is short-term or episodic, but in the sense that attachment between the firm and worker has been weakened. "Loyalty" has become more contingent or opportunistic.

Employment stability: The new model?

"Top companies also plan for and achieve higher turnover rates."[9]

The US Department of Labor's current population survey shows marked declines in employment tenure between 1983 and 2002 for all men over the age of 20, with the most significant drops among men in the age groups over age 45. This is the group that had earlier benefited most from the old psychological contract of long-term employment.

Japan is another country where a dramatic decline in employment security has occurred. Within a generation, the once widely envied model of "lifetime employment" has virtually disappeared, even though it never existed to the extent that many commentators believed. Its demise coincided with the rise in labour market insecurity highlighted in an earlier Chapter 5.

Overall, because of structural changes, employment security has eroded modestly but steadily in most industrialized countries over the past two decades or so.[10] By contrast, China, the Russian Federation and other parts of the former Soviet Union have experienced a rapid deterioration in recent years.

In China, until the 1990s employment security was regarded almost as a right, once a person had entered the state enterprise system. Now this has drastically changed. Chinese workers have been told that they must expect to be laid off or transferred, and millions have felt the full force of labour market restructuring, with many being put on long-term administrative leave or extended lay-off.

6.4 Informalization as employment insecurity

One of the most widespread trends of globalization is the *informalization* of economic activity. In developing countries in the past two decades, the long-expected transfer of labour from agriculture and the urban surplus labour pool to formal employment (as envisaged by the Nobel Prize-winning economist Arthur Lewis) has largely failed to materialize. Informalization of the employment relationship is on the rise in most countries. This is linked to stagnant opportunities for productive employment, and also to the growth of labour contracting and other forms of external labour flexibility.

---

[7]For a review, see G. Standing: *Global Labour Flexibility: Seeking Distributive Justice* (London, Macmillan, 1999).

[8]K. Stone: "Informalization and legal regulation of employment in the United States", in M. Chen et. al. (eds.): *Reconceptualizing Work* (Geneva, ILO, forthcoming).

[9]Towers Perrin: P*erspectives on People: Performance and Rewards* (New York, Towers Perrin, Jan. 2000). See <http://www.towers.com>.

[10]On Australia and the United Kingdom, see A. de Ruyter and J. Burgess: "Growing labour insecurity in Australia and the United Kingdom in the midst of job growth: Beware the Anglo-Saxon model", *European Journal of Industrial Relations*, Vol. 9, No. 2, July 2003, pp. 223–244.

Informalization also extends to the need for people to combine several forms of economic activity — for example, a little on own-account agriculture combined with occasional wage labour — reflecting an existence of insecurity.

There are several reasons for expecting these trends to continue, and even for expecting something similar in industrialized countries where measures to strengthen labour market flexibility have tended to complement enterprise strategies to outsource employment and move away from reliance on regular, full-time labour. One has to be wary about interpreting standard statistics. However, there is an enormous amount of anecdotal and secondary research testifying to the spread of informal and flexible labour relations, which in turn have bred a sense of *precariousness* in employment.

To the extent that this is the case, a basic question is how to provide security to those facing an economic life of precariousness. Another more systemic question is less often posed: If mechanisms to increase labour flexibility and the rollback of protective labour regulations were imposed to accelerate economic growth, what happens if an economic downturn occurs after you have bought growth with flexibility?

It is evident that a large and probably growing number of people are in various forms of "self employment" (Table 6.1), although many of those activities may be disguised forms of wage labour or "dependent labour".

Many of these self-employed lack ownership of means of production and experience limited autonomy in their work. These dependent workers often have a short-term labour relationship with their "customer" as if the customer is their employer, but they do not have any of the rights and benefits that usually accompany an employment relationship.[11] In most developing countries, the proportion of workers classified as self-employed is very high indeed. In Bangladesh and Bolivia, about half the total labour force is so classified, as are about two in every five workers in Colombia.

Table 6.1 Trends in self-employment by region, 1970 to 1990

	% self-employed in non-agricultural employment			% women in non-agricultural self-employment		
	1970s	**1980s**	**1990s**	**1970s**	**1980s**	**1990s**
Developed regions	11.0	12.9	11.5	29.1	29.8	34.5
Africa	27.0	46.2	47.7	20.0	38.2	34.0
Latin America	28.0	28.8	41.8	32.8	33.5	47.4
Asia	28.1	26.2	32.7	17.8	15.0	25.4
World	22.5	27.3	30.9	25.5	28.9	34.5

Source: Charmes (1999a) and (2002).
Note: Non-weighed averages.

In Latin America, it has been estimated that informal labour rose from just over 44% of total "employment" in 1990 to about 48% at the end of the century.[12] Although employment has risen, most of the rise has consisted of poor quality and precarious jobs in an expanding informal economy. According to the *Panorama Laboral* methodology, of every ten jobs created in the 1990s, seven were informal.[13]

More generally, ILO "guesstimates" — and they can be no more than that, given the nature of available data — suggest that most of the 400 million new entrants to labour markets around the world between 2003 and 2010, over half of them in Asia, will be absorbed in informal economic activities.[14]

[11]C. Stanworth and J. Stanworth: "Self employed without employees — autonomous or atypical?", *Industrial Relations Journal*, Vol. 26, No. 3, 1995.

[12]L. Beneria: *Changing Employment Patterns and the Informalization of Jobs: General Trends and Gender Dimensions*, SES Paper No. 6 (Geneva, ILO, 2002).

[13]ILO, *Panorama Laboral 2003: America Latina y el Caribe* (Lima, 2004).

[14]ILO: *Global Employment Trends* (Geneva, ILO, 2003).

This is the most important reality about prospective labour developments. In the immediate future, most people entering labour markets will be entering some form of informal economic activity in which employment protection will be weak.

Informal sector versus informal labour

Debates have raged for many years on the notion of "the informal sector", critics believing that it is a distortion likely to lead to bad policy formulation. The problem is not resolved by moving to another dichotomy of formal versus informal economy.

The reality is that workers all over the world face degrees of informality, the most formal of which have multiple forms of protection, the least formal none at all.

The ILO, through the 17th International Conference of Labour Statisticians, has recently resolved to move to a status-based or "job-based" concept of informality.[15] This is undoubtedly an improvement. But it will be important to avoid falling back into a new dichotomy. There are degrees of formality, and not all forms of informality are bad.

With data collected through the People's Security Surveys (PSS), we are able to present informality as a continuum, and can contrast the picture with notions based on an "enterprise-based concept", such as these used by the ILO's *Key Indicators of the Labour Market* (KLIM), for example. As a continuum, several aspects of informality are taken into consideration. No definition is ideal, but the proxy measure should correspond to the key dimensions of reality that the analyst and policymaker wishes to convey. Labour informality may be defined empirically in terms of five criteria, as follows:

i. *Regularity status:* A value of 1 is given if a person is in regular wage labour, whether full-time or part-time, or in registered self-employment; 0 otherwise.

ii. *Contract status:* A value of 1 if the person has a written employment contract (more than 12 months), 0 otherwise.

iii. *Workplace status:* A value of 1 if the person works in or around a fixed workplace, be it an enterprise, factory, office or shop, 0 otherwise.

iv. *Employment protection status:* A value of 1 if the worker is protected against arbitrary dismissal or entitled to severance pay, 0 otherwise.

v. *Social protection status:* A value of 1 if entitled to paid medical care, whether paid by the employer or by medical insurance, 0 otherwise.

The labour informality continuum has a range of values from 0 to 5. Obviously, the method of simply adding the five elements implies that each element is given the same weight, which is a working assumption. The resultant labour informality spectrum is defined as follows: totally informal = 0 (no criteria met); high informal =1; low informal =2; low formal = 3; high formal = 4; totally formal =5 (all criteria met).

We can use this definition not only to estimate the distribution of workers by degrees of informality, and contrast the pattern with other methods, but also identify which groups are relatively exposed to informalization. For example, according to the KILM estimate, 30% of Chile's workers are in the informal sector. According to the PSS-based method, 66% of workers have less than the five criteria. In Brazil, KILM gives 48%, the PSS method gives 72%.

More interesting, one can provide a richer picture by presenting the workforce in terms of an informality continuum. Figure 6.1 does that for the three Latin American countries covered by the PSS, bearing in mind that this is done for illustrative purposes and covers only urban areas. The figure shows that between 25% and 33% of workers are in fully formal employment and that women are less likely to be in that status, except in Chile.

---

[15]General Report: 17th *International Conference of Labour Statisticians*, Geneva, 24 November—3 December 2003, ICLS/17/2003/1, Report 1, Section 3.1. Statistics of informal employment, 2003, pp. 47–53.

Figure 6.1 Selected Latin American countries: Distribution of workers by degree of labour informality

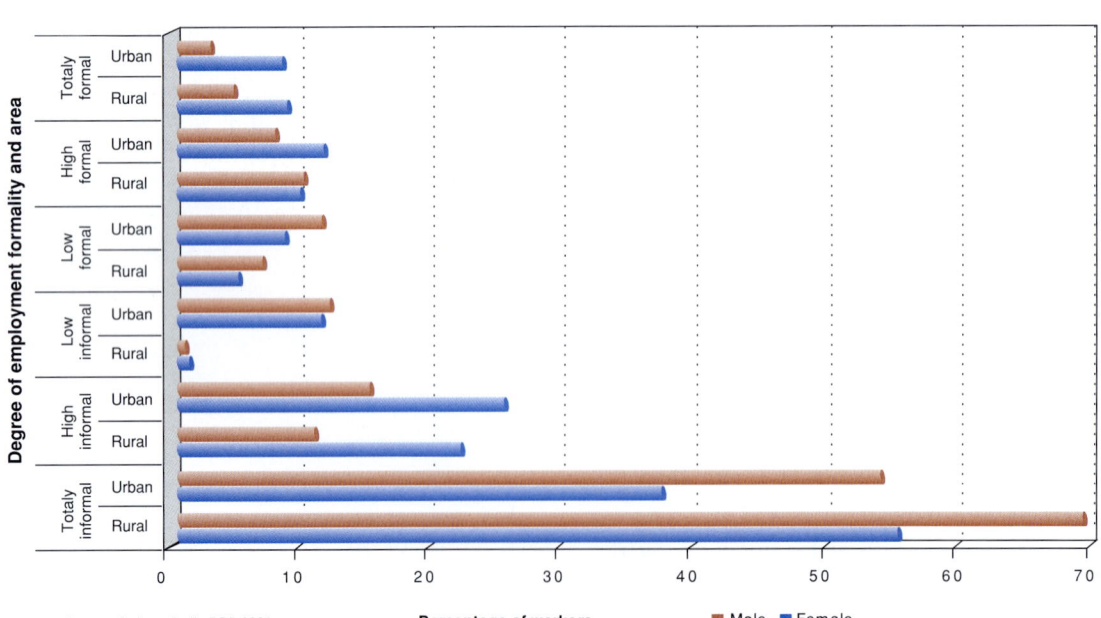

Legend: ■ Totally informal   ■ High informal   ■ Low informal   ■ Low formal   ■ Formal   ■ Totally formal

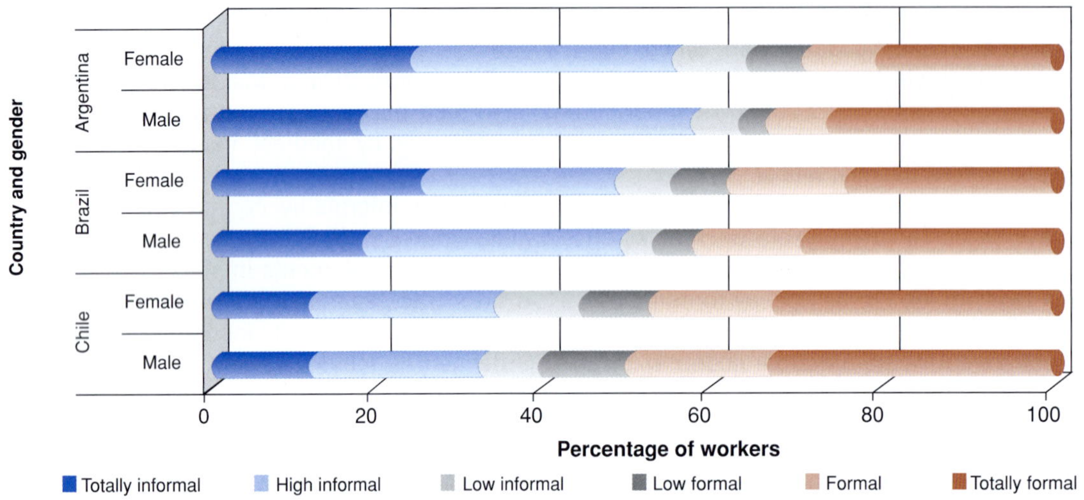

Source: Argentina, Brazil, Chile PSS 2001.

In the course of this and later chapters, we may see whether or not this approach is fruitful in identifying links between informalization (and thus the related notion of employment insecurity) and forms of social and economic insecurity. But at this stage, we can highlight several other patterns derived from application of the informality continuum.

Consider the case of Gujarat, India. Figure 6.2 shows that a majority of both men and women were in highly informal work statuses, satisfying none of the criteria. But the remainder had various degrees of informality.

Figure 6.2 Gujarat, India: Degree of labour informality, by gender and type of area

Source: Gujarat, India PSS 2000.

Percentage of workers   ■ Male ■ Female

In Bangladesh, the picture is similar, most workers being at the low end of the continuum, with women overwhelmingly so (Figure 6.3). There is a tremendous contrast with the situation in China, where the

PSS in three provinces showed a picture of most workers being at the upper end of the spectrum, and with women actually being more likely to be highly formalized (Figure 6.4).

Figure 6.3 Bangladesh: Degree of labour informality of employment, by gender

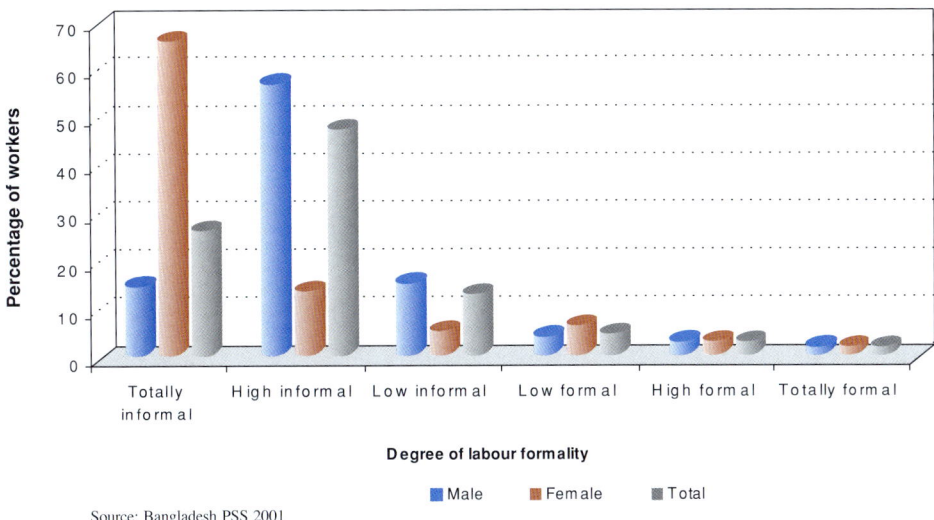

Source: Bangladesh PSS 2001

Figure 6.4 China: Degree of labour informality, by gender

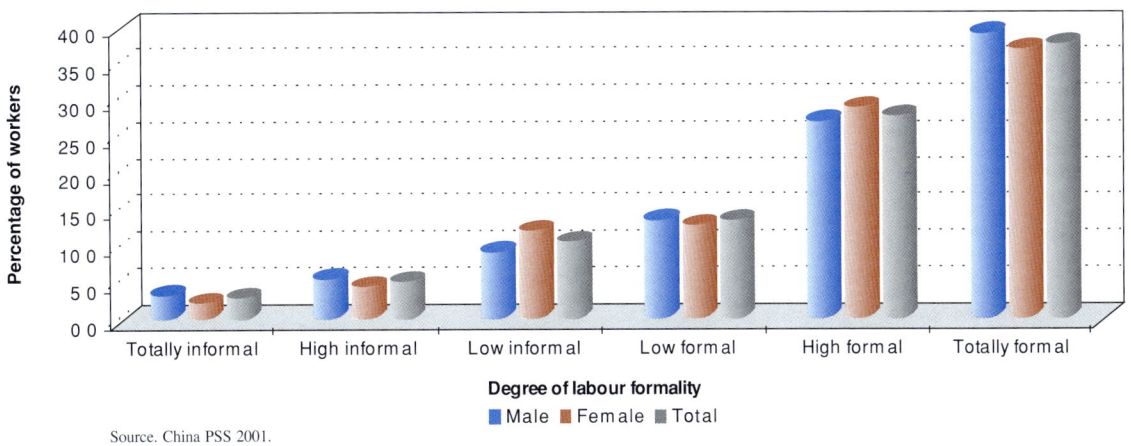

Source. China PSS 2001.

The Chinese pattern is rather similar to that observed in eastern Europe, as should be expected. Thus, the Ukraine PSS shows that a majority of workers are still in highly formal work statuses and that actually more women are in the most highly formal situation (Figure 6.5).

Figure 6.5 Ukraine: Degree of labour informality, by gender

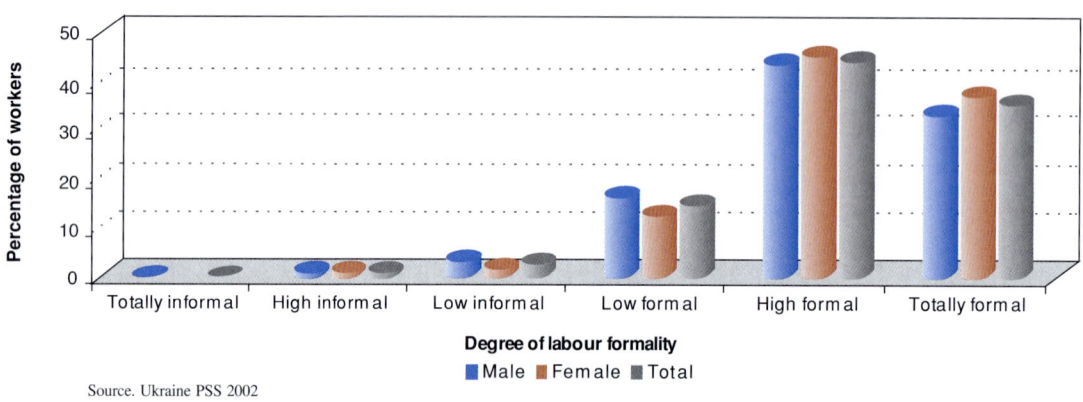

Source. Ukraine PSS 2002

A final example is Ethiopia, where the urban-oriented PSS found that about a third of the workforce were in highly informal work, with women far more likely to be in that situation (Figure 6.6).

Figure 6.6 Ethiopia: Degree of labour informality, by gender

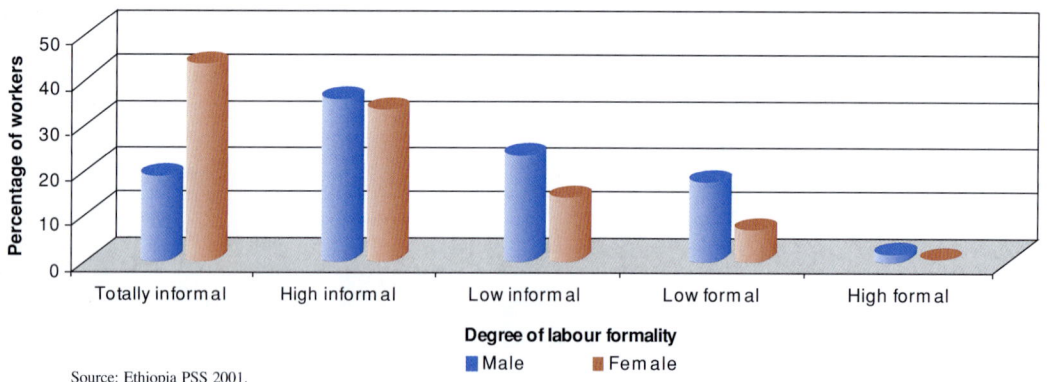

Source: Ethiopia PSS 2001.

It is important to realize that labour informality does not map neatly onto the enterprise-based concept so widely used in reports and by analysts. To give an example, in Ethiopia a majority of workers in relatively large-scale enterprises (or establishments) are rather informal in terms of work status (Figure 6.7).

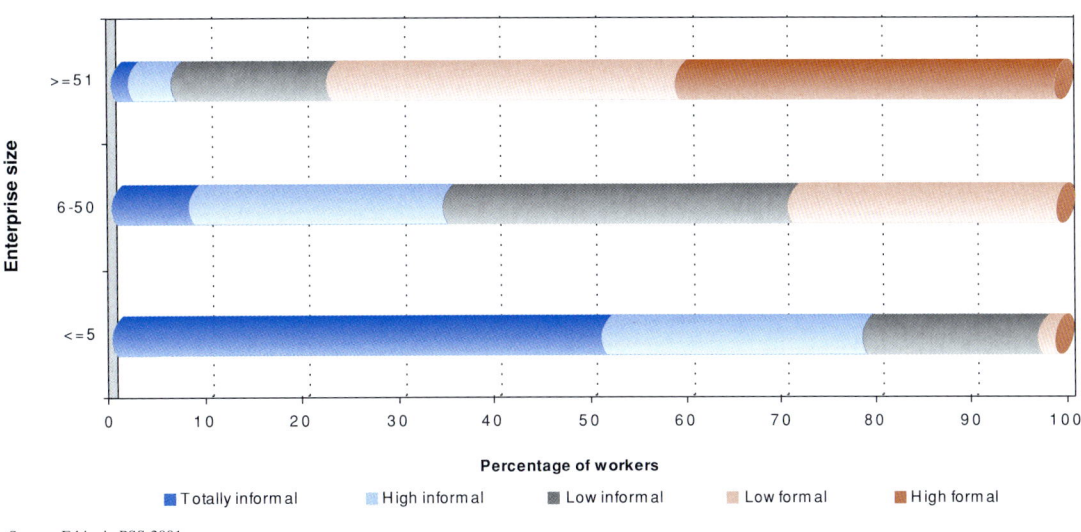

Figure 6.7 Ethiopia: Degree of labour informality, by size of enterprise

Source: Ethiopia PSS 2001.

Another way of bringing out the contrasts between the enterprise-based approach and the work-status continuum approach is by considering Chile, where the PSS data show that 38% of workers in so-called informal enterprises are actually in highly formal labour relations, while 62% of all workers are both in informal enterprises (so-called) and in informal labour as defined in the PSS. Moreover, 42% of workers in so-called formal enterprises (with more than 10 workers) are not in formal labour. In Bangladesh too, only 47% of workers in large firms with more than 500 workers are highly formal, and 27% are low in the scale of formality. Even in China, only 54% of workers in such firms are formal, while 17% of workers in establishments of less then seven workers are formal.

We believe this labour status approach gives a richer picture of labour informalization, avoiding the standard dichotomies and allowing a more realistic assessment of the policy implications, as well as the implications for other forms of work-related insecurities, to which we will return.

almost everywhere. The era of globalization and liberalization has provided a sharp shock to public sector employees in most countries.

In developing countries, structural adjustment policy made it almost mandatory to reduce the "privileges" of public sector employees. In eastern Europe, "shock therapy" did much the same. Combined with rapid privatisation, this led to a sharp deterioration in employment and working conditions, notably for the many thousands of people employed in health care services.[16]

In developing countries, particularly in Africa and South Asia, governments have been urged to "formalize and then flexibilize" their civil services and public social services. They have been expected to impose a discipline on public sector employees, induce a culture of administrative probity and adherence to administrative rules and regulations, and then contract out services and decentralize.

6.5 Public sector: Catching up ... in going down?

For much of the 20th century, the public sector took the lead in providing its workers with strong employment security. It set standards, envied by workers

_____
[16]C.W. Afford: *Corrosive Reform: Health care Workers in Eastern Europe* (Geneva, ILO, 2003).

In the rush to do this, there has been a casualization of public sector employment that has created inefficiencies and a widely reported pattern of "petty" corruption. An end result has been that many more people working in public services have lost any expectation of long-term employment security. Even within public educational services, pressures to make colleges and universities more profit-oriented or efficient have led to outsourcing, leading to casualization and de-unionization, with workers losing entitlements to benefits and receiving lower wages.[17] This seems to be a global trend, albeit more advanced in some parts of the world than others.

6.6 External labour flexibility

There has been a great deal of attention given to external labour flexibility in industrialized countries, as noted earlier.[18] But the same trends have been taking place in both "transition" and "developing" countries. We may give examples of indicators of employment security in firms by drawing on the ELFS. The data for Indonesia show extensive "informal" labour even in so-called formal enterprises (Table 6.2). A similar pattern is seen in the Philippines, as well as in the Latin American countries covered and in Tanzanian firms.

Table 6.2 Establishments using non-regular forms of employment, by country (%)

	Temporary/casual (%)	Contract (%)	Part-timer (%)	Agency-hired (%)
Azerbaijan	19.1	17.6	10.3	n. a.
Brazil	63.3	n. a.	11.7	30.0
Chile	54.8	n. a.	29.4	37.5
China	24.9	52.1	5.2	22.9
Indonesia	34.3	27.5	1.7	2.6
Moldova, Republic of	59.4	54.2	26.3	n. a.
Pakistan	48.0	15.3	9.5	12.3
Philippines	38.6	32.7	10.8	24.5
Russian Federation	65.3	71.4	47.1	n. a.
South Africa	85.5	43.5	26.1	n. a.
Tanzania	51.2	26.5	19.3	5.4
Ukraine	50.5	67.4	49.8	n. a.

Source: ELFS surveys.
n.a. = not available.

As noted in Chapter 5, one form of labour market and employment security brought out in the ELFS that has received insufficient attention in standard statistics is *administrative leave*, or partial or complete lay-off. In transition countries, this took on enormous proportions after 1989, and has remained high in many of them, such as Ukraine (Figure 6.8).

Administrative leave and lay-offs have also been a feature of the extraordinary level of disguised unemployment in China, as well as in the Russian Federation, Republic of Moldova and elsewhere. They give the appearance of employment security, with all those workers hanging on to employment. But in reality the practice of putting workers on administrative leave is merely a way of avoiding having to pay redundancy money to surplus workers.

[17]E. Hartmann, S. Haslinger and C. Scherrer: *Liberalization of Higher Education and Training: Implications for Workers' Security* (Geneva, ILO, 2003).

[18]See also K. Van Eyck: *Flexibilizing Employment: An Overview*, SEED Working Paper No. 41 (Geneva, ILO, 2003).

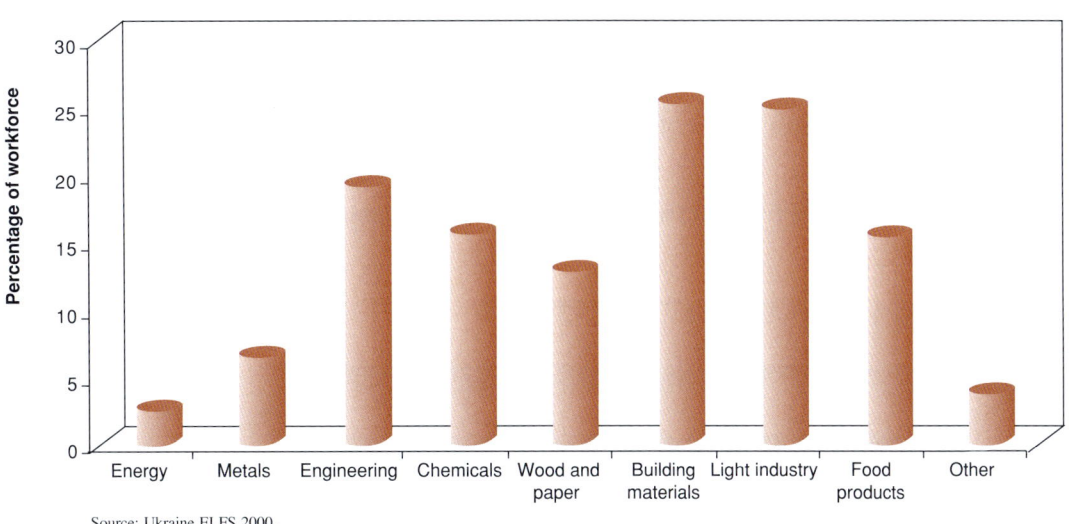

Figure 6.8 Ukraine: Unpaid and partially paid administrative leave, by industry, 2000 (all regions)

Source: Ukraine ELFS 2000.

Employment security at the level of a firm can be measured by the policies or practices pursued by management and by the outcomes. The following box presents two variants of a measure of such se-curity. No doubt these could be modified. But they do capture the essence of what would constitute a relatively decent workplace in terms of its provision of employment security.

A firm-level Employment Protection Security Index

Let us assume that providing its workforce with reasonable employment security is a characteristic of a good firm, or de-cent workplace. Several methods for measuring an Employment Protection Security Index (EPSI) are available in the ELFS. We can present two, which essentially take account of the peculiar phenomenon of unpaid leave in transition economies.

Thus, in Azerbaijan, Republic of Moldova, Russian Federation and Ukraine and in China, the Index is measured as follows:

EPSI = R + N + RB + D + UL

where

R = 1 if the percentage share of the workforce without regular employment contracts was less than 10%, 0 otherwise.

N = 1 if the notice period normally given to workers being retrenched was greater than the statutory minimum, 0 otherwise.

RB = 1 if the firm provided workers being retrenched with any benefits other than severance pay, 0 otherwise.

D = 1 if the number of workers retrenched was less than average for all firms in the previous year, 0 otherwise.

UL = 1 if workers were placed on unpaid leave by the enterprise in the three months before the date of renumeration, 0 oterwise.

In *Brazil, Chile, Indonesia, Pakistan, the Philippines, South Africa and Tanzania*, the Employment Protection Security Index is measured in a similar way, although without the unpaid leave variable and with a modified retrenchment variable:

EPSI = R + N + RB + D

where

R = 1 if the percentage share of the workforce without regular employment contracts was less than 10%, 0 otherwise.

N = 1 if the firm provided workers being retrenched with notice, 0 otherwise.

RB = 1 if the firm provided workers being retrenched with any benefits other than severance, 0 otherwise.

D = 1 if dismissal procedures are covered in the firm's collective agreement, 0 otherwise.

With either variant of the index, the normalized values vary between 0 and 1, and in effect are relative measures. Thus a company with a high score is providing its workforce with a higher value of employment security than one with a low score.

A few results may be sufficient to indicate the main patterns. Thus, according to the ELFS data in China, Chile and Tanzania — three very different economies — there is a clear tendency for employment protection security to be greater the larger the firm (Figure 6.9). There is also evidence that public sec- tors are more likely to promote high levels of employment protection, as indicated in the case of Chile (Figure 6.10). There are often sectoral differences, as can be illustrated in the case of Tanzania (Figure 6.11).

Figure 6.9 China: Firm-level Employment Protection Security Index, by enterprise size

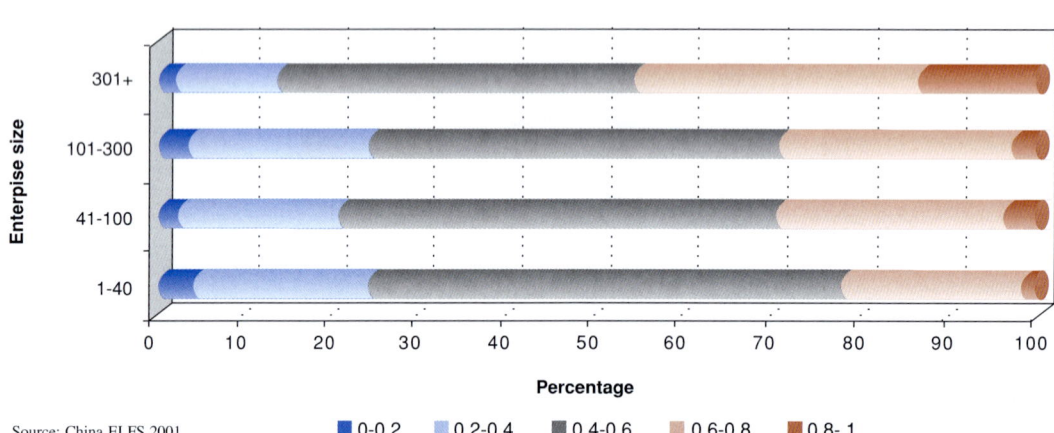

Source: China ELFS 2001.

■ 0-0.2   ■ 0.2-0.4   ■ 0.4-0.6   ■ 0.6-0.8   ■ 0.8-.1

Figure 6.10 Chile: Firm-level Employment Protection Security Index, by property form

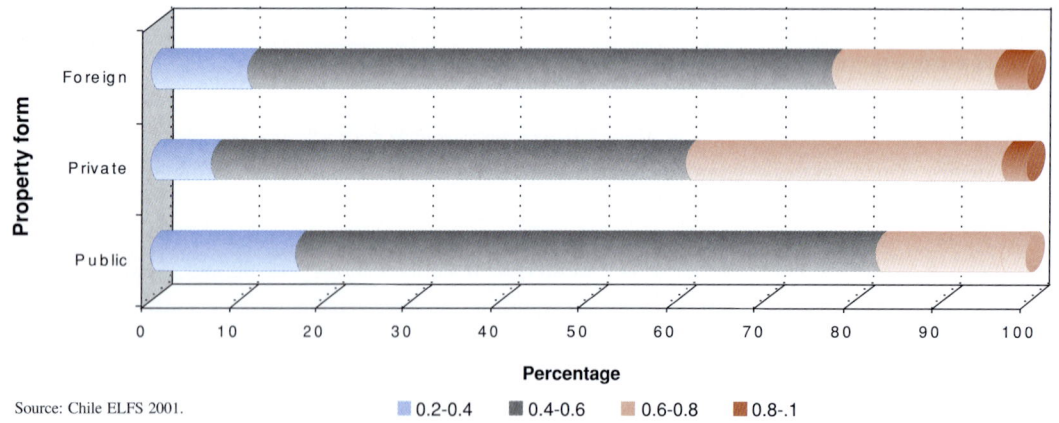

Source: Chile ELFS 2001.

■ 0.2-0.4   ■ 0.4-0.6   ■ 0.6-0.8   ■ 0.8-.1

Figure 6.11 Tanzania: Firm-level Employment Protection Security Index, by industrial sector

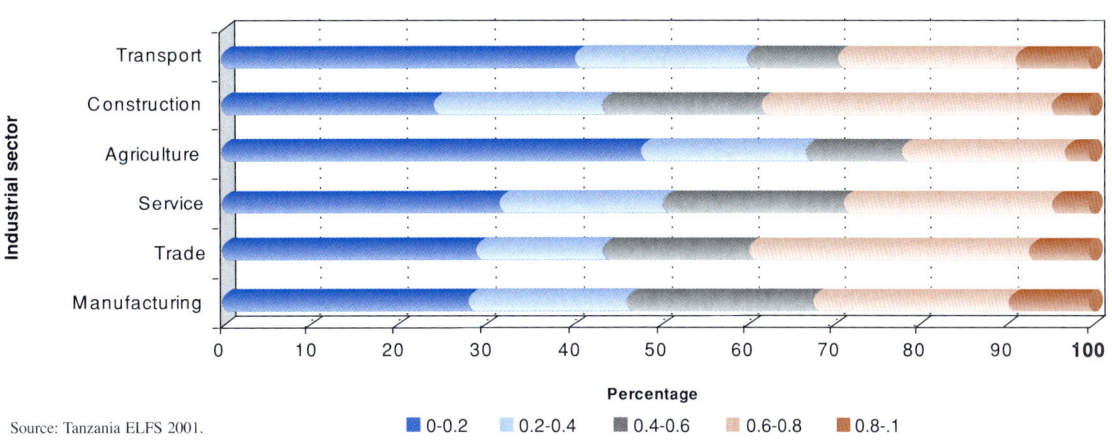

Source: Tanzania ELFS 2001.

■ 0-0.2 ■ 0.2-0.4 ■ 0.4-0.6 ■ 0.6-0.8 ■ 0.8-.1

What is most notable about this firm level on workplace employment security index is, first, that even within sectors and within specific countries, firms practise a very wide variety of employment security systems, and second, there is no obvious relationship between the extent of such security and the performance of firms.

6.7 Evidence from the People's Security Surveys

In developing countries especially, the picture that emerges from the PSS data is one of huge diversity in patterns of employment security across the world. Most workers do not have much protection, most have weak contracts or weakly regulated contracts, and most feel they could lose their employment relatively easily; very few people have strong employment security, while the situation in transition countries has been contradictory. The PSS results highlight some of the key issues.

(i) Employment tenure

In Ukraine, employed workers have been in their jobs for a long time on average. As of 2002, the mean average was 12 years in current employment. This refers to incomplete employment spells and includes all age groups. For those aged 41-50, the mean was 15 years. So, the employment tenure data suggest considerable employment security, or at least retention of employment.

While unemployment has mounted in Ukraine, those in employment have tended to cling to their jobs. Voluntary job-hopping, so characteristic of the false full employment of the Soviet era, has been deterred by the decline in employment. About three in four employed workers had not changed their main employment or income-earning activity in the previous five years, and only 7% had changed twice or more. Men were slightly more likely to have changed employment, but mobility was still low by international standards. Those in their 20s were most likely to have changed jobs, but even in this group a majority had not done so.

Contrast the situation with what is typical of developing countries. In South Africa, the PSS found that a large proportion of wage and salary workers had been in their employment for a short time. But a majority of such workers were under the age of 25. The age structure of the labour force is key. There are lots of young workers, whose turnover rates are high. Sadly, in the case of South Africa and other African countries, another factor in low average tenure is the impact of HIV/AIDS. Many workers do not live active lives long enough to have long-term jobs.

Table 6.3 Average duration in current employment, by age group
(mean average number of years in current employment)

Country	Male			Female			n
	< 25 years	25–44 years	45+ years	< 25 years	25–44 years	45+ years	
Argentina	2.5	7.7	16.8	1.5	6.5	13.2	1 502
Bangladesh	4.2	n. a.	n. a.	3.5	n. a.	n. a.	2 327
Brazil	1.9	6.6	12.6	1.6	5.5	11.8	2 317
Chile	1.8	6.6	15.6	1.2	6.1	10.9	627
China	2.9	9.4	18.1	2.2	9.7	16.7	2 046
Ethiopia	4.4	9.9	8.7	2.2	7.2	8.5	904
Hungary	2.9	7.6	11.9	1.9	7.5	15.3	591
India (Gujarat)	5.2	11.7	19.5	4.1	9.4	16.2	1 236
Indonesia	4.5	10.4	21.3	4.1	10.1	20.2	2 191
Russian Federation	1.5	6.7	12.7	1.8	7.5	14.2	1 515
South Africa	1.6	6.8	12.0	1.6	5.5	11.3	634
Tanzania	3.2	11.2	22.2	3.7	9.7	27.4	1 306
Ukraine	2.0	8.6	17.4	2.1	9.4	18.5	6 400

Source: PSS

(ii) Size of firm

If average tenure data are not particularly reliable indicators of employment security, another indirect indicator of such security is the size of firm in which people are working. Small-scale firms have a higher tendency to go out of existence because they are more prone to bankruptcy or collapse due to personal disasters or random shocks.

Traditionally, most employment in Ukraine has been in large enterprises. Although there has been a decline in the average size of establishment, restructuring has been slow in this respect, as shown in the ELFS carried out in the country annually since 1993. Consequently, most wage employment in Ukraine is still concentrated in large firms.

In China too employment in small enterprises remains low — only 8% of all wage and salary workers were working in firms with fewer than 10 workers. In Hungary, another east European country undergoing large-scale privatization and downsizing, employment in enterprises that employ fewer than 10 workers constitutes 19% of all wage employment.

In developing countries, the figures are much higher. In Tanzania, 30% of all wage and salary workers are engaged in enterprises that employ fewer than 10 workers, while in South Africa such respondents comprised 34% of wage and salary workers. In Ghana, Indonesia and Bangladesh, the great majority were employed in micro-enterprises — 82% of respondents in Ghana, 79% in Indonesia and 56% of PSS wage and salary respondents in Bangladesh.

According to the Indonesian PSS, over three-quarters of all those working were in establishments with five or fewer workers, and only 4% worked in establishments with more than 50 workers. Very small firms were more likely to lay off workers during the crisis of 1998. There is also evidence of lax compliance with regulations, such as minimum wages, in small firms.[19]

The high proportion of micro-enterprise employment in developing countries is linked to work under poor conditions in the so-called informal economy — with no proper contracts, and an employment relationship bereft of rights and benefits.

---

[19] A. Berry, E. Rodriguez and H.M. Sandee: *Firm and Group Dynamics in the Small and Medium Enterprise Sector in Indonesia*, World Bank Institute Working Paper (Washington, DC, World Bank, 2001).

(iii) Employment contract

Another strong indicator of employment security is the existence and duration of an employment contract (Table 6.4). In this regard, workers in Ukraine still have strong employment security. Over three-quarters of the employed claimed to have permanent contracts, with no difference between men and women. Young workers were the most likely to have employment without any contract. But the main predictor of having an insecure employment contract was the size of firm. Nearly 30% of men and 27% of women who were in firms with fewer than ten workers had temporary or casual contracts, compared with 5% of men and 7% of women in firms with more than 1,000 workers.

In Hungary too, another former socialist country, the PSS found that a big majority had "permanent" employment contracts. But it is in developing countries where the challenge is obviously greatest. For example, among wage and salary respondents in Bangladesh, 62% work without a contract, and in Ghana and India over 80% do so.

Table 6.4 Percentage of employed by type of contract, by gender and country

Country	Male			Female			n
	No contract	Short contract	Long contract	No contract	Short contract	Long contract	
Argentina	8.9	6.8	77.0	9.4	10.6	68.5	756
Bangladesh	62.0	0.3	37.6	45.5	1.2	53.3	757
Brazil	15.1	3.8	79.6	18.7	3.6	75.5	1 384
Chile	7.8	12.8	76.2	11.1	14.6	68.1	426
China	17.4	13.2	69.4	17.7	10.5	71.8	1 875
Ghana	83.4	2.2	12.8	85.6	2.0	11.2	1 474
Hungary	3.0	5.2	91.9	2.9	3.3	93.8	514
India	87.9	10.7	1.5	92.2	6.6	1.2	1 236
Russian Federation	7.5	1.6	88.6	6.9	0.6	89.7	1 477
South Africa	55.4	1.4	41.6	57.0	2.2	39.3	617
Tanzania	63.7	5.1	29.9	55.3	2.5	39.7	772
Ukraine	4.5	1.3	88.4	4.4	1.2	88.9	6 400

Note: (1) Fixed term contract, less than a year is included in "Short contract". (2) Verbal more than a month or without limit is included in "No contract".

Source: PSS.

The PSS in some countries also asked if workers were protected against *unfair dismissal*. In Ukraine, about two in five of those employed said that most workers in their workplace had protection against unfair dismissal; a further 11% said some workers were protected. Workers in large firms or organizations were slightly more likely to be protected than in smaller firms. But a majority thought they and their colleagues were unprotected against unfair dismissal. Russians have become more jaundiced, over 40% believing that nobody is really protected. In China, more than four in every five workers said they or most workers in their firms were protected against unfair dismissal. This is a far cry from the situation experienced by workers in Ghana, where 60% re-ported that there was no agreement to protect them against unfair dismissal. The situation was quite similar in South Africa.

National practices also vary widely with respect to notice of redundancy for economic reasons. In Ukraine, nearly a third of all employees thought they could expect more than a month of warning, just over half thought they would receive between a week and a month of notice, and 16% expected it to be a week or less. When asked how much notice they thought *should* be provided, 2% said a week or less, 59% said from a week to a month, 33% said from one to two months, and 6% said more than two months. In China, there is less dispersion — three

151

out of every four workers believe they would receive between a week and a month of advance notice. Since written employment contracts are still very rare in developing countries, the vast majority of employees do not have protection against dismissal. Thus, for example, in Ethiopia, only 9% of urban employees had a written agreement that protected them.[20] In Pakistan, 84% of male wage-workers said that their employers could dismiss them at short notice, and were able to do so without cost because there were ample replacements easily available.[21]

In Ghana, the PSS showed that over three-quarters of rural and nearly two-thirds of urban respondents had no contractual relations with any employer.[22] About two-thirds of wage workers believed they could be laid off without even so much as a day's notice. By contrast, among those in wage employment in South Africa the modal notice period was one month.

(iv) Expectation of continued employment

Another indicator of employment security is the subjective expectation that the person will retain his, or her, employment. The PSS show that there is a widespread lack of confidence in this respect. In eastern Europe, expectations have deteriorated in recent years. Now, merely 28% of Ukrainian workers are reasonably confident; workers in industry were more likely to be confident they would keep their main job over the next 12 months compared with agricultural workers, and public sector workers were most confident of all.

Interestingly, Table 6.5 shows that, first, in many countries women are just as confident as men about keeping their job and, second, the "self-employed" do not necessarily feel more insecure.

Table 6.5 Percentage of workers expecting to stay in current employment over next 12 months, by country and gender

Country	Male		Female		n
	Employed (%)	Self-employed (%)	Employed (%)	Self-employed (%)	
Argentina	57.7	47.6	59.1	42.4	1 466
Bangladesh	73.9	84.6	71.8	92.0	2 323
Brazil	56.2	51.5	60.5	52.6	2 306
Chile	59.3	52.2	63.5	58.3	613
China	75.8	74.0	70.7	69.1	1 907
Ghana	78.9	82.1	82.5	78.1	1 160
Hungary	56.1	62.0	59.8	60.0	567
India	91.1	90.1	95.4	83.5	1 236
Indonesia	56.9	46.0	47.9	42.9	2 154
Russian Federation	69.3	77.8	68.1	66.7	1 514
South Africa	71.4	66.7	67.4	69.0	504
Tanzania	28.1	46.5	33.0	40.8	1 291
Ukraine 2003	22.0	16.8	25.9	14.9	9 000

Source: PSS.

[20]D. Rahmato and A. Kidanu: *Vulnerable Livelihoods: People's Security Survey of Urban Households in Ethiopia*, paper presented at ILO workshop on Economic Security and Decent Work in Africa, Dar-es-Salaam, May 2003.

[21]A. Sayeed and S. Javed: *People's Security Survey — Pakistan*, SES Paper (Geneva, ILO, forthcoming).

[22]N.A. Apt: *Highlights of the Ghana People's Security Survey*, paper presented at ILO workshop on Economic Security and Decent Work in Africa, Dar-es-Salaam, May 2003.

Table 6.6 Women's share of various types of employment, selected countries, 1997–2000

India	India	Kenya	South Africa	Tunisia	Mexico
Agriculture	32.1	54.4	50.7	23.5	13.6
Informal employment	20.0	60.3	53.2	18.5	39.0
Informal sector	20.2	42.0	44.9	14.6	40.1
Undeclared workers	19.6	79.2	60.8	22.3	37.8
Home workers	44.3	34.9	37.9	43.3	
Formal employment	16.8	30.9	38.7	28.5	38.3
Total employment	27.0	53.4	46.9	23.5	34.1
Non-agricultural employment	19.4	51.9	46.1	23.5	38.7

Note: The author's definition of informal sector is based on "residual method" of estimation. Employment, in this paper, includes own-account work, unpaid family work and all forms of wage labour.

Source: Charmes, 2002, and ILO, 2002c.

In many countries, home-working is still disproportionately concentrated among women, who are in effect in "disguised" labour.[24] Within informal types of employment, women's share is particularly high in all forms of undeclared work, as observed in Kenya, Tunisia and South Africa, and in many other countries.

The PSS have shown that women are far more likely than men to be working in small-scale units, in South Africa, Tanzania, Bangladesh, Indonesia, Hungary and Ukraine. They are also more likely to be working without proper or longer-term contracts. However, as shown in Table 6.4, women do not necessarily feel a greater sense of employment insecurity. Perhaps this is because they have been accustomed not to expect it.

6.9 Linking employment security with other forms of security

Loyalty, what loyalty?

"Chances are with our staff turnover, when they get a serious illness, it's not going to be our problem anymore."

— United States employer, 2003.

Employment security is wanted by workers, but employers understandably want flexibility, which typically means less employment security. Reducing employment security is seen as a cost-cutting measure, enabling the level of employment to be adjusted more quickly and overheads to be lowered.

However, weak employment security has implications for other forms of work-related security. Above all, workers in casual labour and in various forms of outwork usually have much less *income security* than those in regular secure forms of employment, as shown in Chapter 3. Not only do they receive lower wages but, probably far more systematically, they receive fewer non-wage enterprise benefits and often fail to gain entitlement to state benefits. Workers with insecure employment also tend to be exposed to more work insecurity, in that they are often not protected by occupational safety and health regulations or mechanisms. There is also ample evidence that workers with insecure employment contracts are less likely to be provided with training.[25]

Nevertheless, strong employment security does not necessarily go with strong income security. The situation in Ukraine might be unusual but is surely not unique. There, no less than 39% of workers reporting that they had strong employment security said their household income was insufficient for their basic household needs.

[24]M. Tomei: *Homework in Selected Latin American Countries: A Comparative Overview*, SEED Paper (Geneva, ILO, 2000); Beneria, 2002, op. cit.

[25]In India, it is the illiterate and those with minimal schooling who are overwhelmingly concentrated in casual and contract labour. Prabhu, 2001, op. cit.

Historically, strong representation security in the form of unionization has gone with relatively strong employment security. Unions have promoted it and have jealously guarded advances made in that respect. This is perhaps the most powerful link between the two forms of security.

If we take the informalization continuum approach outlined earlier, a link with *labour market security* can be discerned. For example, in Argentina the relatively informalized workers are more likely to have experienced a spell of unemployment lasting a month or more in the past two years — 57% of the most informalized, compared with 12% of those in highly formalized statuses. A roughly similar pattern emerges in Brazil and Chile. Contrary to a commonly expressed image, the relatively informal do not in-

dulge in more multiple jobs. What characterizes them most is that they are in constant search for other things to do. In Argentina, almost half of those in highly informal activities were looking for other work, compared with 21% of those in highly formal labour.

Workers in higher degrees of informality may have earnings equivalent to those in formal jobs. As for income security, it is too simplistic to equate informality with poverty, even though more of the relatively informal have low incomes. The examples of Brazil and Chile bring this out. Informality does not map neatly onto income. What seems to be the case is that formality gives greater protection for men than for women, an implication of the patterns shown in Figures 6.16 and 6.17.

Figure 6.16   Chile: Mean adjusted monthly earnings in USD, by level of labour informality and gender

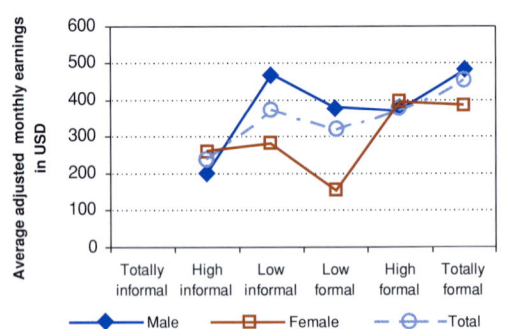

Source: Chile PSS 2001.

Figure 6.17   Brazil: Mean adjusted monthly earnings in USD, by level of labour informality and gender

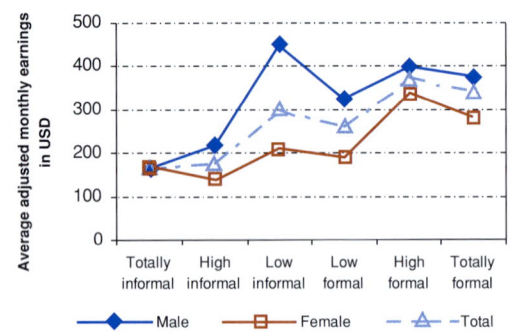

Source: Brazil PSS 2001.

What is key to an understanding of the linkages is that being in an informal labour status means a greater likelihood of income variability and decline. Thus, the Latin American data show that more of the relatively informal had experienced a decline in their income over the past two years (Table 6.7). In

very different circumstances, workers in Ethiopia experienced much the same pattern, with those in highly informal statuses experiencing a much greater incidence of income variability than those with formal jobs, even though the biggest jump seems to come with a very high level of formality.

Table 6.7 Selected Latin American countries: Labour informality and income prior to the survey

| | Level of employment formality | | | | | | |
	Informal	Very low	Low	Medium	Almost formal	Formal	Total
Argentina							
Higher	6.1	7.3	18.8	8.6	17.2	19.0	11.6
About the same	22.7	25.6	37.5	42.9	53.3	53.1	35.8
Lower	68.2	64.2	43.7	45.0	28.0	27.5	50.6
Brazil							
Higher	18.1*	26.0	33.8	32.9	32.8	37.0	29.1
About the same	37.7	36.7	45.9	46.1	43.0	39.6	39.5
Lower	44.3	37.3	20.3	21.0	24.3	23.4	31.4
Chile							
Higher	17.0*	21.9	16.1	27.4	27.7	43.0	29.9
About the same	43.0	33.4	48.3	44.6	50.6	41.6	42.2
Lower	40.0	44.7	35.6	28.0	21.6	15.5	27.9

Source: Argentina, Brazil, Chile PSS 2001.
* Limited number of cases.

The nuanced relationship between labour informality and income security is also brought out in Gujarat (India) where the income advantage only seems to come with very high level of formality (Figure 6.18) and where, as in the Latin American situations, the benefit of formality is gained by men.

Figure 6.18 Gujarat (India): Mean average annual income according to labour formality

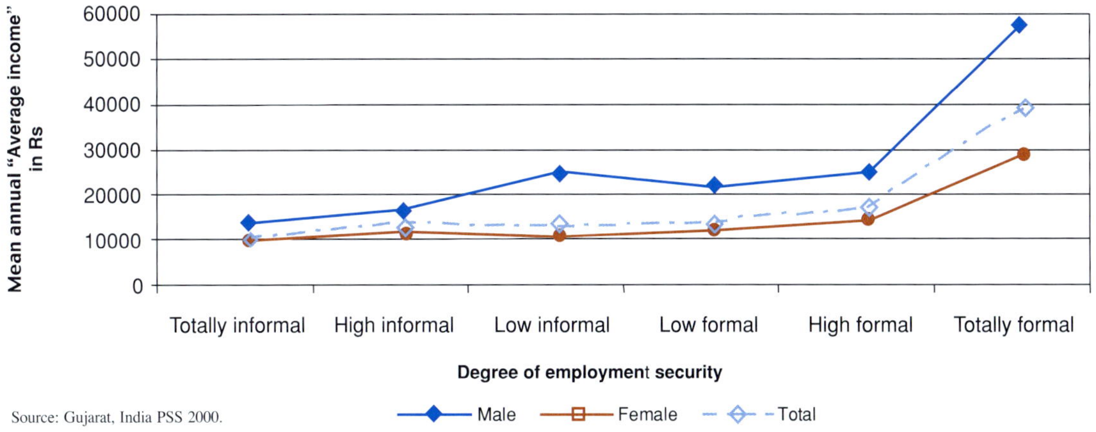

Source: Gujarat, India PSS 2000.

Another link between informalization and income security related to the incidence of financial crisis. The Gujarat situation illustrates the tendency for workers in highly informal work statuses to experience a higher incidence of financial crisis (Figure 6.19), where 13% of those in the most informal status went hungry in the past year, against 6% of those with highly formal status.[26] Finally, conscious of their general insecurity, those in highly informal work statuses worry more than others about what will happen in their old age when they are unable to work.

Figure 6.19 Gujarat (India): Degree of labour informality of employment, by situation of crisis in the last three years affecting income-generation

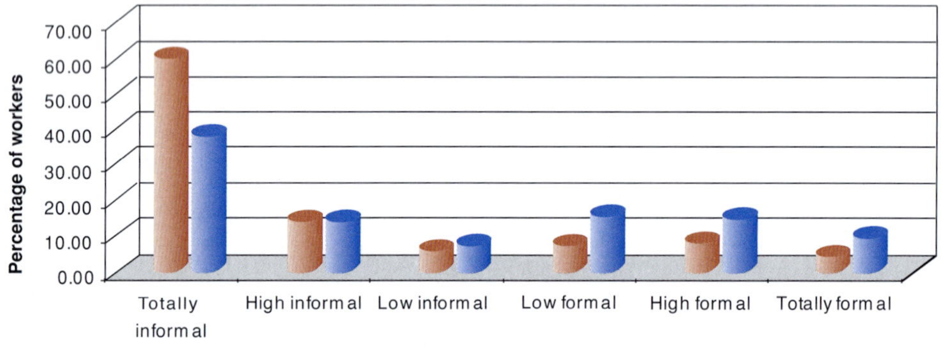

Source: Gujarat, India PSS 2000.

6.10 A national Employment Protection Security Index

Employment security exists where there is protection against unfair and arbitrary dismissal, and where workers can obtain redress if they are subject to unfair dismissal. The strength of employment security is also a function of the type of economy and structure of employment, so that it tends to be stronger where large-scale firms predominate and where the public sector is large.

There have been several attempts to measure something close to employment security and to rank countries in terms of strength of employment protection. In this analysis, we have constructed a national Employment Protection Security Index consisting of sets of *input* indicators (policy commitments made by governments), *process* indicators (measures of existing institutions or mechanisms designed or expected to give effect to policies giving employment security) and *outcome* indicators reflecting actual security levels.

Input indicators
There are three input indicators. The first is whether or not the country has ratified the ILO's Termination of Employment Convention, 1982 (No. 158), which provides that employment shall not be terminated unless there is a valid reason for doing so; a value of 1 is given if the country has ratified it and 0 if it has not. It is notable that only a minority of countries have ratified this Convention. The second indicator is the existence of national legislation on employment protection, dealing with average notice period prior to redundancy, severance pay and definition of unfair dismissal. The third, also based on a national instrument, concerns the degree of protection on collective redundancies and includes aspects such as the obligation to consult prior to dismissal, to follow administrative procedures, etc.

Process indicators
These indicators evaluate workers' access to institutions protecting them from loss of employment or ensuring that legal provisions of employment security are applied. Specifically, the two indicators used are the proportion of workers covered by collective bargaining agreements and the statutory existence (or absence) of independent labour tribunals.

---

[26]This pattern was brought out even more strongly in Ethiopia.

Outcome indicators

These indicators relate in principle to the notion of secure employment, defined as full-time, regular wage or salaried employment, associated with rights and benefits. Insecure employment takes in part-time or temporary wage work and various activities covered by the term "self-employment". Because of lack of data for industrializing countries, three proxy indicators were selected. The first two are the shares of wage and public sector employment in total employment, these being regarded as the most secure forms of employment. The third, to take account of the gender dimension, is the ratio of female to male wage employment.

The Employment Protection Security Index (EPSI) covers 99 countries (Table 6.8). Of these, only 16 come out as "Pacesetters", all of them in western Europe, with the exception of Mauritius. This is because Mauritius has maintained a relatively large public sector, has an employment structure with a majority of wage workers, and has a roughly equal number of men and women in protected employment.

Twenty-one countries emerge as "Pragmatists" — the cluster displaying satisfactory employment security outcomes but scoring less well on the input or process indicators. In most cases, this is due to non-ratification of ILO Convention No. 158 on Termination of Employment, 1982 (which has an overall ratification rate of 17%) and to below-average periods of notice of redundancy. This cluster consists mainly of Latin American countries but includes also some industrialized countries pursuing a liberal economic policy model, such as the United States and the United Kingdom, as well as a few from the Pacific region.

Contrary to other forms of insecurity, employment insecurity is not predominantly associated with the African continent. Countries with overall unsatisfactory performances, in the "Much-to-be-done" cluster, are from all parts of the world. If we include the "Conventionals", two-thirds of all countries, and certainly an even larger proportion of workers, do not have employment security.

Table 6.8 Employment Protection Security Index (EPSI)

	High score on Outcome			
	High score on Input / Process		**Low** score on Input / Process	
Regions	**Pacesetters** Countries		**Pragmatists** Countries	
Africa and Middle East	Mauritius		Algeria	South Africa
			Botswana	Tunisia
			Israel	
Americas			Argentina	Dominican Republic
			Barbados	Mexico
			Brazil	Panama
			Canada	United States
			Costa Rica	
Asia			Australia	Korea, Republic of
			Japan	New Zealand
Eastern Europe and Central Asia			Bulgaria	
Western Europe	Austria	Italy	Switzerland	
	Belgium	Luxembourg	United Kingdom	
	Denmark	Netherlands		
	Finland	Norway		
	France	Portugal		
	Germany	Spain		
	Greece	Sweden		
	Ireland			

	Low score on Outcome				
	High score on Input / Process			**Low** score on Input / Process	
Regions	**Conventionals Countries**			**Much-to-be-done Countries**	
Africa and Middle East	Cameroon Congo, Democratic Republic of Egypt Ethiopia	Gabon Lebanon Morocco Turkey		Benin Burkina Faso Burundi Congo Côte d'Ivoire Gambia Ghana Guinea-Bissau Kenya	Madagascar Mauritania Nigeria Rwanda Senegal Sierra Leone Tanzania, United Republic of Zimbabwe
Americas	Honduras Venezuela			Bolivia Chile Colombia	Ecuador Guatemala Peru
Asia				Bangladesh China India Indonesia Nepal	Pakistan Philippines Sri Lanka Thailand
Eastern Europe and Central Asia	Belarus Czech Republic Estonia Hungary Latvia Lithuania Moldova, Republic of	Romania Russian Federation Slovakia Tajikistan Ukraine Uzbekistan		Albania Armenia Croatia Georgia	Kazakhstan Kyrgyzstan Turkmenistan Western Europe
Western Europe					

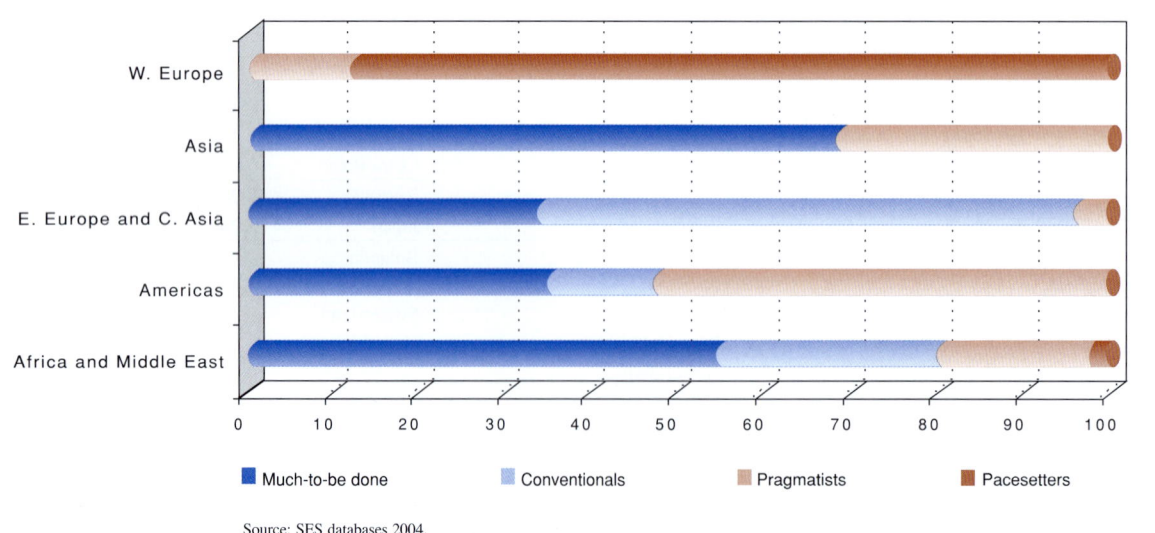

Figure 6.20 Employment protection security index clusters, by region

Source: SES databases 2004.

6.11 Concluding reflections

There should be little doubt that global and competitive pressures have weakened employment security around the world. It was never strong. But employment security seems to be one of those forms of social and economic security that is tradable. In other words, if a person has other forms of security, most notably income security, he or she may feel sufficiently relaxed to accept a moderate degree of employment insecurity.

However, employment security for most workers is definitely declining in an era of labour market flexibility. Between the early 1990s and the end of the decade, employment security scores declined in 16 out of 21 industrialized countries for which comparable data are available.[27] In developing countries, data constraints do not allow such a comparison over that period. But there is enough anecdotal evidence to suggest that there has been no improvement.

A question that will be left open at this stage is crucial for those developing social policy in the early years of the 21st century. If it is a privilege for a minority, should employment security be given a high priority in the general pursuit of economic security? In industrialized countries at least, employment security has remained an important instrumental route to other aspects of economic security. But in many parts of the world it has weakened. If it were further weakened — as mainstream policy-makers and many employers seem to want — then surely other means must be found to ensure those other forms of security.

---

[27] S. Dasgupta and W. Onobogu: *Measuring Employment Security in Industrialized Countries,* SES Paper (Geneva, ILO, forthcoming).

Chapter 7   Work security

7.1 The idea of work security

Most forms of work have their dangers. In some, the dangers are largely physical; in some, they are physical and mental; in some, the hidden dangers are largely psychological. Work security, in the form of occupational health and safety, is immensely complex, and new adversities associated with work and labour seem to be identified almost daily.

Work security is about working conditions that are safe and promote workers' well-being. Although embracing issues traditionally treated under the rubric of "occupational health and safety", work security means more than that. In other words, it is not just about mechanisms to protect workers against occupational hazards, disease and injury; it is also about the so-called modern scourges of *stress, overwork and presenteeism*. And it extends to violence at work and the important area of *harassment* in its various guises.

At the extreme, work can kill. The ILO estimates that over two million workers die each year from work-related accidents and diseases, and that globally this figure is on the rise.[1] As Figure 7.1 shows, fatalities according to these data are particularly likely in certain parts of the world, and once more countries in sub-Saharan African are most severely affected. To complicate the picture, research suggests that work-related factors may play a greater role in worker deaths than has been commonly assumed.[2]

---

[1]ILO: *Conclusions Concerning ILO Standards-Related Activities in the Area of Occupational Safety and Health: A Global Strategy*, International Labour Conference Provisional Record 22, 91st Session (Geneva, 2003).

[2]M. Nurminen and A. Karjalainen: "Epidemiological estimate of the proportion of fatalities related to occupational factors in Finland", *Trade Union News from Finland, June 2001.* <www.artto.kaapeli.fi>.

Figure 7.1 Accident fatality rates, by region (deaths per 100,000 workers)

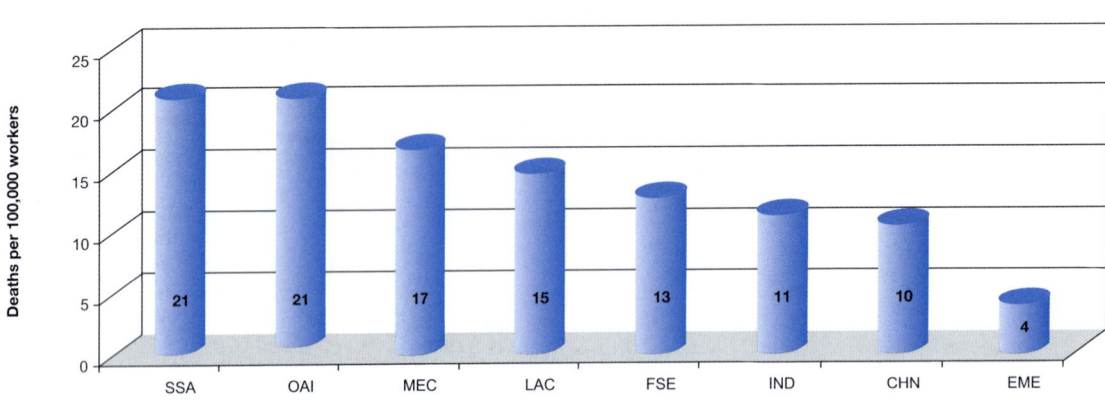

Note: EME= established market economies; FSE= formerly socialist economies of Europe; IND=India; CHN = China; OAI= Other Asia and Islands; SSA = sub-Saharan Africa; LAC= Latin America and the Caribbean; MEC = Middle Eastern Crescent (includes North Africa).

Source: <www.ilo.org/safework>.

A fundamental difficulty with even the most visible and dramatic form of work insecurity — loss of life — is that the available data are scarce and questionable, justifying several ILO initiatives to improve their quality.[3] Indeed, in most countries, the amount of available information on trends in work security is shockingly limited and often unreliable.

The problem is compounded because the statistical picture is almost certainly distorted by bias in the available data. If there were just one message that could be conveyed through this chapter, it would be that this bias results in a systematic understatement of the inequality of work insecurity. That issue is considered in section 7.8. But note that this goes beyond the matter of not having reliable information on all those workers in slums and in impoverished rural areas of developing countries, which is fairly well known. There is also the matter of elusive statistics, highlighted by two examples below.

---

[3] See work being done under the ILO SAFEWORK/STAT project on development of methodologies for information on occupational injuries from sources other than notification systems, including K. Taswell and P. Wingfield Digby: *Accidents Can Happen. Collecting Occupational Injury Data Through Household and Establishment Surveys: An ILO Manual on Concepts and Methods* (Geneva, ILO, forthcoming).

Chinese workers never die: Immortality or elusive statistics?

Have Chinese workers discovered immortality? No, but it appears that some of their foreign employers may have — at least on paper.

Desperate to find employment and improve their lives, many Chinese workers emigrate to Europe. But many in search of basic security for themselves and their families do so illegally, working without documentation, often in textile manufacturing. Typically, several members of the same family may be employed in the same factory. When a fatal occupational accident occurs, it is all too easy and common to cover up the undocumented worker's death by replacing him or her with a documented worker, or a member of the same family using their name and papers. With this convenient system of covering up work-related fatalities, the worker who paid the price with his life never officially died, since he never officially existed in the firm in the first place.

Failure to collect such "elusive statistics" allows workers in many categories to slip through the cracks, to go unrecognized, uncounted, and unaccounted for, never receiving the social protection to which they may be entitled.

To make up for the limitations of occupational health surveillance systems,[4,5] innovative techniques for collecting elusive data are needed. Such techniques exist, and have proven effective.[6]. Developing surveys with trusted local NGOs, and executing them in a culturally appropriate manner, is an effective means of gathering occupational health data from low-wage workers who are not covered by official databases and whose workplaces are not open to researchers. Surveys are particularly helpful for obtaining data in conditions where mortality is low, and can be more sensitive than other data-gathering approaches.

Since innovative techniques for collecting elusive data are not used by national data-collection agencies, it is no wonder that national and international statistics on work security (work-related accidents, injuries, fatalities, diseases) typically are gross underestimations of reality.[7,8]

Innovative data collection methods are useful in countries where official occupational health surveillance excludes large numbers of people, important sectors of the economy, underrepresented groups, or where surveillance does not exist at all.

Techniques effective in developing countries in the investigation of villages and the informal economy have been shown to be effective in industrialized settings. Such techniques apply a public health research model, with participant involvement, for reaching populations traditionally excluded from occupational injury and disease surveillance in industrialized urban areas.

South-east Asian workers in Lowell, Massachusetts, suffer numerous occupational illnesses and injuries, although such incidents are typically not recorded in official statistics. Workers have little access to preventive or curative resources for addressing workplace hazards, and little or no information about mechanisms for compensation. Workers are often "invisible" to existing occupational health surveillance systems due to temporary employment, lack of occupational-health training, low levels of unionization, and use of small clinics for health care.

Providing basic social and economic security to workersis proving to be a significant challenge for most firms and governments today. The task seems nearly impossible if no one knows that the workers existed in the first place.

---

[4]L. Azaroff, C. Levenstein and D.H. Wegman: "Occupational injury and illness surveillance: Conceptual filters explain underreporting", *American Journal of Public Health*, No. 92, 2002, pp. 1421–1429.

[5]E. Pollack and D.E. Keimig: *Counting Injuries and Illnesses in the Workplace: Proposals for a Better System* (Washington, DC, National Academy Press, 1987).

[6]L. Azaroff and C. Levenstein: *Innovations in Monitoring Work Security: A Case Study of Southeast Asian Refugees in Lowell, Massachusetts,* SES Paper No. 21 (Geneva, ILO, 2001).

[7]J. Biddle, K.Roberts, K. Rosenman, and E.M. Welch: "What percentage of workers with work-related illnesses receive workers' compensation benefits?," *Journal of Occupational and Environmental Medicine* Vol. 40, No. 4, 1998, pp. 325–331.

[8]K.D. Rosenman et al.: "Why most workers with occupational repetitive trauma do not file for workers' compensation", *Journal of Occupational and Environmental Medicine*, Vol. 42, No. 1, 2000, pp. 25–34.

7.2 The issue of regulation

As a generalization, across the world for most of the 20th century, the dominant approach to work security was a model of *statutory regulation*, in which governments subscribed to international Conventions and Recommendations on occupational health and safety, passed comprehensive laws setting standards and regulations, established labour inspectorates, and encouraged enterprises to introduce institutional mechanisms such as safety committees and safety departments.

Later, corresponding to the resurgence of neo-liberal thinking, there was a counter-trend towards *market regulation* or *self-regulation*, or to what some observers call "an individual responsibility model". Undoubtedly, in the process, some countries have cut back their regulatory apparatus and state funding for work security.

It is important to understand the implicit or explicit reasoning. The thinking behind the market or self-regulation trend goes something like this: if governments introduce complex comprehensive safety codes, large cumbersome institutional mechanisms, provide "generous" compensation for adversely affected workers, and impose heavy costs on employers, a wide range of *moral hazards* and *immoral hazards* are created. For example, if the rules cover all contingencies there might be a tendency to be careless. If employers have to pay heavy costs for injuries or illnesses of regular workers, they may be inclined to resort more to non-regular workers in precarious contractual arrangements.

The old-style models of statutory regulation are indeed paternalistic. But self-regulation encourages opportunism, inertia and self-exploitation. Our essential argument, which will be developed in the final two chapters, is that the optimum solution is basic income security, which would limit the tendency to self-exploit and ultimately self-destruct, and voice security. The latter would be strengthened by access to relevant information, as advocated in our Barefoot Research Manual,[9] for example, and by bargaining mechanisms in the workplace, in local labour markets, and upwards to the global level.

7.3 Work insecurity as a global challenge

Work insecurity is a global phenomenon, in that the risks and dangers exist everywhere. But they vary from country to country, from industry to industry, from occupation to occupation, and from one type of employment to another.

In developing countries, where the problems are surely greatest, there is also the least information.[10] The voice of ordinary people should be heard, and governments and donor agencies should make sure much more information is gathered on this aspect of work. We have tried to do this in a small way.

Thus, in Tanzania the PSS asked about the realities faced by respondents. One in seven said they worked in dangerous environments.[11] Those in non-agricultural wage jobs were far more likely to report that this was the case. Overall, 40% felt insecure about the health and safety conditions of their workplace, a figure that rose to 80% for casual agricultural workers. Not surprisingly, about one in seven workers had experienced work-related injuries or illnesses.

Among rural workers in Bangladesh, 16% had suffered a work-related injury that required them to miss a week of work.

In Ukraine, according to the PSS, workers live with extreme work insecurity. Over a third said they were exposed to chemical substances, with more women than men exposed to chemicals at work. More than 40% of workers were exposed to unguarded or dangerous machinery, with more men than women facing this problem. And nearly half were exposed to excessive noise on a regular basis. A striking but not surprising fact is that more than 25% of Ukraine's industrial workers said their working conditions were unsafe. In the other countries where the PSS was

---

[9] M. Keith, J. Brophy, P. Kirby and E. Rosskam: *Barefoot Research: A Workers' Manual for Organizing on Work Security* (Geneva, ILO, 2002).

[10] There is also the famous memo sent by the Chief Economist of the World Bank advocating that dangerous and polluting industries should be moved to developing countries where, according to conventional economics, the value of lives was lower.

[11] D. Mushi: *Work Insecurity in Tanzania*, paper presented at ILO workshop on Economic Security and Decent Work, Dar-es-Salaam, May 2003.

conducted, reported exposures to dangerous chemicals with no protections ranged from 6% of casual labourers and wage workers in Gujarat, India saying they were exposed, to 74% of workers in Indonesia.

The Indonesia PSS revealed that nearly one in every five workers said their workplace conditions were poor, over half had no department or committee responsible for health and safety in the workplace, and about 14% said they had been victim of a work-induced injury, with nearly one-third having been absent from work due to accidents.

These findings are repeated in country after country. Nearly half of all wage workers in Bangladesh feel their working conditions are unsafe. In the Russian Federation, 30% of workers consider their work environment "unsafe" or "very unsafe". The same perception exists among 24% of workers in Argentina, 17% of workers in Chile, 17% of Brazil's workers. In Tanzania 80% of casual agricultural workers say they feel insecure about the health and safety conditions of their workplace.

To illustrate the global challenge further, the PSS findings from Gujarat tell a story of extreme insecurity, particularly among rural women where some 30% of women workers missed more than one day of work due to a work-related injury or illness.

7.4 Agricultural workers

The agricultural labour force still represents the largest single occupational group, with 46% of the world's workers, despite the declining share of agriculture in the total workforce in virtually all countries over the past two decades.[12] The agricultural workforce continues to register some of the highest incidences of poverty and has the least access to social protection. These "decent work deficits" are in large part due to the fact that waged agricultural workers are still among the least organized and least represented by trade unions or other organizations.

Agriculture is perhaps the sector most profoundly affected by developments at international level. With the impact of globalization, in many countries it has been transformed into an even more unprotected sector of the economy, with adverse consequences for the workforce.

In many countries where agriculture is a major contributor to the national economy there is little capacity to finance social security. Even in high-income countries, gaps remain for various groups of agricultural workers, who are typically left without any form of social security, including without any protection for workers' health. And in many countries, casual and temporary agricultural workers have long been explicitly excluded from protective schemes, where they exist. In some countries, for example the Republic of Moldova and Slovakia, the situation is compounded by the non-payment of wages to agricultural workers.[13]

Agricultural workers suffer markedly higher rates of accidents and fatal injuries than workers in most sectors. They also figure disproportionately among the more than 160 million workers who are estimated to become ill as a result of workplace hazards and exposures. Ill health and disease are prevalent in agricultural communities. Health data from South Asian countries have consistently revealed that malnutrition, anaemia and maternal mortality rates are higher for plantation workforces than respective national averages.[14] Furthermore, there are very few resources for compensation available to the non-permanent majority of temporary, casual, seasonal or migrant workers.

Every year:

- at least 170,000 agricultural workers are killed as a result of workplace accidents, and some 40,000 of these deaths are from exposure to pesticides;

- 3–4 million people are affected by hazardous pesticides and suffer from severe poisoning, work-related cancer or reproductive impairments;

- in some countries, women account for more than half the total agricultural labour force, and the majority are in regular and casual forms of employment. These are growing and so is the share of women in them;

---

[12]*Decent Work in Agriculture* (Geneva, ILO, 2003), p. 70.
[13]Ibid, p. 54.
[14]Ibid., pp. 54, 60.

- 70% of child labour is employed in agriculture, a large proportion in the worst forms of child labour;

- agricultural workers are among the groups with the highest incidence of poverty in any country;

- only 5% of the world's 1.3 billion agricultural workers have access to any labour inspection system;

- the majority of waged agricultural workers are excluded from social protection;

- less than 10% of the world's waged agricultural workers are organized and represented in trade unions or rural workers' organizations.[15]

Women face particular health and safety problems in agriculture. Much agricultural work is arduous by nature, involving long hours of work with few rest breaks, the lifting and carrying of heavy loads, prolonged bending and stooping, and exposure to extreme temperatures, wind, rain and sun. Unprotected contact with biological and chemical agents, unguarded machinery and poorly designed work tools add to the toll on women's health. Access to health services thus becomes a crucial issue for women workers in what are often remote rural settings, both as a means or preventing ill health and of managing it if it occurs. Nonetheless, reports from Zimbabwe have shown that although women workers on large-scale farms have the highest rates of illnesses, they do not seek health care for fear of losing their jobs, since they are casual employees.[16]

An important source of ill health among women agricultural workers is the close link between their employment status and their living and social conditions. Overcrowded and unhygienic housing surrounding plantation estates is common, perpetuating the spread of infectious diseases, including tuberculosis, cholera and diphtheria as well as sexually transmitted diseases, including HIV/AIDS.

The disproportionate burden of pesticide exposure deserves special mention, particularly as the health impact of pesticide exposure may be greater on women for several reasons. Women in general have more body fat in which certain pesticides have a tendency to accumulate, and malnutrition and exhaustion may make women workers more susceptible to the effects of pesticides. In addition, there is a high risk of adverse effects on the unborn child if a woman is exposed to pesticides during pregnancy.[17,18]

Women's employment status and lack of bargaining power as casual, temporary or seasonal workers weaken their capacity to reduce exposure to occupational hazards and to effectively combat forms of sexual harassment. Male supervisors control decisions concerning work performance and hence remuneration for the "task". They are also the principal perpetrators of sexual harassment at work. Decisions and authorizations can be withheld in exchange for sexual favours, a common practice reinforcing the vulnerability of women workers. As an under-documented "occupational hazard", and serious form of exploitation and sex discrimination, sexual harassment has not yet been taken up seriously by many trade unions in the agricultural sector.

7.5 Work insecurity and enterprise restructuring

While it is well known that occupational safety and health varies by type of industry and type of job, there is also considerable evidence that more flexible labour relations, and in particular the global shift towards *external flexibility* through downsizing, contracting out certain types of labour and so on, have been associated with a deterioration in work security.

A review of 190 studies from 23 countries (including developing countries, transitional economies, and industrialized countries) concluded that about 80% showed a link between increased work insecurity and downsizing, greater employment insecurity, outsourcing and the increased use of temporary and casual labour. Over 140 of these studies showed that precarious employment is associated with higher injury rates, hazard exposures, disease and work-related stress.[19]

---

[15] International Union of Food, Agricultural, Hotel, restaurant, Catering, Tobacco and Allied Workers' Associations: *The WTO and the World Food System: A Trade Union Approach* (Geneva, IUF, 2002), p. 3.

[16] Ibid., p. 61.

[17] Ibid., p. 61.

[18] E. Rosskam: *Your Health and Safety at Work* (Geneva, ILO, 1996).

[19] M. Quinlan: *Regulating Flexible Work and Organizational Arrangements*, paper presented at conference on Australian Occupational Health and Safety Regulation for the 21st Century, Gold Coast, July 2003.

There is also extensive evidence that the more intense work schedules associated with the latest production systems driven by information technology and so-called "Japanese" work methods — "Just-In-Time", "Total Quality Management", "Quality Circles", "Lean Production" and other euphemisms — reduce worker autonomy and individual control of work on the shop-floor, so that the productivity gains come at the cost of worse health and safety of the workers.[20] They result in much greater levels of *cumulative trauma disorders* such as musculoskeletal disorders and repetitive strain injuries, which are caused by repetitive motion, static and/or awkward postures and manipulation of heavy weights.[21] In the United States, such disorders rose from 3.6 per 10,000 workers in 1982 to 27.3 in 1999, an annual growth of nearly 13%. By the turn of the century, they had become the source of the longest absences of work of all safety and health factors.

Beware the euphemisms!

Many terms convey a positive image that could be misleading. These include "Quality Circles", "Total Quality Management" and "team working". Perhaps they do raise productivity, but their downside should be understood.

The evidence shows that they can create cumulative trauma and disorders such as repetitive strain injuries. If they were called labour intensification schemes a negative image would be formed.

One of the effects of globalization is an increased rate of technological innovation under competitive pressures. Workers in the industries most affected, which means mostly in manufacturing, face an increased pace and intensity of work. There is also evidence that the changes in themselves tend to raise work insecurity in the implementation period, resulting in more work-related injuries and illnesses.[22,23]

7.6 The time squeeze and "stress"

The sheer amount of time that some people have to devote to their labour is a major aspect of work insecurity. One cause of work insecurity that has attracted considerable journalistic comment is prolonged working weeks and the re-emergence of long "shifts", even among office workers. This appears to have been greatest in the United States and the United Kingdom, but has characterized labour markets in many other countries.

Related to time pressures and overwork is mental strain. A little-noticed finding of an important report produced by the World Health Organization in 2001 was that depression has become the fourth most serious cause of premature death and disability in the world. Suicide is now seen as a major health problem, with a significantly higher rate among men in many countries. In Japan, *karoshi* (death from overwork) has been spreading. Perhaps the most shocking indicator of social distress in Japan is that in each of the last three years of the 20th century, over 30,000 people committed suicide —three times as many who died from traffic accidents. And it was reported that 5% of all suicide deaths in Japan were "company related".[24]

Time insecurity is a scourge of our age, and is a global phenomenon, though it takes very different forms in low-income schemes and in affluent industrialized economies. In the back streets of Ahmadebad, Gujarat, women outworkers work on average seven hours a day in paid work, but in addition have to wait on the street side for work for another three or four hours, spend one or more hours in travel to and from work, spend three hours in travel to and from the market, and three hours doing basic domestic chores, leaving about seven hours or less for sleep and relaxation each and every day. Such a lifestyle is debilitating.

[20]For examples of research showing these outcomes see R. Delbridge, P. Turnbull and B. Wilkinson: "Pushing back the frontiers: Management control and work intensification under JIT/TQM factory regimes", New Technology, Work and Employment, Vol. 7, No. 2, 1992, pp. 97–106; M. Parker and J. Slaughter: Working Smart: A Union Guide to Participation Programs and Reengineering (Detroit, Labor Notes, 1994).

[21]M.D. Brenner, D. Fairris and J. Ruser: 'Flexible' Work Practices and Occupational Safety and Health: Exploring the Relationship Between Cumulative Trauma Disorders and Workplace Transformation (Amherst, University of Massachusetts, Jan. 2001).

[22]D.I. Levine: Reinventing the Workplace (Washington, DC, Brookings Institution, 1995).

[23]P.S. Adler, B. Goldoftas and D.I. Levine: "Ergonomics, employee involvement and the Toyota production system: A case study of NUMMI's model introduction", Industrial and Labour Relations Review, Vol. 50, No. 3, 1997, pp. 416–437.

[24]Japan Times, 10 May 2003.

The poor have to spend more time on activities that are related to work but do not generate income. To compound the resulting inequality, they usually have to spend more time than richer people in order to obtain access to social services and face a poorer quality of service and treatment. They have to go long distances to find services and then have to wait longer for them.[25] In India, districts with high proportions of lower castes have fewer doctors and nurses, and health care workers are less likely to visit lower-caste and poor households.[26] While this is a matter of *basic security*, it is indicative of how the results of unsafe and debilitating work can be turned into a source of greater inequality.

In many parts of the world, the absence of protective mechanisms results in workers having to work long days and weeks. But what is less appreciated is that they are often obliged to work without breaks, which is particularly onerous. With this in mind, the PSS in Tanzania looked at the links directly by asking workers about work breaks. The data show that those not given breaks during working hours suffer more illness and injury problems than those granted breaks.[27]

In the industrialized world, consumerism produces relentless pressures that are contributing to labour intensification. A recent survey in the United Kingdom found that 42% of adults regularly worked more than 48 hours a week, and concluded that the demands of work, family and commuting made people feel that they were constantly trying to "catch up" with themselves. In 2002, more than 500,000 people said they were affected by stress at work, and 13.4 million working days were "lost" because of stress.[28]

While working time is still higher in South-East Asia than in western Europe, the gap seems to be shrinking, with working time growing in many industrialized countries. In the UK poll, 58% of women and 49% of men said that their long work-weeks made them too tired to enjoy their leisure time, with almost half saying they would like more sleep.

Above all, stress can only be magnified by the combination of labour intensification and precariousness that millions of people have to endure in all parts of the world. And according to epidemiological research, workers with stressful jobs — including jobs involving work in excess of 60 hours per week —

are much more likely to die from heart disease than those with non-stressful work.[29,30] There is also evidence that increases in workload coupled with a reduction in the person's control over his or her work can easily lead to deterioration in mental health.[31] It has even been found that long-term job strain is worse for a worker's heart than gaining 20 kilos in weight or ageing 30 years.[32] Yet, another study found that workers doing meaningless jobs with little or no opportunity for decision-making are more likely to die young than other workers.[33]

Overwork is not just found among the poor or manual workers. It is a malaise that also affects highly paid workers and affluent industrialized countries. Thus, there have been many reports of heart attack and death from overwork in numerous countries, including the United States, United Kingdom, India, New Zealand, Australia, China, the Philippines, Italy, Indonesia, and the Republic of Korea.[34]

---

[25] In El Salvador, for instance, the rural poor have to wait for three hours on average for access to primary health care, according to a World Bank study. M. Lewis, G. S. Eskeland and X. Traa-Valerezo: "Challenging El Salvador's rural health care strategy", *World Bank Policy Research Working Paper Series 2164* (Washington, DC, The World Bank, 1999).

[26] R. Betancourt and S. Gleaton: "The allocation of publicly-provided goods to rural households in India: On some consequences of caste, religion and democracy", *World Development*, Vol. 28, No. 12, 2000, pp. 2169–2182.

[27] Mushi, op. cit., 2003, pp. 12-13.

[28] The ICM Observer Precious Time Poll, reported in *The Observer* (London), 29 June 2003, p. 5.

[29] M. Kivimäki, P. Leino-Arjas, R. Luukkonen, H. Riihimäki, J. Vahtera and J. Kirjonen: "Work stress and risk of cardiovascular mortality: Prospective cohort study of industrial employees", *British Medical Journal*, Vol. 325, 19 Oct. 2002, p. 857.

[30] A. Spurgeon: *Working Time: Its Impact on Safety and Health* (Geneva, ILO, 2003).

[31] The Whitehall II Study, *Work Environment, Alcohol Consumption and Ill-Health* (London, HSE Contract Research Report 422, 2002).

[32] P.A. Landsbergis, P.L. Schnall, T.G. Pickering, K. Warren and J.E. Schwartz: "Life course exposure to job strain and ambulatory blood pressure among men", *American Journal of Epidemiology*, Vol. 157, No. 11, 2003, pp. 998–1006.

[33] B.C. Amick, P. Mcdonough, H. Chang, W.H. Rogers, C.F. Pieper and G. Duncan: "Relationship between all-cause mortality and cumulative working-life course psychological and physical exposures in the United States labour market from 1968–1992", *Psychosomatic Medicine*, Vol. 645, 2002, pp. 370–381.

[34] *Hazards Magazine* (Sheffield, United Kingdom), No. 83, July–Sep. 2003.

Transit stress, not transitory

Stress affecting health and well-being, has only recently begun to be given the attention it deserves in occupational health analysis. Many aspects of life can induce stress, which can lead to a greater susceptibility to illness, given the impact of stress on the human immune system, which can lessen bodily resistance. One contribution to stress is the time required to travel to and from work — commuting time — which, for many people around the world, uses up many hours each day. These "lost hours" obviously limit time for other necessary daily activities, including leisure, rest and sleep.

The table below provides findings from the PSS. Where commuting time exceeds one hour, the onset of stress is heightened. Thus, in the Russian Federation, men and women spend at least one hour per day travelling to and from work, with urban dwellers spending over an hour daily, and rural dwellers spending nearly an hour. In Bangladesh, men appear to spend slightly more time travelling to and from work than women (who spend nearly an hour a day), with rural dwellers spending an hour a day in travel, slightly more than urban dwellers. And as shown in Table 7.1, rural men in Bangladesh spend more time travelling to and from work than other groups, similar to rural men in Indonesia. In Tanzania, men reported spending well over two hours a day travelling to and from work, while women spend nearly two hours. Men in rural areas spend nearly three hours a day in transit, compared with male urban residents who spend nearly two hours each day. Tanzanian women do not fare much better. Both urban and rural female dwellers spend about two hours a day in transit. The figures for Tanzania and Ethiopia are not reported due to small sample sizes of respondents on this question. The situation in Ethiopia appears slightly better, where both men and women travel slightly less than one hour per day.

It is not only the time spent in travel that contributes to stress. The conditions in which one must travel also do so. Walking long distances in a hot climate is onerous and fatiguing. Crowded public transport, exposure to pollution, unforeseen delays, and risk of harassment or violence all contribute to physical stress, anxiety and nervous tension. The urgency with which a person needs to get to work, or return home, and lack of control over travel time and conditions are additional stressors.

Table 7.1 Travelling time to work (round trip), by gender and area, by country (hours spent on travel daily)

	Male	Female	Urban	Rural
Russian Federation	1.2	1.1	1.2	0.8
Ethiopia	0.8	0.8	n.a.	n.a.
Ghana	1.0	1.1	1.1	0.9
South Africa	0.3	0.3	0.3	0.3
Tanzania	2.2	1.8	1.7	2.4
Bangladesh	1.0	0.8	0.8	1.0
Indonesia	0.6	0.4	0.4	0.6

n.a. = not available   Source: SES PSS.

Time spent daily travelling to and from work, and the conditions of travel have a direct impact, usually negative, on one's free time. Sleep is often sacrificed in order to complete daily chores. The PSS in Gujarat provides a glaring example of this condition, where women reported having on average only five hours per day to sleep, after completing their work and family responsibilities, including child-care and preparation of meals. Stress can lead to sleep disorders, which exacerbate the problem, resulting in further loss of sleep.

Some observers, particularly those associated with trade unions, believe that modern technological systems are producing "space-time compression": for example, they claim that "Just-In-Time" delivery systems are eroding terms and conditions of employment and violating fundamental principles of sustainable development.[35] As noted in the last section, these systems tend to increase cumulative trauma disorders. Repetitive strain injuries also seem to go up when working time rises.[36]

The intensity of labour and the tendency to work long hours, whether driven by need, bosses or consumerism, is surely changing the incidence of types of adverse outcome associated with work insecurity.[37,38] Thus, it is widely expected that the top occupational diseases of the 21st century will be heart attacks, suicide and strokes.

The challenge of stress in labour is growing. However, now that it has been recognized as a major issue, corrective reforms will surely move up the policy agenda. In that regard, it is significant that Danish research has suggested a "holistic" approach, which focuses on the overall working environment rather than the narrow individual risk factors in the workplace.[39]

7.7 Society and work security

Societal security conditions work security and vice versa. In societies where violence and lawlessness prevail, or where there is political repression and incarceration, the mores and culture of work security in the workplace are unlikely to be strong.

More information is needed on the links between work and perceptions of personal safety. In Ukraine, the PSS asked a series of questions about physical safety in society. In their *workplace* 18% of industrial workers, 14% of agricultural workers and 13% of service sector workers said they felt insecure, with a further 24%, 27% and 22% respectively saying they were unsure. Only 39% of women said they felt secure at work compared with 42% of men. These figures are not encouraging.

In the *street in daytime*, a majority in Ukraine (60%) said they felt secure, with only 22% saying they felt insecure. There were no noticeable differences between men and women or between age groups. By contrast, in the *street at night*, less than one in four

adults said they felt secure — with merely 18% of urban residents feeling secure. As expected, women were less likely than men to feel secure — nearly two in every three feeling insecure. People mostly felt secure in their *home*, with 70% saying they felt secure there.

This is only one example. Ukraine is unlikely to be among the most insecure societies in this respect. People are generally relatively tolerant and well-inclined towards their neighbours and fellow workers. But these data highlight the fact that security within work and within society should be seen as closely interlinked. Security statistics should focus on those links.

Workplace violence is yet another scourge of present-day working life in countries around the globe (Table 7.2). In the United States, homicide is the second highest overall cause of workplace deaths and is the leading cause of workplace death for female workers.[40] Workplace violence now accounts for 15% of the more than 6.5 million violent acts experienced by US residents aged 12 or older.[41]

[35] W. Gereluk and L. Royer: *Sustainable Development of the Global Economy: A Trade Union Perspective"*, SES Paper No. 19 (Geneva, ILO, 2002).

[36] J. Rinehart, C. Huxley and D. Robertson: *Just Another Car Factory? Lean Production and Its Discontents* (Ithaca, ILR Press, 1997), p. 71.

[37] Institute for Labor and the Community: *Stop Stress at Work* (New York, 1999).

[38] Canadian Union of Public Employees: *Enough Workplace Stress: Organizing for Change* (Ottawa, 2003).

[39] LO Denmark: *Stress Can be Prevented.* <http//www.lo.dk/smcms/English version/News/4458/Index.htm?ID=4458>.

[40] L.B. Anderson and J.E. Smith: *Going Postal: Fact or Fiction?*, Presentation at the Society for Human Resource Management National Conference (Minneapolis, June 1998), pp. 2–9.

[41] R. Bachman: "Violence and theft in the workplace", *National Crime Victimization Survey* (Washington, DC, US Department of Justice, July 1994), pp. 1–2.

Table 7.2 nternational crime victim survey (ICVS) — Prevalence rates of victimization at the workplace, by type of incident, gender and region, 1996 (per cent of labour force)

	Assault Male	Female	Sexual incidents Female
Western Europe	2.7	3.0	5.4
North America	2.5	4.6	7.5
Eastern Europe	2.0	1.4	3.0
Asia	0.4	1.0	1.3
Africa	2.3	1.9	3.7
Latin America	1.9	3.6	5.2

Source: D. Chappell and V. Di Martino: Violence at Work, ICVS survey (Geneva, ILO, 2000), p. 27.

7.8 The inequality of work security

Overall inequality in society and across the world is intensified by the unequal incidence of work insecurity. Those who are disadvantaged in other respects, most notably in terms of income insecurity, also tend to be disadvantaged in this. The poor, those working in "informal" or precarious activities or labour relations, and those in small-scale low-income units of production are all more likely to be less secure. And one feature of work insecurity is that there are distinct gender differences, with women more likely to be disadvantaged in most respects.

The inequality applies to five aspects of work security. Workers are less likely to be *aware of hazards*, to be working in safe types of work (*safety in fact*), to have institutions protecting them (*safety protected*), less likely to be able to obtain compensation if an injury or illness occurs (*insecurity compensated*) and, finally, to be able to cope with adverse outcomes (*coping capacity*).

(i) Awareness

Even within each of those five aspects, inequalities multiply. Thus, the insecure worker is less likely to be aware of the dangers of any type of work, less likely to be aware that he or she is actually exposed to any particular danger, less likely to be aware of the actions that should be taken or not taken, of the opportunities or means of taking the appropriate action, of the means of compensation, and of the best means of coping and recuperating.

Even in industrialized economies, relatively low-qualified workers and migrants are often unaware of the work-relatedness of their ill health or injuries; they may anticipate difficulty in demonstrating work-relatedness of conditions, may assume incorrectly that having a non-benefited job excludes them from workers' compensation, or may assume correctly that their job in the informal economy complicates such coverage.[42] They are also largely unfamiliar with the procedures for obtaining compensation.

(ii) Differential security in fact

In most countries, casual agricultural workers are the least protected from many forms of insecurity and are the main victims of work insecurity, due to work being seasonal, physically demanding and more likely to involve exposure to chemicals. This was revealed to be the case in Tanzania[43] and in Gujarat, India.

Women are also among the least protected from multiple insecurities, including work insecurity. Yet for the reasons following, it is difficult to quantify the factors contributing to women workers' work insecurity compared to that of male workers. Gender-specific data on issues related to work security, particularly data on women workers, are extremely difficult if not impossible to obtain for the majority of countries. Little research exists to date on most jobs performed by women, particularly in

---

[42] Azaroff and Levenstein, 2001, op.cit.
[43] Mushi, 2003, op.cit.

relation to work-related health effects. Research on workers' health tends to concentrate on injuries and illnesses that cause lost work-time and have a clearly defined cause. This results in research generally focusing on traditional male jobs.[44] In most countries, women are concentrated in particular sectors of the economy — in service jobs, in selected areas of manufacturing and in agriculture. Within each of these areas of work there is a concentration of women in the jobs with the lowest pay and the least status. This has led one researcher to conclude that "as a result the impact of waged work on millions of women in both the formal and informal sectors of the global economy, continues to go unrecorded and unregulated".[45] This is despite the fact that many jobs performed exclusively or predominantly by women have an important physical component, which can produce pain and even disability.

Research, recognition and compensation are limited for women's work because the jobs usually assigned to women often lack dramatic, easily identifiable dangers, making women and women's jobs appear "safe".[46] Men have from three to ten times more compensated industrial accidents and injuries per worker than women.[47,48] These statistics are often interpreted to mean women's jobs are safer than men's, which may not be the case upon closer look.[49]

(iii) Differential protection

Most workers in the world lack proper protection in their workplaces. But the further down the income scale the less likely is the person to have access to a protective mechanism.

In general, women workers are in jobs or forms of labour that give them less protection against work insecurity than men.

Actual work security in the workplace starts with the basics. In the Enterprise Labour Flexibility and Security Surveys (ELFS) carried out in 2001-02, questions were asked on the provision of toilet facilities. They showed that a substantial number of firms, even modern so-called "formal" enterprises, do not provide separate toilet facilities for male and female workers, in countries such as Brazil, Chile, China, Indonesia, Pakistan, the Philippines and Tanzania. In Tanzania, 16% of industrial enterprises do not provide separate toilet facilities for male and fe-

male workers, often on the grounds that separate facilities were "too costly". This is a form of work insecurity, and no doubt is a basic source of work-related stress for women, in particular.

In Indonesian enterprises, according to the ELFS, the lack of basic facilities for women workers is oppressive. Thus,

- nearly 45% of enterprises do not have separate toilet facilities for male and female workers;
- 8% of enterprises said providing separate male/female toilet facilities is too costly;
- 5% do not provide separate toilet facilities because they are not required to do so by law;
- for employers providing separate toilet facilities, 10% provided them only because of union demand, or as a response to legislation.

Conditions are equally unsatisfactory in Pakistan, where the ELFS revealed that half of all enterprises do not have separate male/female toilet facilities. In enterprises that do provide separate facilities, 92% provided them as a response to legislation, with a mere 6% providing separate toilets voluntarily.

Meanwhile the Philippines ELFS showed that 12% of enterprises do not provide separate toilet facilities for male and female workers, with 13% of these enterprises saying that separate toilets would be too costly.

One message from these findings is that all countries should adopt legislation requiring that enterprises provide separate sanitary facilities for men and women. Evidence shows that many firms cite the mere existence of such legislation as their main motivation for complying.

[44] L.I. Boden: "Workers' compensation in the United States: high costs, low benefits", *Annual Review of Public Health*, Vol. 16, 1995, pp. 189–218.

[45] L. Doyal: *What makes women sick? Gender and the political economy of health* (London, Macmillan Press, 1995), p. 153.

[46] K. Messing: *One-Eyed Science: Occupational Health and Women Workers* (Philadelphia, Temple University Press, 1998).

[47] A. Pines, C. Lemesch and O. Grafstein: "Regression analysis of time trends in occupational accidents", *Safety Science*, Vol. 15, 1992, pp. 77–95. National Institute for Occupational Safety and Health: *Fatal Injuries to Workers in the United States, 1980–1989* (Washington DC, NIOSH, US Department of Health and Human Services, 1993).

[48] National Institute for Occupational Safety and Health: *Fatal Injuries to Workers in the United States, 1980–1989*, (Washington, DC, NIOSH, US Department of Health and Human Services, 1993).

[49] Messing, 1998, op. cit.

(iv) Differential compensation

When workers are hit by injury or illness at work, some are compensated for the costs but many are not. And those who are least likely to be compensated are those least able to afford the costs.

In many countries, the majority of workers are forced to bear the costs of work-related accidents or illness. According to the PSS, this is the case in Bangladesh, Brazil, Chile, China, India, Indonesia, the Republic of Moldova, Pakistan, the Philippines, Tanzania and Ukraine. Among urban transport workers in Pakistan, nearly all bear the costs of work-related accidents and this is in a context where 30% of workers described themselves as in poor or worsening health.[50] The findings highlight the widespread problem of employers not accepting responsibility for the health of their employees. The problem is also one of governance, where workers have no entitlement to benefits for work-related accidents or diseases.

This is one of the biggest forms of disadvantage faced by workers in developing countries, not recognized in conventional measures of income inequality, conventional data on workers' compensation, conventional occupational health and safety data, nor in enterprise cost analyses of work-related health measures. According to the PSS findings in numerous countries, it would appear that some enterprises could more appropriately be conducting "savings analyses" related to worker health, rather than "cost analyses".

Workers in African countries are among the least likely to have insurance against accidents or injury at work. Thus, in Tanzania the PSS showed that most workers are not insured against wage-work risks; in the event of a work accident 93% would have to pay for treatment themselves, although some thought their employer might help.[51] But even in Tanzania it is those in casual and other irregular labour relations who do worst of all. Thus, in formal enterprises, the probability of being entitled to employment accident and disease benefits from their employer was half as likely for non-regular as for regular workers.

Similar to the findings from Africa, the PSS in Gujarat, India showed that 93% of workers have no insurance against wage-work risks, leaving workers to bear the full cost of treatment for work-related illness or injury. Again emphasizing the inequality of

insecurity, rural women workers and casual workers bear a disproportionate share of this social burden. Where employers do pay for the medical treatment of work accidents, women are once more further disadvantaged compared with their already-disadvantaged male counterparts, with employers shouldering medical costs of 22% of work injuries for male workers, but paying only 7% of costs for women workers.

Among rural workers in Bangladesh, who are among the most insecure, over 80% have to pay out-of-pocket the full costs of treatment for work injuries.[52] In Indonesia, nearly 70% of workers are obliged to pay in full the cost of work-related accidents.

Even where workers are entitled to employer-provided medical services for work injuries or illness, often such services are not available in reality. The PSS in Hungary showed that 60% of workers are entitled to such benefits, but more than 20% never actually receive such services, obliging workers to pay for medical treatment themselves.

(v) Differential coping capacity

Among the poor, the inability to cope with adverse effects of work insecurity is demonstrated by the tendency for sick or injured workers to struggle on without taking leave. Thus, in Ghana, according to the PSS, about 68% of workers in rural Greater Accra, and over 44% of those in rural Ashanti report that they continue to go to work during ill health or injury simply because of fear of losing their income or job.[53] As for having protection at work, about eight out of ten in all areas have no protective clothing or equipment or any department or person responsible for health and safety.

---

[50] A. Sayeed and S. Javed: Work Security Issues Among Urban Transport Workers in Pakistan, SES Paper, (Geneva, ILO, forthcoming).

[51] Mushi, 2003, op.cit.

[52] M.E. Khan, U. Rob, and R. Anker: People's Security Survey in Bangladesh: Some Observations on Work Security in Rural Areas, SES Paper (Geneva, ILO, forthcoming).

[53] N.A. Apt and J.Y. Amankrah: Assessing Ghanaian Insecurities at the Household Level, paper presented at ILO workshop on Economic Security and Decent Work, Dar-es-Salaam, May 2003.

The PSS has revealed that significant numbers of workers in many countries are not entitled to paid sick leave: 40% of workers in Brazil, 29% in Argentina and 14% in the Russian Federation have no such entitlement. With no entitlement to paid leave when ill, workers will often delay seeking medical care for their illness until it becomes too serious to ignore. By that time a longer absence from work is not uncommon, usually bringing with it a greater loss in income and even potential job loss.

The effects of what we refer to as *presenteeism* (the opposite of "absenteeism") are insidious, for workers, co-workers, families and indeed for the public or clients that workers may encounter. In many eastern European countries, health workers come to work when ill because even one day of lost income is a matter of survival.[54] Without the basic security of being able to take the time to recuperate when ill, we need think only briefly to realize the potential for the spread of infection in workplaces, including hospitals, when sick workers are obliged to come to work. Such problems could easily be prevented.

The ELFS further reveals the potential extent of the problem of presenteeism, with non-regular workers, and workers in the informal economy disproportionately exposed to this form of insecurity compared to workers in formal employment. In Pakistan, 86% of firms do not provide paid sick leave to non-regular workers, and 53% do not pay their regular workers if they miss work due to illness. In Tanzania, 12% of firms have no provision for paid sick leave for regular workers and 30% indicated the same for non-regular workers. In the Philippines, 35% of firms do not pay their non-regular workers for missing work when ill.

There is a great deal of disparity in the ELFS on this issue. Findings from other countries where the survey asked about the entitlement to paid sick leave show that in Indonesia, only 5% of firms have no such benefit for regular workers, and 4% do not provide paid sick leave for non-regular workers.[55] Similarly in the Russian Federation, 22% of establishments have no entitlement to paid sick leave for temporary workers, while 5% do not provide such entitlement to part-time workers. In China, as revealed by the ELFS, 4% of workers had their employment terminated due to ill health or work-related accidents (one could imagine that the other 96% continue working when ill or injured in order to safeguard their jobs).

The global trends identified in Chapter 2 appear to be intensifying the inequality of work security. Thus, the informalization of labour relations surely reduces the coverage by proper work security institutions. Distance labour, through outwork and subcontracting, for instance, endangers people through such simple realities as self-exploitation and fatigue.

One stylized fact is that economic liberalization has been associated with a shift away from strongly enforced (if that ever existed) statutory regulation. Firms have been moving away from reliance on union-employer committees, a standard mechanism in ex-socialist countries and also widespread in many other industrialized countries. Similarly, the privatization of state industries and the privatization and liberalization of social services have intensified the inequality of work insecurity. The evidence has stacked up over the past decade.

The privatization and liberalization of health services, for example, have had pronounced consequences both for those providing and those receiving care by causing a marked decrease in health workers' security. The restructuring of health services under the pressure of liberalization has affected female workers disproportionately and created an increase in home care, where workers are mostly female, working part time, earning low wages, and having few health and safety protections. Increasingly, health sector workers are holding multiple jobs — in both the public and private sectors. The increase in the outsourcing of services and the use of flexible contracts has also had numerous detrimental effects.[56,57]

---

[54] C. Afford: *Corrosive Reform: Failing Health Systems in Eastern Europe* (Geneva, ILO, 2003).

[55] This, however, must be qualified. Indonesia is typical of an economy with a large proportion of the workforce in informal jobs. Most wage workers are likely to be in jobs covered by labour laws, providing entitlement to paid sick leave. The trouble is that few workers in Indonesia are in such types of jobs, but in the ELFS sample most firms were registered firms who may have simply indicated their compliance with existing legislation.

[56] J. Lethbridge: *Implications of Health Care Liberalization on Workers' Security*, work in progress, SES Paper (Geneva, ILO, forthcoming).

[57] International Social Security Association Research Programme: *Who Returns to Work and Why? Evidence and Policy Implications from a New Disability and Work Reintegration Study* (Geneva, 2002).

With liberalization comes a reduction of health services staff, increasing pressure on those workers remaining on the job. At the same time new management methods oblige health workers to spend less time with patients and workers often come to work when they are ill for lack of paid sick leave entitlements. All of these recent and growing trends have direct consequences for those receiving care as well.

Developments have been particularly worrying in eastern Europe, where pressure from international financial institutions has resulted in low state and local expenditure on public health services. East European countries spend an average of 5% of GDP on health, compared with the European Union average of 8%.[58] One of the most dramatic outcomes of these reform measures has been the catastrophic fall in life expectancy in countries such as the Russian Federation and Ukraine.

Findings from the region show that health the workers have experienced a widespread fall in their relative wages.[59] Wages are paid at or below minimum subsistence levels (physicians in the Republic of Moldova earn USD15 per month), wage arrears are common, job losses are widespread and "administrative leave" has been extensive, with workers told not to come to work because there is no money to pay them (particularly in Kyrgyzstan, Armenia and the Republic of Moldova). These outcomes have coincided with a significant fall in trade union membership across the region.

The study shows that health workers work under unacceptable working conditions with high levels of stress. They often work excessively long hours, with poor sanitation and infection control, often lacking heat, running water, medicines and food for patients in hospitals. As a result, the quality of patient care has deteriorated alarmingly.

Other reform trends include the introduction of social health insurance. Yet such measures have limited reach, extending only to those who can afford to pay the required contributions. The grim reality is that across the region health services are provided only with a cash or in-kind payment.

The PSS has helped to illuminate the increasingly global nature of this problem. While 88% of families in Ukraine and 82% of families in Hungary are unable to afford basic health care, in Ethiopia, Ghana, South Africa and Tanzania the biggest problem faced by families is the cost of health care. In Tanzania nearly two in every five households have insufficient income to pay for common health care needs.

Such findings are critical in the light of the increasing trend to liberalize health services. The focus of international investment in developing countries' health systems today is on drug-based, high technology care, while the majority of people still need *basic* health services.

Some policy recommendations to reverse the current trends include applying a public health approach, emphasizing prevention rather than drug-based, high technology treatments, focusing on universal access to health care, increasing investment in health care systems, and involving health workers' voice in policy and decision-making.

7.9 Harassment as work insecurity

One form of work insecurity that has received increasing attention is harassment, both physical, sexual and "moral". In general, women experience more of all three.

There is growing evidence and study of these phenomena. More is needed. We may cite just a few findings from the work being done in the ILO. In Tanzania, according to the PSS, women wage workers in the informal economy suffer higher rates of insecurity than men, with 19% suffering harassment often (verbal, physical and/or sexual); employers and supervisors are the main source of harassment.[60]

In many of the other PSS, women respondents reported that they had been subject to sexual harassment by co-workers or managers — Argentina, Brazil, Bangladesh, Chile Hungary, India, Indonesia

---

[58] ILO: *Health Care Privatization: Workers' Insecurities in Eastern Europe*, report of workshop, Geneva, 6–7 Dec. 2001, ILO Socio-Economic Security Programme and Public Services International (Geneva, 2001).

[59] Ibid.

[60] Mushi, 2003, op.cit.

and the Russian Federation. In Bangladesh 11% of women workers reported that they had been subjected to sexual harassment in the workplace. In China one in five female workers reported that they had been victims of verbal harassment or physical touching.

In most countries, it appears that most enterprises do not have specific policies to deal with sexual harassment in the workplace. The ELFS in Brazil, Chile, Indonesia and the Philippines bore this out; none of the firms covered had anything like a committee or department responsible for sexual harassment complaints. According to the PSS, large proportions of respondents in Argentina, Brazil, Chile and the Russian Federation expressed a wish for a workplace policy on sexual harassment.

It is important to recognize that harassment is not merely a matter of inappropriate behaviour by employers and managers towards workers, or women workers in particular. In many countries general workplace violence is a source of worker insecurity, as has been reported in Brazil and Chile; 15% of male workers in the Brazilian PSS reported that they had been victims of violence at work.

Harassment by government or local authority officials or the police, was also reported to be an important source of insecurity for workers in Tanzania, Bangladesh, India, Indonesia and Pakistan. This particularly affects those working in the informal economy as street vendors or outworkers, or those working in small-scale informal premises in urban areas.

7.10 The traumas of work insecurity

Musculoskeletal disorders, or MSDs, are rapidly becoming one of the prime causes of work-related injuries and diseases, affecting every sector of society at every income level.[61] On a global scale, the ILO estimates that musculoskeletal disorders account for 40% of total costs worldwide attributed to work-related injuries and diseases.[62] The European Agency for Safety and Health at Work estimates that 40% of European workers are affected by MSDs.[63] In the United States the number of repeated trauma cases rose steadily from 23,800 in 1972 to 332,000 in 1994 — a 14-fold increase.[64]

Musculoskeletal disorders are the leading workplace hazard in European workplaces today, with more

women workers employed in jobs with a risk of MSD than males.[65] Static loads on the muscles contribute to MSDs.[66] Globally, women workers are the most exposed to static postures, with a higher prevalence among low and unskilled workers.[67]

Stress and muscular tensions result from problems of work organization.[68] Performing monotonous rapid-pace work, with little control over work hours or conditions of employment, has been associated with stress, higher incidence of alcohol-related or gastrointestinal illness, and hospitalization from heart attack.[69] Results of a ten-year study showed that women with "high-strain" jobs were nearly three times more likely to develop coronary heart disease than workers in other jobs.[70,71] A 1993 OECD review of key studies on women's work and health revealed that women are

[61]E. Rosskam: *Working at the Check-In: Consequences for Worker Health and Management Practices* (Lausanne, University of Lausanne Press, 2003).

[62]International Labour Office, InFocus Programme on SafeWork (Geneva, ILO, 1999). This is available on <http://mirror/public/english/protection/safework/cis/oshworld/xvwc/intrep.htm>

[63]European Agency for Safety and Health at Work: *Monitoring the State of Occupational Safety and Health in the European Union — Pilot Study* (Luxembourg, Office for Official Publications of the European Communities, 2000).

[64]United States Bureau of Labor Statistics, 1997.

[65]European Foundation for the Improvement of Living and Working Conditions: *Second European Survey of Working Conditions* (Dublin, European Foundation for the Improvement of Living and Working Conditions, 1996).

[66]S. Snook: "The practical application of ergonomics principles", *Minesafe International*, 1993.

[67]O. Heran-Le Roy and N. Sandret: "Résultats de l'enquête Summer 94: Les contraintes articulaires pendant le travail", *Documents pour le médecin du travail*, No. 71, 3e trimestre, 1997.

[68]For discussion of stress and work organization, see Rosskam, 2003, op. cit.

[69]L. Alfredsson, C.L. Spetz and T. Theorell: "Type of occupation and near future hospitalization for myocardial infarction and some other diagnoses", *International Journal of Epidemiology*, Vol. 14, No. 3, 1985, pp. 378–388.

[70]S. Haynes, A. LaCroix and T. Lippin: "The effect of high job demands and low control on the health of employed women", in J. Quick, R. Bhagat, J. Dalton and J. Quick (eds.): *Work, Stress and Health Care* (New York, Praeger Press, 1987).

[71]A. LaCroix and S. Haynes: "Gender differences in the health effects of work-place roles", in R. Barnett, L. Biener and G. Baruch (eds.): *Gender and Stress* (New York, The Free Press, 1987).

more exposed to monotonous repetitive work than men, and that women's work content often can be characterized as high in demand but with a low level of control by workers. Also revealing is that in typically male-dominated jobs the workplace is designed for male body size and male norms, including most work-tables and workstations where women work.[72]

In the United States women make up 46% of the workforce and 33% of those injured at work. Yet they bear a disproportionate burden, 63%, of repetitive motion injuries that result in lost work time (47,408 injuries out of 75,188). Musculoskeletal disorders account for nearly half of all lost work-time injuries and illnesses among women.

Table 7.3. United States: Ergonomic injuries among women, 1997

Description of injury	Number of injuries causing lost work time to women
Carpal tunnel syndrome	20 584
Tendonitis	11 054
Injury due to repetitive motion	47 408
Injury due to repetitive typing or keyboard entry	10 131
Injury due to repetitive placing/grasping	14 950
Injury due to repetitive use of tools	5 117

Source: United States Bureau of Labor Statistics: Lost Work time Injuries and Illnesses, 1997.

7.11 A Workplace Work Security Index

How should we measure work security at the workplace? We can estimate a composite *workplace work security index*, which is an attempt to create a benchmarking system for how well firms are doing, relatively, in providing work security to a country's employed population. One of the main input indicators in establishing such a measure should be the existence of a department or committee in the workplace dealing with occupational health and safety. The main outcome indicators should be something like the number of *accidents* per 100 workers in a year and the number of *workdays* lost due to accidents, injuries and work-related ill health.

It should be a standard policy requirement that all registered firms should collect and report such information in easily understood and easily accessible forms. This should also be part of the corporate social responsibility (CSR) movement; firms preparing CSR reports should not only report their own accidents and occupational illnesses but also exert moral suasion on their suppliers to do the same.

[72]K. Messing (ed.): Integrating Gender in Ergonomic Analysis: Strategies for Transforming Women's Work, (Brussels, European Trade Union Confederation, Technical Bureau for Health and Safety, 1999).

A Workplace Work Security Index

In all the countries covered by the ELFS, there are data on firms' mechanisms and outcomes on work security. There have been some differences in the degree of detail covered, and account has been taken of national institutional differences. The Workplace Work Security Index (WWSI) was defined, for example, in the case of China where there was a more detailed set of questions on occupational safety and health than in other countries where the survey was conducted. The WWSI has been calculated in the following way:

WWSI = SAFETY + ACCID + ACC.CL + ACC.D

where

SAFETY = 2 if there was a safety committee and safety department,

1 if there was a safety committee or department, but not both, 0 otherwise;

ACCID = 1 if the number of work accidents as a proportion of the workforce was less than the mean average, 0 otherwise.

ACC.CL = 1 if there was any accident in the past year that resulted in the closure of the establishment for one day or more, 0 otherwise.

ACC.D = 1 if there were any accidents at work that resulted in one or more deaths, 0 otherwise.

For eastern Europe, only the first two indicators were used. For Brazil, Chile, Indonesia, Pakistan and the Philippines a more simplistic calculation was required due to the limited number of questions on work security in the surveys there. It gave a value of 1 for firms that had a below-average number of work-related accidents in the past year expressed as a percentage of total employment, 0 otherwise. In Tanzania, an approach was designed to take account of the more "informal" nature of many establishments. For example, the most basic sign of concern for health and safety is the presence of a toilet on the premises. An indicator for this was supplemented by an indicator on the presence of a childcare facility and of a health clinic in the establishment.

Questions related to work security from the ELFS in China, Tanzania, the Russian Federation and Brazil exemplify key trends in work security in four regions of the world. First, as illustrated in the case of China in Figure 7.2, firms that pay relatively high wages also tend to provide a high degree of work security. Second, firms scoring higher on the work security index in China have higher unionization rates. As noted earlier in this chapter, unionized workplaces tend to be safer workplaces.

Figure 7.2 China: Average wage, by work security index (all regions)

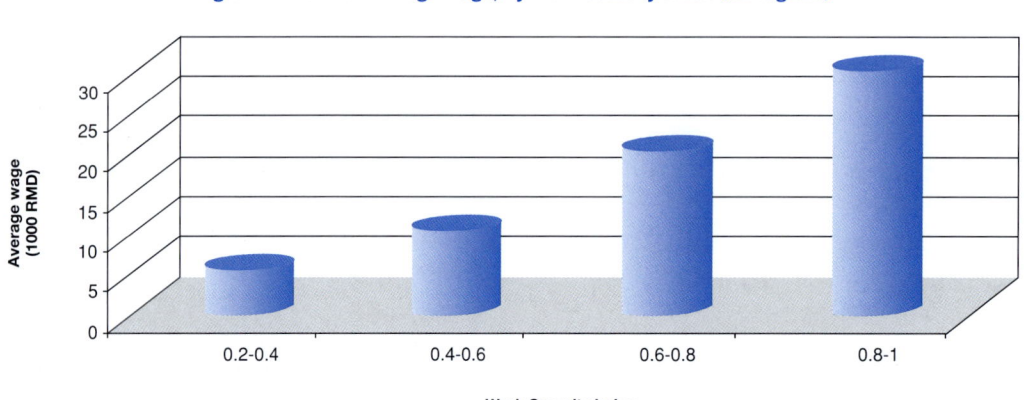

Source: China ELFS 2001.

Third, firms that are entirely or majority publicly owned tend to pay greater attention to work security, a pattern found most strongly in the Brazil and Tanzania ELFS where publicly owned firms scored higher on the work security index than private and foreign-owned firms.

Fourth, larger firms tend to be safer firms because they are able to operate departments or committees devoted to safety. This was revealed in the China and the Russian Federation ELFS, where firms of over 300 and 500 employees respectively scored higher on the work security index compared with firms having fewer employees. Results from the Tanzania ELFS showed less of an association, probably due to the relatively small size of most firms in that country.

Fifth, in Tanzania, China and Russian Federation, firms attributing a higher percentage of their total production costs to labour tended to score higher on the work security index. Basically, this means that those firms trying to pay as little as possible for the cost of labour, as a way to reduce the total cost of production, also tend to provide worse overall working conditions. Thus, the percentage of the total cost of production dedicated to labour appears to be positively associated with the quality of working conditions overall.

Sixth, as revealed most strikingly in Brazil, firms in services (finance, trade, business services) tend to score higher on the work security index than other industries. These industries are well known to have less onerous working conditions than manufacturing, construction and mining.

In sum, we can say that firms paying higher average wages, having high unionization rates, that are publicly owned, that have a large number of employees, that attribute a higher percentage of their production costs to labour, and firms in certain industries, tend to pay greater attention to work security and provide better working conditions than firms not having these characteristics.

7.12 The national Work Security Index

Although it is impractical to imagine a Work Security Index (WSI) that takes account of all the issues raised in this chapter, it is possible to estimate a national index that captures the essentials. Governments and other policy-driving groups could use such an index to identify how best to target efforts aimed at improving work security. The WSI can help to rationalize the use of scarce resources by seeing where their allocation might make the greatest impact. Examining the outcomes for countries in the same region, with similar conditions, could help them gain information and even tips on how to make significant improvements in their own work security outcomes.

The national Work Security Index estimated for this report consists of 11 input indicators, seven of which are the relevant ILO Conventions. The other four input indicators are relevant national laws on occupational safety and health (OSH) and other laws requiring the establishment of occupational health services, protecting disabled workers from discrimination, limiting hours of work, restricting night work, providing maternity protection and guaranteeing paid leave. Note that a country may have a national law requiring the existence of occupational health services without having ratified the corresponding international Convention. Note also that the ILO Conventions outline the minimum protections prescribed but it may well be that a law is not as protective as it may need to be.

Then there are three process indicators, namely, the level of government expenditure on workers' compensation, the existence of disability or invalidity benefits provided to workers injured in work-related accidents, and the existence of bipartite or tripartite occupational safety and health boards or committees.

Outcomes are represented by the five following indicators: the work-related fatal injury rate;[73] a categorical variable with five codes corresponding to estimated levels of fatal injury under-reporting; the share of wage employment in total employment, used as a proxy for the proportion of the population having guaranteed compensation for occupational injury; the average reported working time; and average annual paid leave (vacation days) corrected by the relative size of wage employment.

---

[73]This refers to the number of fatal injuries per 100,000 workers. Some regional estimates have been made to reduce the number of missing values.

The following paragraphs provide a more in-depth description of and justification for the indicators used in the Work Security Index.

Input indicators

1. *Existence of a national law on occupational safety and health:* mandating government regulation of occupational safety and health is a fundamental starting point for the protection of workers against work-related hazards. The elements of the law vary, but countries taking worker protection seriously and with responsibility consider the enactment of such a law primordial.

2. *Existence of a national law requiring the establishment of occupational health services:* such a law is indicative of a more advanced level of worker protection. Since all of the developed countries have today a basic OSH law, we have used this variable as a means of discriminating between countries having only the "bare minimum" (i.e. a law but no further provisions to protect workers' health) and those having established more sophisticated systems. The legal mandate for occupational health services is found among countries with the better systems of worker protection in place. Workers injured on the job, or ill due to workplace exposures, deserve health services dedicated to their care, with health providers specially trained in diagnosis and treatment of work-related illnesses. Workplace-based or community-based occupational health services are also a proven means of preventing adverse work-related health outcomes.

3. *Existence of a national law to protect disabled workers from discrimination:* workers who become disabled due to work injuries, accidents or work-related disease, or who are disabled for other reasons, such as handicaps from birth or from non-work related accidents, are often subject to discrimination, overt or covert, making it more difficult or even impossible to secure employment. Without a means of generating income, disabled workers can quickly fall into a poverty trap, which often catalyses wider impacts on families and society who bear the costs in one form or another. Legal protection for such workers is a minimum and fundamental element of work security. Workers should not be penalized for any disability, whether work-induced or otherwise. They are entitled to the same human rights as any other citizen, and deserve special protection.

4. *Existence of a national law limiting hours of work:* regulating working hours is the basis of the very first Convention adopted by the International Labour Conference. Legal restriction on how much an employer may demand of a worker is fundamental to protecting workers' health and well-being. History demonstrates that without such regulations workers are left exposed to extreme forms of exploitation. A legal limit on working time is one of the fundamental measures of a civil society.

5. *Existence of a national law restricting night work:* night work is proven to be less healthy than day work. Night work is contrary to human biorhythms, and is considered unsocial in terms of working hours. It is often accompanied by numerous adverse health consequences and is associated with family and social problems. Women are particularly vulnerable during night work, requiring special protections to ensure their safety, including travelling to and from work. The regulation of night work has become more complex and more difficult with increases in production and consumption in many countries.

Management techniques that have evolved together with these market tendencies further complicate the enforcement of night work. In particular, "Just-In-Time" policies, work intensification, zero-stock policies, and more intense marketing and competition all contribute to the justification by management of employing workers around the clock. Simultaneously, a vast array of social services, from health care and law enforcement to the availability of food and other consumer goods, have evolved in parallel with the increase in shiftwork.

6. *Existence of a national law mandating paid maternity leave:* pregnant workers require legal and financial protection to cover periods during and after pregnancy, to protect them from work environments that may be hazardous to their health or the health of the foetus, and to protect them from discriminatory actions resulting in job loss due to maternity.

7. *Existence of a national law guaranteeing paid leave:* societies plagued by overwork and lack of paid leave for rest periods, with a minimum of income security, experience high rates of ill-health and social malaise. Without laws guaranteeing workers the right to paid leave, extreme exploitation of

workers is a likely occurrence, with consequences for individuals, families, employers, governments and society. Ill health is a direct outcome of the lack of paid leave entitlement, resulting in overwork. The mere existence of a law mandating the provision of paid leave does not necessarily mean that the law is as protective as it may need to be. ILO Convention No. 132 "Holidays With Pay (Revised), 1970" outlines the minimum protections prescribed and internationally agreed upon.

National laws regulating paid leave should provide at least the minimum amount of paid leave outlined in Convention No. 132. A country may have a national law guaranteeing the provision of paid leave, without having ratified Convention No. 132. Paid leave is available primarily to workers in the formal economy, and is often lacking for workers in many types of work found in the informal economy. We have used the percentage of wage workers as an attempt to equalize the measure of paid leave.

Process indicators

1. *Level of government expenditure on workers' compensation, as a percentage of GDP.* Prevention is the first line of defence against work-related accidents, injuries and diseases. However, where work-induced adverse health outcomes or accidents do result from work-related exposures, adequate compensation for affected workers is a key means of protecting their basic security.

The level of government expenditure on workers' compensation is higher where GDP is higher, although the generosity of benefits per capita and per injury/illness varies greatly among countries. Higher government expenditure on workers' compensation does not necessarily indicate a higher rate of accidents, injuries, illnesses, or a weaker or relatively unhealthy population. Rather it is more often indicative of the existence of an operative structure, whereby workers can make claims, and where a list of covered injuries/illnesses is established nationally.

Conversely, a low level of government expenditure on workers' compensation is not usually indicative of a low level of accidents, injuries and illnesses. It is more indicative of a low level of GDP, which acts as a barrier to the government paying benefits to injured workers. It may also indicate a lack of reporting/notification structures or, where such mechanisms exist, a lack of effective implementation. Low expenditure on workers' compensation may further indicate the absence of trade unions or other organizations for workers, such that workers may not be aware that a compensation system exists, or how to use it. Finally, low government expenditure on workers' compensation also may reflect a preponderance of low-risk activities, such as subsistence farming, in which dangerous machines and chemicals may not be commonly used.

2. *Existence of labour-management, tripartite or bipartite occupational safety and health boards or committees.* To ensure that laws translate into protection of workers' health, a variety of mechanisms are needed to reach employers and workers at the level of the workplace. One of the most fundamental mechanisms is a tripartite or bipartite board or a labour-management safety and health committee. Where these mechanisms exist, usually requiring a legal mandate, social dialogue and consultation are used as means of addressing and solving problems both locally and nationally. Such methods are well established as efficient and cost-effective for employers, workers and governments. Worker participation in implementing health and safety regulations is, furthermore, an element of a just society, for where consultation with workers is systemic and systematic, the rights of workers are more likely to be recognized and respected, and productivity is usually higher.

Furthermore, workers are shown to be healthier when they are able to participate in decision-making. Conversely, when workers are not included in decision-making about workplace exposures, and how work is organized and carried out, ill health and reduced productivity are demonstrated outcomes, bringing with them negative consequences for employers, workers and society. Additionally, joint labour-management or tripartite OSH mechanisms are an effective means of monitoring the implementation of national laws and regulations. Such monitoring can ultimately reduce the numbers of penalties imposed on employers through sanctions for infringement of protective laws.

3. *The existence of disability or invalidity benefits provided to workers injured in work-related accidents.* This is a measure of how well workers

are protected in the event they are injured at work. Where workers are not provided with disability or invalidity benefits following a work-related accident, insecurity is almost guaranteed to follow. However, the fact that benefits are provided does not indicate whether the benefits are sufficient or even whether they are commensurate with the incident. A token benefit for the loss of an eye or limb, for example, is further injustice to a worker who has already suffered the gross injustice of disability or invalidity caused by his/her work, particularly considering that all accidents are preventable.

There is a strong element of social justice associated with this particular variable, as the responsibility to protect workers' health rests first and foremost with the employer, as defined by Convention No. 155 "Occupational Safety and Health, 1981, and agreed upon by the member States of the ILO.

Outcome indicators

1. *The work-related fatal injury rate*[74] is a simple fraction of the number of fatal injuries per 100,000 workers. Work-related fatality data, as reported by a number of countries, have been used. For countries still lacking such reporting, fatal injury rates have been estimated based on neighbouring countries of a similar size, and with similar conditions, in a given region.

2. *The estimated level of under-reporting of fatal injuries* is a categorical variable, with five codes corresponding to estimated levels of fatal injury under-reporting. This is based on the knowledge that most countries lack the means of collecting and recording injury data, including fatal injury data, in a systematic and reliable manner. Countries with large informal economies, in particular, have thus far found it difficult if not impossible to collect and register such data.

An additional difficulty is the recognition of many fatalities as work-related. While this may be obvious in the case of a sudden traumatic event, such as a fall from a height, in many cases some investigation is needed to make the causal association (vehicle-related accidents, poisonings, death from fire sparked off in the workplace, and so on). In countries without a system for reporting such incidents to a competent authority, or where trade union structures are weak, the likelihood of

such investigations being conducted is low. Many countries also lack trained workers (medical, legal, or otherwise) to carry out such investigations. Given the large scope for under-reporting of work-related fatalities, estimates were developed to correct for the expected degree of under-reporting of individual countries.

3. *Proportion of the population guaranteed coverage by workers' compensation for work injury.* The share of employees out of the total number of workers performing income-earning activity is used as a proxy for this. The more coverage of workers' compensation is extended throughout the active labour force in a society, the more security is afforded to workers. This variable is not a measure of what percentage of a population is currently collecting workers' compensation. Rather it is a measure of the extent of protection extended to society at large, in the event such compensation is needed. Non-coverage of significant groups in society, such as those working in the informal economy, or older workers and child workers, leave workers extremely vulnerable if they suffer a work-related incident.

4. *Average reported working time* is a means of gauging how well countries are doing in respecting their own working time laws, where laws exist. With or without a law, average working time will indicate the degree to which workers are being overworked and exploited. Working 45 hours per week is considered the limit, above which damage to physical and psychological health has been demonstrated. Data on working time are often expressed in different ways ("hours worked", "normal", "actual" and "usual" hours of work). In order to gather enough data for this variable, a combination of these expressions of working time has been adopted, excluding "usual hours" as this conflicts with the other definitions which are either the same or very close in measurement.

5. *Average paid leave (vacation days) taken by workers* is a measure of the importance given to the physical and psychological well-being of workers. Workers in countries that are more oriented towards social benefits are entitled to and take more paid vacation days, to rest and

---

[74]Some regional estimates have been made to reduce the number of missing values.

recuperate from the cumulative effects of work. Where workers are not provided with paid vacation days, loss of income may create severe hardship and be a strong deterrent to taking time off from work to rest and refresh the mind and body. Family and community well-being are associated with allowances for time off from work. As this protection applies mainly to employees, the indicator was corrected for the relative size of wage employment.

In all, 95 countries are covered by the Work Security Index. The work security performance of these countries and the measure of their performance in protecting workers' health and well-being is presented in Table 7.4. Several comments can be made on the results of the WSI.

As expected, western European countries have the highest scores, making up entirely the cluster of "Pacesetters". Top performers are Luxembourg, Norway, Sweden, Finland and Denmark. There are no "Pacesetters" in any other region. Eastern Europe and the Americas are the regions having the best performing industrializing or transition economies: Argentina, Barbados, Chile, Czech Republic, Estonia, Hungary, Latvia, Lithuania and Slovakia. These countries are classified as "Pragmatists". As such, by definition, they have relatively weak legislation related to work security, or on mechanisms to ensure the application of the laws, but still achieve good results in the outcome measures.

By contrast, however, over two-thirds of the countries in our list have unsatisfactory levels of work security. The latter are classified as "Conventionals" or "Much-to-be-done", in almost equal numbers. These two clusters contain countries from all regions (except western Europe) and all countries from Africa and Middle East (except Israel, which is a "Pragmatist") as well as from Asia (except Asian OECD countries, which are also "Pragmatists").

The "Conventionals" could be considered as "average" performers in that they have satisfactory institutional or legislative mechanisms and/or satisfactory mechanisms for implementing those norms, but nonetheless perform rather poorly on the outcome measures. Probably for historical reasons the majority of African and Latin American countries come under this label.

Finally, the most critical cases are in the category of "Much-to-be-done", which takes in the most deprived countries from the African continent, Asia and eastern Europe. The countries of eastern Europe have a history of strong legislation on the various aspects of work security, including nearly 100% trade union membership until the fall of communism. Some of the other countries, particularly those in Asia, have more recently upgraded what were basic factory acts carried over from colonial periods to include other laws on work security. Yet the results show that, while laws and mechanisms may exist, alone they are insufficient to protect workers' health.

Table 7.4 Work Security Index

	High score on Outcome			
	High score on Input/ Process		**Low** score on Input/ Process	
Regions	**Pacesetters Countries**		**Pragmatists Countries**	
Africa and Middle East			Israel	
Americas			Argentina Barbados Canada	Chile United States
Asia			Australia Japan	New Zealand
Eastern Europe and Central Asia	Slovenia		Czech Republic Estonia Hungary	Latvia Lithuania Poland Slovakia
Western Europe	Belgium Denmark Spain Finland France Germany Iceland	Italy Luxembourg Netherlands Norway Portugal Switzerland Sweden	Austria Greece	Ireland United Kingdom

	Low score on Outcome			
	High score on Input/ Process		**Low** score on Input/ Process	
Regions	**Conventionals Countries**		**Much-to-be-done Countries**	
Africa and Middle East	Algeria Benin Burkina Faso Burundi Congo Côte d'Ivoire Egypt Ethiopia	Ghana Lebanon Madagascar Morocco Nigeria Senegal Sierra Leone	Guinea-Bissau Mauritania Mauritius Rwanda	South Africa Tunisia Turkey Zimbabwe
Americas	Brazil Colombia Costa Rica Ecuador	Mexico Peru Venezuela	Dominican Republic Honduras	Panama Saint Kitts and Nevis
Asia	Bangladesh Korea, Republic of	Pakistan	China India Indonesia Nepal	Philippines Sri Lanka Thailand
Eastern Europe and Central Asia	Azerbaijan Belarus Croatia Kyrgyzstan	Russian Federation Tajikistan Ukraine	Albania Armenia Bulgaria Georgia Kazakhstan	Moldova, Republic of Romania Turkmenistan Uzbekistan
Western Europe				

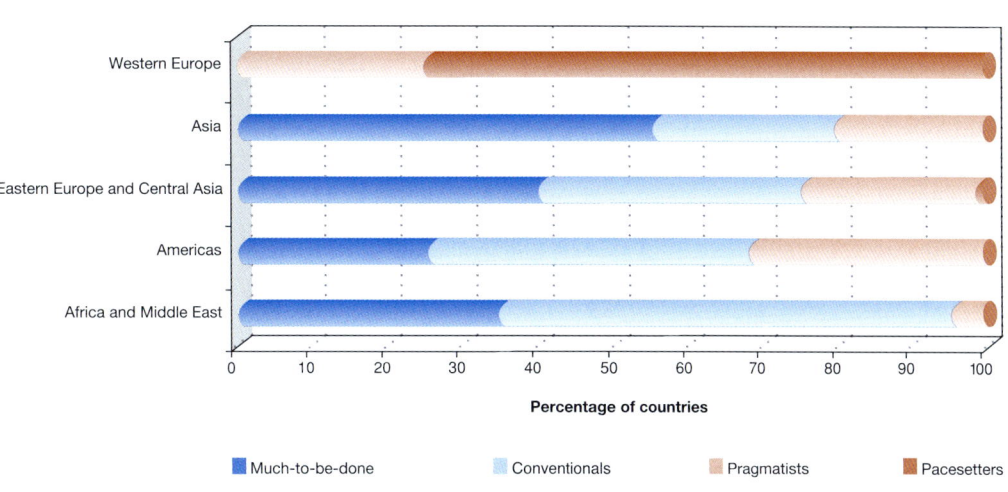

Figure 7.3 Work security index: clusters by region

■ Much-to-be-done   ■ Conventionals   ■ Pragmatists   ■ Pacesetters

7.13 Conclusions

Work security remains among the world's great aspirations. It seems a long way away. In the poorest areas of the world, the deprivations associated with poverty and the disasters that people face daily feed into chronic insecurity in the spheres of work and labour. In the industrializing countries economic liberalization, privatization and many other aspects of globalization have brought new challenges that have scarcely been met. In the affluent countries consumerism and workaholism have induced crises of stress often verging on self-destruction in labour through suicide and heart disease, in particular.

Many, many people — almost certainly more than ever before — are unprotected against workplace risks. Yet this is quite unnecessary and entirely preventable, since the costs of ensuring safer conditions are not onerous. It is possible, feasible and cost-effective to do better.

It is scarcely alarmist to conclude that new strategies are needed for dealing with well-known hazards and risks, such as those from dangerous substances, machinery and tools, and manual handling, as well as for emerging issues, such as biological hazards, psycho-social hazards and musculoskeletal disorders. What is also clear is that most countries in the world could also do much better in adhering to strategies that have been moderately successful in those Pacesetter countries identified in this chapter.

Chapter 8

Skills security

8.1 Introduction

Skill reproduction security is considered as a situation where there is a wide range of opportunities for training, apprenticeship and education to acquire and refine knowledge and competencies. It means assured access to basic education as well as vocational training, with the aim of enabling people to develop their capacities and acquire the qualifications needed to exercise a socially and economically valuable occupation. Another way of looking at it is to say that a person has skills security if he or she has ownership and control over the property rights in competencies.

The idea of *educational poverty* has emerged in recent years, with definitions of absolute and relative educational poverty. This has led to the concept of *precarious educational poverty*, where a large part of the population of a country hover just above an educational poverty line. In many respects, the idea of skill reproduction security echoes that way of thinking.

Skills security is also related to two of the Millennium Development Goals and the *Education for All* (EFA) commitment made at the World Education Forum in Dakar, Senegal, in April 2000, reaffirmed in the Millennium Declaration in New York in September 2000. These goals are to achieve universal primary education for all and to eliminate gender disparities in primary and secondary schooling by 2015.

This chapter first considers the major trends in education under the impact of globalization. It then looks at some relatively unnoticed aspects of skills, in particular through the People's Security Surveys (PSS), before presenting the results of a national Skills Security Index as applied to the 139 ILO member countries for which data are available.

8.2 Education, schooling and "human capital"

The words "human capital" have crept into the English language and into policy-making with deceptive ease. Too often this term and "schooling" are treated as synonymous with *education*. The latter term must be rescued. To be educated is more than to be able to obtain, perform and retain a job. In thinking about skill and capability, we must avoid thinking simply or solely about credentials attained through formal schooling.

In this respect, since he is so often used as a reference point, it is noteworthy that the father of economics, Adam Smith, regarded education very differently from the modern neo-classical economist. He saw education as the means of helping people understand their society and culture. It was not to make money. This is a modern preoccupation.

Basic education is first of all about the capacity to *survive functionally*, the capacity to *understand*, to create and take *opportunity*; the capacity to *develop*, the capacity to cope with adversity, and the capacity to *recover* from it. "Human capital" is the capacity to be employed, to make money, to compete, to win. It is the capacity to be opportunistic. An educated person is someone to whom somebody in need would turn, for assistance, for advice or for comfort. Educated people are more "free".

Skill is not just about obtaining a job, or making more money; it is about providing other forms of security, including the capacity to live. Thus, literacy leads to better decision-making and to greater awareness and practice of good health.[1] Learning about culture may not increase earnings, but it teaches how to enjoy the beauty of the world and how to survive in it.

Education and skill must be rescued from "human capital". The global trends suggest that this should be the most pressing task and challenge for those wishing to see basic security for all. Moreover, it should be recognized that the world's experts simply do not know about the size of the world's pool of skills. No country has good statistics on the level or distribution of skills, and the proxy measures that have to be used are crude.

Is skill security increasing?

With all the emphasis on the need for more schooling and more training, and with the Washington Consensus view that there should be a shift from social protection spending to "human capital" enhancement, the answer to this question might be expected to be "yes".

In fact, we simply do not know. Statistical information on quality of education and on the possession of "skills" is remarkably crude or absent altogether.

This information is improving. UNESCO is producing an annual "Education for All" Monitoring Report. And for industrialized countries the PISA data are an important means of monitoring educational poverty.[2]

8.3 Globalization and "human capital"

Education is a "trust good". This means that a person seeks to obtain it without knowing what will be received, and usually without being able to determine what is received. If sold as a "service" such a good becomes a "commodity of trust". Those receiving it do not have a clear idea of its utility or quality, and must trust the provider. Thus anyone trying to obtain an educational service, even if he or she does not pay for it directly, faces a risk, and because a risk implies a lower value for the service on offer, that will lower demand for it. If commodified through privatization or user fees, demand will fall further.

Moreover, if competition is fostered between education providers, potential students will have to decide between competing providers and also between educational services and other uses of their time. The resultant transaction costs will be a disincentive to the pursuit of education.

In that context, both the Washington Consensus and globalization have had profound effects on the development of education and skills development more generally. Cuts in government spending resulted in cuts in educational spending in many countries, even though there was encouragement for a shift to edu-

cation from other spheres of social policy. Thus, for example, there were cuts in welfare expenditure and cuts in public education in South Africa, both as shares of the overall government budget and in real terms.[3]

The World Bank's role has been pervasive. Until the 1960s, it stayed out of education, rejecting all requests for loans. Since then, it has become the largest multilateral donor agency in education. Although lending for education started with the creation of the International Development Association in 1960, the policy took off in the 1970s when the Bank became the lead player. Whereas UNESCO, the body supposedly setting the international agenda, had promoted the right to education, the Bank

---

[1] See, inter alia, P. Glewwe: "Why does mother's schooling raise child health in developing countries? Evidence from Morocco", *Journal of Human Resources*, Vol. 34, No. 1, 1999, pp. 124–159.

[2] Data from PISA (Programme for International Student Assessment) allow international comparative assessments of basic competencies. See, for example, J. Allmendinger and S. Leibfried: "Education and the welfare state: The four worlds of competence production", *Journal of European Social Policy*, Vol. 13, No. 1, Feb. 2003, pp. 63–81.

[3] L. Van der Walt: "GEAR versus social security", *South African Labour Bulletin*, Vol. 24, No. 5, 2000.

focused on human capital and rates of return on "investment". Initially, it was required to take account of UNESCO's studies, but this soon faded.[4] Later, it set up a central education unit, which focused on efficiency and rates of return, leading to promotion of privatization, liberalization and cost-cutting.

The World Bank's policy on education crystallized in 1986 with the publication of its *Financing Education in Developing Countries: An Exploration of Policy Options*. This had three policy prescriptions: (i) government spending should be redirected to basic education, implying *inter alia* that costs should be recovered from higher education, primarily through fees; (ii) a credit market should be developed for loans and scholarships for students from low-income families; and (iii) management of public education should be decentralized. Later, the Bank also encouraged governments to de-link the teaching professions from civil service pay scales and to use non-union teachers.[5] Many believe that the Bank has thereby encouraged a tendency to casualize teachers' working conditions.[6]

The OECD followed suit, advocating tuition fees, a market-oriented approach and outcome-based quality assessment. It encouraged the removal of the divide between higher education and vocational training, arguing that the supply of education should match the demand patterns of the labour market. It even advocated the replacement of the term "higher education" by "tertiary education", to include various forms of post-secondary schooling and training.

Mirroring the OECD, the World Bank in 1994 argued that donor funds should be provided only if countries had a policy framework encouraging competition and a differentiation of institutions, with an emphasis on private providers and cost-sharing with students.[7] And then UNESCO adopted the rate of return approach in a joint report with the World Bank in 2000.

Thus, two leading international bodies have encouraged the increased commodification of education. But once a service is commodified, providers seek new income-generating devices and rationalization becomes attractive, through economies of scale and standardization, which favour transnational template schooling. Within the new focus on "governance", performance indicators have become the main mechanism of accountability.[8]

The *liberalization of education* is a global trend. Although other forces have also pushed in that direction, it is being accelerated by the WTO's General Agreement on Trade in Services (GATS), which aims to ensure that, if private provision of a service is allowed, foreign suppliers are given equal opportunity with national private providers.[9] Consequently, in many developing countries and some others, multinational educational services are growing, bringing with them an "Americanization" of schooling, particularly at tertiary level and to a lesser extent at secondary level.

The questions raised by this global trend are enormously important. Will it produce standardization? Will it produce a narrowing or a broadening of education? Will it narrow educational differences or widen them, between societies and between groups within society?

---

[4]P. Jones: *World Bank Financing of Education* (London and New York, Routledge, 1992).

[5]K. Mundy: "Retrospect and prospect: Education in a reforming World Bank", *International Journal of Educational Development*, Vol. 22, No. 5, 2002, pp. 483–508.

[6]E. Hartmann, S. Haslinger and C. Scherrer: *Liberalization of higher education and training: Implications for workers' security*, SES Paper (Geneva, ILO, forthcoming), p. 24.

[7]World Bank: *Higher Education: Lessons of Experience* (Washington, DC, World Bank, 1994).

[8]M. Henry, R. Lingard, F. Rizvi and S. Taylor: *The OECD, Globalization and Education Policy* (Amsterdam, Pergamon, 2001).

[9]C. Scherrer and G. Yalcin: *The Globalization of Higher Education: The Trade Regime Dimension*, paper presented at workshop on globalization of social services, Dubrovnik, Sep. 2002, organized by the ILO's Socio-Economic Security Programme and Globalism and Social Policy Programme.

The globalization of schooling?

Cultural diversity and identity are part of existential security. Is that being threatened by the transnationalization and commercialization of "education"?

The liberalization of tertiary schooling is accelerating. There are six types of provider of transnational education: corporate universities, private commercial providers, media publishing companies, international consortia of educational institutions, educational brokers, and public institutions. Among the several thousand of the first are McDonald's Hamburger Universities and Walt Disney University.

Competition between providers is creating a global market. Student mobility is being fostered by such devices as transfers of education credits and modularization of programmes, as well as the multinationalization of "production" through establishment of subsidiaries in various countries. Educational service providers are also pushing for more access to foreign markets within the ambit of the WTO's General Agreement on Trade in Services (GATS). This looks likely to remain part of the long-term liberalization agenda and the "Americanization" of tertiary (and lower levels of) schooling.[10] Particularly in developing countries, there are fears that pressures and financial inducements will lead to "education imports" that hinder the development or maintenance of independent national academic systems.[11]

In short, educational and skills security is being profoundly affected by globalization. Public schooling has been giving way to private (and semi-private) schooling, and multiple providers have become the norm at all levels. To some extent, particularly at tertiary and secondary level, schooling is being converted from a *public good* into a commodified service, for which parents (or pupils) must pay. This has implications for inequalities and for the opportunities for low-income families to support schooling. Privatization and liberalization of education are leading to multi-tiered access. At one end, elite schools and colleges are virtually reserved for those who can afford tuition and other fees, while most students are directed into underfunded, overcrowded public institutions, or into private schemes of dubious quality.

The emphasis on labour market flexibility has meant that the "returns" to skill acquisition can be distorted, acting as a disincentive to skill acquisition and a source of insecurity for workers. Skills insecurity can also result when workers acquire skills but do not receive the "rewards" from the increased productivity, as illustrated in the by-no-means unique case of Mexico (see following box).

---

[10] Hartmann et al., 2003, op. cit., pp. 31–32.

[11] P.G. Altbach: "Higher education and the WTO: Globalization run amok", *International Higher Education*, Spring 2001. <http://www.bc.edu/bc_org/avp/soe/cihe/newsletter/News23/text001.htm>.

A Mexican wave?

In Mexico, as in much of Latin America, globalized economic reforms produced a break in the historical trend between real wages and productivity growth.

From 1950 to 2000, two periods can be identified in the relationship between these variables (Figure 8.1). First, up to and including the Echeverría Government (1970–76), the effect of the traditional distributive policy of the PRI (the party in government throughout this period) is visible: wages grew at a pace similar to productivity. Through bargaining power and gradual institutional change, labour had gained the property right to share in the benefit of productivity growth.

In the second period, starting in 1976, and in particular since the economic crisis of 1982, which consolidated political and institutional change in Mexico (and in most of Latin America), a growing gap emerged between productivity and wages. By 2000 this had become substantial. While average wages were still 10% below the level of 1976, productivity had risen by nearly 20% — and the fall in wages occurred while GDP had grown by 88% and income per capita by a quarter.

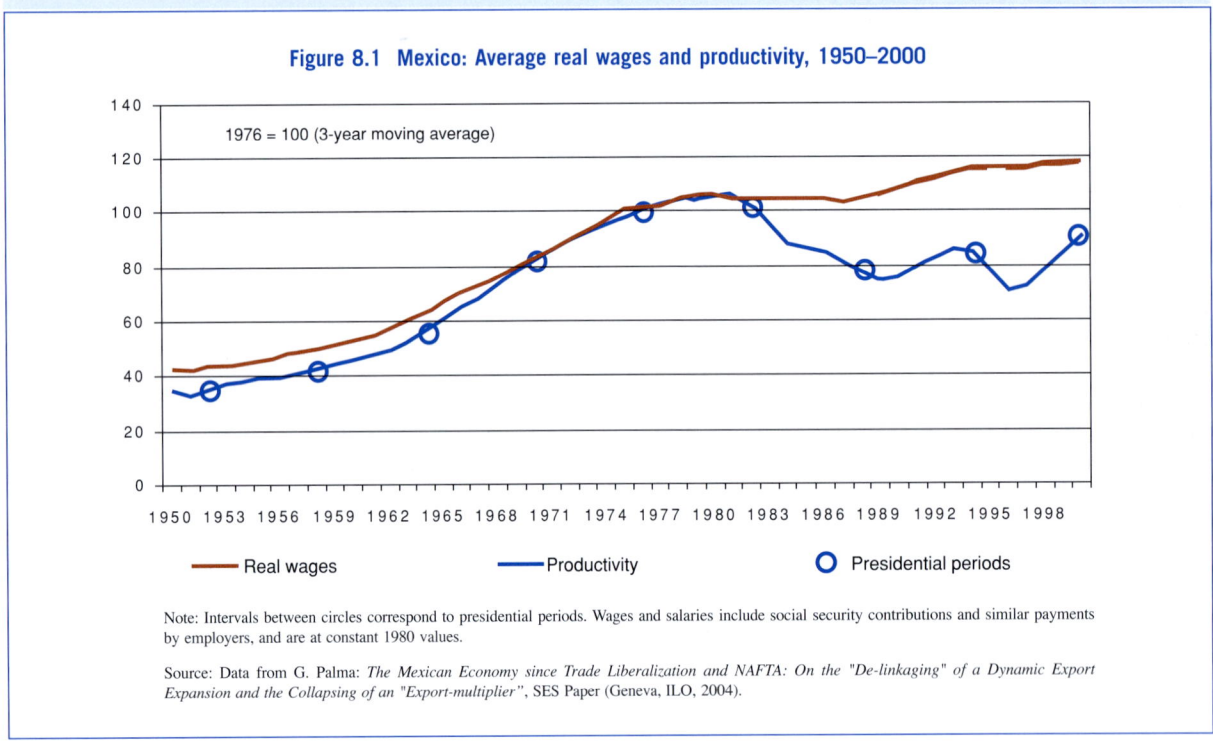

Figure 8.1 Mexico: Average real wages and productivity, 1950–2000

1976 = 100 (3-year moving average)

Real wages   Productivity   O Presidential periods

Note: Intervals between circles correspond to presidential periods. Wages and salaries include social security contributions and similar payments by employers, and are at constant 1980 values.

Source: Data from G. Palma: *The Mexican Economy since Trade Liberalization and NAFTA: On the "De-linkaging" of a Dynamic Export Expansion and the Collapsing of an "Export-multiplier"*, SES Paper (Geneva, ILO, 2004).

Mexico highlights a double irony of labour market flexibility. If capital can squeeze more out of labour via shrinking wages, it will be less inclined to invest in technological innovation. And if workers cannot expect to gain from increased productivity, they will have little incentive to invest in skill improvements. In effect, workers lose their "property rights" over skill. The system of incentives is perverse and cannot be good for long-run growth and development.

The long-term development of skills security is also threatened by crises and shocks. As emphasized in Chapters 1 and 2, lurches in macroeconomic policy, collapses of economic systems and natural disasters set up vicious cycles that cannot be dealt with through conventional mechanisms of mitigating and coping with *idiosyncratic risk*.

What does this mean for skill reproduction security? In developing countries, economic shocks have a powerful adverse effect on child nutrition. This leads to lower school attendance and achievement, and a lower lifetime capacity to learn and maintain skills. The evidence for this chain of events is very strong, as has been shown in Brazil, Mexico and India.[12] And there is a strong relationship between national income volatility and secondary school enrolment rates.[13]

There is a contrary stream of research suggesting that school enrolment rates could rise in a crisis period, because the opportunity cost of attending school goes down even though there is an offsetting income effect (need to complement decline in wages and parental income). Be that as it may, ensuring basic educational security in crisis periods will help to reduce income inequality in the future.

Education for all? — The "Fast Track Initiative"

In June 2002 the World Bank launched an initiative to achieve basic educational goals — the "Fast Track Initiative" (FTI) — targeted initially at 23 selected low-income countries. Designed to support countries that had "sound" educational policies within an approved macroeconomic policy framework, it represented a new type of conditionality. Other donors were encouraged to support those countries that satisfied the approved policies.

Early evidence shows that donors have redirected funds to countries that complied, and officials from those countries have been seconded to FTI in the World Bank. But the Bank has expressed concern that resources are not reaching NGOs and faith-based schools.[14] Others question whether an international financial agency should be directing international resources to faith-based schools.

8.4 Skills security: Personal assessments

Rather than try to give an overall picture of global trends in skill reproduction security, it may be useful to indicate how the process can be monitored at the individual level. Essentially, the key elements that provide security are: access to school (basic capabilities), access to skills training, perceived adequacy of training, use of training, perceived adequacy of skills for the future, and expected access to skills in the future if needed.

A society could be said to provide relatively high skills security if a large proportion of the population has had access to post-primary schooling and access to training opportunities, can use those skills in their work, and see a future in which they either have adequate skills or can obtain them if needed.

The following sections provide a few pointers on those elements, drawing from the People's Security Surveys (PSS) and Enterprise Labour Flexibility and Security Surveys (ELFS). The intention is not to give a comprehensive picture but to highlight certain tendencies.

(i) Access to schooling

How do we measure whether someone has a high or low level of *skills security?* First, it reflects the acquisition of a capacity to learn and a knowledge base. This is the sphere of general education, such as functional literacy and numeracy. Access to schools and to training are the standard measures of skills security.

---

[12] S. Duryea: *Children's Advancement Through School in Brazil: The Role of Transitory Shocks to Household Income*, Working Paper No. 376 (Washington, DC, Inter-American Development Bank, July 1998); E. Skoufias and S.W. Parker: *Labour Market Shocks and Their Impacts on Work and Schooling: Evidence from Urban Mexico*, IFPRI-FCND Discussion Paper No. 129, (Washington, DC, IFPRI-FCND, Mar. 2002); H. Jacoby and E. Skoufias: "Risk, financial markets and human capital in a developing country", *Review of Economic Studies*, Vol. 64, No. 3, 1997, pp. 311–335.

[13] K. Flug, A. Spilimbergo and E. Wachtenheim: "Investment in education: Do economic volatility and credit constraints matter?" *Journal of Development Economics*, Vol. 55, 1998, pp. 465–481.

[14] World Bank, *World Development Report 2004: Making Services Work for Poor People* (Washington, DC, 2003), p. 28.

Conventionally, the main indicator of education and skill is level of schooling attained. In this respect, the global "stylized facts" are startling enough. Millions of people never go to school. Of the 680 million children of primary school age, 115 million are not in school, 65 million of them girls. About 860 million of the world's population of 6.2 billion — one in seven people — are illiterate.[15] It may be more, since lapsed literacy is widespread. Adult literacy is only just over 50% in the so-called least developed countries. The literacy rate for girls in many countries is much lower than for boys, simply because more girls are not provided with the opportunity to learn to read. Basic education has been defined as a basic human right. Many of the world's poor would not understand that; they have not had the education.

A useful way of understanding the basic education story is to consider the *process* of schooling. For illustrative purposes, the following table contrasts two "ideal type" societies. The first is what one might expect in a relatively affluent country; the second is an imaginary developing country. In country A, 100% of children of primary school age are enrolled in primary school, and thereafter a gradually diminishing proportion of the age cohort makes it onward and upward. Compare the situation in country B, where not only does a smaller proportion make it to the starting line but the rate of attrition is much faster. An initial disadvantage becomes a gulf.

	Country A	Country B
Enrol in primary school	100	80
Attend primary school	100	60
Complete primary school	95	30
Enrol and attend secondary school	85	20
Complete secondary school	70	10
Go on to tertiary education	50	5

This stylized process highlights a chain of events pointing to educational success or failure. Within countries, a similar comparison could be made between the rich and the poor, boys and girls, urban and rural. A lack of other forms of security, as well as other barriers to progress, is often what contributes to the sharp attrition rate of the more disadvantaged groups.

Access to primary schooling is where it all begins. It is widely presumed that low rates of enrolment in schooling and lower rates of school attendance reflect the incidence of child labour. This may not be the main factor. In some cases, child labour may be incidental, while non-attendance at school is due to barriers of cost, transport, ignorance or simple incapacity of parents to send children to school. In Gujarat, India for instance, the PSS showed that 28% of children who were not attending school were involved in income-generating activities; the remainder were not attending school for other reasons.

PSS data in Ghana revealed that although one-fifth of all children aged 7 to 15 were not attending school, only 12% of the non-attenders could be described as "child labourers", the remainder being inactive.[16] Those most exposed to child labour were not the direct children of the head of the household in which they were living, which may have been connected to the tendency of orphans of AIDS victims to move into households of more distant kin.

It was noted in Chapter 4 that child labour is a familiar coping mechanism in response to income insecurity that, while often having long-term adverse effects, may not always interfere with schooling (and might even benefit it). In several countries, this was explored further through a direct question. In Bangladesh, just over a third of adult respondents in the PSS, all non-wage workers, said that their

---

[15] UNESCO: *Education for All: Global Monitoring Report* (Paris, 2002).

[16] J.-P. Zoyem: *Labour Market Security and Child Labour in Ghana*, paper presented at ILO workshop on Economic Security and Decent Work in Africa, Dar-es-Salaam, May 2003. This also observed that child labour was greater in rural areas, and greater in Accra than in Ashanti.

children helped them in their work, more doing so in rural areas. But only just over a quarter said that work interfered with the child's schooling. In Tanzania, where about a third of the adults said their children helped in some family work, only 12% said that work interfered with the child's schooling. Now, of course, there may have been some rationalization, or the parents may have been ignorant of the effect. But it should not be presumed that child work does impede school attendance or performance.

Skills insecurity may be due in part to a particular form of paternalism failure. In many countries, primary schools mainly prepare young pupils for secondary schools, whereas most children cannot expect to go on to secondary school. They are left ill-prepared for the working life ahead of them. This familiar point leads to uncomfortable dilemmas and choices. If primary schools are limited to preparing youngsters for semi-skilled manual labour, they risk becoming *dumbing-down* institutions. It is not our intention to go into this in detail, but it is important to emphasize again that education is not just about preparation for existing jobs.

In Gujarat, India, the PSS revealed that 41% of adults were illiterate but that 48% of those with some formal schooling felt their education had not helped them in their main economic work.[17] Even so, a large proportion of all respondents said a lack of education and skills made it difficult for them to move into alternative activities.

Access to school varies fairly systematically. For instance, people living in rural areas are less likely to have access to all levels of schooling. And the poor have lower access, and often more expensive access, than the more affluent. The PSS data bring out these patterns, most notably in Gujarat, India and Ethiopia. This is not just a developing country phenomenon, since similar patterns were observed in the Russian Federation and Ukraine, as well as in China.

In addition, girls have lower access than boys (although this is not a universal pattern). In Gujarat, India, women were much more likely to be illiterate, indicating a lack of completion of even the most basic education. The disadvantage was much greater in rural areas. When asked for the reason for non-attendance, the main reasons given were domestic chores and looking after siblings. In Ethiopia, women were nearly twice as likely to be illiterate as men.

In most parts of the world, barriers to schooling are the distance from home to school, cost of transport, and cost of schooling, rather than the demand or need for child labour. In some places, cultural factors play a part; in others, lack of authority by parents, or absence of parents altogether, is important; in others, parents and children doubt the usefulness of schooling.

These barriers surface in the PSS data. Financial constraints are uppermost, although cultural factors play a part in the difference between males and females. Physical access also plays a part. Children of less educated parents, particularly if they are illiterate, are less likely to go to school. And, as shown in Gujarat, India, children of casual labourers are less likely to go to school than children of those in regular wage or salaried labour.

In many countries, parents regard their children's schooling as a form of investment in their future security. In Ethiopia, the PSS data suggested that nine out of every ten saw this as important, and in Indonesia almost 80% of parents did so.

A factor in education is the level of schooling that parents, children and the community have as their *target* or expectation. In Gujarat, India, for instance, most parents aimed higher for their children than they had themselves attained, but the intended levels were lower in rural areas and lower for girl children.

The adaptation of aspirations means that there is an inbuilt tendency to reproduce inequalities, with less educated parents having lower aspirations, especially for girls. In Gujarat, India, almost half of those who were illiterate intended that their girl children should have no more than primary schooling whereas only 15% of their boy children were expected to stop at that level.

(ii) Access to training

Obviously, skills or capability security depends on access to skill refinement opportunities beyond school, which include various forms of vocational

---

[17]J. Unni and U. Rani: *Insecurities of Informal Workers in Gujarat, India*, SES Paper No. 30 (Geneva, ILO, 2002).

training. In general, countries with more of their population completing higher levels of general schooling are likely to have more facilities for skills training, both institutional and on-the-job.

In the PSS, the main questions relating to access to training by individuals refer to past access to training, use of training, barriers to training, and aspirations with regard to skill acquisition.

There is a strong link between access to formal schooling and access to training and type of training. The principal result is that inequalities are compounded rather than compensated. As with school,

skill reproduction is a matter of reproducing privileges and disadvantages.

Consider some examples. In Gujarat, India, 7% of all respondents in the PSS had received some formal training, all of whom came from among those with most formal schooling. In Brazil and Chile, the more schooling a person had received the greater the probability of having had some vocational training. In Brazil, not only was this true, but a significant number of people with low education reported that they had not acquired training because of a lack of opportunity (Figure 8.2).

Figure 8.2 Brazil: Receipt of formal training, by highest level of schooling

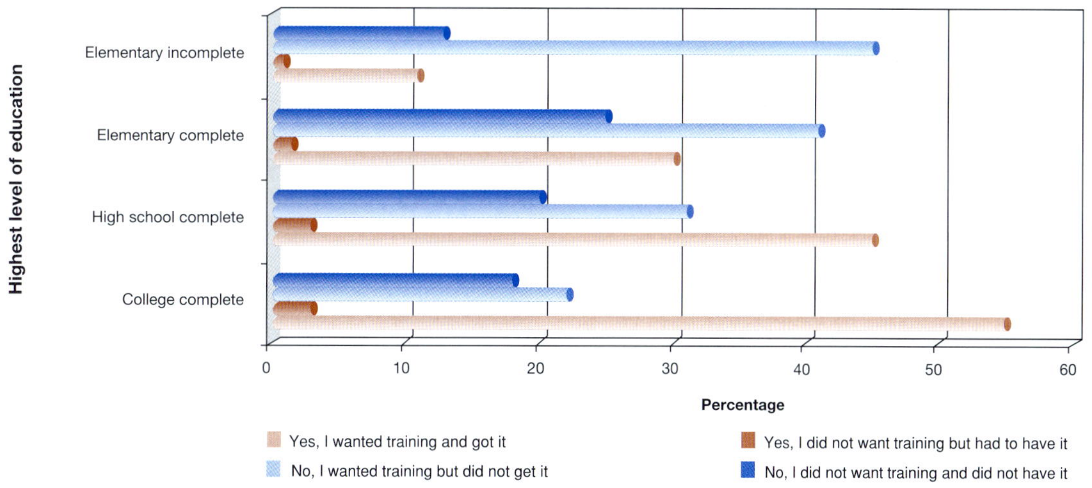

Source: Brazil PSS 2001.

Ironically, in various countries people with low levels of schooling were the most likely to report that they had not received any training because they did not want or need it. Although this may be a rationalization of their situation, people with less schooling appear to be the least aware of the usefulness or need for skills training.

In Brazil, those who most benefit from training are white better-educated men, suggesting that the government's Professional Qualification State Plan (PEQ), introduced in 1996 to upgrade the skills of vulnerable groups, has had only limited success.

In Ukraine, over three-quarters of all respondents in the PSS — 80% of men, 73% of women — had received some formal work-related training.[18] But most who had received training said this was in

[18]L. Zsoldos and G. Standing: *Coping with Insecurity; The Ukrainian People's Security Survey 2002*, SES Paper No. 17 (Geneva, ILO, 2002).

educational institutions (85%), including college, university and vocational schools, so some respondents may have regarded their general schooling as "training".[19] Only 4% said they had served an apprenticeship, while 7% said they had received manual on-the-job training, and 1% said they had received on-the-job training in clerical work. Interestingly, over nine in ten of those who reported that they had received training said that they had done so because they wanted to obtain more education or an occupational profile, whereas 8% said they did so because they were obliged to.

In the Russian Federation, men were slightly more likely than women to have access to training, and those who received it were more likely to be in state or ex-state enterprises. Far fewer workers in new private firms had received any training. Whether cause or effect, or coincidental, those with greater employment security were more likely to have received training. And whereas 78% of those working in large firms had received training, only 37% of those working in small-scale firms had.

In China, about half the workers had received some training, with no difference between men and women. But the greater the person's level of schooling, the more likely he or she was to have received training. The likelihood was greater the larger the firm in which the person was working.

In Gujarat, India, 95% of the minority who had received any training said it had been provided informally, with the rest acquiring it from government extension services (4%) or an NGO (1%). Training was mainly on-the-job or provided by family or friends. Those in formal jobs and those with more schooling were more likely to have had formal training.

In Indonesia, where fewer than a third of working people had received any training, the main form was informal training by older workers. Once again, it was the more educated who were most likely to benefit from formal training.

As expected then, access to training is an advantage for those with other advantages, such as more schooling or employment security.

(iii) Use of training

Another less noted aspect is *utilization* of existing skills and training. Indeed, it may be said with some confidence that the skills possessed by working populations are chronically underestimated by conventional statistics, which report the distribution of existing jobs, classifying people by the skill level required of those jobs.

In this regard, the PSS have relevant findings on the *under-utilization* of "skills". The PSS asked whether or not the person's current main work enabled him or her to use their qualifications and skills. This is indicative of a certain type of underemployment. In many countries, large numbers of people are in that situation. For instance, in Indonesia, only a minority are in jobs in which they can use the skills they possess. More men said they had work that enabled them to use their qualifications (Table 8.1). And those with more schooling were more likely to do so. Women with secondary schooling were particularly disadvantaged, whereas women with tertiary education were more likely to be using their qualifications than their male equivalents.

---

[19]However, more women than men reported that they had received some on-the-job training in the past two years. Women were also much more likely to have received institutional training "with certification", whereas men who had received training were more likely to have picked it up on the job.

Table 8.1 Indonesia: Income-earners believing they use their qualifications or skills
in their main work, by area, type of workplace, establishment size, ownership
and occupation, by gender (percentage responding "Yes")

| | Using qualifications | | Using skills | |
	Male	Female	Male	Female
Type of area				
Urban	62.1	41.7	79.6	76.6
Rural	49.2	42.3	68.8	63.6
Workplace				
Home	73.9	51.5	89.6	72.3
Factory	75.0	50.0	92.0	70.6
Store/shop	50.0	35.9	78.3	60.5
Office	91.4	94.1	89.9	100.0
Street	48.9	30.8	66.4	90.5
Field	38.9	31.4	61.2	56.2
Establishment size				
1–5	48.0	37.9	68.9	66.5
6–10	69.7	73.3	79.5	75.0
11–20	79.3	54.5	75.4	81.3
21–50	79.1	55.6	83.7	73.9
51+	76.5	75.0	84.6	87.5
Work status				
Own account	46.9	34.8	69.0	62.5
Wage				
Private (<5 employees)	43.5	34.1	61.1	66.2
Private (5+ employees)	70.8	58.7	86.7	65.0
Public	80.6	81.0	81.7	96.0
Cooperative	(100.0)	(100.0)	(100.0)	(100.0)
Occupational				
Agricultural	38.5	30.0	60.7	56.4
Non-agricultural	65.7	51.1	80.0	72.2

Note: Figures in parentheses are based on fewer than 10 observations. Source: Indonesia PSS 2001.

In Bangladesh, most of the minority of workers who had received any training reported that they used the associated skills in their main work, although men were more likely to say this. More than nine in ten workers thought their skills were adequate for the work they did. But over 14% thought they were overqualified for their main job, while about 5% thought they were underqualified.

In Gujarat, India, almost a third of respondents said they did not use their education or training in their main work. In Tanzania, among the 19% who had received training, only 70% thought they used what they had learned in their main work, with rather more women reporting they used their skills.

In China, about three-quarters of all those who had received training consider that in their main work they are using the acquired skills or qualifications. More of those who had not received formal training felt that they were not using their skills in their job. As in other countries, workers in large firms and in the public sector, and workers with high levels of skill security in general, are more likely to be actually using their skills. There is also a strong positive relationship between degree of labour formality and use of skills possessed.

In Ukraine in 2002, while most workers who had training reported that they used the resultant skills in their main job — 60% a great deal, 9% somewhat, 13% not very much — 18% did not use their skills/training at all. About half of the employed felt that they would continue to use their skills over the next five years. In the Russian Federation, in the areas covered by the PSS, over 13% of the employed said they did not use their skills at all in their jobs, and only about half of the employed felt that they used them fully. Ironically, the less educated who had training were more likely to report that they did not use their skills fully or to a large extent.

In Hungary, a stranger pattern emerged. About 45% of the employed thought they used their skills fully in their job, but 31% said they did not use them at all (Figure 8.3). It was suggested that industrial apprenticeships do not match the needs of the labour market. There was no significant difference between men and women in this respect. As for expected use in the future, only just over a third of workers were confident that they would be able to use their skills fully over the next three years, while just over a quarter were convinced that they would not be able to do so.

Figure 8.3 Hungary: Use of skills in current job, by level of education and gender (percentage of those in jobs)

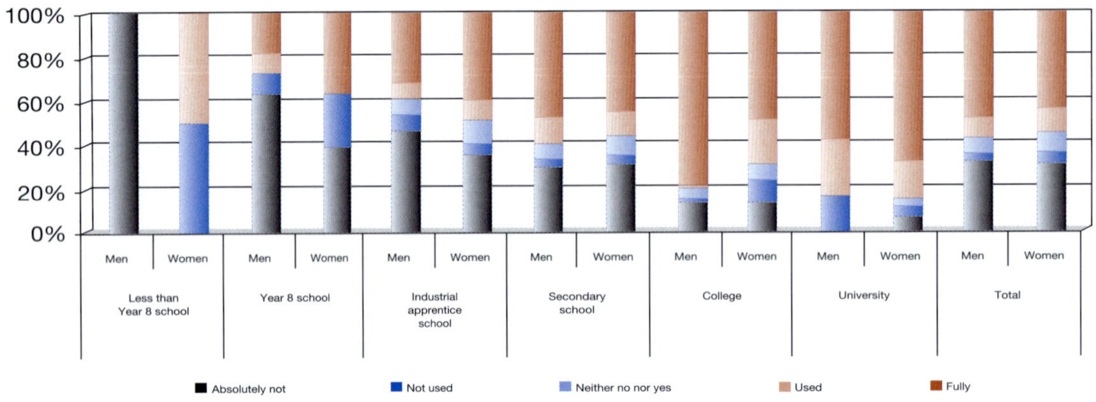

Source: Hungary PSS 2000.

Use of skills and reward for skills are clearly related. If there is little relationship between the "investment" in skill and the income received from the labour expended, there is scarcely an incentive to acquire the skills or to use them if acquired.

(iv) Perceived adequacy of skills

Most people have a reasonable idea of whether or not the skills they possess are adequate for the work they are doing. Someone in a job for which he or she feels under-qualified is likely to feel insecure in several respects.

In Tanzania, most of those doing a main economic activity thought their qualifications and skills were adequate for the tasks, with 31% thinking they were insufficient and 5% thinking they were greater than needed. The more educated were the least likely to believe their skills were adequate, and more likely to think they were over-qualified or had insufficient skills for the work they were doing (Table 8.2).

Table 8.2 Tanzania: Whether qualifications and skills are greater than, adequate for or insufficient for main work (percentage of those in economic activity)

	Greater than needed	Adequate (roughly sufficient)	Insufficient
Male	5.1	65.6	29.3
Female	4.8	62.8	32.4
Total	5.0	64.4	30.6
Illiterate	3.7	74.1	22.2
Literate but no schooling	—	78.9	21.1
Primary	3.9	62.1	34.0
Secondary	7.8	66.9	25.2
University	18.2	54.5	24.3
Regular wage/salary	5.3	69.1	25.6
Casual wage	6.2	71.9	21.9
Non-wage	4.8	62.8	32.4

Source: Tanzania PSS 2001.

In Ukraine, most workers (79%) who had received some training regarded it as roughly *adequate* for the work they were doing (Figure 8.4). But 12% regarded their training as inadequate, while 9% said their training was greater than required for the work, presumably because they were doing jobs requiring little training. There were differences between men and women in this respect; although there was no difference in perceived use of their skills, more men thought their qualifications were inadequate for their job and more thought they were overqualified for their job.

Figure 8.4 Ukraine: Workers' view of adequacy of skills for their job, by sector and gender (percentage of those with training)

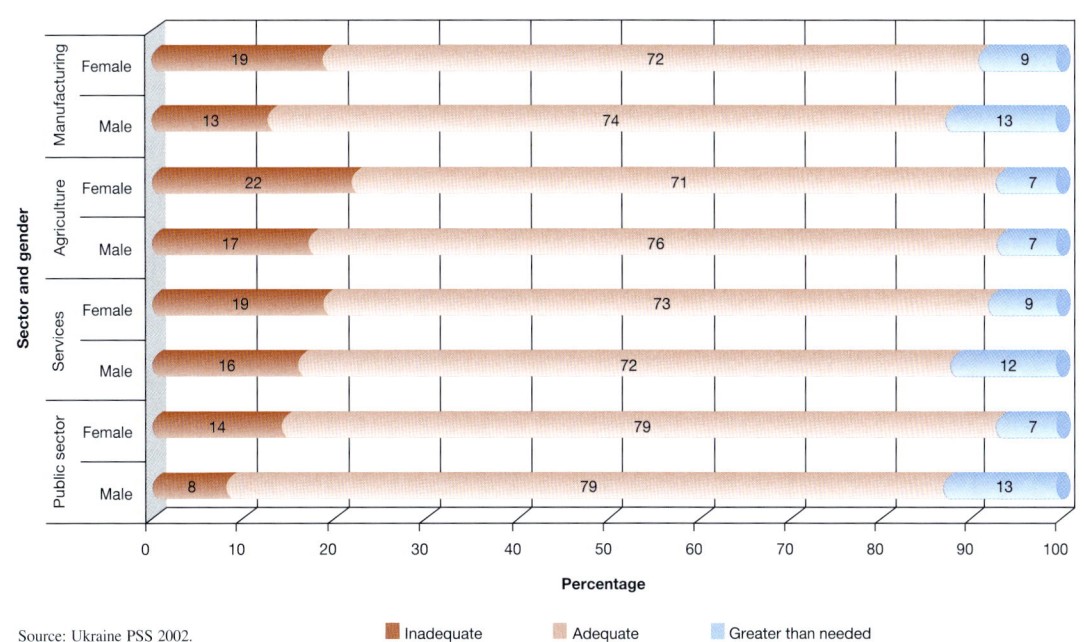

Source: Ukraine PSS 2002. ■ Inadequate ■ Adequate ■ Greater than needed

China is an extreme case of where workers perceive that their skills are underused in the work they are required to perform. More than three-quarters of respondents in the PSS thought their skills and qualifications were greater than required for their jobs. Women were just as likely to think this as men. The proportion was higher for more educated workers, and was greater among those working for large state enterprises than for other firms.

In sum, more attention should be given to the underutilization of skills rather than solely to the possession of them.

(v) Perceived need for training

Do people perceive a personal need for training or retraining? If they do, are they confident they could obtain it? This subjective perspective is an aspect of skill reproduction security, and was explored to some extent in the PSS.

In many cases, workers do feel a need to have some training or retraining. But often a majority do not think like that.

In Brazil and Chile, where over two-thirds of workers said they had not had any training in recent years, about half of those said they had not wanted to obtain any. In Argentina, the share not wanting it was over half. One can only speculate on the reasons for the lack of interest in acquiring skills. The share of those not interested was greater among the less educated.

In Tanzania, over 60% of those who had not acquired training said that it was not required for their jobs, that being more common among women. A similar pattern emerges in Bangladesh – no need, no interest. But here a major difference in attitude was shown between rural and urban workers, more of the latter seeing a need for training.

In Ukraine, for example, in spite of pessimism about prospective upgrading in their current jobs, noted in the next section, 10% of all workers thought it "very likely" that they would need to acquire new work skills in the next five years, and 25% thought it "likely"; 35% thought it was unlikely or very unlikely that they would need to do so. As shown by Figure 8.5, a majority of young workers thought they needed to upgrade their skills, suggesting a willingness to learn.

Figure 8.5 Ukraine: Perceived need to acquire new work skills in next five years, by age and gender (percentage of those with jobs)

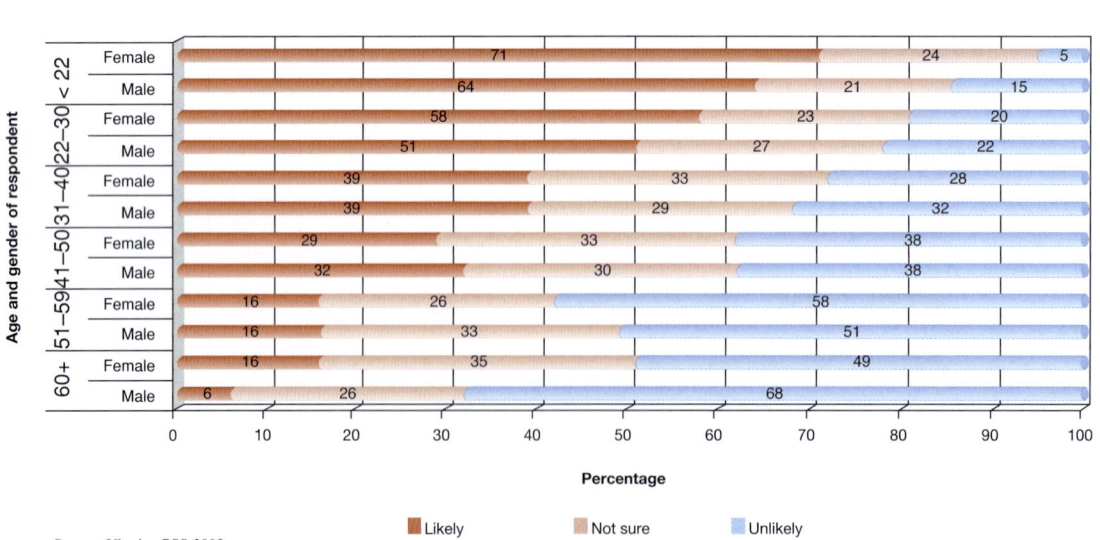

Source: Ukraine PSS 2002.

A majority of workers (53%) were not confident that they could obtain training or retraining at their workplace, with women being less confident. However, slight majorities of younger age groups thought they could obtain workplace training. The lack of training possibilities corresponds to the picture given by managements in the Ukraine ELFS, where many firms have reported giving up their traditional training facilities. It confirms the impression of a collapse of any "training culture" in the country.

Women and men in manufacturing or public sector jobs were more likely to think they could obtain training if needed, as Figure 8.6 suggests. Half those thinking they could not obtain training in their workplace attributed that to a lack of funds within the enterprise, while 29% attributed it to their age and 20% to the lack of a training institution. As for access to training or retraining *outside the workplace*, 53% thought it was not possible, for similar reasons.

Figure 8.6 Ukraine: Perceived likely access to training if needed at workplace, by sector and gender (percentage of those with jobs)

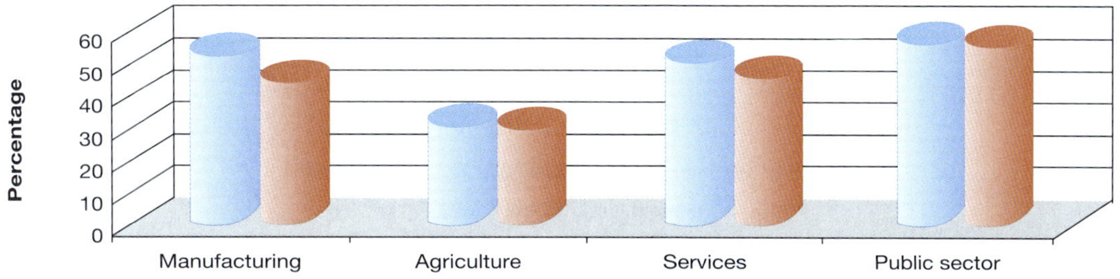

Source: Ukraine PSS 2002

■ Male ■ Female

Questions for monitors of educational security

- Do people perceive incentives to acquire skills?

- If needed, do people think they would be able to obtain training?

- If not, what barriers do they think exist?

- Do people anticipate a need to acquire new skills?

(vi) The digital divide

A great deal has been written and said about the impact of computers on working patterns and opportunities. An indicator of work capacity is the ability to use a computer. In many countries, only a minority have the opportunity to do so.

In several of the PSS, access and use of computers were explored. In Ukraine, when asked,[20] a quarter of respondents said they could use a computer (25% of women, 24% of men). As expected, the reported capacity to use a computer was concentrated among younger adults and the most educated (Figure 8.7). Obviously, this ability will be essential in the future. Unfortunately, very few Ukrainians actually had regular access to a computer — 4% having access to one at home only, 11% at work only, 2% at work and home, leaving 83% without direct access to a computer at all (Figure 8.8). This is in sharp contrast with what would be found in any western European country.

---

[20]The question was sufficiently vague to allow many people to say they could use a computer when their actual skills might be limited.

Figure 8.7 Ukraine: Ability to use a computer, by age and gender
(percentage of respondents)

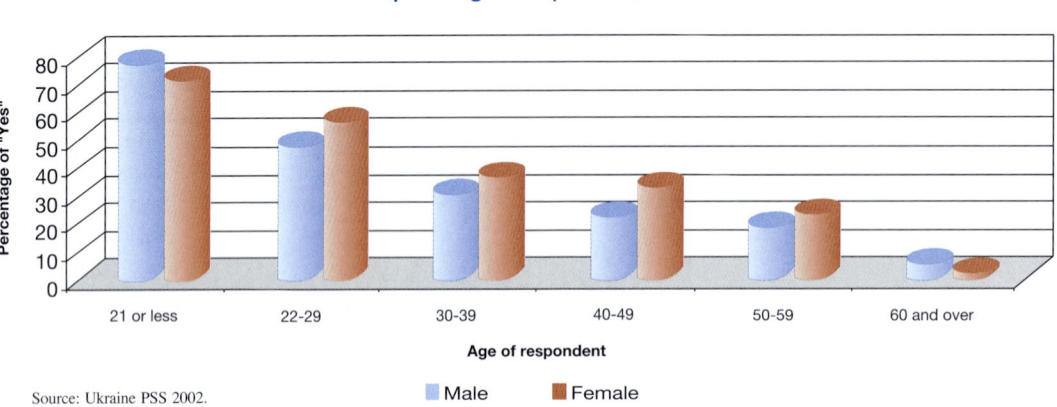

Source: Ukraine PSS 2002.

■ Male ■ Female

Figure 8.8 Ukraine: Access to computer, by age and gender
(percentage of respondents)

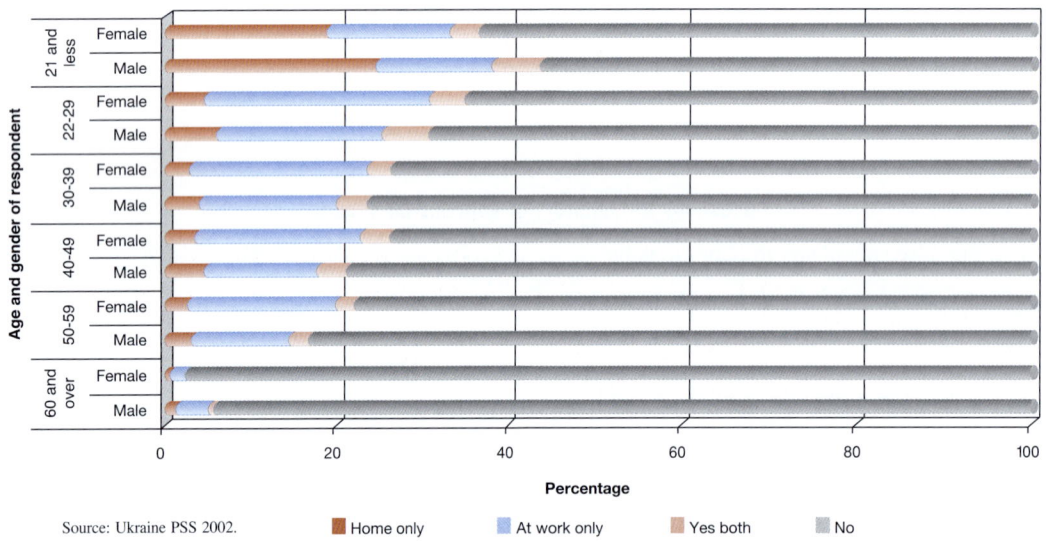

Source: Ukraine PSS 2002.

■ Home only ■ At work only ■ Yes both ■ No

In Hungary, the proportion of adults who can use a computer is higher than in Ukraine, with more women able to do so (Figure 8.9), and access to a computer is greater. In the Russian Federation, capacity to use and access to a computer were lower than in Hungary but greater than in Ukraine. In China, as in all the countries in which the relevant questions were asked, access to and use of computers were much greater in urban areas, and slightly more women could use them, presumably a reflection of their type of employment.

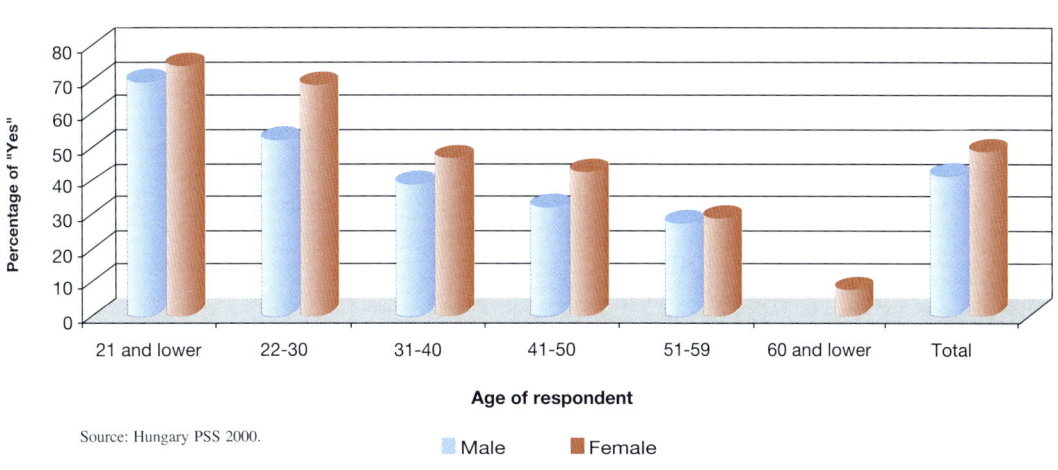

Figure 8.9 Hungary: Ability to use a computer, by age and gender (percentage of respondents)

Source: Hungary PSS 2000.

■ Male   ■ Female

(vii) An individual-level Skills Security Index

Any individual obtains capabilities by diverse means, and neither formal schooling nor any other single measure can capture a person's acquired competencies. We cannot hope to measure the full range of those competencies. However, in the following box an initial exploratory index is presented, which will be used later.

PSS individual Skills Security Index

The individual Skills Security Index combines two types of indicator: some measure basic education, which is clearly an important asset for further access to training, as demonstrated earlier; and some relate to training both in terms of access and type of training and retraining.

Individual Skills Security Index = 2*ED + ((TR + TRF) + (RETR + RETRF))

where the components are defined as follows:

ED: Highest level of schooling

TR: Access to training: TR = 1 if undergone any vocational training, 0 otherwise;

TRF: Type of training: TRF = 1 if TR was apprenticeship or off-the-job training in classroom or institute, 0 otherwise;

RETR: Opportunity to obtain training: RETR = 1 if possible to obtain training or retraining in present workplace if needed, 0 otherwise.

RETRF: Type of possible training/retraining: RETRF = 1 if possible to obtain training or retraining outside workplace if needed, 0 otherwise.

Before normalization, the individual SSI has a value between 0 and 6, with a zero value meaning that the person does not have any skill security. The index implies that each level of training is given equal importance, but formal training is given twice as much weight as informal training.

Figure 8.10   Individual SSI: Ukraine urban

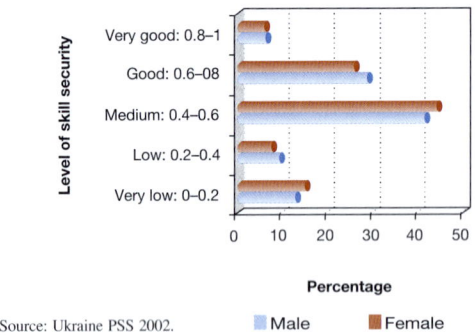

Source: Ukraine PSS 2002.   ■ Male   ■ Female

Figure 8.11   Individual SSI: Ukraine rural

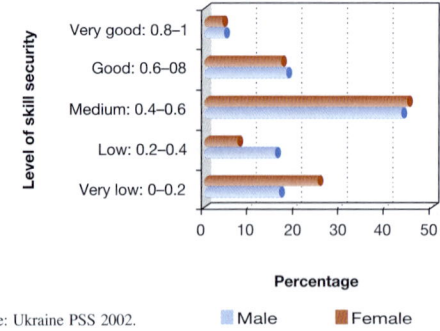

Source: Ukraine PSS 2002.   ■ Male   ■ Female

Figure 8.12   Individual SSI: Gujarat (India) urban

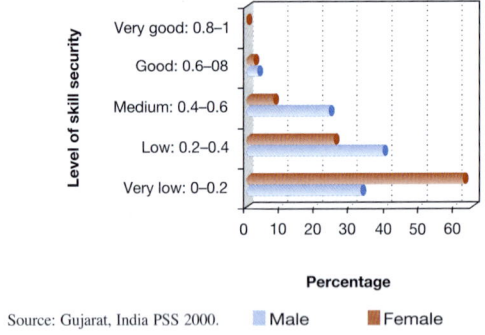

Source: Gujarat, India PSS 2000.   ■ Male   ■ Female

Figure 8.13   Individual SSI: Gujarat (India) rural

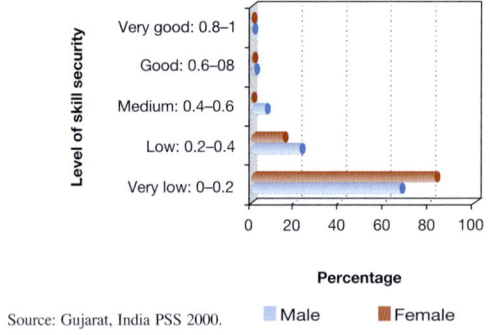

Source: Gujarat, India PSS 2000.   ■ Male   ■ Female

Figure 8.14   Individual SSI: Tanzania urban

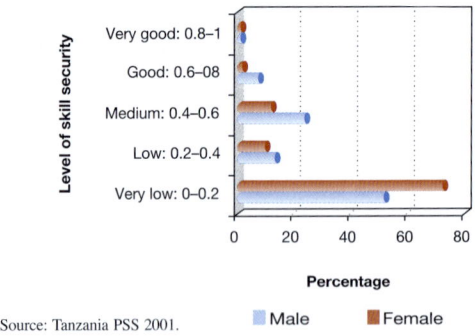

Source: Tanzania PSS 2001.   ■ Male   ■ Female

Figure 8.15   Individual SSI: Tanzania rural

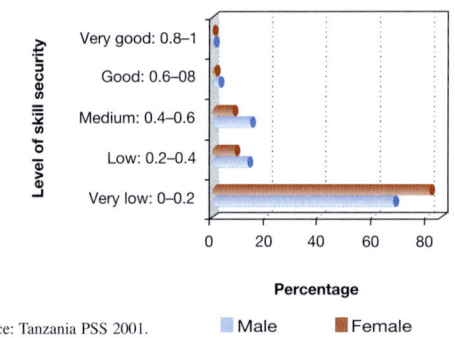

Source: Tanzania PSS 2001.   ■ Male   ■ Female

The general picture that emerges from the PSS data is one of diverging experiences that shape attitudes and behaviour. Early access and continued access to schooling leads to access to training and a greater appreciation of what training may bring. But it also shows that a substantial number of people with skills are not able, or perhaps not willing, to use them in their jobs.

8.5 Skills security in the workplace

Another picture of training comes from what happens in firms in various countries. In the ELFS, information was gathered on three levels of training — entry-level for new recruits, retraining for job performance and retraining for upgrading.

(i) Job training in workplaces

National patterns vary considerably. Many firms provide no training, and in most countries only a tiny minority provides all three levels. Making it hard to assess what is happening is that national traditions can be deceptive. Take, for instance, the reality in eastern Europe. In the old days, much of the formal training was a form of perk. The situation has been changing. For instance, in Ukraine in 2002, three-quarters of firms provided some training for newly hired workers. This was down on 1994 but, in any case, in over two-thirds of all firms providing it, the training was merely informal and on-the-job. Only 13% provided classroom training and 9% provided such training off the premises. Similar trends have occurred in the Russian Federation and the Republic of Moldova.

Corporate social responsibility and training

In relation to assessing and monitoring companies' commitment to skill formation, the Global Reporting Initiative (GRI) has proposed as its relevant core indicator "average hours of training per year per employee by category of employee" and as additional indicators a "description of programmes to support the continued employability of employees and to manage career endings" and "specific policies and programmes for skills management or for lifelong learning".[21]

These are attractive reporting principles. But one cannot realistically expect such detailed information from many small and medium-sized firms; indeed, the GRI proposals may be more appropriate as indicators of accounting practices than of labour practices.

A "decent workplace" should provide opportunities for skills acquisition, ideally providing a *voluntary learning environment*. While there is much talk about making firms centres of learning, this is surely an exaggeration, since firms' commercial interests are likely to shape the extent, type and distribution of training. One must also be careful about idealizing training. The notion of *lifelong learning*, or continuous learning, is not unambiguously good, especially if it entails job insecurity (as discussed in the next chapter). The thought of having to learn new competencies every few months could be unsettling and a source of discordant performance, deterring workers from trying to become excellent in particular skills.

Nevertheless, provision of training by firms is normally preferable to its absence. Emphasis should be on *opportunities* for learning, coupled with reasonable prospects of a personal "reward" from investment in training. And there must be a *voluntary* culture of learning, in that those opting not to train or acquire new skills will not be penalized (other than by losing the opportunity to move or upgrade to jobs requiring those skills).

---

[21] Global Reporting Initiative: *Sustainability Reporting Guidelines* 2002 (Boston, MA, 2002). p. 53. See also <http://www.globalreporting.org>.

Skill formation: The "decent workplace"

A decent workplace is one where there is an environment of skills security, where there are opportunities to learn and apply competencies, and to maintain them. For current purposes, it is proposed that the basic indicators of an orientation to skill formation are the three layers of training, namely:

- entry-level training for newly recruited workers,

- retraining to improve performance or to transfer a person to other jobs with similar skills,

- retraining for upgrading workers or promotion.[22]

Account must also be taken of type of training. If a firm gives just informal, on-the-job training, that deserves less weight than if it involves "classroom" and structured training, including apprenticeship. Accordingly, for each level, a distinction is made between "informal" and "formal" training, with the latter being presumed to have greater value, which is usually if not always the case. Although the difference between formal and informal may be exaggerated, concentrated training involving a quantifiable cost should be preferable to "on-the-job, pick-it-up-as-you-go" training.

Finally, an indicator is included to measure whether or not the establishment pays for training directly, by funding a training institute or by paying the training fees to an institute where it sends workers for training or by giving stipends to workers who go on training courses.

Thus, the model for the workplace skills security index is constructed by a simple addition of the indicators:

$$DWP1 = (TR + TRF) + (RETR + RETRF) + (UPTR + UPTRF) + TR.INST$$

where the components are defined as follows:

TR = 1 if training was usually provided to newly recruited workers, 0 otherwise;

TRF = 1 if TR was apprenticeship or off-the-job training in classroom or institute, 0 otherwise;

RETR = 1 if there was training provided for established workers to improve job performance or transfer between jobs of similar skill, 0 otherwise;

RETRF = 1 if that retraining was formal, in class or institute, 0 otherwise;

UPTR = 1 if training was provided to upgrade workers, 0 otherwise;

UPTRF = 1 if that retraining for upgrading was in class or institute, 0 otherwise;

TR.INST = 1 if the firm paid for trainees at institutes, directly or indirectly, 0 otherwise.

Before normalization, the DWP1 index has a value between 0 and 7, with a zero value meaning the firm gave no training. What the index implies is that each level of training is equally important, and that formal training has twice the weight of informal training.

---

[22]Possibly, the second and third forms of training deserve greater weight than the first. Yet, perversely, in most labour market analyses only the first is considered.

Figures 8.16 to 8.25 present results for the various countries where the enterprise surveys have been conducted. Thus, in Indonesia, only 7% of firms had a normalized value of 0.8 or more, while over 80% were poor performers in terms of skill provision. The results for Chile, the Philippines and South Africa suggest that in all three countries firms were more inclined to train workers than their counterparts in Indonesia.[23]

The pattern for Tanzania is what one would expect for a low-income African country, with the vast majority of firms having low scores. But the pattern for Pakistan shows a bleak picture there as well.

In eastern Europe, the results for the Republic of Moldova, the Russian Federation and Ukraine indicate that, in terms of formal training, firms still score reasonably well. Finally, the distribution for China suggests that there the pattern is distinctively bimodal, with a large proportion of firms scoring very low and a large proportion very high.

Figure 8.16   Indonesia: Distribution of DWP1

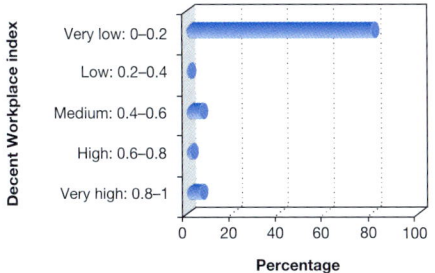

Source: Indonesia ELFS 2001.

Figure 8.17   Chile: Distribution of DWP1

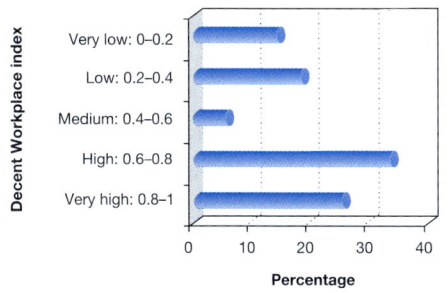

Source: Chile ELFS 2001.

Figure 8.18   Philippines: Distribution of DWP1, (all regions)

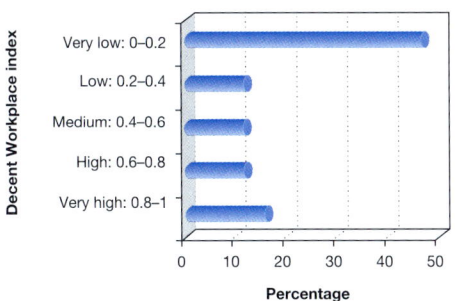

Source: Philippines ELFS 2000.

Figure 8.19   South Africa: Distribution of DWP1

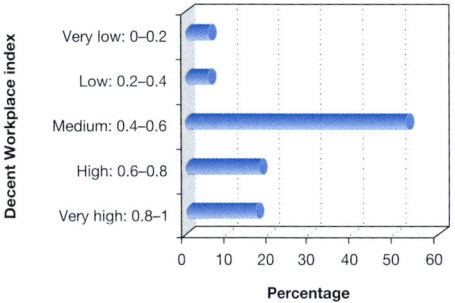

Source: South Africa ELFS 2001.

[23]At this stage, comparisons are cited merely for possible interest. More considered judgments would require multivariate analysis and due account for differences in sample and survey design.

Figure 8.20   Tanzania: Distribution of DWP1 (all regions)

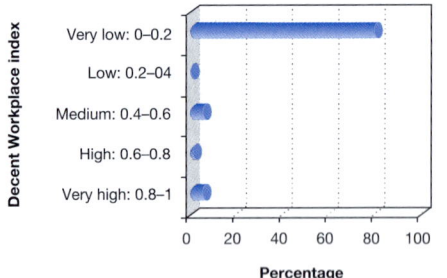

Source: Tanzania ELFS 2001.

Figure 8.21   Pakistan: Distribution of DWP1

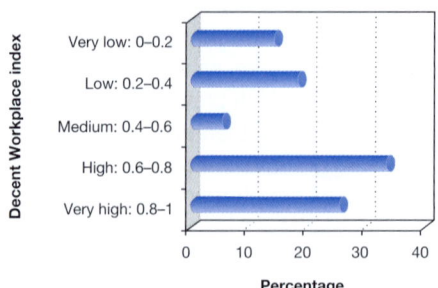

Source: Pakistan ELFS 2001.

Figure 8.22   Republic of Moldova: Distribution of DWP1 (all regions)

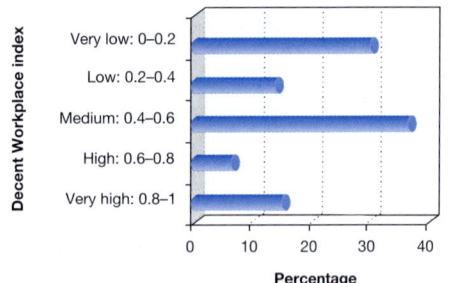

Source: Republic of Moldova ELFS 2000

Figure 8.23   Russian Federation: Distribution of DWP1

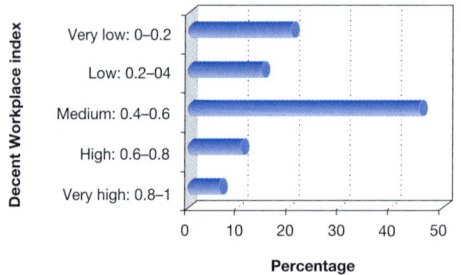

Source: Russian Federation ELFS 2002.

Figure 8.24   Ukraine: Distribution of DWP1 (all regions)

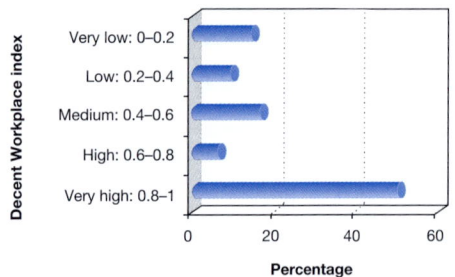

Source: Ukraine ELFS 2002.

Figure 8.25   China: Distribution of DWP1 (three regions)

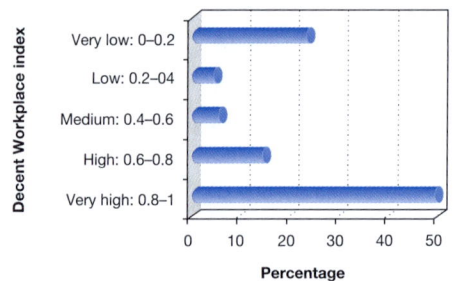

Source: China ELFS 2001.

(ii) Why small may not be beautiful

Across the world, large-scale enterprises have a much greater tendency to provide training and retraining to workers. This was brought out in both the enterprise surveys and the PSS. Thus, workers in Argentina, Brazil and Chile were more likely to have had training in the past two years if they were working in larger firms.[24] In Ukraine, large firms were much more likely to provide training.

Large-scale firms also tend to provide formal rather than informal training, leading to identifiable skills and credentials. Indeed, those who argue that policy should boost small-scale business should note that these are least likely to provide an environment of skill formation, contrary to the image of the craftsmanship model.

In China, ELFS data suggest that training is more likely in larger firms, and is most likely in foreign firms. If a comparison is made for provision of basic training for recruits and for all forms of training combined (initial, retraining and upgrading) the differences between firms become greater. Thus, whereas 45% of firms with fewer than 40 workers provide basic training compared with 80% of firms with more than 300 workers, only 20% of small firms provide all three levels of training against 56% of the large firms.

For illustrative purposes, Figures 8.26 and 8.27 show that in Ukraine and Brazil the larger the firm, the more likely it is to score highly in terms of skill formation. This pattern exists in all countries for which we have data. But in developing countries the difference between small and large firms is on average greater than in eastern Europe.

In Indonesia, the larger the firm the more likely it is to have a working environment oriented to skill development, with initial training, retraining and relatively formal methods of training, as measured by the index of skill development. This is a funding reproduced in most other countries.

Perhaps more interesting than the findings on size of enterprise is the evidence that foreign firms in developing countries are much more likely to provide training than local private firms for Indonesia, the Philippines and in several other countries.

People working in *public sector* enterprises are also more likely to receive training than those working in private firms, as shown in Tanzania, for example. And those who are self-employed or working in the "informal economy" are the least likely to have obtained training, as was found in Argentina, Brazil and Chile.[25] In Ukraine, privatization and restructuring have contributed to the decline in training, because it is less often provided in private and small-scale firms.

Figure 8.26   Ukraine: DWP1 by employment size

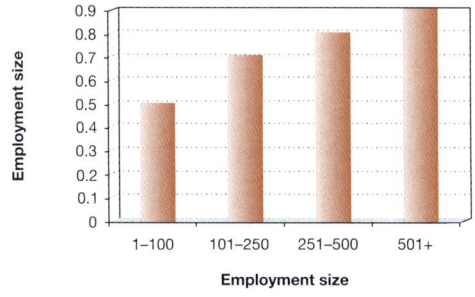

Source: Ukraine ELFS 2002.

Figure 8.27   Brazil: DWP1 by establishment employment size of establishment

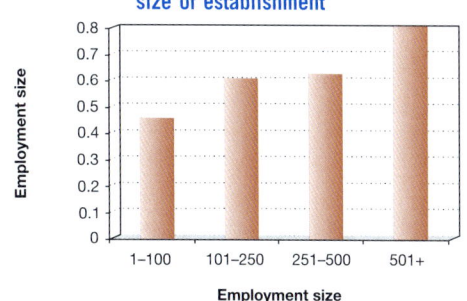

Source: Brazil ELFS 2001.

---

[24]M. Jeria Caceres: "More training, less security? Training and the quality of life at work in Argentina, Brazil and Chile", *International Labour Review*, Vol. 141, No. 4, 2002, pp. 359–384.

[25]Ibid., p. 364.

In short, skill formation is more likely in large-scale firms, in public sector firms and in foreign-owned firms. Policy should presumably wish to encourage small private local firms to enter the process, perhaps by facilitating the operation of training pool schemes.

8.6 Skills security linked to other forms of security

It is often presumed that schooling and education lead to a life of lower levels of other forms of insecurity. In many respects, this may be true. Thus, there is overwhelming evidence that more schooling is associated with higher incomes and greater income security.[26] This was further borne out by the results from the PSS in Argentina, Brazil and Chile.[27] There is also extensive evidence that employer training has similar effects.[28]

One apparently contradictory finding in many developing countries is the tendency of people with more schooling to have a higher incidence of open unemployment, or *labour market insecurity*. This well-known phenomenon was found in the PSS in Ghana.[29] It may reflect a reluctance to take jobs requiring much lower skill levels. It may simply be that the more educated are young, who are more likely to experience open unemployment, and/or concentrated in urban areas, where labour market insecurity more often takes the form of open unemployment.

There is an association between *employment security* and access to training. Those in regular or long-term wage or salaried employment have greater access to training opportunities than those in casual labour or own-account activity. The results from Tanzania (Figure 8.28) are fairly representative of other developing countries — only those in regular wage or salaried employment have high skills security.

Figure 8.28 Tanzania: Individual Skills Security Index, by employment status

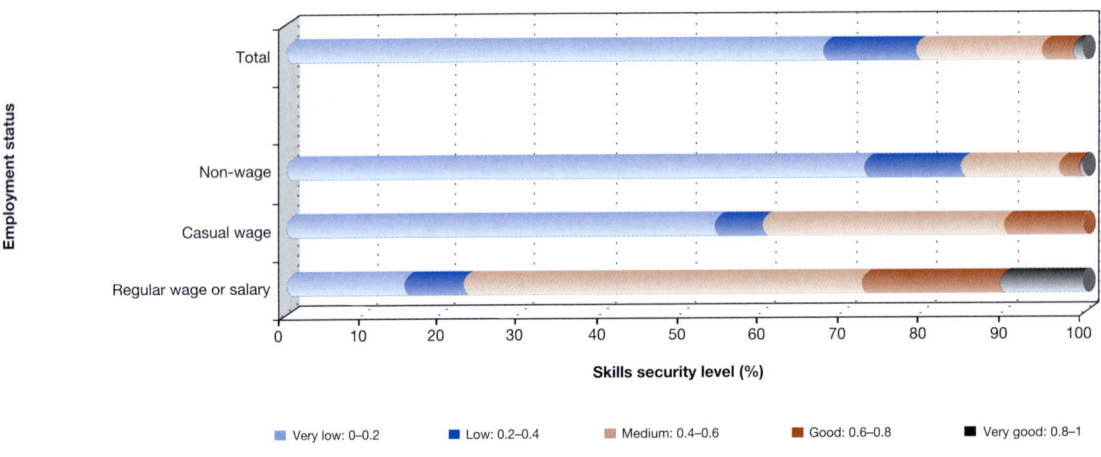

Source: Tanzania PSS 2001.

---

[26]This might be weakening in rich countries where personal services place heavy emphasis on presentation skills and personal appearance. M. Jackson, J. Goldthorpe and C. Mills: "Education, employers and class mobility", in *Research in Social Stratification and Mobility* (London, Elsevier, 2004).

[27]Caceres, 2002, op. cit., pp. 378-379. The results for Chile were non-linear, in that only those with higher education appeared to have better outcomes in terms of incomes and working conditions. Obtaining secondary schooling was not enough.

[28]See, inter alia, P. Schone: "Analysing the effect of training on wages using combined survey-register data", *International Journal of Manpower* (Bradford), Vol. 22, No. 1/2, 2001, pp. 138–158.

[29]Zoyem, 2003, op. cit.

That result is also supported by the finding that those working in larger firms were more likely to have a high value of skills security than those working in small units. The association between skills security and employment security is scarcely surprising. But it implies that the global pursuit of flexible labour relations may weaken the propensity of enterprises to provide workers with training. If this is so, it will be essential for governments to take corrective action, either directly or by regulations or incentives.

Another link comes out between labour informalization and skills security. Recalling the continuum variable devised for the PSS, some examples may illustrate this point. In Gujarat, India, about three-quarters of the highly informal do not have any skills security as defined in this chapter, compared with 13% of those in highly formal labour statuses. Some 96% of the highly informal had not received any training, compared with 60% of the highly formal.

In Ethiopia, as expected, the less educated are concentrated in the more informal work statuses, and the vast majority of them do not meet any of the five criteria used to define formality. As in Gujarat, India, most in such statuses have not had any training. Much the same emerges in the very different economy of China, where those in relatively informal labour statuses are far less likely to have access to training.

There is a positive link between skills security and income, leaving out a well-established positive relationship. Those who score high on skills security tend to have higher incomes. But the results for Ukraine (Figure 8.29) show that the positive relationship is stronger for men than for women. In Gujarat, India, the overall positive relationship holds, but the income reward does not increase with level of skills security.

Figure 8.29 Ukraine: Individual Skills Security Index, by income and gender

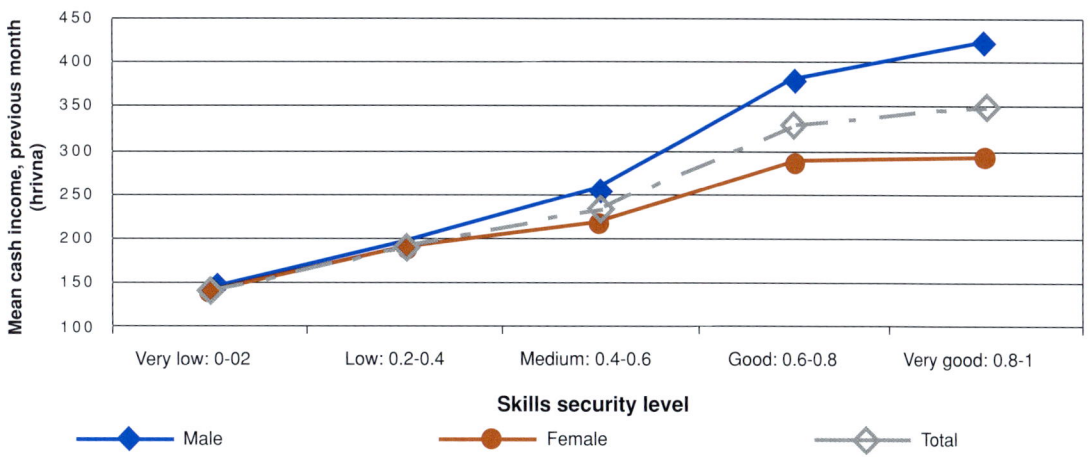

Source: Ukraine PSS 2002.

Finally, there is a positive correlation between skills security as measured by our skills security index and involvement in organizations providing some sort of representation security. Thus, for instance, whereas only 17% of respondents in the Gujarat (India) PSS with low scores on skills security belonged to any organization representing their interests in work, no less than 90% of those with high scores belonged to one. In Tanzania, the respective figures were 2% and 56%; in Ukraine, they were 38% and 67%. It seems reasonable to suppose that belonging to a union helps an individual worker to obtain or to retain his or her skills.

In the ELFS, most results showed a positive relationship between other forms of security and skill reproduction security as measured by the Decent Workplace Index (DWPI). In Chile, the results were mixed. Average earnings were not higher in firms promoting skill development among workers, nor was employment security associated with skills security. But firms giving workers representation in bargaining were more likely to provide high skills security. Voice and skills seem to go together.

In Tanzania (a rather different type of economy), average earnings are much higher in firms that provide internal skills development, and skills security is higher in firms that give workers voice in bargaining. Employment security also tends to be greater in firms providing skills development. In Indonesia, earnings were higher in firms providing skills security, and other results also resembled those for Tanzania. Indeed, in all the surveys these positive associations were broadly supported.

These are merely illustrations, borne out in other countries. The main objective of this section is to indicate that, as with so many spheres, there are cumulative advantages and cumulative disadvantages. A person with a low level of skill security is likely to suffer from other forms of socio-economic insecurity, and vice versa.

8.7 A national Skills Security Index

International data on skills are weaker than might be thought. As noted earlier, there is no information on the global distribution of "skills", for example. Even "schooling" data should be treated with reservation, particularly with such measures as "years of

school completed" and "literacy"; the former may be artificially inflated by drop-out and "repeat" years (as in South Africa), the latter by widespread "lapsed literacy".[30]

For our purposes, a national Skill Security Index (SSI) is built using the following indicators.

Input indicators

The fact that an ILO Convention related to education or training has been ratified by a particular country is an indication of its commitment to skills security and should therefore be rated positively in the calculation of the SSI. Three main ILO Conventions are relevant to this form of security. One is Convention No. 142 on Human Resources Development, 1975, which focuses on vocational guidance and training, emphasizing that policies should enable workers, without any sort of discrimination, to develop their capabilities for work in their own interest and own aspirations. Second is Convention No. 138 on Minimum Age, 1973, which orients governments to take action to abolish child labour and raise progressively the minimum age for employment. Last is Convention No. 140 on Paid Educational Leave, 1974, which has a relatively low ratification rate, but stipulates a proposition which, in the current context of rapid technological change and need for continuous learning, is gaining relevance. As a way of developing skills, this Convention states that leave — during working hours — should be granted to workers for educational purposes with adequate financial compensation.

A fourth indicator takes account of a national instrument in the form of a law on the number of compulsory years of schooling. The range is rather wide — from 5 to 12 years — and is in our understanding a fair proxy for the value that a society attributes to (basic) education.[31]

---

[30] Vinod Thomas has developed indices of education for a sample of 80 countries, for the World Bank.

[31] As indicated in Section 2 (III) of the introduction of Part II, there is a rule in the calculation of the Input scores which says that indicators representing international instruments should not have a greater impact or weight than national ones. In this case 50% was given to compulsory schooling while the other 50% to the three Conventions as a whole, by taking their average ratification record.

Process indicators

These indicators focus on the supply side of the educational. They are intended to reflect how policies and broad orientations and principles adopted by governments are being implemented. A major although incomplete measure — it does not include the private sector — is public expenditure on education. When deflated by the population in schooling age (5–24 years) it indicates the per capita US dollars (current at PPP) used for the development of skills in a particular country, positioning it relatively to others in terms of the amount of available public resources. Complementarily, we introduce the public expenditure on education as a percentage of GDP — also deflated by the population aged 5 to 24. This is to differentiate between countries according to what share of their public funds they spend on education. While the first expenditure indicator gives a measure of "wealth", the second one is an indication of priority among the set of other social sectors spending. Finally, aiming at a proxy of how knowledge is delivered the usual pupil-per-teacher ratio (at primary school level) is used. In spite of its well-known limitations, it aims to reflect the quality of the basic education system.

Outcome indicators

The indicators are proxy measures for the actual level of skills security. They are based on estimates of educational attainment, as portrayed by the educational profile of the adult population (aged 25 to 64) most likely to be economically active. Lack of data on training in developing countries has not allowed us to include indicators in this respect. Although this is a major limitation, as shown earlier in this chapter, the analysis of PSS data clearly demonstrates the strong link between education and training. All three indicators refer to the population aged 25 to 64 and represent basic and higher educational levels. The first two provide two different estimates of basic education.[32] One is the literacy rate, the other the median number of years of schooling. For higher education, the proportion of this population group that has completed at least post-secondary schooling has been retained. Post-secondary was preferred to secondary completed because, among countries in transition and industrialized countries, the secondary level does not represent a high level of education and is less discriminatory.

All these *outcome* indicators are introduced in the calculation of the index in two different forms: total and by gender. The latter is defined as the ratio of the rates for females over those for males. Such ratios with values around one reflect a gender balance in skills security while those with values greater than one indicate more security to female relatively to male and the reverse for values smaller than one.

Data on the above indicators exist for 139 countries. As with other indexes, the results can be summarized by grouping countries in clusters (Table 8.3 and Figure 8.30). A clear divide appears between regions and levels of skills security. All western and eastern European countries are either "Pacesetters" or "Pragmatists". By contrast, no countries from Africa or the Middle East provide satisfactory skills security, with the exceptions of Lesotho and Israel. A similar situation predominates in Asia where a majority of countries also have unsatisfactory levels of skills security, with exceptions from the Asia-Pacific region.

Countries of Latin America and the Caribbean are represented in almost equal numbers in the "Pragmatists", "Conventionals" and "Much-to-be-done" clusters, indicating the absence of a common regional pattern. The case of Cuba should be highlighted as it is the sole country from the region to be a "Pacesetter". It is also the industrializing country with the highest and most satisfactory skills security score.

---

[32]The reason for having two indicators is based on the assumption that their respective deficiencies could in this way be somewhat overcome. Deficiencies are particularly relevant in the context of international comparisons because biases resulting from the effects of the demographic profiles on the literacy rates as well as those resulting from the effects of the varying "grade repetition" rates on the median number of school years can be significant.

Table 8.3 Skills Security Index

Regions	High score on Outcome			
	High score on Input / Process		Low score on Input / Process	
	Pacesetters Countries		Pragmatists Countries	
Africa and Middle East	Israel		Lesotho	
Americas	Cuba		Argentina	Panama
			Canada	Saint Vincent and the Grenadines
			Chile	Saint Kitts and Nevis
			Costa Rica	United States
			Dominican Republic	Uruguay
			Jamaica	
Asia	Australia		Japan	New Zealand
			Korea, Republic of	Philippines
Eastern Europe and Central Asia	Belarus	Poland	Azerbaijan	Latvia
	Czech Republic	Russian Federation	Bulgaria	Moldova, Republic of
	Georgia	Slovakia	Estonia	Romania
	Hungary	Slovenia	Kazakhstan	Turkmenistan
	Lithuania	Ukraine		
Western Europe	Belgium	Luxembourg	Austria	
	Cyprus	Netherlands	Italy	
	Denmark	Norway		
	Finland	Portugal		
	France	Spain		
	Germany	Sweden		
	Greece	Switzerland		
	Iceland	United Kingdom		
	Ireland			

	Low score on Outcome			
	High score on Input / Process		**Low** score on Input / Process	
Regions	**Conventionals Countries**		**Much-to-be-done Countries**	
Africa and Middle East	Algeria	Kenya	Benin	Mauritius
	Bahrain	Kuwait	Burkina Faso	Morocco
	Botswana	Malta	Burundi	Mozambique
	Congo	Tunisia	Cameroon	Niger
	Jordan		Central African Rep.	Nigeria
			Congo, Dem. Rep. of	Rwanda
			Côte d'Ivoire	Senegal
			Egypt	Sierra Leone
			Ethiopia	South Africa
			Gambia	Sudan
			Ghana	Swaziland
			Guinea-Bissau	Syrian Arab Republic
			Iran, Islamic Rep. of	Tanzania, United Rep. of
			Lebanon	Togo
			Madagascar	Turkey
			Malawi	Uganda
			Mali	Zambia
			Mauritania	Zimbabwe
Americas	Barbados	Guyana	Bolivia	Mexico
	Brazil	Nicaragua	Colombia	Paraguay
	Dominican Republic	Saint Lucia	Guatemala	Peru
	Ecuador	Venezuela	Honduras	Trinidad and Tobago
	El Salvador			
Asia	China	Singapore	Bangladesh	Pakistan
	Indonesia	Thailand	Fiji	Papua New Guinea
	Kiribati		India	Sri Lanka
	Malaysia		Myanmar	Viet Nam
			Nepal	
Eastern Europe and Central Asia	Armenia	Kyrgyzstan	Albania	
	Croatia	Tajikistan	Uzbekistan	
Western Europe				

Finally, it is useful to compare the provision of skills security as a whole with a composite measure of gender inequality in schooling, using the outcome sub-index. Some countries provide high overall skills security and a good gender balance. But many do not. For example, there are as many as 23 countries, all from Asia and Africa, which perform badly on both counts, delivering low skills security overall combined with large schooling differences between men and women. By contrast, many countries from Europe achieve high skills security with minor male-female differences.

There is one group of 14 countries in which skills security is low and where the gender differential is large. This is mostly a Latin American phenomenon. Another group, also consisting of 14 countries has high overall skills security but a relatively wide male-female differential. This group consists mostly of countries from central Europe, notably Switzerland and Germany, and from South-East Asia, such as the Republic of Korea and Japan.

Figure 8.30 Skills security index - Clusters by region

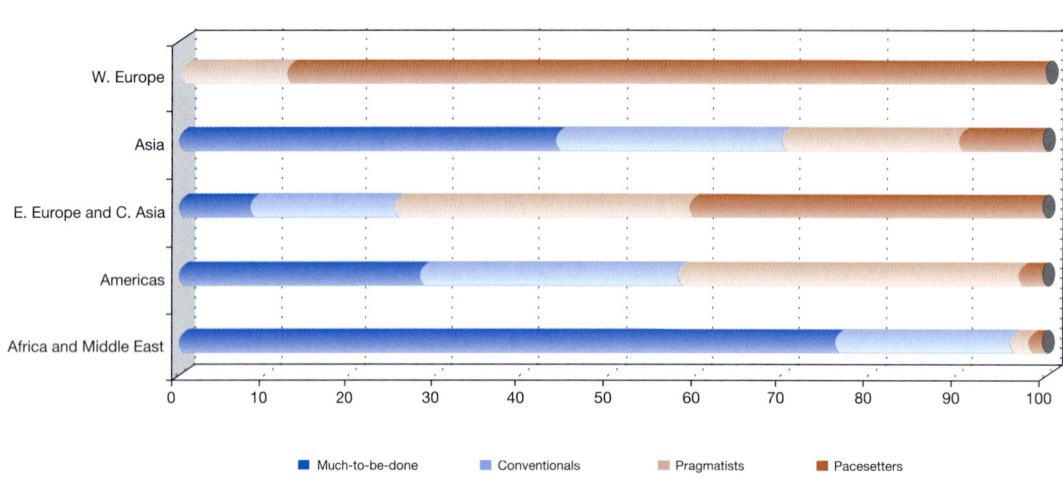

Legend: ■ Much-to-be-done ■ Conventionals ■ Pragmatists ■ Pacesetters

8.8 Concluding reflections

"High school is simply a way of building up a tolerance for stress."

— 14-year-old girl student in the United States [33]

The acquisition and the use of competencies are rightly perceived as crucial to social and economic security. But giving empirical shape to skill reproduction security is hard, in part because the concepts are complex, in part because the statistics on these issues are poor. It is to be hoped that the effort made in this chapter will encourage others to give more attention to those conceptual and statistical issues.

Skills security comes from possessing the capability to learn, which comes from universal basic schooling and a removal of inequalities in the course of subsequent schooling. At the moment, too many inequalities are accentuated by the complex system of education and training, which reproduce society's deeper inequalities. In the pursuit of the Millennium Development Goals, correcting those inequalities will be essential.

The findings that come from the PSS deserve further exploration. Too little attention is given to the *non-utilization* of skills and capabilities. Typically, social scientists focus on the non-development of capabilities, and this is understandable. However, a major sadness is that many, many people are

unable to use the skills and competencies that they do possess, and often worked hard to acquire.

Among the several insights from the national index, is that there is a group of countries that perform well in terms of skills security but which perform quite badly in some other respects, notably income security. It is surely no coincidence that these are among the countries from which there has been extensive and continuing "brain-drain" out-migration.

As we will see, skills security does not necessarily translate into better welfare or greater life satisfaction or personal happiness. This is something that is taken up in Chapter 11, in looking at interrelationships between the various forms of security and other social and economic factors. However, the most vital message is that education is deeper than technical knowledge, which improves productivity and makes for more "efficient consumers".[34] It is about the security of human being.

---

[33]Quoted in *The Observer* (London), 15 July 2001, p. 8.

[34]J. Somavia: *People's Security: Globalizating Social Progress* (New York, 1999), p. 155.

Chapter 9

Job security

9.1 The concept of job security

Job security is the possession of a niche in work, allowing some control over the content of a job, what the worker actually does and the opportunity he or she has of building a career. A worker could have employment security but no job security, when, for instance, within the same firm his tasks undergo unwanted, stressful or unpredictable changes that force him to adjust or to discontinue his job or to change occupations. This form of security is related to both employment and skills security, but differs in that it refers to the worker's own development over his or her entire active life. Again, another way of presenting job security is to refer to *property rights* in a person's work.

In other words, whereas employment security refers to the sense of attachment to a current enterprise or establishment, *job security* refers to the sense of attachment to a particular job or range of tasks. One may have strong employment security but weak job security, or both may be weak or strong, or one may be perceived as strong. Conceptually, the differences are fairly easy to appreciate. However, empirically finding a way to assess job security is much harder, and this aspect of labour-related security has been less studied than employment security.

There is one preliminary point to bear in mind. Job security can be a mixed blessing. Being stuck in a narrowly defined job can be stultifying, hindering a person's development, health and happiness, as well as his or her productivity. Too often in the 20th century, *job demarcation* practices were used as a defensive device to the detriment of workers' development.

Although this chapter will not go into the issue of job security in detail, the subject of a future analysis, it may be useful to indicate a few issues at the workplace and individual level, drawing on the People's Security Surveys (PSS) and Enterprise Labour Flexibility and Security Surveys (ELFS). The final section presents a Job Security Index as measured for 94 countries.

Having a niche in work and access to what is often called a career, is what decent work is or should be all about. In the PSS, efforts have been made to ascertain the characteristics of job security, with questions about discrimination at work, perceived *work satisfaction* and about the breadth of tasks and mobility within work.

9.2 Discrimination as job insecurity

If job security is about having a secure niche in the production process, one measure is whether the person can have a reasonable prospect of retaining his or her job without being arbitrarily transferred to another or being confronted with a situation where the tasks or skills have become obsolescent. A further measure is whether or not the person has a reasonable prospect of enhancing his or her position in terms of status, skill or income. Another is whether or not the person faces discrimination or institutional barriers to work opportunities, including mobility.

Discriminatory labour markets and labour practices cause economic insecurity for those directly involved and for those who think they may be affected. This extends to groups, or forms of behaviour, that are not regarded by the mainstream of society as legitimate. A society that tolerates one or certain forms of discrimination is likely to tolerate others, and thus the insecurities will spill over beyond the groups currently facing discrimination.

Job security entails equal opportunities, which means no unfair discrimination. This opens up sensitive issues, epitomized by the agonizing over "affirmative action" to rectify past discrimination, be it racial, gender, disability, religious, or some other form. The matter can be put starkly. Whenever an employer chooses to appoint one person rather than another, a discriminatory judgement is made. Rarely is the decision made purely on the basis of proven technical competence. Usually, it is "unfair" in some way or another.

Consider the classic case of discrimination against women. A woman may face a lower probability of being selected for a job, or keeping it, because the manager believes women are less "suited" to the job, or have a lower probability of staying in it, or even because of some evidence that on average women have lower productivity in that type of job. Or the action may be based on some gender viewpoint – a belief that women should not be working, for example. Policies to correct for such unfairness would promote women's job security and on this there is probably widespread agreement. But we should not forget that policies and practices designed to rectify past unfairness may unfairly jeopardize the job security of others, in this case men, especially where technically more qualified men are passed over (just as many women have been) in favour of "gender balance". The key point here is that both

discrimination and correcting for past discrimination can induce job insecurity.

There are three main forms of discrimination that affect job security. Categorical discrimination is where visible or identifiable groups are excluded or treated less well than others. Statistical discrimination is where employers discriminate based on group norms, as when the average person of a group is expected to behave in some adverse way. Inferential discrimination arises from application of a general criterion that results in disadvantage to a particular group that happens to fail that criterion. In practice, all three forms of discrimination take place and have proved hard to combat.

(i) Personal awareness

People vary in their perception or awareness of discrimination. In Latin America, for example, in some countries workers are aware of gender discrimination to a greater extent than in others, and in some they see racial or disability discrimination as more pervasive. Thus, in the PSS, workers in Chile say they are aware of discrimination against women to a greater extent than workers in Argentina (Figure 9.1). By contrast, workers in Brazil are more aware of racial discrimination, from which it appears that combating racial discrimination should be given top priority. Of course, perceptions may not correspond to actual practices, but they are probably reasonable guides to what is going on.

Figure 9.1 Argentina, Brazil and Chile: Percentage of workers witnessing discrimination related to race/nationality, gender, homosexuality or serious illness

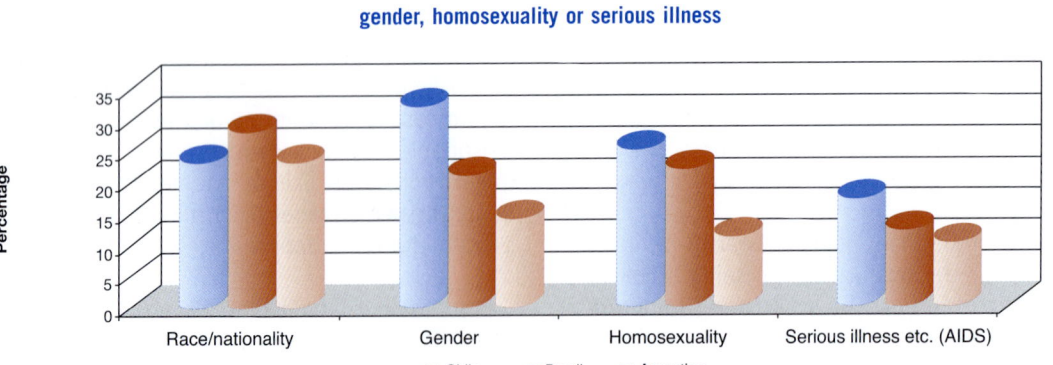

Source: Argentina, Brazil and Chile PSS 2001..

In other countries, race, religion and migrant status tend to be the greatest barriers to equitable treatment in labour markets. In Gujarat, India, those barriers and gender discrimination are widely observed by both men and women (Figure 9.2). In Ethiopia, workers think that migrants face the greatest barriers, as is the case in China.

Figure 9.2 Gujarat, India: Percentage of workers witnessing discrimination against ethnic or religious minorities, migrants or women, by gender

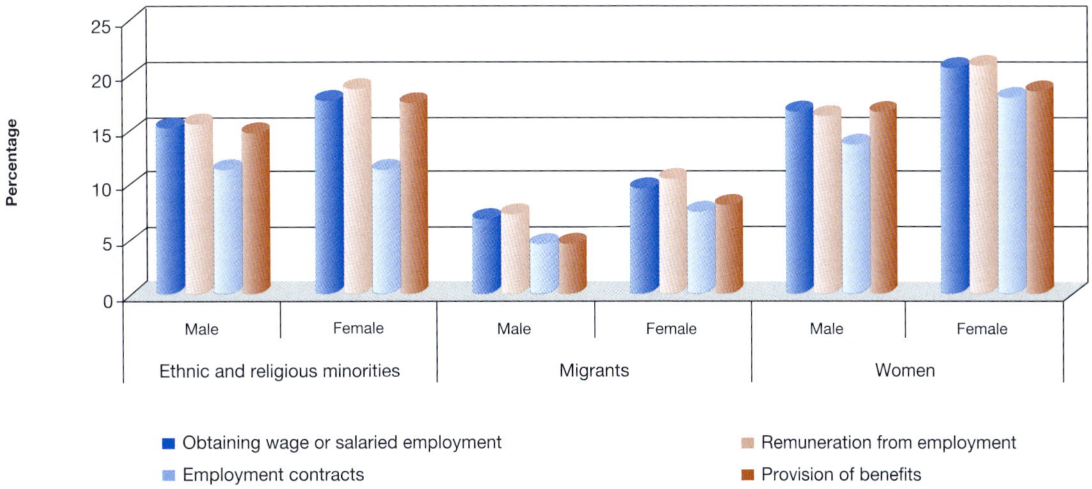

Source: Gujarat, India PSS 2000.

(ii) Workplace discriminatory practices

The data collected from managements in the ELFS reveal widely varying patterns of discrimination around the world. Employers tend to prefer to recruit men rather than women in a wide range of production jobs, while almost everywhere women are preferred in clerical jobs. The greatest inter-country variation in recruitment practices occurs in professional and technical jobs.

In eastern European countries, such as the Russian Federation and Ukraine, more managers prefer women for these types of jobs, although privatization has been accompanied by a shift towards a preference for men. In China, about one in every five firms said they preferred to recruit women as production workers, whereas nearly one in three said they preferred men. For clerical, sales and service workers, 40% said they preferred women, 6% said they preferred men. By contrast, in Chile only 2% of firms said they preferred women as production workers, compared with 43% that preferred men; for clerical, sales and service workers, 7% preferred

men, 7% preferred women; and for professional and technical jobs, 16% preferred men, 2% women. In Tanzania, more firms prefer men as production workers and for professional and technical jobs; whereas for clerical, sales and service jobs, slightly more prefer women. Only to a small extent could the countries' sectoral and occupational structures possibly explain these national or cultural differences.

In every country covered by the ELFS, discriminatory recruitment practices against women are more common among small firms, and greater in private than in public (state) enterprises. One possible explanation is that small private firms are under less regulatory scrutiny, and are less likely to be unionized. As emphasized in Chapter 12, the presence of a union is associated with a lower probability of discriminatory labour practices.

Policies on equality of opportunity often neglect what happens once workers enter firms. Discrimination is often greater in the provision of training opportunities than in recruitment. For instance, in Ukraine the female share of employment is greater than the female share of workers provided with training. But discrimination goes all the way through the employment relationship, with respect to pay, access to fringe benefits, training, mobility and redundancy.

In China, although the great majority of firms said they did not have any preference in laying off workers, more said they preferred to lay off women.

Equal employment opportunity policy

In Tanzania, 41% of firms covered in the ELFS said they had a policy of equal employment opportunity (EOP) for men and women. This was most likely in state enterprises, and least likely in small private firms. Firms operating an Equal Opportunity Policy (EOP) said the main reason was that it created "better relations between workers and clients".

The trouble is that such policies do not always reflect management desires in practice. Most Tanzanian managers did not plan to increase the number of women they employed, even though women were in a minority.

In the Philippines, where also two in every five firms also said they operated an EOP, many firms still expressed preferences for men or for women when recruiting. And two-thirds said they did not plan to increase women's share of employment, even though women had only a minority of jobs.

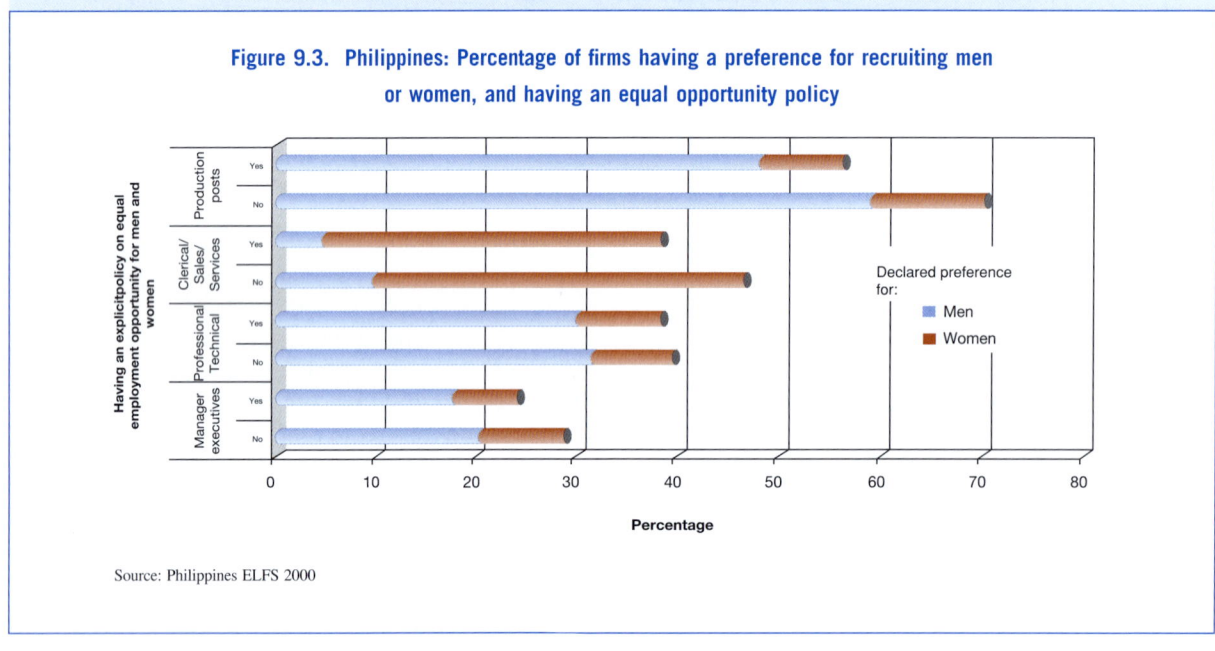

Figure 9.3. Philippines: Percentage of firms having a preference for recruiting men or women, and having an equal opportunity policy

Source: Philippines ELFS 2000

Ukraine: Women disadvantaged by training practices?

Ukraine is one of those transition countries forced to restructure employment to revive their economies. For women to retain their high share of employment, they need to have equal access to vocational and job training, within and outside enterprises. But women may suffer from a mix of structural disadvantage (through being concentrated in firms or sectors not providing training) and overt discrimination in the allocation of training, coupled with behavioural adaptation on the part of women workers themselves.

In Ukraine, firms show a slight tendency to discriminate against women in training. On average the share of women among those having received training in the previous year (36%) was less than their share of employment, and the share had declined since 1995. Although the overall difference was small, the low share in some industries should be a concern (Figure 9.4). However, in terms of overt discrimination, it was at least encouraging that few managers (12%) said they preferred to provide men with training; an even smaller number (3%) said they preferred to give training to women. So, overtly there was little sign of gender discrimination. But these figures reflected a slight increase in pro-male discrimination since earlier rounds of the survey.

Figure 9.4 Ukraine: Female share of workers trained, female share in total employment, and ratio

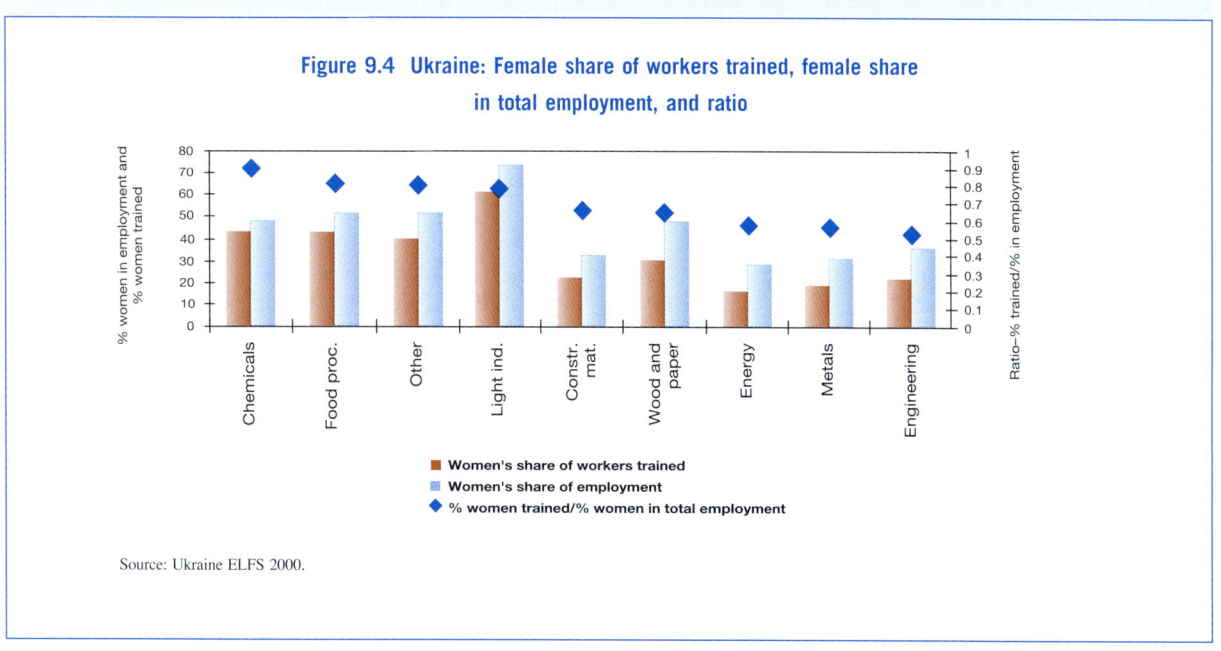

Source: Ukraine ELFS 2000.

Non-Discrimination Index: Application to the Russian Federation, Republic of Moldova and Indonesia

For social equity, non-discriminatory labour practices are essential in identifying a good firm.[1] To be exemplary, an enterprise should act in ways that reduce or avoid segregation based on personal characteristics such as race, gender or disabilities. Although measuring discrimination and disadvantages is notoriously difficult, at a minimum, both employer attitudes (preferences) and outcomes should be taken into account. Neither preferences nor outcomes alone would be sufficient. For instance, one might have a "preference" but not put it into effect, or have no preference yet discriminate by hiring on the basis of characteristics that had the (perhaps inadvertent) effect of excluding certain groups from various jobs.

What is needed is a set of easily understood indicators of social equity. For this reason, in the enterprise surveys, attention is focused on the equitable properties of hiring and training practices. In the ELFS, the main indicators of non-discrimination are related to gender, although this could be adjusted to include other groups. In the case of South Africa, race was also taken into account.

First, in terms of recruitment, if the management reported having no preference for either men or women, this was regarded as a positive factor. It is neutrality that is equitable. Just as it would be inequitable to give a positive value if a firm stated it had a preference for men, it would be inequitable for men if a positive value were given if the management said they preferred to recruit women rather than men, as was the case in some factories. However, we are primarily concerned with redressing the typical case of discrimination against women.

A second input indicator of non-discrimination is a stated commitment to provide training opportunities equally to men and women. Preferences here are also likely to be revealed, where there is no law against discrimination in such matters. Thus, there was a readiness on the part of managements to admit to a discriminatory preference for men and in some cases for women.

In this sphere of enterprise policy, stated preferences — or input indicators — are weak proxies, sometimes being rationalizations of what has happened, and more often being norm-induced. To ignore preferences altogether would be unjustifiable, yet it is important to complement the preference factor with indicators of actual outcomes.

Accordingly, a first outcome indicator of sex discrimination relates to the actual share of employment taken by women. The indicator selected was the percentage of higher-level "employee" jobs taken by women. If that was greater than 40%, the firm was given a positive score in the index. This measure is not ideal, because an outcome could reflect differences in the supply of men and women. However, it does focus on the better type of jobs and identifies relatively good performance in a key area of discrimination.

One could modify the threshold level to be sectorally specific, giving a positive score in the index if a firm had a relatively high percentage of women in training relative to the average for all firms in the sector. This could be justified because the ratios vary by sector _ but it also allows for gender-based industrial segregation of employment.[2] Accordingly, we do not take that route.

[1] Kofi Annan, United Nations Secretary General, in promoting the Global Compact, gave particular attention to the need to make "sure hiring and firing policies did not discriminate on grounds of race, creed, gender or ethnic origins".

[2] For instance, it would be inappropriate to give a positive score to a firm in the energy sector in which merely 12% of its higher level "employees" were women just because the industry's average was 10%.

Besides gender variables, another indicator of discrimination is whether or not the firm was employing workers with registered disabilities. Coupled with the gender variables, this yields an index of non-discrimination, as follows:

ND = Rs + Ts + Tfem + FWC + D

where ND is the index of non-discrimination, and

Rs = 1 if the management has no preference for either men or women in recruiting production workers, 0 otherwise;

Ts = 1 if management stated it had no preference for either men or women in providing training for production workers;

Tfem = 1 if women's share of workers trained is equal to or greater than their share of total employment, 0 otherwise;

FWC = 1 if the female share of employees (managerial, specialist or general service workers) was greater than 40%, 0 otherwise;

D = 1 if the firm employed workers with disabilities, 0 otherwise.

For illustration, Figure 9.5 shows that firms in Russian industry mostly score badly, epitomizing the fragmented and unregulated nature of Russian enterprises in the past decade or so. Only 5% of all firms had a value of non-discrimination of 0.8 or more. Similar patterns emerged in the Republic of Moldova.

In Indonesia (Figure 9.6), no firm had the maximum value of non-discrimination, and more than 60% were in the lowest range of the scale.

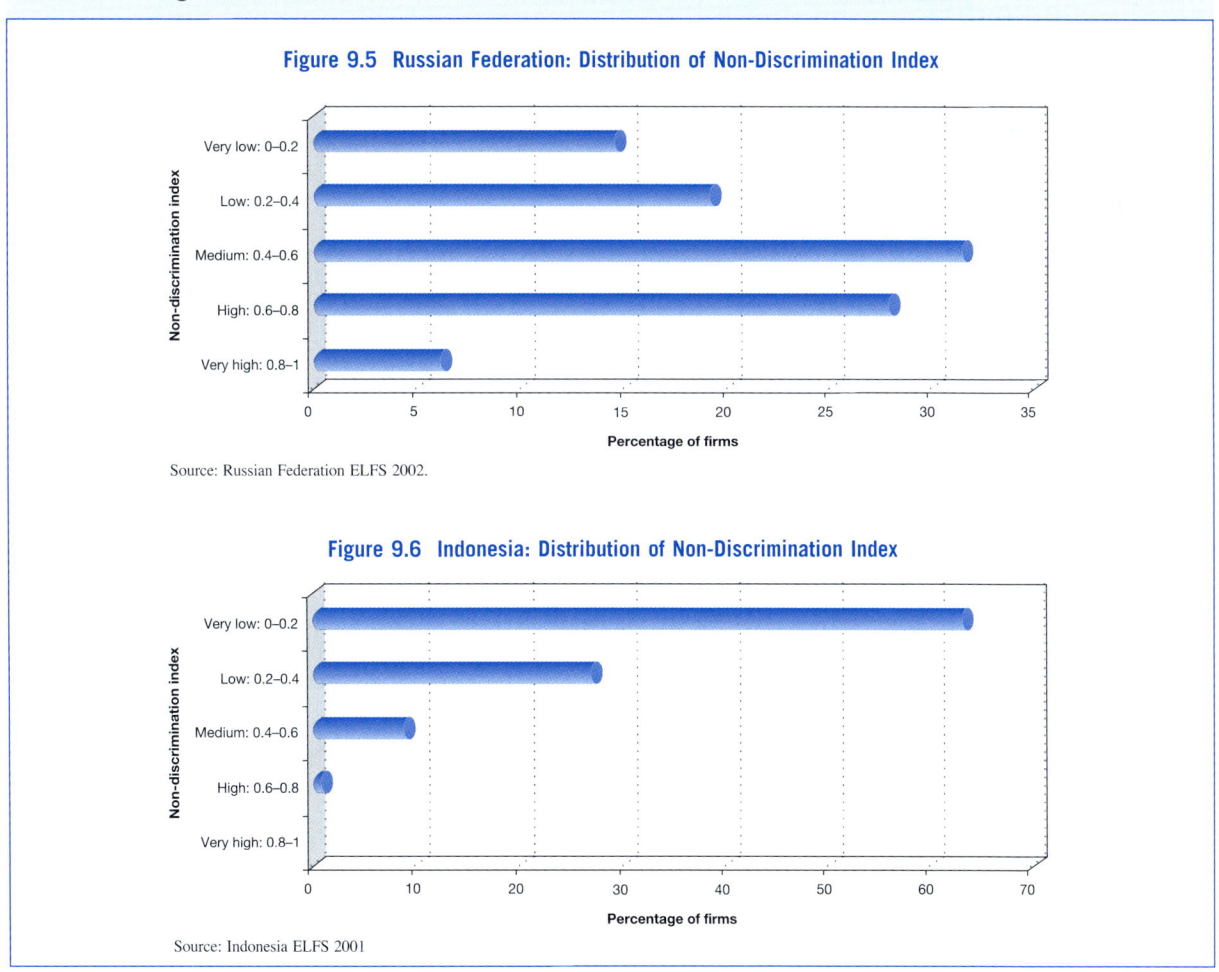

Figure 9.5 Russian Federation: Distribution of Non-Discrimination Index

Source: Russian Federation ELFS 2002.

Figure 9.6 Indonesia: Distribution of Non-Discrimination Index

Source: Indonesia ELFS 2001

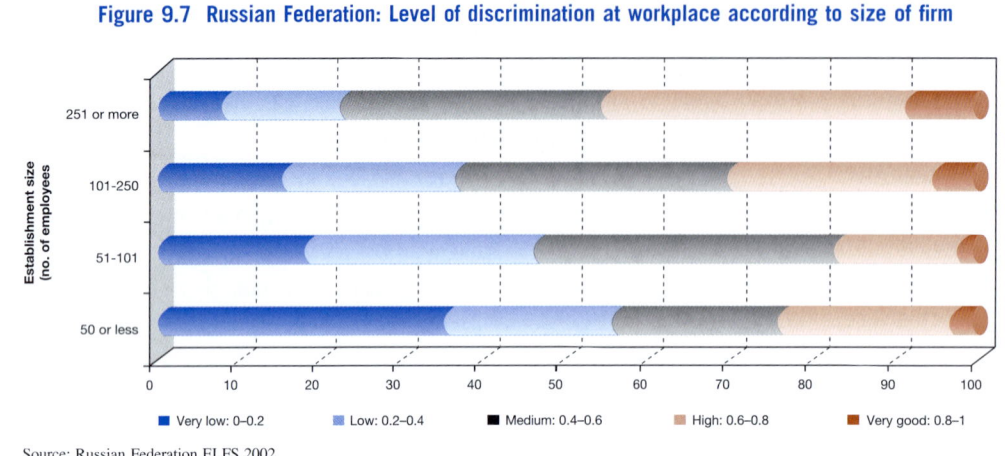

Figure 9.7 Russian Federation: Level of discrimination at workplace according to size of firm

Source: Russian Federation ELFS 2002

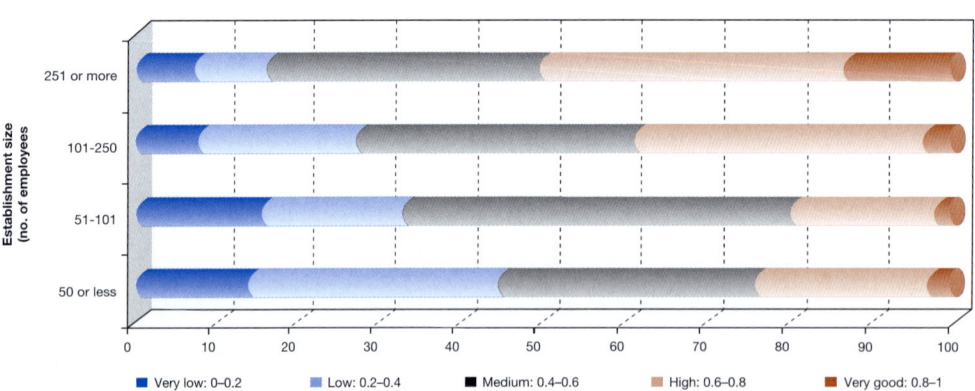

Figure 9.8 Republic of Moldova: Level of discrimination at workplace according to size of firm

Source: Republic of Moldova ELFS 2000.

Level of discrimination depends on the size of the firm, with greater discrimination in smaller firms as shown in the Russian Federation (Figure 9.7) and in the Republic of Moldova (Figure 9.8). It also depends on workers' representation security in the firm, the existence of a trade union as well as a collective agreement having a positive impact on discrimination, as shown in Tables 9.1 and 9.2 for the Russian Federation and the Republic of Moldova respectively.

Table 9.1 Russian Federation: Discrimination index at the workplace
(percentage of firms in specified range)

	Very low %	Low %	Medium %	High %	Very high %	Total %
Acting trade union						
Yes	9.9	20.4	31.4	30.6	7.8	100
No	26.7	16.7	32.7	21.3	2.7	100
Collective agreement						
Yes	11.7	18.3	31.3	30.5	8.1	100
No	22.7	22.0	32.6	21.3	1.4	100
Total	**14.7**	**19.3**	**31.7**	**28.1**	**6.3**	**100**

Source: Russia Federation PSS 2002.

Table 9.2. Republic of Moldova: Discrimination index at the workplace
(percentage of firms in specified range)

	Very low %	Low %	Medium %	High %	Very high %	Total %
Acting trade union						
Yes	8.5	10.8	37.5	34.1	9.1	100
No	14.7	32.0	32.0	21.3		100
Collective agreement						
Yes	15.9	30.5	28.0	22.0	3.7	100
No	7.7	10.7	39.6	34.3	7.7	100
Total	**10.4**	**17.1**	**35.9**	**30.3**	**6.4**	**100**

Source. Republic of Moldova ELFS 2000.

(iii) Pregnancy and job security

For women, one aspect of job security is their ability to have a child without risk of losing their job. This is a matter of discrimination and the ability to pursue a career. In the PSS, workers were asked how likely a woman was to lose her job if she became pregnant at their workplace. In China, 18% of women and 13% of men thought a woman would lose her job, one-quarter were uncertain, and 62% thought it unlikely. In Indonesia, nearly a quarter of all women in wage jobs thought they would lose their jobs, whereas over two-thirds thought it unlikely. In Ethiopia, among the small minority of women in jobs, 19% thought it was very likely they would lose their jobs, and more than a third of those in the younger age groups thought so.

This aspect of job security is related to *employment security,* as measured by employment tenure. In China, women were much less likely to think they would lose their job on becoming pregnant if they had a "permanent" contract (78% felt safe, compared with 61% of those in temporary jobs of less than a year, and 38% of day workers), or had been employed for some time. Those in the public sector also felt relatively secure. Similar patterns were found in Indonesia and in Ethiopia. In all countries, women working in small firms feel relatively insecure in this respect.

In both China and Indonesia, there is also a positive relationship between a woman's education and her expectation of keeping a job on becoming pregnant. Whether that is due to the education itself is doubtful; it rather reflects the type of job obtained by more educated women.

The ELFS shows that management's concern over women workers subsequently taking maternity leave are used by many firms to discriminate against hiring young women. This varies by type of firm. In China, small firms are much more likely to report that regulations on maternity leave discourage them from recruiting women – this is seen as a barrier in 18% of firms with fewer than 25 employees, compared with 8% of those with more than 500 employees. As in so many ways, small is not beautiful in this respect. And private firms are much more likely to discriminate for that reason. In addition, almost one quarter of the smaller firms, compared to 5% of large firms, do not allow women to take maternity leave, with or without pay.

Similar patterns emerge in the Philippines. But there, legislative change might not help. Some 87% of all firms said they would not employ more or fewer women if the labour regulations on maternity leave were removed. Firms are rather rigid. Thus, over two-thirds of firms do not allow women with a new baby to work on a part-time basis (less than 40 hours a week). Larger firms are more willing to offer that kind of arrangement, 37% of firms with more than 100 workers being prepared to do so, compared with 27% of firms with fewer than ten workers.

9.3 Job satisfaction

One way of trying to capture job security is to ask about subjective perceptions of a person's work, such as the perceived opportunity to develop competencies, the chances of upward (and downward) mobility and the degree of *satisfaction* with a job. Satisfaction relates to many aspects of work, and a high level of satisfaction with regard to one aspect, such as income, might be offset by a low degree of satisfaction with regard to another, such as opportunity to develop a career or work security. Moreover, satisfaction may reflect the absence of a gap between reality and *expectations* and/or *aspirations*. If a job is regarded as purely or largely instrumental, a person may be more inclined to express satisfaction as long as the income is acceptable.

The subject of job satisfaction has been extensively studied in affluent societies, and in several industrialized countries large data sets have been assembled to trace patterns and trends. The PSS has attempted to develop a set of questions that could allow more widespread monitoring. Here, we extend the analysis of the resultant PSS data that has already been carried out for Argentina, Brazil, Chile, Hungary and Ukraine.[3]

---

[3] .J. Ritter and R. Anker: "Good jobs, bad jobs: Workers' evaluations in Five countries", *International Labour Review*, Vol. 141, No.4, 2002, pp. 331–384. On Ukraine, see L. Zsoldos and G. Standing, 2002: *Coping with Insecurity: The Ukrainian People's Security Survey 2002*, SES Paper No. 17 (Geneva, ILO, 2002).

Incentives and job security

Incentives work — they incentivize people to want more incentives

Just as advertisements generate dissatisfaction by creating desires and needs that people did not know they had, so incentives commonly foster dissatisfaction, frustration and a sense of personal failing. Psychologists have long understood that job satisfaction is not the opposite of job dissatisfaction. According to a perceptive point made long ago by Frederich Herzberg, job satisfaction comes from factors intrinsic to the work — the range of tasks, a sense of achievement, recognition, responsibility, the creativity allowed, and so on.

By contrast, dissatisfaction comes mainly from extrinsic factors, such as the company's or organization's general policies, the pay structure, working conditions, and so on. Poor pay demotivates more than good pay motivates. Wage incentives can cover up, partially at best, for an unrewarding job. They are like a drug; a person adapts to one, and wants more. In the end, their existence is frustrating. Security comes from doing something in which one believes.

This is why the latest "human resources" [sic] strategies emphasize the need to let people "customize" their jobs to suit their lifestyles and ambitions.[4] Good work creates and enhances commitment — but this is not docile or subordinated loyalty.

In all Tayloristic approaches to job structures and labour relations in the past century, priority was given to explicit factors, such as employment security and wage incentives. Industrial unions contributed to this through their vigorous promotion and then defence of job demarcation boundaries, which accommodated "scientific management", but at the cost of inhibiting internal flexibility, upward mobility and work diversity. Ultimately, therefore, scientific management and the responses to it merely intensified insecurity.

Occupational security is the desired future. The world has a long way to go. But the very recognition that in most jobs there is no "long term" — no job or employment security as in the Taylorist–Fordist model — is an advance. Only with that recognition can policies focus on creating an environment of economic security in which livelihood security can evolve.

Job satisfaction tends to be greater in the three Latin American countries than in the two transition countries, although this partly reflects the fact that people in urban areas are more likely to have a greater degree of satisfaction, and only urban areas were covered in the Latin American countries.

The situation in Ukraine might seem to be reasonably good, in that many workers are moderately satisfied with their jobs. However, satisfaction or dissatisfaction may reflect low or high expectations. A worker may regard all available jobs with such low expectations that even a poor job may be regarded as acceptable. With that in mind, in Ukraine more workers expressed themselves satisfied than dissatisfied with their wages, benefits, nature of work, and degree of autonomy in their work, opportunities to improve skills and opportunities for promotion. If anything, except in the instrumental and important areas of wage levels and benefit entitlements, women were more likely to express satisfaction.

Only in the spheres of nature of work and opportunities for improving skills did a majority express satisfaction — two-thirds in the case of "nature of work" and just about half for skills improvement op-portunities. In relation to opportunity for promotion, more expressed dissatisfaction than satisfaction. A related aspect is the perceived difficulty of obtaining another comparable job. Accordingly, the PSS asked workers how difficult or easy they thought it would be to obtain another job with similar income, or working conditions, or equally suitable for their skill level. In Ukraine, the results may be a clue to those "satisfaction" outcomes, since a majority thought it would be difficult or very difficult in all three respects.

Results from other PSS also show that people mostly adapt to the realities confronting them. In Indonesia, all those with work for pay or profit or family gain were asked about the degree of satisfaction or dissatisfaction with their work in terms of income, benefits and type of work. As shown in Figure 9.9, a slight majority was dissatisfied with their incomes, most had no benefits, and a majority (58%) was satisfied with the type of work they were doing.

---

[4]B. Tulgan: *Winning the Talent Wars* (London, N. Brealy Publishing, 2001), pp. 155–157.

Figure 9.9 Indonesia: Degree of satisfaction with income, benefits and type of work, by gender

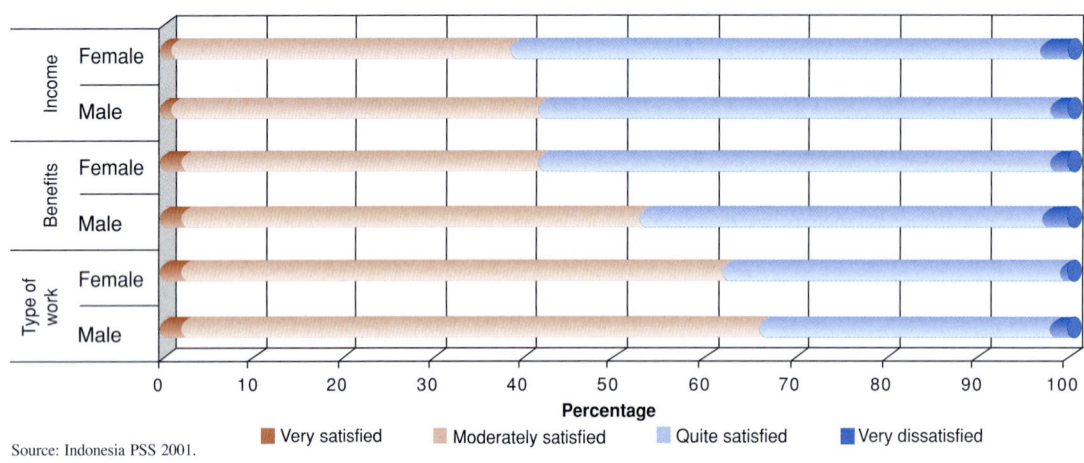

Source: Indonesia PSS 2001.

In Tanzania, in terms of *type of work* being done as their main activity, the picture was more favourable than for income, with 43% of men and 41% of women being reasonably satisfied, and 45% of men and 47% of women being dissatisfied. The more educated were more likely to be satisfied.

In Ghana, among those in employment, there was a remarkable degree of satisfaction with aspects of income-earning work. Over two-thirds of men and nearly two-thirds of women in employment expressed satisfaction with the type of work they were doing, with merely 11% of men and 13% of women expressing dissatisfaction. And nearly three-quarters of workers were satisfied with the degree of autonomy in their work, presumably reflecting the fact that many were doing own-account work of some kind. Over 54% expressed satisfaction with the opportunity to improve their skills through the work they were doing. Ghanaian workers, both men and women, were also mostly satisfied with the length of their working weeks. Basically, the majority was satisfied with the amount of freedom and independence in their work. This result is relevant for interpreting the high score the country achieves on general happiness, discussed in Chapter 11. The high work satisfaction was in contrast with a general lack of satisfaction with income earned from that work and with the non-wage benefits received. In this respect at least, there is something in common with findings in rich countries, where autonomy in work — or the ability to use initiative — is associated with relatively high job satisfaction.[5]

In terms of the prospects of obtaining another job paying them a similar income, in Tanzania most people were pessimistic. Thus, only 10% of men and 12% of women thought that if they lost their current income-earning activity they could find another one paying a similar amount easily. By contrast, 59% of men and 71% of women thought it would be difficult to find one. A majority of people with an income-earning activity believed that it would be difficult to find another activity that would be suitable for their skills — 58% of men and 62% of women.

In Ghana, there was also pessimism about obtaining better work if they left their present activity. Thus, over half thought it would be difficult or very difficult to obtain any job, about 59% said it would be difficult or very difficult to obtain one paying about the same as they were earning over 60% said that about non-wage benefits, and it was similar for access to work suitable for their skills. Although the differences were small, women were slightly more pessimistic about their chances than men.

In Latin America, both men and women seem more satisfied with the nature of the work they do than with opportunities for upward mobility (Figure 9.10). However, dissatisfaction is greater among those with less schooling. In Argentina, for example, 62% of the least educated are not satisfied with opportunities for promotion, against 32% among the most educated. This pattern is also found in Brazil and Chile.

---

[5] A.E. Clark: "What really matters in a job? Hedonic measurement using quit data", *Labour Economics*, No. 8, 2001, pp. 223–242.

Figure 9.10 Latin American countries (Argentina, Brazil and Chile): Satisfaction with nature of work, extent of autonomy/ independence, opportunity for improving skills and for promotion (percentage of responses on each dimension)

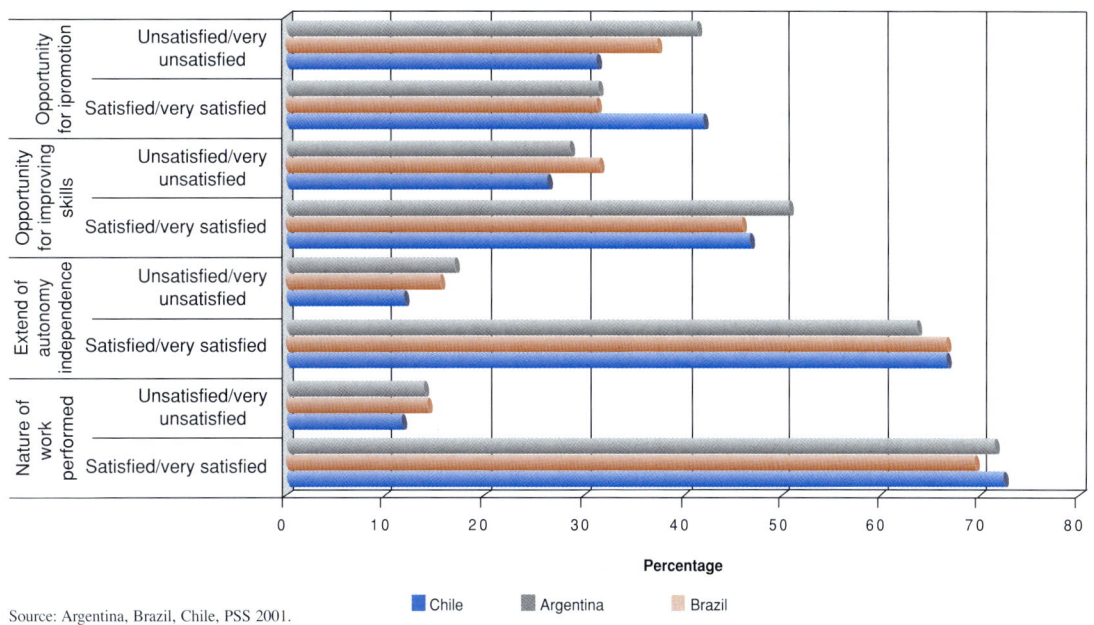

Source: Argentina, Brazil, Chile, PSS 2001.

In China, neutrality is the common feeling regarding satisfaction of both wages and degree of autonomy in the job, training and promotion (Table 9.3). Dissatisfaction is greatest with respect to wages and non-wage benefits, rather than with aspects of the work they are required to do. Again, this may reflect a greater awareness of financial need than with what work could offer.

Table 9.3 China: Satisfaction with wage and non-wage benefits, nature of work, extent of autonomy/ independence, opportunity for improving skills and for promotion (percentage of responses on each dimension)

	Wage level or income	Non-wage and benefits entitlements	Nature of work performed	Extent of autonomy/ independence	Opportunity for promotion skills	Opportunity for improving
Very satisfied	2.2	1.3	3.7	2.9	1.4	0.8
Satisfied	22.9	18.0	47.4	34.5	20.4	12.2
Neutral	40.2	38.0	39.0	46.9	40.4	48.5
Dissatisfied	28.4	34.8	8.9	13.7	30.3	28.6
Very dissatisfied	6.2	7.9	1.1	1.9	7.5	9.9

Source: China PSS 2001.

Similar results emerged in Hungary, where both men and women tended to be more dissatisfied with their wages and non-wage benefits than with the nature of their job (Figure 9.11). In the Russian Federa-

tion as well, dissatisfaction was most common with respect to earnings, ranging from 45% of workers in Moscow to 65% in Samara and 70% in Invanovo.

Figure 9.11 Hungary: Satisfaction with wage and non-wage non benefits, nature of work, extent of independence, opportunity for training and upgrading, by gender

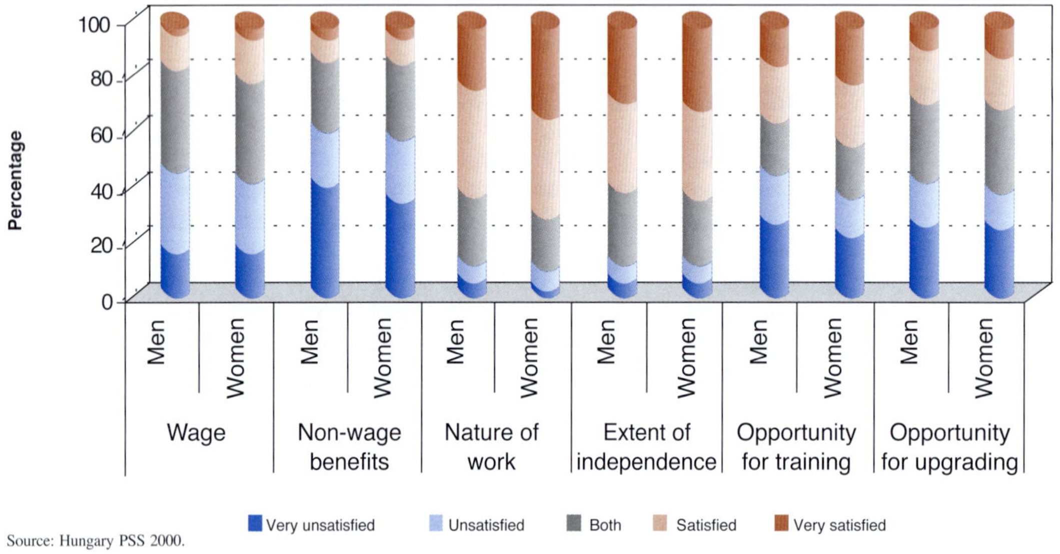

Source: Hungary PSS 2000.

In industrialized countries, there is anecdotal evidence that job satisfaction has declined in many sectors in the last quarter of a century. This may reflect increased education and aspirations that have outstripped improvements in job characteristics.

There is also evidence that job satisfaction is lower for more educated people, who are also likely to have lower life satisfaction.[6] This is scarcely an argument for reducing education or skills. It seems the link is with stressful and prolonged working time, which has been a growing phenomenon among "white-collar" workers in many countries.

In the United Kingdom, for example, the worsening job satisfaction of recent years has been associated with an increasing incidence of stress and psychological ill-being.[7] This corresponds with the arguments about work insecurity made in Chapter 7.

Job satisfaction should not be regarded as synonymous with "happiness" or with an absence of "stress" in work. In many countries, the occupations

that are growing are more demanding in some senses, and there is a statistical association showing that many of these involve more stress and less "happiness" than many old-style manual jobs.

There is also a sensitive gender issue thrown up by the links between stress and job satisfaction. It seems that empirically women are more likely to report stress in their jobs, but are less likely to report job dissatisfaction. One possible explanation is that women are less dominated by their paid job, but are under stress from having too much to do.

---

[6]J. Gardner and A. Oswald: *How Does Education Affect Mental Well-Being and Job Satisfaction?* (Coventry, University of Warwick, 2002, mimeo).

[7]J. Gardner and A.J. Oswald: *What Has Been Happening to the Quality of Workers' Lives in Britain?* (Coventry, University of Warwick, 2001, mimeo).

9.4 Job mobility

An aspect of job security and of the related phenomenon of occupational security is the probability of upward mobility inside one's workplace and job. The PSS asks about past *promotion* and expectations of future promotion.

(i) Past promotion

In all countries, probability of past promotion or upward mobility is positively linked to education, and to the person's skill security level. Schooling, as shown in Chapter 8, is positively associated with access to training, and these feed through to job security. There is also a positive link between job security, as measured by upward mobility, and employment security: workers in small firms and with precarious employment contracts have little or no job mobility.

In Ukraine, about one in four of the employed had been promoted at some time during the past five years, with possibly more women reporting this. The highest probability of promotion was among those in their 20s and 30s. Promotion was particularly likely for those working in the public sector. And, as expected, probability of promotion was greater in large firms.

During the same period, 8% reported that they had been "downgraded", either in occupational grade or skill, or in terms of salary scale. This seemed slightly more likely to have happened to men (10% compared

with 6% for women), and to workers in their 40s and 50s. Downgrading was more likely to have occurred in large firms.

In the Russian Federation, the picture is similar, with some upward mobility but with most being stuck. Two out of every three workers had no upward mobility in the previous three years.

In Latin America, only one in four workers reported upward mobility in the previous two years of their employment, with women and those with little schooling being less likely to have benefited, particularly in Chile. Women's lower probability of upward mobility in the job is common across the world.

In all countries surveyed, there was a strong positive link between level of schooling and upward mobility in jobs. Schooling enhances access to training, and this leads to upgrading. This is well known, but the strong linear relationship means a process of cumulative advantage or disadvantage. In passing, we note that this is a justification for the choice of proxy variables in the national Job Security Index reported at the end of this chapter.

An interesting finding is that the greater the skills security obtained at the individual level, the greater the probability of upward mobility through promotion during the past five years, which holds even when account is taken of age and type of sector. This is shown for Ukraine, where it is also implied that for women the relationship is less strong than for men (Figure 9.12).

Figure 9.12 Ukraine: Promotion in the last five years, by skills security level

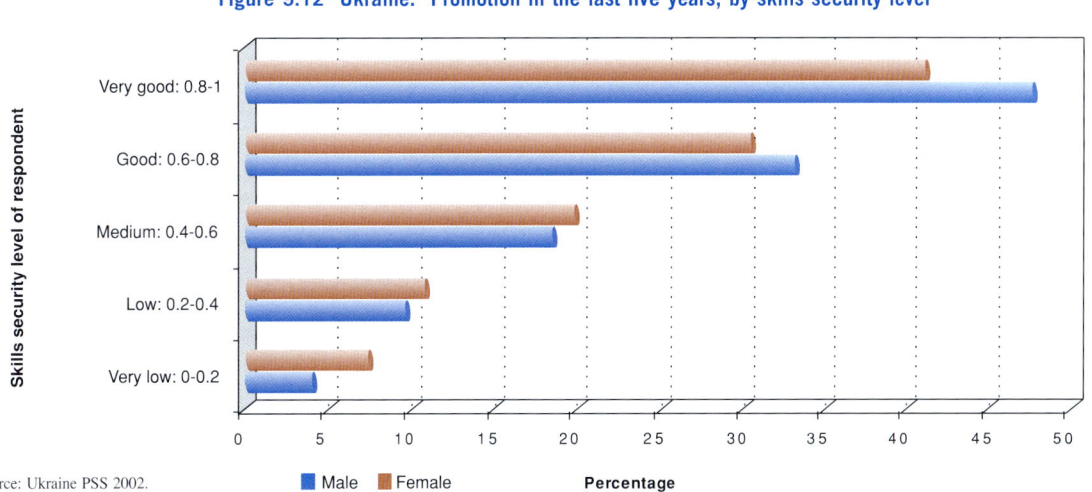

Source: Ukraine PSS 2002.

235

In Indonesia, 43% of workers said they had experienced a rise in income in the past five years, with women slightly less likely to have benefited. The probability of increased responsibility was less, with women again disadvantaged. But while these figures are impressive, only 16% of men and 12% of women thought they had improved their status or occupation in the period. As shown in Figure 9.13, upward mobility is positively associated with level of schooling.

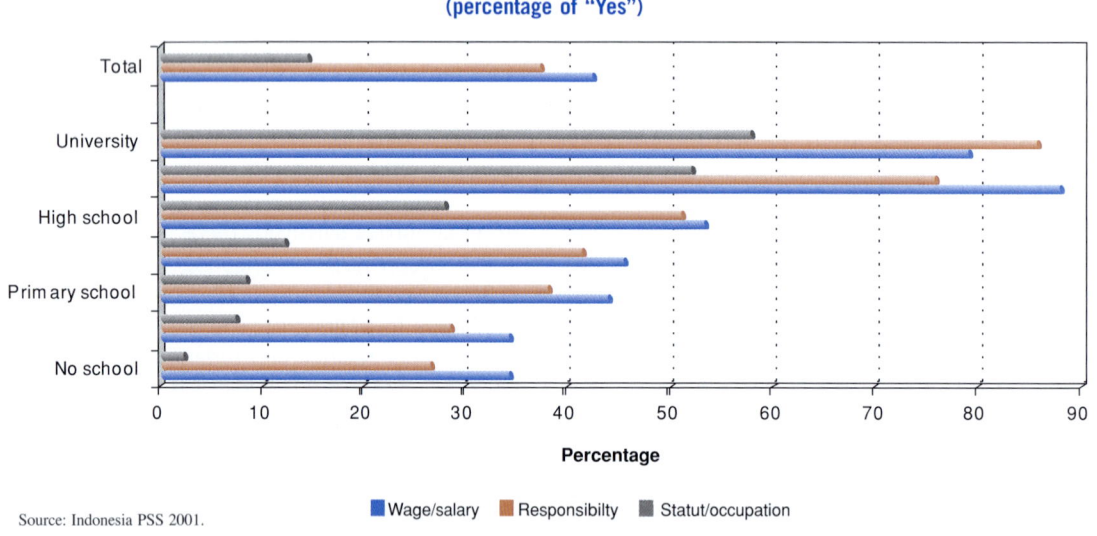

Figure 9. 13 Indonesia: Have you made a "career" advance in the past five years in the type of work you do in terms of wages, responsibility and status by level of education (percentage of "Yes")

Source: Indonesia PSS 2001.

In most countries, probability of upward mobility in the past is greater for men than for women, and what should not be overlooked is the tendency for women to be downgraded to a greater extent. The results for Ethiopia are illustrative of this double pattern (Figure 9.14). The probability of past advance is lower for women whatever the dimension considered. And the probability of downward change is greater.

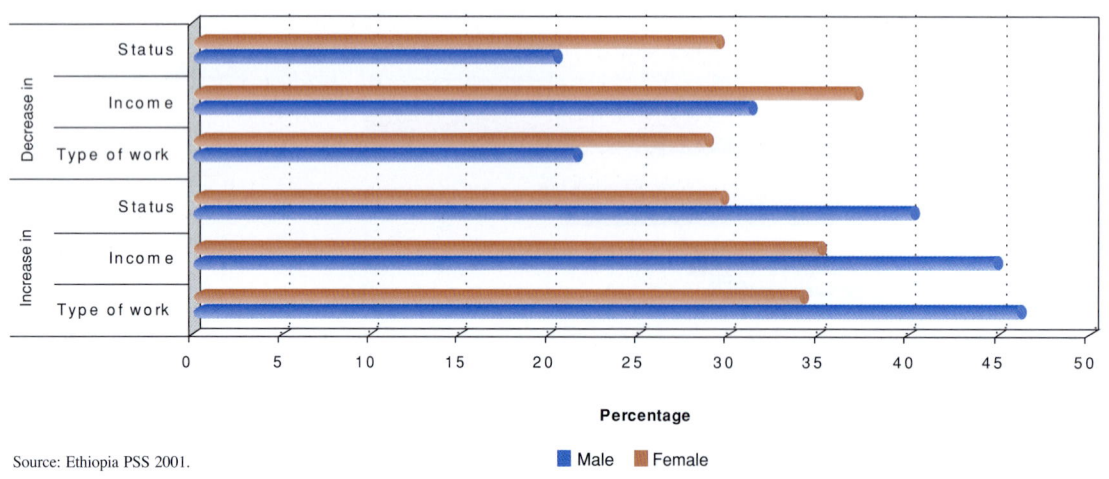

Figure 9.14 Ethiopia: In last three years have you made a career advance or did you see a decrease in terms of type of work, income and status, by gender (percentage of "Yes")

Source: Ethiopia PSS 2001.

(ii) Job mobility expectations

Finally, job security relates to the expectation of upward or downward mobility. The PSS data suggest that optimism or pessimism in this respect varies considerably, being positively related to previous upward mobility and to skills and employment security. But a first point to note is that, in low-income societies, most people rarely think about the longer term, being too preoccupied with daily survival.

A day-to-day view more than a short-term view

In Gujarat, India, thousands of men and women were asked, "Have you thought about what work you will be doing five years from now?"

Nearly three out of every four (72%) had not done so. This applied equally to men and women, and regardless of age or work status. Over 71% of salaried workers had not thought about it. For most, work is a day-to-day means to live or to survive. Only a minority anticipated their future, and most of them anticipated a continuation of what they were doing now.

However, in other societies many people do have a vision of what the future may hold. In Latin America, most workers were extremely pessimistic, the vast majority in Argentina, Brazil and Chile expected no improvement in the next two years, the period specified in the PSS. Again, women are more pessimistic than men, and those with more schooling were more optimistic than others.

In the Russian Federation, the great majority of workers do not expect their jobs to improve: 61% of the respondents do not expect any change in their job in the near future, while less than one in five had hopes of upward mobility. As expected and justified while considering past promotion, people under 35 years of age are more confident about a possible advance in their career (31% against less than 5% among those more than 45 years old).

In Ethiopia, less than one in four workers expected an improvement in the type of work over the next three years, with women being significantly less likely to have any positive expectation. The pattern was similar with respect to expected improvement in income. Expectations are linked to past experience, skills and employment security, but most workers do not expect much to change. Similarly, in Tanzania, only one in three wage workers expect some improvement over the next three years in terms of income and skills, and own-account workers are even less optimistic.

The likelihood is that most workers in most parts of the world, if they can see their future at all, do not expect improvement in their jobs. Stability is the best they hope for.

(iii) Technological change and job security

A full assessment of job security would have to take account of the nature of technological change and the ways firms, workers and social institutions shape such change. Although this set of issues must be studied fully, some tentative information has been collected through the ELFS from a wide range of countries. A few pointers are worth noting.

In China, a large proportion of the industrial enterprises surveyed in the ELFS had introduced new technology in recent years, including new products, new equipment and new working arrangements. The changes are most common in large-scale establishments, and above all in foreign corporations. We asked about the impact of those changes. The perception of managements was that they were having more impact on aspects of job security than on aspects of employment security. As shown in Figure 9.15, managers mostly reported that the changes had increased the complexity of work, requiring more retraining and an upgrading of skills to increase job mobility.

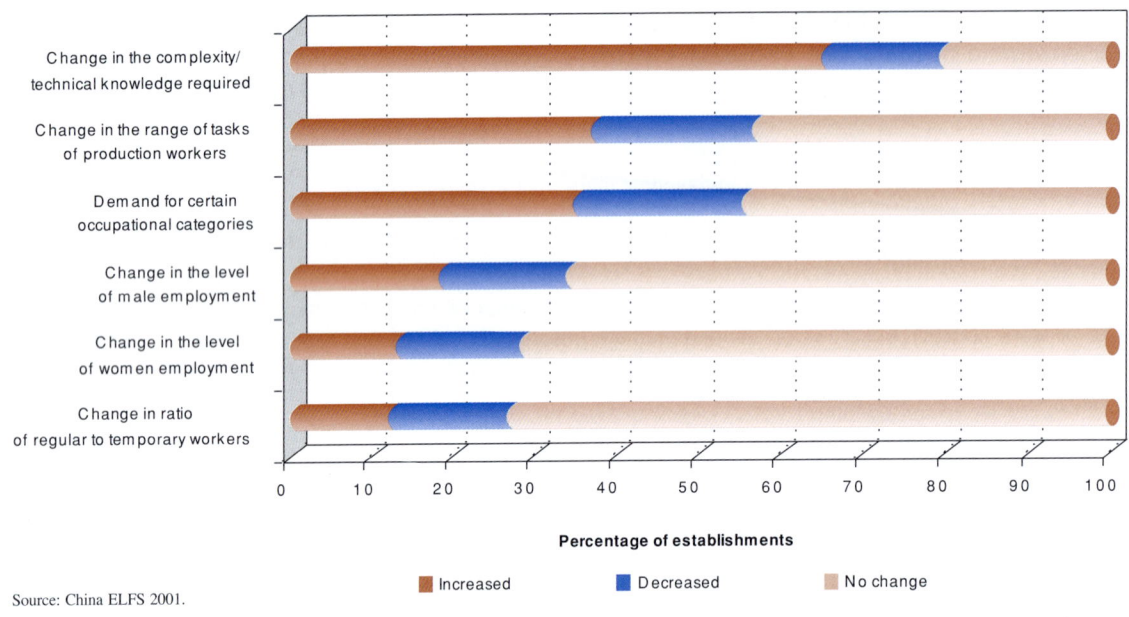

Figure 9.15 China: Consequences/ impact of technological change on job and employment security

Change in the complexity/ technical knowledge required

Change in the range of tasks of production workers

Demand for certain occupational categories

Change in the level of male employment

Change in the level of women employment

Change in ratio of regular to temporary workers

0   10   20   30   40   50   60   70   80   90   100

Percentage of establishments

■ Increased   ■ Decreased   ■ No change

Source: China ELFS 2001.

In the Philippines, fewer firms had made technological changes than in China, but proportionately as many reported that the changes had increased the complexity of work, which required retraining. Many had also introduced changes in work organization, more often than not increasing the range of tasks for production workers, and usually giving as the main reason that this was in response to more intense competition. New products mostly involved an upgrading of jobs. So the overall effect of innovations seemed to be a net upgrading of tasks in the jobs.

In Chile, two-thirds of firms had introduced new technologies, including computerization and line automation. Most said that these changes had not had much effect on the level of employment, but many reported that they had increased the overall complexity of production. More significantly, many more said that the changes had resulted in a decrease in the range of tasks of production workers than said the reverse. If workers are required to perform only a limited range of tasks (the essence of Taylorism), their sense of alienation and loss of connection with the production process will be strengthened.

Technological advances are part of all forms of production. But there is a strong presumption that they are more radical and extensive in the era of globalization than in earlier times, reflecting not just the electronics revolution but the impact of competition. Firms and workers have to adapt. But the accelerated pace of change surely erodes a sense of job security among the majority who have to face the prospect of retooling themselves, with uncertain prospects of doing so successfully.

9.5 An individual Job Security Index

Job security has both objective and subjective elements, and any composite measure should contain information on actual and potential mobility and information on whether the job or niche corresponds to a person's aspirations, expectations and capabilities. The very richness of the idea of job security means that any measure will be partial and less than ideal.

At the individual level, we define a Job Security Index as a combination of two sets of indicators. The first captures job mobility – past mobility, including promotion and upgrading, as well as expectations of future mobility and a person's "transferability". The second captures those aspects of satisfaction that helps express the subjective side of job security – the nature of work, degree of autonomy or independence, and the satisfaction in the prospect of promotion. We would have liked to include measures of discriminatory barriers, but the information in the PSS relates only to perceived discrimination against others.

The individual Job Security Index is measured as follows:

JSI = SAT1 + SAT2 + SAT3 + PROM1 + PROM2

where

SAT1:   If very satisfied or satisfied with nature of work = 1; otherwise 0

SAT2:   If very satisfied or satisfied with autonomy/independence = 1; otherwise 0

SAT3:   If very satisfied or satisfied with opportunity for promotion = 1; otherwise 0

PROM1:   Promotion in terms of Use of skills = 2 if yes, 1 if "neither promoted nor downgraded", 0 if downgraded

PROM2:   Opportunity for future promotion in terms of Use of skills = 1 if yes, 0 otherwise

A value of 1 is described as extremely low, 2 as very low, 3 as low, 4 as medium, 5 as high and 6 as very high.

Combining the two sets of factors in a job security index, we can illustrate the results by looking at just two countries. Thus, in Tanzania, job security in general is low, with rather more women than men having a very low level (Figure 9.16). Most workers with little or no schooling have very low job security scores. The big jump comes with secondary schooling and, as expected, most people with a tertiary education have strong job security (Figure 9.17). Not shown, high job security goes with high skills security, and vice versa. And in general, but far from always, strong job security goes with strong employment security. Also, while job security tends to be higher in the public sector than in the private, only 48% of public sector workers have high job security. Also, as one would expect, the probability of high job security rises with size of establishment. Finally, it is notable that those who belong to a trade union tend to have higher job security than those who do not.

Figure 9.16 Tanzania: Individual job security, by gender

(percentage distribution by score on index)

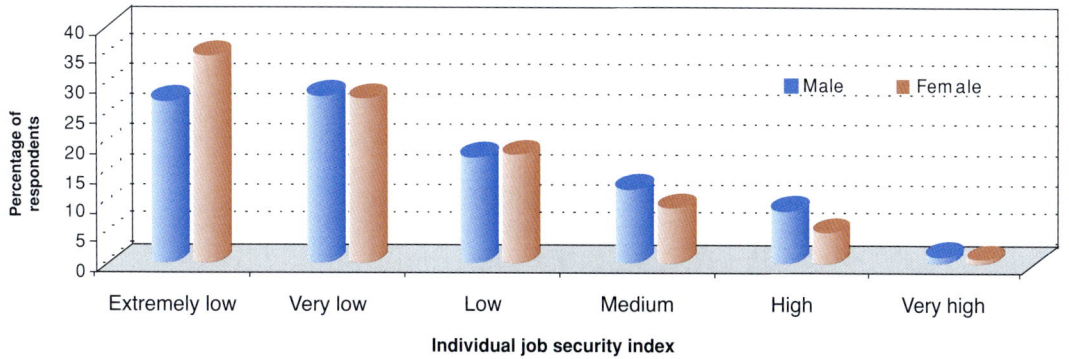

Source: Tanzania PSS 2001.

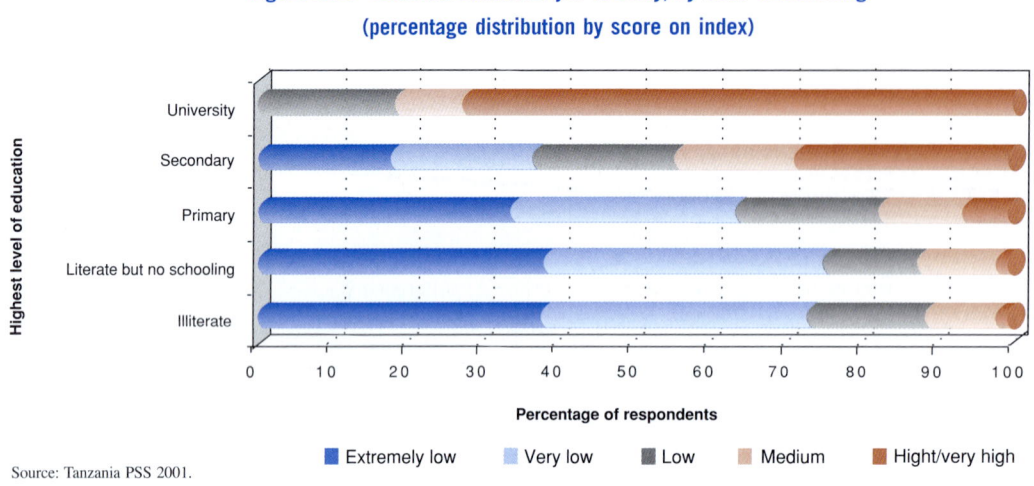

Figure 9.17 Tanzania: Individual job security, by level of schooling
(percentage distribution by score on index)

Source: Tanzania PSS 2001.

In China, job security seems to be higher on average, and the gender difference is less pronounced. The link between skills security and job security is also strong (Figure 9.18). And job security is positively related to income security (Figure 9.19). But in China, there is no difference between public and private sector jobs, while the existence of a union at the workplace does not seem to make much difference to prospective job security

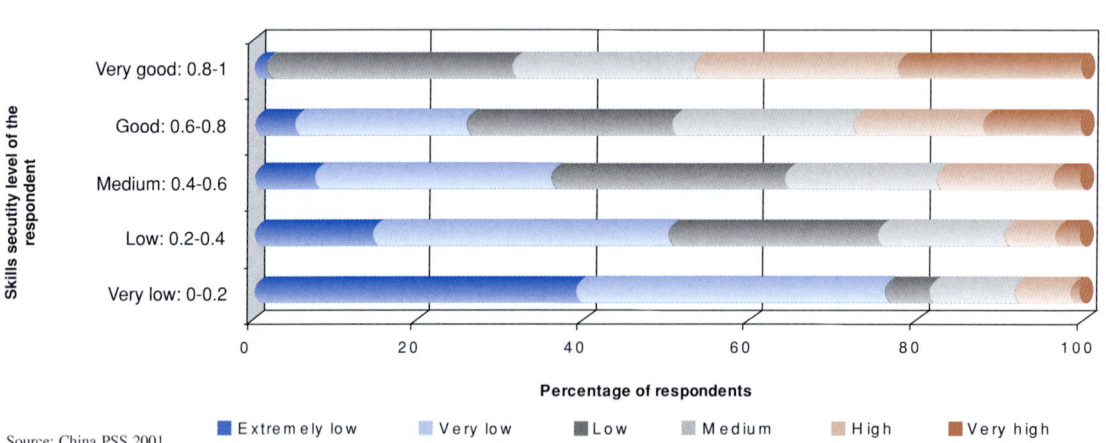

Figure 9.18 China: Individual job security, by skills security index
(percentage distribution by score on index)

Source: China PSS 2001.

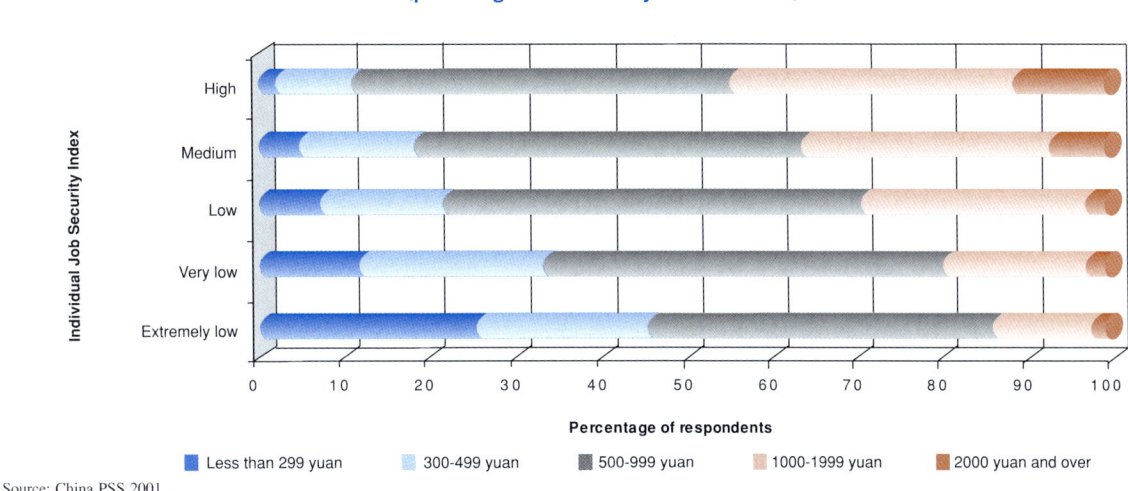

Figure 9.19 China: Individual job security, by income
(percentage distribution by score on index)

Source: China PSS 2001.

9.6 Job security and other forms of security

The evidence from both the PSS and ELFS indicates that those with more education and in jobs with more training are more likely to have job security — to face less discrimination, to have greater opportunities for upward mobility and, in the case of women,

to be more likely to be able to take maternity leave without losing their jobs.

In China, for example, the degree of satisfaction with the work that a person is required to do is positively associated with skills security, as shown in Figure 9.20.

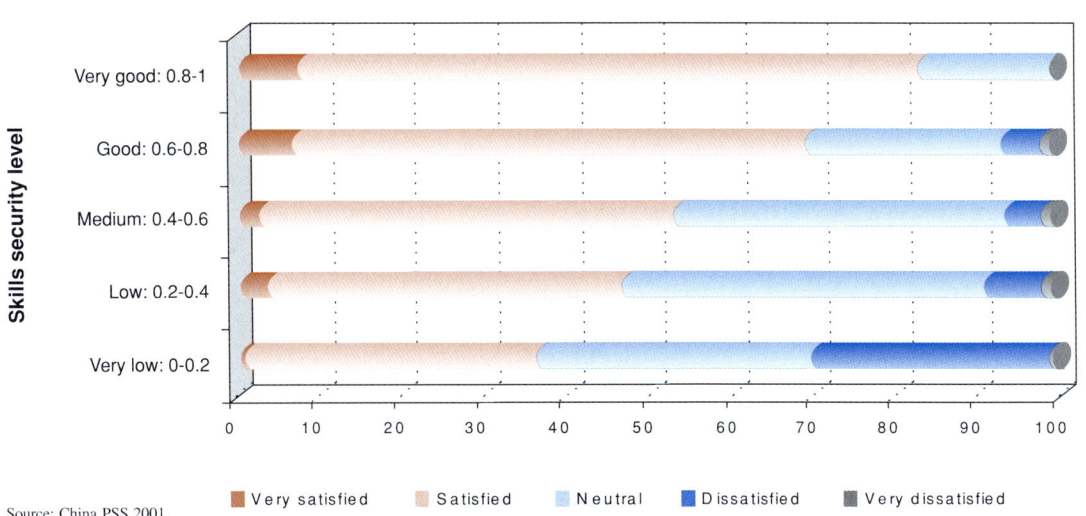

Figure 9.20 China: Satisfaction with current main income activity in terms of nature of work

Source: China PSS 2001.

It was pointed out earlier that those with relatively strong employment security tend to have relatively strong job security. The former might be interpreted as almost a necessary condition for job security. But there is no reason to presume that. Not only could many with employment security have no job security, but also many with employment security may be trapped in stultifying jobs — a sort of employment compact involving a trade-off of several types of security.

However, there is a tendency for those with secure employment to have a greater chance of upward mobility, as was found, for example, in Ethiopia, where regular wage workers and those in the public sector were relatively likely to have experienced upward mobility.

One should be careful about presuming that informalization goes with lack of job security, although it often surely does. Using our status informalization spectrum, it appears that in Brazil there is no difference in income satisfaction by degree of formality, even though the more formal tend to earn higher wages. This contrasts with the situation in Chile, where income satisfaction goes with formality.

Those with income security also tend to have more job security. Research in industrialized countries has found that job satisfaction is determined by a person's *relative income* rather more than by his or her absolute income.[8]

Perhaps above all, those with strong representation security are more likely to have good job security. In other words, job security tends to be positively correlated with most other forms of security. The advantages are cumulative, as are the disadvantages.

9.7 A national Job Security Index

Of all forms of work-related security, data on job security are the most difficult to collect and the most rarely collected, even in affluent countries. Recall that job security is interpreted as the possession of a "niche" at work, allowing some control over job content, i.e. what the worker actually does and the opportunity he or she has to build a career and enjoy a sense of self-realization. A worker could have employment security but no job security when, for instance, within the same firm his/her tasks and skills

undergo such changes as to force him/her to adjust or even discontinue the job or change occupations. This form of security is related to both employment and skills security, but it is different in the sense that it refers to the worker's own development over his or her entire working life.

Accordingly, a national Job Security Index (JSI) must be calculated on the basis of more indirect proxy measures than the others, focused on access to relatively "skilled" jobs and measures to combat discrimination in job opportunities.

Input indicators

A combination of international and national instruments protecting workers against discrimination constitutes the set of *Input* indicators for job security. The variables representing these instruments are coded 1 if they exist or if they have been ratified and 0 otherwise.

- At the international level, ILO Convention No.100 on Equal Remuneration, 1951, establishes the principle of equal remuneration between men and women for work of equal value. It is complemented by Convention No. 111 on Discrimination (Employment and Occupation), 1958, which encourages governments to promote policies and instruments guaranteeing equality of opportunity and treatment in employment and occupation, including access to training, advancement, tenure of job and conditions of work. Convention No. 159 on Vocational Rehabilitation and Employment (Disabled Persons), 1983, extends this principle to discrimination against workers with disabilities. Finally, Convention No. 156 on Workers with Family Responsibilities, 1981, aim at creating effective equality of opportunity and treatment between men and women with family responsibilities.[9]

---

[8]A. Clark and A. Oswald: *Satisfaction and Comparison Income* (Coventry, University of Warwick, 1995).

[9]The most important is Convention No.111 on Discrimination (Employment and Occupation), 1958, which is one of the most widely ratified of all ILO Conventions. This covers issues of *procedural* and *substantive* justice, including equality of opportunity and acceptability of special measures to assist disadvantaged groups.

- At national level, the selected indicators reflect the existence (or non-existence) of laws or regulations guaranteeing equality of employment opportunity between men and women, in recruitment, occupation, promotion and wages. A law banning discrimination against workers with disabilities is also included.

- Finally, another set of twin indicators, the existence of laws on paid maternity leave and one on paid parental leave complements the overview of national mechanisms that guarantee equality in employment between men and women.

Process indicators

- Skills are treated in the JSI as an instrumental component in the sense that the higher the level, acquisition and access to skills the higher the job security. It is assumed that workers with better education, access to information and representation can also better plan their careers and defend their interests and occupation. The situation of women relative to men is also explicitly considered.

- Two indicators of educational level are selected, in total and by gender. The first is the literacy rate, a proxy measure for basic education. It is mainly intended to discriminate among less developed countries. The second focuses on high-level skills. The indicator is the proportion of adults who have completed post-secondary education. This is meant to estimate the probability of workers being able to develop a career on the premise that the higher their educational level the greater are their chances of succeeding and taking advantage of occupational opportunities. Ideally indicators of vocational training should also have been included but data are not available for industrializing countries.

- Finally, assuming that employees have the most secure status in employment and therefore potentially more job security, the share of wage employment in total employment has been used.

Outcome indicators

- Direct measures of the effectiveness of the rules and mechanisms designed to ensure job security are not available, not even in developed countries. Proxies are also difficult to identify and options debatable. One single variable has been retained which is the proportion of workers in "professional" occupations in total employment,

overall and by gender. It is also supposed here that the worker in such high skilled occupations is most likely to possess a "niche" where he or she can realize his or her personal professional potential and derive a sense of security.

- Finally, a corrective variable is included to take account of the fact that, mainly in countries in the former Soviet bloc, large numbers of employees have been put on unpaid administrative leave, whatever their skill level. In countries where such procedures have been extensively used and careers interrupted, in the absence of effective protective mechanisms, insecurity even among the more educated must have grown relatively to countries where such procedures were not pursued.

There are 94 countries covered by the JSI. Two distinctive features of this index are that, first, it indicates rather clearly that most countries in eastern Europe and Central Asia are concentrated in the "Conventionals" cluster, meaning they have the means of providing job security but do not succeed (Figure 9.21). Probably this result from the institutional protective mechanisms they inherited from socialist regimes, which can no longer be financed because of changes in priorities and lack of resources or resource allocation.

Second, most of Latin America provides satisfactory job security, falling into the "Pragmatists" cluster, which is somewhat surprising. A deeper examination of the components of the index shows that these countries not only do not resort to massive administrative leave, which has a negative effect on job security scores, but perform relatively well in terms of the participation of women in high-skilled professions, which has a positive effect on scores.

Western and northern European countries are mostly "Pacesetters", with Finland leading the group. It is surprising to find Argentina, Bulgaria and Lithuania in this cluster. This can partly be explained by their formal commitments to job security and high educational level combined with favourable ratios for female workers in professional occupations.

However, some European countries, such as Switzerland, Ireland, the United Kingdom, Italy and Greece, also provide satisfactory levels of job security but are in the "Pragmatists" cluster, reflecting the fact that they give relatively little attention to the formal or instrumental aspects of the provision of security. The worst exception is Portugal, which is in the cluster of "Conventionals", failing to provide satisfactory job security in spite of having the necessary formal instruments.

As with other forms of security, African and Asian countries have the lowest scores and are concentrated in the "Much-to-be-done" cluster, the exceptions being South Africa and the Asian OECD countries. As shown in Table 9.4, the latter classify as "Pragmatists".

Table 9.4 Job Security Index

	High score on Outcome			
	High score on Input / Process		**Low** score on Input / Process	
Regions	**Pacesetters Countries**		**Pragmatists Countries**	
Africa and Middle East			Egypt	South Africa
			Israel	Tunisia
Americas	Argentina		Barbados	Panama
	Canada		Chile	Saint Kitts and Nevis
			Colombia	United States
			Costa Rica	Venezuela
			Dominica	
Asia	Japan		Australia	
			New Zealand	
Eastern Europe and Central Asia	Bulgaria		Estonia	
	Lithuania		Georgia	
Western Europe	Austria	Luxembourg	Greece	Switzerland
	Belgium	Netherlands	Ireland	United Kingdom
	Denmark	Norway	Italy	
	Finland	Spain		
	France	Sweden		
	Germany			

Regions	Low score on Outcome			
	High score on Input / Process		**Low** score on Input / Process	
	Conventionals Countries		Much-to-be-done Countries	
Africa and Middle East	Côte d'Ivoire		Algeria	Madagascar
			Benin	Mauritania
			Burkina Faso	Mauritius
			Burundi	Morocco
			Congo	Nigeria
			Congo, Dem. Rep. of	Rwanda
			Ethiopia	Senegal
			Ghana	Sierra Leone
			Guinea-Bissau	Turkey
			Lebanon	Zimbabwe
Americas	Brazil		Ecuador	Mexico
	Peru		Honduras	
Asia	India		Bangladesh	Nepal
	Philippines		China	Pakistan
			Fiji	Sri Lanka
			Indonesia	Thailand
			Korea, Republic of	
Eastern Europe and Central Asia	Armenia	Moldova, Republic of	Albania	
	Azerbaijan	Romania	Kazakhstan	
	Belarus	Russian Federation		
	Croatia	Slovakia		
	Czech Republic	Tajikistan		
	Hungary	Turkmenistan		
	Kyrgyzstan	Ukraine		
	Latvia	Uzbekistan		
Western Europe	Portugal			

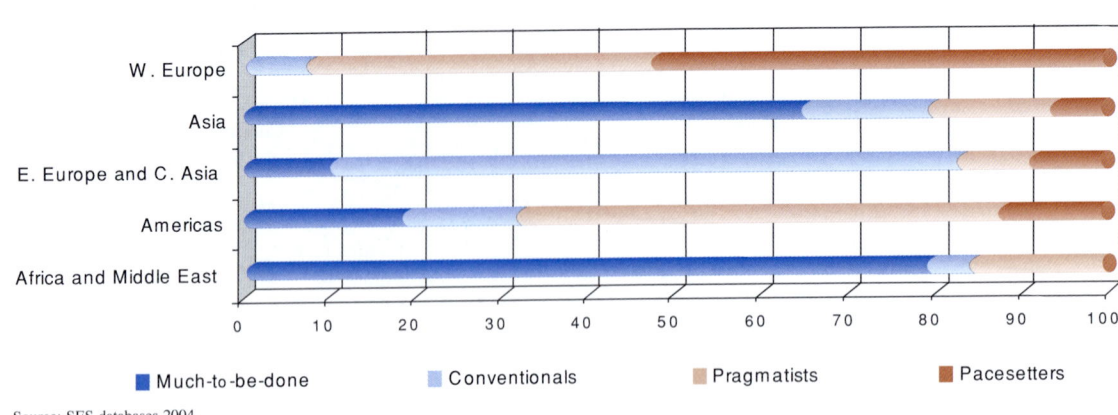

Figure 9.21 Job Security Index — Clusters by region

Legend: ■ Much-to-be-done □ Conventionals ■ Pragmatists ■ Pacesetters

Source: SES databases 2004.

9.8 Concluding remarks

When measured in terms of work satisfaction, job security is good for well-being, not only being associated with happiness in life in general, but with lower levels of coronary heart disease.[10] But static job security is not synonymous with satisfaction or personal development.

Much has been claimed about *job satisfaction*. Some have seen it as the clue to life satisfaction, but applied research suggests that the relationship runs mainly from life satisfaction to job satisfaction.[11] If a person is satisfied with life in general, with his or her personal relationships, income and support networks, he or she is more prepared to put up with unsatisfying work.

Job security should be seen as a matter of inequality, and thus greater insecurity for those with multiple forms of disadvantage. A recent Danish report has graphically shown this. It finds that job autonomy varies with income and qualifications, and that those with the highest qualifications and highest incomes enjoy the greatest degree of job autonomy and general security. The study concludes that non-financial inequalities are more important than monetary ones.

The national Job Security Index focuses largely on issues of discrimination. Not surprisingly perhaps, it is positively correlated with the Skills Security Index. But as pointed out earlier, the possession of skills and education is by no means strongly associated with a sense of job satisfaction.

As will be shown in Chapter 11, the national Job Security Index is related to the Gini measure of income distribution, and there is a view that societies in which income and other forms of inequality are substantial excite wider feelings of dissatisfaction, including a sense of frustration and insecurity in available work. This is an issue that deserves further reflection and empirical investigation.

---

[10] J. House: "Job dissatisfaction as a possible risk factor in coronary heart disease", *Journal of Chronic Diseases*, Vol. 23, 1971, pp. 861–873; Clark, 2001, op. cit.

[11] T.A. Judge and S. Watanabe: "Another look at the job satisfaction-life satisfaction relationship", *Journal of Applied Psychology*, 78, 1993, pp. 939–948.

Chapter 10

Voice representation security

10.1 What is voice?

Representation security is about having voice. This is an instrumental need, in that having Voice is the optimal way of advancing and defending an interest. But it is also a substantive need in its own right, since having a voice is intrinsic to defining one's identity as a human being. Voice is required for many purposes in the sphere of work, the most notable being to negotiate over wages, benefits and working conditions. It is also needed for *monitoring* working practices, for *information-gathering*, and for *evaluating* the impact of work practices or policies. Voice is essential at all levels of social policy, from design to implementation to monitoring and evaluation.

Without access to an organization that can represent their interests, most people are likely to be vulnerable to economic and social insecurity. They need "voice", in the sense of belonging to a body capable and willing to bargain for rights and entitlements, and access to institutions that can enforce and enhance such rights.

Ideally, the idea of representation should combine both *individual representation* and *collective representation*. The former is primarily about *rights*, typically enshrined in laws and individual access to institutions of individual choice. The latter means that any individual or group must have the effective right to be represented by a body that can bargain on their behalf. In practice, it requires that any individual have access both to institutional bodies and processes that give him or her individual rights and to a collective body that can and will represent his or her interests effectively, and which is sufficiently

large, sufficiently independent and sufficiently *competent* to do so.

People need voice for a variety of reasons, which will be considered in the following sections. This chapter will concentrate on trade unions as the primary vehicle for worker voice for the past century and more. Chapter 13 will consider emerging forms of voice. Underlying the analysis is an overriding concern that, in the era of globalization, the capacity for voice mechanisms to influence policies and outcomes has been eroded in countries where it was relatively strong, and has been weakened or prevented from growing in many places where it was already weak. There is a further and related concern, which is that *litigation* is displacing voice *regulation* in social and economic relationships.

10.2 International representation Conventions

Internationally, representation rights are enshrined in ILO Conventions, particularly Convention No. 87 on "Freedom of Association and Protection of the Right to Organise, 1948" and Convention No. 98 on "Right to Organise and Collective Bargaining, 1949". As of 2003, 141 countries had ratified ILO Convention No. 87 and 152 had ratified ILO Convention No. 98. Ratifying countries are required to submit information to show their observance of the Conventions every two years, when unions and employer organizations are invited to comment. The information and comments are then evaluated by the ILO, and by the ILO's Committee of Experts where complaints have been lodged (usually against a government) for non-observance of all or part of a ratified Convention.

In addition to these two main Conventions, the ILO has other Conventions and Recommendations that promote collective voice mechanisms and procedures, ratified by many ILO member States.

Since 1998, the ILO has been promoting the *Declaration on Fundamental Principles and Rights at Work,* which includes the two main Conventions among the core principles to which all member States must adhere. This does not mean that all ILO member countries make it equally easy for workers to organize and join trade unions. But it does mean that most accept that union membership is legally permitted.

10.3 Unions and representation security

Representation security has long implied membership of trade unions. But the dominant models within which representation security has been pursued have changed dramatically over the past century.

The roots of the form and the problems of modern trade unionism stem from the Industrial Revolution. In the 19th century, early labour protection was directed at protecting vulnerable groups, such as women and children, not adult male workers, who were depicted as entering "free contracts of employment". Women and children were "protected" because they were not seen to be full citizens.[1]

Free contracts were of course a mirage, because individual workers were competing not just with employers over wages and working conditions but with other workers wanting to displace them and have their jobs. In those circumstances, the right to collective bargaining arose to fill a vacuum, creating a sort of *industrial citizenship*. This provides employees with labour-based forms of security, to the extent that it is successful. But, being confined to workers, it does not create *social citizenship*, which depends on the character of the welfare state and the extent of public education.

In the United Kingdom and countries that adopted its traditions, voice as part of industrial citizenship entailed liberties rather than rights, through the gradual formation of "negative immunities". Workers could not be stopped from joining unions or going on strike. These immunities were never fully realized anywhere, and some have been curtailed in recent years. But the essence of voluntarism meant that it was left to

workers themselves to want to exercise voice and to find the space in which to do so.

This was less the case in continental Europe, where governments legitimized the voice of labour by incorporating unions into the State and by delegating many means of providing labour-based security to unions. The resulting collective labour rights constituted a positive right of employee voice through trade unions or workplace representative mechanisms. This produced stronger industrial citizenship security, even though it was still based firmly on the performance of labour.

It has been observed that the strength of industrial citizenship does not necessarily imply a corresponding strength of political citizenship. But the entrenchment of collective labour rights has meant greater bargaining scope on behalf of labour interests with the State, particularly in promoting union roles in the areas of pensions, unemployment benefits, health care benefits and other welfare issues so vital to the security of workers.

In the United States, in the wake of the violent struggles to establish trade unions at the beginning of the 20th century, employers tended to adopt what has become known as *welfare capitalism*. This was a paternalist labour system in which efforts were made by firms and government authorities to introduce *company unions*, under the control of managements and employers. The subsequent struggle in the United States and elsewhere over types of union has coloured the development of representation security ever since. The relevance here is that any unionization rate statistic may reflect very different union structures with different bargaining and representation capabilities.

Trade unions have always varied in the degree to which they are representative and responsive to their members' needs and aspirations. Some have been little more than mechanisms of management, or have been divisive bodies giving particular groups of workers privileges and benefits denied to others outside or on the edge of the unions. Now, as labour markets become more flexible and informal, the desirable character of trade unions is changing, making it more important that they represent workers as citizens, rather than just inside the factory or office.

---

[1] T.H. Marshall: *Citizenship and Social Class* (Cambridge, Cambridge University Press, 1950).

Approaching the twilight?

"It is generally agreed that the trade union movement has fallen on hard times."

— ILO: World Labour Report, 1997, p. 6.

In recent years, across the world there has been widespread *de-unionization*, particularly in industrialized market economies, although the rate of decline has probably been most rapid and extensive in the so-called transition countries of eastern Europe.[2] There has also been an erosion of the strength of freedom of association.[3] Some countries have made it harder to organize or to bargain collectively, many have chipped away at bargaining rights, and many have pushed collective bodies such as unions to a more marginal role in social policy. This has accentuated a *vicious circle*. To appeal to workers, unions rely on their capacity to bargain successfully and on their appeal as vehicles of social justice in a wider sense. If they become *social partners* with powerful interests or governments, they lose their appeal to those who wish to see them as an insurgent voice and as strong bargainers. If they focus largely on *bread-and-butter* workplace issues, they lose their appeal as civil society organizations. Related to this, as Flanders so memorably put it, "trade unions have always had two faces, sword of justice and vested interest".[4] But as unions became established in the middle decades of the 20th century, they became more of a bureaucratic mode of representation, a *social partner* rather than a socially insurgent voice. Whether fairly or not, this is how many people perceive unions in the early years of the 21st century. Put cruelly, are unions in a vicious circle of declining relevance and effectiveness?

To compound the problem for unions, it is hard to organize and retain members in many of the new or re-emerging types of labour relationships. This applies most of all to the vast informal economy so characteristic of developing countries. But it also applies to services and "new forms" of employment in industrialized countries. For instance, the Trades Union Congress (TUC) in the United Kingdom reports that call centres are particularly hard for unions to penetrate. Although union membership figures have risen slightly in the United Kingdom in the last few years, due mainly to union recognition deals, membership is particularly low among part-timers (only 21% of whom were unionized at the turn of the 21st century, compared with 32% of full-time workers). Similar difficulties have been reported in many other countries.

Unions tend to be weaker, and less inclined to push hard for high wages and benefits, in industrial sectors that are open to international competition.[5] Since globalization has meant that more sectors in more countries are open to such competition, that in itself must have tended to erode the impact of unions. Indeed, unionization has become increasingly concentrated in *public social services*.

In developing countries, unions have been particularly weak, with a few exceptions, the most notable being South Africa, where unions played a prominent part in the successful struggle against apartheid. In most other parts of the world, unions have been feeble, and have been further weakened by government action, sometimes supported by international agencies.

---

[2] In some where restructuring has been slow, union decline has also been slowed. But even in countries like Azerbaijan, as the PSS there showed in 2002, unionization has fallen considerably.

[3] For an extended review, see G. Standing: *Beyond the New Paternalism: Basic Security as Equality* (London, Verso, 2002).

[4] A. Flanders: *Management and Unions* (London, Faber, 1970), pp. 15–16.

[5] See, for instance, R.J. Franzese: "Institutional and structural interactions in monetary policy and wage/price bargaining", in P. Hall and D. Soskice (eds.): *Varieties of Capitalism: The Institutional Foundations of Comparative Advantage* (Cambridge, Cambridge University Press, 2001), pp. 411–434.

The collective action dilemma

Would a rational individual freely participate in collective action? This was the dilemma posed famously by Mancur Olson.[6] In a large group, one person's individual contribution would not make much difference and the outcome would be uncertain, but the cost of participation would be high and certain, while the personal risk might also be high. So, calculating individuals would "free ride".

The point can be put more prosaically. An individual worker will not make much noise because he could lose his job. To be effective, voice must be collective. But if an individual tries to organize, he is likely to be singled out to lose his job.

If so, all would lose, since the benefits of collective action would not occur. What should a union do to overcome the dilemma? Offering selective benefits to attract members would require a prior degree of union capacity. Trying to impose a closed shop would be resented by individuals who might prevent it emerging.

Some observers have tried to resolve the Olsonian dilemma by claiming that because they have similar roots workers perceive themselves as part of a group, with distributional norms, imbued with a collective identity. Others have suggested that the collective action dilemma explains why collective organization has only emerged strongly as a result of social turbulence, as a vehicle of protest against perceived injustice. Many have pointed to the vital need for governments to promote collective voice, recognizing the potential positive effects on efficiency, equity and security.

The dilemma has sharpened in the era of globalization and flexible labour relations because pressures to be individualistic seem to be overwhelming the sense of collective identity. The adverse side is the loss of social and economic benefits that could come from collective action. If it is true that a surge in collective representation comes in the wake of more intensified social injustice, perhaps a new surge will be stimulated by the insecurities of globalization. But will it take the shape of the last time round?

Employer security and voice

Employers face a collective action problem as well as workers. Individual employers compete with one another and with workers. But they want industrial and social peace in which to carry out their business. Social peace is a collective good. In Germany, employers collectively accepted co-determination and related practices for reasons of solidarity, without statutory underpinnings.[7]

Globalization, and the transnational character of many firms, has eroded loyalty to such normative principles. Employers have become less inclined to accept collective social compromises that impose burdens on individual employers.

It is generally accepted that one fundamental cause of low unionization is labour informalization. In industrialized countries, casual labour has rarely been well organized, nor have part-timers, outworkers, contract workers and agency workers. In developing countries, it is the vast numbers of informal workers who are least organized, and it is an irony that many formal unions have treated organizations that have tried to represent the interests of informal workers with suspicion if not outright hostility. There are good and bad reasons for this simmering conflict. To some extent, those trying to organize informal workers bridle at the so-called privileged treatment of formal workers; they want to overcome the dualism that typically exists. To some extent, those representing formal workers worry about losing the advances gained over the years for their members.

Organizing the numerous types of informal worker is notoriously difficult, but as argued later this is vital if overall representation security is to be strengthened. In some cases, there may be resistance by the workers themselves. In others, what they want or

[6]M. Olson: *The Logic of Collective Action: Public Goods and the Theory of Groups* (Cambridge, MA, Harvard University Press, 1965).

[7]W. Streeck: "German capitalism: Does it exist? Can it survive?" in C. Crouch and W. Streeck (eds.): *Political Economy of Modern Capitalism* (London, Sage, 1997).

need may not be what they perceive trade unions as offering. The issue of emerging forms of voice will be considered later (in Chapter 13). However, it might be instructive to reflect on attitudes expressed by self-employed transport workers in Pakistan interviewed for the People's Security Survey (PSS).

They were asked whether or not transport workers should form a union. About a quarter (24%) thought they should. But 35% were against the idea, while 41% did not know what they thought. If a union for transport workers were to exist, 15% of the respondents said they would join. The remainder would refrain from joining because they did not think that unions could resolve their problems (22% of the total said this), or because they felt that, even if unions could resolve their problems, union personnel would in practice do nothing to help workers (16%), or because they thought membership would be a waste of time (31%), or because they felt they did not have the time to belong to a union (22%).

Finally, it was apparent that the workers mostly did not think unions could be very effective, since 57% thought they were not responsive to workers' needs, and 21% thought they could not protect workers' security needs, leaving just over one in five thinking a union could protect them. When asked about their attitude towards unions in general, 9% said they

strongly believed in trade unions, 12% saw unions as important, and 79% expressed indifference. For anybody believing in the necessity of voice, these figures are deflating.

In many developing countries, the first hurdle for those wanting to organize is simply a lack of awareness. In some, awareness is even lower than might be expected. For example, in Gujarat, India, only 20% of respondents knew about unions, and only 16% of women knew about them.

According to the Bangladesh PSS in 2002, 38% of workers knew about organizations like trade unions, while 9% of respondents belonged to an association or union organization that represented worker interests (women 10%, men 9%). Of the latter 94% described themselves as active members with an opportunity to vote (women 82%, men 97%). Bangladesh may not be typical, since it is well known to be a society with a proud history of collective organization. But even so, the low level of participation is the most relevant variable.

It is also true that unionization is concentrated in just a few sectors of the economy, often being mostly strongly entrenched in the public sector. This is brought out, for example, by the PSS in Argentina and in Chile (Figures 10.1 and 10.2).

Figure 10.1 Argentina: Presence of unions as reported by workers, by sector

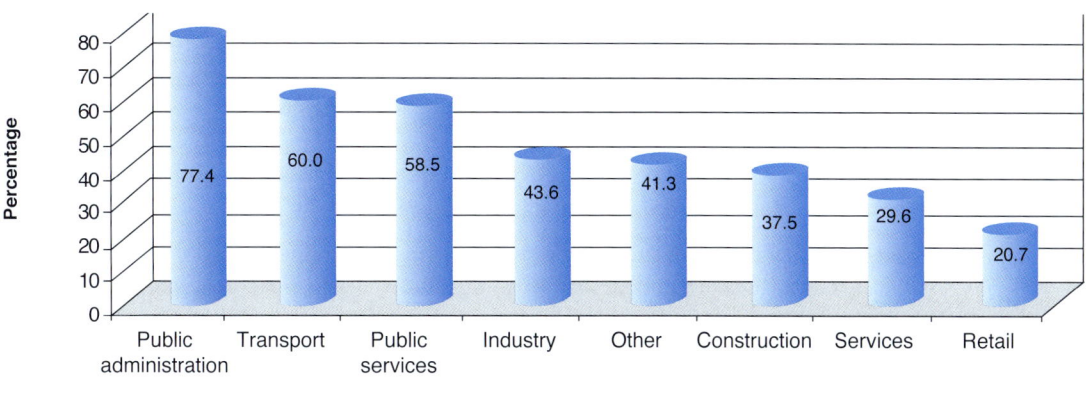

Source: Argentina PSS 2001.

Figure 10.2 Chile: Presence of unions as reported by workers, by sector

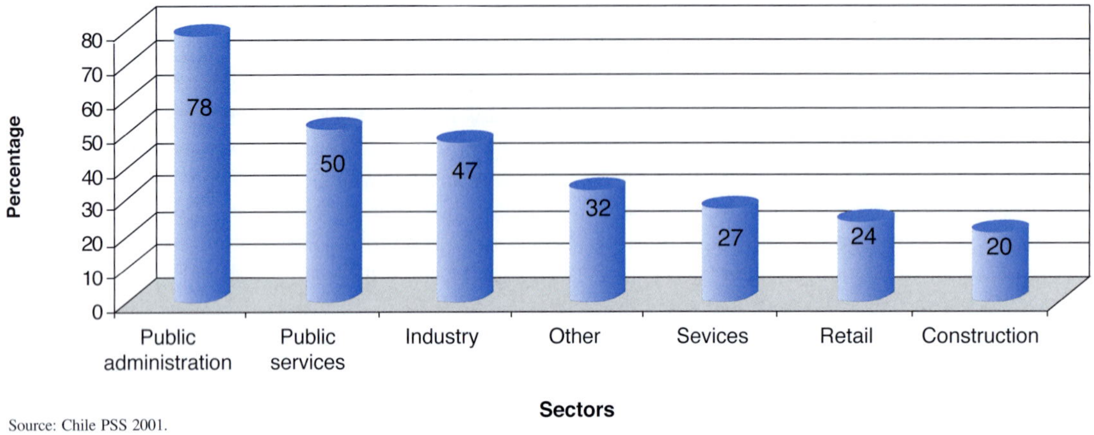

Source: Chile PSS 2001.

A region of the world where a peculiar paradox has arisen is eastern Europe. In the Soviet era, there was almost universal unionization of the labour force, since membership was almost mandatory and the means to obtain wages, benefits and services. Since 1989, all that has changed, at least in most parts of the region. Unionization has fallen very sharply indeed. But paradoxically, in some respects real representation may have increased.

According to the Russian Federation PSS of 2002, just under a third of Russian workers were members of a trade union, far less than a decade earlier. In Ukraine, according to the PSS carried out in 2002, 53% of all the employed still belonged to trade unions, which was also well down on Soviet levels. Men were slightly more likely to be members than women, but the difference was small. Older workers were more likely to belong. Both men and women were far more likely to be union members if working in medium or large-scale firms than in those with fewer than 50 workers.

De-unionization in eastern Europe has had profound adverse consequences for public social services. All sorts of labour-related insecurities have intensified for health care workers, as a series of surveys carried out for the ILO showed. A similar pattern has emerged in public schooling, where teachers have had to resort to secondary jobs in order to survive. The problems have been compounded by the lack of union strength to demand that incomes are paid, working conditions are improved, and threats to workers' lives from infection are reduced. It constitutes one of the saddest chapters of the story of the "transition" in the region.

Health care workers in eastern Europe

Throughout central and eastern Europe, sharp falls in union membership among health care workers — for example, by 70% in Armenia and the Czech Republic, and 80% in Lithuania and Poland — plus a growth of professional associations, notably among physicians, has left workers without a body to represent their interests and needs, adding to their already severe workplace insecurities.[8]

---

[8]C. Afford: *Corrosive Reform: Failing health systems in Eastern Europe* (Geneva, ILO, 2003).

Why do workers and citizens not join trade unions? A standard answer is *false consciousness*. But this can be simplistic. There are all sorts of other reasons. We may note here the reasons given in several of the PSS. A simple one is that workers are not *aware* of the existence of unions, or aware they could be representing their interests. For instance, in Gujarat, India, less than one in four of the "informal workers" were aware of unions; men were more aware than women.[9]

The issue of *trust* will be considered later. But in Brazil one in four urban workers who were not in unions said they did not join because they "had no trust" in unions, one in four said that they did not know enough about them, and one in four said they were not interested.

What of workers' overall attitudes toward trade unions? Findings from the PSS reveal the degree to which workers have positive (or negative) attitudes towards unions, and whether such attitudes are different among men, women, and workers of different age groups.

In Ukraine, more people had a "mostly positive" attitude towards unions than a negative one, with about a third reporting that they had a "mixed opinion". While there was no difference between men and women in this respect, older workers were more likely to be positive, whereas the young often tended to have a mixed opinion. This result should be interpreted by union leaders as a warning but also as a sign of hope, indicating that potentially a majority of youth are still open to trade unions.

In the Russian Federation in 2002, according to the PSS, only 21% of adults had a positive attitude to unions; 40% were indifferent towards them; 6% were "mostly negative", and 33% had a completely negative attitude. Women tended to have a more positive attitude towards unions than men. Paradoxically, nearly 60% of respondents expressed the view that unions are needed, indicating that if the appropriate type of organization was to emerge, and the evident alienation could be reversed. There may be a basis for organizing or re-building collective strength.

In Hungary, also in contrast to Ukraine, the PSS data show that only about one in six adults have a positive attitude to unions. This has been attributed to the legacy of union-government alliances and the deep employment crisis of the 1990s.

Beyond these special cases, there seem to be several generalizations about the propensity to belong to trade unions. Unless blocked by legislation or government pressure, unionization tends to be relatively high among public sector workers, higher among those in regular full-time jobs than among those in non-regular and part-time jobs, usually higher among men than among women and, because of the steep decline of unionization in the past two decades, relatively high among older workers.

These patterns were found in most of the PSS, even though there were very different absolute levels of unionization in the various countries. Thus, they applied to Bangladesh, Brazil, Hungary and Tanzania, although in Hungary women were as likely to be union members as men.[10]

Attitudes to unions vary by group in a fairly predictable way. However, one generalization does fail to stand up to close scrutiny; this is that men are more likely to have a positive attitude to unions, which are often seen as "male-dominated". Thus, in Bangladesh (Table 10.1 a) women are slightly more positive than men.[11] Beyond that, public sector workers are generally more positive than other groups, and higher-income earners are less likely to be positive. The vast majority thought that trade unions focused mainly on protecting workers' interests.

In Gujarat, the attitude towards trade unions was predominantly positive, with women being slightly more likely to be that way inclined (Table 10.1 b).

---

[9]J. Unni and U. Rani: *Insecurities of Informal Workers in Gujarat, India*, SES Paper No. 30 (Geneva, ILO, 2002).

[10]S. Dasgupta: "Attitudes towards trade unions in Bangladesh, Brazil, Hungary and Tanzania", *International Labour Review*, Vol. 141, No. 4, 2002, p. 417.

[11]Ibid., p. 429.

Table 10.1 Attitudes to unions, by gender (percentage of respondents)

(a): Bangladesh:

Bangladesh	Positive toward unions	Negative toward unions	Indifferent toward unions	Don't know
Male	72.6	15.4	8.9	3.1
Female	82.7	8.6	4.9	3.8
Total	**73.8**	**14.6**	**8.4**	**3.2**

Source: Bangladesh PSS 2001.

(b): Gujarat, India

Gujarat	Strongly believe in unions	Consider unions important	Indifferent toward unions	Do not believe in in unions	Don't know
Male	45.1	28	4.9	22.0	0.0
Female	47.5	32.5	6.9	12.5	0.6
Total	**46.7**	**31.0**	**6.2**	**15.7**	**0.4**

Source: Gujarat, India PSS 2001.

In China, the attitude to trade unions was mainly positive, with just under two thirds expressing a positive opinion, and only about 5% expressing a negative one. A positive attitude was much more likely among older workers.

In Indonesia, only a minority strongly believed in unions, and in general there was uncertainty, with women less likely to be positive (Figure 10.3). Indeed, it is the general lack of interest among women that testifies to the sense of alienation from collective voice in the sphere of work.

Figure 10.3 Indonesia: Attitudes towards trade unions, by gender

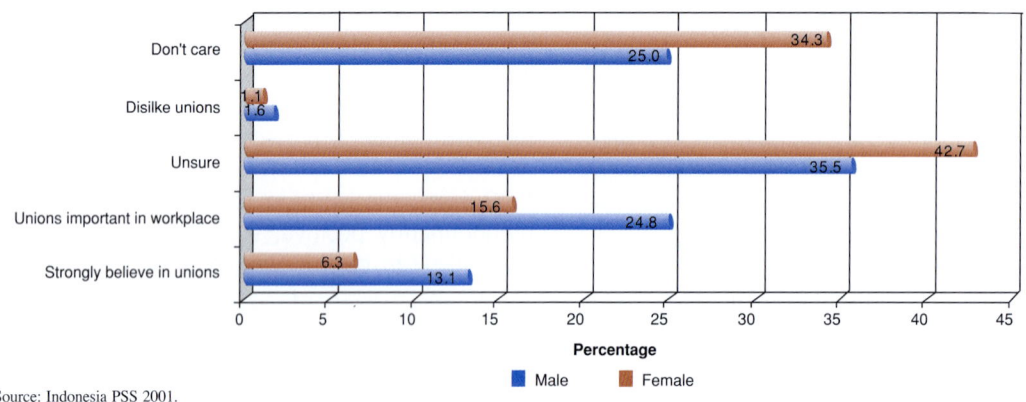

Source: Indonesia PSS 2001.

In urban areas of Ethiopia, 43% of respondents said their attitude to unions was mostly positive, compared with only 8% who said they disliked them and 4% who did not care. The most common answer (45%), as one might expect, was that they did not know what they thought about unions, almost certainly because they had not experienced conditions in which unions operated. In Ethiopia, men were much more likely to have a positive attitude, while women mostly (58%) did not have an opinion at all.

When asked about reasons for their attitude, the main one for being positive (47%) was the feeling that unions could provide employment and income security for workers. As for what unions should focus on doing, about two in five workers could not say (a third of the men and over half of the women). For the remainder, the most commonly stated objectives were protection of members' rights and their employment security. Very few indeed thought their main function should be to improve their members' incomes.

In Ghana, people's attitude to trade unions was more positive than in many countries, with 53% having a mainly positive attitude, men and women being equally likely to have that view. Only 7% expressed a negative view, with 39% not knowing what they thought. Perhaps one reason for the balance of opinion is that 52% of respondents thought that belonging to a union would be of help in obtaining a job.

In Tanzania, about a third of PSS respondents had a mostly positive attitude to unions, a quarter was mostly negative, and 22% were indifferent. Women were significantly more likely to be positive, and less likely to be negative.

In South Africa, 27% of PSS respondents regarded trade unions as mostly positive, men being more likely to feel that way; 9% were mostly negative toward unions; 22% had a mixed opinion; and 41% did not know what they thought about them, with women much more likely to be in that position. A remarkable feature of the situation in South Africa is that people think that the level of unionization is much higher than it is, testifying to the public stature of COSATU, the main national federation of unions, and union figures in general.

However, while many workers expressed the view that unions were helpful in enhancing their employment and income security, nearly as many thought they were ineffective in that respect and just over 5% of workers saw unions as "disruptive".

Another worrying feature in South Africa, which is approximately replicated in other countries, is that the least educated are the least likely to have an attitude towards unions (Figure 10.4). Thus they are least likely to be aware of advantages that could be gained from union membership, making them the least likely to join or to participate. Women are also far more likely to be unaware. The irony is that the least educated and disadvantaged groups that include women are the most in need of powerful collective voice to combat the many forms of insecurity that they face.

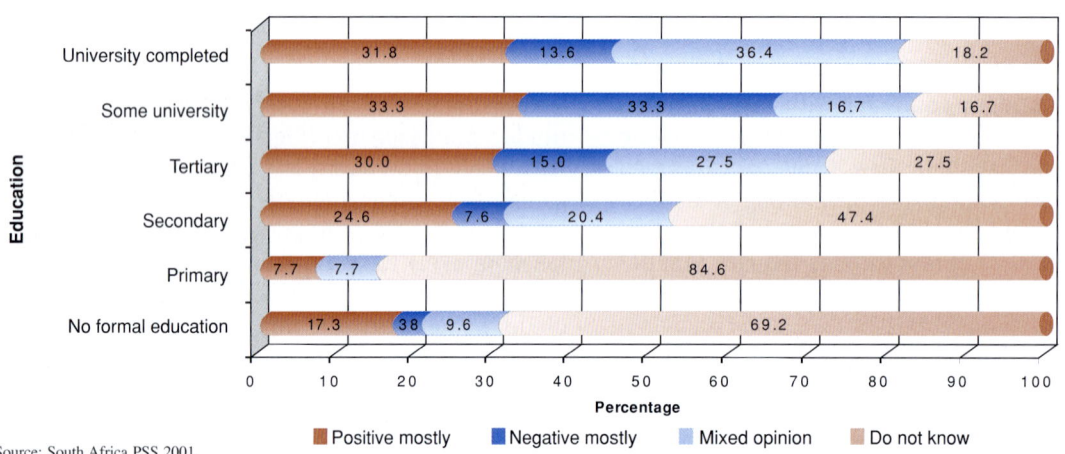

Figure 10.4 South Africa: Attitudes to trade unions, by schooling and gender

(a) Men's attitude to trade unions, by education

Source: South Africa PSS 2001.

Figure 10.4 South Africa: Attitudes to trade unions, by schooling and gender

(b) Women's attitude to trade unions, by educationn

Source: South Africa PSS 2001.

Another question pursued in some of the PSS is whether or not people believe unions represent workers' interests in practice. Remarkably, and worrying for the unions, in Brazil only about 18% of all wage workers "fully agreed" that they did so, while 23% said they disagreed.

In Chile, 18% believed that unions adequately represented their interests; 29% partially agreed that they did so; 19% did not have an opinion one way or the other; and 22% felt that unions did not adequately represent their interests.

In Argentina, even though a relatively large proportion of workers were in trade unions, scepticism about their effectiveness as representative bodies was evident. Thus, only 6% believed that unions adequately represented their interests; 12% thought they only partially did so; 11% had no opinion; and a remarkable 66% felt that they did not adequately represent their interests.

In sum, a picture that emerges is that a great many working people, particularly in developing countries, are not aware of unions, are not drawn to belong to unions and are not aware of advantages that they could provide. These findings may be an important basis for global awareness-raising and organizing campaigns, raising the level of workers' voice representation, targeting issues of priority to workers in specific countries.

11.4 Trade unions and economic security

In spite of the previous conclusion, voice, and collective representation in particular, is surely vital for other forms of work-related security. Unions have been credited with having many positive effects — and some negative — both at the macroeconomic and enterprise levels. But simply in terms of their impact on the securities of workers, the ledger is strongly positive.[12] Overall, whatever their limitations, they have been a *sword of justice.*

Fundamental rights, still a fundamental fight

Workers' most fundamental rights, enshrined in International Labour Conventions,[13] are flouted in countries around the world, depriving millions of working people of their rights to fair wages, trade union representation and decent working conditions. Violations of these fundamental rights range from provisions in national legislation restricting legitimate trade union activity, through outright bans on freedom of association, to intimidation, wrongful detention, torture and murder of trade unionists.

During 2002, no region of the world was without such violations. Serious violations of workers' most fundamental rights have been reported in Latin America (in particular Colombia, where trade unionists continue to be murdered systematically), North America, and Europe including the transition countries of eastern Europe, Asia, Africa and the Middle East.

Efforts to organize free trade union activity were repressed, often with violence, in China, while anti-union repression increased in Venezuela and Zimbabwe, and remained a feature in several other countries in Africa, the Americas and in Asia-Pacific. All forms of trade union activity remained illegal in virtually every Gulf State.

Globalization, in the absence of mechanisms to ensure full respect for ILO standards, is leading to international competition based on a 'race to the bottom'. Restrictions and deficiencies in law deprive millions of workers in export processing zones and in agriculture of their rights. Conditions in export processing zones are generally extremely exploitative, with women workers suffering the most. Rural workers in a number of countries have been denied trade union rights and faced repression by employers and governments.[14]

Numerous cases have been brought before the ILO concerning restrictions contained in provincial-level legislation in Canada. Also brought before the ILO have been numerous examples of US employers discriminating against trade unionists and repressing union organizing efforts, in both private and public sectors.

Certain countries appear year after year in the ICFTU's *Survey of violations of trade union rights,* often for recurring violations of the same nature, with repeated cases brought before the ILO in some instances. The ongoing refusal of these countries to respect fundamental labour standards calls for stronger promotion and guarantees of workers' rights everywhere.

---

[12]The classic study, which has generated many others, is R. Freeman and J. Medoff: *What Do Unions Do?* (New York, Basic Books, 1984).

[13]Fundamental ILO Conventions include Convention No. 29 on Forced Labour, 1903; Convention No. 87 on Freedom of Association and Protection of the Right to Organise, 1948; Convention No. 98 on Right to Organise and Collective Bargaining, 1949; Convention No. 100 on Equal Remuneration, 1951; Convention No. 105 on Abolition of Forced Labour, 1957; Convention No. 111 on Discrimination (Employment and Occupation), 1958; Convention No. 138 on Minimum Age, 1973 and Convention No. 182 on Worst Forms of Child Labour, 1999.

[14]*Annual Survey of Violations of Trade Union Rights 2003* (Brussels, International Confederation of Free Trade Unions, 2003)

Thus, the presence of unions in workplaces has been shown to improve *income security*, by raising wages in general, by narrowing wage differentials (notably between men and women), by increasing enterprise benefits for workers and by reducing the likelihood of non-compensated layoffs and redundancies. After many of its reports had taken an opposite view, even the World Bank has issued a study that shows many of these findings.[15]

The most widely accepted result is that unions raise wages of their members compared with other groups of workers.[16] To some extent there are externalities, in that where unions bargain successfully for higher wages, they tend to drag up the wages of other groups as well.[17] However, many studies show that, controlling for personal and other characteristics, there is a "union premium". This has also been shown at the individual level from the PSS data for

Bangladesh, Brazil and Tanzania, even though the extent of union membership is very limited in Bangladesh and Tanzania.[18]

A "union premium" has also been found for firms, where those firms with unions tend to pay higher wages than non-union firms, controlling for other factors. One might question the causal relationship; this has been shown in various developing countries, as well as in industrialized market economies. The effect of unions on wages has so far been hard to detect in Eastern Europe but it is evident in countries like Malaysia, Indonesia and the Philippines. In the Philippines, according to the ILO ELFS, average wages were perhaps three times what they were in non-union firms (Table 10.2). And wage differentials between managerial employees and unskilled workers were much narrower in unionized firms.

Table 10.2 The Philippines: Monthly average wages and earnings in union and non-union firms, 2001 (in pesos)

	Non-union	Union	Union type Company	Affiliated
Average wage	129 420	378 740	168 700	437 230
Average earnings	174 320	540 220	244 880	618 230

Source: Philippines ELFS 2002.

Regression analysis of wages in the Philippines ELFS showed that, controlling for the effect of industry, size and ownership (public, private), unionized firms had significantly higher average wages. And affiliated and independent unions had a bigger positive effect than company unions. In Indonesia too, a similar regression function showed that the average wage was positively and significantly related to the presence of a union, although there was no difference between types of union.

The most common arguments that governments and certain international agencies have used for curbing the rights of unions around the world are that they have raised labour costs and contributed to rigidities in employment and working practices. There are some theoretical reasons and empirical evidence to permit scepticism on many of these claims.[19] But the fact is that in many countries legislative

moves have curtailed union capacities in recent years.[20]

[15]T. Aidt and Z. Tzannatos: *Unions and Collective Bargaining: Economic Effects in a Global Environment* (Washington DC, World Bank, 2002).

[16]Among the many country studies, see J. Budd and I.-G. Na: "The union membership wage premium for employees covered by collective bargaining agreements", *Journal of Labor Economics*, Vol. 18, No. 4, 2000, pp. 783–807.

[17]T. Boeri, A. Brugiavini, L. Calmfors et al.: *The Role of Unions in the 21st Century* (Oxford, Oxford University Press, 2001), p. 17.

[18]Dasgupta, 2002, op. cit., p. 426.

[19]For instance, there is evidence that strong worker voice inside firms tends to produce higher levels of productivity, making it possible to pay higher wages without raising labour costs.

[20]For a review of the arguments, see Standing, 2002, op. cit.

[20]Cumulative trauma disorders are muscle or nerve damage caused by repetitive work — see Chapter 7 on work security.

Besides the complex series of effects on income security, unions have also had a complicated effect on *work security*. It seems that there is a positive (inverse) statistical relationship between the presence of unions in a firm and the level of cumulative trauma disorders[21] — unionized firms fare better. However, this seems to be due to the tendency of firms with unions to report (and possibly to recognize) such disorders,[22] which is a common finding in the literature on workplace health and safety more generally.[23]

Unions can be an effective means of ensuring attention to safety. This is an area in which unions have made some of their most substantive inroads into traditional management rights, winning measures of democracy through participatory voice mechanisms, such as joint workplace health and safety committees.[24] Thus, although there has been scepticism about the effectiveness of unions in Ukraine, workers who belonged to trade unions were more likely to report that they had safety departments or committees in their workplace.[5]

One area of concern where collective action can be highly effective is in the generation and use of *information*. This is too often regarded as a matter of accumulation and sifting of factual knowledge. Often, it is said that workers should be "given" information by management or by "policymakers". This is to mistake the nature of knowledge. What a worker needs or wants to know is often quite different from what a manager or policymaker needs or wants to know. And how information is gathered, and by whom, can make a big difference to the interpretation of any particular reality. Similarly, *monitoring* and *evaluating* knowledge is rarely purely objective.

This recognition of how information is generated and used leads inexorably to the need to ensure that all sides of any social relationship should have the opportunity and incentives to collect, collate, analyse and use the data they want. In the sphere of work security, a practical manual on information gathering has been prepared for use by workers, by unions and by those working with them.[26] Use of Voice to inform workers about work security is still rare, but an example of the type of initiative needed is the *London Hazards Centre,* which provides workers with information on potential health problems associated with various types of work and operates a free telephone advice line, databases, training services for community groups and so on.

Comprehensive national surveillance systems are crucial to the recognition, treatment and prevention of occupational injuries and diseases, and can be used for targeting resources and interventions to worksites, industrial processes or populations. These require involvement of those directly affected, or at least representatives of their interests.[27]

The presence of trade unions in plants and enterprises is also associated with a greater degree of *skills security*. In a large survey of Malaysian manufacturing firms, it was found that firms with unions were more likely to provide workers with training, and firms with independent unions were more likely to do so than those with "company unions".[28] In the Philippines, as shown by the enterprise survey, not only were unionized firms more likely to provide training, but independent and affiliated unions were more likely to do so than firms with company unions. In Indonesia, unionized firms were also more likely to have training for workers than non-union firms.

In South Africa and Tanzania, unionized firms were far more likely to operate equal opportunity recruitment practices (no preference for men in recruitment), and were more likely to provide training.

---

[21] Cumulative trauma disorders are muscle or nerve damage caused by repetitive work — see Chapter 7 on work security.

[22] D. Fairris and M. Brenner: "Workplace transformation and the rise in cumulative trauma disorders: Is there a connection?", *Journal of Labor Research*, Vol. 22, No. 1, 2002, pp. 15–28; Brenner et al., 2001, cited in Chapter 7 on work security.

[23] D. Fairris: "Compensating payments and hazardous work in union and non-union settings", *Journal of Labor Research*, Vol. XIII, No. 2, Spring 1992, pp. 205–21.

[24] W. Gereluk and L. Royer: *Sustainable Development of the Global Economy: A Trade Union Perspective*", SES Paper No. 19 (Geneva, ILO, 2002).

[25] L. Zsoldos and G. Standing, 2002, op. cit. Whether or not there is a causal relationship is an issue that deserves further inquiry.

[26] M. Keith et al.: *Barefoot Research: A Workers' Manual for Organizing on Work Security* (Geneva, ILO, 2002).

[27] L. Azaroff and C. Levenstein: *Innovations in Monitoring Work Security: A Case Study of Southeast Asian Refugees in Lowell, Massachusetts*, SES Paper No. 21 (Geneva, ILO, 2002).

[28] G. Standing: "Do trade unions impede or accelerate structural adjustment?", *Cambridge Journal of Economics*, Vol. 16, No. 3, 1992, pp. 327–354.

Unions have also been associated with some improvement in *employment security*. In Ukraine, workers who belonged to trade unions were more likely to report that all or most of the workers in their firm were protected against unfair dismissal.[29] But it should not be always presumed that unions stand resolutely in favour of employment security for all groups of worker. In Brazil, for example, a study found that unions mostly did not object to firms resorting to non-standard labour contracts, on the grounds that these were better than nothing and that, if firms could not do so, they would not create jobs.[30] In South Africa, according to the PSS data, many workers thought unions did improve employment security, but many others did not.[31]

In the Philippines, firms with unions were likely to give longer notice periods than non-union firms when laying off workers, and were more likely to have a notice policy; in both respects firms with independent unions gave more employment security than firms with company unions. Similar results were found in Indonesia.

Where the effect of unions has been most controversial is in the realm of *job security*. In many countries, unions have been strong defenders of existing job titles and structures, often resisting technical redivisions of labour and "functional flexibility" in the name of combating "deskilling". What is less clear is whether, in doing so, they have helped make job structures rigid and static.

This issue aside, however, there can be little doubt that, taken overall, trade unions have been a powerful means of strengthening worker securities. The problem is that they have been losing force and effectiveness. The question is whether they or some other form of collective organization can revive those positive effects.

Agricultural workers without voice

Less than 10% of the world's waged agricultural workers are organized and represented in trade unions or rural workers' organizations. The potential for meaningful negotiation at both national and enterprise levels is thus severely constrained, and the reality is that negotiation or even discussion tends to be the exception rather than the rule.

Rural agricultural workers in a number of countries face both de facto and de jure obstacles to becoming organized. Violations of freedom of association among agricultural workers are frequent, demonstrated by cases examined by the ILO Committee on Freedom of Association. Such violations range from regulatory restrictions and anti-union practices to physical violence, repression and even the assassination of trade union leaders. The situation is even more critical for indigenous workers, who are often denied the right to set up or join such organizations.

Indeed, traditional forms of voice representation and regulation are in some cases no longer effective. There is a need for new approaches and strategies to address the critical problems faced by agricultural workers, including strategic alliances at international, national and local level.

At a time of declining memberships for many trade unions in the agricultural sector, the question of "relevance" is important. Addressing issues of specific concern to particular groups of workers, such as women waged agricultural workers, can help improve organization, boost membership and build capacity. "Relevance" can thus strengthen workers' organizations. This process also helps to identify "decent work deficits".

10.5 Bargaining, types of union and coordination

There is a vast academic literature on the effectiveness of different bargaining structures. The most common tendencies in the era of globalization have been that centralized bargaining has declined, if not disappeared altogether, while more limited plant-level bargaining has been maintained in some form, or been actively promoted by governments and international agencies.

The extent of coordination at national level has undoubtedly shrunk, even though some studies have suggested that coordinated structures perform better in some respects.[32] In many cases, decentralization has been pursued as a means of weakening union bargaining power. But some unexpected outcomes have been observed. A study in Brazil found that decentralized wage bargaining had raised wages by increasing the "insider" power of unions.[33]

Most observers refer to *trade unions* as if there was only one type in existence, and one type that is possible. Historically, this is far from the case. There are craft unions, descended from guilds established in the Middle Ages; there are industrial unions, usually operating on a sectoral and national level; there are general unions, often mainly focused on the needs and aspirations of manual workers in one or several sectors; and there are "independent local unions" and "company unions". Difficulties with independent local unions and unaffiliated unions include their financial *vulnerability*, and a tendency to suffer from the "golden handcuffs" technique of management.[34]

However, it is notable that in the period of globalization many governments have favoured bargaining decentralization and, partly reflecting the influence of the Japanese model of industrial relations; company unions have become far more widespread. The capacity of these to provide effective voice security remains dubious.

10.6 Union voice and action

Voice can be a whisper, because it has no strength, or because those who need to use it are unaware of the means of doing so. The evidence is overwhelming that often people do not join collective representation organizations because they are not aware of their existence or are unaware that they could join or are unaware of the benefits of joining. It should be a public social service to break down those barriers, in the interest of social solidarity and societal security.

However, effective voice depends in part on the willingness of people to act to promote or defend their rights and interests. Consider some examples. Let us start with pointers from some of the poorest societies in the world.

In Ethiopia, respondents were asked whether they supported workers going on strike to improve working conditions. Less than a third agreed, while 29% said they should not do so, the remainder being undecided. The rather negative attitude was common across all age groups. Once again, women were relatively prone to be undecided, which may be because women were less informed of union activities. But the findings did not mean that there was a lack of willingness to use voice, since an overwhelming majority stated that they would be prepared to demonstrate over work-related grievances. One way of interpreting the findings is that people found it hard to identify with the available type of institutions for representing their interests, as shown by the fact that most said they would not appeal to any organization for action.

In Indonesia, opinions on what unions should or should not do were intriguing. When asked what they thought of workers going on strike, 21% agreed that they should do so to pursue their interests, 16% were uncertain, 53% disagreed and 10% did not have any opinion. There were no significant differences between men and women in this respect, although rather more women had no opinion. The point is that most people were hostile or indifferent to the idea of collective industrial action.

---

[32] See, inter alia, P.A. Hall and R. Franzese: "Central bank independence, coordinated wage bargaining, and European Monetary Union", *International Organization*, Vol. 52, Summer 1998, pp. 505–535; D. Soskice: "Wage determination: The changing role of institutions in advanced industrialized countries", *Oxford Review of Economic Policy*, Vol. 6, 1990, pp. 36–61.

[33] F. Carneiro and A. Henley: "Wage determination in Brazil: The growth of union bargaining power and informal employment", *Journal of Development Studies*, Vol. 34, No. 4, 1998, p. 133.

[34] Standing, 1999, op. cit., p. 385.

By contrast, nearly three quarters of the sample believed that, if there were grievances about work or incomes, people should demonstrate; many more men agreed with this than women. The small difference between striking against an employer and making a social demonstration may indicate a sense of dependency on the state and society in general to address social injustice. So, not surprisingly, many more respondents said people should complain to government institutions about work grievances rather

than take direct action against their employers. They were also more likely to think that they should turn to non-governmental organizations.

In Gujarat, India, respondents in the PSS were asked what they thought was the best means of representing workers' interests at work. The answers highlight the diversity of appropriate means of pursuing work-related interests.

Table 10.3 Gujarat, India: Best means of representing work-related interests, by gender (percentage of respondents)

Gender	Collective action	Through corporation	Through contractor	Union	Written application	Direct representation to employer	Not going to work
Male	10.4	26.1	13	13.9	7.0	22.6	7.0
Female	15.6	22.7	14.9	6.1	1.7	35.1	3.9
Total	**14.8**	**23.3**	**14.6**	**7.4**	**2.6**	**33.0**	**4.4**

Source: Gujarat, India PSS 2000.

In Bangladesh, in response to a neglect of labour safety codes in the workplace, many workers said they would be most inclined to take part in meetings or demonstrations, with women expressing this more often than men. Turning to a trade union was the second most common response. Scarcely anybody said they would go to a government agency; one in seven thought it best to appeal to the courts. One in five thought nothing could be done. Perhaps surprising was that male youths were relatively inclined to be passive, feeling that nothing could be done.

In the face of an increase in the price of raw materials, fuel or anything affecting production, evidence suggests that most workers in Bangladesh feel helpless. If the price of raw materials increases, or if the authority decides to enforce rules affecting their work (as opposed to a violation of the collective agreement), they feel that nothing can be done to stop such events from happening.

No less than 70% said they were powerless to do anything in response to the authorities deciding to

enforce rules and laws affecting their work through access to the workplace or licensing requirements. In Tanzania, people were slightly less pessimistic, although even there 42% said they thought they were powerless to do anything in such circumstances, with no difference between men and women. About one in five would go to a government agency, and 17% would appeal to the law, leaving merely 1% going to unions.

By contrast with low-income societies relatively unfamiliar with institutions that have been linked to industrialization and formal employment, societies that had a prolonged period of state socialism could be expected to view standard voice options with a rather jaundiced eye, rather than one based on lack of awareness.

In Ukraine, the PSS asked workers what issues they thought would lead to protest or action in their enterprise. A predominantly passive attitude emerged both in general and on specified issues. We first asked: "What type of attitude characterizes the majority of workers in your enterprise?" About 61% of the men and 56% of the women said the attitude was "passive". Perhaps surprisingly, industrial workers were more likely than service workers to perceive their fellow workers as passive.

When asked what attitude best characterized themselves, only 28% of men and 30% of women said they were passive. About themselves, the most common answer was "consensual with management", with nearly half of all men and women giving that answer. This might reflect how they see themselves, when the same attitude would be described more pejoratively when seen in others!

Respondents were then asked what issues would lead to protest or to direct action by workers in their enterprise. Again, a mainly passive attitude emerged. Thus, only about one in four workers said there would be action if wages were perceived as "unfair", and only a third said action would occur if wages were low or delayed. In almost every instance, women workers were more passive in their attitude.

What these figures suggest is a lack of faith or awareness of active protest. Most workers were effectively saying they would take a relatively passive approach, with large numbers admitting a sense of apathy. This applied to men and to women, and to workers of all ages. Although there were signs of willingness to participate in collective action, there was a lack of faith in, or awareness of, the role of active protest. Most workers were effectively saying that they would take a relatively passive approach, with large numbers admitting a sense of apathy. This applied to men and to women, and to workers of all age groups.

Lack of militancy might strike some observers as a favourable feature of a workforce. An alternative view is that passivity means an absence of pressure to improve working conditions, productivity and enterprise dynamism.

Very few Ukrainians interviewed for the PSS in 2002 knew of any organization besides trades unions that might represent workers' interests. This is both a worrying sign, and an encouraging one for trade unions, in that they remain the only feasible source of worker representation. Meanwhile, over two out of every five knew of organizations to represent the interests of the self-employed, presumably including employers. But only a minority of the self-employed actually belonged to any such organization.

In Ukraine, worker attitudes towards employers or managers varied a great deal. About 60% of all the employed said their employer provided opportunity to discuss claims and personal issues. And 48% said they trusted management to look after their welfare, but only in the service sector did a majority trust management.

By way of exploring attitudes to collective agency and collective action, respondents in the Ukrainian PSS were asked how they would react to certain labour market contingencies. In the case of *wage arrears* lasting three months or more, few workers saw government as the source of support, only a small minority thinking it worthwhile applying to a government agency. Two in every five thought they would take the employer to the courts, one in seven thought they would go to their trade union, and a handful would strike or demonstrate. A tiny minority would take no action whatsoever, presumably reflecting lack of faith in any of the available channels of protest.

In response to systematic neglect of *work security* (or *labour safety*), nearly a third were inclined to turn to trade unions, with the next most common reactions being applications to the courts, no action, application to government agencies, demonstration and strike.

In the case of unfair dismissal of other workers, court action was the preferred response for nearly a third of workers; with a quarter thinking it would be best to rely on the unions to contest it. Application to the courts was also the most popular reaction to *violations of a labour law or collective agreement* — one third saying this. The second most popular reaction was appeal to the union, followed by application to government agencies. Only 3% said no action should be taken.

In response to *price increases on food and other basic consumption goods*, one in five thought it most appropriate to lobby a government agency for help. Nearly 12% said that no action was appropriate. Going on strike was a more common response than applying to the courts. But nearly a third of all adults said they did not know what they would do in this respect.

In response to *price increases in local transport* — another basic need in Ukraine — the most popular action was to apply to government agencies, followed by public demonstrations, no action, strike, application to the courts, and application to trade unions. Some of these perceived responses might seem fanciful and unlikely to go very far, but they do show a pattern of perceived options to social pressures.

In response to any *disconnection of water supply, gas or heating*, protesting to government agencies was again the most popular reaction, followed by application to the courts, demonstrations, no action, strike, and appealing to trade unions.

In response to an *increase in crime,* easily the most popular reaction, as expected, was to look to government agencies, presumably demanding more police protection, although nearly as many said they would not know what to do.

Table 10.4 Ukraine: Anticipated reactions to various labour market and social crises
(percentage of respondents)

Reaction	Wage arrears	Neglect of work security	Unfair dismissal	Violation of labour law collective agreement	Basic goods price increase	Local transport price increase	Disconnection of utilities	Increase in crime
Apply to the courts 41.6	22.3	31.6	33.6	6.0	4.3	12.8	16.9	
Seek government support	9.1	11.1	7.7	7.9	21.3	25.5	32.6	35.8
Appeal to trade union	13.4	31.8	24.6	27.6	2.6	3.0	1.4	1.7
Demonstrate	3.5	2.9	3.1	2.4	14.2	12.5	5.6	8.3
Strike	4.4	2.4	2.4	2.1	6.5	6.2	2.1	3.9
No action	5.0	4.0	5.2	3.5	11.9	12.4	6.7	5.1
Other	4.7	4.8	4.3	3.7	5.1	5.2	6.3	4.8
Do not know	18.2	20.8	21.1	19.3	32.3	30.8	32.3	23.5

Source: Ukraine PSS 2002.

In Hungary, when asked what was the most appropriate action for workers to take in circumstances of non-payment of wages for three months or more, a majority of all workers, including those in unions, said that going to the courts was a better option than going to a trade union, which was the second most popular option among both unionized and non-unionized workers.[35] Interestingly, going to a union was the most popular option among both groups in the face of a violation of the safety code. In the case of a violation of a collective agreement, recourse to the union was the main response, but going to the courts was almost as popular. Indeed, the picture that emerges is that many workers are beginning to see the courts as the alternative to direct action through a collective body.

In the Russian Federation, among both men and women, the main response to extended non-payment of wages, unfair dismissal, violation of safety standards and violation of a collective agreement was going to court. This was the case for all age groups, but was greatest among older workers.

In developing countries, going to the courts is less likely to be an attractive option. In Bangladesh, among unionized workers, the main response to violations of the safety code or a collective agreement was to go to the union, followed by going on a demonstration; among non-unionized workers (the vast majority), demonstrating was seen as the best option, followed by going to a court and then going to a union.

In Tanzania, going to a union was the main response among unionized workers, followed by going to a court. But among non-union workers, going to a government agency was the most popular choice in cases of violations of the safety code, followed by going to a court. In cases of violations of a collective agreement (which would rarely be applicable), going to court and then going to a government agency were seen as the main options.

---

[35] Dasgupta, 2002, op. cit., p. 436.

In South Africa, when asked how they would react if wages were not paid for a month or more, going to a trade union was the most popular option (25%), followed by going to court (15%); 12% said they would strike, 11% said they would go to a bargaining council (a South African mechanism), and 8% said they would go to the police.

What these data imply is that, even in the perception of the most appropriate response to standard forms of work-related insecurities, groups and countries differ. In many countries, workers feel there is simply no option. Thus in Bangladesh, one in four non-unionized workers said that they would do nothing in response to safety code violations or an employment agreement. But there was also minimal trust in government agencies, in that scarcely anybody said they would go to them in adversity. This brings us to a major area of governance.

In China, although many workers do belong to a trade union, according to the PSS carried out in 2001, only a minority would go to the union in the case of any of the mentioned risks. The really revealing point is that 35% would not do anything in the case of wages not being paid for three months or more.

Table 10.5 China: Preferred actions of workers in case of difficulty (percentage of respondents)

	Go to union	Go to court	Appeal to government agency	Take part in demonstration	Not do anything	Other
Wage arrears	13.7	1.2	15.5	1.5	35.1	33.0
Non-observance of labour safety rules	18.6	2.1	14.3	3.5	25.9	35.6
Unfair dismissal of fellow worker	14.0	3.4	17.1	1.3	26.0	38.2
Violation of collective agreement	12.4	7.5	17.5	2.5	24.1	36.0

Source: China PSS 2001.

In the case of non-observance of labour safety rules, a mere 3.5% would engage in collective action while again one quarter would not do anything.

In the case of unfair dismissal of a fellow worker, one quarter of workers said they would not do anything. This may reveal a strong lack of social solidarity, even among unionized workers, a high level of fear in standing up for fellow workers, or passive resignation to decisions made by figures of authority, even when seen as unfair.

In the case of a violation of a collective agreement, 12% would turn to a trade union, while one quarter would not do anything.

Collective action starts with collective meeting

In China, over three quarters of workers still belong to trade unions. But according to the China PSS, only one in four regularly attend and less than a third occasionally attends union meetings. About one in ten does not attend any meeting, and an equal number claim that there are no meetings to attend.

Compare these responses with those to similar questions in the Russian Federation. There, when asked how they would respond to prolonged wage arrears, merely 6% said they would turn to a trade union; 13% would go on strike; 15% would appeal to their director; 6% would turn to the labour disputes committee; 31% would appeal to a court; 6% believed that collective action would be best. Hardly anybody said they would simply leave their job. But for 15% of workers, there was no point in doing anything because action was regarded as ineffectual.

In response to unfair dismissal, 10% would turn to a union; 2% would go on strike; 10% would appeal to their director; 12% would turn to the labour disputes committee; 46% would appeal to court; 2% believed in collective action. In this case, 13% thought that all forms of action would be ineffectual.

In response to violations of a collective agreement, 10% would turn to the union; 2% would go on strike; 11% would appeal to their director; 18% would turn to the labour disputes committee; 38% would appeal to a court; 3% would use collective action; 11% thought employee action was ineffectual and would not do anything.

In response to violations of safety rules, 15% would turn to a trade union; 2% would go on strike; 16% would appeal to their director; 1% would merely inform the management; 16% would turn to the labour disputes committee; 26% would appeal to a court; 3% believed in collective action; 11% thought all employee action was ineffectual and would do nothing; and just 0.2% would leave their job if their working conditions or safety were jeopardized.

In many ways, these statistics are perturbing, suggesting a passivity and sense of anomic adjustment to realities perceived as undesirable, if not dangerous. Strengthening Voice in such circumstances would be for the benefit of workers and society, and of the firms and communities in which those workers live and work.

Voice and fatalism

In South Africa, people seem to have a balanced view of how their life chances are influenced by their own self-determination and the role of outside forces. Thus, 25% believe that living standards and opportunities are mostly determined by the individual; 14% believe living standards and opportunities are determined by outside forces; and 42% think both individual and outside determination are equally important in determining living standards and opportunities. Women were more likely to think living standards are determined by individual action.

Compare the situation in the Russian Federation, where respondents were asked a similar set of questions. There nearly 50% of adults still think that their welfare is determined by outside forces, a fatalism that tallies with the perceived lack of any body to protect their interests.[38]

Collective bodies can give meaning to an individual's existence, helping him or her to have a balanced view that recognizes that, while there are constraints, well-being or its opposite can be shaped by group and individual action.

A Chinese puzzle

Faced with problems as serious as non-payment of wages and employer non-observance of labour safety codes, most Chinese workers would not take any action. This may reveal passivity embedded in the culture when it comes to workers taking action against their superiors, or it may reveal a lack of confidence in any results being obtained.

Nonetheless, this is curious given that over half of Chinese workers feel they have reasonable opportunities to express grievances and raise personal concerns in the workplace.

Having the opportunity to express Voice may not correlate with workers' actually using their voice in many cultures. The findings also indicate a lack of feeling of solidarity, as workers reveal they would not stand up for fellow workers who are unfairly dismissed, and would not act on violations of a collective agreement.

[13] See section 13.5 on trust in Chapter 13.

10.7 Unions as women's voice

It is often claimed that women are secondary citizens in union movements. Are they less likely to be union members, less likely to feel their interests are pursued, and less likely to take leadership positions?

The general picture is something of a paradox. While women are often less likely to be unionized, and while unions have been dominated by men, there is empirical evidence that not only have women benefited from unionization but that in some respects at least they have benefited more than men. This latter finding may reflect the fact that without unions women as workers are in a more vulnerable position than men. Nevertheless, it suggests that women would benefit from joining unions — even if the latter could do rather better as promoters of gender equality.

Women in trade union management

In the Voice Representation Security section of the SES questionnaire, correspondents were asked:

"For the 3 largest unions, how many top officials are men and how many are women?"

Assuming that an equal number of men and women as top union officials is a desirable goal, only 6 out of 61 countries achieved anything like that goal. Nine out of every ten trade unions do not have any women among senior officials. This under representation is found in all regions. However, the OECD has the largest regional share of women among top union officials, even though the share is still quite low, averaging about 26% and ranging from none at all to over 60%. Eastern European and Central Asian countries had rather similar patterns.

Finally, union managements in Asia (represented by only six countries) have female shares of around 10%, similar to the shares in the Middle East and North Africa. In sub-Saharan Africa and in Latin America, women's participation in union management is marginally better, averaging about 16%. That is one woman in any team of six senior officials.

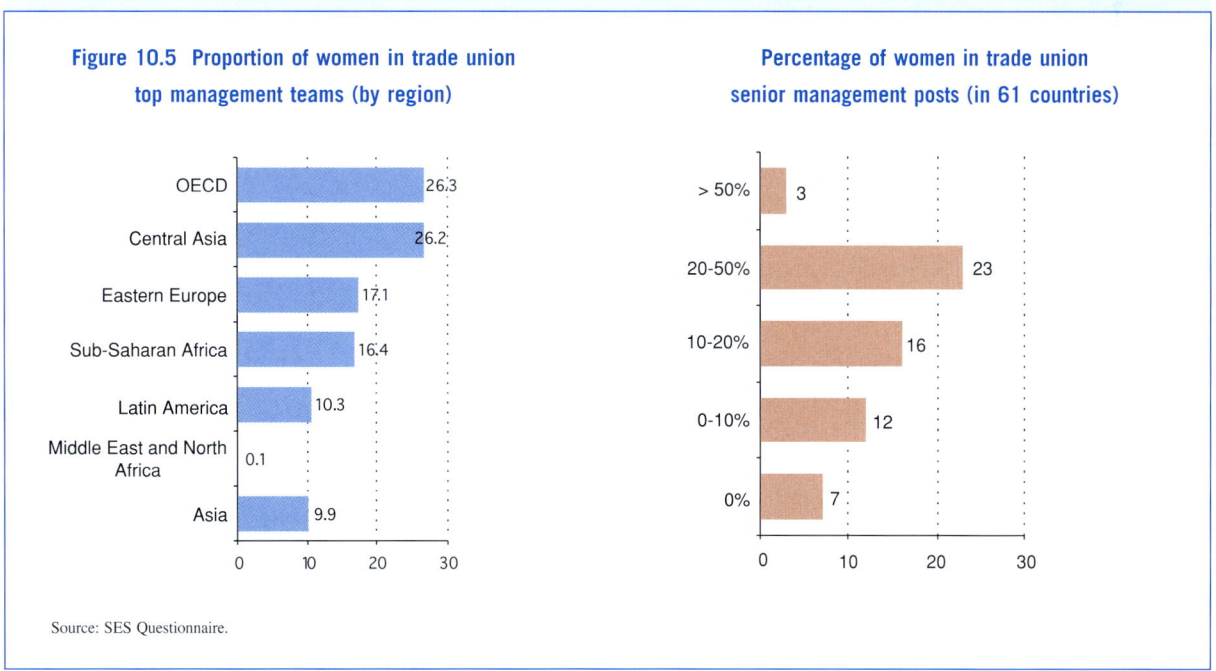

Figure 10.5 Proportion of women in trade union top management teams (by region)

Percentage of women in trade union senior management posts (in 61 countries)

Source: SES Questionnaire.

Women tend to be excluded from unions because of the work they are doing. Thus, more women than men are doing various types of "informal" activities, which are rarely unionized. But the disparity goes through the labour market. Thus, in Chile, according to the PSS, women are not only less likely to be in firms that have unions but are less likely than men to be in the unions in unionized firms.

In eastern Europe, women and men tend to have similar attitudes to unions, although it was notable that in Hungary a larger share of women had a positive attitude to unions and were slightly more likely to be union members.

In Indonesia, almost all the minority of firms in the ELFS that had a union reported that there were no women in the union. The PSS data confirmed that women were less likely to be unionized than men, but this was mainly because they were in informal labour activities. As shown earlier, men were more likely to believe in trade unions and to think they helped workers.

10.8 Shades of voice and muted voice

As noted earlier, unions take many forms. Where they developed as insurgent voice, through "struggle", they have tended to have an independence of purpose oriented to "adversarialism". But one response in the early 20th century by managers and corporations, replicated in slightly different form in Japan and elsewhere much later, was to try to encourage a less adversarial model through institutionalizing "company unions".

In the same way, employers and managers have fostered notions of "human resource management" and "employee involvement", which have, deliberately or otherwise, tended to co-opt workers, encouraging them to believe that aggressive independent unions are unnecessary or destructive. Many observers believe participation along those lines amounts to a subversion of real voice. Others might argue that even pseudo-participation raises the consciousness of what real participation could achieve.

A related issue concerns a tendency for managements and governments to institutionalize several forms of voice, at different levels or dealing with different sets of issues. The dual system of industrial relations in Germany is the classic example, prompting the question of whether the division between works councils and unions is a source of representation weakness or strength. In the abstract, multiple layers of voice raise questions about tensions between loyalties to units, companies and sectors and broader notions of social solidarity.

This is not the place to try to make an assessment of these particular debates. However, it might be useful to take note of some of the findings from the PSS and ELFS that prompt questions for future reflection.

No doubt, in many parts of the world, a majority of employers oppose unions and would like to see them disappear. But in many countries opinions are mixed and, among those employers who are opposed to "actually existing" unions, some would like to see a mechanism to ensure workers' voice is heard.

Chile has been an influential case in which unions have been transformed, for better or for worse. According to the enterprise survey, about one-fifth of managements believed that unions were no longer relevant, about three in ten thought they were still relevant for protecting workers' rights, and just over that proportion thought unions should reorganize to be more socially and economically useful. Among those favouring change, many wished to see unions become more like social clubs, a few wished them to become more like cooperatives, and about 18% wished them to become employee associations.

What is clear is that managements were co-opting workers within the firm, most notably by so-called labour-management cooperative schemes. As of 2000, over a quarter of industrial firms operated some form of labour-management cooperative scheme, which in the main were either of the quality circle variety (45% of the total) or labour-management discussion groups (34%). By far the main issue covered by these initiatives was "productivity" (41%), followed by "work organization" (21%) and "wages" (10%). Not surprisingly, managements thought that the main effect of their cooperation scheme had been an increase in productivity. But they also stressed that it had induced workers to identify more with the firm.

In Brazil, about 12% of industrial managers said that they thought unions were no longer relevant, about a third thought they were relevant, and 48% thought they should reorganize. About one in five of those dismissive of unions thought cooperatives were the most appropriate form of labour organization, over 29% thought they should be social bodies, and one-third thought they should be employee associations.

One-fifth of Brazilian industrial firms operated a labour-management cooperative scheme, the main type being a "labour-management discussion group" (over half having this), followed by a quality circle scheme (32%). The main issue covered in Brazilian schemes has been work organization, followed by productivity. As in Chile, the main effect of the scheme was perceived to be improved productivity (30%), followed by improved identification with the firm (25%).

On the other side of the world, in the Philippines, many employers said that they also thought unions irrelevant. This was the perception of about 39% of ELFS respondents; they tended to believe that co-operatives or employee associations were the most appropriate form of labour organization. Many firms had resorted to labour-management cooperative schemes, the main type being characterized as "labour-management discussion groups", followed by quality circles, with productivity improvement being the main objective.

In Tanzania, a quarter of industrial firms' managers thought unions were not relevant, but over a third thought they could help protect workers' interests. About 13% thought unions should reorganize, while another quarter had no opinion.

Of those against unions, about 17% thought workers should organize as cooperatives, 54% thought labour organizations should be mainly for social purposes and 27% thought employee associations would be most appropriate. About 18% had some sort of labour-management cooperative scheme, the main one being a discussion group, the main objective being to raise productivity, the main effect being to do so.

In Indonesia, managements of industrial firms were mostly inclined to think that unions were relevant and could promote workers' security; only 2% thought they were irrelevant. But more firms operated some labour-management cooperative scheme

(33%) than had unions in them. Admittedly, the main type of scheme was a discussion group of some kind. Overwhelmingly, the main objective of the scheme was to raise productivity.

In Pakistan, just over a quarter of the managements interviewed in the enterprise survey said they thought unions were not relevant. Only 9% said they thought they were able to protect workers, and nearly two-thirds thought they should reorganize. Most thought unions should focus on social issues, and one in five managers thought employee associations were the most appropriate form of labour organization. Too few firms had some sort of labour-management co-operation scheme to merit interpretation of the data.

10.9 A national Representation Security Index

To design a national index of representation security, it was decided to take a fairly conventional approach, focusing on standard aspects of freedom of association. As with other security indexes, there are sets of input indicators, process indicators and outcome indicators, which are combined into a single representation index.

Input indicators

Desirable input indicators should refer to the legal and regulatory framework, as well as the existence of collective bodies to which workers could belong. In essence, input indicators assess the formal commitment of the state to representation security. The input measures might include indicators such as whether or not the country has ratified well-established international freedom-of-association "Conventions", and whether or not there is a law allowing trade unions and making it easy for them to organize. They could also include measures of bargaining scope and freedom to bargain, freedom to strike, to picket and so on.

Five input indicators were selected. Three take account of the country's ratification of the most relevant ILO Conventions. Thus, a value of 1 is given if the country has ratified Convention No. 87 on Freedom of Association and Protection of the Right to Organise, 1948, and 0 otherwise; a value of 1 is given if it has ratified Convention No. 98 on the Right to Organise and Collective Bargaining, 1949, 0 otherwise, and a value of 1 is given if it has ratified Convention No. 141 concerning Rural Workers'

Organisations, 1975, and their role in economic and social development, 0 otherwise.

Fourth, a value of 1 is given if the country's laws have no restriction on the type of union that can be formed. The reason for this is that national and sectoral unions provide a greater degree of collective representation than is possible when only local or plant-level unions are allowed.

Fifth is the existence and coverage of a law on collective bargaining. This has three possible values: 0 if there is no law or other formal instrument on collective bargaining in the country, 1 if such a law exists but with a limited coverage, and 2 if there is a law with near-general coverage.

Since we did not wish to give a disproportionate weight to the most formal and international components of the input index, the five input indicators are divided into two sets. The first set includes the three Convention ratification indicators and is given only half the weight of the second, which is the national law component.[37]

Process indicators

Process indicators are mechanisms for strengthening voice; four indicators were selected. First, a value of 1 is given if there is a national tripartite board or council dealing with labour and social policies, 0 otherwise. Second, a value of 1 is given if the country's legislature allows non-governmental organizations to operate to promote worker interests, 0 otherwise.

Third, a scale is used for the percentage of total employed covered by collective agreements, adjusted by multiplying the number by the percentage of the workforce in wage and salaried employment. In some countries, actual figures exist on this, but in many others the estimate is crude. Accordingly, we have had to use secondary information, and have estimated a five-point range (insignificant, low, medium, high, and very high). Last is the share of employees in total employment as a measure of the potential public for voice representation.

Outcome indicators

Devising appropriate *outcome* indicators is relatively difficult for representation security, and yet these deserve more weight in the overall index than either the input or the process indicators, privileging indicators on effectiveness over those on formal arrangements.

Four indicators were selected. The standard outcome indicator of collective representation security is the *unionization* rate, i.e. the percentage of the workforce belonging to trade unions. Unfortunately, even assuming that it is a valid proxy for representation security, this is hard to measure satisfactorily. In some countries, the figure comes from the reports submitted by the unions themselves, in some it comes from sample surveys (the most reliable method, in principle) and in some it comes from establishment surveys.

Estimated unionization rates are from the ILO's *World Labour Report* and from the SES Primary Database. There are several conceptual and measurement difficulties, and there is much to be done to improve international data in this respect. What we have done is treat the very high figures recorded for ex-Soviet Union countries as misleadingly high, in part because until the late 1980s or early 1990s, all workers were required to belong to unions, formally at least. There is a legacy here, so we have halved the values for all of these countries — which still puts most of them in the high-level bracket. The unionization figures for all countries have also been adjusted by multiplying the recorded rate (or half of it in the case of the countries of the former Soviet Union) by the percentage of the workforce in wage and salaried employment.

Second, we use an estimate of the change in unionization during the 1990s. Because of data reliability and because we had to rely on "guesstimates" in a few cases, we put these estimated changes into several groups — big fall, small fall, little or no change, small increase and big increase. The most common outcome in the decade was a big fall in unionization, followed by countries with small declines.

---

[37]For an alternative or complementary approach to a measure of freedom of association and collective bargaining, which relies on coding information from ICFTU reports, US Department reports and reports from the ILO's Committee on Freedom of Association, see D. Kucera: *The Effects of Core Workers' Rights on Labour Costs and Foreign Direct Investment: Evaluating the Conventional Wisdom*, IILS Discussion Paper (Geneva, International Institute for Labour Studies, 2001).

Third, we take the Civil Liberties Index developed by the non-profit organization Freedom House, which has a scale of 1 (highest in terms of freedom) down to 7.[38] For the purposes of the representation index, the numbering is reversed, since larger numbers are given a greater weight. Finally, because an improving or deteriorating situation shapes security, a measure is included for the change in the Civil Liberties Index between 1990 and 1999, expressed as a ratio of the two values.

Calculations were carried out for 99 industrial and industrializing countries for the year 1999. Several comments can be made on the results (Table 10.6). As expected, the Nordic countries and other western European countries have the highest scores. Top performers are Sweden, Finland, Denmark and Norway. There are no "Pacesetters" in the Americas or Asia. Africa is the continent having the best-performing developing country, South Africa. It happens to have been one of the very few countries where the unionization rate rose quite strongly in the 1990s. Its position thus comes as little surprise. The only other non-western European country classified as a "Pacesetter" is Bulgaria. It has reached this position mainly due to its outstanding achievements in terms of the legislation and other norms established to guarantee and promote the voice representation of workers.

The next best voice security providers — the "Pragmatists" — are mainly countries from the Americas, East Asia and the Pacific, and the higher income eastern European countries plus the Russian Federation (Figure 10.6). Outsiders in this cluster, in decreasing order of security provision, are Switzerland, Mauritius, the Philippines and China.

By contrast, almost two-thirds of the countries have unsatisfactory levels of representation security, and over one in every two of these come under the "Much-to-be-Done" label. Almost all countries in Africa and the Middle East fall into either the "Conventional" or "Much-to-be-done" categories. The latter group also includes large Asian countries such as India and Indonesia, and the Central Asian republics.

The average performers — the "Conventionals" — come mostly from Africa and Latin America. Surprisingly, France and Greece also enter this cluster, the former mainly because it has a very low unionization rate and the latter because of a large decline in unionization over the 1990s.

---

[38]The Civil Liberties Index includes indicators of "association and organization rights", "freedom of expression and belief", "rule of law and human rights", and "personal autonomy and economic rights". Freedom House: *Freedom in the World: The Annual Survey of Political Rights and Civil Liberties* (New York, various years).

Table 10.6 Voice Representation Security Index

	High score on Outcome			
	High score on Input / Process		**Low** score on Input / Process	
Regions	**Pacesetters Countries**		**Pragmatists Countries**	
Africa and Middle East	South Africa		Mauritius	
Americas			Barbados	Santa Lucia
			Brazil	Saint Vincent and
			Canada	the Grenadines
			Chile	United States
Asia			Australia	Korea, Republic of
			China	New Zealand
			Kiribati	Philippines
Eastern Europe and Central Asia	Bulgaria		Czech Republic	Lithuania
			Estonia	Romania
			Hungary	Russian Federation
			Latvia	Slovakia
Western Europe	Austria	Italy	Switzerland	
	Belgium	Luxembourg		
	Denmark	Netherlands		
	Spain	Norway		
	Finland	Portugal		
	Germany	Sweden		
	Ireland	United Kingdom		

	Low score on Outcome			
	High score on Input / Process		**Low** score on Input / Process	
Regions	**Conventionals Countries**		**Much-to-be-done Countries**	
Africa and Middle East	Algeria	Israel	Burundi	Morocco
	Benin	Madagascar	Congo, Dem. Rep. of	Nigeria
	Burkina Faso	Senegal	Egypt	Rwanda
	Congo	Sierra Leone	Ethiopia	Tanzania, United Rep. of
	Côte d'Ivoire	Tunisia	Guinea-Bissau	Turkey
	Ghana		Lebanon	Zimbabwe
			Mauritania	
Americas	Argentina	Mexico	Colombia	Peru
	Costa Rica	Panama	Ecuador	Venezuela
	Dominican Republic	Saint Kitts and Nevis	Honduras	
Asia	Japan		Bangladesh	Pakistan
			Fiji	Papua New Guinea
			India	Sri Lanka
			Indonesia	Thailand
			Nepal	
Eastern Europe and Central Asia	Belarus	Moldova, Republic of	Albania	Kyrgyzstan
	Croatia	Tajikistan	Armenia	Turkmenistan
			Azerbaijan	Ukraine
			Georgia	Uzbekistan
			Kazakhstan	
Western Europe	France			
	Greece			

Figure 10.6 Representation Security Index — Clusters by region

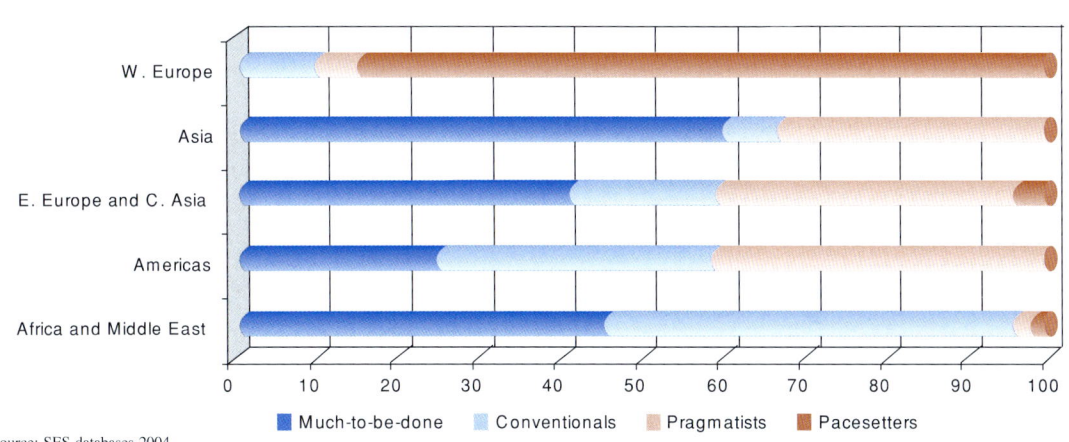

Source: SES databases 2004.

In conclusion, these results are consistent with other social indicators and relevant sources of information. They also tell a story about how voice is treated and distributed around the world, suggesting countries fit into one of three types, or groups that are relatively balanced in terms of number of countries. The first type consists of 36 countries out of the 99 under study, which have all neglected or rejected this aspect of security.

The second cluster includes 24 countries that, apparently convinced of the need for voice, have taken steps to secure it, without succeeding so far. They include countries from all continents and political regimes. Common to them appears to be a lack of financial resources and/or political will.

A third type consists of 39 countries that have in common the fact that they have provided "voice security" but differ in the nature of the model chosen. One way, which is predominantly found in western Europe, secures voice in an explicit way, reflecting a rights-based and state-based approach. The other, cutting across geographical areas, provides equivalent levels of representation security, but has adopted a liberal perspective, where a major role is played by the private sector and where only weak formal guarantees exist.

10.10 Future directions

This chapter has focused on worker representation security, but has also taken account of certain other developments. The worries about the strength of representation security associated with unions,

highlighted in the first part of the chapter, must be appreciated in the context of the positive value that such security can have in societies at all levels of economic development.

The Representation Security Index is significantly correlated with a number of important social and macroeconomic indicators. Briefly, it is most highly positively correlated with income security. It is also highly positively correlated with — in descending order of significance — work security, employment security, job security and labour market security, as measured by the respective indexes summarized in earlier chapters.

As might be expected, given the link with income security, the Representation Security Index is inversely related to the Gini coefficient of income distribution, implying that it is associated with lower levels of inequality. And it is positively and statistically significantly correlated with the UNDP's Human Development Index.

These are indeed encouraging signals that worker representation security remains a strong and instrumental form of economic security. What is worrying is that there has been a powerful erosion of the main forms of voice in the world of work in the era of globalization. Are there emerging forms that should give hope for the future? This is an issue that is addressed in Chapter 13.

---

[39]The Pearson rank correlation coefficients with the other indexes are 0.851 (income security), 0.829 (work), 0.822 (employment), 0.799 (job), 0.744 (labour market) and 0.724 (skills), all being statistically highly significant.

Chapter 11   Economic security and "Decent Work"

11.1 The idea of "Decent Work"

The ILO began the 21ˢᵗ century with a new concept, decent work. From the perspective of this report, decent work means creating an environment of basic economic security in which an increasing number of people in all societies can pursue their own sense of occupation, requiring good and improving social and economic security as defined in the preceding chapters.

The starting point is the claim that for everybody in society, in the workplace and as individuals, decent work requires equal basic security. Although there are seven forms of security in the sphere of work, primacy should be given to basic income security and basic representation security, as proposed in Chapter 1. Without reasonable income security, people lack real freedom to make rational choices and be socially responsible. Without collective and individual voice, the vulnerable will remain that way.

At the aggregate (macro) level, the objective may be defined as the creation of laws, regulations and institutions that enable a growing number of people in all societies to work without oppression, in reasonable security and with steadily improving opportunity for personal development, while having enough income to support themselves and their families. At the workplace (meso) level, a decent work environment is one that provides adequate security for workers while fostering the dynamic efficiency of their enterprises. At the individual worker (micro) level, decent work consists of having good work opportunities with adequate levels of all forms of work-related security.

In a sense, decent work can be said to exist when individuals have a decent level of income security, decent representation security, decent work security, and the real freedom to pursue whatever of the other forms of work-related securities they desire.

We propose that it is the combination of securities that make up economic security, and that this constitutes a decent work environment. In that spirit, the next section combines the seven security indexes into a macro-level Economic Security Index, which is measured for 90 countries.

After considering the links between economic security and globalization, the chapter then considers possible links with other aspects of social development, notably the extent of societal "happiness". Section 11.3 briefly describes an approach to measuring an economically secure workplace, and Section 11.4 defines what might be called a secure or decent work status for individuals.

11.2 The national Economic Security Index

In recent years, there has been a proliferation of performance indexes, many being attempts to identify "good practices" and "good performers".[1] Here, we

---

[1]The GDP and GNP are themselves indexes, which have been widely criticized. A refinement is Net National Product (NNP), which is GNP less depreciation. Some economists have suggested that all of these should be adjusted by measuring depletion of natural resources, including the value of goods and services produced outside the economic system (for example, care and voluntary work), reclassifying certain activities now counted as consumption as investment, taking account of polluting expenditures and weighting NNP by extent of inequality.

measure economic security, by combining the normalized values of the seven socio-economic security indexes to yield a composite measure designated the Economic Security Index (ESI). The ESI is defined as a weighted average of the scores of the seven forms of security, in which double weight is given to income security and to representation security, for reasons stated in Chapter 1, that basic income security is essential for real freedom to make choices and that representation security is essential to enable the vulnerable to retain income security.

The idea of economic security is that people need a combination of forms of social and work-related securities in order to flourish and develop. In a sense, economic security is an abstract asset, although crucially, as defined, it encompasses legal and institutional safeguards that make it a very real phenomenon.

A country's ESI score indicates the country's extent of economic security, in a relative sense. A high score indicates that a country is providing more security than one with a low score. But a high score does not necessarily imply that the country is providing a very strong environment of economic security, merely that it is doing better than many others. It is a relative measure, not an absolute one.

The ESI is estimated for all those 90 countries for which the component indexes could be estimated with the data available.[2] The 90 countries account for 86% of the world's population, although they comprise just over half the ILO's total member States. The ESI scores are by definition constrained to a value between 0 and 1. A check on the distribution of these scores indicates that countries are reasonably close to being normally distributed.[3] As Figure 11.1 shows, there is no polarization of values around the extremes of the distribution.

Figure 11.1. Distribution of the 90 countries by the ESI scores.

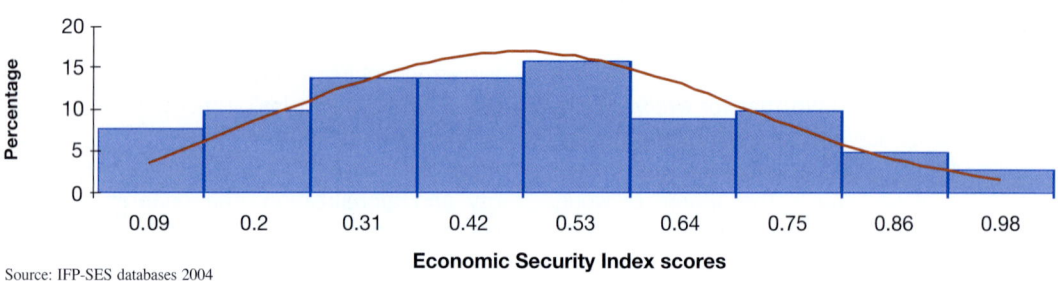

Source: IFP-SES databases 2004

Applying the classification criteria based on the scores of the *Input, Process and Outcome* sub-indexes, countries are grouped into four clusters. As with the individual securities, the "Pacesetter" cluster consists of countries that score high on all three sub-indexes; the "Pragmatists" consist of those doing well in terms of outcome, but less well in terms of either *Input* or *Process* or both sub-indexes; the "Conventionals" are those that have high scores in terms of *Input* and/or *Process* but somehow have a less satisfactory *Outcome* sub-index; the "Much-to-be-done" cluster consists of those countries doing poorly in all sub-indexes.

Table 11.1 presents the four clusters of countries (the individual scores are presented in the Appendices B1 to B8). Although the overall scores are approximately normally distributed, the sub-indexes are not. For that reason the two largest clusters are the "most insecure" and "most secure" countries. Together, the "Pacesetter" and "Much-to-be-done" clusters account for over two-thirds of the 90 countries, respectively 24 and 41.

---

[2] For four of the 90 countries one of the seven security scores could not be estimated. It is assumed that this would not alter significantly their final score and their ESI was therefore based on the normalized value calculated from the other six security scores. These four countries are Azerbaijan, Congo (Democratic Republic), Senegal and Turkmenistan.

[3] The Kolmogorov-Smirnov test shows that the hypothesis of normal distribution of the ESI scores cannot be rejected.

Table 11.1 Economic Security Index

	High score on Outcome			
	High score on Input/ Process		**Low** score on Input/ Process	
Regions	**Pacesetters** **Countries**		**Pragmatists** **Countries**	
Africa and Middle East	Israel		Mauritius	South Africa
Americas	Canada		Barbados Costa Rica	Chile United States
Asia	Japan		Australia Korea, Republic of	New Zealand
Eastern Europe and Central Asia	Bulgaria Czech Republic Hungary	Latvia	Estonia Lithuania	Slovakia
Western Europe	Austria Belgium Denmark Finland France Germany Greece Ireland Italy	Luxembourg Netherlands Norway Portugal Spain Sweden Switzerland United Kingdom		

	Low score on Outcome			
	High score on Input/ Process		**Low** score on Input/ Process	
Regions	**Conventionals** **Countries**		**Much-to-be-done** **Countries**	
Africa and Middle East	Burkina Faso Congo		Algeria Benin Burundi Congo, Dem. Rep. of Côte d'Ivoire Egypt Ethiopia Ghana Lebanon Madagascar	Mauritania Morocco Nigeria Rwanda Senegal Sierra Leone Tunisia Turkey Zimbabwe
Americas	Argentina Brazil Ecuador	Panama	Colombia Honduras	Mexico Peru Venezuela
Asia	Philippines		Bangladesh China India Indonesia	Nepal Pakistan Sri Lanka Thailand
Eastern Europe and Central Asia	Azerbaijan Belarus Croatia Moldova, Republic of	Russian Federation Tajikistan	Albania Armenia Georgia Kazakhstan	Kyrgyzstan Romania Turkmenistan Ukraine Uzbekistan
Western Europe				

Source: IFP-SES database 2004.

"secure" countries and high in the "insecure" ones.[6] This implies that the result in terms of overall economic security is associated with the way achievements are reached at the level of each of the seven forms of security, whether they are achieved in a balanced or unbalanced way.

Although there is no statistical reason for this to be the case, the best performing countries have high scores in all forms of security. This indicates that they have pursued a consistent set of policies. In other words, good overall performance goes together with comprehensive and balanced policy approaches towards the various forms of workers' security. Sweden, the most economically secure country, has high scores in all forms of security, as reflected in the lowest coefficient of variation (0.6%). By contrast, among countries that perform poorly, one finds situations in which, say, high work security coexists with medium representation security and low levels of other forms of security. Lack of policy coordination, limited resources and/or sectoral inefficiencies may cause such imbalances. Thus, Bangladesh, the third least economically secure country, has the highest coefficient of variation (94%).

Second, there is a strong positive correlation between all the forms of security.[7] This does not mean that all countries with high scores on one form have high scores on all others, but often good scores on one go with good scores on various others. All coefficients of correlation are highly significant.[8] This corresponds to the idea that the notion of decent work is best understood as a system of complementary forms of social and economic security, each form contributing to the others. We will return to this point shortly.

Third, as argued in Chapter 1, income security and representation security can be expected to play a prominent role in shaping other aspects of economic security. Regressions show that if representation or income security is very low, all other forms of security are low. But, as shown in Table 11.2, income security emerges as more important than representation security as a determinant of other forms of security, being positively associated with all work-related securities.

Table 11.2. Regression results of linkages between forms of security[1]

	Representation security	Beta coefficients Income security	Intercept	R^2 (adjusted)	No. of countries
Labour market security	0.159	0.725 ***	0.064 **	0.740	87
Employment protection security	0.269 ***	0.651 ***	0.075 ***	0.788	88
Job security	0.390 ***	0.481 ***	0.155 ***	0.695	89
Work security	0.250 ***	0.663 ***	0.110 ***	0.780	88
Skills security	0.123	0.707 ***	0.168 ***	0.655	89

[1] These results are derived from 5 bi-variate linear models where the dependent variable is one of the other forms of security and the independent variables are representation and income security.

Note: *** = significant at 0.01; ** = significant at 0.05; * = significant at 0.10.

---

[6] The coefficient of variation is a measure of dispersion defined by the ratio of the standard deviation to the mean. In this case, for each country, it measures the variation among the seven security scores.

[7] Each of the seven security indexes is based on a set of between ten and 20 indicators; in all, a total of 108 different indicators are used. Only ten of those enter more than one index and of these only two enter more than two indexes. Co-linearity can therefore be regarded as small.

[8] The correlation coefficients are significant at the 1% level, 2-tailed, and range from 0.723 to 0.879.

As should be expected from the analysis of Chapter 9, job security is the most positively affected by representation security and the least affected by income security. This does not mean that the causal relation is simply one way. But it does suggest that where unions and collective bargaining have been most successful, job security has been most strengthened, at least in the 20th century sense of that term.

Indeed, these exploratory findings suggest that representation security as developed in the 20th century may have achieved more in terms of *job, work* and *employment* security than in terms of either *labour market* or *skills* security. In the globalization era, all commentators seem to agree that it is skills security that is crucial for social, economic and cultural development.

What do the indexes show in connection with the traditional relationship between skills and income? First, the correlation coefficient between the two indexes is high and significant (0.814), confirming the usual postulate on the close relationship between economic and knowledge development. This relationship holds at high levels of economic development but not to the same extent at very low levels of development. Looking at the top 20 countries in terms of skills and income security, the richest countries are also top performers in skills security. There are two exceptions: unsurprisingly, Hungary is in the "Pacesetter" cluster of skills, although it is not in terms of income security; surprisingly, Austria is only in the top cluster of income security. The first corresponds to the well-known excellence of the Hungarian education system, and the country's current economic situation. As for Austria, its skill security level is reduced by the fact that the country scores low in terms of its input indicators. Contrary to many of its neighbours, it has not ratified ILO Conventions No. 140 on Paid Educational Leave, 1974, and Convention No. 138 on Minimum Age, 1973.

Looking then at the 20 countries most insecure in terms of skills and income, the picture is more differentiated. Only 13 of the 20 countries are represented in both lists. Central Asian Republics are illustrative of this differentiation, as they are not on the list of the skills-insecure countries but are on that of the income-insecure. Other poorer countries with a similar pattern are Colombia, Peru, Congo, Zimbabwe and Indonesia. Finally, there are countries that are not among the poorest but lack skills security. Not surprisingly, they are all sub-Saharan countries: Benin, Burkina Faso, Ghana, Madagascar, Rwanda and Senegal. Egypt is also a part of this group but the only one outside that subregion.

(ii) The impact of globalization on economic security

Various factors were identified in Chapter 2 to suggest that globalization, and policies associated with it, would have a strong impact on economic security and the several forms of work-related security. Without going into a detailed examination of the determinants of economic security, it may be useful to consider several hypotheses in terms of the several indexes.

Before doing so, it is worth noting that, while the ESI is positively correlated with other measures of social and economic development, it is not merely another way of expressing the same thing. It is positively correlated with the UNDP's Human Development Index and with GDP per capita. But at the simple correlation level, it is not significantly related to economic growth.

It was suggested earlier that globalization is best seen as a steady opening of national economic systems. While economic openness may have a beneficial effect on economic growth it could have a disruptive effect on economic stability and economic security, particularly at a low level of economic development, when institutional safeguards may be relatively weak.

Economists have debated the possible links between openness and economic growth, openness and income inequality and openness and poverty. There is no consensus on any of these, apart perhaps for the finding that financial liberalization in developing countries must be handled slowly, with prudential regulation and only on attainment of stable macroeconomic conditions.

Is economic security related to economic openness?

The correlation between trade openness — adjusted for level of development - and economic security was -0.275 and statistically significant.

Two models were tested. One is based on a quadratic relation suggesting that economic security declines sharply as trade openness increases from very low levels ($R^2 = 0.455$), then levels off and subsequently increases but only at very high levels of openness. The second model is a semi-log function, which suggests that the higher the extent of trade openness the lower is economic security ($R^2 = 0.524$).

These results suggest that economic security is inversely related to openness, except for extreme cases where trade "openness-development" ratios are either very large (as in Congo, Burundi, Madagascar and Nigeria, for example) or very small (as in Argentina, Australia, Japan and the United States). In such exceptional cases, there is no significant relationship between openness and security.

To test this, a measure of a country's economic openness is constructed to include both trade and capital account openness. Trade openness is defined as the sum of exports and imports as a share of GDP, which is the standard measure.[9] Capital account openness is measured by the Capital Account Openness Index, derived from the IMF's 13 categories of international transactions.[10]

To convert these variables to measures of openness relative to level of economic development, both are divided by the country's GDP per capita, giving two "openness-development" ratios. In terms of simple correlations, both these ratios are negatively related to economic security, the "capital-ratio" having a higher negative correlation (-0.302) than the "trade-ratio" (-0.275).[10] This result implies that when openness is large relative to the level of development, economic security is reduced. However, it could be affected by the influence of other variables. Accordingly, we created an Openness Index by averaging the normalized values of the trade and capital account openness ratios, and have estimated a multiple regression function that takes account of other possible influences.

The first of these is economic growth, the supposition being that high and sustained economic growth could be expected to improve economic security and the component forms of security, while low or erratic growth would have the reverse effects. As a measure of this, the total growth rate for the 20 years up to the end of the century is taken as an independent variable.

A second control variable and influential factor in its own right is the government's commitment to so-

cial policy. This is measured by the percentage share of GDP spent on social security. It is hypothesized that the higher this share the greater the level of economic security and the greater the level of the various forms of work-related security.

There are also good reasons for believing that political freedom and political democracy promote a social environment where various aspects of economic security are strengthened. To measure the impact of these factors, the Freedom House Civil Liberties Index is used. Since prior creation of political freedom could be expected to have an effect on economic security later, the value attained in 1990 is used as one independent variable. A second variable is the change recorded between 1990 and 1999, the expectation being that if freedom improved so would economic security.

[9]Some observers claim that only the export share of GDP should apply, since changes in imports do not appear to affect economic growth. P.A. Yotopoulos: *Exchange Rate Parity for Trade and Development: Theory, Tests and Case Studies* (New York and London, Cambridge University Press, 1996). Some have used "input" measures. Thus, Rodriguez and Rodrik used an index of tariff and non-tariff barriers and found that countries with more restrictive systems did not have slower growth than others. F. Rodriguez and D. Rodrik: Trade policy and economic growth. A sceptic's guide to the cross-national evidence", in B.S. Bernanke and K. Rogoff (eds.): NBER *Macroeconomics Annual 2000* (Cambridge, MA, The MIT Press, 2001).

[10]World Bank: *The Quality of Growth* (New York, Oxford University Press, 2000).

[11]These two correlation coefficients are statistically significant at the 0.01 level (2-tailed).

While more complex modelling is in order, a set of multiple ordinary least squares regressions was run, with the Economic Security Index and individual forms of security expressed as functions of economic openness, social policy, economic growth and political freedom, as just defined.[12] The results are presented in Table 11.3.

Table 11.3 Explaining economic security: Exploratory models[1]

Security Indexes	Beta coefficients					R^2 (adjusted)
	GDP growth 1980–2000	Civil liberties index 1990	Civil liberties index 1999/90	Social security % GDP 1999	Trade and capital openness 1999	
Economic security	0.043 *	0.459 ***	0.149 ***	0.453***	-0.045 **	0.978
Labour market security	0.114 ***	0.504 ***	0.134 ***	0.373 ***	-0.084 ***	0.954
Employment protection security	0.069 *	0.512 ***	0.141 ***	0.383 ***	-0.058 *	0.956
Job security	0.024	0.516 ***	0.180 ***	0.360 ***	-0.010	0.957
Work security	0.025	0.491 ***	0.129 ***	0.425 ***	0.001	0.969
Skills security	-0.008	0.595 ***	0.182 ***	0.314 ***	-0.053	0.956
Representation security	0.039	0.379 ***	0.206 ***	0.450 ***	0.021	0.951
Income security	0.045 *	0.447 ***	0.140 ***	0.470 ***	-0.050 **	0.974

[1] These results are derived from eight multi-variate linear models (N = 74) where the dependent variables are the various security indexes and the independent ones are those described above in the text.

Note: *** = significant at 0.01; ** = significant at 0.05; * = significant at 0.10.

What do these results suggest? They indicate, quite clearly, that operating in a democratic setting and having an effective commitment to the social sphere are the two most conducive elements to economic security. This holds true for economic security as a whole and for its different components.

More precisely, "democracy" is important for all forms of securities, including of course representation security. But a closer link is found with skills security. The direction of the causal relationship, if any, is unclear as one could equally argue that greater democracy is a function of higher education levels, and that higher and more equal access to skills can only be achieved in a society where the majority of the population is effectively represented.

Economic security is also positively associated with the share of national resources allocated to the social sector. Thus, social spending by governments has a strong positive effect on economic security, and on all forms of work-related security. As expected, the most significant impact of social expenditure is on income security, very probably reflecting the role of pensions in social security expenditure. Its least significant impact is on skills security, possibly because the private sector and other influences play a major role in this area.

More controversially, economic performance and openness seem to play a minor role. They have a significant overall impact on economic security – the first a positive and the second a negative one – but they only relate selectively and significantly to specific forms of security, namely to labour market, employment protection and income securities.

A straightforward interpretation is that growth sets the scene for an increase in job opportunities as well as for higher and more regular earnings from work, enhancing income security. A less obvious relation is between growth and employment protection. More dynamic economies may be more inclined than stagnant or declining economies to cover work-related risks and implement schemes based on solidarity. Additionally or alternatively, strong employment protection may enhance, and is certainly no impediment to, economic growth.

[12] Several variants were also tested, including a semi-log form and an equation that included dummy variables for the various regions of the world.

On openness, it appears that too much of it at early stages of development leads to more insecurity in these three same aspects. Economies opening "excessively" to foreign capital and/or trade may inhibit domestic job creation and incomes, and induce more employment flexibility or precariousness, generating a decrease in the country's overall economic security.

(iii) Economic security and "happiness"

"What is the highest of all goods achievable by actions?... both the general run of man and people of superior refinement say that it is happiness... but with regard to what happiness is, they differ."

— Aristotle, Nicomachean Ethics, Book 1, Chapter 4.

Policy-makers might find it useful to know the relationship between economic security and other measures of welfare. For many years, Erasmus University has measured overall "happiness" in various countries and monitored happiness trends. The happiness measure is the ratio of the level of life satisfaction – on a scale from 1 to 10 – to the dispersion of such levels within the country, the reference period being the 1990s.

For those 49 countries for which both the Economic Security Index and the Happiness Index exist, there is a statistically significant positive correlation (0.555). This suggests that economic security induces greater happiness.

Happiness is obviously a subjective concept. There is a positive relationship between income and happiness as income rises at low levels. But richer people do not become happier when they become even richer.[13] In affluent countries increases in per capita income have not produced any observed increase in happiness or "life satisfaction".

Indeed, in recent years overall "life satisfaction" has declined considerably in several countries for which the happiness index has been measured for some years. They include Denmark and Belgium, even though Denmark (with the Netherlands) has the highest proportion of its population expressing themselves as "very satisfied" with life among all European Union countries. The relationship between economic growth and life satisfaction seems to be weak or non-

existent. One possible explanation is that a combination of increased inequality and growing education without commensurate increases in opportunities to use that education in work or other activities has induced a growing sense of relative deprivation and dissatisfaction.

Accordingly, a model is tested in which the happiness index is the dependent variable, and the various security indexes are the independent variables. Dropping the statistically insignificant variables, the results suggest that the level of income security has a powerful positive effect on national happiness (see Table 11.4). We know from other research that, for individuals, national income has a positive effect on happiness up to some fairly high level, while income inequality has a negative effect on it.[14] Both of these factors are taken into account in the Income Security Index.

The results bear out what many believe, and what a wise observer concluded early in the 20th century:

Human happiness requires security – know what to expect under given circumstances.[15]

---

[13] See, for example, M. Argyle: "Causes and correlates of happiness", in D. Kahnemann, E. Diener and N. Schwarz (eds.): Well-Being: The Foundations of Hedonic Psychology (New York, Russell Sage Foundation,1999). On research showing a positive relationship between happiness and level of GDP and economic growth, see R. Di Tella, R.J. MacCulloch and A.J. Oswald: The Macroeconomics of Happiness, (Coventry, University of Warwick, 2001, mimeo).

[14] Inequality is associated with lower life satisfaction in Europe, but not in the United States. The most popular explanations for this apparent difference are that greater social mobility in the United States checks unhappiness due to inequality — more people think they will reach the heights — and that many of the American poor are immigrants, or children of immigrants, whose sense of relative deprivation is limited because their reference is their lower-income nations of origin. A. Alesina, R. Di Tella and R. MacCulloch: Inequality and unhappiness: Are Europeans and Americans different?, NBER Working Paper 8198 (Cambridge, MA, National Bureau of Economic Research, 2001).

[15] L.T. Hobhouse: The Elements of Social Justice (London, George Allen and Unwin, 1922), p. 16.

Table 11.4. The impact of economic security on happiness[1]

Explanatory Variables	Beta coefficients
Intercept	2.195 ***
Income security	0.701 ***
Skills security	- 0.679 **
Job security	0.546 **
R^2 adjusted (N=49)	0.378

(1) These results are derived from a multivariate linear regression model where the dependent variable is the happiness index and the various securities are the independent ones.

Note: *** = significant at 0.01; ** = significant at 0.05; * = significant at 0.10.

Less predictably, there is a negative relationship between skills security and happiness. This should not be interpreted to mean that education is bad for you. Rather it suggests that as education levels rise, adjustments should be made in the way work is organized and life is lived. Otherwise, frustrations build up. This interpretation also corresponds to other research, which has shown that once income, health and access to social institutions are taken into account, there is no correlation between education and life satisfaction.[16]

Skills security may not produce more happiness because happiness derives primarily from what activities the person is able to do and what the person aspires to do. An increase in education may generate feelings of dissatisfaction if the quality of work opportunities does not increase commensurately. A Tayloristic job structure is unlikely to be acceptable for people with the higher expectations that usually accompany education. In industrialized countries, recent evidence shows that, while more schooling yields higher income, which should be conducive to greater happiness and life satisfaction, it also leads to more hours of work, which have the reverse effect.[17] The stress and unhappiness outlined in Chapter 7 is a predictable outcome.

Finally, there is a positive link between job security and happiness, as should be expected in light of the considerations discussed in Chapter 9. Job security gives an individual a sense of being in control over his or her life, which has been shown to have a positive effect on a person's happiness. It is no coincidence that job satisfaction has been associated with less risk of heart disease.

(iv) Income distribution versus security distribution

Income is unequally distributed around the world, and so is security. But can we say that security is more or less unequally shared? By way of an answer, there is a teasing finding on the relation between income and economic security that we produce for reflection, and no more than for that reason.

We may compare the distribution of global income, as measured by the sum of the GDP of all the 90 countries included in the analysis, with the distribution of global economic security, as measured by the ESI. To measure global economic security, the ESI score is multiplied by the country's total population. The sum of national security levels of the 90 countries is defined as *global economic security*, i.e. the "pie" of security to be shared out.

It turns out that income is much more unequally distributed among countries than economic security. For example, the average income of the top quintile of countries (the richest) is 21.6 times that of the lowest, while for economic security this multiple is only 4.6 (Table 11.5 and Figure 11.4).

[16]E. Diener, E.M. Suh, R.E. Lucas and H.L. Smith: "Subjective well being: Three decades of progress", *Psychological Bulletin*, Vol. 125, No. 2, 1999, pp. 276–302; R. Inglehart and H.-D. Klingemann: "Genes, culture, democracy and happiness", in E. Diener and E.M. Suh (eds.): *Culture and Subjective Well Being* (Cambridge, MA, MIT Press, 2000).

[17]J. Gardner and A. Oswald: *How Does Education Affect Mental Well-being and Job Satisfaction?*, (Coventry, University of Warwick, 2002, mimeo).

Table 11.5 Distribution of global security and global income, by income quintile, 1999
(absolute numbers and percentages in parenthesis)

Quintile[1]	Global security[2] million units (%)	Security per capita (average) unit	Global income[3] USD billion (%)	GDP per capita (average) USD	Population[4] million (%)	Pearson correlation: ESI and GDP per capita
1 (poorest)	99 (4.9)	0.155	845 (2.0)	1 324	638 (12.2)	0.008
2	423 (21.1)	0.272	4 183 (10.0)	2 692	1 554 (29.6)	0.011
3	665 (33.2)	0.373	8 458 (20.3)	4 749	1781 (33.9)	0.238
4	259 (12.9)	0.529	5 648 (13.7)	11 536	490 (9.3)	0.575
5 (richest)	559 (27.9)	0.709	22 533 (54.0)	28 598	788 (15.0)	0.028
Total	**2 005 (100.0)**	**0.381**	**41 667 (100.0)**	**7 936**	**5 251 (100.0)**	**0.883**

[1] Quintiles are defined according to the ranking of countries by GDP per capita. [2] Global Security is defined as the sum of the country's ESI score multiplied by its population. [3] Global income is defined as the sum of the GDPs. [4] These figures correspond to the population of the 90 countries under study.

Source: IFP-SES database 2004 and World Bank, World Development Indicators, 2003.

Figure 11.4. Distribution of global security and global income, by income quintile, 1999

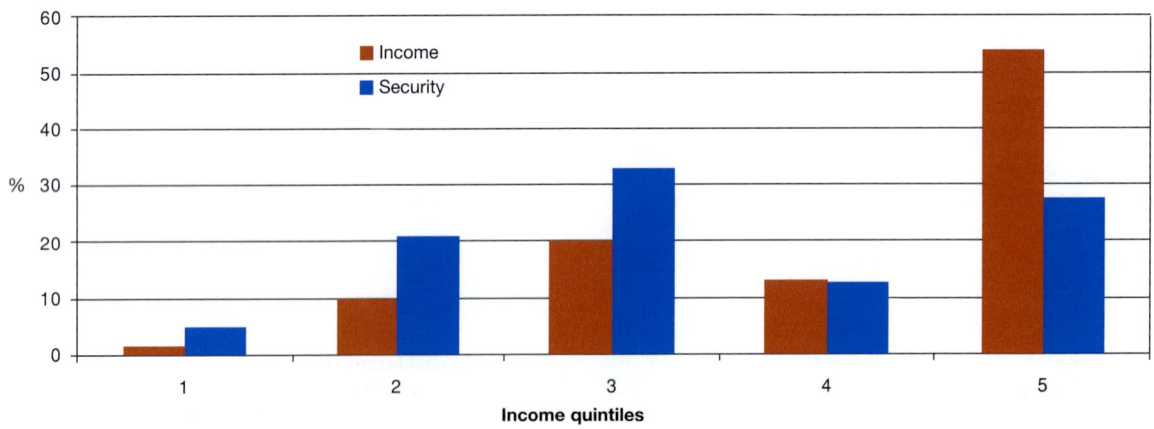

Source: IFP-SES database 2004 and World Bank, *World Development Indicators*, 2003.

Weaker correlations prevail at both ends of the distribution (1st, 2nd and 5th quintiles), while strong links exist for countries with an income per head of between USD4,000 and USD20,000 (the 3rd and 4th quintiles of income). For countries with per capita income of below USD4,000, as well as for the richest (beyond USD20,000), economic security is not correlated with income.[18]

What do these relationships mean? A first interpretation is that, in the richest as in the poorer societies, economic resources are a relatively less dominant factor in the provision of security. It looks as if, at some point of the development process, economic security is affordable or regarded as a priority. From this point on, economic security improves in parallel with increases in income. Once some "satisfactory" level of development (and security) is reached, income loses importance. The statistical evidence suggests that the richest countries do not always deliver top-level economic security because other factors come into play. This is also true in countries with low incomes since levels of security among them vary significantly. A low level of resources does not necessarily imply high economic insecurity.

Another interpretation, based on seeing how each component of economic security relates to income, is that some higher-income countries – such as the United States, Canada, Australia, New Zealand, Switzerland, United Kingdom and Italy – have been relatively disinclined to ratify international conventions or to institutionalise strong protective laws, and therefore have low *Input* scores. This weakens the correlation of income per capita with the Input sub-index, which in turn weakens the correlation with the overall Economic Security Index. We believe that both these interpretations are acceptable and are relevant to the analysis of the security-to-income relationship.

Because most of the countries in the upper decile are in the OECD, the distributions of security and income by region have some similarities. In the OECD, as in the upper decile, the shares of income appropriated are much greater than those of security. By contrast, in all other regions (or deciles) the reverse is true (Figure 11.5), and income shares are smaller than those of security. But there are also differences between these distributions.

Leaving the OECD aside, one can distinguish two distinct groups of countries (Table 11.6). A first group includes middle-income regions such as Latin America, eastern Europe, North Africa and Middle East, where similar shares of global income and global security are appropriated. For example, Latin America has 8% of global security and 6% of global income. By contrast, the other group, which includes lower income regions such as Asia and sub-Saharan Africa, receives a much larger share of security than of income. For example, in South Asia, the respective shares are double: 14% for security and 7% for income. This pattern supports the view that security relates to regional development levels.

[18]This is supported by the fit of a quadratic relationship between ESI and income. The parameters of the quadratic regression are: R^2 (adj.) = 0.942; Beta coefficients: GDP per capita = 1.97 (significant at the 0.01 level) and GDP per capita^2 = -1.10 (significant at the 0.01 level). It should also be noted that statistically the association between security and income varies non-linearly with development level, and corresponds graphically to an inverted U curve.

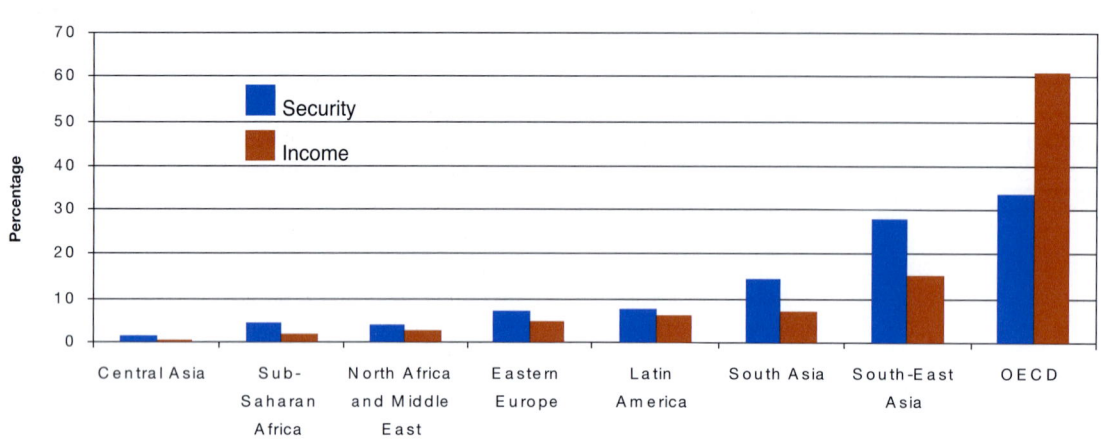

Figure 11.5. Distribution of global security and global income by region, 1999

Source: IFP-SES database 2004 and World Bank, *World Development Indicators* 2003.

Table 11.6. Distribution of global security and global income, by region, 1999
(absolute numbers and percentages in parentheses)

Regions[1]	No. of countries	Global security[1] million units (%)	Global income[2] USD billion (%)	Population million (%)
OECD	24	672 (33.5)	25 438 (61.1)	998 (19.0)
Latin America	11	154 (7.7)	2 540 (6.1)	341 (6.5)
Eastern Europe	15	147 (7.3)	2 132 (5.1)	286 (5.5)
Central Asia	7	23 (1.1)	228 (0.5)	69 (1.3)
Sub-Saharan Africa	17	93 (4.6)	767 (1.8)	387 (7.4)
North Africa and Middle East	7	77 (3.9)	1 175 (2.8)	214 (4.1)
South East Asia	4	554 (27.7)	6 418 (15.4)	1 626 (31.0)
South Asia	5	284 (14.2)	2 969 (7.1)	1 330 (25.3)
Total	**90**	**2 004 (100.0)**	**41 667 (100.0)**	**5 251 (100.0)**

[1] Regions are defined by the list of countries under study. For details see Table 11.1. The OECD region in this table includes Mexico and the Republic of Korea and omits Iceland.
[2] Global security is defined as the sum of the ESI scores multiplied by the population size of the countries.
[3] Global income is the sum of the GDPs of the countries.
Source: IFP-SES database 2004 and World Bank, *World Development Indicators*, 2003.

A more detailed comparison of these two distributions shows that in most cases the relative performance of countries in the production of income and in the provision of security is similar.[19] Those that do relatively well in one also do well in the other. Over two-thirds of countries (63) belong to the same quintile for income and security distributions, showing a consistency between social and economic achievements. But the remaining 27 countries show interesting deviations, having either less or more security than could be expected from their income level.

For example, in Europe, while Italy is the only country that provides less economic security than could be expected from its resources, Spain and Portugal provide more. The same is true for some eastern European and central Asian countries. Thus, Bulgaria, Croatia, Lithuania, Latvia, Republic of Moldova, Ukraine, Azerbaijan and Tajikistan all rank higher in terms of security than income.

By contrast, countries in Latin America (Argentina, Chile, Mexico, Colombia and Peru) provide less security than could be expected given their relative income level. This is also the case for large countries in Asia, such as China, India, and Indonesia, and for the Russian Federation.

11.3 A Decent Workplace Index

In preceding chapters, patterns and trends in workplace securities have been considered, and indexes for various types of labour security have been proposed. In the same spirit, could we measure what might be called the characteristics of a secure or decent workplace? Indeed, is it too fanciful to envisage a set of practices and outcomes that would constitute a *Decent Workplace Index?*

This could not apply to informal enterprises, and the best that could be hoped is that good managements in medium and large firms and organizations will establish practices to be emulated, to the extent possible, by small-scale informal firms.

Any such idea should be seen as a set of "good practices", not as a route to statutory regulation and standard setting. It should also be interpreted in relative terms, i.e. vary according to a country's overall standard of living and institutional strength, and perhaps relative to the size of firm and type of sector.

There are those who believe that decent work is only a macroeconomic issue, and that it is invalid to try to measure decent work practices at the level of a firm or workplace. Others believe that, somehow, if there were such a measure, it might be used by opponents of trade unions to claim there would be no need for unions. Both these positions seem untenable and unnecessarily defensive. If you do not have an idea of what is a *decent workplace*, then the concept of decent work is rather hollow.

There is a great deal of interest in corporate codes of conduct and voluntary initiatives around corporate social responsibility. What is proposed in this section is consistent with the spirit of the best of those initiatives. Essentially, a decent workplace is defined as one in which there is relatively good worker security in the firm or organization, as long as whatever is provided is compatible with dynamic efficiency.

To measure a Decent Workplace Index (hereinafter DWPI), we draw on data from the ELFS, which is a survey of managers that examines their attitudes, practices and outcomes. The method of constructing the DWPI is analogous to that used for the macro-level indexes described earlier, and is calculated by combining sets of indicators of the main forms of security identified in the preceding chapters, in this case excluding labour market security, which is obviously not relevant at the level of an individual workplace. The normalization procedure is used for each sub-index, but in this case the method is to build up an index by steps along the lines shown in Figure 11.6.

---

[19]This comparative analysis was carried out using a two-entry table grouping countries by quintiles of income on the one hand, and economic security on the other. Countries in the diagonal of the table are those belonging to the same quintile, meaning that in relative terms those countries do similarly well whether in terms of income or security. Countries above the diagonal do relatively worse in security than in income terms and those below the opposite.

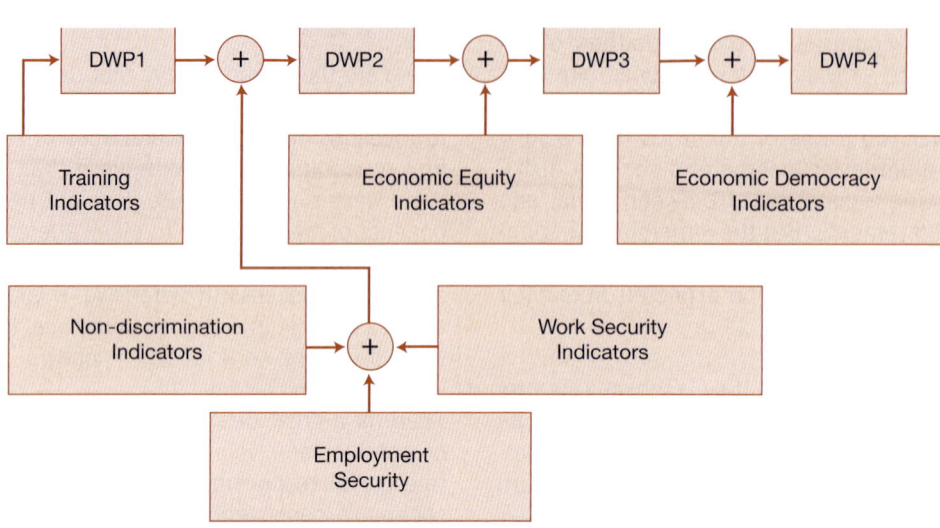

Figure 11.6. Hierarchy of Decent Workplace Indexes

To identify a DWPI, we need indicators of the principles (input), practices (process) and outcomes that deserve to be promoted. Inevitably, this means there is some subjectivity and pragmatism, due to absence of data or difficulty of obtaining measurable information on some issues. As many who have tried to judge what firms should do have discovered, appropriate performance indicators are hard to identify and measure.

We start with the idea that a decent workplace is one that promotes skill reproduction security among its workers. The *input* indicators are whether or not the firm provides entry-level training for newly recruited workers, retraining to improve job performance or to transfer workers to other jobs with similar skills, and retraining for upgrading workers or for promotion.

The *process* indicator is the type of training provided. For example, if a firm only gave informal, on-the-job training, that would deserve less weight than if it gave "classroom" and structured training, including apprenticeship. Accordingly, for each of the three levels, a distinction is made between "informal" and "formal" training, with the latter being presumed to have greater value, which is usually (though not always) the case. Although differences between formal and informal may be exaggerated, concentrated training that involves a monetary cost should be preferable to "on-the-job, pick-it-up-as-you-go" training.

The selected *outcome* indicator is whether or not the establishment actually pays for training directly, by funding a training institute, by paying the training fees to an institute where it sends workers for training, or by giving stipends to workers who go on training courses.

Beyond skill security, a decent workplace might be expected to provide its workers with adequate *employment security*. This index is calculated by the extent to which a firm provides workers with regular employment contracts, whether it provides predetermined notice periods in situations of retrenchment, whether it provides benefits to workers being retrenched, and whether it has dismissal procedures covered by a collective agreement.[20]

As far as work security is concerned, the indicators include a positive value if there was a safety committee or department in the firm, a positive value if the number of work accidents as a proportion of the workforce was less than the mean average, and a positive value if there were no accidents resulting in a closure or any death in the firm. In some surveys, most notably in Tanzania, we also have data so that

_____

[20] As noted in earlier chapters, in eastern Europe and in China, where ELFS were conducted, a variable was added giving a negative value if the firm was putting workers on "administrative leave".

we can give a positive value if the workplace has separate toilets for men and women, a positive value if there are childcare facilities on the premises and a positive value if there is a health clinic.

A third dimension is related to the notion of job security and involves an *index of non-discrimination*. For social equity, non-discriminatory labour practices are essential. To be exemplary, an enterprise should act in ways that avoid labour segregation based on personal characteristics such as race, gender or disabilities. Although measuring discrimination is notoriously difficult, both employer *attitudes* (inputs) and *outcomes* should be taken into account. Neither would be sufficient alone. For instance, one might have a "preference" but not put it into effect, or have no preference yet discriminate by hiring on the basis of characteristics that had the (perhaps inadvertent) effect of excluding certain groups from various jobs.

What is needed is a set of easily understood indicators of social equity. For this reason, in the enterprise surveys, attention focuses on the equitable properties of hiring and training practices. The main indicators are related to *gender*, although they can be adjusted to include other groups, as in South Africa where *race* was also taken into account.[21]

In terms of recruitment, if management reported that there was no preference for either men or women, this was taken as a positive factor, *neutrality* being regarded as equitable. Just as it would be inequitable to give a positive value if a firm had a preference for men, it would be inequitable for men if a positive value were given if management preferred to recruit women, as is sometimes the case. However, we are *primarily* concerned with redressing the typical case of discrimination against women.

Another *input* indicator is a stated commitment to provide training equally to men and women. Preferences here are likely to be revealed, especially where there is no law against any discrimination. But one must recognize that stated preferences may be rationalizations, or norm-induced. To ignore preferences would be unjustifiable, yet one must complement them with indicators of actual outcomes. One *outcome* indicator is the share of employment taken by women. If the percentage of higher-level "employee" jobs taken by women was greater than 40%, a positive score was given. Al-

though this is not ideal, because the outcome could reflect differences in the supply of men and women, it does focus on the better jobs and identifies relatively good performance in a key area of discrimination.[22] Another outcome variable is the share of all workers trained who are women; if greater than or equal to women's share of total employment, a positive value is given.

Besides gender variables, another indicator of discrimination is whether or not a firm employs *workers with registered disabilities*. So, a positive score is given to a firm employing any workers with disabilities. Coupled with gender variables, this results in an index of non-discrimination suitable for all workplaces.

Adding the work security, employment security and non-discrimination indexes to the skills reproduction index gives what we might call the *socially decent workplace.*

A decent workplace is, we reason, one in which there is reasonable income security. The literature on economic equity is vast, yet scarcely any discusses the issue in relation to the microeconomics of the firm. What is an economically equitable firm? It is surely one in which the differences in earnings and benefits between its members are minimized to the point where efficiency is not jeopardized. This might be called the *Principle of Efficient Inequality*. As that is rather utilitarian, one should add a Rawlsian caveat — with priority given to improving the situation of the "worst off" workers.

An economically equitable workplace should have few if any workers paid a small fraction of the average in the firm. We need a proxy for that principle.

---

[21] The approach does not deal with training discrimination between higher-level and lower-level workers. There is international evidence of intra-firm discrimination against those with less "skill". With respect to training, under the diminishing marginal utility principle, a social welfare function might weight desirable characteristics for those at the "bottom" of the firm more than for others.

[22] One could make the threshold sectorally specific, giving a positive score if a firm had a high percentage of women in training relative to the average for all firms in the sector. But this is not as justifiable as it might appear, since it allows for gender-based industrial segregation.

So, the minimum wage received by the lowest-paid full-time workers acts as the initial yardstick. If less than 5% of workers receive this wage the firm is given a positive score on economic equity. A positive score is also given to any firm in which the minimum amount paid was equal to or greater than 50% of the average wage. These are only proxy measures, yet seem reasonable.

Another indicator is whether the average wage itself is equitable relative to that paid in other firms. Here, a sectorally relative measure is used, to reflect technological and market factors. If the average wage in the firm is greater than the industry average then a positive score is given.

Finally, economic equity is improved if the firm provides benefits and entitlements that provide security against various contingencies and enhance workers' standard of living. As wages and incomes are only part of the remuneration system, a positive value is given if the firm provides production workers with more than eight types of specific non-wage benefits. We move next to devise and incorporate a representation security index into the proposed decent workplace measure. This is most controversial. However, in the 21st century democracy in the workplace will surely be seen as essential for decent work and

also be recognized as essential for dynamic efficiency and sustainable corporate governance.

We measure representation security with a variety of indicators, depending on the type of economy and structure of industrial relations. The core factors are straightforward. A positive value is given if the firm recognizes a union, and if more than 50% of the workforce is unionized. A positive value is given if there is a collective agreement operating in the firm, covering wages and other labour matters. A positive value is given if there is a joint management-worker committee of some sort, such as a Work Forum in the South African case. A positive value is also given if the workers possess more than 10% of the shares of the firm, and if there is a bargained profit-sharing payment scheme for workers.

Of course, one could improve on these indexes. However, they surely capture the essence of decent workplaces. Adding them together and normalizing them yields interesting results. We have estimated the DWPI for 14 countries. Just for illustrative purposes, the distribution of the resultant scores for Tanzania is given in Figure 11.7, showing that no firms scored above 0.8. In other countries, the distribution is close to a diamond, tapering so that just a few firms have very high values, and with the bulk in the middle ranges.

Figure 11.7 Tanzania: Distribution of firms according to DWPI scores, 2001, all regions

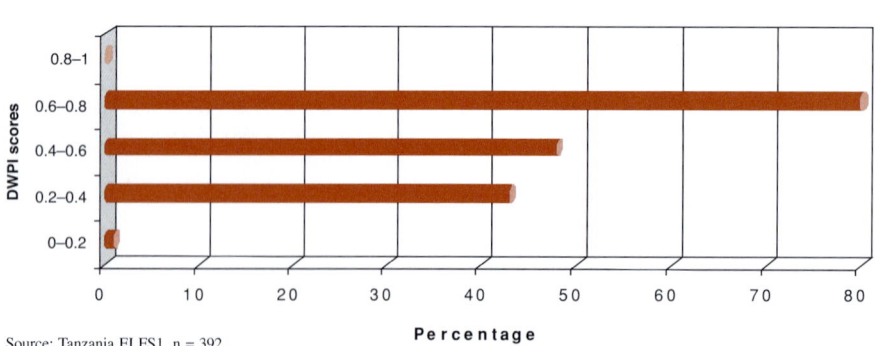

Source: Tanzania ELFS1, n = 392.

What is most instructive about use of the decent workplace index is that it shows a positive relationship with economic, or commercial, performance of the firm. This corresponds with what astute observers have claimed about the impact of good work practices. For instance, PriceWaterhouseCoopers, the consultancy firm, carried out a "Global Human Capital Survey" in 2002, covering over 1,000 companies in 47 countries. While the survey's methodology is dubious (there being too few firms from each of the countries to be reliable), it is worth noting one key finding: "taken in isolation, participation in training, management development, or performance appraisal show no links to profit margins or revenue per employee. This is consistent with the view that it is the overall system that is important, not the individual elements".[23]

Similarly, a survey carried out by Business in the Community (BITC) in 2002 found that a large majority of chief executives in Europe believed socially responsible practices improved competitiveness, innovation and profitability.[24]

Encouragingly, the ELFS shows that, controlling for the influence of other factors, firms that provide a decent workplace as we have defined it do better than others in several respects. In country after country, there is a significant positive correlation between DWPI and various measures of workplace performance, such as productivity and employment growth, as was found in a comparison of firms in China.[25] While we could debate the nature of the causal relationship, this suggests that at the very least, decent workplace practices are compatible with profitable performance. Another example is on Ukraine for which Figure 11.8 shows that those firms with low workplace security are also those losing workers and having the highest turnover of workers. Finally, the case of Indonesia (Figure 11.9) indicates that the share of labour costs in total costs tends to be smaller in establishments which provide workplace security to their employees.

Figure 11.8 Ukraine: Percent employment change by DWPI, 2002

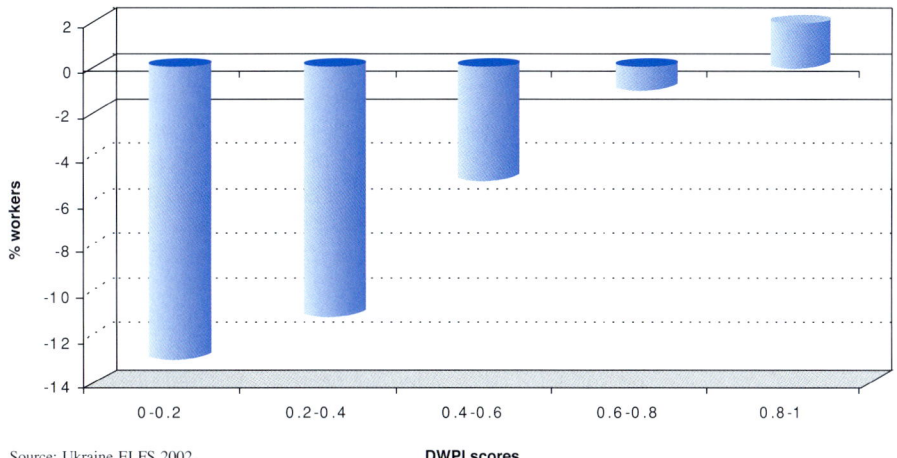

Source: Ukraine ELFS 2002.

DWPI scores

---

[23]PriceWaterhouseCoopers: *Global Human Capital Survey 2002/3*, Executive Briefing (London, 2002), p. 6. This attracted more uncritical media attention than it deserved.

[24]Reported in "FT Management: Focus on corporate social responsibility", *The Financial Times*, Dec. 10, 2002, p. 1.

[25]Standing, 2003, op. cit, p. 60.

Figure 11.9   Indonesia: Labour cost share of production costs by DWPI, 2000

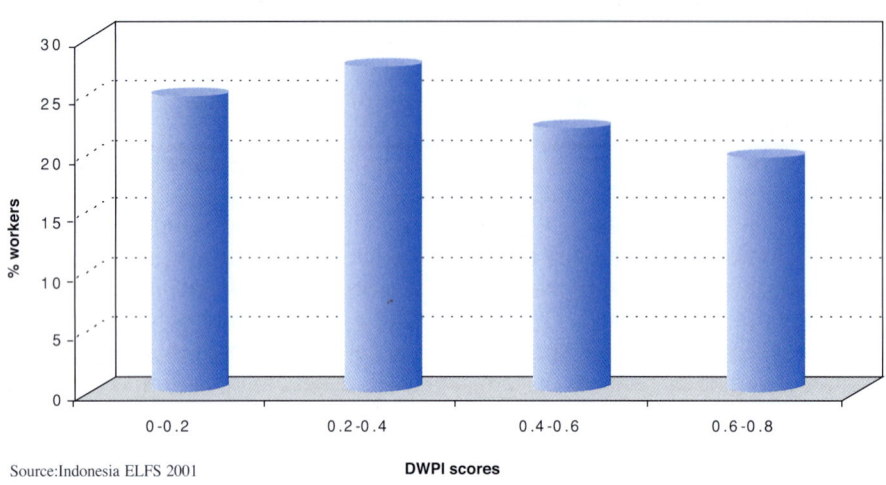

Source:Indonesia ELFS 2001   **DWPI scores**

Many analysts now argue that treating workers well enhances a firm's performance, and correlations between the Decent Workplace Index and commercial performance indicators bear that out.

11.4 A Decent Work Status Index

At the aggregate level, as stated earlier, "decent work" can be defined as the creation of laws, regulations and institutions that enable a growing number of people in all societies to work without oppression, in reasonable security and with steadily improving opportunities for personal development, while earning enough to support themselves and their families.

At the micro (individual) level as at the macro-level, security can be seen as a proxy for decent work. If a person has good income security, good skill reproduction security, good occupational security, good representation security, and good work security, he/she could be said to have decent work — and to be extremely fortunate. To these could be added good employment security and labour market security. However, they could be regarded as having lower priority than the others, and as instrumental needs rather than desirable attributes of decent work. In what follows, employment security is included, labour market security excluded.

We merely note here what is included in the individual Decent Work Status Index (DWSI), which is

the equivalent at the micro level of the national Economic Security Index.[26] Labour market security is treated as a contextual variable, and is thus excluded, so the DWSI is based on indexes of the six other forms of security. For those, there are *subjective* and *objective* indicators.

For the *employment security* index, the subjective indicator is the degree of security felt by the person about retaining his or her current main work; the objective indicators are measures of contract status and size of unit in which the person is working. For the *job security index*, the subjective indicator is whether or not the person anticipated having a good job in a year's time; the objective indicators are whether or not the person had experienced a rise in income from work over the past five years, whether or not he or she had a job in which responsibilities had increased, and whether or not an advance in grade or occupational title had been achieved.

For the *work security* index, the subjective indicator is whether or not the person feels safety and health conditions in his or her work are good; the objective indicators are whether or not the person had a safety committee or department at his or her workplace,

---

[26]For a fuller description, see G. Standing: "From People's Security Surveys to a Decent Work Index", *International Labour Review*, Vol. 141, No. 4, 2002, pp. 441–454.

and whether or not he or she worked with dangerous equipment or chemicals. For the *skill reproduction security index*, the subjective indicators are partly objective, and are whether or not the person used the qualifications and skills he or she possessed; the objective indicator is whether or not the person had received formal training.

For the *representation security index*, the subjective indicator is whether or not the person believes available organizations represent his or her interests in work matters; the objective indicators are whether or not the person belongs to a union, whether or not a union is operating in his or her workplace, and whether or not there is another organization representing the person's interests.[27]

Finally, for the *income security index*, the subjective indicator is whether or not the person feels "well off" by comparison with other people living and working locally; the objective indicators are mea-sures of income adequacy and income stability, and whether or not the person has access to income-supplementing or income-replacing benefits or entitlements.

Normalizing each of these indexes separately, using the standard formula, and aggregating them gives a DWSI with a range of values from 0 to 1. We can show the distribution of decent work statuses for all working respondents in any People's Security Survey. The Indonesian PSS is used as illustrative. As expected, it shows that women tended to have lower decent work status and that both men and women in poor and vulnerable households were less likely to be in decent work situations (Figure 11.10).[28]

In Tanzania, one also finds that the women's distribution of decent work statuses is to the left of men's, and is worse in rural than in urban areas. Migrants tend to have a lower DWSI value than non-migrants in the area.

Figure 11.10. Decent work status: Indonesia — Distribution of households with greatest vulnerability, by gender, 2001

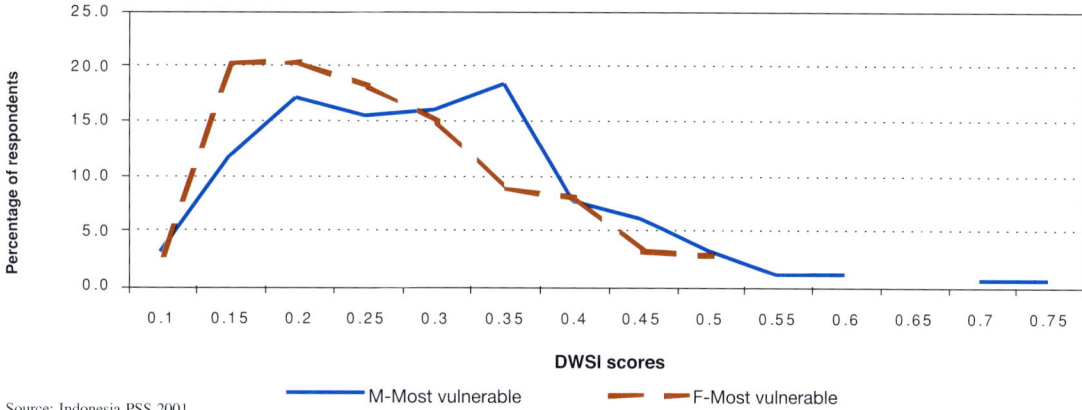

Source: Indonesia PSS 2001.

—————

[27] In some of the surveys, the subjective indicator was not included.

[28] In the Indonesian PSS, vulnerable households are defined in terms of poor housing conditions and the absence of any person with more than primary schooling.

Table 11.7. Decent work status index Regression results[1]

Independent variables	Beta coefficients Bangladesh	Brazil	China	Tanzania	Ukraine
Intercept	0.520 ***	-0.04 ***	0.350 ***	0.129 ***	-0.223 ***
Age	0.184 *	1.269 ***	0.355 ***	0.558 ***	2.444 ***
Age	-0.177 *	-1.342 ***	-0.486 ***	-0.524***	-2.456 **
Male	0.037 **	0.166 ***	0.040 **	0.124 ***	0.045 ***
Rural	-0.474 ***	n.a.	n.a	-0.158 ***	-0.105 ***
Black	n.a.	-0.019 ***	n.a	n.a	n.a
Mixed, Asian, Indian	n.a.	-0.044 ***	n.a	n.a	n.a
Migrant	0.008	-0.033 ***	0.111 ***	0.207 ***	0.019 **
R-square (Adjusted)	0.229	0.091	0.031	0.113	0.222
N	3 157	4 000	3 345	1 004	9 400

Notes: (*) = significant at 0.10 level; (**) = significant at 0.05 level; (***) = significant at 0.01 level, n.a. = corresponding variable not available in the country.

1. These results are derived from multivariate linear regression models where the dependent variable is DWSI. The independent variables are defined as follows:

Age- Years completed; Male = 1, Female=0; Black = 1, Other = 0; Mixed, Asian, Indian = 1, Other = 0; Migrant = 1, Non-migrant = 0.

Source: PSS Brazil 2001, Bangladesh 2001, China 2001, Tanzania 2001, Ukraine 2002.

Although more analysis of the determinants of decent work status is required, it is worth noting that multivariate regressions show that in all countries covered by the PSS men are more likely to have a high score, controlling for various other factors. Table 11.7 shows results for a selection of countries. It is also apparent that decent work status tends to rise with age, before turning down in later years, probably varying by type of economy. This pattern occurs almost everywhere, although not in Bangladesh, where older workers apparently do not experience a decline. As expected, in countries where there are racial minorities (or in the case of South Africa, a long-disadvantaged racial majority), these on average have a lower level of decent work, as shown to be the case in Brazil.

Those living in rural areas tend to have a lower level of decent work than those in urban areas, as shown in countries as dissimilar as Bangladesh, Tanzania and Ukraine. More interesting perhaps is the finding that migrants, defined as those who moved as adults into an area where they work, typically attain a higher work status than non-migrants. An exception is Brazil, where adult migrants in urban areas have a lower work status.

11.5 Conclusions and reflections

In general, Scandinavian countries perform relatively well on all aspects of social and economic security, and consequently emerge as the leading Pacesetters in terms of economic security. Since this is a relative measure, it should not be taken as implying that in absolute terms these countries have reached some sort of ideal. But they are setting standards for others to emulate or surpass.

Among the most important policy messages to emerge is that income security is a major determinant of other forms of labour-related security. A key factor is the extent of income inequality, which is inversely related to overall economic security. The correlation coefficient between the Gini measure of inequality and the ESI is -0.474, and between the ESI and the share of the upper decile of the income distribution it is -0.493. The message is that highly unequal societies are unlikely to achieve much by way of economic security or decent work.

At the level of the firm, it is possible to compile a reasonable index of economic security or a decent workplace index. The most important findings here are that this is positively related to economic performance of companies and that decent workplace practices are not a hindrance to company success. At the level of the individual worker, we offer merely the first approximation of what would seem to constitute a decent work status index. This suggests that most people are denied a reasonably good status, and that women are, as expected, more disadvantaged in this respect.

Economic security is positively related to national happiness. Recently, the World Economic Forum organized a survey in various parts of the world that enabled the Forum secretariat to conclude that on balance more people expect that the coming generation will live in a less safe world, that international security is "poor" and that people are gloomy about it.[29] The survey also found extensive anxieties about security in old age. These results, although very heuristic, add weight to the concerns about the central role of economic security. Those countries where a high level of economic security is attained deserve to be regarded as pointing the way to a better world.

Economic security fosters social happiness, and happier people are more likely to make responsible citizens, with healthier lifestyles. That in itself is reason enough for governments and the international organizations to give a much higher priority to the promotion of economic security than has been apparent in the recent past.

---

[29]"Global survey finds ordinary people feel 'unsafe, powerless and gloomy' about the future security and prosperity of the world" (Geneva, World Economic Forum, Jan. 2004). <http://www.weforum.org/ securitysurvey>.

Policies for Economic Justice

"It is more important to adopt the right way, to pursue the right means, than even to have the right objectives, important as that is".

— Jawaharlal Nehru

Part III

Chapter 12

Attitudes to economic justice and security

12.1 Introduction

It is evident that globalization and related developments have created more economic insecurity, and that some countries have nevertheless achieved much greater security than others. But has the growth of insecurity and the changing perspectives guiding social and economic policy altered what people think their governments should do? Can we discern people's normative perspectives, in relation to principles of security and social justice? What do they want for their fellow citizens? And do their governments pursue policies consistent with these values and with what they want?

Too often policymakers *presume* to know what people want and need – the classic paternalistic twitch. Too often, subtle and not-so-subtle tactics are adopted to shape opinions. But it is surely instructive to take into account the views of "ordinary people", as well as to consider the impact of economic insecurity on those views. That is the task of this chapter.

12.2 What we (they) want: Attitudes to social justice

Globally, within numerous countries, over the past two decades inequality has increased. There should be no doubt about that. It has done so in many guises, as noted in Chapter 3. Most people have an opinion on inequality, one way or another. It is both a political-philosophical issue and an instrumental-economic issue. It is about morality and fairness, and it is about efficiency.

As far as efficiency is concerned, one could imagine that if all incomes were equal, or if overall differentials were very small, economies would stagnate and motivation would be removed. But one could equally imagine that, with extreme inequality, workers would be unmotivated and unable to labour, while the incentive to invest and save among the rich would be neutralized.

What do people think? Most have an idea about what is fair, and adhere to some principle of *equity*. They also have some idea of what should be equalized in society, and thus adhere to some principle of *equality*. And they have some idea of what they and their fellow citizens need to survive and flourish in decency. Attitudes to social justice thus break down into those relating to *equity*, those relating to *equality* and those relating to *need*.[1] Inequity arises from a sense that people are not receiving appropriate rewards, and is relative to what if any discriminatory practices are legitimate. Attitudes to equality relate to perceptions of the appropriateness of distributions of rewards. Attitudes to need relate to what people need to avoid poverty or to lack of capacity to exist as a human being.

---

[1] R. Stock: *Socio-Economic Security, Justice and the Psychology of Social Relationships*, Socio-Economic Security Paper No. 8 (Geneva, ILO, 2002).

Table 12.1 Agreement with an upper limit on income, by country and gender

	Yes (%)	No (%)	Don't know (%)	Male: Yes (%)	Female: Yes (%)
Hungary	46.8	50.9	2.3	42.3	51.1
Russia Federation	32.1	45.9	22.0	30.3	33.6
Ukraine	30.1	47.5	22.4	28.7	31.0
Ethiopia (urban)	18.6	61.3	20.1	17.8	20.4
Ghana	25.1	38.6	36.2	27.7	23.1
South Africa (mainly urban)	43.7	38.4	17.9	45.8	42.2
Tanzania	20.3	52.2	27.6	21.4	19.4
Bangladesh	23.3	74.9	1.8	24.7	19.7
China	39.5	38.7	21.9	38.4	40.7
Gujarat, India (mainly women)	51.9	44.0	4.0	53.3	51.7
Indonesia	41.3	43.1	15.6	38.6	43.9
Argentina* (urban)	34.8	n.a.	n.a.	33.7	35.9
Brazil* (urban)	36.6	n.a.	n.a.	39.3	34.2
Chile* (urban)	35.0	n.a.	n.a.	33.9	36.1

n.a. = not available

Note:*Latin American survey results adjusted by adding those selecting "upper and lower limits", as well as just an upper limit.

Source: SES PSS.

The percentages for the South American countries are misleadingly low, since respondents in these countries were asked to choose between different redistributive options, and as will be evident later, many chose an even more egalitarian option, particularly in Brazil. There should be no presumption that there is weak support for redistribution in these countries.

The initial picture of opinions in eastern Europe also deserves comment. The level of agreement in Hungary suggests there has been a decline in redistributive values in the 1990s, since the earlier ISJP survey found that 58% of Hungarians favoured an upper limit on incomes. Opinion in the Russian Federation showed little change (32% against 34% previously).

A feature in most countries is that many people find it hard to form a clear opinion on this redistributive view, as reflected in the proportion of "don't knows" in many countries. This probably reflects the fact that in no country is there an official upper limit (and very few have effective upper limits through taxation now). As more detailed analyses of the responses show, it also reflects a link with education – those with relatively little formal education are more likely to be undecided, although most do have a view.

What do people think about the desirable dispersion of incomes? A substantial minority in the seven countries where this question was asked thought that there should be a limit on the spread of incomes (Table 12.2). The figures are impressive, since in most cases the question, like that of the ISJP, used a personal/individual frame of reference by talking about what someone can earn.

Table 12.2 Agreement with upper and lower limits, by country and gender

	Yes (%)	No (%)	Don't know (%)	Male: Yes (%)	Female: Yes (%)
Russian Federation	34.5	34.0	31.4	31.7	36.9
Ethiopia	24.9	55.3	19.8	24.3	26.0
Gujarat, India	51.1	0.5	48.5	52.8	50.7
Indonesia**	59.6	32.8	7.7	58.8	60.3
Argentina*	26.6	n.a.	n.a.	25.1	28.0
Brazil*	24.9	n.a.	n.a.	27.6	22.7
Chile*	25.7	n.a.	n.a.	25.8	25.6

n.a. = not available

Note: * As respondents were asked to select a preferred option, the residuals cannot be interpreted as " no" or " don't know".

** In Indonesia, respondents were asked whether there should be restrictions on the spread of incomes.

Source: SES PSS.

Thus the psychological response to being asked about placing a limit on a person's income was probably different in Indonesia, where respondents were asked whether they agreed or disagreed with the principle:

"There should be restrictions to limit the difference in income between the richest and poorest."

In further evidence that this way of putting the issue commands more support for redistribution, 55% of those Indonesians who agreed that there should be an upper income limit also agreed there should be a restriction on the range of incomes. But 47% of those who disagreed with an upper limit also supported a restriction of income differentials.

The Indonesian findings correspond with several ISSP surveys in the Philippines. Those found that a large proportion of the population believes differences in incomes there are too large, and that conflicts between rich and poor are more significant than conflicts between managers and workers, the unemployed and employed or any other social divide.[11]

In general, the PSS results suggest that gender does not play a strong role in differentiating opinions on the desirability of a narrowing of the dispersion in incomes, with only Hungary and the Russian Federation demonstrating significant differences between men and women. But when people were asked specifically whether differences should be restricted (as in Ethiopia and Indonesia) or whether

there should be an upper and a lower limit, the picture changed. This lends rather more support to a finding from other research, which suggests that in general women are more egalitarian than men.[12]

In sum, while some groups may be more supportive than others, the overall proportions supporting a reduction in inequality range between 25% and almost 60%. There seems to be a strong groundswell of support for limiting inequality, what has been called "near-equality".[13] Thus, despite two decades of globalization and efforts to legitimize inequality, a large number of people in a wide range of types of society favour a reduction in inequality.

(i) Where are the egalitarians?

When we turn to pure income equality (*everyone should have a similar income*), few countries demonstrate much support. Proportions supporting this old-style egalitarian principle range from 3% in Hungary to

[11] Social Weather Stations Inc.: *ISSP 1999 Module on Social Inequality III in the Philippines: Data and Documentation* (CD-ROM) (Manila, Social Weather Stations Inc., 2000); L.L. Guerrero: *Social Inequality in the Philippines*: The 1992 ISSP Survey, SWS Occasional Paper (Manila, Social Weather Stations, Inc., 1993).

[12] B. Major: "From social inequality to personal entitlement: The role of social comparisons, legitimacy appraisals and group membership", *Advances in Experimental Social Psychology* (San Diego), Vol. 26, 1994, pp. 293–355.

[13] J. Kelley and M. Evans: "The legitimation of inequality: Occupational earnings in nine nations", *American Journal of Sociology*, Vol. 99, No. 1, July 1991, pp. 75–125.

43% in Brazil. This last figure may appear puzzling. Was this indeed a remarkable result or does it reflect a survey problem? It did not appear to be the latter, but it does raise questions that merit further exploration.

In other countries, proportions of around 20% (South Africa, Tanzania, Argentina and Chile) indicate that quite a large number of people are highly egalitarian. Support was least in the post-communist countries, where opinion against equality was overwhelming (78–93%). In the African countries by contrast, there were large proportions of "don't know". It may well be that the ex-communist countries associate this type of equality with the loss of freedom they had experienced. In other countries, equality may be a less familiar possibility. Support for full equality may not be in the ascendant in the current ideological climate, but nor has it been forgotten.

Statistically significant differences in support for equality between men and women were found in all three Latin American countries, in the expected direction. More women than men were egalitarian.

(ii) Where are the inegalitarians?

In four countries (the Russia Federation and the three South American countries) respondents were asked whether they favoured no limits on incomes at all. Only a small minority did so, but in Chile a little over 20% were openly inegalitarian. In all four countries,

more men than women said they thought there should be no upper or lower limit, and it also seemed that older people were more likely to think that way.

However, the key point is that everywhere only a small minority is in favour of no limits on incomes. The great majority are simply not that way inclined.

(iii) Inequality with social protection

Several studies have shown that inequality can be acceptable if it is coupled with a strong needs-based distribution system or the provision of a minimum income.[14] It has also been shown that support for a minimum income can be combined with tolerance of a considerable spread in incomes.[15]

In seven countries, rather than asking about inequality *per se* (in the form of no limits on income) the PSS asked about support for no limits on income if there were policies to help the poor. The question posed was whether or not they would support the following:

"There should be no limit on a person's income but there should be policies to improve the situation of the least well-off."

Although the question makes no mention of a minimum income *per se*, the answers could be expected to give an impression of people's attitudes to poverty alleviation. In a sense, this is a test of a person's disposition to *charity* rather than to social consciousness and an interdependence of social groups associated

Table 12.3 Agreement with no limit on income if policies to support least well-off, by country and gender

	Yes (%)	No (%)	Don't know (%)	Male: Yes (%)	Female: Yes (%)
Hungary	69.5	27.7	2.8	67.1	71.9
Ukraine	54.9	15.6	29.5	54.3	55.3
Ethiopia	n. a.	n. a.	n. a.	n. a.	n. a.
Ghana	46.7	17.6	35.7	48.7	45.2
South Africa	63.5	22.2	14.3	63.8	63.3
Tanzania	73.6	11.3	15.2	73.6	73.5
Bangladesh	92.4	6.8	0.8	92.3	92.6
China	66.8	14.4	18.8	68.2	65.2

n.a. = not available   Source: SES PSS.

[14]Stock, 2002, op. cit.
[15]Kelley and Evans, 1991, op. cit.
[16]de Swaan, 1988, op. cit.

with universal values. The one view need not be in contradiction with the other, but a positive view on charity has tended to precede the development of a positive disposition towards redistribution.[16]

The principle that inequality is acceptable where there is government support for the least well-off could be taken as an approximation to Rawls's Difference Principle, that if there is any increase in inequality it must benefit the least well-off to be acceptable.[17] While in the mainstream of political thinking in industrialized market countries, it finds support in developing and "transition" countries as well. In six of the seven countries in which this question was asked there is an outright majority, and in the seventh, Ghana, support runs at 47%, substantial in any electoral calculation.

Conveniently, it seems there is acceptance of inequality, but not, as is often argued, as long as there is genuine equality of opportunity (which neo-liberals conveniently presume is the case), but only when there are policies to alleviate poverty. Far from accepting an absence of social protection, people in these countries firmly believe there is a role for policy to help those at the bottom of the ladder.

12.4 Support for a basic income

"Yet the true friend of the people should see that they be not too poor, for extreme poverty lowers the character of the democracy. Measures therefore should be taken which will give them lasting prosperity; and as this is equally the interest of all classes, the proceeds of the public revenues should be accumulated and distributed among its poor, if possible in such quantities as may enable them to purchase a little farm, or, at any rate, make a beginning in trade or husbandry."

— Aristotle, *Politics*, Book 5, Chapter 6

The attitudes revealed with respect to inequality may be linked to the belief that being poor is a punishing experience, which is generally unacceptable. It seems to be a widely held view that people should not be impoverished. In a range of laboratory-type experiments, one research project conducted in various places across Canada, the United States and Poland found that most people opted for the view that a minimum "floor" amount of income should be provided to everybody in society, as a *right*. It also found that support for this grew if people de-

liberated about it and about alternative principles of justice.[18] Another empirical study asked people how much someone should be paid in various occupations. It found that there was a consensus that no occupation should receive less than a reasonable minimum.[19]

The first large-scale surveys to examine this question, within the ISJP, demonstrated that there was near-universal consensus within and across countries that there should be some kind of minimum, although there was variation in what that minimum should be. In all countries covered by the ISJP surveys similar support for a minimum income has been found. Even in the United States, often considered the least egalitarian of cultures, there is substantial support for income to cover basic needs.[20]

The PSS asked whether there should be a lower limit for people's income, sufficient to cover their basic needs. In order to compare the results of the Latin American countries and the others, Table 12.4 shows the share of adults in the Latin American countries supporting a minimum income by including those who support both an upper and a lower limit. Even so, levels of support in Latin America are lower than elsewhere, which probably reflects both the single best-choice format and, particularly in the case of Brazil, extensive support for the egalitarian option. In the three South American countries, when those who said there should be a lower and an upper limit and those who opted for "equal incomes" are added, over 98% supported a minimum income in Argentina, 88% did so in Brazil, and 93% did so in Chile, bringing their results very much in line with the other countries covered by the PSS.

In general, putting aside the minority who were uncertain ("don't knows"), the results show that in all countries covered, perhaps with the exceptions of Tanzania and Ghana, support for a minimum income floor was strong.

---

[17]Rawls, 1973, op. cit.

[18]N. Frohlich and J. Oppenheimer: *Choosing Justice: An Experimental Approach to Ethical Theory* (Berkeley, CA, University of California Press, 1992). For a discussion of the implications, see Standing, 2002, op. cit., Chapter 11.

[19]Kelley and Evans, 1991, op. cit.

[20]J. R. Kluegel and E.R. Smith: *Beliefs About Inequality: Americans' Views of What is and What Ought to Be* (New York, Aldine de Gruyter, 1986).

Table 12.4 Support for lower limit (minimum income), by country and gender

	Yes (%)	No (%)	Don't know (%)	Male: (%) Yes	Female: (%) Yes
Hungary	84.0	15.3	0.7	83.5	84.6
Russian Federation	83.3	6.2	10.5	82.7	83.8
Ukraine	61.1	20.5	18.5	62.9	59.7
Ethiopia	67.3	20.4	12.2	68.3	65.1
Ghana	41.5	23.1	35.3	42.9	40.5
South Africa	57.0	27.5	15.5	57.4	56.7
Tanzania	41.3	33.8	25.0	41.9	40.7
Bangladesh	63.7	35.1	1.2	63.5	64.1
China	82.1	5.2	12.7	82.5	81.7
Gujarat, India	98.1	1.5	0.5	98.1	98.0
Indonesia	67.3	25.5	7.2	63.6	70.9
Argentina*	51.4	n.a.	n.a.	53.3	49.7
Brazil*	35.0	n.a.	n.a.	38.6	31.9
Chile*	49.8	n.a.	n.a.	53.0	46.7

n.a. = not available.

Note: *Latin American survey results adjusted by adding those selecting "upper and lower limits", as well as just a lower limit. As respondents were asked to select a preferred option, the residuals cannot be interpreted as "no" or "don't know".

Source: SES PSS.

In China and in "transition" countries, there was strong support for the floor of basic income security. The results in eastern Europe indicate that the essence of solidarity is still alive in that part of the world. In Ukraine, a majority said that the government should provide a minimum income, with women and men roughly equally inclined to support this, and younger age groups more inclined to do so than older.[21]

In the Russian Federation, a high proportion supported a minimum income, with the more educated possibly most inclined to agree. In Hungary, support was also very high, bearing out the results of the ISJP, which found that commitment to social solidarity principles was higher in Hungary than in other countries covered in that project.

The ISJP surveys also took place in Hungary and the Russian Federation, which allows direct comparison. Attitudes in favour of a guaranteed minimum standard of living received levels of support similar to those found in the PSS of between 50% and 80%, with the United States an outlier at 27%. Over 81% supported a guaranteed income in Hungary and 64% in the Russian Federation. They also asked about a needs-based minimum but this was linked to a rider about redistribution, which, with the exception of the two parts of Germany, brought support down considerably. In the Russian Federation, 47% supported it and in Hungary 65%.

Pessimistic egalitarianism?

In Hungary, according to responses given in the PSS, people feel that inequality is too great, yet they think it is increasing. They may be pessimistic about reducing that by a great deal.

However, a majority of respondents thought there should be a minimum income for everybody.

---

[21] The extent of support was actually less than observed in the first round of the Ukrainian PSS. But not too much should be made of this since the sampling was different, with the first round being restricted to employees. On the first round, see D. Levison, J. Ritter, R. Stock and R. Anker: "Distribution of income and job opportunities: Normative judgments from four continents", *International Labour Review*, Vol. 141, No. 4, 2002, pp. 385–411.

Comparing these results with those for *"no limits but policies to support the least well off"* for the seven countries where both questions were asked, support for a minimum income seems less than that for the "justified-inequality" principle in Bangladesh, Tanzania, Ghana and South Africa. In Hungary, Ukraine and China, it was higher.

Even so, in all countries support for a minimum income to meet basic needs is widespread. There is an outright majority in all but two of the countries. The percentages agreeing with a minimum income are also higher than the equivalent normative question asked in the ISJP, where comparison was allowed.

Another point to bear in mind is that these widely held views in favour of providing basic security for everyone may not mesh with attitudes on redistribution. People can have ideas belonging to more than one belief system, and they can endorse contradic-

tory ideas or even parts of ideas.[22] Indeed, a study of affluent groups in the United States, Japan and Sweden found there was strong sympathy with the plight of the less well-off, expressed in a desire to see their absolute position improve, but this was coupled with a desire to maintain the gap between them and other social groups.[23]

In the three Latin American countries, where support for a minimum actually seems to be very strong, a separate question was also asked: *"Should the government provide the poor with a minimum income?"* This too attracted overwhelming support (79% in Argentina, 86% in Brazil, 85% in Chile). But a majority also said that the poor should have to fulfil certain conditions. The most popular conditions were that either the adult should work or the children should go to school (Table 12.5). However, only a minority of those supporting the introduction of a minimum income want a work condition.

Table 12.5 Whether minimum income should require conditions and type of condition, Argentina, Brazil and Chile (percentage responding "Yes")

Alternative source of financial support	Argentina	Brazil	Chile
Minimum income, % believing condition should be applied	59.1	67.6	57.4
Conditions, if required:			
Adults should work	32.3	16.2	45.0
Parents should send their children to school	20.6	39.4	49.8
Mother should stay home to look after children	5.9	10.2	25.3
Community work	14.6	10.1	26.6
Take job offered by government	23.3	20.3	49.0
Other	3.3	3.7	3.7

Note: In Argentina and Brazil, only one condition could be chosen, whereas in Chile several conditions could be selected.

Source: Latin American PSS.

[22] See, e.g., Hochschild, 1981, op. cit.; Stock, 2002; P. Converse: "The structure of belief systems in mass public", in D. Apter, (ed.): *Ideology and Discontent* (New York, Free Press, 1964).

[23] S. Verba, with S. Kelma, G.R. Orren, I. Miyake, J. Matanuki, I. Kabashima and D.G. Ferree: *Elites and the Idea of Inequality: A Comparison of Japan, Sweden and the United States* (Cambridge, MA, Harvard University Press, 1987), p. 263.

While the eastern European data indicate more support for a minimum income than has been found before in those countries, the results for Africa and Asia are the first of their kind. In effect, there is a global groundswell of support for a minimum income, a universal recognition of the principle of need, even though the degree of support varies between countries.

For policy-makers seeking to build social cohesion, these results are encouraging, since support for the principle of need is known to be associated with nurturant attitudes and behaviour.[24] The PSS findings are also clear in terms of policy implications. This is important because it appears that abstract and concrete examples of values can elicit quite different responses.[25]

12.5 Who most supports basic security and redistribution... and who does not?

Overall, the PSS data — and the ISJP data for industrialized affluent countries — show widespread support for the principle that everybody in society should be provided with a minimum income sufficient to cover their basic needs. Are certain groups more or less likely to support the minimum income principle?

Various groups in society have been shown to have different attitudes to distributional issues. Researchers working within the tradition of the theory of social representation argue that social position affects personal perspective. People see the world from different vantage points, and this mediates responses.[26] A similar claim is that views on distributive issues are affected by the person's own view of his or her class position rather than the actual technical classification.[27]

Running through these arguments is the idea that people support what benefits them, and that as a result, self-interest is the primary motive in distributional issues. This must be of concern to those whose aim is to ameliorate some of the increasing insecurity and inequality of the last few years: if people only support distributions that benefit themselves, how is the social solidarity to be built that will allow redistribution of resources, and of security itself? Perhaps even more importantly, how are policy-makers to address problems that require some restraint on the part of individuals for the collective good (such as increased taxation to improve the population's health) or some sacrifice in the short term for longer-term goals (such as reduced car use)?

Are some groups more likely to support the minimum income principle than others? As far as *gender* differences are concerned, research elsewhere has found women to be more needs-oriented than men in their preferred income principles, although cross-cultural variations exist.[28] In the PSS, in Argentina and Brazil women were slightly more supportive of the minimum income principle, although the level of support was high among both men and women, once support for other redistributive options are taken into account. In other countries, there was no significant difference, particularly if the "don't knows" are excluded. Only in Hungary, the Russian Federation and Bangladesh do the differences amount to more than five percentage points.

Among age groups too, there is not much difference in strength of support.[29] As for differences among those with different levels of *schooling*, the more educated were slightly more likely to support the minimum income principle in Argentina, Brazil, Chile, Ethiopia, South Africa, Bangladesh and Ukraine, but not in Hungary. One must be cautious about interpreting these patterns, since, as the results for Ethiopia suggest, much of the difference between those with different levels of schooling stems from a tendency for the least educated to have no clear opinion.

---

[24] On attitudes, see Stock, 2002, op. cit.; on behaviour, see M. Deutsch: *Distributive Justice* (Yale, Yale University Press, 1985).

[25] J. Huber and W. Form: *Income and Ideology: An Analysis of the American Political Formula* (New York, Free Press, 1973).

[26] J.C. Abric and J.P. Kahan: "The effects of representations and behaviour in experimental games", *European Journal of Social Psychology*, Vol. 2, 1972, pp. 129–144.

[27] A. Swift, G. Marshall, C. Burgoyne and D. Routh: "Distributive justice: Does it matter what the people think?", in Kluegel, Mason and Wegener, 1995, op. cit., pp. 15–47.

[28] V. Murphy-Berman, J. Berman, P. Singh, A. Pachauri and P. Kumar: "Factors affecting allocation to needy and meritorious recipients", *Journal of Personality and Social Psychology*, Vol. 46, No. 6, pp. 1267–1272; Swift et al., 1995, op. cit.

[29] Levison et al., 2002, op. cit., p. 398, on South Africa, Bangladesh, Hungary and the first round in Ukraine.

There is considerable variation in the influence of some other structural factors, most notably type of area of residence. Even though it is known that income differentiation is usually less there than in urban areas, people who live in rural communities are more likely to support redistributive principles. For instance, in Indonesia rural dwellers were more likely to endorse an upper limit than urban residents (73%, compared with 60%).

It might be of interest to compare the patterns in two African countries, Ghana and South Africa (Table 12.6). In Ghana, compared with their urban counterparts, those living in rural areas are more inclined to support having an upper limit but are less likely to support either a minimum income or *no limits with help to the poor,* and in both Ghana and South Africa rural dwellers are more inclined to support the egalitarian option of similar incomes for all. This *pattern* of support suggests that the rural population is more egalitarian than urban dwellers.

In Ghana, those with least schooling, usually a proxy for class, are most likely to be egalitarian, while the more educated are most likely to favour the charity option of "no limits but policies to help the poor". Indeed, in both Ghana and South Africa, support for "no limits but policies to help the poor" is stronger among the more educated. Those with more schooling can expect to reach higher income levels than those with fewer qualifications.

What is most striking about the pattern in South Africa, not shown in the table, is the different attitudes in the various racial groups, obviously a legacy of apartheid and of the persistent race-based inequalities in the country. Blacks were far more likely to favour equality and an upper limit on incomes, and whites were strongly against an upper limit. What is rather encouraging is that a majority of both main racial groups favour a minimum floor income, corresponding to the widespread popularity of the proposed basic income grant in the country, which is considered in the final chapter.

Information on income level is only available for some countries, but where it is, as in Ghana, support for a lower limit guarantee actually increases with income level. Support for the charity principle of "no limits but policies to help the poor" also increases, and the biggest step-change is between the poorest and the next income band. A similar pattern is evident in South Africa, which may indicate the role mentioned above, of a needs-based minimum in legitimizing inequality. In both countries, support for equality was significantly higher among lower-income groups. This could be taken as a "self-interested" choice, benefiting those who have most to gain, but in the context of the other results brute self-interest is by no means the only process going on.

	Ghana			
Principle	Upper limit (%)	Lower limit (%)	No limits but policies to help the poor (%)	Similar income for all (%)
Education level				
No schooling	38.7	59.1	63.0	22.4
Primary	32.7	60.3	68.9	21.6
Secondary	36.0	60.2	68.7	17.5
Tertiary	40.4	63.0	71.5	16.1
Sex				
Male	38.7	60.1	68.4	19.0
Female	34.3	60.2	67.2	19.1
Region				
Urban	30.8	64.3	73.9	11.8
Rural	40.9	56.7	62.6	25.0
Income level (cedis, monthly)				
0–50 000	34.8	51.1	53.0	24.2
51 000–100 000	34.3	54.5	63.2	17.7
101 000–200 000	36.3	63.4	70.5	18.6
201 000–400 000	37.6	55.2	71.4	24.8
401 000+	41.0	69.4	69.7	13.1
Income for health care				
More than sufficient	32.0	60.4	65.3	16.3
About adequate	36.2	61.7	69.4	17.0
Insufficient	36.6	59.2	66.6	20.6
Income for food				
More than sufficient	42.6	61.1	62.3	15.4
About adequate	34.8	60.6	69.2	18.1
Insufficient	36.5	59.6	67.0	20.8
Total	**36.3**	**60.2**	**67.7**	**19.0**

Source: GPSS1. N = 2081.

South Africa

Principle	Upper limit (%)	Lower limit (%)	No limits but policies to help the poor (%)	Similar income for all (%)
Education level				
Primary	44.5	55.5	60.5	30.2
Secondary	42.2	60.1	69.8	26.4
Tertiary	42.5	65.0	77.5	17.5
Sex				
Male	45.8	57.4	63.8	27.6
Female	42.2	56.7	63.3	29.7
Region				
Urban	52.1	53.4	58.3	31.1
Rural	45.9	50.5	58.7	46.7
Income level (rands, monthly)				
1–200	44.3	47.6	50.4	33.6
201–600	50.9	56.9	57.2	36.5
601–1 600	44.7	58.8	70.4	28.4
1 600+	44.2	64.3	72.1	17.2
Income adequacy for health care				
More than sufficient	41.8	50.3	70.3	23.3
About adequate	46.0	60.7	63.8	32.8
Insufficient	41.8	55.4	60.4	26.3
Income adequacy for food				
More than sufficient	40.3	53.1	69.4	23.7
About adequate	45.8	61.1	63.5	31.2
Insufficient	42.7	53.5	60.1	28.4
Total	**43.7**	**57.0**	**63.5**	**28.8**

Source: SAPSS.

12.6 Economic insecurity and attitudes to social justice

A potentially important issue is the link between personal economic insecurity and the personal attitude to equity and to inequality. Although economic insecurity can be measured in several ways in the PSS, just three measures were taken: (i) whether or not family income is adequate for health care needs (a measure of income security), (ii) the degree of confidence that the person feels in retaining his or her current main source of income over the next year (a measure of employment security), and (iii) whether or not the person, if working, is satisfied with the income received from income-earning activity (a measure of job security).

The hypotheses we propose to test are that people who are insecure are more likely to favour a *needs-based* justice principle than those feeling secure, and that the insecure are more likely to favour a *progressive redistribution* (cutting inequality) principle. An alternative view would be that support for these principles derives not from envy or fear but from a sense of civility and an appreciation that society must foster a sense of social solidarity.

The results are presented in Table 12.7. Bearing in mind the differences in samples, these suggest cultural and national differences that need further study. Those feeling economically secure in Ghana and in South Africa, for example, were no less likely to sup-

313

port principles of *equality* than others. But, although not shown here, support for upper limits was greater for those in food insecurity in South Africa, Hungary and Ukraine, defined in terms of incomes perceived as inadequate for food needs. And in Latin America, people in food insecurity were more likely to favour a minimum income for the poor.

The relationship between perceived employment insecurity and income distribution principles is not very clear, although for most countries the more insecure are more likely to support redistribution. The countries where this is not shown are the Russian Federation and Tanzania, and the Indian State of Gujarat. The findings in Argentina, Brazil and Chile can be interpreted through looking at support for the three redistributive principles combined. Elsewhere the picture is clearer. For instance, in Hungary and Ukraine the employment-insecure are more likely to favour an upper limit on income. In Ghana, the stronger support for "similar income" levels implies greater support for redistribution; in Ethiopia and

South Africa, there is stronger support for both upper limits and narrower differentials among the employment insecure. In China and in Indonesia, they are more likely to support an upper limit.

People's satisfaction with their income seemed more closely related to support for distributive principles. For instance, in both the Russian Federation and Hungary, those dissatisfied with their earnings were more likely to favour an upper limit on incomes than those who were satisfied, but in Ukraine it was the other way round. The only principle where all the countries having significant differences were in the same direction is the *charity principle* – the more satisfied with their own income were more likely to support the view that while there should be no limits there should be policies to help the poor.

This suggests that it does indeed function as a justification for inequality since those satisfied with the *status quo* (who will mainly be those who benefit from it) are more likely to endorse it.

Table 12.7 Percentage believing in income security principles, by economic security status and country

| | Income for health care | | Security in main work | | Satisfied with income | |
	Adequate	Inadequate	Secure	Insecure	Satisfied	Dissatisfied
Hungary						
Minimum Income/Lower Limit	n. a.	n. a.	84.8	74.1	84.8	87.1
Upper Limit	n. a.	n. a.	38.4	51.2	34.6	47.2
No limits, but help the poor	n. a.	n. a.	70.8	65.9	75.0	70.4
Russian Federation						
Minimum Income/Lower Limit	85.9	90.8	89.1	90.1	89.2	91.2
Upper Limit	30.1	41.3	38.1	32.9	28.6	38.2
Limit Differential	32.8	45.8	39.1	37.9	30.5	42.9
Similar Income	6.8	13.3	7.7	7.9	5.8	10.0
No limits	29.1	22.1	23.9	25.5	29.6	25.1
Ukraine						
Minimum Income/Lower Limit	63.2	60.6	68.2	65.0	61.6	60.1
Upper Limit	28.8	30.3	25.1	30.5	29.0	24.0
Similar Income	6.0	6.7	3.4	5.6	5.4	5.2
No limits, but help the poor	56.0	54.7	51.1	51.8	51.5	46.9
Ethiopia						
Minimum Income/Lower Limit	62.0	77.6	78.8	67.9	66.4	70.3
Upper Limit	18.7	22.3	18.7	22.6	21.2	20.6
Limit Differential	24.3	30.0	24.3	28.8	35.2	25.5
Ghana						
Minimum Income/Lower Limit	61.6	59.2	60.5	57.7	61.7	52.0
Upper Limit	36.1	36.6	35.9	35.1	37.3	34.4
Similar Income	16.9	20.6	15.8	26.0	16.6	22.5

	Income for health care		Security in main work		Satisfied with income	
	Adequate	Inadequate	Secure	Insecure	Satisfied	Dissatisfied
No limits, but help the poor	69.2	66.6	66.8	72.9	67.8	63.3
South Africa						
Minimum Income/Lower Limit	58.0	55.4	64.3	74.2	64.6	59.6
Upper Limit	44.9	41.8	45.5	48.5	47.7	42.6
Similar Income	30.4	26.3	23.1	24.2	24.9	27.7
No limits, but help the poor	65.5	60.4	72.3	74.2	70.5	69.7
Tanzania						
Minimum Income/Lower Limit	42.4	45.1	40.9	40.0	32.8	43.7
Upper Limit	18.5	24.7	20.0	19.7	20.5	19.7
Similar Income	15.8	25.1	18.1	19.6	21.3	17.7
No limits, but help the poor	81.3	61.5	77.8	65.9	77.4	71.2
Bangladesh						
Minimum Income/Lower Limit	63.9	63.3	n.a.	n.a.	68.3	60.3
Upper Limit	21.9	27.0	n.a.	n.a.	24.3	22.5
Similar Income	7.3	13.1	n.a.	n.a.	9.5	8.9
No limits, but help the poor	92.4	92.5	n.a.	n.a.	92.2	92.7
China						
Minimum Income/Lower Limit	83.5	87.8	87.3	92.1	86.2	88.6
Upper Limit	36.8	48.6	39.0	48.4	38.0	50.9
Similar Income	8.7	16.7	13.0	13.2	12.1	14.8
No limits, but help the poor	70.5	69.7	74.4	73.7	73.0	70.1
Gujarat, India						
Minimum income/Lower limit	99.0	97.9	98.2	98.2	98.2	97.2
Upper Limit	48.5	52.6	53.2	45.6	52.2	49.7
Limit Differential	48.5	51.5	52.4	43.9	51.4	48.3
Indonesia						
Minimum Income/Lower Limit	76.7	77.5	76.0	80.4	74.0	94.1
Upper Limit	51.4	54.7	51.1	60.2	50.5	75.0
Limit Differential	66.3	74.3	69.1	71.2	69.8	91.2
Argentina*						
Minimum Income/Lower Limit	53.3	49.0	55.2	48.7	53.4	52.5
Upper Limit	34.7	35.2	35.6	35.8	36.0	36.0
Limit Differential	26.8	26.4	28.4	25.9	27.9	27.9
Similar Income	20.3	26.4	17.6	24.3	19.5	22.3
No limits	18.5	15.8	19.9	17.1	18.9	17.1
Brazil*						
Minimum Income/Lower Limit	40.3	29.6	39.3	30.4	39.3	33.0
Upper Limit	39.6	33.3	41.3	32.6	41.7	36.2
Limit Differential	28.0	21.8	27.6	22.0	28.4	23.2
Similar Income	36.7	48.4	34.8	48.8	36.0	41.7
No limits	11.5	10.4	12.3	10.2	11.5	12.3
Chile*						
Minimum Income/Lower Limit	52.5	37.3	54.5	56.3	48.6	57.4
Upper Limit	37.1	27.3	33.6	48.7	30.3	37.6
Limit Differential	28.2	15.8	25.3	42.3	23.2	29.5
Similar Income	18.4	21.1	12.4	11.5	13.9	10.7
No limits	20.2	30.0	24.8	25.7	30.4	23.8

n.a. = not available.

* Latin American survey results adjusted by adding those selecting "Limit Differential" to Lower and Upper Limit.

Source: PSS.

What is really needed is analysis that can take account of several influences – gender, education, insecurity, income and area of residence. Accordingly, we may conclude this preliminary investigation by looking at the patterns of support for the various justice principles by means of logistic regressions, in which the dependent variable is the probability of agreeing with the specific principle.

Some results are worth highlighting. In Indonesia, for instance, it was found that when controlling for other influences, women were significantly more likely to favour a minimum income than men. Neither schooling nor age had any effect one way or the other. But those living in rural areas were significantly more likely to support the principle, as were those in income-earning work compared with others. What came out most strikingly was that, when controlling for all these other factors, those in income insecurity, as defined by having an income inadequate for their health care needs, were significantly more likely to support the principle.

In Brazil, to give another example, the same relationship held for women. The more educated were less likely to support a minimum income, as were those in jobs compared with those who were not. Again, the income-insecure were more likely to support it. We must recall that the questions were posed differently in the Latin American surveys. However, in this case the dependent variable is taken to be agreement to either a lower limit or a lower and an upper limit.

From most of the countries, the data suggest that personal insecurity strengthens a needs-based view of distribution, and strengthens a belief that the government should take steps to reduce earnings inequality. These findings should surely be an important consideration in policy design.

"Individualists" versus "fatalists"?

People look on life as a mix of luck, effort and talent. Some are inclined to think everything depends on "fate" or "God" or some other outside force; some believe that one's position is largely determined by one's skills and hard work; others think it is a mix of luck, talent and hard work.

Does this mental state make a difference to a person's attitude to social justice principles? The PSS asks whether people think their personal situation in life is determined mainly by their individual capacities, or by outside forces, or by both about equally. We might call the first group the "individualists" and the second "fatalists". In some countries, fatalism was much stronger than in others. But what effect, if any, does this have on attitudes to normative principles of justice?

In Tanzania, men and women who were individualists were twice as likely as fatalists to favour a minimum income for everybody. Those who thought both individual and social forces were equally important tended to be closer to the individualists.

In Bangladesh, men individualists were more likely to favour a minimum income than the fatalists, but no relationship existed for women. Unlike Tanzania, where there was not much difference, the individualists were much less likely to favour an upper income limit than the fatalists.

In South Africa and in Ukraine, men individualists were marginally less inclined to support a minimum income (although a majority did so in both cases), but women individualists were in both countries more likely to support a minimum income than the fatalists.

These findings are quite encouraging. Since modernization involves a move towards thinking that life is determined by one's own efforts and capacities, one might expect that selfishness would be stronger among individualists. The evidence suggests that this dismal expectation is not supported.

12.7 Support for the poor

We saw earlier that when posed as the charity principle, many people believe government policies should assist the poor. In some of the countries, the PSS also probed for the degree of support that people think should be given.

In the African countries, respondents were asked to what extent government should provide remedial assistance for poverty alleviation. In Ghana and in Ethiopia, there was overwhelming support for this. In Ghana, 34% favoured "complete assistance" and 60% "partial assistance". Although there were no differences between men and women in this respect, those living in rural areas, and the poor in general, were most likely to support full assistance.

There was also strong support for the charity principle in South Africa, but here a majority favoured "complete assistance", rather than partial. That the beliefs were widely shared points to a sense of social solidarity. Thus, even though more of the poor supported assistance, a majority of the more educated and the non-poor did so as well.

The altruism held up to a large extent even when South Africans were asked a rather strong leading question:

"Supporting the poor costs money. Do you think more support should be given to the poor even if it means that taxes must be increased for everybody earning money?"

The question is not ideal, in that people may have different views on what is implied by "more". They may also imagine that much is being done at the moment. And the idea of more taxes for everyone may have conjured up an image of themselves being hit, and if on the borderline, imagining that extra taxes would be a serious burden.[30]

In spite of the discouraging way the question was posed, 46% of all respondents still said that "complete assistance" should be given, i.e. that the poor should be raised out of poverty by government transfers or services, and a high proportion of the remainder were merely uncertain in the face of a prospective tax rise. Support for a tax-based income support policy also seemed widespread among all social groups. Thus, while more than 50% of those with only primary schooling favoured raising taxes, still about a third of those with university education did so.

In Ghana, respondents were asked a less strict version of the question used in South Africa, being asked simply whether or not taxes should be increased to enable the government to take care of the poor. There, 71% said they should be increased. There was no difference in attitude between men and women, but it seemed that among men the proportion saying taxes should go up rose with age.

These results lend further support to the view that people, even when living in economically poor environments, want more help to be given to the poor in their societies, and that this applies even if they anticipate being made slightly worse off in seeing that come about.

In China, where there was strong support for both a minimum income and for policies to assist the poor, additional questions probed for people's degree of satisfaction with existing policies, bearing in mind that this is a period of upheaval in the country's social protection policies. Evidently, there is fairly strong dissatisfaction, with more dissatisfaction with specific policies than with the general one on poverty alleviation (Table 12.8).

---

[30] In future PSS, we plan to modify the question to specify that tax increases would be limited to middle-income and rich citizens.

Table 12.8 China: Degree of satisfaction with government policy
(percentage distribution of views on area of policy)

	Satisfied (%)	Fairly good (%)	Dissatisfied (%)	Don't know (%)
Policy:				
Poverty alleviation	9.5	36.3	36.6	17.6
Urban minimum income guarantee	7.3	34.1	43.1	15.6
Social security	7.1	34.6	45.5	12.9
Public employment service	7.0	30.2	48.4	14.4
Living allowances for laid-offs	5.9	31.3	45.4	17.4

Source: CPSS. 2001.

12.8 Whither private philanthropy?

Poverty is widespread, inequality grows, the rich become richer, and the State is depicted as "withering" as a social force. Somehow, private philanthropy is expected to fill the vacuum. Many of the rich make ostentatious gestures, disbursing large amounts, even though they may be tiny fractions of a growing income, and largely written off as tax deductible.

Nowhere is *philanthropy* more needed as an immediate source of support than in Africa, where

government institutions for social support are fragile and mostly poorly funded. It seems that this is what its people expect, since there was a generally positive sentiment about the need for the rich to give charitable support to the poor. In Tanzania, most people thought the non-poor should give some of their income each year to support the poor — 71% of men and 74% of women. The less-educated were, perhaps, more likely to say this (Table 12.9).

Table 12.9 Tanzania: "Should the rich give income to the poor?",
by schooling of respondent (percentage responding "Yes")

No schooling	75.8
Primary	73.1
Secondary and above	67.0
Total	**72.6**

Source: TPSS1, n = 1503.

This sentiment should be considered in the light of the findings reported in Chapter 4 suggesting that inter-household income transfers are less widespread than is commonly believed. The image of richer households helping out those in economic difficulty may comfort those who wish to downplay the needed role of state institutions. Those informal mechanisms are apparently quite weak, but there is a popular belief that they are a proper part of society.

A problem may be that those who seem rich in a local community may relate their income and wealth to an outside reference community, and feel themselves anything but rich. This interpretation is consistent with a finding that comes across in all the PSS where the questions were asked, which is that far more people think their income is below average than above average.

12.9 Response to social disasters and personal crises

The attitudes of ordinary people on principles of economic justice summarize the moral bindings of society, setting the contours for a real if tenuous sense of community. In thinking about basic security, people were asked what they want the government to do in terms of giving assistance to those in specific situations of distress or insecurity.

The first of these was:

"Should the government provide complete, some or no assistance to help people affected by a natural disaster?"

In African countries, the answers suggest a very high degree of communal solidarity. For example, in Ghana over a third say they should be fully assisted and nearly two-thirds say there should be some assistance. In Ethiopia and in South Africa, over two-thirds of respondents thought the government ought to compensate people fully for the effect of natural disasters, and about a quarter in both thought it should provide partial compensation. In Ethiopia, given the poverty of that drought-affected country, this was perhaps unrealistic. However, the popular opinion testifies to a healthy belief that the State should play a major role in social protection.

In terms of *health care* problems, a similar set of views emerges. In Ghana, for instance, there was overwhelming support for government assistance, a finding common to all social groups. The same was true for support for those suffering from some sort of *disability*. In South Africa, a strong majority (58%) favoured complete assistance to those hit by ill health, and a third supported partial assistance. A similar pattern held in Ethiopia.

In some of the countries, questions were asked about whether the government should compensate people for other personal mishaps. In Ghana, for instance, nearly 90% said that it should provide at least partial compensation for unemployment. Four out five also thought victims of riots or sexual attack should be compensated.

In Indonesia, the PSS asked respondents whether or not they thought the government should provide financial assistance to those affected by various difficulties. The results are summarized in Table 12.10. In general, they reflect a set of sentiments in favour of social solidarity. However, attitudes to assistance for disability varied according to disability, with many more thinking the physically handicapped should be assisted with their daily needs than the mentally handicapped.

Table 12.10 Indonesia: Percentage believing government should assist in hardships, by sex of respondent (percentage wanting complete or some assistance)

Assistance	Male Complete	Some	Female Complete	Some	Total Complete	Some
Hardship:						
Natural disaster	57.3	38.1	56.9	38.9	57.1	38.5
Poverty	43.1	53.5	42.3	54.5	42.7	54.0
Ill health	35.2	59.3	35.6	57.6	35.4	58.4
Old age	47.1	46.8	46.3	48.3	46.7	47.6

Source: Indonesian PSS1, n = 3202.

The key point is that many people in all types of society believe that their government should provide assistance to those hit by diverse forms of personal disaster. This is a standard view.

12.10 Support for the elderly

Attitudes towards support for the elderly also reflect the extent of social solidarity. In most countries, it is a widely held view that the State should provide some income security for its elderly. But, as indicated in Chapter 3, old-age income security is strong in only a few countries of the world. What do people in countries where it is not strong think their governments should do?

In Indonesia, as shown above, there was strong support for assisting the elderly. In Ghana, there were similar levels of support for government assistance to the elderly, although the share favouring "complete assistance" was lower. A similar picture emerged in the urban areas of Ethiopia covered in the survey.

Indeed, in all countries there was strong support for state help for the elderly. This is clearly not seen as an area for private or family provision alone. The support for state assistance for the elderly is so universal that we need not look at variations of attitude between various social groups. Inter-generational solidarity to that extent remains a feature of social solidarity in developing countries and in transition economies.

12.11 Support for care work

Everywhere in the world, care work takes up more time than any other form of work, a disproportionately large part being done by women. Yet it is unremunerated and uncompensated by most governments, and largely ignored in policy-making. It is underpaid when done for income, partially because it is uncompensated in general. In some countries, this is changing, because it is being recognized that good care work is vital for the long-term economic growth and social welfare of society. The ILO has recently begun to address this issue more systematically.[31]

In the PSS, respondents were asked about their attitude to *income security for those providing care* to family and community members. First, they were asked for their view on whether or not the government should compensate fully, partially or not at all the time parents (or their surrogates) put into the *care of their children under the age of five* years.

The popular view in eastern Europe was very clear. For instance, in Ukraine, in the PSS of 2002 (and in other years as well), nearly two-thirds said parents should be fully compensated, and a third thought they should be partially compensated. There was no difference between women and men, or across age groups. With respect to *caring for elderly relatives*, nearly two in five said people should be fully compensated, just over half partially. In providing *care for disabled persons*, around two-thirds said carers should be fully compensated, just over a quarter partially. Overall 90% or more agreed with compensation for care of the elderly in Hungary, the Russian Federation and Ukraine.

They were also asked about those doing *voluntary work for their community*. Whereas Hungarians showed a similar level of support to those caring for the elderly, in Ukraine a little less than two-thirds agreed with compensation (a fifth thought they should be compensated fully, two-fifths partially). In the Russian Federation, nearly 60% agreed with such compensation.

In Africa, perhaps surprisingly – and encouragingly – popular sentiments are also rather clear. In Ghana, two-thirds of all respondents, men and women, were of the opinion that the government should provide some compensation to parents to cover care for their own children under the age of five. Over 70% said that the government should provide support for people having to work caring for elderly relatives, and an even higher percentage said it should do so for those caring for sick relatives. These recognize that in all three respects people, mostly women, have to devote a considerable amount of time to care activities that could otherwise be spent on income-earning activities.

---

[31] M. Daly (ed.): *Care Work: The Quest for Security* (Geneva, ILO, 2002); K. Dixon-Fyle: *Social Policy with Respect to Care: A Perspective for Sub-Saharan Africa*, SES Paper No. 27 (Geneva, ILO, 2002).

More than a third of respondents in Ghana felt that people doing *voluntary community work* should also be compensated. Such work can be important in any society where social and economic institutions are undeveloped or overstretched. It is as much work as any counted as such in labour force statistics, and is often more important for providing individuals, families and communities with security.

Once again, we find a strong universal view in favour of government compensation for those doing activities that are not often taken as deserving of such help by those preoccupied with market risks and market activities.

Ranking risks for state compensation

At this stage, one might ask: Do people have a ranking of lifetime risks for public compensation? The PSS ask people whether they think victims of various forms of risk should be compensated through government assistance, and whether they should be fully or partially compensated. Are some risks perceived as "deserving" of compensation more than others? Do people's attitudes correspond to the priorities implicit in the allocation of public assistance? The summary Table 12.11 suggests that most people, even in low-income countries, believe that government should assist people affected by income-threatening shocks or events. In South Africa, for example, a majority in each case said that the government should give full assistance, with many of the remainder opting for partial assistance. Over 90% believed government should provide assistance in the case of poverty, old age, natural disasters, disability, ill health and unemployment, in that order. Perhaps more interesting is that old age and natural disasters are the two areas where most people believed full assistance was desirable. This may well reflect a phenomenon often observed in European countries, that where a person is considered responsible for their plight they are seen as less deserving.[32] Usually, no responsibility is attributed to a person suffering from either disaster or old age.

What is also significant is that a majority believed government should compensate people for childcare, caring for elderly relatives and for voluntary community work, and nearly as many believed that compensation should be given for community care as for some of the standard contingency risks.

These figures are potentially significant for the system of social protection, for they imply that it would be hard to justify focusing resources on one or several of the range of social needs, or on policies that require labour or the promise to perform labour as a condition for government assistance or entitlement.

12.12 Economic insecurity and attitudes to support of hard-hit groups

We have seen that there is considerable popular support for policies to help those hit by shocks. The question considered in this section is whether personal insecurity affects people's attitudes to such policies.

This section gives a few examples. In Indonesia and in Ethiopia, as shown in Tables 12.12 and 12.13, the PSS suggest that people in insecure positions are more likely to support policies giving full support for social victims. One interpretation is that those who are insecure themselves are more likely to empathize with those affected by hardships. In the case of Ethiopia, however, only assistance for the poor was associated with insecurity in one's main work.

---

[32] K.Y. Tornblom, S.M. Muhlhausen and D.R. Jonsson: "The allocation of positive and negative outcomes: When is the equality principle fair for both?", in R. Vermunt and H. Steensma (eds.): *Social Justice in Human Relations* Vol. 1: *Societal and Psychological Origins of Justice* (New York: Plenum, 1991), pp. 59–100.

Table 12.11 Percentage believing in total and partial support for specific contingency risks

Support	Disasters		Disability		Ill health		Old age		Unemployment	
	Total	Partial	Total	Partial	Total	Partial	Total	Partial	Total	Partial
Hungary	n.a.	n.a.	73.8	25.8	80.3	19.6	78.3	21.7	74.8	15.0
Gujarat, India	98.3		99.0		98.9		94.0		n.a.	n.a.
Indonesia	56.6	38.9	47.1	48.3	34.9	58.8	46.4	47.8	74.1	
Ethiopia	63.8	26.6	73.4	17.1	63.0	26.9	67.8	22.4	n.a.	n.a.
Ghana	34.0	63.6	32.3	65.3	29.9	66.7	38.1	58.0	23.4	66.4
South Africa	68.0	23.9	66.7	27.3	58.3	33.7	73.5	22.0	63.7	28.0

Support:	Poverty		Childcare		Elderly care		Community care	
	Total	Partial	Yes	No	Yes	No	Yes	No
Hungary	n.a.	n.a.	98.2	1.8	97.8	2.2	98.2	1.8
Russian Federation[33]	n.a.	n.a.	93.3	2.3	89.5	3.2	58.7	15.9
Ukraine	n.a.	n.a.	62.7[f] / 32.6[p]	1.8	38.5[f] / 52.7[p]	4.1	21.5[f] / 42.5[p]	16.3
India, Gujarat		99.1	92.0	7.8	n.a.	n.a.	n.a.	n.a.
Indonesia	42.4	54.2	n.a.	n.a.	n.a.	n.a.	n.a.	n.a.
Ethiopia	41.3	46.1	n.a.	n.a.	n.a.	n.a.	n.a.	n.a.
Ghana	28.2	65.6	66.5	30.9	71.8	26.5	35.4	61.8
South Africa	62.4	30.4	54.8	37.2	62.1	30.3	64.7	27.4
Argentina	79.2		78.6	21.4	83.0	17.0	71.6	28.4
Brazil	86.1		80.7	19.3	88.1	11.9	81.4	18.6
Chile	84.5		72.8	27.2	77.0	23.0	57.0	43.0

n.a. = not available.
Note: [f] Full support - [p] Partial support
Source: PSS.

[33] In the case of the Russian Federation, respondents were asked whether they favoured full compensation, partial compensation, or no compensation for the work of caring for children, for elderly relatives and for voluntary community work. The figures given refer to "full compensation" and "not at all". The figures for partial compensation were 34.5%, 47.2% and 34.9% respectively.

Table 12.12 Indonesia: Support for complete assistance for social shocks, by personal insecurity (percentage "Yes")

	Security in main work		Satisfaction with income	
	Secure	Insecure	Satisfied	Dissatisfied
Full assistance for:				
Ill health	29.6	41.6	29.9	43.2
Disabled	45.1	50.4	46.5	59.5
Poor	38.1	44.2	40.3	56.8
Single parents	50.2	49.1	51.4	67.6
Natural disasters	52.4	57.1	52.7	78.4
Old age	42.7	46.7	45.3	73.0
Benefit for job loss	70.9	80.5	73.1	59.5

Source:Indonesia PSS.

Table 12.13 Ethiopia: Support for complete assistance for social shocks, by personal insecurity (percentage "Yes")

	Security in main work	
	Secure	Insecure
Full assistance for:		
Ill health	61.4	62.6
Disabled	70.0	73.4
Poor	35.3	44.6
Single parents	56.5	57.0
Natural disasters	60.4	64.3
Old age	63.8	65.7
Benefit for job loss	86.5	87.2

Source: Ethiopia PSS.

Examining the effect of the insecurity and dissatisfaction with income across countries, Indonesia turns out to be the country with the most widespread effects on these attitudes. Where information is available on the endorsement of full as well as partial support for these contingencies, total support is high in all countries, almost always more than 90%. This total support does not vary with either insecurity or dissatisfaction with income. What does change is the proportion supporting total versus partial support. People who are insecure are considerably more likely to favour full support as opposed to partial support.

12.13 Discrimination: Should people be treated equally?

Do people think all groups in society should have basic security and that all groups should have the *same* security? What are people's attitudes to fairness at work, and in particular to whether or not different groups should be treated the same or more or less favourably? A great deal of policy and analytical attention is given to patterns of discrimination. But relatively little is given to ordinary people's attitudes to principles of "selectivity" (discrimination). The PSS probe to ascertain some of the more important discriminatory views.

Table 12.14 shows responses to questions about three forms of discrimination. From the extensive work that has been done on discrimination against women, we know that there are two principal dimensions: equality of access to opportunities and equality of reward or pay in work.[34] Other research has suggested that people can have conflicting views on these two aspects, with greater endorsement of equality of access to jobs than to equal pay.[35]

Table 12.14 Percentage agreeing with recruitment and wage discrimination against specified groups, by country and gender

	Women Male	Female	Migrants Male	Female	Ethnic minorities Male	Female
Hungary						
Hiring	6.9	8.5	5.0	6.9	2.9	3.9
Wages	8.6	9.2	25.5	27.9	10.2	9.1
Russian Federation						
Hiring	11.4	3.1	64.7	60.5	n.a.	n.a.
Wages	4.0	1.6	46.7	42.7	n.a.	n.a.
Ukraine						
Hiring	12.7	11.7	28.8	28.1	n.a.	n.a.
Wages	5.4	3.2	18.5	17.3	n.a.	n.a.
Ethiopia						
Hiring	37.8	37.7	40.3	39.8	n.a.	n.a.
Ghana						
Hiring	27.0	27.0	24.8	28.4	n.a.	n.a.
South Africa						
Hiring	20.3	7.0	57.9	59.5	n.a.	n.a.
Wages	19.9	6.6	56.5	57.4	n.a.	n.a.
United Republic of Tanzania						
Hiring	26.8	9.7	n.a.	n.a.	n.a.	n.a.
Wages	26.9	14.1	n.a.	n.a.	n.a.	n.a.
Bangladesh						
Hiring	46.9	19.9	n.a.	n.a.	n.a.	n.a.
Wages	27.5	10.9	n.a.	n.a.	n.a.	n.a.
China						
Hiring	4.5	6.3	11.5	11.5	n.a.	n.a.
Wages	4.1	4.1	16.5	13.4	n.a.	n.a.
Gujarat, India						
Hiring	17.0	21.1	7.5	10.1	16.0	18.1
Wages	16.5	21.2	8.0	10.7	16.5	19.0
Indonesia						
Hiring	37.9	23.7	29.2	24.3	n.a.	n.a.

n.a. = not available
Source: SES PSS.

[34]Psychological studies suggest that a common perception that it is "fair" for women to receive lower wages has helped in the legitimization (or acceptance) of sex-based wage differentials. See, for instance, Major, 1994, op. cit.

[35]C. Burgoyne, A. Swift and G. Marshall: "Inconsistency of beliefs about distributive justice: A cautionary note", *Journal for the Theory of Social Behaviour* (Oxford), Vol. 23, 1993, pp. 327–342; R. Stock: *Explaining the Choice of Distribution Rule,* paper presented at 8th Biennial Conference of the International Society for Justice Research (Tel Aviv, Sep. 2000).

In the countries covered by the PSS, there seems to be strong popular support for gender equality. In four countries, discrimination against women (in both access and rewards) is supported by less than or near 10% of the sample: Hungary, the Russian Federation, Ukraine and China. Notably, these are all ex-communist countries.

In no country was there an outright majority in favour of discrimination against women, but with respect to access (equality in hiring) Bangladesh showed that 47% of men were prepared to see women be disadvantaged in pay and substantial proportions (over 25%) of men in four other countries showed similar attitudes. It should be remembered that there may be a "social desirability" response here: respondents, whether presenting themselves in the best possible light or simply adhering to accepted norms, may agree with attitudes they do not hold. These results may well overstate opposition to gender discrimination (and other forms as well). However, if non-discrimination has become a prevailing norm to which people think they should be seen to agree, then surely that is a step forward for those seeking to redress the bias against women.

The questions did not simply ask about discrimination against certain groups. They also asked about support for no discrimination either way (an equality rule) and discrimination in favour of the group concerned (positive discrimination). Again, the east Europeans show a deeper respect for equality than elsewhere. In Hungary, no less than 92% favoured that. Elsewhere, the picture is rather different. Thus, in Bangladesh, in addition to the 27% favouring men in hiring practices (i.e. discrimination against women) 65% said there should be no difference and 8% said women should be favoured. Positive discrimination against women was always in the minority, but the persistent 10-15% who supported it could be a base from which to work for support for such policies. In South Africa, remarkably one of the more egalitarian countries in this respect, 75% backed equal treatment, 10% said women should be favoured, 13% said men should. In Ghana, although 26% said men should be favoured in hiring, 14% said women should be given preference; 60% said men and women should be treated equally. The distribution of responses was similar for men and women.

If we consider the use of an equality rule, then Ethiopia is less egalitarian even than Bangladesh. Only 47%

said that men and women should be treated equally in recruitment, while 31% thought men should be given preference. This pro-male bias was as strong among women as among men, and was actually stronger among the more educated than among those with little education.

Overall, there is strong support for an equality rule, although support for positive discrimination in favour of women is quite small. It is encouraging that support for open discrimination against women is low, notwithstanding the fact that this will not necessarily reflect actual behaviour.

In terms of the young relative to *older workers*, a favourable attitude to equality of treatment was again the dominant rule, but there were some national differences, which may have something to do with the age structure of the countries or reflect cultural differences.

In some countries there was strong support. For instance, in South Africa, 73% said there should be equal treatment, and 17% said younger workers should be preferred. In Ghana, just over 50% said there should be no age preference, with a roughly equal number saying the young should be preferred as the opposite. However, the equality rule did not always apply; many said the more educated should be given preference – 70% saying that for similar work the more educated should be preferred. Not surprisingly, a similar result emerged for the more "skilled" relative to the "unskilled".

Nor were all countries as supportive of equality. In Ethiopia, only 28% favoured equal treatment of young and old, whereas 45% thought youth should be given preference over older workers. In Bangladesh, only 43% said there should be equal treatment for younger and older workers, and 52% said preference should be given to young people.

In eastern Europe, where population ageing is pronounced, attitudes towards older workers remain positive. For instance, in Ukraine, in 2002 over two-thirds thought workers in their 50s should have opportunities equal to those of younger workers, and three-quarters thought there should be no difference between the middle-aged and younger workers in their 20s. These results show that where support for equality is reduced it is often the young who benefit by increased support: to give preference to those presumed to be fitter and more able to work may be regarded as a sensible option, particularly if the family structure means that those young people support their elders.

What about recruitment discrimination with respect to minorities and migrants? In general, attitudes are much less tolerant and the proportions in favour of discrimination ranging from 5% in Hungary to 65% in the Russian Federation. Another worrying case is South Africa, where only 39% of respondents supported equality and 59% said those born in the country should be given preference. In Ethiopia, 43% favoured equality, but 31% thought local Ethiopians should be given preference.

In other countries, there was less evidence of discriminatory views and more support for equality, again with eastern Europe standing out. In Ukraine, in the 2002 sample, 68% favoured equal treatment for immigrants and native-born workers, while 27% thought Ukrainians should be given preference. In

Hungary, 94% thought Hungarians and "guest workers" should be treated equally, 6% thinking Hungarians should be preferred.

In general, there is far more support for direct discrimination against migrants, and much less support for equality. This is to be expected in any situation where people perceive themselves as in competition in various ways, notably for scarce jobs (or scarce jobs with a decent income). In these conditions, the psychology of distributions predicts that an unequal distribution will seem appropriate and acceptable.

Support for this can vary between women and men. In Tanzania, whereas over two-thirds said that men and women should be paid the same wages for similar work, 27% of men and 14% of women said they thought men should receive higher wages. Overall, however, acceptance of a principle of gender equality in the labour market seems widespread across a wide range of cultures.

Equality of opportunity for those with disabilities

In Ghana, people were asked whether in job recruitment decisions a preference should be given to workers with disabilities or to those who were "able bodied" or whether they thought there should be no preference one way or the other.

Only 37% favoured the equal opportunity option, 25% said preference should be given to someone with a disability, and 38% said preference should be given to those without disabilities. It turned out that men were more likely to think that there should be discrimination in favour of those without disabilities, and this view was more likely the older the man.

In Indonesia, a majority of people felt that the physically disabled should have the same opportunity to obtain a job as others — 63% (with no difference between men and women); only 21% disagreed. Even more agreed that those with hearing problems should have equal opportunities (69%), and a similar share said those with speech defects should have them (69%). The responses on the blind were less clear — 57% saying they agreed with equal opportunities. Perhaps some of those expressing reservations were thinking about practicalities. This comes across even more in attitudes to equal opportunity for the mentally impaired — merely 24% agreed.

What is encouraging is that the vast majority believed that all public buildings should provide facilities for the disabled, and even more agreed with the idea of mobilizing social resources to help the disabled and giving financial support for their health care. As for places to rehabilitate or assist the disabled, 21% knew of such places, and of those who did so, 17% thought they were good quality, 4% that they were fair, while 78% did not know. Some 13% knew of a training centre for the disabled; most of those who knew of a government training centre (68%) thought such facilities were good, and 52% thought the private centre known to them was good. Finally, a majority were against the proposition that the disabled should beg for money — 44% strongly disagreeing, and 21% disagreeing on balance.

Attitudes to equality of treatment of married and single people are more varied. In Tanzania, over two-thirds of men and women thought that married workers should be paid the same as single workers, most of the others saying they should be paid higher wages. In Bangladesh, almost all thought they should be paid the same, with only 8% thinking married women should be paid less. By contrast, in Hungary and Ukraine (second round), 29% and 38% respectively thought married women with children should be paid more than single women. This may be attributable to the long tradition of giving women with children prolonged paid maternity leave and is usually evidence of a need rule being applied. A similar example is in Ukraine, where younger respondents and women in general, were more likely to think they should be paid more. Besides self-interest, presumably financial need dictated this.

The attitude to age discrimination is also stronger in some countries than in others. In South Africa, more than three-quarters said there should be no age preference per se, with an equal number favouring higher wages for younger workers as for older. In Bangladesh, 91% said there should be no difference, whereas in Hungary 65% favoured equal treatment while 26% thought younger workers should receive lower wages than older workers. In Western countries a proportional number feels that preferences to status/seniority rule should be the norm in the workplace but people doing the same work should be paid equally.[36] Support for discrimination here may actually represent the combination of these rules. The proportions favouring equality were in fact substantial indicating, an "equal pay for equal work" attitude.

Attitudes to wage discrimination with respect to minorities and migrants are often more sensitive indicators of social tolerance. Thus in South Africa only 41% of the sample said that immigrants should be paid the same as nationals for doing similar work, while 57% said South African nationals should be paid more. But precisely which minority is in question can make a difference. In Hungary, although 90% said that *Romas* should be paid the same as others, 9% said they should be paid less. However, whereas 73% said "guest workers" should be paid the same as Hungarians, 25% said they should be paid less.

There was only limited evidence of xenophobia in Ukraine, since 77% said that immigrants should be paid the same as those born in Ukraine. However, 23% of men and 20% of women said they should be paid less, and this attitude was strongest among the young. There should be concern about this, although the generally civilized perspective in the very difficult economic circumstances of that large country is encouraging.

Discriminatory attitudes against migrants are a more general concern. In three countries (the Russian Federation, Ethiopia and South Africa), a belief that there should be discrimination against migrants was over 40%. In Hungary, Ghana and Indonesia it was over 25%. Globally, this is a well-known serious issue, borne out by the responses in a wide variety of cultures.

12.14 Personal insecurity and attitudes to discrimination

It is sometimes argued that people who feel insecure in their personal lives and threatened by adversity become more intolerant and less supportive of equal treatment of others. Are the insecure more likely than others to favour discrimination against minorities or "others", strangers or those they would like to regard as their social inferiors? Although we cannot hope to answer this stark issue definitively, the PSS data do provide information useful for assessing the insecurity-intolerance thesis.

The key attitude shown so far is discrimination against migrants. In this respect, there are very clear national differences in general. But it is hard to see any clear pattern by degree of insecurity (Table 12.15). In China, it seems that those feeling insecure about their jobs are more likely to favour discrimination against migrants, and in the Russian Federation those not satisfied with their earnings seem more inclined to favour discrimination. But in neither country is there much difference. More worrying was the overall high degree of xenophobia displayed among Russians, comparable to that observed in South Africa. The key may be that in those countries where insecurity is very extensive, the relatively most insecure will become more intolerant.

---

[36] Stock, 2000, op. cit.

Attitudes to discrimination against women also show no clear pattern. In Indonesia, those feeling insecure about their jobs are more likely to favour discrimination in recruitment practices. And those dissatisfied with their earned incomes were much more likely to favour discrimination. But in most other countries there was no apparent relationship.

Table 12.15 Support for discrimination against migrants, by country and economic security status
(percentage favouring wage or hiring discrimination)

Discrimination against migrants	Income for health care		Security in main work		Satisfied with income	
	Adequate	Inadequate	Secure	Insecure	Satisfied	Dissatisfied
Hungary						
Hiring	n. a.	n. a.	5.7	8.3	7.4	3.2
Wages	n. a.	n. a.	21.8	17.3	27.5	22.8
Russian Federation						
Hiring	60.3	65.2	60.9	64.5	59.4	63.8
Wages	43.4	46.1	38.7	45.0	42.8	43.9
Ukraine						
Hiring	32.1	27.7	33.7	30.6	33.2	32.4
Wages	21.2	17.2	17.2	19.2	21.1	19.0
Ethiopia						
Hiring	38.4	41.6	42.9	34.0	35.4	42.1
Ghana						
Hiring	29.0	25.6	27.3	20.0	26.9	31.7
South Africa						
Hiring	61.0	55.5	65.4	72.7	63.5	64.9
Wages	58.0	55.6	60.2	68.2	55.8	64.4
China						
Hiring	11.3	11.7	10.9	12.7	10.1	13.2
Wages	14.0	15.9	12.3	14.7	10.4	16.8
Gujarat, India						
Hiring	7.0	10.1	9.0	10.5	9.2	12.6
Wages	8.5	10.6	9.6	14.0	9.8	14.0
Indonesia						
Hiring	27.9	26.4	27.2	26.0	29.2	33.3

n.a. = not available.
Source: SES PSS.

Table 12.16 **Support by men for discrimination against women, by country and economic security status**
(percentage favouring discrimination in recruitment or wages)

	Income for health care		Security in main work		Satisfied with income	
	Adequate	Inadequate	Secure	Insecure	Satisfied	Dissatisfied
Hungary						
Hiring	n. a.	n. a.	7.3	4.8	8.3	5.7
Wages	n. a.	n. a.	4.1	4.7	7.3	2.4
Russian Federation						
Hiring	7.9	5.9	6.2	5.7	6.0	5.3
Wages	2.9	2.3	2.5	2.5	4.6	1.7
Ukraine						
Hiring	14.3	11.7	12.5	14.1	12.9	12.7
Wages	5.3	3.9	3.4	3.1	3.6	2.9
Ethiopia						
Hiring	30.8	42.9	42.4	33.3	31.5	40.7
Ghana						
Hiring	27.8	27.8	28.0	30.0	26.6	28.0
South Africa						
Hiring	12.3	12.6	11.5	12.1	14.0	12.8
Wages	11.8	12.4	12.7	13.6	11.9	11.2
Tanzania						
Hiring	18.8	17.8	18.5	17.3	20.7	17.0
Wages	18.7	21.7	18.9	22.4	23.6	18.9
Bangladesh						
Hiring	36.3	46.5	n. a.	n. a.	39.6	41.6
Wages	19.2	32.0	n. a.	n. a.	23.0	23.8
China						
Hiring	4.9	5.9	4.8	6.0	6.1	6.1
Wages	3.4	5.0	3.1	4.6	3.0	5.8
Gujarat, India						
Hiring	16.5	21.1	19.9	22.8	19.8	25.2
Wages	17.0	21.0	20.0	21.1	19.6	26.6
Indonesia						
Hiring	33.8	30.2	29.6	36.2	29.3	54.1

n.a. = not available.
Source: SES PSS.

12.15 Support for civil rights

Finally, although not studied in most of the PSS, it is perhaps of interest to note the results from a series of questions addressed to respondents in the second round of the Ukrainian PSS in 2002. The section on social justice began by asking people about their attitudes to various aspects of social justice and personal liberties. All respondents were asked to indicate the importance they attributed to specific social values, giving a ranking of between 1 and 7, with 1 being low importance and 7 being very high importance.

Intriguingly, *people's rights* tended to attract large proportions with high values, with two-thirds giving it a value of 5 or more. In terms of the percentage of the total giving values of 5 or more, this was followed by *freedom, personal independence, adherence to law, equality, responsibility*, and, a long way behind, *active participation in government* (on which two-thirds gave a value of 1). Not surprisingly, younger age groups gave a particularly high value to freedom and independence.

What is a signal of wider relevance to this analysis, those suffering from greatest income insecurity tended to give lower value to freedom than those who felt income secure. But in other respects, there were no significant differences. Support for a guaranteed minimum income, for example, was just as strong for those giving a high value to personal independence as those giving a lower value to that. This is further evidence that people with widely differing views on other aspects of society and social environment share a commitment to basic income security.

12.16 Concluding reflections

Although public attitudes are malleable, underneath the surface is a widely shared human commitment to fairness, social solidarity and tolerance. Although social and economic insecurity may weaken that commitment to some extent, they make people realize the value of basic security as a human need.

This is a major message that comes across from the People's Security Surveys and from other research on social justice being conducted around the world. Do policies correspond to it? And how could they become more compatible with it? These are issues that will figure in the final chapter.

By way of conclusion, it is worth recalling the important findings from the fascinating psychological experiments mentioned earlier in the chapter. The study found that when the redistributive policy of providing a minimum income and taxing others to pay for it was put into effect, it did not have a negative effect on production. Indeed, productivity increased after the transfer was made.[37] And the recipients of the transfer increased productivity sharply when the decision was made democratically.

The message is that if economic security is provided, productivity will increase. And recipients will become more productive if the decision is made democratically. This is surely a powerful and optimistic message.

There is one point that should be put aside for reflection. There is evidence that attitudes to different aspects of social justice vary according to national cultures and socio-economic structures. In particular, there seems to be a tendency for people in the United States to believe government should give a lower priority to "guaranteeing no one is in need"

than in other rich countries and much higher priority to providing individuals with "freedom to pursue goals".[38] In other words, the country setting the model for others to follow, through the Washington Consensus and other means, is one in which guaranteeing economic security is given relatively low priority.

That aside, the normative values expressed by people across the world continue to reveal a sense of social interdependence, a belief in the desirability of limiting inequalities and in the need to help people who are poor or who are less fortunate than themselves, and a belief in the desirability of compensating those who perform socially vital functions, private and social, that have traditionally not been compensated in market economies. The normative values that come through are not in favour of rampant individualism, but of basic security for all, regardless of capacities or labour market status.

In that context, one subject not discussed in this chapter is how to achieve a shift to an income distribution system that gives priority to basic security for all, accompanied by some reduction in inequality. A clue to future policy may lie in a key finding of psychological economics, which is that people generally value modest losses in income about twice as much as they value equivalent gains.[39] What this implies is that it would be better, and easier socially to implement, if the aim of basic security were pursued from growth, making sure that most of the accumulated gains were allocated to the goal of basic security. That way, relative losses by the relatively well-off would not be seen as absolute losses.

It would be a gross misrepresentation to believe that people's attitudes reflect "interest group economism". That key premise of so much that goes for "public choice" theorizing is an insult to the human spirit. People believe that their fellow citizens should have a similar level of basic security as they want for themselves and for their families.

---

[37]Frohlick and Oppenheimer, 1992, op. cit., p. 132.

[38]"A survey of America", *The Economist*, 8 Nov. 2003, p. 4.

[39]A. Tversky and D. Kahneman: "Rational choice and the framing of decisions", *Journal of Business*, Vol. 59, No. 4, Oct. 1991, pp. S251–S278; M. Rabin: "Psychology and economics", *Journal of Economic Literature*, Vol. XXXVI, Mar. 1998, pp. 11–111.

Chapter 13   Emerging forms of voice representation security

People in poverty want for their children… education, good health, security and opportunity. They want voice. They do not want charity. They want a chance to make better lives for themselves. They want respect for their human rights."

— James Wolfensohn, President, World Bank.[1]

13.1 The 21st century dilemma

Representation security is fundamental to basic security. Old-style trade unions are in trouble. They know it. And they are looking at all possible ways of strengthening their appeal to workers, reaching types of workers they have traditionally failed to reach or have ignored, and looking at ways of organizing more effectively. Yet the view has to be entertained that the forms of voice that are going to predominate in the 21st century will look very different from the trade unions of the 19th and 20th centuries.

There is little doubt that new forms of voice are required at all levels, from the global to the local. There is also growing realization that "coalitions of organizations" can exert far more influence than can be achieved by the sum of the parts.

One of the interesting aspects of globalization is that multinationals in many sectors are wishing to establish their credentials with "socially conscious consumers" in their main markets, such as the United States and the countries of the European Union. Partly because of this, some have actually become promoters of trade unions in developing countries.

Thus, Reebok, the US sportswear company, in 1998 organized seminars for workers in one of its sub-con-tractor firms, a Republic of Korea factory in Indonesia, on how to organize and bargain collectively. This represents the fourth phase in the reaction of multinationals to pressure by human rights advocates over "sweatshop" production. The previous three were, first, denial (which could not be maintained against the evidence); second, pressure on suppliers to respect worker rights (which failed largely because of inadequate monitoring); then third, making inspections more credible by hiring independent monitors.

This example demonstrates just one of the many tensions emerging as people learn to react to the insecurities unleashed by globalization. But by themselves trade unions cannot provide adequate representation security. The national governance structures based on national *tripartism* and neo-corporatist regulation of social and economic matters, which for many years provided or promised labour-based security, are very unlikely to be resurrected. New mechanisms of representation security are needed at every level of policy-making. This chapter will consider just a few examples of new initiatives to promote economic security in which voice security is crucial.

---

[1] J. Wolfensohn: *Building an Equitable World*, Address to the Board of Governors, Prague, Sep. 2000, p. 4.

331

13.2 From thin democracy to real democracy

The past two decades have seen a trend to political democratization. According to Freedom House, by 2003 more than half the world's population was living in politically democratic societies, up from a third in 1983. This is the good news. However, there is a contradictory aspect. Increasingly, decision-making is more distant and less transparent while elites appear to control the character of this political democracy and its outcomes. Power seems to be slipping to undemocratic groups, including financial institutions and tiny cliques who control the media. And political democracy seems rather *thin*, as reflected in falling voting levels in all forms of elections in many parts of the world. Democratic accountability also looks thin. Culpable failures by the powerful are not matched by appropriate responses from elected politicians, who are too beholden to their interests.

The cities of voice?

Porto Alegre, Florence, Mumbai, Barcelona, and where else? A range of cities where two generations of "civil society" congregate in many thousands under the banner of the World Social Forum. The older generation fought for human rights, for women, for sustainable development and for indigenous movements. The younger generation are resolutely opposed to the dominant ideology of "globalization". The widening and disparate agenda has hindered establishment of a common voice for change.

The World Social Forum is a giant "Voiceplace". The 2002 Forum had 1,714 panels and seminars, a whirlwind of activities. Mumbai in 2004 was bigger still. But one could also say that there is an atomization of dialogue, a lack of focused energy. Voice is not sensibly measured in numbers, but in coherence and impact.

Where will all this voice lead?

To give modern meaning to democratization, there is a need to combine strong *individual* voice security – rights in work, capacity to pursue them at low financial, emotional and social cost – with a strong *collective* voice for all legitimate interests in society and in the international economic system. All such interests must have roughly equal strength of voice. And we must remember that voice without resources is a whisper, rarely heard, easily ignored.

Thin democracy may be described as the almost-ritualistic voting for carefully packaged "candidates". Real democracy may be described as the democratization of life and work through active involvement, participation and control. Thin democracy does not contribute to economic security, thick democracy may and should do.[2]

There are fears that democracy is a term being used to rationalize a great deal of non-democratic action, and that it is increasingly built on what Bobbio called "descending" rather than "ascending" power, from real participation at local levels, in communities, workplaces or occupations, schools and so on.[3] Some see a corrosion of the democratic spirit. One sign of this is public dissatisfaction with democratically elected governments, as shown, for example, across Latin America.[4]

Another fear concerns a tendency – perhaps increasing – for groups in the electorate to vote for their own interests, rather than in the interests of social solidarity. In response, some propose modifying the electoral process to protect minorities from a "tyranny of the majority". Perhaps the most bizarre suggestion is in the following box.

---

[2]It could be said that the United States is at once the most democratic society and among the least democratic of the democracies, in that about one million elections take place in each four-year period, but voter turnout in all forms of election is among the lowest. "A survey of America", *The Economist*, 8 Nov. 2003, p. 3.

[3]N. Bobbio: *The Future of Democracy* (Cambridge, Polity Press, 1987).

[4]The *Latinobarometro* opinion polls found that in 2002 less than one-third of Latin Americans were satisfied with their governments, and 80% believed corruption had increased.

Weighted voice?

In Germany, some people have proposed that the voting age should be lowered to zero. The reason? Because of ageing, the interests of older voters are becoming dominant, so that old-age income security is being protected while the security needs of the young are neglected. So, the idea goes, if children were given a surrogate vote, which would be exercised by their parents, their security needs would be taken more into account.

There are other variants of the idea. In Singapore, it was once suggested that working parents should have extra votes, on the grounds that they would be the most likely to vote in the interests of future generations.

Why stop there? Well, there are some objections. Perhaps generational gerrymandering is only one of them.

13.3 Global governance for security

At the global level, there has been much talk in recent years about a need to *rearrange the architecture*, a euphemism for restructuring the system of institutions that emerged at the end of the Second World War. This report will not try to deal with this sensitive and highly charged set of issues, other than to make a few points of principle that must be borne in mind if socio-economic security is to be enhanced. In particular, whatever is done should be assessed in terms of whether or not it increases accountability, transparency, democracy and equity.

The original Bretton Woods institutions – the IMF and the World Bank – were set up to deal with post-war reconstruction in the late 1940s. They were supposed to assist in stabilizing economies and managing the international payments system. But, though lacking a clear mandate to do so, they evolved to deal with "structural adjustments" and assist in the development process. Fair enough, some commentators would say. However, others believe they are ill-adapted to deal with economic instability and insecurity. It is partly a matter of *governance*.

The orthodox policies preached by the international financial agencies include democratic accountability. It is essential that they should practise that themselves, perhaps by extending their accountability from just finance ministries and central banks. At the very least, as a first step, ministries of social welfare and labour should be involved, and be included in evaluations of IMF and World Bank programmes.

One idea, proposed by the Vice-Chancellor of Delhi University, Deepak Nayyar, is that there should be a *Global People's Assembly*, modelled on the European Parliament, running parallel to the UN General Assembly to serve as the voice of global civil society. Another idea is that there should be an *Economic Security Council*, within the United Nations. This would be an institutional mechanism for debate on global economic and social policies and for the collation of information to be made available to the whole world.

In some areas, there are advances taking shape, for instance, in the extension of the international justice system with the establishment of the International Criminal Court and regional human rights courts such as the newly created African Court on Human and People's Rights. In the economic sphere, as the Commission on Human Security recognized, "the creation of an independent adjudication authority for disputes in the World Trade Organization provides an example of a recent advance in the regulation of interdependence."[5]

In the sphere of social policy, globalization poses a challenge for coordination to prevent *social dumping*. Many commentators have claimed there is a "race to the bottom" in social policy and social and labour regulations, as countries compete to become more attractive for foreign capital.[6] Others believe there is a tendency that could be described as a "race to the middle", in which advances in affluent industrialized countries are being rolled back at the same time as advances are being made in at least some developing countries.[7]

---

[5] Commission on Human Security: *Human Security Now* (New York, 2003), p. 12.

[6] Among the many commentators arguing in this vein, see D. Rodrik: *Has Globalization Gone Too Far?* (Washington, DC, Institute of International Economics, 1997); R. Mishra: *Globalization and the Welfare State* (Bristol, Edward Elgar, 1999).

[7] J. Alber and G. Standing: "Social Dumping: Catch-up or convergence?", introduction to Special Issue of *Journal of European Social Policy*, Vol. 10, No. 2, Mar 2000, pp. 99–119.

Proposals to link labour standards to trade have been consistently rejected by most WTO members. However, there may be a need for an international mechanism to deter or discourage countries from *lowering* their institutional and policy standards protecting social and economic security. Without coordination, a race of some kind could continue to erode all forms of security. But it will be essential for the voices of all interests and groups likely to be affected by shifts in social policy to be incorporated into any new institutional regulation.

13.4 National governance for security

"Without government human progress is impossible – because government provides the structures and the security which underpin trust."

—John Browne, Chief Executive, BP[8]

In the era of globalization, the dominant thinking on the role of government first moved away from "big", in the sense of a "mixed economy" in which public ownership was expected to move steadily from the "commanding heights" to many other spheres of economic activity, and in which statutory regulation was extensive and public social services regarded as the advancing norm.

The dominant thinking then moved to "small", through privatization of economic activities and the privatization and liberalization of social policy, and "deregulation", which meant in fact a shift to regulations intended to promote market competition. But the discourse has shifted to a more nuanced interpretation. Now the conventional wisdom seems to be that government at national and local levels must be strengthened in order to provide an effective counterweight to the adverse impacts of globalization. On this view, governments need to impose a fair system of rules as well as create equality of opportunity in a market economy.

However, coexisting with this view, national policy has reflected a tendency to "de-politicize" monetary policy (making central banks "independent", for example) and to accept international convergence of fiscal policy and many facets of social policy, a convergence dictated by an apparent need to adhere to market forces and internationally agreed competition rules.

As far as social and economic security is concerned, three aspects of governance trends pose dilemmas for policy-makers. First is the emerging regime of *subsidiarity*, in which governance is supposedly left to the lowest level possible. The rhetoric of decentralization has clouded the reality that this can lead to fragmentation and structural inequalities.

There is much talk about "empowering" local communities and sharing experiences between networks of local actors. But local communities have limited powers because they have a limited range of fiscal options. Big cities are struggling to come to terms with the limits and many are experimenting with new social policies, some of which are considered in this chapter and the following one. There is the fanfare of mayors coming together to share experiences. As long as these exercises do not become expensive sequences of glad-handing events, they may prove useful. But it is small and medium towns, and neglected rural communities, that are least able to operate in this pyramid of subsidiarity, unless fiscal and social policy is made more solidaristic. The values of social solidarity must drive all these initiatives if they are to prove valuable for the long-run development of basic security.

The second aspect is the disappearance of institutionalized collective voice. In the days of "big" government, *corporatism* was the dominant ethos, in which employer organizations and unions were regularly consulted and given an active role in governance at every level. Collective voice was central and, although the collective voices tended to become less representative of broader social groups as time went by, the bargaining between interests was reasonably balanced. For better or worse, this has gone. What has taken its place? And what should take its place? At this stage, all we can do is pose the questions and indicate some promising signs of emerging voice.

The third issue goes to the heart of the matter. It is an underlying theme of our analysis that a society in which basic economic security is regarded as a *right* requires that the values of social solidarity are kept at the forefront of policy. There are plenty of commentators who dismiss the value of social

---

[8]Speech at Chatham House, and article in *The Independent* (London), 1 Mar. 2002, p. 4.

solidarity, and there are plenty who see the issue for what it is and want to suppress it in favour of other goals they regard as overriding. We dismiss both those perspectives.

Policy-makers must instead confront the dilemma that there is a tension between rules that demand respect for market competition and policies that promote social solidarity. This is particularly relevant in the sphere of social protection rules, where the essence of many systems developed in the 20ˢ century was a solidaristic sharing of risks and reciprocity of contributions and compensation.

By way of example of the difficulties these dilemmas pose for regional economic integration and the principle of subsidiarity, consider developments in the European Union (EU). The European Court of Justice (ECJ) has responsibility for jurisprudence on EU social policy. The EU is mainly about market integration. Social and tax policy is supposedly left to the national level. The ECJ, which is supposed to define a common line, has ruled that *basic* social protection should be allowed to adhere to social solidaristic principles while *supplementary* schemes should adhere to market competition rules standardized at EU level. But what is the difference?

In practice, the attempt to answer this has been left to interpretation by lawyers at the ECJ because there has been no effective EU initiative in the area of social protection. This has left room for social policy to be fashioned by lawyer opinion, rather than by citizens' voice (see following box). The problem starts with the legalistic interpretation of basic social security schemes, the ECJ ruling that they must have compulsory membership.[9] According to the ECJ, voluntary schemes are not solidaristic and thus must

---

Solidarity versus market rules? The European Union social protection model

Will what is happening in the European Union be a paradigm for other regional blocs?

In France in the late 1980s the Mutualité Sociale Agricole (MSA), which provides basic social security for French farmers, was granted the exclusive right to operate a supplementary old-age pension scheme (COREVA) for farmers based on voluntary contributions. The Fédération française des sociétés d'assurances (FFSA), the French federation of insurance companies, claimed to the ECJ that the MSA's monopoly was an unfair distortion of EU competition rules and the ECJ agreed.[10] The French government was obliged to introduce new legislation opening up the sector to competition and granting all providers the same tax privileges.

In another example, the Dutch government brought in legislation to make compulsory industry-wide pension, non-profit pension schemes run by employers and union representatives, which had been established by collective agreements. In 1999 the ECJ decided that since these were compulsory and did not involve risk selection they qualified as solidaristic and were not subject to EU competition rules.[11] The decision implicitly recognized the role played by employers and unions in social protection.

However, non-profit schemes have no legal status under EU law, meaning that many such schemes risk falling foul of EU competition rules if they operate on a voluntary basis, even when their method of operation is solidaristic. For instance, non-profit schemes based on occupation, industry or other common feature may aim to provide protection for all members without risk selection, while profit-making institutions may charge differential tariffs depending on degree of risk. And because they do not have shareholders, non-profit schemes can be managed with reference to long-term viability and the interests of their members (who may also have a voice in their administration). An ECJ ruling against such schemes on the grounds that they were "abusing a dominant position" could thus conflict with the common good.

Since EU countries provide varying levels of social protection through a variety of different institutions, public and private, the dichotomy in EU law between public "solidaristic" schemes and private "competitive" schemes is inappropriate. By leaving the legal status of many solidaristic non-profit institutions in doubt, the EU has handed policy-making on key aspects of social protection to lawyers rather than to citizens and democratically elected governments.

---

[9]See the ECJ rulings on Poucet and Pistre, dated 17 Feb. 1993, and Garcia, dated 26 Mar. 1996.

[10]ECJ ruling on COREVA, 16 Nov. 1995.

[11]ECJ ruling on Brentjens, Albany and Maatschappij (C-115/97, C-116/97 and C-117/97).

operate under rules of competitive markets. Since many schemes in this era of social policy pluralism and liberalization are voluntary, the supranational rules are effectively limiting solidarity.

In devising rules encompassing different levels of government, at regional, national and local levels, policy-makers may easily overlook these three dilemmas. Subsidiarity must not be a route to socio-economic fragmentation, deregulation must not be a cover for de-legitimizing social interests and collective voice, and market rules must not be a means of denying citizens the choice of social solidarity.

13.5 Trust and institutions

To function effectively, institutions must engender a spirit of trust — or at least this is the current conventional wisdom. This report will not go into the role of trust and loyalty in detail. But clearly there is a connection between trust and security.

People feel more secure if they trust those with whom they are working, those employing them, those representing them as bargainers or politically, those providing them with services, those selling to them or buying from them, those supplying them with information. In each case, the trust may be misplaced or deserved, contrived or well tested.

Voice institutions are valuable or not to the extent to which they give confidence to the citizen that his or her interests are being respected and given their due. We saw earlier that there is some shortcoming in this respect with regard to trade unions. This section will merely highlight some comparisons.

In Brazil, for example, the church emerged as the most trusted institution — 60% of all respondents believed the church was trustworthy, compared with 30% who believed the unions were. Respondents also trusted neighbourhood associations more than trade unions. A consolation for unions is that political parties were even less trusted. And women were more likely to trust unions than men. Higher-income and more educated respondents were less likely to trust unions than others.

The lack of trust in unions in Brazil may reflect a feeling that workers' voice has been "obliterated", and contrasts with the much higher levels of trust in all forms of institution a few years earlier.[12]

In Argentina, the PSS found that people mostly had trust in local institutions. Thus, over 52% expressed trust in parents' associations, and about 47% had trust in churches and other religious institutions, about the same as had trust in students' associations. About 44% had trust in neighbourhood associations. Perhaps surprisingly, over 41% trusted the press. About a third had trust in NGOs in general.

By contrast with these relatively positive views, only 15% had confidence in the judicial system, 14% in the police, and 11% in labour unions. A mere 8% had faith in Congress, and only 6% viewed political parties as trustworthy.

In Chile, perhaps reflecting the socially and economically calmer times, there was generally more trust in the spectrum of institutions, but with some dissimilarities in the ranking. Most trusted was the church. Thus, 59% felt they could rely on churches and other religious institutions. Over 40% trusted parents' associations and a similar percentage believed in students' associations, with nearly as many having confidence in neighbourhood associations. Interestingly, 39% felt that the Chilean police were reliable. More encouraging for unions, 32% trusted them.

Institutions in which the citizenry had relatively little trust were the press (23%), the judiciary (21%), NGOs (20%), Congress (19%) and, far in the rear, political parties (8%).

In Ukraine, many more people have little or no trust in *government agencies* dealing with social matters. In 2002, only 5% said they had full trust in them, 37% had not much trust, and 47% had no trust at all. The only good point about those figures is that they reflected a marginally less negative attitude than a year or so earlier. Those in urban areas were less likely to have any trust than those in rural areas, and industrial workers were much less likely to have any trust in government agencies, perhaps reflecting recent experience with wage and other arrears, noted elsewhere in this report.

In the Russian Federation, loss of faith in institutions has gone a long way. From PSS data, it appears that workers trust only themselves to protect their

[12] A. Cardoso: *Workers' Representation Security in Brazil: Global Forces, Local Stress*, SES Paper No. 28 (Geneva, ILO, 2002).

interests, and lack confidence in institutions that should protect their interests. Thus, according to the PSS conducted in 2002, a third of the Russian Federation workers believe no one is protecting their interests; 39% feel that only they as individuals are protecting their interests; for 18% of workers, their interests are protected by their family; 8% feel that the State protects their interests; 2% believe that trade unions protect their interests; no workers reported that NGOs protect their interests; 0.1% believe that religious organizations protect their interests; 0.2% feel that their manager/supervisor protects their interests; no workers reported that their employer protects their interests. This is a remarkable litany of societal alienation.

Only a minority of adults regarded the municipal institutions dealing with social protection as trustworthy. Just over a third (36%) thought welfare offices were trustworthy in dealing with the payment of assistance and child benefits; about half thought those dealing with pensions were; about a quarter thought those dealing with unemployment benefits were trustworthy; and about a third (31%) thought the offices dealing with the disabled were reliable.

13.6 Civil society and representation: Emerging voice?

"Natura vacuum abhorret"[13]

The main 19th and 20th century forms of representation, notably trade unions, were great advances for humanity. However, as implied in Chapter 9, they have limits and limitations. Numerous surveys and reports around the world have testified to a widespread dissatisfaction with trade unions – who they represent and what they do and set out to do. This report will not go into whether or not such dissatisfaction is "fair" or "justified". The fact is that there has been dissatisfaction, coming from many quarters, much of it because people feel that unions do not represent their particular interests.

Other forms of voice have been emerging or re-emerging in what some observers have called an *associational revolution*. The decline in old representative bodies, such as unions and the organized church has been offset by the rapid growth of so-called *non-governmental organizations* (NGOs) or civil society organizations (CSOs).[14] NGOs have been shooting up at an incredible rate, revealing a wide-

spread concern about representation gaps and an energy that has not found a niche in traditional representative organizations. Critics say that too many of these NGOs are non-accountable, non-representative, non-transparent and non-democratic. Perhaps this is true of many of them, but such criticisms are equally applicable to many other institutions that are not usually subject to the same scrutiny.

At the top of this pile, there are now more than 30,000 international NGOs, including some major bodies such as the World Wildlife Fund, reported to have 4.5 million supporters, and Amnesty International, reported to have over one million members. At national level, thousands more NGOs have become a force that cannot be ignored. But whose interests are the various types of "NGO" representing?

Undoubtedly, CSOs have become a major social force helping to shape the character of globalization. Some have emerged to fill a near-void; others have done so because people have felt traditional bodies were failing to address their concerns or interests; some have emerged simply to lobby for commercial interests.

Workers' voice for economic security is not just required inside the workplace or in policy-making circles, which is where most attention is concentrated. It is also required in the social community. This is becoming even more necessary given the trend towards outwork and other forms of distance working, in which workers are scattered and less likely to be in one centralized workplace.

For instance, in the Indian PSS conducted in Gujarat — and one may be safe in assuming that circumstances are similar in other parts of India — harassment of informal "outworkers" by police and municipal officials is widespread. More than a third of all outworkers had been victims of such harassment, and one in five was obliged to pay bribes to officials simply to keep the business running. Individually, they could not hope to combat the

---

[13]"Nature abhors a vacuum". Attributed to François Rabelais and to Sir Isaac Newton.

[14]H. Anheier et al.: *Work in the Non-Profit Sector: Forms, Patterns and Methodologies* (Geneva, ILO, 2003).

resultant income insecurity. In both Ethiopia and Tanzania, many respondents said they had to pay government or local authority officials' money to enable them to carry on their activities. Similar findings were found in the other PSS.

What is required is a multitude of *types* of collective organization, to ensure that all legitimate interests in society can be heard effectively. Even then, not all aspects of a particular interest can or should be represented by a particular type of organization. The role of generating information may be performed better by one type than the role of lobbying or monitoring, for instance.

The passivity of survival

People in different societies have very different tendencies to look to the State to provide them with basic security, and the degree of fatalism also varies widely.

In the Russian Federation, 51% of workers believe that the welfare of a Russian citizen depends mainly on the person him/herself, whereas 50% think that it depends largely on the State.

Men aged between 21 and 30 tend to depend more on themselves (13%) than on the State (8%) as far as their welfare is concerned. Dependence upon the State increases with age. Men between 41 and 60 equally rely on themselves and the State (18%). About as many women aged between 21 and 60 believe their welfare depends on the State as much as upon themselves. As with men, dependence upon the State increases with age: women over 60 are more inclined to rely on the Russian State (15%) than upon themselves (6%).

In neighbouring Ukraine, the pattern is quite similar, as successive rounds of the PSS have shown.

In the Russian Federation, workers' representation is weak and citizens know it. When asked what they would do in the face of food price rises, public transport price rises, a rise in crime, regular cuts in electricity, water or gas... in each case the most common response was to say there was no point in attempting to influence the authorities and that action would be ineffectual.

(i) Unaware and unattached

In recent years, NGOs have attracted a great deal of international attention, and have had some spectacular successes. However, it is far from clear how effective they are as vehicles of voice. A rather basic issue is *awareness* of their existence and functions.

In this respect, there is cause for concern. For example, according to the data from the PSS in the Russian Federation in 2002, remarkably few respondents knew of the existence of NGOs. Only 6% knew of the existence of an NGO protecting the interests of the self-employed; 12% were aware of an NGO protecting the interests of business people; 8% were aware of one that represented farmers' interests. And only 2% of those who were aware of any such NGO were members. This suggests that, while numerous, NGOs in such a society may indeed be rather "thin" and thus potentially rather unrepresentative.

In Ukraine, only 9% of respondents knew of an organization other than trade unions that could represent workers' interests, although 43% knew of an organization in their country that represented the interests of the self-employed.

In Ethiopia, according to the PSS, only 5% of respondents (6% of men, 3% of women) knew of organizations other than trade unions that would help them. In China, only 16% of respondents were aware of organizations in their country that could represent workers' interests other than trade unions. By contrast, as befits its high-profile status as one of the centres of NGO activity, in Bangladesh 35% of respondents knew of an organization that represented the interests of the self-employed. In Ghana too, 36% of respondents in the PSS said they knew of an organization representing the interests of the self-employed, and 20% of them belonged to such an organization. By contrast, in Tanzania merely 5% knew of an organization representing the interests of the self-employed. In South Africa, 7% of PSS respondents knew of an organization representing the self-employed, although only a minority of them belonged to one.

In Indonesia, a tiny proportion of respondents (less than 3%) knew of any organization other than trade unions that might help them. Nevertheless, asked what action they would take in response to work-related grievances, nearly half said they would consider appealing to an NGO. Since multiple answers were allowed, it is worth noting that about three-quarters said they would complain to government agencies and about 30% said they would demonstrate, with men more supportive of all of these actions. The responses no doubt reflected recent turbulent political upheavals, in which street protests played a major role in toppling the Suharto regime.

In Argentina, only 6% of adults were aware of any organizations in the country other than trade unions that could represent workers' interests. In Brazil, the corresponding figure was 9%, and in Chile it was 17%.

Quite clearly, awareness of alternative sources of voice representation varies considerably. And yet awareness is only the first part of the story. What is really significant is *participation* in voice institutions other than trade unions.

In Argentina, few workers belong to any association outside of the union in their workplace. This may reveal apathy, a lack of solidarity or a lack of effectiveness and reputation among the various organizations. Contrasting with the expressions of trust cited earlier, no more than 5% of respondents belonged to any collective institution, with 5% saying they were members of a religious body, 3% members of a political party and 0.4% members of an environmental body. About 1% said they were members of a neighbourhood association, parent association, student association, charitable association or an NGO.

In Brazil, there was more participation, but this was mainly because 14% were members of a religious body. Less than 4% belonged to any other type of institution, with neighbourhood associations attracting 3.9%.

In Chile, participation in social bodies was greater than in either Argentina or Brazil. But again, it was quite limited. Some 16% belonged to a religious body,

12% belonged to a parent association, and 11% belonged to a neighbourhood association. Participation in other bodies was a little higher than in the other two countries, but was under 10%.

In Ghana, a surprisingly large number of people said they belonged to a political party (43% of all respondents), with as many women as men being members. But in terms of civil society organizations, only small minorities belonged to other associations. The most common was an ethnic or home-town association, to which 14% belonged, with women slightly less likely to be members. Then, 10% belonged to a neighbourhood association, 10% to a recreation or sports club, 9% to a union, 2% to an NGO, and 1% to a disability-related organization, with women being about as active as men in all cases. This is also not suggestive of extensive participation in "civil society".

In South Africa, over half the respondents belonged to a religious body, with more women than men involved. Otherwise, collective bodies drew rather little active participation. Just over 13% of adults belonged to a community association, 12% to a political party, 10% to a sports or recreation club, 5% to a union, 2% to a health-related body, and 1% to an NGO.

The gender of South African voice

Men and women participate in voice organizations in South Africa. But the pattern varies. Men are more likely to be in sports clubs and political parties, women in religious bodies or community associations. Neither men nor women are likely to be active in other civil society bodies.

In addition to these salutary statistics on lack of awareness and limited participation, more significant in the longer term is the sheer diversity of the alternative sources of voice that are emerging. Recognizing this, in 2000 the ILO's Socio-Economic Security Programme set up a pilot project, *Voicenet*, in order to identify promising new forms of voice representation, including those taking place within traditional bodies such as trade unions.

(ii) The voice of the unorganized

Probably the greatest challenge to improving work-related security in the era of globalization is finding the most appropriate form of voice. Whether fairly or not, trade unions are perceived to represent the interests and aspirations of wage workers in mass production and mass services, as has been the norm in the public sector. The great advances they have achieved have been attempts at societal rent-seeking for their members, in a struggle with the representatives of industrial capital to secure their fair share or in ensuring that the public sector achieves and maintains "best practice" exemplary labour standards and working conditions.

In the era characterized by informalization and flexibility, new forms of organization have emerged or re-emerged in a new guise. Some have come into existence as little more than alternative unions, searching for the appropriate bodies with whom to bargain. Others have been more like what might be called a *total institution*, representing workers qua workers but also seeking to provide them with multiple forms of social income and broad social protection.

Whether narrowly focused or total organizations, they face common difficulties in giving people working informally an adequate voice for security. One of the main obstacles to the organization of workers in the informal economy is the fact that they are not part of the labour force *recognized by law* (especially "own-account" or self-employed workers), as was the case with black South African workers for many decades until 1979.[15] Yet unless workers in the informal economy are brought into the system of voice regulation, labour market inequalities between them and workers in the formal economy will deepen or remain.

Trying to give voice to workers who are legally not recognized by the term "worker" runs up against the bureaucratic hurdle of legitimation. Workers in the informal economy, where not recognized as workers in terms of labour legislation, are penalized in being denied a forum in which to operate. They therefore need to organize not only for improvements in their working and living conditions, but to shape new laws, which recognize and protect them.

Voice coalitions for informals

Workers in the informal economy need to engage in alliances with formal workers and their trade unions, learning what works and what does not, learning what causes divisions between them and how best to address these causes.

Organizations attempting to give voice to those outside the ambit of standard employment have to focus much more on identifying and engaging a variety of people and institutions with which to bargain. Their needs and priorities are scarcely ever easily reduced to workplace issues. One of their likely demands is for a place in formal bargaining channels, at every level.

A first step is to seek and secure accreditation, or a sense of legitimacy, without which they are unlikely to be able to test and prove themselves as accountable and democratic institutions. This can often turn out to be a vicious circle, since lack of demonstrable accountability and representativeness may be used by authorities to justify denying these organizations accreditation. The problem rarely starts there, since the structures of a body trying to represent workers in informal working relations are themselves likely to be relatively diffuse and decentralized. If they were not, there would probably be grounds for suspicion.

Here another problem arises. Many organizations of workers in the informal economy lack the administrative capacity required to be effective, and some look to outside authorities or big business to assist them in capacity building. Such assistance often does not come without influencing the autonomy and independence of the organization, and ultimately its ability to represent the interests of its members, most of all when their interests conflict with those of their benefactors. Opportunistic positioning can easily lead to petty corruption and worse.

---

[15] P. Horn: "Voice regulation and the informal economy", in M. Chen, S. Dasgupta et al.: *Reconceptualizing Work* (Geneva, ILO, forthcoming).

Membership-based organizations: Voice by the "hard to reach"

NGOs. Unions. CSOs. Diverse organizations profess to provide voice for various groups in society. The key words are "providing voice for". Why should organizations provide voice *for* workers, when workers can speak for themselves? Is not true democracy the voice of the people, by the people, and for the people? When considering workers doing informal work, preconceived notions of organization are misleading. A broader form of organization is proposed for such workers: a people's or membership-based organization (MBO).[16]

Workers in the informal economy do not fit into usual structures of representation and bargaining. These presume a fixed employer-employee relationship and a fixed workplace. Trade unions are ineffective when there is no defined employer, no one to bargain with. And outside the union structure, systems do not exist for determining a representative organization for informal workers, with a lack of laws and policies determining how, where and why they can be represented.

According to Renana Jhabvala of SEWA, workers on the "inside" cannot properly represent workers on the "outside". Workers in the formal economy and their unions are not suitable representatives for workers in the informal economy. The only acceptable voice regulation mechanisms for workers in the informal economy are unions and workers' organizations that have organized workers in the informal economy as members and that regularly elect their own representatives.

MBOs take many forms, but their underlying feature is control by the people they serve, with the decision-making body democratically chosen. Control within an MBO can take various shapes. Small organizations can be run, managed and controlled by the members. Bigger organizations would have to hire skilled persons, maybe professionals, but the guiding force should be the workers themselves.

While voluntary action is characteristic of both an NGO and a people's organization, the two differ. An MBO is composed, controlled and run by the people for whom it is intended. An NGO is set up to provide a service to society. It is a voluntary organization without an intended benefit to those who control and manage it. Also, differing from an NGO, a people's organization should be scattered across a country, representing groups in all regions. The people running an MBO are the same people it is serving. And a third feature differentiating MBOs from NGOs is based on the nature of empowerment, which can only come about when people run their own organizations.

What characteristics are common to successful people's organizations? They have agendas that are multi-faceted, dealing with multiple issues and engaging in multiple activities. They are intensely involved in core issues affecting unorganized workers but also address social and economic issues. They intervene in the economy at various levels as well as in social and political processes. And they employ methods of struggle as well as methods of development.

To build up workers' voice in the informal economy, support for their self-governance is needed, and this could begin with NGOs and unions. Typically they have not reached out to informal economy workers. Yet NGOs have a key role to play in the emergence of MBOs, which need financial and moral support for capacity building, and for creating a favourable institutional atmosphere. NGOs can provide this kind of support.

For informal workers to participate in and sustain an effective system of voice, it is necessary for them to form independent, democratic organizations controlled by and accountable to themselves. Such organizations may differ from traditional unions, and require different organizing strategies. Members will need to elect spokespeople to represent them in collective bargaining and in dialogue with various decision-making and power-holding groups.

Changes that benefit the poorest also lead to beneficial effects for those higher up the socio-economic security scale. One could consider this a "trickle-up" principle. Just as worsening conditions for groups at the top levels of society have the effect of pushing down (even further) conditions for those at the bottom, when the poorest segments of society gain improvements, coalitions are formed and conditions also improve for those in middle and upper echelons. In the end, all groups should benefit from efforts to support the least well-off, including workers in the informal economy.

---

[16]For a discussion of MBOs and how they differ from traditional unions and NGOs, see R. Jhabvala: "New forms of workers' organizations: Towards a system of representation and voice", *The Indian Journal of Labour Economics*, Vol. 46, No. 2, April-June 2003, pp. 203–218.

With these important caveats in mind, consider a few examples of promising forms of voice. An outstanding case of a total institution is the Indian Self-Employed Women's Association (SEWA), established in 1972, which has its main base in Gujarat. SEWA, which has nearly 700,000 members, exists to organize women outworkers, and is easily the most advertised organization of its type.

Does SEWA achieve what it sets out to achieve and what it claims? In both respects, the answer is mostly positive. However, in the Gujarat PSS (carried out in collaboration with SEWA), only 21% of all respondents were aware of its existence — 23% of women, 15% of men.

Members perceived SEWA as offering improved security in a wide range of areas. Thus, 97% saw SEWA as offering credit, 86% as offering insurance, 74% as offering training opportunities, 74% as offering housing assistance, 62% as offering healthcare assistance, 58% as offering help with obtaining literacy, and 54% as offering trading opportunities. Less than half the members saw SEWA as offering legal help (49%), childcare (48%), food (47%) and union-type assistance (42%). Nearly all SEWA members had taken advantage of at least one of its services. However, over three-quarters had used its credit facility, while no more than 8% had used any of the other facilities.

Those who belonged to SEWA have apparently gained in terms of an awareness of what matters to them and what they might be able to do about it; this was mentioned by 47% of members as the main advantage. The second most cited advantage, mentioned by 31% of members, was the opportunity to obtain a loan to build up assets, such as housing and equipment for carrying out a small-scale business. By comparison, 8% said that belonging helped build up their confidence, 7% said that it provided employment opportunities, 3.5% said it had helped them to become independent, and 3% did not see any benefit in belonging to it.

The PSS also asked members what they wished SEWA would do that it did not do at present. The most common hope was that it would promote household-based activities, followed by the hope that it would provide basic infrastructure, improve wages for those doing carework, and promote the interest of women in disadvantaged situations.[17]

SEWA as women's voice

Does belonging to SEWA reduce the perception of insecurity? Or do women suffering from intense insecurity join SEWA? Or do those who belong to SEWA come to understand that they suffer from insecurity?

The PSS in Gujarat suggested that membership of SEWA did not enable the women to earn more money than those who did not join. The reasons for joining seemed more broadly social, membership giving the women confidence and a sense of social solidarity. A majority of the women had debts, and many were worried about their capacity to repay those debts. To that extent SEWA had not been able to relieve their financial hardships. But the social benefits were quite evident.

In South Africa, there is a much smaller but nevertheless active Self-Employed Women's Union (SEWU). It exists primarily to promote the interests of women street-traders and is concentrated in the city of Durban.[18] Another significant women's organization of this type is Community, Women and Development (COWAD) in Nigeria, which has been a means of supplying micro-credit and advisory services to women working in informal economic activities.[19] In spite of very difficult political circumstances, it has continued to operate with some redistributive effect.

Apart from women's organizations, there have been various somewhat successful cases of organizations

---

[17]A study of responses to the 2001 Gujarat earthquake found that SEWA performed better than leading UK aid agencies. Its help was judged faster, more effective and better targeted, and better linked to longer-term development concerns. International Federation of Red Cross and Red Crescent Societies: *World Disasters Report* 2003 (Geneva, 2003), p. 138.

[18]Horn, 2004, op. cit.

[19]J. O. Jeminiwa et al.: *Civil Society and Workers' Security: Community, Women and Development* (COWAD) Nigeria, SES Evaluation Report (Geneva, ILO, 2002, mimeo).

of loosely knit groups of workers such as Self-Help Groups in India, and the headload workers in Kerala and Maharashtra.[20] These are examples of collective action, but are mostly limited to what security they can provide to their members.

A different example of an alternative voice organization is VivaRio, a body mainly for providing work and security for young labour force entrants in Rio de Janeiro, though it has also been active in other parts of Brazil.[21] It targets poor youth, the group deemed to be at greatest risk of urban violence and social exclusion, with projects to integrate youth socially by bolstering vocational training and increasing schooling and involvement in local communities and groups.

VivaRio

In the favelas and slums of Rio de Janeiro, an organization has taken shape to give youth avenues to organize their lives, develop skills and become more socially integrated in a non-paternalistic way.

A striking feature of VivaRio is its capacity to reach low-income communities and channel resources to them, marking a break with the traditional paternalism and cronyism that have dogged Brazilian social policy. All its projects are implemented through partnerships with government (federal, state, municipal), private firms and local organizations, as well as with communities themselves and their representatives (churches, neighbourhood associations, etc.). It mediates between funding agencies and programme users, by qualifying demands and adapting projects to local realities and needs. These projects are normally outside government programmes, such as schooling for youth and adults, special types of credit, and information via the Internet.

VivaRio could be seen as an example of a voice organization oriented to strengthening *skill security*. It has established an Internet course, called Tele-Course that provides education to disadvantaged youth, using distance learning videos in classrooms and in their neighbourhoods, supported by instructors. Operated in partnership with the Ministry of Labour, this has been a first step towards the democratization of Internet use, reducing the digital divide between low-income communities and the rest of society. Such has been its perceived success that a similar scheme

is being launched by VivaRio in the Democratic Republic of Timor-Leste.

VivaRio also runs a micro-credit scheme, the first of its kind in Brazil to operate without government funds. It is too early to say whether this has been a success. But it stemmed from a realization that social integration would only occur if slum communities could be economically included in city life.

A major challenge for organizations such as VivaRio is to assemble a representative and professional structure, capable of forming alliances with the community without letting itself be contaminated by the pressures and demands of local politics.

Many community organizations are fledgling trade unions, but the extent to which they contribute to the improvement of work-related security varies considerably. Among promising schemes are the Workers' Fund in the Philippines, and the slum-dwellers' federation in Mumbai, which is organized around housing and public social services, as well as in production.

(iii) *Voice for labour market security*

In many industrialized countries, early labour unions existed primarily as a means of organizing workers in a particular trade to supply their labour in a relatively orderly and secure manner, to check abuses and exploitation. In flexible labour markets, there are signs that this role has been reviving.

An interesting example of how an NGO can become a means of strengthening labour market security and voice simultaneously is the *Korean Construction Workers' Job Centre* (KCWJC) in Seoul, which emerged to help construction workers find decent jobs.[22]

---

[20] R. C. Datta: "Public action, social security and unorganized sector", *Economic and Political Weekly*, Vol. 33, No. 22, 1998; M.S. Pillai: "Social security for workers in the unorganized sector: Experience in Kerala", *Economic and Political Weekly*, Vol. 31, No. 3, 1996, pp. 2098–2107.

[21] B. M. Alasia de Heredia, T. Juvenal, M. Sa Correia and M. Arretche: *Civil Society and Workers' Security: VivaRio*, SES Evaluation Report (Geneva, ILO, 2002, mimeo).

[22] J.-W. Cho et al.: *Civil Society and Workers' Security: Korean Construction Workers' Job Centres*, SES Evaluation Report (Geneva, ILO, 2002, mimeo).

Of the Republic of Korea's 13 million workers, 1.2 million are in construction, over three-quarters of whom are contingent, working as day labourers or as temporary contract labour. These workers live with precariousness, and were hard hit by the Asian crisis of late 1990s, suffering from high unemployment, labour intensification, an absence of even basic social protection and fewer opportunities for part-time work among older workers.

The KCWJC was created to assist construction day labourers through employment placement and job creation. It acts as a labour broker, linking unemployed workers with jobs in construction, using a nationwide infrastructure of job centres, while maintaining close ties with regional unions. It has organized construction workers and has provided advisory services to members, particularly in the sphere of their labour rights.

A main activity is representing individual workers having difficulties on work sites, such as wage arrears and arbitrary dismissal and those suffering workplace accidents. It also administers welfare programmes during periods of crisis, and it lobbies employers to improve working conditions and to protect ageing workers. The long-term *goals* include reforming the industry's employment structure, maintaining skills, helping jobseekers to find jobs, persuading employers to hire more workers, preparing for self-help employment programmes, and protecting the workers' rights. A *policy* aim is elimination of the gang-based contracting practices that dominate the Republic of Korea's labour market.

The construction industry is unique in its form of subcontracting, and complete reliance on foremen to recruit and maintain a workforce, which is nearly entirely tied to gangs. By externalizing responsibility for workers on site, the main contractor can cut labour and management costs. The foreman-based system allows firms to cut wage costs and shift responsibility for workers during recessions. The system allows unethical practices to continue unchecked, including kickbacks and bribes, while middlemen take commissions, further impoverishing workers at the bottom of the pyramid.

Working in conjunction with the construction workers' union to address workers' rights, the centre has achieved a reduction in working time for day labourers — from 12 hours to 9 hours per day. It

has proved effective in placing construction workers in jobs, in 1999-2000 alone placing over one million. But perhaps KCWJC's main advantage lies in its combination of non-profit NGO status with union-like activities to defend workers' interests. It provides a model for building labour market security, which could be applied to other industries characterized by high job turnover.

(iv) *Voice for basic security: Its role in social protection*

For much of the 20th century, workers were expected to have an influential voice in the provision of social protection through tripartite governance structures overseeing social security schemes, and through collective bargaining with employers and government authorities. In some countries, workers' organizations were more directly involved in providing social benefits, in extreme cases being responsible for the collection of contributions and for the disbursement of benefits.

In industrialized countries, such arrangements are rarer these days. But in developing countries many experimental schemes have been giving some role to collective voice organizations, either in policy-making or more commonly in implementing policy as a provider. However, this latter role risks blurring the principal-agent distinction.

The context is crucial. Social policy is evolving rapidly, with numerous selective schemes reaching out to the poor, the insecure and their communities. Many fail to reach their targets, as shown in this report and many others. We oppose conditional means-testing of social security. But if selective schemes are to work half-decently, involving collective bodies of actual or potential users should improve their efficiency and equity. Thus, *participatory poverty assessments* can improve the targeting of benefits, an approach that has had some success in parts of Africa.

In the past decade, *decentralization* has been a new feature of the dominant ideology. Unbundled, the concept involves *delegation* and *devolution* of responsibilities, and a distinction between *political*, *administrative* and *fiscal* decentralization. The idea is that decentralization gives greater scope for participation by local interests, and thus ideally increases the likelihood of reaching the most insecure groups.[23] The trouble is that the potential benefits are seldom realized.[24] Decentralization fails often because of inadequate capacity, poor fiscal control and a lack of accountability to local citizens.[25] Democracy at any level presupposes effective voice, or it is subject to various forms of capture. It presupposes access to information, an effective media, and transparent procedures of government, weak clientelism and much else. Otherwise, decentralization can mean merely "repression being brought closer to the people".[26]

Are voices of the poor poor voice?

The new orthodoxy is that the poor must be consulted and must be heard. This populist assertion, while attractive morally, should not go unquestioned. Almost by definition, a poor person has a weak voice. It is a populist position to imagine or claim that the poor can articulate a long-term view. If they could, they might not be poor. A poor uneducated person is unlikely to appreciate the virtue of learning about mathematics. A poor person is unlikely to understand the evil of gross inequalities, and may imagine that this is the natural order of life. The poor in most of history have been pacified and passive, more anomic than radical. This is not a call for cynicism about the new orthodoxy. It is a call for realism and a recognition that the main call should be for social solidarity based on the principle that policy should be based on "do unto others as you would have them do unto you".

Populist inclusion of the voices of the poor in development or policy-making processes is dangerous, in that it could lead to a false sense of pro-poor consensus. Coached voices are not unknown, and it is often easier to coach someone to ask for something you want him to ask for, if he needs a meal and needs to feel he is liked and will be welcomed back.

Community-based initiatives reduce crime – and fear of crime

The fear of crime is directly related to economic, social and political insecurities. Such findings have been supported by research from Chile, in particular by the UN Development Programme (UNDP).

Community-based initiatives in Chile to reduce crime provide a model for many countries. They contrast favourably with crime control policies based on brute force (policies known as *mano dura*) in other countries in South America. There is evidence that as cities rely more on community-based initiatives to fight crime, citizens' fear of crime decreases. Indeed, it has been shown that citizens who participate in any type of community organization manifest levels of fear that are significantly lower than those who do not participate at all.[27]

---

[23] H. Blair: "Participation and accountability at the periphery: Democratic local governance in six countries", *World Development*, Vol. 28, No. 1, 2000, pp. 21–39.

[24] See, for example, R. Crook and J. Manor: *Democracy and Decentralization in South-East Asia and West Africa: Participation, Accountability and Performance* (Cambridge, Cambridge University Press, 1998); P. Francis and R. James: "Balancing rural poverty reduction and citizen participation: The contradictions of Uganda's decentralization programme", *World Development*, Vol. 31, No. 2, pp. 325–337.

[25] C. Johnson: "Local democracy, democratic decentralization and rural development: Theories, challenges and options for policy", *Development Policy Review*, Vol. 19, 2002, pp. 521–532.

[26] C. Cross and M. Kutengule: *Decentralization and Rural Livelihoods in Malawi*, Working Paper No. 4 (Norwich, University of East Anglia, 2001), p. 6.

[27] L. Dammert and M.F. Malone: *Public Insecurity and Crime Control in South America*, SES Papers (Geneva, ILO, forthcoming).

In *community-managed systems*, governments or donors from abroad encourage local communities to take over or develop a particular sphere of social or infrastructural policy. In several countries, such as Ghana and India, local communities have been delegated responsibility for the design, operation and maintenance of local water supplies. This is appealing. What are the risks?

One is that local communities will not have the expertise to fulfil those responsibilities. Another is that such delegated decentralization may accentuate regional inequalities; the poorest areas may have a relatively weak sense of community or may lack an adequate number of people with education or leadership capacities. Another is elite capture, which may be easier in a highly decentralized system, since local groups are unlikely to be monitored by donors or national policymakers. Another is group capture since, even if initially involved, minorities are easily "crowded out".[28]

Social funds have often emerged in response to social crises, although they have also been stimulated from outside, for instance, by donor agencies. Social funds will be considered in the following chapter. But to have any lasting success, it is essential that the voice of the community play a central role in disseminating fund money and in monitoring its use.

Another admired system is *participative budgeting*, developed in Brazil. Although it existed in other Brazilian cities before Porto Alegre and Belo Horizonte, these are the best known examples.[29] Although there is no single "model", participative budgeting has been widely praised as an attempt to achieve "good" government by involving local people in formulating and implementing decisions on public expenditure. It is seen by its advocates as an important step in building democratic institutions, especially suitable for recently redemocratized countries.

In unequal societies, participative budgeting could be one of the few means of transforming public spending decisions from favours into rights. It could increase the capacity of disadvantaged minorities to influence investment decisions and improve their access to basic urban services. It could also make local democracy more effective in redistributing resources to the poor and insecure, given the traditional power of elites.

Participative budgeting can also improve local democracy by bringing in representatives of social groups from low-income areas that previously had no chance to make decisions regarding their living conditions. But it is salutary to recognize that in the two best-known cases, Porto Alegre and Belo Horizonte, the social and economic conditions were above average for Brazilian cities. This allowed their local governments more room for increasing local taxes, thus giving them more revenue to redistribute through participative budgeting schemes. In both cities, success was greater than in other cities because the local governments managed to be re-elected so that the process could be sustained.

In Belo Horizonte, mass mobilization was achieved by a strategy of allowing participation of individuals and of existing associations, even if seen as clientelist. Regional and thematic plenary assemblies gather in different parts of the city to participate in the budget-writing process. There are two rounds of plenary assemblies in each region, and on each thematic area, for each state. It is not the whole budget that is at stake, and decisions are mostly on alternative infrastructural investment. Thus, the share of total investment laid aside for the participative budget in Porto Alegre's municipal budget has varied from 10% to 17%. In Belo Horizonte, in the first year the participative budget represented only 5% of the total budget.

In Porto Alegre, resources allocated through the participative budget are destined mainly for street paving, sewerage, housing and community equipment. In Belo Horizonte, preferences are for sewerage, street paving, shantytown urbanization, health and education. Both cities have established criteria to assure a progressive distribution of resources so poorer areas receive more funding than richer areas. The process revealed that the citizens' priorities differed from those established or imagined by local government. In the first year in Porto Alegre, the administration thought the poor's priority would be public transport, but what they voted for was water supply and sewerage.

---

[28]L. Pritchett, A. Wetterberg and V. Alatas: *Voice Lessons: Evidence on Social Organizations, Government Mandated Organizations and Governance from Indonesia's Local Level Institutions Study* (Boston, Kennedy School of Government, Harvard University, 2001).

[29]C. Souza: *Participatory Budgeting in Brazilian Cities: Limits and Possibilities in Building Democratic Institutions*, SES Evaluation Reports (Geneva, ILO, 2002, mimeo).

Inhabitants in Porto Alegre have a higher rate of associational activity, political awareness and communal trust compared with inhabitants of most Brazilian cities. Participants have been a balanced group of men and women with an average age of 41. In Belo Horizonte, women represented 45% of delegates to the participative budgeting process, and a majority of delegates were aged between 31 and 40. In both cities, one-third of delegates had not completed primary school, with most participants coming from the poorest sections of society. In both cities, roughly 40% of the people expressed their belief in civic associations of some type to defend their interests, although in both communities scepticism was higher than trust.

In Porto Alegre, an estimated 16,000 people belonging to 300 grassroots movements have participated in the participative budgeting process. In Belo Horizonte, 15,700 people participated in 1994, and 52,900 in 1995, representing 800 grassroots movements. In Porto Alegre, participative budgeting is well known among the local population and over 50% of participants in regional and thematic assemblies claim to have benefited from it. In Belo Horizonte, 85% of delegates approved of participative budgeting, claiming it allowed people to decide how to invest government money. However, half said that the main problem was the limited amount of resources.

Participative budgeting has had an impact beyond the budgeting process itself, affecting other government and social practices and institutions. It is a way of tackling a tradition of secrecy in public budgeting and making decision-making more transparent. The levels of public resources and expenditure are disclosed to participants and to the media, thus discouraging negotiations based on vested interests, such as those facilitating clientelism and corruption. But success requires several preconditions, including the political will to cede power to associations, a rejection of clientelism, a willingness to delegate some financial control, and the capacity to allocate adequate resources. With these preconditions, participative budgeting could become generalized in municipal administration.

There is wide agreement that in Brazil the process has been able to reflect the priorities of the poor. In increasing transparency, accountability and credibility, it can be a way of challenging clientelism,

authoritarianism and paternalism. It is changing the political life of both cities, and is an innovative instrument for reconstruction of public life, allowing a new relationship between local public power, popular organizations and society to address the demands of the poorest groups; it encourages more urban associationism and a stronger relationship between community associations and district dwellers. Being a relatively equitable means of deciding on resource allocation, it can be seen as a way of advancing basic security.

Another model is the *panchayat* system in India. The *panchayats* are village councils, whose administrative and fiscal authority has been enhanced through amendments to the Indian Constitution. Nowhere is their new-found authority more evident than in the southern state of Kerala, where hundreds of thousands of women have mobilized themselves under the *panchayat* umbrella, helping in the organization of work, the provision of credit and much else.[30]

In many poor communities and poor countries, one of the most basic needs of all is *voice for sanitation*. The lack of community infrastructure combined with poor habits can have devastating effects on the welfare of whole communities. It is recognized that the "supply-driven approach", in which public or private commercial agencies install sanitation systems, is often unsuccessful or only partially successful because the community is not mobilized.[31] Sanitation is a social solidarity issue. A campaign around the slogan "Voice for sanitation" may not be very attractive, but it could save millions of lives, especially if built around what is called the *total sanitation approach*, involving community-based initiatives.

---

[30] T.M.T. Isaac, M. Williams, P. Chakraborthy and B. Thampi: *Women Neighbourhood Groups: Towards a New Perspective*, paper presented at an ILO seminar on Decentralization, Sustainable Development and Social Security, Mararikulum, Kerala, India, May 2002.

[31] A celebrated example occurred in Maharashtra, India. It changed from a latrine subsidy scheme, which had a high failure rate, to a scheme that rewarded communities for good sanitation, which resulted in a rapid adoption of total sanitation.

Another innovation of recent years is the use of report cards, by which clients are encouraged to participate in monitoring service delivery. These have been used with apparent success in India.[32] Monitoring as an integral part of social protection policy seems to be part of the countervailing strategy for security, with various initiatives giving voice to citizens as clients.[33] If citizens are involved in collecting and using information themselves, better and more equitable decision-making should result.

(v) Faith-based voice

Strongly encouraged by several governments of advanced industrialized countries, a growing phenomenon has been for religious organizations to become informal or formal agencies for dispensing benefits and services for the poor.[34] While some 20th century initiatives have thrived and become important contributors to community welfare,[35] the new growth areas of "faith-based" activity are rather different. Two types of body predominate, which can be called *evangelical* and *faith-based*. The former is more sectarian, in that it exists for those of the chosen faith, and requires beneficiaries to subscribe to that faith. The latter may bring together people of a certain faith, but does not require members or clients to subscribe to it.

Since membership of churches and religious bodies remains more extensive than membership of any other civil society organization in many countries, as the data cited earlier demonstrated, it is not surprising that they are a convenient and still widely used means of providing economic security. In contexts characterized by a failed or withered State, it is equally unsurprising to find that the poor and insecure turn more to such bodies for help and to find that international donors look to them as a viable means of reaching the poor.

Faith-based NGOs may offer more service than state counterparts, although this may reflect a shortage of funds and staff in the latter. They may also pay lower wages to their staff and charge clients less. They may also reach some groups that would not be reached by public or commercial bodies.

However, there are problems. They are almost certainly highly paternalistic and also prone to attach behavioural and other forms of conditionality. There are well-known reasons for wanting a separation of "church" and "state", and there is always a danger, however small in many societies, for religious sectarianism to be encouraged if there is excessive reliance on religious bodies to operate social policy.

They are likely to be selective in choosing whom they help and whom they do not, a practice that is not conducive to an equitable set of social policies. Finally, although many faith-based NGOs may appear to be the most altruistic type of body for dispensing social benefits and services, altruism cannot be presumed.

(vi) Voice versus corruption

Poverty, income insecurity and economic stagnation are worsened by many forms of corruption. The extent to which these practices accentuate social and economic insecurities is almost certainly underestimated. And almost certainly the pattern of financial transfers contributes to a worsening of income

---

[32] P. Samuel: *Making Voices Work: The Report Card on Bangalore's Public Service*, World Bank Policy Research Working Paper Series 1921 (Washington, DC, World Bank, 1998).

[33] L. Gilson et al.: "Strategies for promoting equity: Experience with community financing in three African countries", *Health Policy*, Vol. 58, No. 1, 2001, pp. 37–67.

[34] L. Gilson et al.: "Should African governments contract out clinical health services to church providers", in S. Bennet, B. McPake and A. Mills (eds.): *Private Health Providers in Developing Countries: Serving the Public Interest?* (London and New Jersey, Zed Books, 1997).

[35] See, for instance, S. Eliesh et al.: *Combating Labour Insecurity in Egypt — Do "NGOs" have a Significant Role to Play*, SES Evaluation Reports (Geneva, ILO, 2002, mimeo).

inequality. The poor are not only more likely to have to pay bribes but are likely to have to pay a larger proportion of their incomes, as has been observed in Romania, for instance.[36]

Collective voice can be a crucial means of combating many of these practices. Risk of exposure by such groups may deter some petty corruption. It may also block some types of behaviour, such as demands from middlemen for payments from hired workers. If one individual refuses, the middleman can turn elsewhere. If the group refuses, the bribe pool dries up.

The biggest drawback of relying on voice organizations as a bulwark against corruption is that they can become an easy target for the corrupters. They can do good, but not too much should be expected of them.

(vii) NGOs: Empty vessels or swords of justice?

Should NGOs be the new providers of security? They should surely have a vital role in giving voice to citizens by exposing abuses, by providing the material for *self-regulating*, and by identifying and disseminating information that can be used by citizens politically and as clients, policymakers and service providers. It is when NGOs go beyond that, either voluntarily or by being co-opted to be providers of services that problems are most likely to arise.

A crucial challenge is to ensure that voice organizations do not become *rent seekers*, looking after their special interests to the detriment of others. The more powerful the voice, the more likely that will be a tendency. Several analysts have shown that vociferous urban groups have been able to steer resources to their needs, even though other groups endured greater hardships.

NGOs can, however, promote basic security by playing a *supportive* role in the implementation and operationalization of social policy. They can help break down taboos or inertia. Since they may be held accountable, the *shadow of the future* hangs over them when they undertake this role, which should minimize opportunistic lobbying for special interests. Among examples of perceived success in this role has been the activity of the Bangladesh Rural Advancement Committee (BRAC), whose community

workers are trained to find the extremely poor in their communities.[37] Others include the numerous NGOs in India that have assiduously sought out children doing labour and helped arrange for them to go to school and providing innovative education for street children. These efforts can only be saluted, even if some might be amateurish.

Using voice organizations for direct *service provision* is more problematical. It can work.[38] But problems *of moral hazard* and *immoral hazard* do arise. To maximize the resources they receive, organizations may exaggerate the plight of their communities, and they may have a perverse incentive to ensure continuing transfers. In addition, there is the perennial tendency for *elite capture*, by which rich or well-placed minorities obtain the funds or services provided.

(viii) Voice for information

Access to information is part of basic security. In this supposedly "linked-up" era, more and more people should be enabled to find out about policies and institutions that could improve their social and economic security, and how to obtain services and redress against wrongs.

Coupled with the Internet, NGOs around the world have become marvellous vehicles for collating information needed to enhance various forms of security. The difficulty is that the ratio of noise to substance has risen too. Each interest requires a specialized *information service*. The notion of an international financial agency, such as the World Bank, becoming what it said it wished to become, "the knowledge Bank", is a frightening prospect, because of the high risk of monopolizing information and dominance of policy analysis.

---

[36]J. Anderson, D. Kauffman and F. Recanatini: *Service Delivery, Poverty and Corruption — Common Threads from Diagnostic Surveys*, paper for the World Bank's World Development Report (Washington, DC, 2004).

[37]A. Hadi: "Promoting health knowledge through microcredit programmes: Experience of BRAC in Bangladesh", *Health Promotion International*, Vol. 16, No. 3, pp. 219–228.

[38]Examples include the Bamako Initiative and the community-led health programmes in Peru. See, for example, S. Mehrotra and S.W. Jarrett: "Improving basic health service delivery in low-income countries", *Social Science and Medicines*, Vol. 54, No. 11, 2002, pp. 1685–1690.

Among the initiatives that deserve to be replicated and refined is the one mentioned in Chapter 10, known as the *London Hazards* Centre, which collates and disseminates information on work security. Something similar should be developed in every country.

At the other end of the development scale, in India an example of a successful voice-for-information initiative was the *Mazdoor Kisan Shakti Sangathan* (Organization of Labourer and Peasant Power, MKSS). Set up in 1991 to organize "public hearings", this had the aim of exposing "ghost projects" – that is, government schemes for providing social and economic security for which funds had been allocated but which somehow did not exist. The voice was heard, in that retributive justice was meted out to corrupt officials. But the best outcome was a Right to Information Act in the state of Rajasthan, where the MKSS had its base.

(ix) Voice for care work

It is a fundamental tenet of this report that all forms of work should be conducted in conditions of basic security. This must include the vital work of *care*, which encompasses a wide array of tasks conducted by more people than any other form of work in all parts of the world, a disproportionate amount done by women.

It is a shocking indictment of 20th century labour policy that there was little or no representation security for this type of work, for those doing it and for those on the receiving end of care.

What is needed is a voice for those receiving care,[39] a voice for those providing care and a voice for those in the middle, the intermediaries.[40] One of the most exciting developments in recent years has been the emergence of national organizations to represent caregivers, a promising example being the Irish Careworkers' Association. Others are the United Kingdom carers' movement, and various bodies in the United States, such as the Service Employees' International Union.[41]

Even in developing countries, there is scope for involving communities and groups of "care-givers" in defending the rights and interests of those working to care for children, the elderly and others.[42] As will

be shown in the final chapter, there is considerable popular sentiment that such work should be compensated and supported.

13.7 Pension funds and worker voice

The global shift to defined-contribution pension schemes puts workers at risk. So it is only fair to ensure that the workers who contribute to the schemes should have a voice, if not the final say, in how the funds are invested and distributed. The US Steelworkers Union has argued that workers should have more control over their own pension funds, which should diversify pension fund assets to help restructure regions where steel production is shrinking.[43] The steelworkers are not alone. In effect, millions of workers are shareholders in pension funds but do not have control over assets that are in their name.

At present, company pension plans are mainly controlled by employers, who appoint trustees and fund managers. None is normally accountable to the workers, who are both dependent on the scheme for pensions and are nominal shareholders, giving rise to what has been called a "double accountability deficit".[44] Workers' insecurity is intensified and their voice is ignored. Although this may seem to be largely a concern for workers in industrialized countries, private pension schemes are spreading and the need for proper voice everywhere will grow rapidly.

As with all forms of representation, whatever emerges must be more than tokenism. Those whose

[39] For papers on this, see M. Daly (ed.): *Care Work: The Quest for Security* (Geneva, ILO, 2001).

[40] E. Collins-Hughes: "Caring for carers: An example from Ireland", in ibid, pp. 211–218.

[41] M. Barnes: "From private carer to public actor: The Carers' Movement in England" in ibid, pp. 195–210; J. Walsh: "Creating unions, creating employers: A Los Angeles home-care campaign", in ibid, pp. 219–233.

[42] K. Dixon-Fyle: *Social Policy with Respect to Care: A Perspective for Sub-Saharan Africa*, SES Paper No. 27 (Geneva, ILO, 2002).

[43] A. Fong, T. Hebb and J. Rogers (eds.): *Working Capital: The Power of Labor's Pensions* (Ithaca and London, Cornell University Press, 2001).

[44] A. Sykes: *Capitalism for Tomorrow: Reuniting Ownership and Control* (Oxford, Capstone, 2000).

contributions go into pension funds should be able to obtain full information on what is done with the money, and should be able to influence decisions on investments. In some cases, pension funds (including government funds) have paid out rather low pensions and have "over-invested" in long-term assets or have diverted funds to questionable uses. The capacity to monitor and to audit must be developed in compliance with standard principles of accountability.

This is scarcely a marginal issue. At the outset of the 21st century, the assets of US pension funds were more than USD7 trillion. And pension funds have been growing very rapidly in many parts of the world. It is encouraging that some "activist shareholders" are emerging, most notably Calpers, one of the largest pension funds in the world, managing over USD150 billion of assets and employing many other fund managers. In February 2002, it announced that it would withdraw from all investments in Indonesia, Malaysia, the Philippines and Thailand, because of its concern over social conditions there and its decision to revise its "permissible countries" criteria to give weight to labour standards as well as to market regulation, investor protection and accounting transparency.[45]

Was this genuine or "tokenism" or "disguised protectionism"? Workers without rights, in export processing zones in particular, must hope that it will be a force for good. Evaluations by independent monitors are required, but this is an example of how pension funds could become a force for security.

13.8 Corporate social responsibility and "stakeholder" voice

Trust in managers

In Ukraine, nearly half the workers (47%) say they would trust management to look after their welfare, with women being slightly more trusting than men.

In Hungary, only one in four workers said they trusted their employer to look after their interests one in three men and one in five women. About one in seven felt they could express grievances and raise personal issues with their employer.

In Tanzania, 78% of workers trust management to look after their welfare. In South Africa, that figure is 45%, although over 50% feel they are able to express grievances to their employer.

In recent years, attempts to guide companies to behave "socially" and "responsibly" have spawned a virtual industry in *corporate social responsibility* (CSR). This has been due, in part, to the growth of multinational and transnational investment, in part to a loss of faith in statutory regulations (pushed by the World Bank, IMF and others in the 1980s, in particular), in part to growing concern over ecological sustainability, in part to the growth of "civil society", and in part to the liberalization drive led by GATT and then the WTO. The result has been a plethora of "codes of conduct", CSR "reporting systems" and third-party "social auditing" proposals.

A criticism of *codes of conduct* is that by no means all firms that claim to have them share compliance information with the public (less than one in four), and even fewer subject themselves to third-party auditing.[46] Perhaps because they allow for a wide array of interpretations, codes have proliferated, without consensus on what they should include or on how they might be used to best effect. It has been said, correctly, that "making a code fully operational takes years. Management systems are still in their infancy, which makes it hard to assess the effectiveness of these private initiatives. Clearly, the intense code activity of recent years has kept a spotlight on undesirable practices."[47]

As far as CSR *reporting is concerned*, there has been an extraordinary growth in its incidence, focused on environmental and social issues. A survey found that, in 2002, 45% of the world's largest 250 companies produced such reports, up from 35% in 1999.[48] But there are many sets of guidelines on what such reports should contain, and much of what has been done is public relations. As one CSR consultant put it, "The increase in reporting is good news. But there's still too much fluff about".[49]

---

[45]"Calpers on Asian retreat: A victory for ethics", *Financial Times*, 22 Feb. 2002.

[46]J. Ruggie: "Managing corporate social responsibility", *Financial Times*, 25 Oct. 2002.

[47]B. Fliess: "Better business behaviour", *OECD Observer*, No. 229, Nov. 2001, p. 53.

[48]KPMG: KPMG *International Survey of Corporate Sustainability Reporting 2002*. See <http://www.globalreporting.org>.

[49]Peter Knight, director of Context, quoted in report on "Sustainable business", *Financial Times*, 23 Aug. 2002, p. VIII.

At the global level, the most newsworthy development has been the UN's *Global Compact*, launched in Davos in January 1999, and formalized in New York in July 2000. This advocates what has been called *voluntary corporate citizenship*. All of those three words raise awkward questions.

There are advantages in a voluntaristic approach. After all, there are laws and institutions that aim to ensure compliance with minimum standards. An advantage of a voluntary approach is that *aspirations* can be set higher; a second is that it is easier to obtain *consensus* on principles and practices to espouse. A downside of a voluntary approach compared with a mandatory one is that there may be a higher probability of "window dressing" (or "bluewash", as it has been called), because everything depends on moral suasion and the appeal of belonging to a club of laudable people.[50] Moreover, there is a "free rider" problem in that firms that do not adhere to a voluntary code of conduct may be able to lower their costs and out-compete those that do.[51]

The view that CSR should be voluntary has been subject to extensive criticism. Thus, in the early 1990s the G77 (Group of 135 developing countries) had a dispute with the OECD, the G77 wanting a binding code, the OECD advocating a non-binding one. Later, spokesmen from developing countries came to suspect any proposal for mandatory schemes as a disguised form of protectionism.

Rather than discuss this further, we may just recall that the Global Compact requires companies wishing "to embrace universal principles to make globalization more stable and inclusive by embedding markets in shared values" to commit themselves to *nine principles,* covering protection of human rights (supporting them in general and ensuring their own firms respect them in particular), core labour standards (on freedom of association, child labour, forced labour and anti-discrimination), and environmental protection (supporting a "precautionary approach", undertaking environmental initiatives and encouraging "environmentally friendly technologies"). There has also been talk of adding a tenth principle, on opposing corruption. By early 2004, over 1,200 companies in more than 70 countries had signed up to the Global Compact.

The Global Compact is an effort to move from abstract principles "downwards" to firms. This is a potentially good feature, although it imposes a responsibility on those driving the strategy to make the requirements sufficiently specific. However, there is a danger of elitism — enlisting big-name executives of brand-name corporations who can meet at Davos and at other attractive venues, and do little more.[52] The Compact has no capacity to check whether or not a chief executive's stated commitment to the nine principles actually changes company behaviour. The hope is there, and the UN's unit dealing with the Compact believes that through it "United Nations' values are penetrating the texture of leading companies".[53] The trouble is that the Compact has no monitoring or regulatory function.[54]

---

[50] Among organizations pushing for mandatory multilateral rules to enforce labour and environmental standards are Friends of the Earth and Greenpeace. The British charity Christian Aid has even proposed there should be a "global regulator" to enforce a code of conduct. It is often presumed that opposition to voluntarism comes exclusively from unions and NGOs. However, some executives are against it. Sir Geoffrey Chandler, former Shell executive and senior civil servant, told a public meeting that "voluntarism never works". Cited in supplement on CSR, *The Observer* (London), 2 Feb. 2003, p. 6. More often, the scepticism comes from spokespeople for the trade unions. Thus, David Coats of the UK's Trade Union Congress asserted: "Much of the CSR stuff companies do is little more than a smokescreen to avoid statutory legislation. Most corporate responsibility programmes do not involve workers' rights. These tend to be dealt with separately". The Observer (London), 8 July 2001.

[51] E.V.K. FitzGerald: *Regulating Large International Firms*, UNRISD Technology, Business and Society Programme Paper 5, (Geneva, UNRISD, 2002).

[52] It was unfortunate that the person appointed as special adviser on the Global Compact, the former chief executive of ABB, withdrew after a year when it was revealed that he had received about USD50 million in pension benefits, some of which he was asked to repay. *Associated Press*, 1 Mar. 2002.

[53] Quoted in "Making a commitment to corporate citizenship", *Financial Times*, 12 Feb. 2003.

[54] At its annual session in spring 2004, the UN Commission on Human Rights is due to consider adopting *Norms on the Responsibilities of Transnational Corporations and Other Business Enterprises with Regard to Human Rights*. The draft norms codify company responsibilities under existing international human rights laws and standards, and endorse independent monitoring and other review mechanisms to hold firms accountable

Another problem is the uncritical view of globalization that seems to underlie it. According to the executive head of the UN's Global Compact Office, "poverty is caused by too little globalization, not too much", while the Compact "tries to stay away from politics — we are beyond ideology". Since ideology is about values and ethics, only by staying in the abstract realm of overarching principles can one be "beyond" it.

Another global activity is the *Global Reporting Initiative* (GRI), conceived in 1997, and launched by the US-based Coalition for Environmentally Responsible Economies in partnership with the United Nations Environment Programme. An ambitious attempt to induce companies to report on "the triple bottom line", the GRI is "an international multi-stakeholder effort to create a common framework for voluntary reporting of the economic, environmental and social impact of organization-level activity".[55] As demonstrated in its *Sustainability Reporting Guidelines,* it is very complicated. The Guidelines are not intended to be a code or set of principles of conduct, or a performance standard, or a management system[56] Such a venture will require sensitive handling. The only way to do justice to the GRI's scope is to study the extensive documentation it has generated. According to GRI's chief executive, Allen White, by mid-2002 more than 2,500 corporate environmental or sustainability reports had been published. As of 2003, the GRI required reporting on 57 "core indicators" of performance and 53 "voluntary indicators".

The complexity highlights a difficulty inherent in this sort of initiative. It tries to cover all the angles, and is thus in danger of being choked with detail and bureaucratization under the weight of the offsetting voices steering the initiative. Perhaps unfairly, it has also been criticized for apparently proposing a "one-size-fits-all" reporting framework, applicable to all sectors, all sizes of firm and so on.[57] These issues may have been taken into account by the people driving the GRI. However, it is apparent that applying the GRI can be very expensive.[58]

To some extent, the GRI and other initiatives have built on guidelines established by the OECD and the ILO in the late 1970s. The OECD issued its *Guidelines for Multinational Enterprises* in 1976, which it revised in 1991 and 2000; the ILO issued its *Tripartite Declaration of Principles concerning Multinational Enterprises and Social Policy* in 1977 (revised 2000).[59] The OECD Guidelines encouraged corporations to adhere to standards of *disclosure, labour relations, environment, bribery, consumer interests, competition, taxation and technology.*[60] A significant change following the 2000 revision was the establishment of *national contact points* (NCPs) to monitor the voluntary Guidelines, which the ILO believes has strengthened their implementation.[61] At the time it was agreed, the US government representative said that the revised Guidelines would promote "a race to the top" in standards of corporate behaviour.

The *European Commission* has also become more active in promoting CSR. In 2001 it published a Green Paper (consultative document), followed in July 2002 by a Communication in which "the Commission presents a EU strategy to promote CSR".[62]

---

[55] *Global Reporting Initiative.* See also <http://www.globalreporting.org>.

[56] Global Reporting Initiative: *Sustainability Reporting Guidelines 2002* (Boston, GRI, 2002), p. 8.

[57] For instance, BP has argued that the GRI over-aggregates data from across the company, and has thus not used the GRI guidelines. In response to such criticism, one GRI board member has claimed, "We are in year five of a 30-year process." A. Maitland: "Businesses are called to account", *Financial Times*, 28 Mar. 2002, p. 11.

[58] One company that compiled a report using the GRI guidelines, Baxter International, the healthcare company, stated that its exercise cost USD625,000 over the two years it took to complete it. A. Maitland: "Pressures mount for greater disclosure", *Financial Times*, 10 Dec. 2002.

[59] Other codes of conduct for multinationals have included the *Global Sullivan Principles*, drafted in 1976 for employment practices in South Africa, the *UN Draft Code of Conduct for Transnational Corporations*, drawn up in 1977 and abandoned in 1992, and the *Caux Round Table Principles*, drafted in 1986 by a coalition of business executives from North America, Europe and Japan.

[60] At the time of its revision, the government of Mexico objected strongly, claiming that although the guidelines were voluntary and not legally binding, it believed such voluntary standards had deprived Mexico of investment from other members of NAFTA. *Financial Times*, 24 June 2000.

[61] Working Party on the Social Dimension of Globalization: *Information Note on Corporate Social Responsibility and International Labour Standards*, fourth item on the Agenda, ILO Governing Body (Geneva, ILO, Mar. 2003), p. 11. The ILO has also established a Business And Social Initiatives database (BASI), see <http://www.ilo.org/basi>.

[62] European Commission, Directorate-General for Employment and Social Affairs: *Corporate Social Responsibility: A Business Contribution to Sustainable Development* (Luxembourg, The Office for the Official Publications of European Communities, 2002). This can be accessed via <http://europa.eu.int>.

This is a succinct statement of mainstream views on the subject, placing emphasis on the *voluntary* nature of CSR (contrary to the position advocated by trade unions and various other non-governmental organizations), and a need for *transparency* and *credibility*. It advocates a "balanced and all-encompassing approach to CSR", recognizes the special situation of small and medium-sized enterprises, and commits the European Union to support the ILO's core labour standards and the OECD's Guidelines for Multinational Enterprises.

The "strategy" the European Commission proposes is impressive — to increase knowledge of the impact of CSR, develop an exchange of information on good practice, promote management skills in CSR, facilitate convergence and transparency of CSR practices, and integrate CSR into EU policies. It has launched a *Multi-Stakeholder Forum on CSR* at EU level.[63] In this, as in so much of the CSR movement, the biggest challenge will be to move beyond abstract principles to practical measures. It is relevant to note that when the European Commission launched consultations on rules to guarantee "socially intelligent restructuring" of companies and sectors at the beginning of 2002, it ran into heavy opposition from UNICE, the European employers' federation.[64]

The World Bank has also stepped up its interest. It initiated a programme called *Business Partners for Development* (BPD) to encourage firms, governments and community groups to pool expertise to tackle social issues in developing countries.[65] And its International Finance Corporation (IFC) has established an *IFC corporate citizenship facility*, in part to help its clients and private firms in emerging markets to identify appropriate investment opportunities. The IFC has developed a framework for measuring private investment sustainability, which includes assessment of workers' health, safety and welfare. Actions that companies are asked to take include compliance with ILO Conventions, paying "somewhat higher wages than average" and meeting the ILO Code of Practice on HIV/AIDS.

Not to be outdone, the *World Economic Forum* launched the WEF's global corporate citizenship initiative in 2002, and focused on the need to "rebuild" trust at its 2003 Davos meeting. The 31 chief executives included in its survey all said they were developing measures and targets for their "leadership teams" on CSR or corporate citizenship. A majority said there was a merging of the corporate citizenship and corporate governance agendas in their companies, no doubt due to the loss of trust engendered by the Enron and other corporate scandals of the recent past.

There have also been numerous national initiatives. In the United States, the CSR movement, spearheaded by the GRI, was boosted by the establishment of *Business Strengthening America* (BSA) in December 2002, whose aim is "to encourage civic engagement and volunteer service in corporate America". This had the support of President George W. Bush and some high-profile corporate executives. Early signs are that it is designed to improve the image of corporations in the wake of business scandals and to encourage businesses to "do well by doing good". It does not seem to be a means of focusing on what is appropriate to do in their own domains, and thus may exist outside the reporting frameworks.

A relatively promising tendency in the United States has been shareholder activism in favour of CSR, led by pension funds. Another recent trend has been for leading companies to invest in the monitoring process by non-governmental organizations. In 1999, Nike gave USD7.7 million to the International Youth Foundation to set up the Global Alliance for Workers and Communities to monitor the practices of subcontractors.

In the United Kingdom, there is the government-backed Ethical Trading Initiative (ETI), a tripartite body consisting of employers, unions and campaigning groups, which developed a code based on ILO Conventions.[66] *Business in the Community* (BITC) sets out to help companies quantify performance on

---

[63] Although the Communication on the Forum does not mention involvement of non-EU organizations, it seems there will be observer status for the ILO, OECD and the UN's Global Compact Office.

[64] As UNICE Secretary-General, Philippe de Buck, stated in January 2002: "When Anna Diamantopoulou [EU Social Affairs Commissioner] calls for a long discussion on corporate restructuring, we say 'Stop'."

[65] <http://www.bpdweb.org>.

[66] For a good review of the ETI and difficulties of implementation, see R. Crowe: "Hard labour to put code into practice", *Financial Times*, 12 June 2001.

a set of indicators covering the marketplace, environment, workplace, community and human rights.[67] In March 2003, the BITC issued a Corporate Responsibility Index, which perhaps comes closest to what the ILO's Socio-Economic Programme is proposing. But its scope is different, as is its methodology.[68] It sets out to measure firms' performance in terms of five "divisions" – environment, employment, community, human rights and consumer issues. It is thus very broad in scope. It is also, so far, very limited in the number of companies it covers, only 122 as of March 2003. It also seems to be a tool for pointing out poor or "irresponsible" performance.

The Danish Ministry of Social Affairs has developed a social index, intended to measure the social responsibility of companies. Enterprises that obtain verification will receive an "S-label". The Danish Confederation of Trade Unions (LO) has proposed that to obtain this, companies should be measured by actual performance.[69]

Among the many national-level and more informal initiatives, one can mention AccountAbility's 1000 (AA1000) framework.[70] Presented by its designers as an auditing complement to the GRI, this has been well advertised, and is designed to improve the accountability of organizations by increasing their social and "ethical" accounting, auditing and reporting. Like the GRI (and others), it espouses a "multi-stake-holder" approach, and covers a broad range of issues.[71]

Another approach is the *ISO model, notably SA8000*.[72] In January 2003, the International Organization for Standardization (ISO) established a CSR Advisory Group (with the ILO, the International Organization of Employers and the International Confederation of Free Trade Unions on board) to consider a CSR management standard. In February 2003, it recommended that ISO should conduct a survey of the worldwide state of the art on social responsibility codes and guidelines and consider preparation of "a management system guideline standard that specifically includes a process for the self-declaration of conformity by organizations and excludes conformity assessment involving third-party certification".[73]

The broad range of issues covered by such "standards" as the ISO model and the AA1000 framework raises a familiar problem of lack of rigour and sharpness. This may be lessened by approaches that are more focused on labour standards per se, such as the proposals of the *Fair Labor Association*, which has conducted "anti-sweatshop" campaigns, and *Social Accountability International*. But in all such cases, heavy demands are placed on inspection and auditing, which seem to be left largely to international consultants and accounting firms, again raising problems of conflict of interest.[74]

Ethical behaviour can pay

Being ethical can pay, at least in Umbria, Italy. There, companies certified under the SA8000 ethical workplace standard have been given preferential treatment when bidding for local government contracts. The Umbria region has introduced a law that allows SA8000-certified firms — of which there are 26 in Italy — to join a dedicated SA8000 register. Providing they are competitive on cost and quality, firms on the register will receive priority when companies are chosen to run franchises or operate contracts on behalf of the local government. Umbria says it has introduced the measures to promote *"a wide spread of knowledge of the importance of the social responsibilities of companies and consumers"*.

[67] See <http://www.bitc.org.uk/corporate-impact>.

[68] For its Business Impact Self-Assessment Tool, see <http://www.business-impact.org/review/>.

[69] Danish Confederation of Trade Unions: *Corporate Social Responsibility — A Discussion Paper* (Copenhagen, LO, 2002), p. 19. The LO has also proposed a "Workplace Knowledge Index".

[70] AccountAbility: *AccountAbility 1000 (AA1000) Framework: Standards, Guidelines and Professional Qualification* (London, Institute of Social and Ethical AccountAbility, 1999).

[71] For a review of multi-stakeholder monitoring initiatives, see M. Urminsky (ed.): *Self-Regulation in the Workplace: Codes of Conduct, Social Labeling and Socially Responsible Investment*, Working Paper Series on Management Systems and Corporate Citizenship No. 1 (Geneva, ILO, 2001), pp. 28–34.

[72] This is based on ISO9000, an auditing technique specifying corrective and preventive actions.

[73] ISO Press Release, 19 Feb. 2003. The group was chaired by a senior vice-president of Alcan.

[74] For discussion of these dilemmas, see G. Standing: "Ratcheting labour standards", in A. Fung, D. O'Rourke and C. Sabel (eds.): *Can We Put an End to Sweatshops?* (Boston, Beacon Press, 2002).

Interestingly, there is a widespread impression that the CSR reporting movement has made less progress on labour and work issues than on environmental and economic issues. As the *Information Note* for the ILO Governing Body of March 2003 concluded, "the labour and employment information disclosure in this type of report is generally quite weak."[75]

In reviewing the issues that are most typically reported, it added: "The subjects least frequently reported on included equal remuneration (a fundamental category), job security, the effect of technology on employment quality and quantity, disciplinary practices and establishing linkages with national enterprises."

The CSR movement is related to the proliferation of *corporate governance initiatives*, which were in part stimulated by the protracted debate on the relative appeal of the continental European "stakeholder" model and the Anglo-Saxon "shareholder" model. No doubt, the characterization of these two types was somewhat simplified and even misleading.[76] Nevertheless, since the late 1990s there has been a period of agonizing over what should constitute good corporate governance.[77] Among the outcomes were the Cadbury Commission and the Turnbull Report in the United Kingdom, the King Report in South Africa, the OECD's *Principles of Corporate Governance*, and the World Bank's *Corporate Governance Forum*.

In several countries, a link has been made between new codes of corporate practice and stock market regulation. Thus, the Johannesburg Stock Exchange requires all listed companies to adhere to the King Report's Code of Corporate Practices and Conduct.

While consultancies and international groups are competing to set guidelines and standards for CSR reporting, the pressure to adhere to CSR principles is coming mainly from the growth of investment funds and related pressure groups for *Socially Responsible Investment* (SRI). There are *funds* that have been established to steer investment to highly rated companies; there are elaborate *ratings*; and there are indexes. But so far there is no evidence of convergence on one type of SRI, one type of SRI fund, one type of rating or one type of index.[78] Nevertheless, the sheer scale of the phenomenon is impressive. In the United States, SRI already accounts for one in nine dollars under professional investment management, amounting to over USD2 trillion.[79]

Many SRI funds have been set up by big commercial funds, and many belong to the *Social Investment Forum*, a non-profit membership organization set up to promote SRI. Many of these funds, not yet a majority, include labour relations criteria and a big majority include equal opportunity and non-discrimination criteria.[80] Some ratings agencies include the full range of the ILO's core labour standards.[81] Many of the funds have been given exotic names; among the more intriguing are the Domini Social Equity Fund in the United States, which "seeks to invest in companies that involve employees in day-to-day operations" (whatever that means), and the Social Awareness Fund of Friends Ivory, which "favours companies that provide excellent workplaces and strong benefits to increase employee loyalty".

---

[75]ILO, 2003, op. cit., p. 8. It draws on work by the ILO's Multinational Enterprises Programme on corporate social reports.

[76]*The Economist* has written a robust defence of the Anglo-Saxon model, claiming it is "far from heartless". *The Economist*, Special Report, 4 Dec. 2002.

[77]The notion of balancing the interests of "multi-stakeholders" is fuzzy. What does "balance" mean in this context? There is no principle by which a manager can guide decisions, nor benchmark on which to judge the outcome. See R.R. Ellsworth: *Leading with Purpose: The New Corporate Realities* (Stanford, CA, Stanford University Press, 2002)

[78]For instance, some SRI funds focus mainly on "sustainability" of financial returns, investing in companies that at best have a positive impact on society and the environment, and at worst are "broadly neutral". See, for example, the report on the SRI part of Morley Fund Management in the supplement on CSR in *The Observer* (London), 2 Feb. 2003.

[79]Social Investment Forum: *2003 Report on Socially Responsible Investing Trends in the United States* (Washington, DC, Social Investment Forum, 2003). See <http://www.socialinvest.org.>

[80]Ibid. This reported that investments using one or more SRI criteria had risen in the United States from USD40 billion in 1984 to over USD2.34 trillion in 2001.

[81]These include EIRIS (Ethical Investment Research Service) and PIRC (Pensions and Investment Research Consultants). For reference to others, see ILO, 2003, op. cit., p. 7.

Finally, there are the "sustainability stock market indexes", the two most well-known of which are the *FTSE4Good Index*[82] and the *Dow Jones Sustainability Index*. The latter was set up in 1999. The FTSE4Good Index was launched in 2001 and screens companies on a wide range of issues, from human rights to their ecological record.[83] Whereas the Dow Jones Index compilers invite companies to apply, the people responsible for compiling the FTSE4Good Index study about 2,200 companies and exclude some sectors and types of producer, in effect excluding about 55% of all companies registered on the FTSE All-Share Index. This has made it somewhat controversial among major pension funds.

Less well known are the indexes used to guide purchasing practice, such as the *Co-op Bank's Ethical Purchasing Index* in the United Kingdom. These indexes are generating other activities. Thus, the consultancy Sustainable Assets Management (SAM) has carried out a survey for the Dow Jones Sustainability Index to determine how many companies are taking account of CSR performance in determining remuneration. In the United Kingdom, there were plans in early 2003 to launch an Ethical Exchange, a kind of alternative stock market for what are being called Alternative Public Offerings.

The promotion of CSR has become part of government policy in a growing number of countries, including Belgium, Denmark, France, the Netherlands and the United Kingdom. There is now a UK minister with responsibility for CSR, and UK law requires pension funds to disclose how they view social, ethical and environmental issues in their investment decisions. The government-backed *Ethical Trading Initiative* brings together unions, companies and NGOs to draw up codes of conduct on labour rights. And the UK's Department for International Development is working with the Canadian International Development Agency to promote CSR in development. In France, the amended *Nouvelles régulations économiques* (NRE) require all nationally listed corporations in France to report to shareholders and stakeholders on various sustainability issues from 2003 onwards.

In sum, Corporate Social Responsibility is so entrenched as a slogan that its immediate future is assured. According to an international survey conducted by PriceWaterhouseCoopers in 2002, 70% of executive directors of global corporations believe that CSR is vital to their company's profitability. And an Environics International survey in 2002 suggested there was widespread support for the view that companies should go beyond "financial philanthropy" to solve "social problems".[84]

Some corporations are even using CSR or corporate citizenship performance to determine executive remuneration explicitly. Is the following a sign of things to come? Olav Fjell, chief executive of Statoil, Norway's largest oil company, linked CSR to his contract:

Indicators related to health, safety, environment and employee satisfaction are included, among others, in my performance contract and are thus used for determining my bonus and form part of my performance review. So far, there are no indicators covering bribery and corruption, security and human rights and community development – but these topics are on the board's agenda and are thus indirectly part of the review of the CEO.[85]

Doing good socially has become part of the executive's job. However, it is far from clear whether the power to do good should be extended to the point where firms become the instrument of many aspects of social policy. The critics should not be dismissed as cynics or unethical apologists.[86] There has been a tendency for rhetorical abstraction to swamp practical, operational measures.

Most CSR advocates recognize that society and the environment depend on responsible behaviour to a

[82] FTSE: *FTSE Develops Standard for Socially Responsible Investment* (2001), available on <http://www.ftse4good.com>.

[83] Companies in some sectors are excluded altogether, such as tobacco and weapons manufacturers. Others are screened by EIRIS, an ethical specialist firm, on environmental sustainability, positive relationships with "stakeholders" and human rights.

[84] Cited in "The financial case for behaving responsibly", *Financial Times*, 19 Aug. 2002, p. 6.

[85] "Tools to build a reputation", Financial Times, 20 Jan. 2003; O. Fjell: "Corporate citizenship: Statoil", *New Solutions: A Journal of Environmental and Occupational Health Policy*, Vol. 13, No. 1, 2003, pp. 43–48.

[86] Not all critics come from "the left" or from disappointed ecologists wanting a mandatory approach. Some economists argue that CSR is doing harm and is part of what the former chief economist of the OECD has called "global salvationism". D. Henderson: *Misguided Virtue: False Notions of Corporate Social Responsibility*, Hobart Paper No. 142, (London, Institute of Economic Affairs, 2001).

much greater extent than can be captured by detailed legislation and complex regulations. Realism requires a balance between idealism and common practice — the realm of decency.

Companies should not be expected to take over responsibility for social policy, and should avoid becoming paternalistic. As Kofi Annan, UN Secretary-General, told a meeting of the Swiss business community in March 2001, "clearly business is about making profits, and public policy is the responsibility of states. If the 20th century taught us anything, it is that when one tries to do the other's job, all sorts of things go wrong."[87]

This statement is tantalizing, since the first part seems to contradict the essence of the CSR movement and the Global Compact. But it returns us to a dilemma emphasized at the outset of this section, the danger that corporate welfare and "social responsibility" could exceed as well as fall short of desirable boundaries. All those working in this field need to keep that in mind.

Our primary interest in all the activity around corporate social responsibility and governance is whether it is promoting voice for social and economic security. This may become clearer in the years ahead.

13.9 A Charter for interest associations?

If the emerging forms of non-governmental organization are to provide an effective voice for the enhancement of security, they must adhere to certain general principles concerning accountability, transparency, democracy and equity. They have to avoid *moral hazards* and *immoral hazards*.

What would a Charter for NGOs look like? It would require all NGOs to take an approach to their own

---

Civil society and human security

"With more than 30,000 international non-governmental organizations and many more local and national NGOs, they are emerging as a visible, credible and accountable force in advancing human security."

— Commission on Human Security[88]

To set up an NGO is not very difficult. But that does not mean that it is an instrument for the advancement of security. A fancy name, an office in a capital city of a rich country, and access to World Bank contracts may not add up to a "credible and accountable force" for social or economic security. To give just one example, NGO-controlled micro-credit organizations are rarely accountable to public scrutiny or to local governments.[89]

---

affairs that they demand of others. Many do this already.[90] However, they need to ensure accountability, transparency, democracy, real participation for their members, and they need to provide information on their sources of funds, the uses to which such funds are put, and the evidence that independent objective auditing, monitoring and evaluation are carried out. Civil society would be greatly strengthened if those principles were respected and if umbrella organizations ensured that they were respected, and where not, that those abusing them were openly identified.

[87]United Nations Office at Geneva, 28 Mar. 2001. Also <http://www.unog.ch>. *The Economist* put it more sharply, "It is no advance for democracy when public policy is 'privatized', and corporate boards take it upon themselves to weigh competing social, economic and environmental goals. That is the job for governments, which remain competent to do it if they choose." *The Economist*, 17 Nov. 2001, p. 84.

[88]Commission on Human Security, 2003, op. cit., p. 88.

[89]V.K. Ramachandran and M. Swaminathan: *Does Informal Credit Provide Security? Rural Banking Policy in India*, SES Paper No. 12 (Geneva, ILO, 2002).

[90]For an account of efforts by humanitarian agencies to develop clearer ethical principles, minimum technical standards and greater accountability to beneficiaries as well as donors, see International Federation of Red Cross and Red Crescent Societies, 2003, op. cit., pp. 135–155.

13.10 Concluding recommendations

Voice is active and can combat a tendency for the passage of time to legitimize the status quo. As David Hume noted in the 18th century, the persistence of any practice over time "reconciles (men) to any authority, and makes it seem just and reasonable".[91] Voice exists to challenge and to propose alternatives, to excite the imagination and to foster the pursuit of justice. It was ever thus, but is more vital in the era of globalization than at any time in human history.

As far as the emerging forms of voice are concerned, the *associational revolution* that is taking place in the world should be seen as a healthy sign of human energy. Of course, traditional vested interests feel under threat, and powerful interests resent their intrusion into their comfort zones. Undoubtedly, there is a lot of chicanery out there. But undoubtedly too, a strong desire to see improvements in the human condition is driving much of what is happening. The greatest challenge is to transform the previously cited assertion from the Commission on Human Security into a reality.

Harnessing the energy for good is the challenge ahead. In that regard, voice remains as important as ever in providing people with a sense of social solidarity and security, an end in itself and an instrument for the attainment of other forms of security.

---

[91] D. Hume: *A Treatise on Human Nature* (1739-40), Book III, Section X.

Chapter 14

Seeking income security

"Until we are a world that recognizes that we have to share, as families share, we will constantly be surprised that there are huge pockets of resentment, of anger, and that a few seem to benefit from globalization and the rest have to pay a very, very heavy price."

— Desmond Tutu, former Archbishop of Cape Town, winner of the 1984 Nobel Peace Prize, December 2001.

14.1 The challenge

Globalization is producing the prospect of pervasive income insecurity everywhere. Is this what we want the 21st century to mean? Surely not. Fortunately, it is also a time of constructive experimentation across the world in addressing the challenge of income insecurity, even though the attentions of mainstream policy-makers and international agencies are diverted elsewhere.

It is clear that income insecurity is the norm everywhere, even in industrialized countries, and that this reflects open economies, flexible labour markets, economic informalization and the abandonment of anything approaching an idealized world of Full Employment based on people being in full-time jobs with contingency benefits.

What are the new policies that promise to improve the situation? Before addressing this question, we first recall what people think should be the principles of just income security and then consider orthodox or mainstream approaches in that light. Finally, we look at promising alternative approaches to the promotion of universal income security, some of which are already in operation on a small scale and others that are under consideration by policy-makers.

14.2 Recalling the policy principles for basic security

Clearly, as shown in Chapter 12, around the world there is a yearning for basic economic security, a popular set of sentiments that together express the view that policies should focus on principles of social and distributive justice. We should search for measures that satisfy both of the policy decision principles enunciated in Chapter 1 — to give priority help to the most insecure and to eschew paternalism in all spheres of social and economic policy.

The preliminary assessment of attitudes to social justice can be helpful. There is widespread support for a needs-based approach to income distribution, demonstrated in the support for a minimum income. This is reason enough to support policies that move societies in that direction. But there is also a suggestion that income insecurity induces people to be more supportive of that principle, more supportive of a progressive redistribution of income, and more supportive of policies to assist the unemployed.

However, people who feel insecure are also more likely to be intolerant and favour discriminatory practices. If it is true that insecurity is growing, policy-makers should be encouraged to favour a needs-based set of policies that are also redistributive, and should do so for the additional reason that this approach would be a means of reducing intolerance and discrimination.

In this regard, the international community could launch a commitment to socio-economic security around the world. This would complement the Millennium Development Goals, but would focus more on economic security and the criteria for assessing policy decisions before they are made. If the United Nations can give so much attention to a Global Compact for business corporations, it should be able to do something similar on economic security. Similarly, if developing countries can form an alliance on trade negotiations, perhaps there is scope for a "Southern" network to drive a social policy agenda. The essential starting point is the need for **public provision** as part of economic security.

A charter on economic security

A good society is one that guarantees all its members equal basic economic security. This requires at least a minimal income on which to survive in decency, and equal voice representation security for all groups in society. The one without the other would be inadequate. However attained, basic income security is essential for real freedom. Collective voice representation is essential to enable the socially vulnerable to have their interests and aspirations taken into account. Without collective voice, there can be no basic socio-economic security.

Development should be assessed by movement in the direction of attaining those two meta-needs. For this, one should add something like the Rawlsian Difference Principle, rephrased as the *Security Difference Principle*:

Policies, regulations and institutional changes shall be deemed socially just only if they improve, or at least do not worsen, the socio-economic security of the least secure groups in society.

This should be coupled with what might be called the *Paternalism Test Principle*, defined as follows:

Policies, regulations and institutional changes are just only if, they do not impose controls on some groups that are not imposed on the most free groups in society.

It is crucial to regard security in positive terms. Security should not be interpreted merely as protection against the consequences of risk (the approach taken by the World Bank's Social Protection Division and presented in the Bank's *World Development Report* for 2001). Security should include a steady "negation of the negation"; it can be advanced only if the diverse controls inhibiting real freedom are systematically removed or made innocuous. For instance, a bonded labourer may have security in some narrowly defined sense, but the controls exercised by a moneylender, a landlord or a trader deny real human security.

Finally, and most crucially of all for the future, in this era of globalization, rapid technological change, flexible labour processes and economic informalization, it is essential that policies, institutions, regulations and new representative organizations should promote *occupational security*. This means creating an environment in which individuals and communities can develop and apply their human competencies and aspirations in real freedom. In sum, social protection and other policies must be assessed not only by whether or not they protect people against contingency risks but by whether or not they give them freedom, incentives and opportunity to develop their own sense of occupation.

There is a further complication that must be kept in mind in assessing the appropriateness of any policy. As indicated in Chapter 2, globalization, global warming and environmental degradation are producing more frequent and more severe crises, shocks and natural disasters. In consequence, informal mechanisms for mitigating and coping with risk are increasingly ineffectual, particularly those that are *group-based*.[1] This is one reason why informal voice institutions are so fragile and why they often can survive only if injected with regular doses of outside financial assistance. If a group of "informal workers" in a local area pools funds, it is reasonable to hope that reciprocal transfers can continue. But if suddenly the whole community is hit, the mechanism is unlikely to survive unless propped up, which may be prohibitively expensive if expanded on any large scale.

---

[1] J. Morduch: "Between the state and the market: Can informal insurance patch the safety net?", *World Bank Research Observer*, Vol. 14, No. 2, 1999, pp. 187–207.

However, the shift to a greater incidence of covariant risk also means that the classic welfare state policies are increasingly inappropriate. They were created to deal with what is known as *idiosyncratic risk* (individual contingencies) rather than *covariant risk* (mass shocks). In the latter case, mass claims on an insurance mechanism in a crisis are likely to lead to collective insurance failure.

For any policy, it is important to consider whether or not it can resolve the *sustainability dilemma*. Often, evaluations of particular mechanisms are carried out in non-crisis periods, making it likely that the results will be biased in a positive direction.

14.3 Orthodox schemes for income security

An enormous amount of money is spent on poverty-reduction schemes, and yet there are probably more people than at any time in human history in poverty and economic insecurity. Instead of a constant refrain to spend "more", attention should focus on how funds for poverty relief are being spent.

Consider the case of India. Annually, the Indian government spends about USD5.5 billion on poverty-reduction programmes.[2] These include transfers to the poorest through the many food distribution schemes (food subsidies, in effect), the National Housing Scheme and the National Old Age Pension Scheme. They also include asset-building schemes (effectively more subsidies), such as the Accelerated Rural Water Supply Programme and the Drought Prone Areas Programme, as well as employment and self-employment promotion schemes. In addition to the USD5.5 billion, a further USD5 billion is spent by other government departments on poverty relief, the biggest programme being that run by the Public Distribution Scheme to provide subsidized food through a national network of "fair price shops".

The amount of expenditure and the sheer range of schemes of selective support are impressive. And yet much of that spending never reaches the poor and economically insecure. The Indian Ten-Year Plan estimated that leakage from the numerous Centrally Sponsored Schemes was between 20% and 70%.

In Brazil until recently, pensions (mainly for civil servants) accounted for two-thirds of social spending, and other programmes that scarcely reached the poor

accounted for most of the remainder. Assistance specifically for the poor amounted to only 0.4% of GDP.[3] This was at a time when various estimates had concluded that about 40 million people were living on less than 240 *reals* (USD80) a month and when 23 million of those people were regarded as living in extreme poverty.

Any other dimension that is too rarely taken into account in assessing the opportunity to provide economic security as a citizenship right is the vast extent of government and donor subsidies to all sorts of interests. Economists know that *subsidies* distort choices, encourage inefficiency and damage the environment. Yet they attract little criticism compared with small transfers to the poor and unemployed.

Some observers have suggested that worldwide subsidies amount to "at least USD2,000 billion a year".[4] This is 3.5 times the amount proposed at the Rio Earth Summit's budget for sustainable development, which governments dismissed as unfeasible. Moreover, subsidies create or strengthen powerful interests that then lobby and cajole to maintain them. Unless those subsidies are substantially reduced and also reallocated, there is little prospect of attaining a world of basic security for all.

---

[2]J. Farrington, N.C. Saxena, T. Barton and R. Nayak: "Post offices, pension and computers: New opportunities for combining growth and social protection in weakly-integrated rural areas?", *ODI Natural Resource Perspectives 87* (London, Overseas Development Institute, 2003). This paragraph draws on the ODI review.

[3]*The Economist,* 16 Aug. 2003, p. 38.

[4]N. Myers and C. Tickell: "The no-win madness of Catch-22 subsidies"; *Financial Times,* 28 July 2003.

End subsidies as we know them!

The world is awash with subsidies. The trouble starts with the fact that they mostly go to the rich.

When the assertion is made that a country or government "cannot afford" to provide its citizens with basic economic security, the first place to look for potential funds should be the subsidy pool, to determine whether or not subsidies are efficient and equitable, or indeed contributing to public welfare.

Agricultural subsidies in the European Union and the United States are notorious, and scarcely need further comment.[5] They harm the income security of poor farmers everywhere, including those in their own countries. Agricultural subsidies comprise about half of the total budget of the EU.

Examples are almost invidious, since hefty subsidies to affluent interests are so widespread. But studies have shown that they are substantial and wasteful in many countries, including Japan, Poland, Ireland, Israel, the Republic of Korea, Sweden and the United States.[6]

In Latin America, the incidence of subsidies has been a major factor in the ecological decay taking place across the continent. As one critic has observed tersely, the subsidies have gone to powerful elites:

"These are the groups that have become enormously rich by benefiting from tax exemptions, tax holidays, financial grants, cheap public credit, free access to natural resources, almost unlimited effective rights to pollute air, water, etc."

Most subsidies are transfers to private firms rather than to private citizens, let alone private poor citizens. Subsidies, according to basic economics, always induce inefficiency.[7] They are bad economies. They are bad social policy.

(i) Food subsidies

Food subsidies have always had backing among those wishing to relieve poverty. Possibly the biggest single programme is the Indian Public Distribution Scheme, in which over 450,000 "fair price shops" provide some 160 million Indian families with subsidized food. This hugely expensive programme involves a complex storage and acquisition scheme.

When some observers claim that only a tiny percentage of the Indian population are "covered" by social security, and call for an "extension" so that a larger percentage are "covered", they are implicitly overlooking the existence of this and a number of other forms of "social protection". It is precisely for that reason that it is necessary to look at the system overall rather than just at conventional schemes of social security.

Food subsidies are intrinsically paternalistic. They also involve considerable transaction costs that gobble funds ostensibly allocated for poverty relief. As noted above, according to analysis of the Indian scheme, at least 20% of the funds disbursed through fair price shops fail to reach the poor, and for some schemes the leakage is as high as 70%.[8] Subsidy programmes tend to be subject to similar failings

wherever they operate, and these tend to be greater and more damaging the less developed the administrative structures, the more undeveloped the economy and the poorer the population. They are too complex, and they are vulnerable to misappropriation. Thus, in India resources tend to be diverted to political supporters, and while local

---

[5] Among the biggest US beneficiaries of subsidies has been the Boswell family, the world's largest cotton grower, which became very wealthy "harvesting government subsidies" ranging from crop insurance, set-asides, payments in kind, marketing loans, export subsidies, flood-control benefits and cheap irrigation water. M. Arax and R. Wartzman: *The King of California: J.G. Boswell and the Making of a Secret American Empire* (New York, Public Affairs, 2003).

[6] See, for example, R. Beason and D. Weinstein: "Growth, economies of scale and targeting in Japan", *Review of Economics and Statistics*, Vol. 78, No. 2, pp. 286–295; F. Bergstrom: *Capital Subsidies and the Performance of Firms*, Working Paper No. 285 (Stockholm, Stockholm School of Economics, 1998); G. Fournier and D. Rasmussen: "Targeted capital subsidies and economic welfare", *Cato Journal*, 1986, pp. 295–312.

[7] R. Lopez: "The policy roots of socio-economic stagnation and environmental implosion: Latin America 1950-2000", *World Development*, Vol. 31, No. 2, 2003, p. 273.

[8] J. Farrington and N.C. Saxena: "Protecting and promoting livelihoods in rural India: What role for pensions?", *ODI Annual Report 2002/2003* (London, Overseas Development Institute, 2003), p. 20.

officials expect and receive "special payments", the subsidized items often go to those not needing or not entitled to them. Moreover, contractors typically distort procedures to divert surplus to themselves or to share with local officials.

Direct food provision in India for midday meals in schools has had a positive effect on school attendance, but the programme is expensive. Each rupee's worth of food costs more than one rupee to distribute — due to transport, corruption, illicit sales and recycling of the food.[9] And it seems there is a regressive distributional bias, since it is easier to reach urban areas.

In Brazil, the issue of food subsidies has been given a renewed emphasis with the launch by the new government of *Fome Zero* (Zero Hunger). This is a national scheme that combines emergency food aid with "structural measures", such as the construction of water wells in drought-prone areas. As the scheme took shape in 2003, an attempt was being made to produce an integrated anti-poverty approach, combining it with income-transfer schemes, and giving poor families a small transfer payment with which to purchase food. While it is too early to pass judgment on this initiative, it does raise standard questions about paternalism and about the effective targeting on the most economically insecure.

In Indonesia, in a context of pervasive economic insecurity, the PSS was used to probe ordinary people's perceptions of the impact and adequacy of selective government interventions introduced in the wake of the 1997 crisis, known as the JPS (*Jaring Pengaman Sosial,* or social safety net). A major "safety net" measure was the *subsidized rice* scheme, the OPK (*Operasi Pasar Khusus*). In the PSS in 2001, about 18% of respondents had received it (20% in rural areas, 14% in urban), and a further 7.9% said that others in their households had received it.

However, those households reporting that their income was sufficient to pay for their food needs were as likely to have received the subsidized rice as those reporting that their income was inadequate for their food needs (24% compared with 25%). Those reporting that their income was "just enough" for food were, if anything, more likely to have received it (29%). Clearly, the selective targeted subsidy scheme was poorly targeting the needy.

Earlier assessments of the government's OPK scheme to distribute subsidized rice to poor households also identified considerable leakage and inadequate targeting. The PSS data in Table 14.1 show that over 70% of all households, including the most vulnerable, did not receive any subsidized rice. Although a slightly higher proportion of the "most vulnerable" rural households received this rice (29%), as compared to less vulnerable urban households (21%), those classified as "more vulnerable" were scarcely more likely to receive it than the "less vulnerable" category.

Table 14.1 Indonesia: Receipt of subsidized rice by the most vulnerable and less vulnerable urban and rural households

Receipt	Urban				Rural			
	Most vulnerable		Less vulnerable		Most vulnerable		Less vulnerable	
	No.	%	No.	%	No.	%	No.	%
Yes, personally	26	19.0	81	13.0	128	22.0	311	19.0
Yes, others in household	10	7.0	49	8.0	42	7.0	138	8.0
No	97	70.0	477	78.0	401	70.0	1 209	72.0
Missing value	6	4.0	7	1.0	4	1.0	10	1.0

Source: Indonesian PSS1, 2001.

[9]P. Deshingkar and C. Johnson: *State Transfers to the Poor and Back: The Case of Food-for-Work Programme in Andhra Pradesh,* ODI Working Paper (London, Overseas Development Institute, 2003).

Another indicator of poor targeting is that house-holds reporting that they had insufficient money for healthcare were no more likely to have received the subsidized rice than those able to pay for it (Table 14.2). And those who regarded their income as adequate for their general basic needs were as likely to have received the subsidized rice (26%) as those whose income was inadequate (23%). Furthermore, 16% of those who thought they were well-off compared with other people living locally were receiving the subsidized rice, compared with 26% of those who thought their income was about average and 23% of those who felt it was below average.

Table 14.2 Indonesia: Receipt of subsidized rice, public works and food donations, by perceived income adequacy for food, money for healthcare, adequacy of cash income and relative income

Receipt of	Subsidized rice %	Public works %	Food donations %
Income for food			
Sufficient	23.6	2.4	5.1
Just enough	28.7	2.7	7.2
Insufficient	24.9	2.5	7.5
Money for healthcare			
Yes	26.3	3.1	9.4
No	25.6	2.2	5.0
Cash income			
More than adequate	14.7	0.0	5.9
Adequate	26.1	2.4	8.1
Less than adequate	23.4	2.3	5.8
Relative income			
Above average	15.8	0.9	2.3
Average	26.4	3.3	7.2
Below average	23.4	1.5	6.6

Source: Indonesian PSS, 2001.

In short, the selective food subsidy programme in Indonesia illustrates the typically weak capacity of such schemes to target the most insecure and poor. But of course it is the administrative and other forms of leakage that make them both expensive and inefficient. Food subsidies typically do not pass the paternalism and security difference tests.

(ii) Targeting and means-tested benefits

Although the failings of the various forms of selectivity have been documented very extensively, this has not stopped the re-growth of selectivity and the drift to the use of means-testing and behavioural conditionality, as shown in Chapter 3.

The argument starts from the claim that selectivity is necessary to make sure limited resources reach the most needy or the most "deserving". Immediately, this poses a moral dilemma. Who are the most needy? Are some people in need less deserving of basic security and assistance than others?

Then there are the forms of selectivity and targeting. The main form is means-testing, which usually depends on either income or a proxy for income, such as assets. Some observers refer to *administrative targeting,* whereby local officials determine who should receive assistance by checking on proxy indicators of income or means, such as livestock ownership, land ownership, age and gender. Each of these proxies will be at best only a crude indicator of need. And application of a multitude of implicit tests of need and deserving status will set up unfairness, incentives for deception, bribery and petty corruption, and openly discretionary behaviour by the administrators.[10]

Administrative targeting can take place at various levels of government, national or local. It has been found that central government is better able to identify poor communities, while local bodies are better at identifying poor households and poor individuals.[11]

Some form of selectivity is probably appropriate when used in response to natural or social disasters, or "crisis" situations, when simple rules are essential for rapid action. In these cases, the key selectivity variable is usually *location*, in that assistance is rushed to an area devastated by an earthquake, war or other disaster. To use means-testing in such circumstances would look rather ridiculous, and would almost certainly be chaotic and counter-productive.

However, in response to *chronic* poverty and income insecurity, most forms of selectivity are open to criticism. The classic policy is to resort to use of a *poverty line*, decreeing that those living below it should be given assistance. In reality, the poverty line measurement is usually crude and often based on out-of-date and inadequate statistical data (as noted in Chapter 3).

Among the difficulties that arise in trying to use a poverty line to determine eligibility for income support are (i) it is often difficult to identify a person's income, (ii) income often drifts above and below any such line over the course of the period selected, (iii) official lists of eligible persons and households are mostly out of date. Because of the difficulties, means-tested schemes relying on *poverty lines* allow substantial discretion for local bureaucrats, with all the problems that entails, and are prone to Type A and Type B errors, such that some non-eligible people receive benefits and many eligible people do not.

Income instability is an important part of income insecurity. In developing countries, most people's income is irregular, as Chapter 4 showed. A substantial proportion of the population is constantly on the margins of poverty, moving above or below any poverty line.[12] This is often compounded by inflationary circumstances that make adjustments very hard to put into effect. Thus any short-period assessment of income could be thoroughly misleading

as a measure of average income. And any longer-term averaging of income would suffer from recall and other errors. Using assets as a proxy for income in means-testing might be just as erroneous. And use of means-testing during or just after a crisis or natural disaster is likely to be particularly costly, difficult and unreliable.

Other forms of targeting, based on criteria such as area of residence, age, family status or identifiable group (such as caste), are likely to avoid some of the failings of means-testing. However, these forms are also likely to suffer from Type A and Type B errors, benefiting some who are not in need and not giving to some who are in need. For example, a popular form of selectivity is gender, the argument being that assistance given to women will be more likely to have beneficial outcomes for children, as well as for the women receiving it. But what happens to the minority of men supporting children or in chronic need of assistance?

So-called *self-selection or self-targeting* is sometimes used as a means of targeting the needy, as in food-for-work and public works schemes, discussed below, and more coercively in *workfare* schemes. The idea is that some condition or combination of conditions is imposed as necessary for entitlement. For example, a public works scheme may set wages so low that only someone desperate for income or the food provided would step forward. That is not a very moral way of proceeding.

The self-selection procedure for the *bono solidario* social assistance scheme in Ecuador involves applicants making a sworn declaration at a Catholic or Evangelical church, after which the social security administration checks on background information.

---

[10]For a general critique of selectivity and targeting, see Standing, 2002, op. cit.

[11]G. Mansuri and V. Rao: *Evaluating Community Driven Development: A Critical Review of the Research* (Washington, DC, World Bank, 2003).

[12]In Pakistan, a five-year panel survey found that most of the poor moved above and below the designated poverty line. B. Baulch and N. McCulloch: *Being Poor and Becoming Poor: Poverty Status and Poverty Transitions in Rural Pakistan*, IDS Working Paper No. 79 (Brighton, Institute of Development Studies, 1998).

It does not seem to work very well, since a survey found that about a third of those receiving the benefit were really non-eligible, while 18% of those who were eligible did not receive it.[13]

Another form of selectivity is *community-based targeting,* where the community makes decisions on the eligibility of households for, say, food aid. This may have populist appeal, but it presumes a very special set of circumstances, including a homogeneous community and a democratic process that avoids bureaucratic capture, clientelist practices and the like. Such a system could also put onerous pressure on decent people. What would happen if they

had to decide on giving food aid between someone who was ill or someone who was angrily demanding it, or between those who could "contribute" to the community and those most in need? Voice for targeting is not a prescription for tranquillity.

Ultimately, selectivity and means-testing fail because *take-up* is low and often perverse, so that not only do more of the poor fail to receive the benefit but those who do are not among the most needy. These failings are shown in the People's Security Surveys. In Tanzania, for instance, most people are *unaware* of the existence of the selective schemes on offer (Table 14.3).

Table 14.3 Tanzania: Awareness and receipt of selective government schemes of social protection, by level of schooling of respondent

Scheme	No schooling %	Primary %	Secondary and above%	Total %
Small credit				
Aware	44.9	57.5	59.8	56.0
Receipt	4.2	9.7	12.0	9.3
Food for work				
Aware	5.9	6.7	5.3	6.3
Receipt	0.8	2.3	0.0	1.7
Food donations				
Aware	16.9	24.8	13.5	21.6
Receipt	9.3	10.1	3.8	8.9
Cash grant for school attendance				
Aware	2.5	9.9	9.0	8.6
Receipt	2.5	2.7	0.0	2.2

Source: Tanzania PSS, 2001.

In terms of awareness of the "small credit" scheme, for example, 52% of men and 63% of women said they were aware of it, with the more educated more likely to be informed. Only 9% said their households had received assistance from the scheme. Nobody under the age of 26 had received any help. But the more educated the person, the more likely he or she was to have received credit. Since the educated tend to be more affluent, the targeting is scarcely working. Overall, the more affluent seemed more likely to be aware of the existence of selective anti-poverty schemes, and had been more likely to have access to small-scale credit.

In Ghana, just over a third of men and women said they were aware of a small credit scheme; the less educated were no more likely than the more educated to know. But only 6% of men and 5% of women had actually received any credit; the more educated were slightly more likely to have done so. Those whose household incomes were inadequate for their food or healthcare needs were not more aware of any

---

[13]M.D. Velasquez Pinto: *The Bono Solidario in Ecuador: An Exercise in Targeting,* Extension of Social Security Paper No. 17 (Geneva, ILO, 2003), Table 5, p. 7.

selective anti-poverty scheme than the more affluent households and were not more likely to be beneficiaries.

In South Africa, only a minority was aware of the main poverty relief schemes run by the government, and very small proportions of the sampled population in Western Cape and Durban had been reached by them. There was also no evidence that the "targeting" was appropriate in terms of awareness or access to such schemes. Thus, for example, compared with low-income households, more affluent households were more likely to be aware of the ex-

istence of public works, selective poverty alleviation schemes or unemployment benefit schemes. This suggests they are unlikely to be effective in addressing insecurity or income poverty.[14]

In Ethiopia too, remarkably few people seem aware of government programmes to reduce poverty (Table 14.4), suggesting that selective schemes there scarcely make a dent on poverty or economic insecurity. Only one in four thought government anti-poverty programmes were having any success in reducing poverty, whereas over half thought they were unsuccessful.

Table 14.4 Ethiopia: Awareness of government financial support programmes, by personal characteristics (percentage responding "Yes")

	Pension fund	Training and education	Health fund	Family planning programme	Social security net/poverty alleviation	Other
Schooling level						
No schooling	1.3	0.6	0.2	0.0	0.2	0.6
Primary	3.0	0.3	1.1	0.0	0.3	1.1
Secondary and above	2.4	1.0	0.7	1.5	1.5	0.7
Sex						
Male	2.0	0.8	0.7	0.8	0.8	0.6
Female	2.3	0.4	0.2	0.0	0.4	1.0
Household income level (in Birr)						
1-150	1.5	0.4	0.0	0.0	0.0	0.4
151-250	5.5	1.8	0.6	1.2	0.0	0.6
251-500	6.8	1.0	1.9	1.0	1.0	1.0
501+	1.9	1.9	1.3	2.5	0.0	0.6
Income adequacy for healthcare						
Sufficient	1.4	0.9	0.5	0.5	0.5	0.5
Adequate	0.7	0.9	0.7	0.7	1.1	1.1
Insufficient	3.0	0.5	0.5	0.5	0.5	0.6
Income adequacy for food						
Sufficient	0.0	3.3	0.0	1.6	1.6	1.6
Adequate	1.1	0.6	0.6	0.8	0.8	0.8
Insufficient	3.1	0.6	0.6	0.3	0.6	0.7
Total	**2.1**	**0.7**	**0.6**	**0.6**	**0.7**	**0.7**

Source: Ethiopia PSS

[14]For reasons, see G. Standing, J. Sender and J. Weeks: *Restructuring the Labour Market: The South African Challenge* (Geneva, ILO, 1996). For a pro-public works perspective, see A. McCord: *Public Works as a Response to Labour Market Failure in South Africa*, SALDRU/CSSR Working Paper (Cape Town, University of Cape Town, Oct. 2002).

In Bangladesh, the majority of people were aware of one or other of the various selective schemes being operated by the government, and the poorer households were more likely to be aware of most of them. The exception was knowledge of the ration card for subsidized food, about which over nine out of every ten persons did not know anything. This relatively favourable situation almost certainly testifies to the success of non-governmental organizations in Bangladesh, highlighting the need for voice to make income support schemes have some chance of success.

One should not be too sanguine even then. Where the problem arises is in *access*. Only a minority had been reached by any of the selective schemes, and although more of those reporting that their household income was inadequate for their food needs and inadequate for their healthcare needs were being reached by one scheme or another, almost as many of the more affluent households were receiving assistance as the number of poor households who were not being reached. For example, while 30% of the households with income inadequate for their food needs had benefited from the small-credit scheme, 20% of those with adequate income had been beneficiaries.

In Gujarat, the situation seems even more perverse. Defining poor households as those reporting that they did not have enough income for their food needs, the PSS showed that the poor were significantly less likely to be aware of pension schemes, among others. And they were significantly less likely to have been reached by various selective measures, including school-help schemes.

Although the results are not conclusive, they highlight two failings characteristic of selective schemes. These are that (i) awareness of their existence is often limited, and may often be misinformed, and (ii) those most in need tend to be the least aware of their existence, and thus relatively unlikely to apply for assistance through them.

In this respect, the data support the claim made in one assessment of the social security system in Tanzania, which asserted that the constitutional right to social security for all citizens had not been realized, in part, "because of a lack of awareness on the part of the members of society".[15] This is the reality in many, many countries.

Once again, the targeting of selective schemes fails the double test, failing to help the most insecure and being rather paternalistic.

(iii) Food-for-work

One type of targeted basic security programme consists of *food-for-work* schemes, which distribute food on condition that the person participates in some form of public works. These are likely to have easy political appeal, since they can be used to show to the public that action is being taken. And they rely on a high degree of *self-selection*, since it is reasoned that only those needing food would wish to participate in the labour.

Some countries have placed a great deal of faith in such schemes. The government of Ethiopia has devoted 80% of its food assistance to food-for-work schemes, and its official policy is that no able-bodied person should receive food aid without working on a community project; free food is reserved for those deemed to be unable to work.

A further factor shaping these schemes is the view that it is preferable to focus on women, in part because women are considered more likely to ensure that the food reaches children. Thus, the World Food Programme, the major food donor to Ethiopia, decided that it would require women to control family entitlement to food in 80% of WFP-handled and contracted projects.[16]

However, in practice these schemes have structural shortcomings. Often — particularly as the labour is usually manual and is conducted in the heat — the calorific value of the food provided is less than the energy expended. It is well known that physical labour imposes additional nutritional burdens,[17] all

---

[15] A.S. T. Mchomvu, F.S.K. Tungaraza and S. Maghimbi: "Social security systems in Tanzania", *Journal of Social Development in Africa*, Vol. 17, No. 2, July 2002, p. 17.

[16] C.B. Barrett: "Food security and food assistance", in B.C. Gardner and G.C. Rausser (eds.): *Handbook of Agricultural Economics* (Amsterdam, Elsevier Science, 1999).

[17] See, e.g., P. Higgins and H. Alderman: "Labor and women's nutrition: The impact of work effort and fertility on nutritional status in Ghana", *Journal of Human Resources*, Vol. 32, 1997, pp. 577–795.

the more so when the physical condition of the aid recipient is already debilitated. So, food-for-work schemes may actually be detrimental for adult and family health.[18] In India and Nepal, targeting food-for-work on women led to excessive work by women, affecting their health, and less to work by men – so-called female empowerment at the cost of increased drudgery.[19]

This may be particularly the case if the adult performs the labour in order to obtain food to meet the needs of children. The opportunity cost of the participation in the labour is reflected in part in neglect of domestic activities, which has a deleterious effect on child health. Moreover, even where the woman receives the food, girls are less likely to benefit, simply because boys are seen as the better "investment" for the longer-term security of adults.[20] Ironically, in Ethiopia free distribution of food, without conditions, led to an improvement in girls' nutrition, while the food distributed via the food-for-work programme led to better nutrition of boys.

Another drawback of food-for-work schemes is simply that those in need are unaware of them. For example, in Tanzania, only 7% of men and 4% of women were aware of the "food for work" scheme, with no difference by education. Scarcely anybody had benefited from it — 2% of men, 1% of women. In Ghana, the situation was not much better — 14% of men and 12% of women were aware of a food-for-work scheme, with again no difference by age or level of schooling. And only just over 1% of households said they had benefited from any such scheme.

In Tanzania, compared with other selective schemes, more people knew of the "food donations" programme — 25% of men, 15% of women — and the less educated were slightly more likely to be aware of it. Some 11% of men and 4% of women said they had received assistance. This may have been relatively "well targeted" in that those with less schooling were possibly more likely to receive it. In Ghana, 16% of both men and women said they were aware of such a scheme.

In sum, as is the case with so many benevolent paternalistic schemes, what seems a good idea may turn out to have very poor outcomes. All such schemes fail the double test.

(iv) Public works

For many decades, emergency public works or just plain public works have been a standard instrument for responding to high unemployment and mass poverty. Such projects aim to create "socially useful" work for poor people, mostly building infrastructure such as roads, irrigation ditches and community facilities. A vast amount has been written and said about them, which we will not attempt to summarize. The key claims made on their behalf are that (i) they put funds to productive use, (ii) they match spending with obligations, and (iii) they are effective as a targeting mechanism, because they operate on the basis of self-selection.

The most famous right-to-employment scheme is the Maharashtra Employment Guarantee Scheme (MEGS). It has been widely eulogized. But many have criticized it as administratively unwieldly, with multiple application forms and complex wage determination formulae. This leaves it open to bureaucratic capture — discretionary and untransparent decision-making by officials.

There should be no presumption that public works are well targeted. In Indonesia, which we may take as an example, public works were stepped up in the wake of the Asian crisis.[21] In the PSS, questions were asked about people's awareness of and involvement in them. Their reach was even less than the subsidized rice scheme of the same period, with merely 1.4% of respondents saying they had benefited from them, and 1.1% saying that other members of their household had done so. But the

[18] A.R. Quisumbing: "Food aid and child nutrition in rural Ethiopia", World Development, Vol. 31, No. 7, 2003, pp. 1309–1324.

[19] S. Osmani: Empowerment and Drudgery: Trade-Offs for Poor Rural Women, paper presented at workshop on Gender Differentials in Work Intensity, Sustainability and Development, University of East Anglia, Norwich, 1997.

[20] A.R. Quisumbing and J.A. Maluccio: "Resources at marriage and intrahousehold allocation: Evidence from Bangladesh, Ethiopia, Indonesia and South Africa", Oxford Bulletin of Economics and Statistics, 2003.

[21] Several programmes came under the term "public works", and were generally described as padat karya (labour intensive). For a critique, see S. Sumarto, A. Suryahadi and L. Pritchett: Safety Nets and Safety Ropes: Who Benefited from Two Indonesian Crisis Programmes – The "Poor" or the "Shocked"? (Jakarta, World Bank, East Asia and Pacific Region, Sep. 2000).

immediate point is that it was not well targeted; 2.4% of households reporting that their income was sufficient for their food needs were working on public works schemes while 2.6% of those whose income was insufficient for food were on them.

The PSS data also show that, however one assesses income adequacy, public works were poorly targeted if the objective was to reach the poorest. They did not reach the more vulnerable households any more than the less vulnerable. In urban areas, only 4% of the more vulnerable and 3% of the less vulnerable were reached, while in rural areas the respective figures were 1% and 3% — the opposite of what those favouring targeted schemes would predict.

Public works are usually intended to reach the very poor, and as such have tended to involve simple manual labour. Their supporters reason that the schemes would thus attract only the poor, and so constitute a good form of "safety net". However, to make sure this is the case, the wage rate is set below the market rate, a measure often rationalized on the ground that public works should be less attractive than private alternative jobs. So, immediately, the public works scheme sets up an unfairness. Why should someone lifting bricks on a public works scheme be paid less than someone lifting bricks on a private building site?

Public works tend to be stigmatizing, which often deters the poor from applying. There is no reason to suppose that public works offer participants "self respect and independence".[22] They also tend to be selective of men, because much of the labour required is heavy manual work. Ironically, when schemes have introduced gender quotas in an attempt to increase female participation, the unintended negative consequences have harmed women. As with any workfare scheme, they have added to time pressures, exacerbating women's "time famine", with short-term and longer-term adverse effects on their health and capacity to function.[23] As a means of poverty relief, they tend to discriminate against "labour-constrained" households, which often means families headed by women.

Other criticisms of public works as a means of providing basic security for all are that they are stigmatizing, they are usually too small to have a great effect, and tend to involve high administrative costs that imply major leakages.[24] Unquestionably,

they are paternalistic, and it is doubtful if they satisfy the other policy decision rule either, that of reaching the most insecure. Not only will the "take-up" rate be affected by the stigma of participating in a very open form of poverty revelation but the really poor may have neither the clothes nor financial means to be able to present themselves at the "entrance" of the public works. Many of the poorest simply cannot afford to pay for the transport.

A relatively rich country in which public works have grown to be an integral and corrosive part of the State is Japan. There, they account for 8% of GDP, over twice as much as in other industrialized societies. It has been acknowledged that the schemes have been determined by party political objectives. The rising amount allocated to keep constituency support has pushed up local government debt to 36% of GDP, while the service charges have "crowded out" welfare services — a case of active policy squeezing out protective policy.

In sum, public works have long appealed to those concerned with poverty and unemployment. They are frequently used in developing countries, and are often presented as the means of creating public infrastructure, generating jobs and "targeting" the poor. Unfortunately, there are reasons for scepticism about the wilder positive claims made for public works. One is that they use up a lot of scarce resources, and result in low-productivity work being done. Another is that they are not very good at "targeting". The poorest and most insecure are likely to be at the end of the queue for these casual jobs. Yet another is that such schemes are prone to political corruption. And perhaps above all, they have to be massive schemes if they are to have much effect on the incidence of poverty and economic insecurity.

---

[22] A. Sen: "The political economy of targeting", in D. van de Walle and K. Nead (eds.): *Public Spending and the Poor* (Baltimore, Johns Hopkins University Press, 1995).

[23] S. Jackson and R. Palmer-Jones: *Gender, Work Intensity and Wellbeing*, UNRISD Occasional Paper (Geneva, UNRISD, 1998); S. Devereux: *Social Protection: What are the International Lessons with Respect to Programmes Targeted at the Poor?* (London, Department for International Development, 2001).

[24] For a critique of public works in South Africa that brings out these and other failings, see Standing, Sender and Weeks, 1996, op. cit.

(v) Public subsidy for private interest

The boundaries between public and private provision of social services are fuzzy. In every part of the world, enormous subsidies have been provided by governments and donor agencies to private providers, while public services have turned increasingly to market mechanisms and both formal and informal payments.

What is the purpose of those hefty subsidies? And what are their effects? Economists are usually critical of subsidies, on the grounds that they encourage inefficiency and distort markets. And yet there has been rather little criticism of the growing propensity to provide substantial public subsidies to private firms. Perhaps they serve the poor and reduce citizens' insecurity. But in practice the subsidies are going to the "haves" rather than the "have nots".

Increasingly, in many countries social services are becoming little more than government-subsidized private services. Even in China, it has been estimated that public hospitals receive more than 80% of their revenue from patients' "co-payments".[25] Uganda provides subsidies to "not-for-profit" service providers. And in most countries there has been a steady informal marketization of public services, with citizens being required to make under-the-table payments (that are not taxable) and formal user fees.

There ought to be a full assessment of these global trends. There must surely be a *prima facie* case for arguing that subsidies to private providers are misguided. The sums involved must be very large indeed. A subsidy provided to a private firm encourages the firm to be less efficient in the allocation of resources and in the delivery of "service". To avoid the worst outcomes in these respects, a strong public regulator is required, which raises administrative costs and bureaucratic inefficiencies. A subsidy given to one type of service or provider effectively discriminates against others. A subsidy given to a relatively affluent group is regressive.

A subsidy given in any direction is paternalistic, since it decrees implicitly that this is what is wanted and citizens cannot be trusted to make up their own minds. The alternative to subsidies to providers is transfers to the potential "clients", who can then make up their own minds.

(vi) Micro-credit

Micro-credit has had a good run for its money in recent years, and a great deal of money has been invested in it. It has been seen as a means of reducing the income insecurity of the poor. From their religious origins in the Raiffeisen Funds in Germany, micro-credit institutions and rotating community loan funds have been diffused across much of the world. Those institutions receiving most attention since the early 1980s are in South and West Africa, South-East Asia, American inner cities (e.g. in Chicago), and above all Bangladesh. They have also flourished recently in eastern Europe, and have evolved too in China.

Rotating savings-credit associations are local, autonomous, informal mutual funds that lend small sums of less than USD100, primarily to women, as start-up capital for a small business or for educating children. Its advocates claim that reimbursement rates are high because of trust and peer pressure within the group. A similar principle guides local credit unions, NGO intermediaries and micro-credit banks, which, if capitalized with external aid, can subsidize interest rates on slightly larger loans. Group lending is seen as more suitable than bank loans for poor borrowers who lack collateral. In effect, the group itself serves as collateral. Unlike loans to individuals, loans to groups pool individual risks at a lower common equilibrium interest rate.

Micro-credit has been regarded as suitable for dealing with *idiosyncratic risk*, enabling the poor to smooth their consumption in the face of fluctuating incomes, or appropriate for the poor to deal with the standard contingency risks, such as illness and unemployment. In this regard, there are reasons for reservation, because micro-credit tends to involve groups with similar types and degrees of risk. Increasingly, as noted in earlier chapters, communities suffer from *covariant risk*, that is, all households suffer from similar adverse events, making micro-credit schemes of limited value.[26]

---

[25]G. Bloom: *China's Rural Health System in Transition: Towards Coherent Institutional Arrangements?*, paper presented at conference on Financial Sector Reform in China, Harvard University, Boston, 2001.

[26]M.R. Carter: "Environment, technology and the social articulation of risk in west African agriculture", *Economic Development and Cultural Change*, Vol. 45, No. 3, 1997, pp. 557–590.

What are micro-credit schemes supposed to achieve? First, they have been used to encourage so-called "micro-enterprise" and self-employment. Where financial capital is scarce and outside investment inadequate, local communities are considered as assets to be deployed for development.

Second, they are seen as a means of reducing poverty. The Grameen Bank in Bangladesh reduces poverty to some extent by making very small loans to five-member groups of the poor for income-producing, non-agricultural businesses at an interest rate of 18% for one year and a 2% risk-fund charge. The Grameen Bank, the Bangladesh Rural Advancement Committee, and the Bangladesh Rural Development Board's PD-12 project are reported to have had positive effects on income, production and employment, especially in the rural non-farm sector. Own-account work has risen at the expense of wage employment, raising wages. But to have a large impact on wages would require restructuring of the entire rural economy to raise productivity.[27]

The Grameen Bank has served as a model for micro-credit initiatives elsewhere in the world, but it is not always transferable. For example, the Philippine government initiated two micro-credit projects for poor women in 1994, but they had only a marginal impact on women's situation, partly due to insufficient outreach.[28] Likewise, the *Lik Lik Dinau Abitore* Trust created in Papua New Guinea in 1994 had problems enforcing loan conditions, was slow in implementing projects, and had relatively low repayment rates compared to the Grameen Bank. Local conditions that impeded success included geographical isolation, linguistic diversity, local cultural and economic issues, and high levels of violence.[29]

Micro-finance schemes in general fail to reach the really poor, who are operating in what has been called the "mini-economy" in which transactions are very small and irregular, making it hard for financial institutions to charge standardized administrative costs or monitor activities.[30] And there are reasons for the really poor to exclude themselves, including a fear that micro-credit bodies would merely replace older dependency relationships with one based on an NGO.[31]

It seems that, to have much effect on poverty, micro-credit should be part of more integrated programmes. For example, health programmes are being tied in-

creasingly to anti-poverty strategies. Teenagers in Lusaka, Zambia, receive health and safe-sex education as well as micro-credit and training in business skills.

Third, micro-credit has been extensively advocated as a means of *empowerment of women*, seen as improving *agency*. Does micro-credit, and micro-finance generally, provide women with improved income security? The evidence is at best mixed. One of the difficulties in reaching a balanced assessment of actual schemes is that often they have been part of a more general set of interventions, including family planning, schooling, health practices and so on. There is evidence that micro-credit in rural Bangladesh has helped women, though not men, to improve the nutritional well-being of their children.[32]

Donors and NGOs have played a major part in promoting micro-credit. Thus, Oxfam gives women in West Africa small loans to improve their bargaining status in the household with respect to reproduction and expenditure decisions. Grants are used to capitalize revolving credit funds, and contacts are made with credit management organizations. Oxfam claims that the groups were used to train members and network so that women's literacy improved.

[27] S.R. Khandker, H.A. Samad and Z. Khan: "Income and employment effects of micro-credit programmes: Village-level evidence from Bangladesh", *Journal of Development Studies*, Vol. 35, No. 2, 1998, pp. 96–124.

[28] *Asia-Pacific Journal of Rural Development*, 1995.

[29] *Pacific Economic Bulletin*, 11, Nov. 1996, pp. 23–38.

[30] I. Matin, D. Hulme and S. Rutherford: *Financial Services for the Poor and the Poorest: Deepening Understanding to Improve Provision*", Finance and Development Research Programme Working Paper Series No. 9 (Manchester, University of Manchester, 1999); D. Hulme and P. Mosley: *Finance Against Poverty* (London, Routledge, 1996).

[31] N. Kabeer: *Safety Nets and Opportunity Ladders: Addressing Vulnerability and Enhancing Productivity in South Asia* (Brighton, Institute of Development Studies, University of Sussex, 2001).

[32] M.M. Pitt and S.R. Khandker: "The impact of group-based credit programmes on poor households in Bangladesh: Does the gender of the participants matter?", *Journal of Political Economy*, Vol. 106, No. 5, 1998, pp. 958–996.

Fourth, one of the beneficial effects associated with micro-credit schemes is that they have fostered "group formation". This was the original feature of the Grameen Bank, copied by many others including Opportunity International's "Trust Banks" in eastern Europe. But criticisms have accumulated: group loans require group participation in time-consuming meetings; group pressures hold back the most entrepreneurial; borrowers collude against the bank's use of social collateral; and group lending can be costly to implement.[33] These reasons have been used to encourage a shift to more individualistic lending, which has tended to mean a shift towards less poor groups in society.

As recent emphasis has been to make micro-credit more *minimalist*, that is, focused specifically on the provision of credit, the social mobilization function may weaken. A major reason for the minimalism is concern about the financial sustainability of micro-credit schemes that spread their social functions. But, short of its broader aims, how is micro-credit to bring about social change?

The minimalist perspective sees micro-credit as providing financial services for the poor, which if directed mainly at women will lead to their having greater control over their well-being, and thus their children's. But this has been challenged.[34] Women face many other barriers, and control over income is not necessarily derived from having access to credit. Indeed, some have argued that micro-credit has reinforced patriarchal subordination of women.[35] It has been suggested that women have an additional burden of becoming "debt collectors" for micro-finance organizations, inducing stress, a worse time-squeeze for themselves and/or an increased labour burden as they try to put the credit to productive use.

Other observers are more sanguine. They argue that women can use the credit to increase intra-family leverage, even when they give the money to their husbands, which in a country like Bangladesh may be almost the only means of enabling the money to be used productively.[36] In circumstances where strict cultural subordination of women is the norm, so the argument goes, independent decision-making by women may be sub-optimal for the women. A reasonable defence of micro-credit is that it is a means of providing a "pre-condition" for choice, a means of providing "agency" and a means of achieving

better security and welfare.[37] Or as one conceptual approach would put it, micro-credit may increase women's "material" empowerment, their "cognitive" empowerment (through encouraging them to recognize their skills or their capacity to acquire skills), their "perceptual" empowerment (how others see them and treat them) and their "relational" empowerment.[38]

There must be a doubt. It has been claimed that fewer than 10% of micro-finance institutions worldwide are financially sustainable, most depending on extensive subsidies.[39]

The point has been made that to be active is not necessarily to be *independent*, the implication being that agency depends on being active and that the degree of independence is of secondary importance.[40]

---

[33] B.A. de Aghion and J. Morduch: "Microfinance beyond group lending", *Economics of Transition*, Vol. 8, No. 2, 2000, pp. 401–420; see also, among others, T. Besley and S. Coate: "Group lending, repayment incentives and social collateral", *Journal of Development Economics*, Vol. 46, No. 1, pp. 1–18.

[34] L. Mayoux: "Questioning virtuous spirals: Micro-finance and women's empowerment in Africa", *Journal of International Development*, Vol. 1, No. 7, 1999, pp. 937–954.

[35] A.M. Goetz and R. Sen Gupta: "Who takes the credit? Gender, power and control over loan use in rural credit programmes in Bangladesh", *World Development*, Vol. 24, No. 1, 1996, pp. 45–63; R. Montgomery, D. Bhjattacharya and D. Hulme: "Credit for the poor in Bangladesh", in D. Hulme and P. Mosley (eds.), *Finance Against Poverty* (London, Routledge, 1996), pp. 94–176; A. Rahman: "Microcredit initiatives for equitable and sustainable development: Who pays?", *World Development*, Vol. 27, No. 1, 1999, pp. 67–82.

[36] S.M. Hashemi, S.R. Schuler and A.P. Riley: "Rural credit programmes and women's empowerment in Bangladesh", *World Development*, Vol. 24, No. 4, 1996, pp. 635–653; N. Kabeer: "Conflicts over credit: Re-evaluating the empowerment potential of loans to women in Bangladesh", *World Development*, Vol. 29, No. 1, 2001, pp. 63–84.

[37] N. Kabeer: *The Conditions and Consequences of Choice: Reflections on the Measurement of Empowerment*, United Nations Research Institute of Social Development Discussion Paper DP108 (Geneva, UNRISD, 1999).

[38] M. Chen and S. Mahmud: *Assessing Change in Women's Lives: A Conceptual Framework*, BRAC-ICDDRB Joint Research Project, Working Paper No. 2, Matlab, Dhaka, 1995.

[39] J. Morduch: "The microfinance promise", *Journal of Economic Literature*, 1999, pp. 1569–1614; J. Morduch: "The microfinance schism", *World Development*, Vol. 28, No. 4, 2000, pp. 617–630.

[40] S. Mahmud: "Actually how empowering is micro-credit?", *Development and Change*, Vol. 34, No. 4, Sep. 2003, p. 590.

This may be the case. But a difficulty with micro-credit is that the women (and men) who use it are likely to be the more active in any case, and thus to be relatively advantaged, so that the incidence of micro-credit use could be regressive.

Are micro-credit schemes really sustainable, without continuous outside assistance? One aspect is the ability to receive repayment of loans. In spite of setbacks caused by floods and other acts of nature, most micro-credit schemes achieve high repayment rates. But this could reflect a selectivity bias. One criticism of micro-credit programmes in Bangladesh is that female participants are largely self-selected from those most likely to succeed. They are more educated, have more educated husbands, are more often wage workers, have more freedom, are more likely to use contraception, and have higher aspirations for their daughters. They face pressure from others in the group and from the bank to repay loans quickly. This ensures the viability of the loan fund and allows rapid refinancing and loan recycling. But there are social costs of such peer pressure in disciplining rather than protecting the poor involved in micro-credit. It can give rise to new sources of gender inequality in the household, as women are dependent on their families to repay the loans in case of default.[41]

Attention has focused on micro-credit's economic development outcomes to the neglect of the lending process itself, which can be oppressive and exploitative. Poor debtors are vulnerable to pressures that come with any borrowing. And often the borrowers have demands placed on their loans that are not anticipated in the loan arrangement. There is evidence from Bangladesh that micro-credit does not crowd out more costly informal borrowing (loan sharks), since households resort to "cross-financing" when they cannot meet payment schedules. To avoid such problems, many poor people prefer to continue to rely on "patron moneylenders".[42]

One lesson from the considerable sympathetic research devoted to micro-credit in recent years is that to achieve anything like the goals so widely anticipated, micro-credit requires *collective agency* or "voice" at all points of the credit service chain. An individual woman (or man) entering the credit chain is too vulnerable and insecure to avoid a high probability of an adverse outcome. By contrast, the potential benefits if combined with voice security are positive, at least for dealing with idiosyncratic risk.

Micro-credit has been recommended for assisting households affected by HIV/AIDS. However, treating HIV/AIDS as an idiosyncratic risk is surely inappropriate, since the disease has deep impoverishing implications not just for households but for communities and support networks.

Micro-credit and micro-insurance schemes are often seen as the twin sides of a type of social protection for the poor. Micro-insurance schemes are common in many parts of the world, with local rotating savings schemes, the *tontines* in French-speaking Africa, and many other variants. These have provided local communities with some social protection, and have sometimes been useful in improving accountability of service providers. But they suffer from the same sort of drawbacks that affect micro-credit schemes, most notably the tendency for the "risk pool" to be too small to avoid system vulnerability in times of crisis. Re-insurance has been an option favoured by some in the ILO.[43] However, as critics have pointed out, this is likely to lead to governance problems and to costly interventions that mean it will have limited effect.

The reality of micro-credit schemes has been a drift away from the original narrative — enthusiastically publicized by Muhammed Yunus via the Grameen Bank — of "group lending with joint liability", even though this has remained the popular image among proponents. Increasingly, schemes have allocated more funds to individual borrowers, and in doing so have moved away from lending to the poorest, because they have required collateral. As they have moved in this direction, they have become less oriented to the provision of basic income security for poor groups and poor communities.

---

[41] A. Rahman: "Micro-credit initiatives for equitable and sustainable development: Who pays?", *World Development*, Vol. 27, No. 1, 1999, pp. 67–82.

[42] G. Wood: "Staying secure, staying poor: The 'Faustian Bargain'", *World Development*, Vol. 31, No. 3, Mar. 2003, p. 466.

[43] D. Dror and A. Preker: *Social Re-insurance – A New Approach to Sustain Community Health Financing* (Geneva, ILO, 2003).

(vii) Social funds

Social funds are another well-tried measure for improving income security in developing countries. During the 1980s, when structural adjustment strategies were imposing hardships, social funds were a widely adopted remedial policy, aimed at reducing the vulnerabilities of lower-income groups.

The number of social funds has grown sharply since 1987, when the first was created to respond to emergency conditions among the poor in Bolivia. There are now social funds in almost all Latin American and Caribbean countries and in 24 sub-Saharan African countries. During the 1990s, the World Bank financed 108 social funds in 57 countries in 100,000 communities. While social funds provide finance and technical assistance, poor people and communities decide on their development priorities, select competing contractors (who are often private, small and local), and manage the completed projects.

Social funds provide finance for community projects in which poor people are expected to participate in their own development. The original goal was self-determined project development by communities, focusing on public works. Over the years, the focus has shifted from responses to emergencies towards pursuing "sustainable development". However, in spite of the many millions of dollars from the World Bank and other donors and local governments — for water, sewerage, transport infrastructure, healthcare, nutrition, education, social services, training, micro-enterprise development, and so on — the macroeconomic impact of social funds has been limited. Only Nicaragua has had a social fund that spent over 1% of GDP. In Latin America, less than USD10 per year per poor person is spent, with even lower sums in the Middle East and North Africa.[44]

There is evidence from Bolivia and Honduras that social funds have helped the very poor. In those cases, use of supported health clinics rose, and child mortality and disease declined. Construction and equipment in supported clinics and schools were superior and better maintained. Although social funds operate in almost every municipality in the country, only about 30% of the resources go to households in the lowest income decile.[45] Targeting the poor and rural areas has improved, but remote areas are still neglected. There are also trade-offs between rapidity

of response and involvement of the poor, who often need more time for training and experience.

In developing countries, social funds have some advantages over governments in responding to crises, and thus in encouraging decentralization. They mobilize resources where bureaucracies lack capacity. Their partial independence from the public sector avoids "red tape" in implementation. They have lower overhead and administrative costs than governments. They usually hire competent staff and operate with transparency, since they are accountable to outsiders. They can bypass some actors, avoid potential "capture" by special interests, and allow participation by the poor, while coordinating international donors, public and private sectors, NGOs, municipalities and grassroots communities. Projects can be tailored to local needs and can address them comprehensively. They can even build what some observers call "social capital" and "trust in government".

However, social funds do face problems of sustainability, requiring continuous injections of new money, and often outside involvement even when there is a participatory approach. They often lack adequate resources and are poor at "targeting". One evaluation found that often they suffer from the two types of error, supporting those not in need and failing to reach those in need.[46] Many have failed to benefit women directly or indirectly.[47]

Social funds also have other weaknesses. It is unclear whether jobs created by funded projects are sustainable, since local agencies and communities must ultimately take over the projects. Second, credit schemes could create a revolving self-sustaining pool of resources, but social funds have been unsuccessful with micro-credit programmes in Albania and Egypt. Newer funds seem to perform better at lending. Third, social funds are autonomous from, but cannot substitute for, public poverty reduction

---

[44] World Bank, 1999, op. cit.

[45] Ibid.

[46] F. Stewart and W. van der Geest: *Adjustment and Social Funds: Political Panacea or Effective Poverty Reduction?* (Oxford, International Development Centre, Queen Elizabeth House, 1994).

[47] R. Sabates-Wheeler and N. Kabeer: *Gender Equality and the Extension of Social Protection,* Extension of Social Security Paper No.16 (Geneva, ILO, 2003), pp. 32–33.

programmes. Otherwise, communities will be unsure who is in charge of their projects. International and national efforts need to be integrated, and successful models of social funds adopted locally. But, as a World Bank assessment concluded, "*Social funds should not duplicate or overlap other national initiatives, but serve as a specific instrument in the arsenal of social safety net programmes that reach out to isolated regions, ethnically or socially excluded communities, and marginalized groups.*"

While social funds may build partnerships between various social groups, bringing strength to local projects, the scale of these initiatives remains modest. Although capacity-building is a common theme in community-driven development initiatives, doubts remain. NGOs can assist fledgling groups technically and help them network, and small-scale entrepreneurs can be helped with training and credit. But the scale of all this is too small to have much effect.

The social fund approach is largely reactive, with winners compensating losers forced to adjust to market competition. It can become a welfare system encouraging dependency if the funds are not invested to stimulate sustainable development.

Indeed, a look at investment trends in the European Social Fund (ESF) since its establishment over 40 years ago reveals a shift from public infrastructure projects towards investment in "human capital". The ESF is now directed at preparing people for work and developing their "employability", especially in regions that need to upgrade workforce skills, foster entrepreneurship and attract investors. The employability pillar of the European Union's Employment Strategy includes tackling youth unemployment, easing the transition from school to work, preventing long-term unemployment, moving to so-called active measures to encourage work and training, and promoting partnerships. Indeed, unions and employers, voluntary organizations, educators and governments at all levels are involved in implementation, which encourages comprehensive local solutions to local problems.

In sum, "activating" social funds increasingly means shifting to supply-side rather than demand-side interventions. As such, they are likely to become paternalistic and inefficient. Given the likely scale and difficulties of sustainability, the social fund is not an effective instrument for enhancing the economic security of poor communities.

(viii) Vouchers

Vouchers — the provision of a card or credit for a specific use — have become very popular as a means of providing basic security. The main type has been schooling vouchers. These have been introduced in countries as varied as Bangladesh, Chile, Colombia, Côte d'Ivoire and the Czech Republic. Advocates argue that they allow for greater choice of schools among students and their families. Whether vouchers reach the most insecure groups in society is another matter.

Evaluations of the impact of vouchers are still limited, although many are under way. Some observers believe that vouchers have improved student performance among some groups, with lower school repetition rates and higher test results.[48] But there is some evidence that they do not really help low-income groups, in that universal voucher schemes enable students from richer families to concentrate in private elite schools.[49]

Vouchers thus can be instruments for *increased* inequality. Restricting the vouchers to poor or disadvantaged groups avoids this pitfall,[50] but raises familiar questions about the effectiveness of targeting, since all the problems in identifying and reaching the deserving categories arise, as well as the potential stigma associated with being a "voucher student".

[48] J. Angrist, E. Bettinger, E. Bloom, E. King and M. Kremer: "Vouchers for private schooling in Colombia: Evidence from a randomized natural experiment", *American Economic Review,* 2004 (forthcoming).

[49] An example of a voucher scheme that avoided this perverse selectivity is the Colombian PACES, a secondary school voucher scheme, which chooses beneficiaries by lottery.

[50] V. Gauri and A. Vawda: *Vouchers for Basic Education in Developing Countries: A Principal-Agent Perspective,* background paper for the World Bank's *World Development Report* 2004.

(ix) Minimum income integration schemes

One type of policy to increase income security that has attracted considerable attention in industrialized market economies is what is often called, for short, minimum income integration schemes. Although they are unlikely to attract much attention in low-income societies, they just might. What do they offer and what do they do?

Although no doubt there were precursors (there are for most policies), the modern trend to integration schemes is usually associated with the French RMI (*revenu minimum d'insertion*), which has been much studied since its almost-accidental introduction in 1988. The RMI concept — which offers benefits if the beneficiaries undertake to integrate into labour force activity — stemmed from the perception that the major problem in western Europe was *social exclusion*. High unemployment and the changing character of labour markets meant, so it was reasoned, that those who could not enter the formal labour process or who were marginalized as a result of failure were cut off from society and incapable of reintegrating themselves. So, the State had to step in to provide guidance as a complement to financial relief.

There are many aspects of the RMI and similar schemes that have been operating in some other European economies, such as Belgium and Portugal.[51] To the extent that the "compacts" used to guide people into income-earning activities are sufficiently voluntary to leave scope for a wide choice of response, the paternalistic character of such schemes may be held in check. But real voice for the "clients" is needed to ensure that paternalism is constrained. At least one study has shown that integration schemes induce a new form of "dependency", on social workers and on the schemes themselves.[52]

They are really an extension of *active labour market policy*, whereby tighter conditions are placed on the distribution of monetary transfers to the unemployed and working poor. In extreme cases, they merge into workfare.

(x) Workfare

Stemming from so-called "active labour market policy", the performance of labour or participation in a training scheme, the notion of workfare came into vogue in the 1980s. Thinking along the lines of *workfare* has greatly influenced welfare reform in the past decade, most strikingly in the United States, epitomized by the 1996 welfare reform intended "*to end welfare as we know it*".

Many economists believe that unemployment benefits are disincentives to labour. They often produce "unemployment traps", in that going from receipt of a benefit to an available job would result in a decline in income. So, it is convenient for governments to *oblige* the unemployed to take a job or a training place, or lose entitlement to benefit. This seems a strange interpretation of what is nominally an insurance scheme.

Does workfare pass the two policy decision principles tests? Decidedly not. Almost by definition, workfare is highly paternalistic. As with integration schemes, the person at the receiving end is confronted with someone who has an ambiguous role, that of adviser and that of coercer. You can have trust, or you can have coercion. But you cannot have both at the same time.

(xi) Tax credits

The use of fiscal policy as social and regulation policy has been enormously strengthened by the spread of so-called earned income tax credits. So far, these have been exclusively used in industrialized countries, most notably the United States, where they have become easily the biggest income transfer mechanism. But there has been interest among policy-makers and social analysts in developing countries as well.

Tax credits are a means of supplementing low earnings of those in the labour force. To a certain extent, they are being extended to give income credits for those engaged in some other activities such as carework. But they are really "in-work" benefits, rather than a means of reaching the most insecure groups in society.

---

[51]For a critique of national schemes of this type, see G. Standing (ed.): *Minimum Income Schemes in Europe* (Geneva, ILO, 2003).

[52]S. Aho and I. Virjo: "More selectivity in unemployment compensation in Finland: Has it led to activation or increased poverty?", in ibid, pp. 183–208.

One issue that has not attracted much attention so far is that tax credits, being essentially a subsidy to low-wage unskilled labour, may be construed as a labour market distortion. And to the extent that they go disproportionately to labour-intensive sectors that are competing with imports from developing countries, they could be construed as a non-tariff trade barrier, as could other selective subsidy schemes, including some public works or social fund schemes.

(xii) The future of social insurance

Social insurance was the idealized norm for providing income security in the 20th century. Many cling to the hope that it will be the norm during the 21st century as well. But increasingly, even in countries where it was widely used, the insurance principle has been *fictitious* or patched up. The reality is that to work well, it requires the vast majority of workers to be in regular, stable, full-time employment.

In the era of globalization, a rethinking of social insurance is overdue. Liberalized stock markets and foreign exchange markets interact to create greater economic instability. Society needs to be insulated from this, and the standard forms of social insurance do not provide adequate security in such circumstances. Does this imply nationalization of private insurance, in contrast to the World Bank's support for wholesale privatization of insurance? We pose this question as one that deserves extensive research, without implying agreement or disagreement. In the meantime, powerful interests are pushing for social insurance to be phased out, with individual savings accounts being common replacements.

14.4 Promising avenues to universal income security

So far, we have referred to what are broadly orthodox policies that have been used extensively to strengthen income security. In this final section, we will review briefly some more innovative measures that have been gaining ground in the past decade or so and that are likely to become more significant over the next few years.

As before, in each case one needs to ask whether or not the measure satisfies the two policy principles — supporting the most insecure and being non-paternalistic. It should also be recalled that a majority of people believe in the provision of basic security; they want a floor for everybody and think governments should give assistance to the poor, the elderly, the sick, and those who care for them. And they tend to believe in redistributing at least some of the income of the rich to the poor.

In considering alternatives, relatively little attention will be given to alternative means of financing policies to provide greater income security. The pessimism that goes with the view that taxes cannot be raised has not been justified. However, it must always be remembered that the funding of social policy is about *priorities*. Many countries spend a very low share of their national income in providing their citizens with basic economic security, and there is no reason to presume that governments could not increase it. Indeed, economic growth and development would be improved if such spending were to increase. As for how to do that, this is up to the politicians.

(i) Aid for income security

Does the enormous flow of international aid focus sufficiently on providing basic economic security? Can aid be a more effective means of doing so? Four trends have dominated the flow of aid. First, it has fallen as a share of international capital flows. Second, it has become far more conditional in character. Third, there is greater coordination of effort by bilateral donors. Fourth, there seem to be steadily stronger efforts to integrate bilateral aid with multilateral aid, with donors trying to follow the lead of the international financial agencies.

Old-style development aid and technical assistance, which supposedly ignored domestic politics, has given way in recent years to the claims of *coherence*, the belief that aid should go to countries with "good" governments pursuing "good" policies and building "good" institutions. This shift has given rise to fears that the reduction of social and economic insecurity will become subservient to political and "developmental" criteria.

A prime example of coherence is said to be the *New Partnership for Africa's Development* (NEPAD). This states that aid should be made conditional on good behaviour by governments, defined in terms of human rights, democracy and the extension of free trade. These conditions have been extended to discussions of debt relief, highlighting the danger that NEPAD may be merely another pretext for extending conditionality.

Some NGOs have moved to strengthen their humanitarian ethos, through codes of conduct and measures to enhance accountability to aid recipients. Examples include the Humanitarian Accountability Project, the SPHERE Humanitarian Charter of Minimum Standards, and the Quality Project. Meanwhile, however, donor government agencies are developing contractual relationships with NGOs that give the agencies more control over where aid money is directed.[53]

The debate on aid will be invigorated by the emphasis given to the Millennium Development Goals. But there is a danger that, for all the rhetoric about "ownership" and "participation", aid will continue to be largely based on self-interested steering. At present, therefore, much aid fails the paternalism test, especially when backed by concealed forms of conditionality, and fails the test of improving the security of the most insecure groups.

(ii) Social pensions

The world is ageing. Pension systems are creaking. Reforms have been cushioning the wealthy and the salaried, and making the vulnerable more so. But the very crisis that is so much talked about is inducing fresh and promising thinking.

In the rush to create *multi-pillar* pension systems, governments are being encouraged to institute proper universal basic state pensions. In a sense, they have been the basis of the Scandinavian pension systems. One good point is that they were drawn up *before* those countries became rich. Even in developing countries, some old models offer hope for wider replication.

In India, the Indian National Old Age Pension scheme (NOAPS) deserves more attention. It seems to pass the two policy decision principles, in that it helps the most insecure and is non-paternalistic. Unlike many other schemes of poverty relief in India, it has been relatively free of misappropriation and has a low leakage rate.

About USD100 million of central government funds are set aside annually to support the poor aged over 65 through the NOAPS. This comes to about USD1.60 per month, to which is added roughly the same again in transfers from individual states. At present, several methods of payment are used, but it seems the least prone to misappropriation is the simplest monthly payments via the post office or via bank accounts.

Given the huge leakages in other schemes of poverty relief, such as the food subsidies discussed earlier, income security could be greatly strengthened by re-allocating resources to the NOAPS. It has been estimated that if the pension were extended to all below the poverty line and the individual amount quadrupled, the cost would be USD800 million — a small fraction of the amount spent on the wasteful food subsidy scheme that also fails the policy principles.

Those who have studied the system estimate that, at an extra cost of less than USD2 billion, the entitlement age could be reduced to 60, widows' pensions could be made universal and an allowance for single-parent families could be added. For less than USD1 billion, mother and child allowances could be paid. So, the total for an effective universal system of basic income security could be paid by re-allocating about three-quarters of the food subsidy funds.

An additional advantage of building on the NOAPS is its computerized system. This is cost efficient, meaning that more of the money allocated is likely to reach the intended beneficiaries. It would also, rather importantly, reduce the discretion local bureaucrats and politicians currently have over beneficiary selection.

At the macroeconomic level, re-allocating expenditure from in-kind to simple cash transfers would boost spending by the poor on goods that generate work and income for relatively poor communities. Thus, given the high income elasticity of demand for food among the poor, cash transfers to the poor would boost demand for locally produced food and thus improve incomes of the poor.

---

[53]For a range of views, see Insights (Brighton, Institute of Development Studies, University of Sussex, Jan. 2002).

Another well-tried policy for providing income security for the elderly that has been rather successful is South Africa's social pension scheme, regarded as the country's outstanding and almost only redistributive social policy. This is financed out of general tax revenue, rather than from social insurance. Although nominally means-tested, it has been successful primarily because the means test has not been applied. A similar scheme has operated in Namibia since the early 1970s.

The social pension was introduced for several reasons, not all laudable, but, among the unintended benefits, it has been a means by which rural blacks have been able to obtain schooling, since the transfers have skipped generations, being given by "grannies" to grandchildren. Various evaluations have demonstrated its success in this respect and in moderating race-based inequality and poverty.[54]

If the pension is set at about 20% of the average earned income, it is fiscally feasible, and typically would cost between 1% and 2% of GDP in a developing country, or between 10% and 20% of its social expenditure. Bearing in mind that subsidies to richer elements typically come to much more than that, it could not be condemned as financially unaffordable, especially as social protection is often a very low share of GDP and could be raised to the benefit of economic growth. Moreover, at least part of the financing could come from foreign aid, thus facilitating the transition to a full pension system.

Indeed, there is a fledgling movement to launch a Global Social Trust Initiative, promoted by the ILO's Financial, Actuarial and Statistical Services Branch, to elicit contributions from affluent parts of the world to a fund to be used to pay out a modest pension in developing countries. This is a bold, ambitious idea, and could be seen as an exemplary piece of global altruism. This could be construed as consistent with the charity principle as enunciated in Chapter 12.

One key advantage of moving in this direction is that it compares well with the main alternatives mooted by commentators. The first is to "extend" social insurance pensions. The extension model presumes that somehow gradually all or most of the population will come under a self-financing insurance scheme, which is most unlikely given the way labour markets are developing. Moreover, a large proportion

of the social insurance fund is lost in administrative costs, making that route both inefficient and inequitable (since the extension typically goes from middle-income recipients downwards, never reaching the low-income groups). The second alternative is to go down the road of individual private accounts coupled with a means-tested basic tier. This will surely continue to be inequitable and costly, as discussed earlier.

The social pension, as implemented so far, does not fully satisfy the security difference and paternalism principles. Even though the means test is fairly nominal, the take-up rate is far from complete. And as with any targeting scheme, it does raise questions of both social equity and economic efficiency. If a very large proportion of social spending is allocated to social pensions, is that fair? Not all the poor are elderly, and not all the elderly are poor. Moreover, some economists would argue that rather than spend on yesterday's workers, why not allocate the available money to the young, tomorrow's workers, boosting their "human capital", and so on. The only answer to this sort of reasoning is that for economic security and long-term development, policies should involve shifting more of the total to universal social protection.

(iii) Minimum-income-with-schooling schemes

One of the most promising income security schemes is what is known in Brazil as *bolsa escola*, which in its various forms amounts to a monthly minimum income payment paid to mothers on condition that the children go to school. A similar scheme exists in Mexico, which long went under the title of *PROGRESA*, but which has been renamed *Oportunidades*. Somewhat similar schemes exist in Colombia (*Familias en Acción*, and *Empleo en Acción*), in Honduras (*Programa de Asignación Familia (PRAF)*), in Nicaragua (*Red de Protección Social (RPS)*), in Jamaica *(PATH)*, and in Bangladesh *(Food for Education)*.

---

[54]The issues and evidence were summarized in the Committee of Enquiry for Comprehensive Social Security (the Taylor Committee), set up by the Government and consisting of a broad cross-section of interests, which reported in 2003. Earlier assessments, all reaching positive conclusions, include A. Case and A. Deaton: "Large scale transfers to the elderly in South Africa", *Economic Journal*, Vol. 108, No. 450, pp. 1330–1361; Standing, Sender and Weeks, 1995, op. cit., and the references cited therein.

The *bolsa escola* began as a local city initiative, but has become national in scope, paying up to 45 *reals* a month. It was linked to *Projeto Alvorada*, a government scheme combining *bolsa escola* transfers and sanitation measures. Most of the benefits were channelled to the poorest districts, defined as those with the lowest levels of the UNDP's Human Development Index, which meant that states such as Rio de Janeiro, with no districts below the threshold HDI value, were left out. By 2003, it was estimated that about five million families were reached by this programme.

A related scheme is *bolsa alimentaçao*, which went to families on condition that they bring their pre-school children regularly to the local health clinic. Beneficiaries collect their payment from a bank through an electronic card, which contains information on the person that can be used for other purposes. Both schemes require parents to do something that is of direct benefit to their children. This highlights one potential criticism of this type of scheme, which is that it is paternalistic. It states that parents cannot be trusted to send their children to school or to a health clinic voluntarily.

Brazilians do not appear to be too concerned about that. Indeed, it is likely that the condition of school attendance helped legitimize support for the *bolsa escola* among middle-class voters. Potentially more worrying is the political discretion in the way limited funds for such schemes can be steered to particular states and districts. At present, it is too early to know the implications of the priority being given to the government's *Fome Zero*, mentioned earlier, although in October 2003 a new coordinated scheme came into effect (see following box).

The Brazilian *Bolsa Familia* of 2003

On 20 October 2003, the Brazilian President announced the *bolsa familia*, unifying four programmes – the *bolsa escola*, the *bolsa alimentaçao* [Minimum Income and Nutrition scheme), the *cartao alimentaçao*" [National Access-to-Food scheme], and the *auxilio gas* [Gas Help scheme].

All families with an income per head below R50 per month and with children under the age of 15 will have an entitlement to receive between R65 and R95 each month, depending on the number of children up to three.

Families will have to show that children aged 0 to 6 have been vaccinated and are being taken to public health clinics to check on their nutrition. Children aged 7-15 must be attending school. And adults must participate in literacy classes.

The new coordinated scheme will remove the previous obligation to spend the benefit on food.

The government forecast that 3.6 million families would be enrolled in the scheme by the end of 2003, and 11.4 million by the end of 2006.

Although recent changes will need close monitoring, it is possible to take stock of the effects of the implementation of *bolsa escola* in the many cities that introduced a variant during the 1990s — providing low-income women with a monthly income grant conditional on sending their children to school.

Evaluations of these schemes, within the ILO's Programme and elsewhere, have shown four positive effects. They reduce the incidence of women's poverty, as expected and intended. Less predictably, they actually result in a rise in female labour force participation, by enabling women to be able to afford decent clothing and transport to work. In Recife, women's participation rose by about eight percentage points. The schemes also increase school attendance among primary school-age children, with drop-out rates dropping to zero. And they dramatically reduce income inequality.

At the same time, the enthusiasm that should be generated by the positive outcomes associated with these schemes must be tempered by disappointment at the *ad hoc* way they were introduced. There has been a plethora of schemes, some overlapping, some over-complicated, some with high administrative costs. There is also concern about some of the criteria used for establishing entitlement.

Mexico's PROGRESA (now renamed *Oportunidades*) was launched in 1997, partly to improve health and schooling among the poor, based on a *set of transfers*. A cash transfer is provided to poor households on condition that the children regularly attend school between grades 3 and 9. A second transfer goes to the mother to pay for school supplies. A third transfer is provided if the mother (or both parents) attends health education lectures and if children go for regular medical checks and immunizations. Selected families could obtain the benefit for up to three years, after which they have had to reapply.

The scheme, which covers more than 40% of rural families, has increased school enrolment, especially at secondary level and especially for girls. Child nutrition has improved and illness among children has dropped sharply. The result is that basic income security and basic skill security have improved.

Like many transfer schemes, PROGRESA applies selectivity criteria in allocating scarce resources. It operates on the basis of means-testing and specifically targets women. Since women on average experience more economic insecurity than men, the categorical targeting is relatively appealing. But it does risk omitting men in similar situations, and may set up perverse behavioural responses on the part of recipient households.

It has contained a *poverty trap*, since anybody who manages to improve her income to just above the poverty line used to determine eligibility will lose the benefit, leading to a predictable immoral hazard (one conceals the income, or lies) as well as a moral hazard (one does not try to increase income from more work). As such, while it may only moderately offend the paternalism test principle, it will surely be quite inefficient and probably inequitable (especially for those living far from the places where they have had to go to collect the benefit, for whom transport costs may account for nearly half the value of the benefit).[55] Conceptually, it is also closer to being part of the charity principle, rather than an extension of economic rights.

One limitation of cash-for-schooling schemes is that they do not have flexibility to cover households that fall *into* poverty during economic crises. They are unlikely to give help to many households whose income fluctuates around any designated poverty line.

Another limitation is that potential beneficiaries are unaware of their existence, or do not think they qualify. In Tanzania, only 9% of men and 8% of women were aware of the existence of the "cash grants for school attendance" scheme; among the most relevant age group, those aged 26 to 35, the percentage was about 11%. Those with no schooling themselves were easily the least likely to know of its existence. Only 2% of men and women had received it. In Ghana, 15% of men and 14% of women said they were aware of such a scheme. Less than 2% had received any such grant.

Despite these reservations the success of cash-for-schooling schemes in Brazil and Mexico suggests they could be copied and adapted elsewhere. In 2001 the ILO and the United Nations Conference on Trade and Development (UNCTAD) proposed the introduction of pilot schemes in heavily indebted African countries as part of a debt relief package.

The promising aspect of these schemes is that they help some of the more economically insecure and reduce the paternalism in helping children. But they have a long way to go to satisfy the paternalism and security difference tests.

(iv) Freedom and restructuring grants

One of the worst forms of inequality, and thus source of income insecurity, is the grossly unequal distribution of wealth in the form of ownership of assets and property rights. Societies cannot expect to achieve universal basic security if wealth is concentrated overwhelmingly in the hands of a tiny minority. If income security is a goal, this issue cannot be neglected.

The question is how to secure some redistribution of wealth without severe negative social, economic, political and ecological effects.

---

[55]This point was made early in the scheme's evolution. See, for example, Comisión de Desarrollo Social de la Cámara de Diputados: *Informe preliminar de la visita de seguimiento al PROGRESA en el estado de San Luis Potosi* (Mexico City, CDSCD, mimeo., 1998); I. Yaschine: The changing anti-poverty agenda: What can the Mexican case tell us?", *IDS Bulletin*, Vol. 30, No. 2, 1999, p. 56.

One scheme that has attracted favourable attention is the Alaska Permanent Fund, considered later. Would such a scheme work in a country such as Iraq? There are reasons to think that it might and that it would be a valuable way of strengthening social solidarity. More generally, it would seem to have appeal in any country in which natural resources yield a substancial long-term flow of income.

Freedom grants for Iraq?

In the aftermath of the Iraq war in 2003, many Iraqi families faced great hardships. Jobs were scarce and basic necessities hard to come by, potentially generating new forms of extremism and bitterness.

This could be avoided if the powers-that-be ensured that all Iraqis in the very near future had basic social and economic security.

An enlightened policy would be to provide every Iraqi with a small monthly income without conditions — a "freedom grant" or "solidarity grant".

If coordinated with a supply-side macroeconomic policy, this would cut poverty, help to kickstart a distributionally decent market economy and show that the international community wants to enable Iraqis to take control of their own lives. It would promote real freedom, and be less prone to moral hazards than if the same amount was spent on paternalistic measures that have high administrative costs, foster corruption and entail distortionary distributional effects.

Freedom grants could be paid for by a dividend from the sale of Iraqi oil, supplemented by international aid. To some extent, the proposed scheme would be analogous to the Alaska Permanent Fund, which is a success in the United States. So it is not that radical. However, whereas that started slowly, the situation in Iraq requires that an initial lump sum should be invested in a special Iraqi Freedom Investment Fund (IFIF) so that a monthly flow of modest payments could be delivered at this time of greatest need.

Iraq possesses the second largest oil reserves in the world. This largesse is a mixed blessing, since it makes the country a potential victim of "the Dutch disease". By channelling part of the proceeds from oil exports to the populace of Iraq, policy-makers could counteract that tendency. It is no coincidence that Norway and Alaska are the only oil-rich State and region that have managed to deliver sustained benefits from oil, since they have had explicit policies of redistributing the economic gains to their people.

Evidence also shows that an inclusive social protection policy in a post-conflict period can boost economic growth and reduce the rise in mortality rates that usually follows a war, due to disease and traumas.

Unless something bold is done, how many people in Iraq will die in the aftermath of the end of the dictatorship? In that country, as in any other, basic security is real freedom. Life and decent work can flourish only on that foundation.

(v) Revisiting pension funds

Old-age income security seems to be receding all over the world, as was brought out in earlier chapters. The future of pensions and the provision of income security for the elderly are two of the great conundrums of the early part of the 21st century. The idea of social pensions is one way of moving forward, particularly in developing countries. But everywhere governments and experts are looking for new pension systems that are both fiscally viable and equitable. There is no way forward without reforming the pension funds, which have become major factors in patterns of insecurity.

The first requirement is a secure state system. In this regard, there may be merit in moving to a prefunding of public pensions, as proposed by Richard Titmuss in the 1950s. This idea, which has advocates in the United States, United Kingdom and elsewhere, would require a mix of contributions, tax revenue and other sources of funds.[56]

---

[56] See, for example, P. Diamond (ed.): *Issues in Privatizing Social Security*, Report of an Expert Panel of the National Academy of Social Insurance, Cambridge, MA., 1999; P. Orszag and J. Stiglitz: "Rethinking pension reform: Ten myths about social security systems", in R. Holzmann and J. Stiglitz (eds.): *New Ideas About Old Age Security: Towards Sustainable Pension Systems in the 21st Century* (Washington, DC, World Bank, 2001).

One challenging proposal is to use stock options.[57] At present, these are in effect a gift to an elite of salaried employees and executives in major corporations. Why not limit them in general and require that 10% of annual profits of any publicly listed company be issued as shares held by something like a Social Security Trust Fund (an American institution) or by national or regional pension boards?

One problem would be that it would not reach those outside the profitable corporation. Accordingly, they could be placed in community funds. In that way, this would be moving towards a capital grant, considered in the next section. Such a scheme would not affect the firm's cash flow, and legislation could require that such shares be held for a minimum period of, say, five years.

(vi) Capital grants

Wealth provides income security. But wealth is concentrated in the hands of tiny minorities in almost every society. This is why some governments and some social scientists have been enthusiastic about new efforts to universalize access to capital, such as the *baby bonds* introduced by the British government.

The most celebrated variant of capital grants is the Alaska Permanent Fund, which was set up in a small way in 1977, gradually developing into a significant means of providing income security for the citizens of Alaska. Since 2000, it has been able to distribute about USD2,000 per person, via an annual dividend viewed as an entitlement that all Alaskans share.[58]

The Fund was built up by required deposits of royalties collected from the sale of state-owned natural resources, in effect oil. In practice, this has worked out at about 10% of profits. The intention has been to prevent oil revenues from being squandered by opportunistic politicians, by sharing part of the revenue from publicly-owned natural resources among all citizens, regardless of social status. There is no eligibility test other than an intention to remain a resident of Alaska.

Since the Fund was designed as a savings account, and not for a particular sphere of social or economic spending, it gained broad public support. The dividend, which is paid annually, has become a source of *social solidarity*, and appears to have been used mainly to acquire consumer durables to improve living standards. In some parts of the state, it has been estimated that the dividend represents about 10% of household income. That is, on average, for a family of four, the four dividend cheques can amount to about three months of regular income.

One of the perceived positive effects of the Fund is its role as an automatic economic stabilizer, reducing the impact of cyclical fluctuations in incomes associated with commodity price changes. But as the Fund has grown, some politicians have seen it as a potential source of money for infrastructural and other spending. It remains to be seen whether the citizens of Alaska will defend their Fund to retain it for its original purpose as a means of providing modest income security.

(vii) Care work grants

One of the greatest changes in the world of work has been the recognition that *care work* is work. There seems to be widespread support for the principle that all those providing care should be provided with financial security. Some would argue that this would only be realistic in affluent industrialized societies. However, if the principle is accepted that those doing care work are as "deserving" of income security as those doing labour, then it further erodes the legitimacy of schemes that offer basic security only if the individual or household performs specified labour.

One context that might help to legitimize giving basic security to care workers is the scourge of HIV/AIDS. It is becoming clear that the catastrophic social and economic effects of the disease on communities in Africa will be redressed only if a systemic approach to social support policy is adopted. The key to that will be whether or not help is given to those caring for victims and for the relatives of those victims.

---

[57]R. Blackburn: *Banking on Death or Investing in Life: The History and Future of Pensions* (London, Verso, 2002).

[58]O. Goldsmith: "The Alaska Permanent Fund Dividend: An experiment in wealth distribution", in G. Standing (ed.), *Promoting Income Security as a Right* (London, Anthem Press, 2004).

Giving care grants would be a transparent, sensible means of reducing the probability of inter-generational transfer of chronic economic disadvantage, and a means of limiting the damage to community support and productive systems.

It would satisfy the two policy decision principles, being non-paternalistic and helping the most insecure groups. It would also tend to reduce inequality, and would thus be redistributive, in that the poor suffer disproportionately from the worst effects of the disease.

(viii) Basic income as a right

Finally, there is a growing advocacy for policies that would provide a basic income for everybody — or initially for specific vulnerable groups gradually to be extended to all — as a right, without conditions. This report will not review the arguments for and against such a move. Suffice it to state that it is a non-paternalistic means of providing universal basic security, has appeal in both affluent and developing countries, and can be seen as a long-term objective, with schemes such as social pensions, capital grants (Alaska) and care grants counting as moves in that direction.

Brazil has well-known advocates for basic income.[59] There, the *bolsa escola* is seen by some of its supporters as a stepping stone to a more universal and less conditional income transfer system. Peru is also seen as a potential country for such a scheme.[60] In South Africa, there has been a strong campaign to introduce a *Basic Income Grant*. Following the end of *apartheid*, the new ANC government swept into office pledging to restructure South African society so as to reduce poverty and inequality among the black majority. The democratization process was a "political miracle". Sadly, it was not swiftly followed by an economic miracle. The two-nation society soon showed signs of becoming a *four-nation society*, since the extent of income inequality between whites and blacks remained large, while the extent of inequality within both the white and black populations grew.

At the end of the century, the South African government set up a special committee to consider a comprehensive reform of social security. One of its recommendations was a gradual introduction of a Basic Income Grant, which has been advocated by the national trade union confederation, COSATU, by the leadership of the churches in South Africa, by women's groups, by various NGOs and some leading politicians and economists. It is generally accepted that it could dramatically cut poverty and improve economic security, and there is little doubt that it could be afforded.[61] The real challenge is political.

More generally, simple small-scale regular transfers represent *ex ante* risk reduction means of providing basic security. And there is increasing evidence that *ex ante* schemes are in general more efficient than *ex post* schemes, which try to provide assistance to mitigate the outcomes of adverse shocks and help people cope with the consequences.[62] A simple cash transfer scheme not only satisfies the criterion that it would not be paternalistic, but it would be welfare-enhancing and poverty-reducing.

Cash transfers are generally the least costly and most rapid way of helping people in times of crisis. They are also the most transparent and easiest to administer. They have the positive features that are not found with other schemes. Thus, by giving each individual a certain amount they reduce the tendency to channel the benefits to any one person or type of person, as has been observed with food-for-work schemes.

There is a growing sentiment among policy-makers and advisers that there should be mixed provision of basic social services, with private and public providers charging user fees. Those who object typically worry about the distributional impact of such moves. Let us accept, for the sake of argument (and there is evidence to support it), that providers of

[59]E. Suplicy: "Legitimizing basic income in developing countries: Brazil", in A. Khan and G. Standing (eds.): *Income Security as a Development Right* (forthcoming).

[60]M.A. Amparo-Saco: "A basic income for Peru: Can it work?", in Khan and Standing, ibid.

[61]See P. le Roux: "A targeted and affordable South African universal income grant" and M. Samson et al.: "The social, economic and fiscal impact of a basic income grant for South Africa", in G. Standing and M. Samson (eds.): *The Basic Income Grant in South Africa* (Cape Town, University of Cape Town, 2003).

[62]T. Owens, J. Hoddinott and B. Kinsey: "Ex-ante actions and ex-post public responses to drought shocks: Evidence and simulations from Zimbabwe", *World Development*, Vol. 31, No. 7, 2003, pp. 1239–1256.

services are more likely to take care of clients if they have more than moral incentives to do so. If this means introducing or formalizing payments, then the sensible way to avoid the adverse distribution effects is to provide lower-income groups with transfers enabling them to make real choices, and ensure that there are voice mechanisms enabling them to have adequate information and to monitor and hold to account the providers of those services.

14.5 Concluding points

"Oh, the little more, and how much it is!
And the little less, and what worlds away"

— Robert Browning

The world is full of risks, the number and severity of which seem to be increasing, as are the social and economic uncertainties and hazards. This perception of a riskier world attracts a remarkable degree of agreement. Besides the risks of death, starvation or disability, perhaps the greatest risk is loss of a sense of *identity,* a sense of belonging, coupled with a feeling that ideas of *social solidarity* are fading. Not far behind are the "reputational risks", the fear of failure and the fear that some event or action will tarnish the reputation of a brand-name company, an individual worker or a citizen among his or her neighbours. Risks multiply and so do their potential costs.

To build a new social structure that will revive personal security while strengthening social solidarity will require a coherent set of policies that equalizes basic security. For this, a combination of basic representation security and basic income security is crucial.

It is not too much of an exaggeration to state that the major divide in thinking about social and economic policy in the first decade of the 21st century is between those who regard the riskiness of modern existence as something to be welcomed and those who see it as something that must be curbed. There are social policy thinkers who believe that policy should maximize the space for opportunities, giving rewards to those who succeed and telling the losers that their failure is "tough luck". And there are those who wish to see as many risks as possible underwritten, either removed or fully insured. Very few observers would go to either extreme. But most would admit to veering towards one pole or the other.

If all the costs of risks were to be removed, miraculously or by dint of comprehensive compensation for adverse outcomes, the predictable result would be a sea of moral hazards. Individuals, firms and communities would not care enough to curb the risks and would become socially irresponsible. Conversely, if few or no risks were covered, opportunism and bitterness would prevail. In between, a society committed to decency and social solidarity should surely limit the downside costs of risks and uncertainties, and provide its citizens with basic security.

Many currently popular policies are failing to provide basic economic security. Essentially, the emerging orthodoxy is *populist.* It gives a limited role for the state at central level, coupled with increased reliance on "civil society" and on such populist measures as microfinance and individual savings accounts, suitably subsidized. And it involves the State taking a judgmental view, directing those who fail in ways deemed appropriate for their social integration, and ultimately coercing them to do so, if necessary. This combination of policies does not strengthen citizenship *rights,* which are the essence of economic security and social solidarity. Indeed, the orthodox policies have reduced the emphasis on solidarity and pushed the democratic choice towards greater individualism.

Meanwhile, there is a pervasive sense of societal insecurity that seems to be linked to a sense of human smallness in the face of huge global forces. We hear the standard "sound bites" of news filtered through to us, and our perceptions are shaped by powerful special interests. In low-income countries and communities, the shaping is more awesome than elsewhere. Only if real voice security is developed can a capacity to understand the force of special interests be developed, and only then can an agenda for real security be developed. Everybody except a tiny minority of ridiculously privileged people would benefit from this.

Moving towards rather than away from basic security for all must be the fundamental guiding principle of social and economic policy in the 21st century. Although no sensible policy-maker considers that complete equality of incomes and wealth is possible or even desirable, most sensible policy-makers realize that inequality has become intolerable. There is no way that economic security can be assured unless the vast inequalities that characterize the world's economies are addressed.

In the new era, there must be an "assault on closed minds", making society's winners realize that they must make concessions to its many economic and social losers, for their own sake and for social justice. This must include those operating the international financial agencies. The macroeconomic strategy they have supported around the world in recent years has increased the sense of uncertainty.

Real security for all is not advanced by systematic resort to subsidies for relatively affluent interests or by directed social policy for the poor and insecure, relying on a mix of means-testing and stricter conditionality. This is the primary critical message of the second half of this report. The primary positive message is that redirecting the funds used for those subsidies and directive social policies — telling people what they must do and not do — could provide an enhanced degree of basic security for people in every part of the world.

Basic security for all is an equitable principle on which to build society and to enable everybody to live a life in which decent work is a meaningful proposition. To achieve that, governments and international organizations must promote income security and voice security for all legitimate interests. It is surely not too much to hope that many more countries will move in that direction in the next few years.

Appendix A

List of external collaborators

Country	Institute
Argentina	Centro Interdisciplinario para el Estudio de Políticas Públicas (CIEPP), Buenos Aires
Australia	Australian Centre for Industrial Research and Training, Sydney
Azerbaijan	State Statistics Committee of the Government of Azerbaijan, Baku
Bangladesh	Centre for Operations Research and Training (CORT), Dhaka
	Institute for Development Policy Analysis and Advocacy (IDPAA/PROSHIKA), Dhaka
	Population Council (Bangladesh), Dhaka
Belgium	International Confederation of Free Trade Unions (IFCTU), Brussels
	European Federation of Food, Agricultural and Tourism Unions (EFFAT), Brussels
	Department of Philosophy, Université Catholique de Louvain, Louvain-la-Neuve
Brazil	Instituto Universatario de Pesquisas do Rio de Janeiro (IUPERJ)
	Instituto de Pesquisa Economica Aplicada (IPEA), Rio de Janeiro
	Força Syndical, Sao Paulo
	Trade Union Confederation of Brazil (CUT), Sao Paulo
	Fundacentro (National Institute of OSH), Sao Paulo
	Fundaçao VivaRio, Rio de Janeiro

Country	Institute Canada
Canada	Centre for Occupational Health and Safety, Windsor, Ontario
	Groupe d'Analyses Économiques, Quebec
Chile	Deparmento de Estudios, Dirección del Trabajo, Santiago
China	Chinese Academy of Labour and Social Security (CALSS), Ministry of Labour and Social Security, Beijing
	Rural Development Institute, Chinese Academy of Social Sciences (CASS), Beijing
	Ford Foundation, Beijing
	Population Division of the Education, Science, Public Health Committee of the National People's Congress, Beijing
	China-Netherlands Poverty Alleviation Project, Huoshan County
	Institute of Population Studies, Chinese Academy of Social Sciences, Beijing
Colombia	School of Economic Science, Colombian National University, Bogotá
Denmark	Danish General Workers' Union, Copenhagen
Egypt	The National NGO Centre for Population and Development, Cairo
Ethiopia	Forum for Social Research, Addis Ababa
	Miz-Hasab Research Centre, Addis Ababa
Finland	Department of Social Policy and Social Work, University of Tampere, Tampere
	Department of Social Policy, University of Turku,
France	Trade Union Advisory Committee (TUAC) to OECD, Paris
	Public Services International, Ferney-Voltaire
	Institut National de la Statistique et de Études Économiques (INSEE), Centre Lebret, Paris
Germany	Department of Sociology, Humboldt University, Berlin
	Institute for Social Ecology, University of Jena, Thüringen
Ghana	Centre for Social Policy Studies, University of Ghana — Legon, Accra

Country	Institute
Hungary	Institute of Sociology and Social Policy, Eotvos Lorand University, Budapest
	Department of Social Work and Social Policy, Government of Hungary, Budapest
India	Institute of Human Development (IHD), New Delhi
	National Council of Applied Economic Research, New Delhi
	Kerala Health Studies Research Centre (KHSRC), Thiruvananthapuram
	Department of Economics, University of Kerala, Thiruvananthapuram
	Centre for Development Studies (CDS), Thiruvananthapuram
	Centre for Studies in Rural Development (CSRD), Mararikulum
	Gujarat Institute of Development Research (GIDR), Ahmedabad
	Self-Employed Women's Association (SEWA), Ahmedabad, Gujarat
Indonesia	Demographic Institute, University of Indonesia, Jakarta
	Bureau of Statistics, Government of Indonesia, Jakarta
Ireland	Careers Association, Dublin
	Conference of Religious of Ireland, Dublin
Israel	ADVA Centre, Tel-Aviv
Italy	Department of Economics, University of Milan
	Department of Economics, University of Rome
	European University Institute, Florence
Japan	Institute for Science of Labour, Kawasaki
Lebanon	Institut Libanais de Développement Économique et Social, Jal-El-Dib
Mauritius	Department of Economics and Statistics, University of Mauritius, Reduit
Moldova	State Statistics Committee of the Government of Moldova, Chisnau
The Netherlands	Institute of Social Studies (ISS), The Hague
	Department of Cross-cultural Studies, Utrecht University, Utrecht
	International Child Development Initiatives (ICDI), The Hague

Country	Institute
Nepal	New Era, Kathmandu
New Zealand	Centre for Labour Studies, University of Auckland
Nigeria	M. Iwoudou Institute for Labour Studies, Lagos
Norway	Centre for Women and Gender Research, University of Bergen
Pakistan	Pakistan Institute of Labour, Education and Research (PILER), Karachi Lahore School of Economics
Panama	SIAL, Panama
Peru	Pontifica Universidad, Lima
Philippines	Institute of Labour Studies (ILS), Department of Labour and Employment, Manila
Portugal	Portuguese Catholic University, Lisbon
Russia	Centre for Labour Market Research, Institute of Economics, Russian Academy of Sciences, Moscow
Slovakia	United Nations Development Programme (UNDP), Bratislava
South Africa	Research Surveys (PTY) Ltd., Cape Town SALDRU, University of Cape Town Economic Policy Research Institute (EPRI), Cape Town Self-Employed Women's Union (SEWU) of South Africa, Durban Department of Economics, University of Western Cape Black Sash (NGO), Cape Town School of Development Studies, University of Natal, Durban National Labour and Economic Development Institute (NALEDI), Johannesburg STREETNET Association, Durban Industrially Developing Countries Committee, International Ergonomics Association, Grahamstown
South Korea	Korean Labour Institute, Seoul

Country	Institute
Switzerland	International Federation of Building and Wood Workers, Geneva
	School of Management, University of Lausanne
	Global Labour Institute, Geneva
Tanzania	Economic and Social Research Foundation (ESRF), Dar-es-Salaam
	Institute of Development Studies at the University of Dar-es-Salaam
	Research on Poverty Alleviation (REPOA), Dar-es-Salaam
Turkey	Turkish Medical Association, Ankara
Ukraine	State Statistics Committee (GOSKOMSTAT) of the Government of Ukraine, Kiev
United Kingdom	Institute of Development Studies (IDS) at the University of Sussex, Brighton
	Department of Social and Policy Sciences, University of Bath
	Faculty of Economics, Cambridge University
	Queen's College, Cambridge University
	Nuffield College, Oxford University
	Centre for Comparative Labour Studies, University of Warwick, Coventry
	Department of Economics, University of Southampton
	Centre for Civil Society, London School of Economics and Political Science (LSE)
	Centre for the Study of Global Governance, London School of Economics and Political Science (LSE)
	Department of Social Psychology, London School of Economics and Political Science (LSE)
	Department of Economics, School of Oriental and African Studies (SOAS), London
	International Transport Workers' Union, London
	Hazards Magazine, Sheffield
	Globalization and Social Policy Programme (GASPP), University of Sheffield
	European Centre for Occupational, Safety, Health and Environment, University of Glasgow
	International Committee for Social Welfare, London
	Public Services International Research Centre, University of Greenwich, London
	School of Social Sciences, University of Birmingham

Country	Institute
	Department of Politics, University of York
	School of Sociology and Social Policy, Queen's University, Belfast
United States	Economic Policy Institute (EPI), Washington D.C.
	United States-Agency for International Development (US-AID), Washington D.C.
	Kennedy School of Government, Harvard University, Boston
	University of Massachusetts, Lowell
	Department of Economics, University of Massachusetts, Amherst
	Institute of Industrial Relations, University of California, Los Angeles
	Cornell Law School and the Department of Economics, Cornell University, Ithaca
	Rockefeller Foundation, New York
	Ford Foundation, New York
	Department of Sociology, Brown University, Providence
Venezuela	Office of Economic and Financial Affairs, National Assembly of Venezuela, Caracas
Zimbabwe	School of Social Work, Harare

Appendix B1

Labour Market Security Index (LMSI)

Rank	Countries	Scores			
		LMSI	Input	Process	Outcome
1	Norway	0.981	1.000	0.928	1.000
2	Sweden	0.955	1.000	0.857	0.981
3	Ireland	0.930	1.000	0.838	0.941
4	Iceland	0.925	1.000	0.841	0.929
5	United Kingdom	0.909	1.000	0.767	0.935
6	Canada	0.899	1.000	0.821	0.887
7	Netherlands	0.895	1.000	0.940	0.820
8	Denmark	0.879	1.000	0.893	0.812
9	Finland	0.862	1.000	0.779	0.835
10	Austria	0.861	1.000	0.863	0.791
11	Israel	0.848	0.778	0.920	0.847
12	Australia	0.825	0.778	0.852	0.836
13	Japan	0.823	1.000	0.795	0.748
14	Germany	0.808	1.000	0.804	0.714
15	New Zealand	0.799	0.778	0.730	0.845
16	United States	0.793	0.667	0.823	0.841
17	Portugal	0.787	1.000	0.795	0.677
18	France	0.779	1.000	0.830	0.643
19	Belgium	0.772	1.000	0.844	0.622
20	Luxembourg	0.763	0.667	1.000	0.693
21	Korea, Rep. of	0.754	0.778	0.719	0.759
22	Switzerland	0.749	0.667	0.743	0.794
23	Barbados	0.720	0.778	0.688	0.708
24	Hungary	0.701	0.778	0.589	0.718
25	Slovenia	0.685	0.778	0.834	0.565

Rank	Countries	Scores			
		LMSI	Input	Process	Outcome
26	Slovakia	0.685	1.000	0.645	0.547
27	Belarus	0.678	1.000	0.517	0.599
28	Czech Republic	0.667	1.000	0.667	0.499
29	China	0.666	0.778	0.827	0.529
30	Thailand	0.663	0.778	0.573	0.650
31	Latvia	0.662	1.000	0.402	0.623
32	Italy	0.662	1.000	0.761	0.444
33	Poland	0.662	1.000	0.872	0.388
34	Panama	0.641	0.778	0.749	0.519
35	Spain	0.639	1.000	0.754	0.401
36	Kyrgyzstan	0.632	1.000	0.365	0.581
37	Brazil	0.625	0.778	0.622	0.550
38	Republic of Moldova	0.622	0.778	0.261	0.725
39	Greece	0.622	1.000	0.700	0.393
40	Costa Rica	0.622	0.556	0.655	0.638
41	Philippines	0.618	0.778	0.600	0.547
42	Romania	0.616	1.000	0.446	0.509
43	Mauritius	0.603	0.444	0.746	0.610
44	Lithuania	0.593	0.667	0.445	0.630
45	Estonia	0.583	0.667	0.508	0.578
46	Azerbaijan	0.573	1.000	0.356	0.468
47	Uzbekistan	0.570	1.000	0.501	0.390
48	Croatia	0.556	1.000	0.505	0.359
49	Russian Federation	0.552	0.778	0.407	0.511
50	Venezuela	0.545	0.778	0.544	0.429
51	Chile	0.544	0.556	0.682	0.468
52	Tajikistan	0.518	0.556	0.388	0.564
53	Tunisia	0.516	1.000	0.740	0.162
54	Lebanon	0.512	0.556	0.582	0.455
55	Ukraine	0.511	0.778	0.324	0.471
56	Kazakhstan	0.507	0.778	0.382	0.433
57	Honduras	0.500	0.556	0.319	0.562
58	Georgia	0.496	1.000	0.000	0.492
59	Ecuador	0.482	0.778	0.516	0.318
60	Bulgaria	0.475	0.444	0.460	0.498
61	Peru	0.469	0.556	0.594	0.363
62	Turkey	0.460	0.667	0.622	0.275
63	Côte d'Ivoire	0.455	0.444	0.532	0.422
64	Mexico	0.451	0.333	0.649	0.410
65	Colombia	0.450	0.333	0.687	0.390

Rank	Countries	Scores			
		LMSI	Input	Process	Outcome
66	Armenia	0.446	1.000	0.267	0.259
67	Argentina	0.446	0.444	0.612	0.363
68	India	0.443	0.667	0.325	0.391
69	Burkina Faso	0.443	0.444	0.653	0.338
70	South Africa	0.442	0.444	0.621	0.351
71	Albania	0.436	0.667	0.375	0.351
72	Sri Lanka	0.418	0.444	0.361	0.434
73	Algeria	0.418	0.778	0.661	0.116
74	Indonesia	0.407	0.222	0.496	0.455
75	Mauritania	0.386	0.778	0.597	0.085
76	St. Vincent and the Grenadines	0.383	0.000	0.501	0.516
77	Nigeria	0.375	0.222	0.624	0.326
78	Morocco	0.357	0.556	0.570	0.151
79	Ghana	0.346	0.000	0.663	0.361
80	Egypt	0.341	0.222	0.682	0.230
81	Benin	0.327	0.444	0.627	0.119
82	Ethiopia	0.326	0.444	0.515	0.173
83	Dominica	0.321	0.000	0.501	0.391
84	Madagascar	0.297	0.333	0.502	0.177
85	Nepal	0.295	0.222	0.640	0.158
86	Sierra Leone	0.285	0.000	0.297	0.422
87	Congo, Dem. Rep. of	0.279	0.222	0.485	0.205
88	Fiji	0.278	0.000	0.256	0.428
89	Fiji	0.278	0.000	0.256	0.428
90	Bangladesh	0.268	0.333	0.658	0.041
91	Pakistan	0.236	0.333	0.586	0.013
92	Burundi	0.233	0.222	0.000	0.331
93	Rwanda	0.213	0.444	0.219	0.095
94	Congo	0.165	0.444	0.215	0.000

Appendix B2

Employment Protection Security Index (EPSI)

Rank	Countries	ESI	Input	Process	Outcome
			Scores		
1	Finland	0.960	1.000	1.000	0.920
2	Sweden	0.951	1.000	0.833	0.985
3	France	0.884	0.897	0.833	0.903
4	Denmark	0.839	0.691	0.667	1.000
5	Luxembourg	0.790	0.815	0.667	0.839
6	Netherlands	0.767	0.465	0.833	0.885
7	Norway	0.762	0.383	0.667	0.999
8	Portugal	0.755	0.897	0.667	0.729
9	Belgium	0.754	0.424	0.833	0.880
10	Israel	0.747	0.136	1.000	0.926
11	Spain	0.743	0.763	0.667	0.772
12	Germany	0.723	0.383	0.833	0.839
13	Austria	0.720	0.486	0.833	0.781
14	Australia	0.697	0.604	0.500	0.841
15	Ireland	0.692	0.331	0.833	0.803
16	Mauritius	0.690	0.506	0.667	0.794
17	Canada	0.679	0.167	0.833	0.858
18	Italy	0.655	0.486	0.667	0.733
19	Greece	0.635	0.506	0.667	0.683
20	Barbados	0.619	0.249	0.500	0.863
21	Switzerland	0.613	0.321	0.500	0.816
22	Botswana	0.613	0.218	0.500	0.867
23	United Kingdom	0.603	0.218	0.500	0.847
24	Slovakia	0.597	0.486	0.833	0.535
25	Ukraine	0.594	0.578	0.833	0.482

401

Rank	Countries	Scores			
		ESI	Input	Process	Outcome
26	Japan	0.591	0.105	0.833	0.713
27	Tunisia	0.589	0.300	0.667	0.694
28	Argentina	0.576	0.383	0.500	0.711
29	Estonia	0.576	0.588	0.667	0.525
30	United States	0.575	0.115	0.500	0.842
31	South Africa	0.573	0.136	0.667	0.745
32	Bulgaria	0.564	0.244	0.833	0.589
33	Panama	0.553	0.115	0.667	0.716
34	Russian Federation	0.551	0.280	0.833	0.545
35	Dominica	0.546	0.167	0.667	0.675
36	Latvia	0.544	0.630	0.500	0.523
37	Algeria	0.533	0.218	0.667	0.624
38	Brazil	0.532	0.218	0.667	0.622
39	New Zealand	0.528	0.000	0.500	0.804
40	Czech Republic	0.525	0.321	0.833	0.473
41	Belarus	0.515	0.239	0.667	0.578
42	Korea, Republic of	0.503	0.136	0.667	0.605
43	Costa Rica	0.495	0.300	0.333	0.672
44	Sri Lanka	0.487	0.300	0.500	0.574
45	Moldova, Republic of	0.477	0.733	0.333	0.421
46	Lithuania	0.475	0.136	0.667	0.549
47	Morocco	0.475	0.604	0.167	0.565
48	Egypt	0.470	0.424	0.333	0.561
49	Hungary	0.467	0.131	0.667	0.536
50	Venezuela	0.466	0.547	0.167	0.575
51	Turkey	0.464	0.547	0.500	0.404
52	China	0.454	0.218	0.500	0.549
53	Croatia	0.448	0.249	0.500	0.521
54	Tajikistan	0.447	0.321	0.500	0.484
55	Romania	0.417	0.275	0.667	0.363
56	Bolivia	0.415	0.259	0.500	0.450
57	India	0.415	0.300	0.500	0.429
58	Cameroon	0.411	0.630	0.167	0.424
59	Kyrgyzstan	0.408	0.239	0.500	0.446
60	Chile	0.406	0.136	0.333	0.578
61	Philippines	0.402	0.198	0.500	0.455
62	Mexico	0.394	0.033	0.333	0.606
63	Thailand	0.382	0.218	0.500	0.405
64	Uzbekistan	0.371	0.084	0.667	0.366
65	Zimbabwe	0.362	0.300	0.500	0.324
66	Lebanon	0.356	0.321	0.167	0.468

Rank	Countries	Scores			
		ESI	Input	Process	Outcome
67	Honduras	0.355	0.321	0.167	0.466
68	Ecuador	0.352	0.218	0.167	0.512
69	Kazakhstan	0.348	0.136	0.500	0.378
70	Albania	0.343	0.136	0.500	0.367
71	Turkmenistan	0.340	0.084	0.500	0.387
72	Colombia	0.333	0.136	0.167	0.514
73	Mauritania	0.317	0.136	0.333	0.400
74	Georgia	0.316	0.084	0.500	0.339
75	Peru	0.306	0.300	0.333	0.295
76	Armenia	0.306	0.239	0.167	0.409
77	Tanzania, United Rep. of	0.296	0.079	0.167	0.469
78	Gabon	0.291	0.712	0.000	0.226
79	Congo, Dem. Rep. of	0.280	0.630	0.333	0.078
80	Pakistan	0.270	0.053	0.333	0.346
81	Senegal	0.269	0.218	0.333	0.263
82	Nigeria	0.268	0.084	0.333	0.327
83	Guatemala	0.265	0.033	0.333	0.346
84	Kenya	0.251	0.300	0.500	0.103
85	Ethiopia	0.231	0.496	0.333	0.048
86	Madagascar	0.216	0.136	0.500	0.115
87	Indonesia	0.216	0.198	0.167	0.250
88	Côte d'Ivoire	0.182	0.218	0.333	0.089
89	Congo	0.182	0.218	0.333	0.088
90	Burkina Faso	0.178	0.218	0.167	0.164
91	Ghana	0.177	0.136	0.500	0.036
92	Burundi	0.163	0.218	0.333	0.051
93	Gambia	0.153	0.136	0.000	0.238
94	Sierra Leone	0.139	0.053	0.167	0.169
95	Benin	0.139	0.218	0.333	0.003
96	Bangladesh	0.117	0.136	0.333	0.000
97	Nepal	0.114	0.053	0.333	0.035
98	Guinea Bissau	0.110	0.053	0.167	0.109
99	Rwanda	0.055	0.053	0.167	0.000

Appendix B3

Job Security Index (JSI)

Rank	Countries	Scores			
		JSI	Input	Process	Outcome
1	Finland	0.940	1.000	0.957	0.901
2	Belgium	0.929	0.833	0.882	1.000
3	Canada	0.855	0.833	1.000	0.794
4	Netherlands	0.852	0.833	0.833	0.870
5	Ireland	0.821	0.778	0.819	0.843
6	Sweden	0.811	1.000	0.936	0.654
7	Luxembourg	0.781	0.944	0.806	0.687
8	United Kingdom	0.779	0.667	0.872	0.789
9	Denmark	0.771	0.944	0.914	0.612
10	New Zealand	0.755	0.500	0.921	0.800
11	Norway	0.750	1.000	0.917	0.542
12	Spain	0.747	0.833	0.816	0.669
13	France	0.745	1.000	0.877	0.551
14	Greece	0.742	0.833	0.719	0.708
15	Australia	0.741	0.528	0.899	0.768
16	Germany	0.710	0.944	0.804	0.546
17	Japan	0.693	0.944	0.880	0.474
18	Russian Federation	0.685	1.000	0.851	0.445
19	Panama	0.685	0.944	0.727	0.534
20	Italy	0.680	0.944	0.726	0.526
21	Lithuania	0.673	0.944	0.764	0.491
22	United States	0.669	0.417	0.951	0.653
23	Israel	0.668	0.764	0.752	0.579
24	Austria	0.668	0.833	0.764	0.538
25	Bulgaria	0.665	0.833	0.833	0.496

Rank	Countries	Scores			
		JSI	Input	Process	Outcome
26	South Africa	0.663	0.833	0.679	0.569
27	Argentina	0.656	0.833	0.756	0.516
28	Costa Rica	0.647	0.778	0.725	0.543
29	Egypt	0.645	0.667	0.379	0.767
30	Ukraine	0.633	0.889	0.762	0.441
31	Slovakia	0.631	1.000	0.773	0.376
32	Hungary	0.629	0.944	0.776	0.398
33	Switzerland	0.625	0.556	0.772	0.586
34	Portugal	0.624	0.833	0.753	0.455
35	Philippines	0.622	0.944	0.701	0.422
36	Brazil	0.616	0.944	0.613	0.454
37	Latvia	0.615	0.833	0.765	0.430
38	Saint Kitts and Nevis	0.611	0.667	0.768	0.505
39	Belarus	0.602	0.833	0.754	0.409
40	Venezuela	0.599	0.500	0.687	0.605
41	Czech Republic	0.593	0.944	0.741	0.344
42	Estonia	0.591	0.556	0.831	0.488
43	Georgia	0.581	0.667	0.643	0.508
44	Kyrgyzstan	0.580	0.944	0.719	0.328
45	Azerbaijan	0.580	0.944	0.765	0.304
46	Croatia	0.574	1.000	0.704	0.297
47	Chile	0.561	0.500	0.713	0.515
48	Lebanon	0.561	0.778	0.589	0.438
49	Peru	0.551	1.000	0.624	0.291
50	Tunisia	0.536	0.556	0.493	0.548
51	Colombia	0.532	0.556	0.626	0.474
52	Honduras	0.531	0.667	0.519	0.469
53	Dominican Republic	0.527	0.389	0.720	0.500
54	Moldova, Republic of	0.526	0.833	0.648	0.311
55	Tajikistan	0.514	0.944	0.640	0.237
56	Armenia	0.506	0.833	0.639	0.276
57	Mauritius	0.506	0.625	0.549	0.425
58	Ecuador	0.503	0.778	0.669	0.282
59	Uzbekistan	0.496	0.833	0.647	0.252
60	Kazakhstan	0.492	0.667	0.703	0.300
61	Turkmenistan	0.487	0.611	0.733	0.301
62	Romania	0.483	0.833	0.650	0.223
63	Algeria	0.469	0.528	0.416	0.466
64	Korea, Republic of	0.465	0.764	0.700	0.199
65	Barbados	0.454	0.167	0.635	0.508

Rank	Countries	Scores			
		JSI	Input	Process	Outcome
66	Thailand	0.452	0.556	0.611	0.320
67	Mexico	0.437	0.778	0.648	0.161
68	Morocco	0.421	0.667	0.258	0.379
69	Pakistan	0.416	0.667	0.163	0.417
70	Indonesia	0.413	0.667	0.450	0.268
71	India	0.410	0.833	0.313	0.248
72	Congo	0.401	0.667	0.323	0.308
73	Côte d'Ivoire	0.399	0.944	0.169	0.240
74	Albania	0.395	0.667	0.523	0.196
75	China	0.391	0.722	0.528	0.157
76	Turkey	0.389	0.514	0.458	0.293
77	Madagascar	0.357	0.569	0.281	0.289
78	Nigeria	0.349	0.556	0.330	0.254
79	Mauritania	0.336	0.639	0.178	0.264
80	Sri Lanka	0.326	0.278	0.552	0.237
81	Ethiopia	0.323	0.708	0.144	0.219
82	Zimbabwe	0.314	0.653	0.448	0.078
83	Congo, Dem. Republic of	0.290	0.542	0.180	0.218
84	Burkina Faso	0.286	0.778	0.000	0.183
85	Benin	0.276	0.667	0.008	0.215
86	Senegal	0.260	0.444	0.108	0.243
87	Rwanda	0.229	0.319	0.193	0.203
88	Ghana	0.224	0.292	0.268	0.168
89	Burundi	0.206	0.319	0.134	0.185
90	Guinea-Bissau	0.203	0.389	0.047	0.188
91	Bangladesh	0.201	0.556	0.084	0.082
92	Fiji	0.196	0.000	0.584	0.099
93	Nepal	0.126	0.444	0.052	0.000
94	Sierra Leone	0.104	0.000	0.085	0.165

Appendix B4

Skill Security Index (SSI)

Rank	Countries	Scores			
		SSI	Input	Process	Outcome
1	Sweden	0.888	0.714	0.920	0.959
2	Finland	0.863	0.714	0.826	0.956
3	Norway	0.863	0.726	0.853	0.936
4	Denmark	0.850	0.631	1.000	0.886
5	Germany	0.822	1.000	0.685	0.802
6	Canada	0.814	0.476	0.770	1.000
7	Belgium	0.802	0.917	0.537	0.876
8	France	0.799	0.810	0.682	0.852
9	Netherlands	0.791	0.810	0.708	0.824
10	United Kingdom	0.780	0.738	0.638	0.873
11	New Zealand	0.776	0.476	0.696	0.967
12	United States	0.775	0.476	0.683	0.971
13	Spain	0.760	0.810	0.614	0.809
14	Israel	0.758	0.821	0.658	0.776
15	Australia	0.754	0.560	0.630	0.914
16	Poland	0.741	0.714	0.611	0.819
17	Switzerland	0.736	0.631	0.769	0.772
18	Ireland	0.729	0.631	0.601	0.841
19	Hungary	0.726	0.810	0.543	0.776
20	Japan	0.704	0.464	0.543	0.904
21	Iceland	0.703	0.643	0.658	0.756
22	Luxembourg	0.702	0.548	0.740	0.761
23	Portugal	0.701	0.631	0.633	0.770
24	Russian Federation	0.701	0.631	0.407	0.883
25	Azerbaijan	0.697	0.905	0.324	0.780

Rank	Countries		Scores		
		SSI	Input	Process	Outcome
26	Slovenia	0.695	0.619	0.640	0.760
27	Cuba	0.690	0.714	0.477	0.784
28	Lithuania	0.686	0.631	0.516	0.798
29	Italy	0.682	0.536	0.715	0.738
30	Austria	0.676	0.464	0.735	0.752
31	Slovakia	0.675	0.714	0.447	0.769
32	Belarus	0.669	0.631	0.508	0.769
33	Estonia	0.669	0.381	0.619	0.838
34	Argentina	0.663	0.726	0.369	0.778
35	Cyprus	0.658	0.631	0.497	0.752
36	Venezuela	0.657	0.810	0.359	0.730
37	Greece	0.656	0.631	0.481	0.755
38	Ukraine	0.655	0.631	0.454	0.767
39	Malta	0.653	0.738	0.528	0.674
40	Latvia	0.652	0.464	0.557	0.793
41	Czech Rep.	0.649	0.548	0.525	0.761
42	Georgia	0.647	0.631	0.447	0.756
43	Saint Kitts and Nevis	0.645	0.667	0.357	0.778
44	Bulgaria	0.643	0.452	0.411	0.855
45	Dominica	0.642	0.643	0.374	0.775
46	Korea, Republic of	0.632	0.631	0.352	0.772
47	Kyrgyzstan	0.626	0.726	0.342	0.717
48	Barbados	0.625	0.571	0.624	0.652
49	Moldova, Republic of	0.623	0.452	0.564	0.737
50	Kazakhstan	0.621	0.571	0.378	0.768
51	Costa Rica	0.607	0.548	0.374	0.753
52	Malaysia	0.604	0.643	0.400	0.687
53	St. Vincent & the Grenadines	0.604	0.476	0.465	0.737
54	Sainte Lucia	0.601	0.476	0.503	0.713
55	Chile	0.595	0.536	0.296	0.773
56	Guyana	0.592	0.619	0.334	0.708
57	Romania	0.589	0.452	0.387	0.758
58	Croatia	0.587	0.452	0.500	0.697
59	Tajikistan	0.587	0.631	0.268	0.724
60	Ecuador	0.579	0.560	0.303	0.726
61	Armenia	0.577	0.571	0.301	0.717
62	Kuwait	0.575	0.452	0.433	0.708
63	Philippines	0.575	0.452	0.224	0.812
64	Panama	0.568	0.286	0.362	0.811
65	Jordan	0.565	0.631	0.402	0.613

Rank	Countries	Scores			
		SSI	Input	Process	Outcome
66	Uruguay	0.562	0.262	0.365	0.810
67	Dominican Republic	0.555	0.643	0.169	0.703
68	Nicaragua	0.548	0.619	0.221	0.677
69	South Africa	0.547	0.381	0.387	0.710
70	Brazil	0.546	0.452	0.391	0.670
71	El Salvador	0.545	0.631	0.262	0.643
72	Singapore	0.539	0.381	0.421	0.676
73	Bahrain	0.538	0.381	0.421	0.676
74	Kiribati	0.535	0.381	0.512	0.623
75	Lebanon	0.517	0.381	0.325	0.682
76	Turkmenistan	0.514	0.286	0.279	0.747
77	Uzbekistan	0.510	0.286	0.356	0.699
78	Tunisia	0.500	0.631	0.443	0.464
79	Mexico	0.499	0.262	0.340	0.698
80	Fiji	0.497	0.286	0.353	0.674
81	Trinidad and Tobago	0.496	0.190	0.382	0.705
82	Botswana	0.489	0.262	0.411	0.641
83	Jamaica	0.481	0.095	0.364	0.732
84	Indonesia	0.474	0.548	0.254	0.548
85	Thailand	0.474	0.095	0.394	0.704
86	Sri Lanka	0.472	0.381	0.280	0.614
87	Paraguay	0.468	0.095	0.343	0.718
88	Albania	0.467	0.452	0.314	0.551
89	Swaziland	0.461	0.190	0.295	0.679
90	China	0.459	0.548	0.315	0.487
91	Kenya	0.459	0.619	0.305	0.455
92	Lesotho	0.453	0.190	0.130	0.746
93	Mauritius	0.450	0.357	0.371	0.536
94	Peru	0.446	0.095	0.256	0.717
95	Algeria	0.444	0.631	0.319	0.413
96	Congo	0.440	0.643	0.174	0.471
97	Colombia	0.439	0.000	0.317	0.720
98	Turkey	0.437	0.536	0.236	0.489
99	Honduras	0.427	0.262	0.227	0.611
100	Viet Nam	0.426	0.000	0.256	0.724
101	Egypt	0.409	0.536	0.330	0.386
102	Zimbabwe	0.388	0.369	0.167	0.509
103	Zambia	0.382	0.357	0.121	0.524
104	Tanzania, United Rep. of	0.377	0.524	0.148	0.418
105	Bolivia	0.370	0.452	0.324	0.352

Rank	Countries	Scores			
		SSI	Input	Process	Outcome
106	Myanmar	0.359	0.000	0.290	0.573
107	Guatemala	0.340	0.262	0.191	0.454
108	Nigeria	0.325	0.381	0.151	0.384
109	Ghana	0.318	0.286	0.244	0.371
110	Iran, Islamic Rep. of	0.309	0.000	0.300	0.468
111	India	0.290	0.286	0.192	0.340
112	Sudan	0.284	0.286	0.221	0.315
113	Morocco	0.277	0.190	0.319	0.299
114	Syrian Arab Rep.	0.272	0.095	0.276	0.358
115	Ethiopia	0.266	0.262	0.102	0.351
116	Malawi	0.263	0.452	0.070	0.264
117	Uganda	0.261	0.095	0.159	0.394
118	Madagascar	0.258	0.095	0.107	0.416
119	Rwanda	0.257	0.262	0.090	0.337
120	Papua New Guinea	0.237	0.095	0.178	0.337
121	Togo	0.215	0.262	0.242	0.177
122	Cameroon	0.204	0.095	0.000	0.362
123	Côte d'Ivoire	0.201	0.095	0.179	0.265
124	Senegal	0.200	0.262	0.123	0.208
125	Gambia	0.199	0.095	0.265	0.217
126	Mauritania	0.192	0.095	0.213	0.229
127	Congo, Dem. Rep. of	0.186	0.000	0.240	0.253
128	Mali	0.161	0.381	0.003	0.130
129	Mozambique	0.156	0.000	0.013	0.305
130	Pakistan	0.155	0.095	0.124	0.201
131	Burkina Faso	0.154	0.357	0.134	0.063
132	Burundi	0.152	0.095	0.125	0.193
133	Sierra Leone	0.151	0.000	0.189	0.207
134	Nepal	0.132	0.167	0.200	0.080
135	Niger	0.123	0.345	0.143	0.000
136	Guinea-Bissau	0.120	0.095	0.129	0.128
137	Central African Republic	0.111	0.095	0.004	0.172
138	Bangladesh	0.091	0.000	0.050	0.157
139	Benin	0.088	0.095	0.090	0.083

Appendix B5

Work Security Index (WSI)

Rank	Countries	Scores			
		WSI	Input	Process	Outcome
1	Luxembourg	0.944	0.944	1.000	0.915
2	Norway	0.940	0.833	0.931	0.998
3	Sweden	0.938	0.888	0.888	0.988
4	Finland	0.931	0.888	0.834	1.000
5	Denmark	0.902	0.777	0.862	0.984
6	Netherlands	0.892	0.833	0.769	0.983
7	Austria	0.874	0.722	0.766	1.005
8	Germany	0.866	0.833	0.772	0.930
9	Japan	0.866	0.722	0.928	0.906
10	Belgium	0.856	0.777	0.888	0.878
11	France	0.847	0.777	0.883	0.864
12	Switzerland	0.837	0.777	0.819	0.876
13	Australia	0.836	0.722	0.820	0.901
14	Spain	0.823	0.916	0.791	0.792
15	Iceland	0.804	0.777	0.826	0.806
16	Italy	0.798	0.805	0.813	0.787
17	Portugal	0.796	1.000	0.674	0.756
18	Canada	0.784	0.722	0.789	0.813
19	Ireland	0.747	0.833	0.533	0.810
20	Greece	0.727	0.833	0.640	0.718
21	United Kingdom	0.726	0.667	0.482	0.877
22	Israel	0.704	0.722	0.773	0.661
23	Czech Republic	0.698	1.000	0.434	0.679
24	Slovenia	0.692	0.944	0.705	0.560
25	Poland	0.686	0.722	0.690	0.665

413

Rank	Countries	Scores			
		WSI	Input	Process	Outcome
26	Hungary	0.665	0.944	0.553	0.582
27	Lithuania	0.665	0.833	0.599	0.614
28	Slovakia	0.660	0.888	0.600	0.576
29	United States	0.656	0.222	0.761	0.820
30	Croatia	0.646	0.944	0.635	0.503
31	Latvia	0.633	0.805	0.599	0.564
32	Argentina	0.628	0.777	0.603	0.567
33	Barbados	0.609	0.444	0.682	0.655
34	Brazil	0.608	0.916	0.695	0.410
35	Costa Rica	0.608	0.777	0.655	0.499
36	New Zealand	0.605	0.444	0.434	0.771
37	Mexico	0.602	0.833	0.570	0.501
38	Russian Federation	0.601	0.833	0.580	0.496
39	Chile	0.593	0.666	0.581	0.563
40	Belarus	0.592	0.777	0.580	0.506
41	Romania	0.590	0.722	0.614	0.512
42	Ecuador	0.582	0.777	0.594	0.479
43	Bulgaria	0.572	0.722	0.554	0.506
44	Kazakhstan	0.571	0.722	0.535	0.513
45	Ukraine	0.569	0.777	0.549	0.475
46	Kyrgyzstan	0.568	0.777	0.589	0.453
47	Korea, Republic of	0.559	0.722	0.714	0.400
48	Estonia	0.555	0.444	0.690	0.543
49	Egypt	0.540	0.777	0.594	0.394
50	Algeria	0.536	0.667	0.673	0.403
51	Dominica	0.531	0.667	0.531	0.464
52	Tajikistan	0.527	0.777	0.511	0.409
53	Mauritius	0.522	0.667	0.616	0.402
54	Colombia	0.521	0.833	0.580	0.336
55	Morocco	0.516	0.667	0.673	0.362
56	Uzbekistan	0.509	0.722	0.489	0.412
57	Lebanon	0.506	0.777	0.552	0.348
58	Armenia	0.503	0.667	0.509	0.419
59	Peru	0.499	0.777	0.599	0.310
60	South Africa	0.486	0.667	0.590	0.344
61	Venezuela	0.484	0.777	0.155	0.501
62	China	0.479	0.500	0.628	0.394
63	Azerbaijan	0.456	0.777	0.113	0.467
64	Madagascar	0.448	0.777	0.663	0.176
65	Congo	0.435	0.667	0.668	0.202

Rank	Countries	Scores			
		WSI	Input	Process	Outcome
66	Moldova, Republic of	0.432	0.611	0.160	0.479
67	Mauritania	0.430	0.667	0.609	0.221
68	Nigeria	0.428	0.500	0.663	0.276
69	Tunisia	0.425	0.500	0.341	0.430
70	Albania	0.421	0.667	0.192	0.414
71	Côte d'Ivoire	0.416	0.722	0.668	0.138
72	India	0.416	0.722	0.517	0.213
73	Philippines	0.412	0.722	0.628	0.149
74	Georgia	0.411	0.444	0.271	0.464
75	Zimbabwe	0.411	0.722	0.589	0.167
76	Burkina Faso	0.409	0.833	0.603	0.100
77	Panama	0.396	0.722	0.129	0.366
78	Bangladesh	0.395	0.722	0.663	0.099
79	Benin	0.379	0.722	0.663	0.065
80	Turkey	0.366	0.500	0.565	0.200
81	Saint Kitts and Nevis	0.366	0.667	0.000	0.400
82	Indonesia	0.356	0.667	0.549	0.104
83	Honduras	0.330	0.667	0.033	0.309
84	Senegal	0.328	0.444	0.668	0.099
85	Ghana	0.325	0.777	0.235	0.144
86	Ethiopia	0.322	0.777	0.504	0.000
87	Burundi	0.310	0.500	0.663	0.038
88	Sri Lanka	0.307	0.500	0.390	0.169
89	Pakistan	0.306	0.777	0.172	0.138
90	Sierra Leone	0.297	0.444	0.663	0.040
91	Thailand	0.292	0.444	0.525	0.098
92	Turkmenistan	0.268	0.222	0.033	0.409
93	Guinea Bissau	0.206	0.500	0.235	0.044
94	Rwanda	0.188	0.500	0.206	0.023
95	Nepal	0.138	0.000	0.464	0.044

Appendix B6

Representation Security Index (RSI)

Rank	Countries	Scores			
		RSI	Input	Process	Outcome
1	Sweden	0.995	1.000	0.991	1.000
2	Denmark	0.941	1.000	0.892	0.936
3	Finland	0.921	1.000	0.983	0.851
4	Norway	0.910	1.000	1.000	0.821
5	Luxembourg	0.776	0.920	0.898	0.643
6	Ireland	0.764	0.920	0.972	0.582
7	South Africa	0.756	0.920	0.766	0.669
8	Austria	0.746	1.000	0.781	0.602
9	Germany	0.744	1.000	0.784	0.596
10	Netherlands	0.743	1.000	0.785	0.594
11	Canada	0.742	0.759	0.887	0.660
12	Belgium	0.741	0.920	0.973	0.536
13	Hungary	0.720	0.799	0.776	0.652
14	Italy	0.694	1.000	0.848	0.463
15	Spain	0.692	1.000	0.866	0.452
16	Bulgaria	0.688	0.920	0.780	0.527
17	United Kingdom	0.685	1.000	0.783	0.478
18	Switzerland	0.674	1.000	0.680	0.509
19	France	0.667	1.000	0.994	0.338
20	Portugal	0.649	0.920	0.850	0.414
21	Barbados	0.642	0.719	0.879	0.486
22	Japan	0.626	0.920	0.875	0.354
23	Australia	0.621	0.518	0.880	0.543
24	Czech Republic	0.621	0.719	0.875	0.444
25	Slovakia	0.616	0.719	0.484	0.631

Rank	Countries	Scores			
		RSI	Input	Process	Outcome
26	Mauritius	0.612	0.759	0.766	0.461
27	Philippines	0.598	1.000	0.574	0.409
28	Panama	0.593	0.920	0.724	0.364
29	Croatia	0.579	0.920	0.652	0.371
30	Israel	0.573	1.000	0.779	0.257
31	Latvia	0.571	0.518	0.878	0.445
32	Lithuania	0.563	0.719	0.767	0.384
33	Korea, Republic of	0.562	0.598	0.724	0.464
34	Russian Federation	0.548	0.518	0.895	0.390
35	Saint Kitts and Nevis	0.545	0.920	0.564	0.347
36	Greece	0.541	1.000	0.821	0.172
37	Estonia	0.540	0.719	0.587	0.427
38	Ukraine	0.535	0.719	0.667	0.377
39	Romania	0.527	0.518	0.708	0.442
40	Brazil	0.526	0.438	0.710	0.477
41	United States	0.517	0.598	0.589	0.440
42	Costa Rica	0.517	0.799	0.737	0.265
43	Moldova, Republic of	0.516	0.920	0.514	0.315
44	Argentina	0.513	0.719	0.746	0.294
45	Mexico	0.505	0.639	0.724	0.328
46	Benin	0.503	0.920	0.388	0.352
47	Burkina Faso	0.495	1.000	0.524	0.227
48	New Zealand	0.491	0.598	0.560	0.402
49	Tajikistan	0.481	0.920	0.727	0.139
50	Turkey	0.471	0.518	0.692	0.338
51	Chile	0.470	0.317	0.431	0.565
52	Peru	0.470	0.719	0.578	0.291
53	Fiji	0.470	0.719	0.407	0.376
54	Georgia	0.466	0.719	0.577	0.283
55	Ghana	0.466	0.920	0.313	0.315
56	Dominica	0.462	0.920	0.323	0.304
57	Nigeria	0.461	0.518	0.574	0.376
58	Zimbabwe	0.459	0.759	0.563	0.257
59	Tanzania, United Rep. of	0.456	0.518	0.581	0.362
60	Madagascar	0.455	0.920	0.514	0.192
61	St. Vincent & the Grenadines	0.450	0.518	0.240	0.520
62	Côte d'Ivoire	0.449	0.920	0.422	0.227
63	Algeria	0.446	0.920	0.728	0.067
64	Sri Lanka	0.441	0.719	0.412	0.317
65	Belarus	0.435	0.518	0.757	0.233

Rank	Countries	Scores			
		RSI	Input	Process	Outcome
66	Senegal	0.430	0.920	0.422	0.188
67	China	0.426	0.197	0.453	0.527
68	Ecuador	0.425	0.799	0.615	0.144
69	Azerbaijan	0.423	0.518	0.576	0.298
70	Albania	0.407	0.719	0.521	0.195
71	Congo	0.404	0.920	0.322	0.187
72	Saint Lucia	0.398	0.197	0.421	0.488
73	India	0.396	0.478	0.587	0.260
74	Lebanon	0.385	0.357	0.587	0.298
75	Congo, Dem. Rep. of	0.367	0.719	0.389	0.179
76	Kiribati	0.348	0.197	0.185	0.505
77	Tunisia	0.347	0.518	0.734	0.068
78	Indonesia	0.346	0.719	0.239	0.213
79	Sierra Leone	0.344	0.920	0.186	0.134
80	Kyrgyzstan	0.342	0.518	0.463	0.194
81	Burundi	0.317	0.719	0.388	0.080
82	Thailand	0.312	0.000	0.569	0.342
83	Papua New Guinea	0.308	0.116	0.433	0.342
84	Egypt	0.308	0.116	0.616	0.250
85	Turkmenistan	0.303	0.518	0.350	0.173
86	Honduras	0.302	0.518	0.177	0.257
87	Morocco	0.296	0.357	0.576	0.125
88	Kazakhstan	0.294	0.518	0.429	0.115
89	Uzbekistan	0.294	0.357	0.518	0.151
90	Nepal	0.289	0.558	0.209	0.195
91	Colombia	0.288	0.317	0.591	0.122
92	Venezuela	0.274	0.398	0.611	0.043
93	Ethiopia	0.260	0.518	0.192	0.165
94	Armenia	0.257	0.197	0.193	0.319
95	Pakistan	0.256	0.317	0.458	0.124
96	Rwanda	0.224	0.719	0.186	0.000
97	Bangladesh	0.189	0.317	0.201	0.118
98	Mauritania	0.150	0.116	0.354	0.065
99	Guinea Bissau	0.113	0.357	0.000	0.046

Income Security Index (ISI)

Rank	Countries	Scores			
		ISI	Input	Process	Outcome
1	Norway	0.941	0.889	0.951	0.963
2	Netherlands	0.931	1.000	0.942	0.891
3	France	0.923	1.000	0.842	0.925
4	Sweden	0.912	0.667	1.000	0.991
5	Denmark	0.898	0.667	0.925	1.000
6	Switzerland	0.877	0.778	0.874	0.929
7	Finland	0.868	0.556	0.983	0.967
8	Belgium	0.854	0.889	0.821	0.853
9	Austria	0.845	0.889	0.814	0.838
10	Luxembourg	0.836	0.778	0.744	0.911
11	Portugal	0.818	1.000	0.698	0.788
12	Germany	0.811	0.778	0.714	0.876
13	Spain	0.811	1.000	0.720	0.761
14	Japan	0.810	0.833	0.663	0.872
15	Canada	0.783	0.667	0.689	0.888
16	Australia	0.782	0.778	0.674	0.838
17	United Kingdom	0.772	0.667	0.664	0.879
18	Iceland	0.766	0.667	0.570	0.914
19	Ireland	0.764	0.778	0.752	0.763
20	New Zealand	0.759	0.667	0.762	0.803
21	Israel	0.750	0.778	0.560	0.832
22	Czech Republic	0.742	0.667	0.697	0.802
23	United States	0.739	0.556	0.618	0.891
24	Italy	0.713	0.444	0.733	0.837
25	Slovakia	0.708	0.667	0.712	0.726

Rank	Countries	Scores			
		ISI	Input	Process	Outcome
26	Latvia	0.694	0.667	0.700	0.705
27	Poland	0.692	0.667	0.680	0.710
28	Slovenia	0.685	0.556	0.583	0.800
29	Croatia	0.679	0.667	0.847	0.600
30	Hungary	0.672	0.556	0.660	0.736
31	Korea, Republic of	0.666	0.778	0.538	0.673
32	Bulgaria	0.658	0.778	0.708	0.573
33	Mauritius	0.654	0.778	0.666	0.586
34	Barbados	0.653	0.667	0.633	0.657
35	Estonia	0.627	0.333	0.747	0.713
36	Moldova, Republic of	0.624	0.778	0.610	0.554
37	Lithuania	0.622	0.444	0.604	0.721
38	Greece	0.594	0.333	0.600	0.721
39	Argentina	0.594	0.778	0.588	0.505
40	Ukraine	0.590	0.444	0.704	0.605
41	Brazil	0.586	0.889	0.586	0.434
42	Tunisia	0.585	0.778	0.554	0.504
43	Costa Rica	0.581	0.778	0.342	0.602
44	Belarus	0.570	0.333	0.624	0.661
45	Turkey	0.567	0.889	0.424	0.478
46	Chile	0.566	0.778	0.518	0.484
47	Mexico	0.555	0.778	0.524	0.459
48	Albania	0.541	0.556	0.543	0.533
49	Lebanon	0.540	0.889	0.117	0.576
50	Panama	0.538	0.778	0.330	0.522
51	Algeria	0.535	0.667	0.553	0.461
52	Romania	0.514	0.333	0.588	0.568
53	Saint Kitts and Nevis	0.506	0.556	0.167	0.652
54	Venezuela	0.505	0.667	0.489	0.432
55	Egypt	0.505	0.444	0.474	0.550
56	Sri Lanka	0.502	0.667	0.219	0.560
57	South Africa	0.487	0.667	0.516	0.382
58	Ecuador	0.464	0.778	0.450	0.314
59	Georgia	0.460	0.333	0.454	0.527
60	Russian Federation	0.456	0.222	0.511	0.545
61	Burkina Faso	0.447	0.889	0.226	0.336
62	Ghana	0.434	0.667	0.208	0.430
63	Philippines	0.432	0.667	0.207	0.428
64	China	0.428	0.222	0.461	0.515
65	Azerbaijan	0.424	0.333	0.559	0.402

Rank	Countries	Scores			
		ISI	Input	Process	Outcome
66	Senegal	0.421	0.889	0.029	0.383
67	Dominica	0.416	0.333	0.345	0.493
68	Benin	0.414	0.778	0.138	0.370
69	Armenia	0.411	0.111	0.455	0.540
70	Thailand	0.408	0.333	0.199	0.549
71	Madagascar	0.399	0.778	0.069	0.375
72	Uzbekistan	0.389	0.111	0.500	0.472
73	Honduras	0.386	0.667	0.217	0.330
74	Rwanda	0.377	0.444	0.126	0.469
75	Kazakhstan	0.377	0.111	0.409	0.494
76	Tajikistan	0.373	0.667	0.250	0.287
77	Turkmenistan	0.372	0.111	0.520	0.429
78	Kyrgyzstan	0.371	0.222	0.484	0.388
79	Bangladesh	0.365	0.333	0.137	0.495
80	Nigeria	0.363	0.778	0.192	0.240
81	Pakistan	0.360	0.333	0.310	0.398
82	Zimbabwe	0.357	0.222	0.374	0.415
83	Peru	0.356	0.556	0.195	0.337
84	Côte d'Ivoire	0.348	0.778	0.005	0.304
85	Nepal	0.340	0.444	0.000	0.457
86	Colombia	0.335	0.111	0.358	0.436
87	Morocco	0.331	0.222	0.210	0.445
88	Indonesia	0.328	0.333	0.135	0.422
89	Congo	0.317	0.778	0.216	0.137
90	St. Vincent & the Grenadines	0.306	0.333	0.083	0.403
91	Burundi	0.303	0.444	0.138	0.315
92	Mauritania	0.301	0.444	0.191	0.285
93	Ethiopia	0.295	0.556	0.024	0.299
94	India	0.288	0.000	0.329	0.411
95	Congo, Dem. Rep. of	0.280	0.667	0.016	0.219
96	Sierra Leone	0.197	0.778	0.010	0.000

Appendix B8

Economic Security Index (ESI)

Rank	Countries	ESI	Input	Process	Outcome
				Scores	
1	Sweden	0.977	0.909	1.000	1.000
2	Finland	0.947	0.870	0.992	0.962
3	Norway	0.926	0.871	0.967	0.933
4	Denmark	0.910	0.812	0.930	0.949
5	Netherlands	0.865	0.910	0.871	0.840
6	Belgium	0.829	0.845	0.887	0.792
7	France	0.829	1.000	0.914	0.698
8	Luxembourg	0.813	0.801	0.869	0.791
9	Germany	0.793	0.871	0.785	0.759
10	Canada	0.785	0.582	0.853	0.853
11	Ireland	0.782	0.741	0.818	0.784
12	Austria	0.782	0.796	0.821	0.755
13	Spain	0.756	0.976	0.777	0.635
14	Portugal	0.738	0.955	0.751	0.623
15	United Kingdom	0.736	0.681	0.673	0.795
16	Switzerland	0.727	0.661	0.745	0.751
17	Australia	0.724	0.535	0.771	0.794
18	Japan	0.718	0.702	0.814	0.679
19	Israel	0.695	0.708	0.774	0.650
20	Italy	0.681	0.687	0.777	0.629
21	Hungary	0.635	0.628	0.665	0.623
22	Slovakia	0.626	0.722	0.612	0.585
23	Czech Republic	0.622	0.674	0.719	0.548
24	New Zealand	0.614	0.353	0.632	0.735
25	United States	0.612	0.261	0.662	0.762

Rank	Countries	Scores			
		ESI	Input	Process	Outcome
26	Greece	0.592	0.654	0.670	0.521
27	Latvia	0.587	0.591	0.663	0.546
28	Bulgaria	0.582	0.589	0.673	0.534
29	Barbados	0.574	0.396	0.680	0.610
30	Lithuania	0.556	0.493	0.625	0.553
31	Croatia	0.546	0.715	0.629	0.419
32	Korea, Republic of	0.545	0.535	0.615	0.516
33	Mauritius	0.536	0.516	0.635	0.497
34	Estonia	0.525	0.354	0.650	0.548
35	Ukraine	0.524	0.569	0.612	0.457
36	Costa Rica	0.521	0.592	0.498	0.497
37	Argentina	0.521	0.600	0.585	0.449
38	South Africa	0.519	0.509	0.587	0.490
39	Brazil	0.517	0.566	0.598	0.452
40	Panama	0.515	0.615	0.491	0.478
41	Russian Federation	0.503	0.400	0.653	0.479
42	Belarus	0.499	0.431	0.632	0.466
43	Moldova, Republic of	0.495	0.712	0.397	0.435
44	Romania	0.456	0.397	0.568	0.429
45	Philippines	0.455	0.647	0.401	0.387
46	Chile	0.447	0.327	0.429	0.516
47	Azerbaijan	0.425	0.572	0.434	0.347
48	Mexico	0.418	0.412	0.518	0.370
49	Tunisia	0.412	0.500	0.559	0.296
50	Algeria	0.409	0.572	0.565	0.249
51	Tajikistan	0.404	0.643	0.420	0.277
52	Ecuador	0.395	0.619	0.414	0.274
53	Venezuela	0.393	0.493	0.379	0.351
54	Lebanon	0.390	0.452	0.317	0.395
55	Georgia	0.389	0.387	0.363	0.402
56	Turkey	0.381	0.500	0.464	0.280
57	Kyrgyzstan	0.380	0.428	0.423	0.335
58	China	0.356	0.157	0.461	0.403
59	Egypt	0.339	0.182	0.442	0.367
60	Albania	0.339	0.423	0.373	0.280
61	Peru	0.339	0.447	0.364	0.272
62	Sri Lanka	0.330	0.343	0.281	0.348
63	Kazakhstan	0.320	0.249	0.388	0.323
64	Uzbekistan	0.312	0.202	0.467	0.290
65	Thailand	0.287	0.009	0.393	0.373

Rank	Countries	Scores			
		ESI	Input	Process	Outcome
66	Armenia	0.285	0.213	0.235	0.347
67	Honduras	0.276	0.372	0.086	0.324
68	Burkina Faso	0.266	0.644	0.237	0.091
69	Colombia	0.258	0.000	0.398	0.317
70	Nigeria	0.254	0.284	0.321	0.206
71	Zimbabwe	0.254	0.265	0.384	0.184
72	Madagascar	0.249	0.452	0.260	0.142
73	Côte d'Ivoire	0.247	0.542	0.187	0.129
74	India	0.246	0.185	0.333	0.232
75	Morocco	0.237	0.198	0.308	0.220
76	Turkmenistan	0.230	0.012	0.310	0.300
77	Indonesia	0.228	0.296	0.163	0.226
78	Ghana	0.227	0.341	0.216	0.176
79	Congo	0.226	0.579	0.196	0.064
80	Senegal	0.223	0.505	0.136	0.126
81	Benin	0.215	0.493	0.190	0.089
82	Congo, Democratic Republic of	0.148	0.345	0.120	0.065
83	Ethiopia	0.142	0.371	0.078	0.059
84	Pakistan	0.136	0.092	0.210	0.121
85	Mauritania	0.128	0.128	0.223	0.081
86	Burundi	0.098	0.170	0.132	0.044
87	Rwanda	0.073	0.209	0.000	0.041
88	Bangladesh	0.070	0.060	0.140	0.041
89	Sierra Leone	0.060	0.207	0.041	0.000
90	Nepal	0.051	0.033	0.093	0.039

Bibliography

Abric, J. C.; Kahan, J. P. 1972. "The effects of representations and behaviour in experimental games", in *European Journal of Social Psychology*, Vol. 2, pp. 129–44.

AccountAbility. 1999. *AccountAbility 1000 (AA1000) Framework: Standards, Guidelines and Professional Qualification* (London, Institute of Social and Ethical AccountAbility).

Adler, P. S.; Goldoftas, B.; Levine, D. I. 1997. "Ergonomics, employee involvement and the Toyota production system: A case study of NUMMI's model introduction", in *Industrial and Labor Relations Review*, Vol. 50, No. 3, pp. 416–437.

Afford, C. 2003. *Corrosive Reform: Failing Health Systems in Eastern Europe* (Geneva, ILO).

Aho, S.; Virjo, I. 2003. "More selectivity in unemployment compensation in Finland: Has it led to activation or increased poverty?", in Standing, G. (ed.): *Minimum Income Schemes in Europe* (Geneva, ILO), pp.183–208.

Aidt, T.; Tzannatos, Z. 2002. *Unions and Collective Bargaining: Economic Effects in a Global Environment* (Washington, DC, World Bank).

Alasia de Heredia, B. M., et al. 2002. *Civil Society and Workers' Security*: VivaRio, SES Evaluation Report, mimeo (Geneva, ILO).

Alber, J.; Standing, G. 2000. "Social Dumping: Catch-up or convergence?", in *Journal of European Social Policy*, Vol. 10, No. 2, pp. 99–119.

Alesina, A.; Di Tella, R.; MacCulloch, R. 2001. I*nequality and unhappiness: Are Europeans and Americans different?* NBER Working Paper 8198 (Cambridge, MA, National Bureau of Economic Research).

Alfredsson, L.; Spetz, C. L.; Theorell, T. 1985. "Type of occupation and near future hospitalization for myocardial infarction and some other diagnoses", in *International Journal of Epidemiology*, Vol. 14, No. 3, pp. 378–388.

Allmendinger, J.; Leibfried, S. 2003. "Education and the welfare state: The four worlds of competence production", in *Journal of European Social Policy*, Vol. 13, No. 1, pp. 63–81.

Altbach, P.G. 2001. "Higher education and the WTO: Globalization run amok", in *International Higher Education*, Spring 2001, at: <http://www.bc.edu/bc_org/avp/soe/cihe/newsletter/News23/text001.htm>. [27 Feb. 2004]

Alwin, D.; Gornev, G.; Khakhulina, L. 1995. "Comparative referential structures, system legitimacy and justice sentiments: An international comparison", in Kluegel, J., Mason, D. and Wegener, B. (eds.): *Social Justice and Political Change: Public Opinion in Capitalist and Post-Communist States* (New York, Aldine de Gruyter), pp. 109–130.

Amick, B. C. et al. 2002. "Relationship between all-cause mortality and cumulative working-life course psychological and physical exposures in the United States labour market from 1968–1992", in *Psychosomatic Medicine*, Vol. 64, No. 3, pp. 370–381.

Amparo-Saco, M. A. Forthcoming. "A basic income for Peru: Can it work?", in Khan, A.; Standing, G. (eds.): *Income Security as a Development Right*.

Anderson, J.; Kauffman, D.; Recanatini, F. 2004. *Service Delivery, Poverty and Corruption: Common Threads from Diagnostic Surveys*, paper for the World Bank World Development Report (Washington, DC, World Bank).

Anderson, L. B.; Smith, J. E. 1998. *Going Postal: Fact or Fiction?* Presentation at the Society for Human Resource Management National Conference, Minneapolis, June.

Angrist, J., et al. 2001. *Vouchers for Private Schooling in Colombia: Evidence from a Randomized Natural Experiment*, NBER Working Paper 8343 (Cambridge, MA, National Bureau of Economic Research).

Anheier, H. et al. 2003. *Work in the Non-Profit Sector: Forms, Patterns and Methodologies* (Geneva, ILO).

Appadurai, A. 1998. "Dead certainty: Ethnic violence in the era of globalization", in *Development and Change*, Vol. 29, No. 4, pp. 905–925.

Apt, N. A.; Amankrah, J. Y. 2003. *Assessing Ghanaian Insecurities at the Household Level*, paper presented at ILO Workshop on Economic Security and Decent Work, Dar-es-Salaam, May.

Arax, M.; Wartzman, R. 2003. *The King of California: J. G. Boswell and the Making of a Secret American Empire* (New York, PublicAffairs).

Argyle, M. 1999. "Causes and correlates of happiness", in Kahnemann, D., Diener, E.; Schwarz, N. (eds.): *Well-Being: The Foundations of Hedonic Psychology* (New York, Russell Sage Foundation).

Ascher, W. 1999. *Why Governments Waste Natural Resources: Policy Failures in Developing Countries* (Baltimore, Johns Hopkins University Press).

Audley, J., et al. 2003. *Decoding Cancun: Hard Decisions for a Development Round*, Policy Brief No. 26, (Washington DC., Carnegie Endowment).

Azaroff, L.; Levenstein, C. 2002. *Innovations in Monitoring Work Security: A Case Study of Southeast Asian Refugees in Lowell, Massachusetts*, SES Paper No. 21 (Geneva, ILO).

Azaroff, L.; Levenstein, C.; Wegman, D.H. 2002. "Occupational injury and illness surveillance: Conceptual filters explain underreporting", in *American Journal of Public Health*, No. 92, pp. 1421–1429.

Bachman, R. 1994. *Violence and Theft in the Workplace, National Crime Victimization Survey* (Washington, DC, United States Department of Justice).

Bank for International Settlements (BIS). 2000. *70th Annual Report 1 April 1999-31 March 2000* (Basel).

———. 2003. *Overview of the New Basel Capital Accord*, Basel Committee on Banking Supervision Consultative Document (Basel).

Barrett, C. B. 1999. "Food security and food assistance", in Gardner, B. L.; Rausser, G. C. (eds.): *Handbook of Agricultural Economics* (Amsterdam, Elsevier Science), Vol. 2B, Chapter 40.

Baulch, B.; Hoddinott, J. 2000. "Economic mobility and poverty dynamics in developing countries", in *Journal of Development Studies*, Vol. 36, No. 6, pp. 1–24.

Baylies, C. 2002. "The impact of AIDS on rural households in Africa: A shock like any other?", in *Development and Change*, Vol. 33, No. 4, pp. 611–632.

Beason, R.; Weinstein, D. 1996. "Growth, economies of scale and targeting in Japan", in *Review of Economics and Statistics*, Vol. 78, No. 2, pp. 286–295.

Bergstrom, F. 1998. *Capital Subsidies and the Performance of Firms*, Working Paper No. 285 (Stockholm, Stockholm School of Economics).

Bernard, A. B.; Jensen, J. B. 2002. *The Death of Manufacturing Plants*, NBER Working Paper 9026 (Cambridge, MA, National Bureau of Economic Research).

Besley, T.; Coate, S. 1995. "Group lending, repayment incentives and social collateral", in *Journal of Development Economics*, Vol. 46, No. 1, pp. 1–18.

Betancourt, R.; Gleaton, S. 2000. "The allocation of publicly-provided goods to rural households in India: On some consequences of caste, religion and democracy", in *World Development*, Vol. 28, No. 12, pp. 2169–2182.

Bhagwati, J. 1998. *Why Free Capital Mobility May be Hazardous to Your Health: Lessons from the Latest Financial Crisis*, remarks prepared for the NBER Conference on Capital Controls in Cambridge, MA, Nov.

Biddle, J. et. al., 1998. "What percentage of workers with work-related illnesses receive workers' compensation benefits?", in *Journal of Occupational and Environmental Medicine*, Vol. 40, No. 4, pp. 325–331.

Blackburn, R. 2002. *Banking on Death or Investing in Life: The History and Future of Pensions* (London, Verso).

Blair, H. 2000. "Participation and Accountability at the Periphery: Democratic Local Governance in Six Countries", in *World Development*, Vol. 28, No. 1, pp. 21–39.

Bloom, G. 2001. *China's Rural Health System in Transition: Towards Coherent Institutional Arrangements?*, paper presented at the Conference on Financial Sector Reform in China, Cambridge, MA, Harvard University, Sep.

Boadway, B.; Keen, M. 2000. "Redistribution", in Atkinson, A.B; Bourguignon, F. (eds.): *Handbook on Income Distribution* (Amsterdam, North–Holland).

Board of Governors of the Federal Reserve System. 2001. *Flow of Funds Accounts of the United States* (Washington, DC).

Bobbio, N. 1987. *The Future of Democracy* (Cambridge, Polity Press).

Bobbitt, P. 2002. *The Shield of Achilles: War, Peace and the Course of History* (New York, Knopf).

Boden, L. I. 1995. "Workers' compensation in the United States: High costs, low benefits", in *Annual Review of Public Health*, Vol. 16, pp. 189–218.

Boeri, T., et al. 2001. *The Role of Unions in the 21st Century* (Oxford, Oxford University Press).

Boltvinik, J. 2002. *Poverty Measurement Methods: An Overview* (New York, UNDP).

Bonczar, T.; Beck, A. 1997. *Lifetime Likelihood of Going to State or Federal Prison* (Washington, DC, Bureau of Justice Statistics).

Bonnet. F. Forthcoming. *Whither Social Security? A Response Through Indicators*, SES Paper. (Geneva, ILO).

Boyer, R. 2002. *Is there a Welfare State Crisis? A Comparative Study of French Social Policy*, SES Paper No. 26 (Geneva, ILO).

Brenner, M. D.; Fairris, D.; Ruser, J. 2002. *"Flexible" Work Practices and Occupational Safety and Health: Exploring the Relationship between Cumulative Trauma Disorders and Workplace Transformation*, SSRN Working Paper No. 3 (Amherst, MA, Political Economy Research Institute, University of Massachusetts).

Brockner, J.; Adsit, L. 1986. "The moderating impact of sex on the equity satisfaction relationship: A field study", in *Journal of Applied Social Psychology*, Vol. 71, pp. 585–590.

Budd, J.; Na, I.-G. 2000. "The union membership wage premium for employees covered by collective bargaining agreements", in *Journal of Labor Economics*, Vol. 18, No. 4, pp. 783–807.

Burgoyne, C.; Swift, A.; Marshall, G. 1993. "Inconsistency of beliefs about distributive justice: A cautionary note", in *Journal for the Theory of Social Behaviour*, Vol. 23, pp. 327–342.

Canadian Union of Public Employees (CUPE). 2003. *Enough Workplace Stress: Organizing for Change* (Ottawa).

Cardoso, A. 2002. *Workers' Representation Security in Brazil: Global Forces, Local Stress*, SES Paper No. 28 (Geneva, ILO).

Carneiro, F.; Henley, A. 1998. "Wage determination in Brazil: The growth of union bargaining power and informal employment", in *Journal of Development Studies*, Vol. 34, No. 4, pp. 117–138.

Carter, M. R. 1997. "Environment, technology and the social articulation of risk in west African agriculture", in *Economic Development and Cultural Change*, Vol. 45, No. 3, pp. 557–590.

Chahad, J. P. 2002. *Non-Standard Labour Contracts*, paper presented at an SES Seminar, Geneva, Sep.

Chan, K. W. 2000. *Internal Migration in China: Trends, Determinants and Scenarios* (Washington, C, World Bank).

Chang H.-J. 2002. *Kicking Away the Ladder* (London, Anthem Press).

Chen, M.; Mahmud, S. 1995. *Assessing Change in Women's Lives: A Conceptual Framework*, Working Paper No. 2 (Matlab, Dhaka, BRAC-ICDDRB Joint Research Project).

Cho, J.-W., et al. 2002. *Civil Society and Workers' Security: Korean Construction Workers' Job Centres*, SES Evaluation Report, mimeo (Geneva, ILO).

Clark, A. E. 2001. "What really matters in a job? Hedonic measurement using quit data", in *Labour Economics*, No. 8, pp. 223–242.

Clark, A.; Oswald, A. 1995. *Satisfaction and Comparison Income* (Coventry, University of Warwick).

Clarke, S. 2001. *Do Russian Households Have Survival Strategies?* (Coventry, University of Warwick).

Commission on Human Security (CHS). 2003. *Human Security Now* (New York, CHS).

Converse, P. 1964. "The structure of belief systems in mass public", in Apter, D. (ed.): *Ideology and Discontent* (New York, Free Press), pp. 206–261.

Cornford, S. G. 2003. *Socio-Economic Impacts of Weather Events in 2002* (Geneva, World Meteorological Organization).

Cornia G. A.; Court J. 2001. *Inequality, Growth and Poverty in the Era of Liberalization and Globalization* (Helsinki, World Institute for Development Economics Research).

Crook, R.; Manor, J. 1998. *Democracy and Decentralisation in South-East Asia and West Africa: Participation, Accountability and Performance* (Cambridge, Cambridge University Press).

Cross, C.; Kutengule, M. 2001. *Decentralisation and Rural Livelihoods in Malawi*, Working Paper No. 4 (Norwich, University of East Anglia).

Cutler, D. M. 2002. "Equality, efficiency and market fundamentals: The dynamics of international medical-care reform", in *Journal of Economic Literature*, Vol. 40, No. 3, pp. 881–906.

Daly, M. (ed.). 2002. *Care Work: The Quest for Security* (Geneva, ILO).

Dammert, L.; Malone, M. F. Forthcoming. *Public Insecurity and Crime Control in South America*, SES Paper (Geneva, ILO).

Landsorganisationen i Danmark (LO, Danish Confederation of Trade Unions). 2002. *Corporate Social Responsibility - A Discussion Paper* (Copenhagen).

———. 2003. *Stress Can be Prevented*, at: <http://www.lo.dk/smcms/English version/News/4458/Index.htm?ID=4458> [27 Feb. 2004]

Dasgupta, S. 2002. "Attitudes towards trade unions in Bangladesh, Brazil, Hungary and Tanzania", in *International Labour Review*, Vol. 141, No. 4, pp. 413–440.

Datta, R. C. 1998. "Public action, social security and unorganized sector", in *Economic and Political Weekly*, Vol. 33, No. 22.

De Aghion, B. A.; Morduch, J. 2000. "Microfinance beyond group lending", in *Economics of Transition*, Vol. 8, No. 2, pp. 401–420.

Deaton, A. 2000. *Counting the World's Poor: Problems and Possible Solutions, Research Programme in Development Studies* (Princeton, NJ, Princeton University).

De Ferranti, D., et al. 2004. *Inequality in Latin America and the Caribbean: Breaking with History?* (Washington, DC, World Bank).

Delbridge, R.; Turnbull, P.; Wilkinson, B. 1992. "Pushing back the frontiers: Management control and work intensification under JIT/TQM factory regimes", in *New Technology, Work and Employment*, Vol. 7, No. 2, pp. 97–106.

Deshingkar, P.; Johnson, C. 2003. *State Transfers to the Poor and Back: The Case of Food-for-Work Programme in Andhra Pradesh*, ODI Working Paper (London, Overseas Development Institute).

De Soto, H. 2000. *The Mystery of Capital: Why Capitalism Triumphs in the West and Fails Everywhere Else* (New York, Perseus Book Group).

De Swaan, A. 1988. *In the Care of the State: Health, Education and Welfare in Europe and the United States in the Modern Era* (London, Polity Press).

Deutsch, S. 1989. "Worker learning in the context of changing technology and work environment," in Leymann, H.; Kornbluh, H. (eds.): *Learning at Work: A New Approach to the Learning Process in the Workplace and Society* (Gower).

Devereux, S. 2001. *Social Protection: What are the International Lessons with Respect to Programmes Targeted at the Poor?* (London, Department for International Development).

Dhanani, S. 2004. *Unemployment and Underemployment in Indonesia, 1976–2000: Paradoxes and Issues*, SES Paper No. 41 (Geneva, ILO).

Diamond, P. (ed.). 1999. *Issues in Privatising Social Security, Report of an Expert Panel of the National Academy of Social Insurance* (Cambridge, MA, MIT Press).

Diener, E., et al. 1999. "Subjective well being: Three decades of progress", in *Psychological Bulletin*, Vol. 125, No. 2, pp. 276–202.

Di Tella, R.; MacCulloch, R. J.; Oswald, A. J. 2001. *The Macroeconomics of Happiness* (Coventry, University of Warwick).

Dixon-Fyle, K. 2002. *Social Policy with Respect to Care: A Perspective for Sub-Saharan Africa*, SES Paper No. 27 (Geneva, ILO).

Donelan, K., et al.1999. "The cost of health system change: Public discontent in five nations", in *Health Affairs*, Vol. 18, No. 3, pp. 205–216.

Doyal, L. 1995. *What Makes Women Sick? Gender and the Political Economy of Health* (London, Macmillan Press).

Dror, D.; Preker, A. 2003. *Social Re-insurance: A New Approach to Sustain Community Health Financing* (Geneva, ILO).

Duryea, S. 1998. *Children's Advancement through School in Brazil: The Role of Transitory Shocks to Household Income*, Working Paper No. 376 (Washington, DC, Inter-American Development Bank).

Dwivedi, R. 2002. "Models and methods in development-induced displacement", in *Development and Change*, Vol. 33, No. 4, pp. 709–772.

Eliesh, S., et al. 2002. *Combating Labour Insecurity in Egypt–Do "NGOs" have Significant Role to Play*, SES Evaluation Report, mimeo (Geneva, ILO).

Ellsworth, R.R. 2002. *Leading with Purpose: The New Corporate Realities* (Stanford, CA, Stanford University Press).

Emler, N.; Dickinson, J. 1985. "Children's representations of economic inequalities: The effects of social class", in *British Journal of Developmental Psychology*, Vol. 3, pp.191–198.

Ensignia, J. D. R.1997. *La seguridad social en América Latina: Reforma o liquidación?* (Caracas, Venezuela Nueva Sociedad).

Esping-Andersen, G. 1990. *The Three Worlds of Welfare Capitalism* (Cambridge, Polity Press).

European Agency for Safety and Health at Work. 2000. *Monitoring the State of Occupational Safety and Health in the European Union - Pilot Study*, (Luxembourg, Office for Official Publications of the European Communities).

European Commission, Directorate-General for Employment and Social Affairs. 2002. *Corporate Social Responsibility: A Business Contribution to Sustainable Development* (Luxembourg, OPEC).

European Foundation for the Improvement of Living and Working Conditions. 1996. *Second European Survey of Working Conditions* (Dublin).

Fabbri, F.; Haskel, J. E.; Slaughter, M. J. 2002. *Do Multinational Firms have More Elastic Labour Demands?* NBER Working Paper (Cambridge, MA, National Bureau of Economic Research).

Fairris, D. 1992. "Compensating payments and hazardous work in union and non-union settings", in *Journal of Labor Research*, Vol. 13, No. 2, pp. 205–221.

Fairris, D.; Brenner, M. 2001. "Workplace transformation and the rise in cumulative trauma disorders: Is there a connection?", in *Journal of Labor Research*, Vol. 22, No. 1, pp. 15–28.

Fang, C. 2003. *Migration and Socio-Economic Insecurity: Patterns, Processes and Policies*, SES Paper No.36 (Geneva, ILO).

Farrington, J.; Saxena, N. C. 2003. "Protecting and promoting livelihoods in rural India: What role for pensions?", in *ODI Annual Report 2002/2003* (London, Overseas Development Institute).

Farrington, J., et al. 2003. *Post Offices, Pension and Computers: New Opportunities for Combining Growth and Social Protection in Weakly-integrated Rural Areas?*, ODI Natural Resource Perspectives No. 87 (London, Overseas Development Institute).

Filmer, D. 2002. *Fever and its Treatment among the More and Less Poor in Sub-Saharan Africa*, World Bank Policy Research Working Paper No. 2798 (Washington, DC, World Bank).

Financial Times Stock Exchange (FTSE). 2001. *FTSE Develops Standard for Socially Responsible Investment*, at: <http://www.ftse4good.com> [27 Feb. 2004].

FitzGerald, E. V. K. 2002. *Regulating Large International Firms*, UNRISD Technology, Business and Society Programme Paper 5, (Geneva, United Nations Research Institute for Social Development).

Flanders. A. 1970. *Management and Unions* (London, Faber).

Fliess, B. 2001. "Better business behaviour", in *OECD Observer*, No. 229, pp. 226–227.

Flug, K.; Spilimbergo A; Wachtenheim, E. 1998. "Investment in education: Do economic volatility and credit constraints matter?", in *Journal of Development Economics*, Vol. 55, pp. 465–481.

Fong, A.; Hebb, T.; Rogers, J. (eds.). 2001. *Working Capital: The Power of Labor's Pensions* (Ithaca, NY, and London, Cornell University Press).

Fournier, G.; Rasmussen, D. 1986. "Targeted capital subsidies and economic welfare", in *Cato Journal*, Vol. 6, No. 1, pp. 295–312.

Francis, P.; James, R. 2003. "Balancing rural poverty reduction and citizen participation: The contradictions of Uganda's decentralisation programme", in *World Development*, Vol. 31, No. 2, pp. 325–337.

Franzese, R. J. 2001. "Institutional and structural interactions in monetary policy and wage/price bargaining", in Hall, P.; Soskice, D (eds.): *Varieties of Capitalism: The Institutional Foundations of Comparative Advantage* (Cambridge, Cambridge University Press), pp. 411–434.

Freedom House, Freedom in the World. Various years. *The Annual Survey of Political Rights and Civil Liberties* (New York).

Freeman, R.; Medoff, J. 1984. *What Do Unions Do?* (New York, Basic Books).

Frohlich, N.; Oppenheimer, J. 1992. *Choosing Justice: An Experimental Approach to Ethical Theory* (Berkeley, CA, University of California Press).

Furman, J.; Stiglitz, J.E. 1999. *Economic Crises: Evidence and Insights from East Asia*, Brookings Papers on Economic Activity No. 2 (Washington, DC, Brookings Institution).

Gardner, J.; Oswald, A. 2001. *What has been Happening to the Quality of Workers' Lives in Britain?* (Coventry, University of Warwick).

Gardner, J.; Oswald, A. 2002. *How does Education Affect Mental Well-being and Job Satisfaction?* (Coventry, University of Warwick).

Gauri, V. ; Vawda, A. 2004. *Vouchers for Basic Education in Developing Countries: A Principal-agent Perspective*, background paper for the World Bank World Development Report (Washington, DC).

Gereluk, W.; Royer, L. 2002. *Sustainable Development of the Global Economy: A Trade Union Perspective*, SES Paper No. 19 (Geneva, ILO).

Geschiere, P.; Meyer, B. 1998. "Globalization and identity: Dialectics of flow and closure", in *Development and Change*, Vol. 29, No. 4, pp. 873–903.

Gilson, L., et al. 1997. "Should African governments contract out clinical health services to church providers", in Bennet, S., McPake, B. and Mills, A. (eds.): *Private Health Providers in Developing Countries: Serving the Public Interest?* (London and New Jersey, Zed Books).

Gilson, L., et al. 2001. "Strategies for promoting equity: Experience with community financing in three African countries", in *Health Policy*, Vol. 58, No. 1, pp. 37–67.

Gimpelson, V.; Lippoldt, D. 2001. *The Russian Labour Market* (Lanham Maryland, Rowman and Littlefield).

Glewwe, P. 1999. "Why does mother's schooling raise child health in developing countries? Evidence from Morocco", in *Journal of Human Resources*, Vol. 34, No. 1, pp. 124–159.

Global Reporting Initiative (GRI). 2002. *Sustainability Reporting Guidelines 2002* (Boston).

Goetz, A. M.; Sen Gupta, R. 1996. "Who takes the credit? Gender, power and control over loan use in rural credit programmes in Bangladesh", in *World Development*, Vol. 24, No. 1, pp. 45–63.

Goldin, J. 2003. *The Topography of Voice: Dynamics of Belonging*, paper presented at ILO Workshop on Economic security and Decent work, Dar-es-Salaam, May.

Goldsmith, O. Forthcoming. "The Alaska Permanent Fund Dividend: An experiment in wealth distribution", in G. Standing (ed.): *Promoting Income Security as a Right: Europe And North America* (London, Anthem Press).

Goodhand, J. 2003. "Enduring disorder and persistent poverty: A review of the linkages between war and chronic poverty", in *World Development*, Vol. 31, No. 3, pp. 629–646.

Gordon, R. 2002. *Two Centuries of Economic Growth: Europe Chasing the American Frontier*, paper prepared for the Economic History Workshop, Northwestern University, Evanston, IL, Oct.

Gorg, H.; Strobl, E. 2003. "Footloose multinationals?", in *Manchester School*, Vol. 71, No. 1, pp. 1–19.

Gotsch, C. 1972. "Technological change and the distribution of income in rural areas", in *American Journal of Agricultural Economics*, Vol. 54, No. 2.

Government of India, Ministry of Sound Justice and Empowerment. 1999. *First Report of Expert Committee for Devising a Pension System for India* (New Delhi).

Griffith-Jones, S.; Ocampo, J. A. 2001. "Facing the volatility and concentration of capital flows", in Teunissen, J. J. (ed.): *Reforming the International Financial System: Crisis Prevention and Response* (The Hague, FONDAD).

Groshen, E.; Potter, S. 2003. "Has structural change contributed to a jobless recovery?", in *Current Issues in Economics and Finance*, Vol. 9, No. 8, at <http://www.newyorkfed.org/research/current_issues/ci9-8.pdf> [27 Feb. 2004].

Gu, E. 2003. *The Institutionalization of Unemployment in China*, SES Paper No. 33 (Geneva, ILO).

Guan, X. 2000. "China's social policy: Reform and development in the context of marketization and globalization", in *Social Policy and Administration*, Vol. 34, No. 1, pp. 115–130.

Guerrero, L. L. 1993. *Social Inequality in the Philippines: The 1992 ISSP Survey*, SWS Occasional Paper (Manila, Social Weather Stations, Inc.).

Hadi, A. 2001. "Promoting health knowledge through micro-credit programmes: Experience of BRAC in Bangladesh", in *Health Promotion International*, Vol. 16, No. 3, pp. 219–228.

Hall, P. A.; Franzese, R. 1998. "Central bank independence, coordinated wage bargaining, and European Monetary Union", in *International Organization*, Vol. 52, No. 3, pp. 505–535.

Hallerberg, M.; Basinger, S. 1998. "Internationalization and changes in taxation policy in OECD countries: The importance of domestic veto players", in *Comparative Political Studies*, Vol. 31, No. 3, pp. 321–352.

Hartmann, E.; Haslinger, S.; Scherrer, C. 2003. *Liberalization of Higher Education and Training: Implications for Workers' Security*, SES Paper (Geneva, ILO).

Hashemi, S. M.; Schuler, S. R.; Riley, A. P. 1996. "Rural credit programmes and women's empowerment in Bangladesh", in *World Development*, Vol. 24, No. 4, pp. 635–653.

Haynes, S.; LaCroix, A.; Lippin, T. 1987. "The effect of high job demands and low control on the health of employed women", in Quick, J., et al. (eds.): *Work, Stress and Health Care* (New York, Praeger Press).

Health and Safety Executive (HSE). 2002. *The Whitehall II Study: Work Environment, Alcohol Consumption and Ill-health*, HSE Contract Research Report 422 (London).

Heller, P. 2003. *Who Will Pay? Coping With Aging Societies, Climate Change and Other Long-term Fiscal Challenges* (Washington, DC, IMF).

Henderson, D. 2001. *Misguided Virtue: False Notions of Corporate Social Responsibility*, Hobart Paper No. 142 (London, Institute of Economic Affairs).

Henry, M., et al. 2001. *The OECD Globalization and Education Policy* (Amsterdam, Pergamon).

Heran-Le Roy, O.; Sandret, N. 1997. "Résultats de l'enquête Sumer 94: Les contraintes articulaires pendant le travail", in *Documents pour le médecin du travail*, No. 71, 3ème trimestre.

Higgins, P.; Alderman, H. 1997. "Labor and women's nutrition: The impact of work effort and fertility on nutritional status in Ghana", in *Journal of Human Resources*, Vol. 32, pp. 577–595.

Hobhouse, L. T. 2002. *The Elements of Social Justice* (London, George Allen and Unwin).

Hochschild, A. R. 2001. "Global care chains and emotional surplus value", in Hutton, W.; Giddens, A. (eds.): *On The Edge: Living with Global Capitalism* (London, Jonathan Cape).

Hochschild, J. 1982. *What's Fair? American Beliefs About Distributive Justice* (Cambridge, MA, Harvard University Press).

Horn, P. Forthcoming. "Voice regulation and the informal economy", in Chen, M., et al. *Reconceptualizing Work*.

House, J. 1971. "Job dissatisfaction as a possible risk factor in coronary heart disease", in *Journal of Chronic Diseases*, Vol. 23, pp. 861–873.

Hulme, D.; Mosley, P. 1996. *Finance Against Poverty* (London, Routledge).

Hulme, D.; Shepherd, A. 2003. "Conceptualizing chronic poverty", in *World Development*, Vol. 31, No. 3, pp. 403–423.

Hume, D. 1739-40. *Treatise on Human Nature*.

Hussain, A. 2003. *Urban Poverty in China: Measurements, Patterns and Policies*, SES Paper No. 34 (Geneva, ILO).

Inglehart, R.; Klingemeann, H.-D. 2000. "Genes, culture, democracy and happiness", in Diener, E.; Suh, E.M. (eds.): *Culture and Subjective Well Being* (Cambridge, MA, MIT Press).

Institute for Labor and the Community. 1999. *Stop Stress at Work* (New York).

Institute of Development Studies (IDS). 2003. *The Rise of Rights*, University of Sussex Policy Briefing (Brighton, 17 May).

Inter-American Development Bank (IADB). 2000. *Social Protection for Equity and Growth* (Washington, DC).

International Confederation of Free Trade Unions (ICFTU). 2003. *Annual Survey of Violations of Trade Union Rights 2003* (Brussels).

International Federation of Red Cross and Red Crescent Societies (IFRC). 2003. *World Disasters Report: Focus on Ethics in Aid* (Geneva).

International Labour Office. Business and Social Initiatives Database (BASI), at: <http://www.ilo.org/basi> [27 Feb. 2004].

International Labour Office (ILO). 1998. *Cost of Social Security Inquiry* (Geneva, ILO), at: <www.ilo.org/protection/socfas> [27 Feb. 2004].

———. 2000. *World Labour Report 2000* (Geneva).

———. 2001. *Health Care Privatization: Workers' Insecurities in Eastern Europe*, Report of the ILO, Socio-Economic Security Programme and Public Services International Workshop on the Privatization of Health Care Health Care, Geneva, Dec.

———. 2001. *Labour Overview: Latin America and the Caribbean* (Lima).

———. 2002. *ILO Compendium of Official Statistics on Employment in the Informal Sector* (Geneva).

———. 2002. *Women and Men in the Informal Economy: A Statistical Picture* (Geneva).

———. 2003. *Conclusions Concerning ILO Standards-related Activities in the Area of Occupational Safety and Health: A Global Strategy*, International Labour Conference, 91st Session, 2003, Provisional Record 22 (Geneva).

———. 2003. *Decent work in agriculture* (Geneva).

———. 2003. *Information Note on Corporate Social Responsibility and International Labour Standards* (Geneva, Working Party on the Social Dimension of Globalization).

———. 2004. *Global Employment Trends 2003* (Geneva).

———. 2004. *Investing in Every Child: An Economic Study of the Costs and Benefits of Eliminating Child Labour* (Geneva, International Programme on the Elimination of Child Labour).

International Monetary Fund (IMF). 1998. *World Economic Outlook: Financial Crises: Causes and Indicators* (Washington, DC).

———. 1999. *World Economic Outlook 1999* (Washington, DC).

———. 2002. *World Economic Outlook 2002* (Washington, DC).

International Social Security Association (ISSA). 1999. *Social Security Programs Throughout the World* (Geneva).

International Union of Food, Agricultural, Hotel, Restaurant, Catering, Tobacco and Allied Workers' Association (IUF). 2002. *The WTO and the World Food System: A Trade Union Approach* (Geneva).

Isaac, T. M. T., et al. 2002. *Women Neighbourhood Groups: Towards a New Perspective*, paper presented at the ILO Seminar on Decentralization, Sustainable Development and Social Security, Mararikulum, Kerala, India, May.

Jackson, M.; Goldthorpe, J.; Mills, C. 2004. "Education, employers and class mobility", in *Research in Social Stratification and Mobility* (London, Elsevier).

Jackson, S.; Palmer-Jones, R. 1998. *Gender, Work Intensity and Well-being*, UNRISD Occasional Paper (Geneva, United Nations Research Institute for Social Development).

Jacoby, H.; Skoufias, E. 1997. "Risk, financial markets and human capital in a developing country", in *Review of Economic Studies*, Vol. 64, No. 3, pp. 311–335.

Jeminiwa, J. O., et al. 2002. *Civil Society and Workers' Security: Community, Women and Development (COWAD) Nigeria*, SES Evaluation Report, mimeo (Geneva, ILO).

Jeria Caceres, M. 2002. "More training, less security? Training and the quality of life at work in Argentina, Brazil and Chile", in *International Labour Review*, Vol. 141, No. 4, pp. 359–384.

Johnson, C. 2002. "Local democracy, democratic decentralisation and rural development: Theories, challenges and options for policy", in *Development Policy Review*, Vol. 19, pp. 521–532.

Jones, P. 1992. *World Bank Financing of Education* (London and New York, Routledge).

Judge, T.A. and Watanabe, S. 1993 "Another look at the job satisfaction-life satisfaction relationship", in *Journal of Applied Psychology*, 78, 1993, pp. 939–948.

Kabeer, N. 1999. *The Conditions and Consequences of Choice: Reflections on the Measurement of Empowerment*, UNRISD Discussion Paper DP108 (Geneva, United Nations Research Institute of Social Development,).

———. 2001. "Conflicts over credit: Re-evaluating the empowerment potential of loans to women in Bangladesh", in *World Development*, Vol. 29, No. 1, pp. 63–84.

———. 2001. *Safety Nets and Opportunity Ladders: Addressing Vulnerability and Enhancing Productivity in South Asia* (Brighton, Institute of Development Studies, University of Sussex).

Khan, A.; Standing, G. (eds.). *Forthcoming. Income Security as a Development Right.*

Khan, M.E.; Rob, U.; Anker, R. Forthcoming. *People's Security Survey in Bangladesh: Some Observations on Work Security in Rural Areas*, SES Paper (Geneva, ILO).

Kaminsky, G.; Schmukler, S. 2003. *Short-run pain, long-run Gain: The effects of financial liberalization. IMF Working Paper 03/34* (Washington, DC, International Monetary Fund).

Karshenas, M. 2003. "Global poverty: National accounts-based versus survey-based estimates", in *Development and Change*, Vol. 34, No. 4, pp. 683–712.

Kaufman, H. 2000. *On Money and Markets: A Wall Street Memoir* (New York, McGraw Hill).

Keith, M., et al. 2002. *Barefoot Research: A Workers' Manual for Organising on Work Security* (Geneva, ILO).

Kelley, J.; Evans, M. 1991. "The legitimation of inequality: Occupational earnings in nine nations", in *American Journal of Sociology*, Vol. 99, No.1, pp. 75–125.

Khandker, S. R.; Samad, H. A.; Khan, Z. 1998. "Income and employment effects of micro-credit programmes: Village-level evidence from Bangladesh", in *Journal of Development Studies*, Vol. 35, No. 2, pp. 96–124.

Kivimäki, M., et al. 2002. "Work stress and risk of cardiovascular mortality: Prospective cohort study of industrial employees", in *British Medical Journal*, Vol. 325, pp. 857–860.

Kornai, J. 1994. "Transformational recession: The main causes", in *Journal of Comparative Economics*, Vol. 19, No. 1, pp. 39–63.

Korzeniewick, R. P.; Moran, T. 1997. "World economic trends in the distribution of income, 1965–1992", in *American Journal of Sociology*, Vol. 102, pp. 1000–1039.

KPMG. 2002. *KPMG International Survey of Corporate Sustainability Reporting 2002* (Amsterdam).

Kucera, D. 2001. *The Effects of Core Workers' Rights on Labour Costs and Foreign Direct Investment: Evaluating the Conventional Wisdom*, IILS Discussion Paper (Geneva, International Institute for Labour Studies).

Kwa, A. 2001. *Agriculture in Developing Countries: Which Way Forward?* Occasional Paper No. 4 (Geneva, South Centre).

LaCroix, A.; Haynes, S. 1987. "Gender differences in the health effects of work-place roles", in Barnett, R.; Biener, L.; Baruch, G. (eds.): *Gender and Stress* (New York, The Free Press).

Landsbergis, P. A., et al. 2003. "Life course exposure to job strain and ambulatory blood pressure among men", in *American Journal of Epidemiology*, Vol. 157, No. 11, pp. 998–1006.

Laurell, A.C. 2003. "What does Latin American social medicine do when it governs? The case of the Mexico City government", in *American Journal of Public Health*, Vol. 93, No. 12, pp. 2028–2031.

Leiser, D.; Zalsman, J. 1990. "Economic socialization in the kibbutz and in the town in Israel", in *Journal of Economic Psychology*, Vol.11, pp. 557–565.

Le Roux, P. 2003. *A Targeted and Affordable South African Universal Income Grant* (Cape Town, University of Cape Town).

Lethbridge, J. Forthcoming. *Implications of Health Care Liberalization on Workers' Security*, SES Paper (Geneva, ILO).

Levine, D. I. 1995. *Reinventing the Workplace* (Washington, DC, The Brookings Institution).

Levison, D., et al. 2002. "Distribution of income and job opportunities: Normative judgments from four continents", in *International Labour Review*, Vol. 141, No. 4, pp. 385–411.

Lewis, M.; Eskeland, G. S.; Traa-Valerezo, X. 1999. *Challenging El Salvador's Rural Health Care Strategy*, World Bank Policy Research Working Paper Series 2164 (Washington, DC, World Bank).

Lindert, P. 2000. "Three centuries of inequality in Britain and America", in Atkinson, A. B.; Bourguignon, F. (eds.): *Handbook on Income Distribution* (Amsterdam, North-Holland), Vol. 1, Chapter 3.

———. 2000. "When did inequality rise in Britain and America?", in *Journal of Income Distribution*, No. 9, pp. 15–25.

Lopez, R. 2003. "The policy roots of socio-economic stagnation and environmental implosion: Latin America 1950-2000", in *World Development*, Vol. 31, No. 2, pp. 259–280.

Mackenzie, E. 1994. *Privatopia: Homeowner Associations and the Rise of Residential Private Government* (New Haven, CT, and London, Yale University Press).

Mahmud, S. 2003. "Actually how empowering is microcredit?", in *Development and Change*, Vol. 34, No. 4, pp. 577–605.

Majid, N. 2003. *Globalization and Poverty*, Employment Paper 2003/54 (Geneva, ILO).

Major, B. 1994. "From social inequality to personal entitlement: The role of social comparisons, legitimacy appraisals and group membership", in *Advances in Experimental Social Psychology*, Vol. 26, pp. 293–355.

Mansuri, G.; Rao, V. 2003. *Evaluating Community Driven Development: A Critical Review of the Research* (Washington, DC, World Bank).

Marshall, T.H. 1950. *Citizenship and Social Class* (Cambridge, Cambridge University Press).

Marti-i-Sala, M. 2002. *The World Distribution of Income*, NBER Working Paper Series No. 8933 (Cambridge, MA, National Bureau of Economic Research).

Matin, I.; Hulme, D.; Rutherford, S. 1999. *Financial Services for the Poor and the Poorest: Deepening Understanding to Improve Provision*, Finance and Development Research Programme Working Paper Series No. 9 (Manchester, University of Manchester).

Mayhem, P.; Van Dijk, J. 1997. *Criminal Victimization in 11 Industrialized Countries* (The Hague, Netherlands Ministry of Justice).

Mayoux, L. 1999. "Questioning virtuous spirals: Micro-finance and women's empowerment in Africa", in *Journal of International Development*, Vol. 1, No. 7, pp. 937–954.

Mbembe, A. 1999. Notes on the Postcolony (Berkeley, CA, University of California Press).

McCord, A. 2002. *Public Works as a Response to Labour Market Failure in South Africa*, SALDRU/CSSR Working Paper (Cape Town, University of Cape Town).

McGillivray, W. 2001. "Contribution evasion: Implications for social security pension schemes", in *International Social Security Review*, Vol. 54, No. 4, pp. 3–22.

Mchomvu, A. S. T.; Tungaraza, F. S. K.; Maghimbi, S. 2002. "Overview of social security systems in Tanzania", in *Journal of Social Development in Africa*, Vol. 17, No. 2, July 2002, pp. 11–28.

Mehrotra, S.; Jarrett, S. W. 2002. "Improving basic health service delivery in low-income countries", in *Social Science and Medicines*, Vol. 54, No. 11, pp. 1685–1690.

Merrill Lynch and Cap Gemini Ernst and Young. 2003. *World Wealth Report 2003* (Dublin, Ireland).

Messing, K. 1998. *One-Eyed Science: Occupational Health and Women Workers* (Philadelphia, Temple University Press).

Messing, K. (ed.). 1999. *Integrating Gender in Ergonomic Analysis: Strategies for Transforming Women's Work* (Brussels, European Trade Union Technical Bureau for Health and Safety).

Milanovic, B. 1999. *True World Income Distribution, 1988 and 1993: First Calculation Based on Household Surveys Alone* (Washington, DC, World Bank Development Research Group).

———. 2000. *A New Polarization Measure and Some Applications* (Washington, DC, World Bank).

Ministry of Labour and Social Security of China. 2000. *Vocational Training and Employment in China* (Beijing, Ministry of Labour and Social Security).

Mishra, R. 1999. *Globalization and the Welfare State* (Bristol, Edward Elgar).

Montgomery, R.; Bhjattacharya, D.; Hulme, D. 1996. "Credit for the poor in Bangladesh", in Hulme, D.; Mosley, P. (eds.): *Finance Against Poverty* (London, Routledge), pp. 94–176.

Moore, M. 1999. "Politics against poverty? Global pessimism and national optimism", in I*nstitute of Development Studies Bulletin*, Vol. 30, No. 2.

Morduch, J. 1999. "Between the state and the market: Can informal insurance patch the safety net?", in *World Bank Research Observer*, Vol. 14, No. 2, pp. 187–207.

Morrison, N.; Moore, M. 1999. "Elite perceptions of poverty: Bangladesh", in I*nstitute of Development Studies Bulletin*, Vol. 30, No. 2, pp. 106–116.

Mundy, K. 2002. "Retrospect and prospect: Education in a reforming World Bank", in *International Journal of Educational Development*, Vol. 22, No. 5, pp. 483–508.

Murphy-Berman, V. 1984. "Factors affecting allocation to needy and meritorious recipients", in *Journal of Personality and Social Psychology*, Vol. 46, No. 6, pp. 1267–1272.

Mushi, D. 2003. *Work Insecurity in Tanzania*, paper presented at the ILO Workshop on Economic Security and Decent Work, Dar-es-Salaam, May.

Myers, N.; Kent, J. 2001. *Perverse Subsidies: How Tax Dollars can Undercut the Environment and the Economy* (London, Island Press).

Nagaraj, R. 2000. "Indian economy since the 1980s: Virtuous growth or polarization?", in *Economic and Political Weekly*, pp. 2831–2839.

National Institute for Occupational Safety and Health (NIOSH), United States Department of Health and Human Services. 1993. *Fatal Injuries to Workers in the United States, 1980-1989* (Washington, DC).

Nattrass, N. 2003. *The Moral Economy of AIDS in South Africa* (Cape Town, University of Cape Town Press).

Nurminen, M.; Karjalainen, A. 2001. "Epidemiological estimate of the proportion of fatalities related to occupational factors in Finland", in *Trade Union News from Finland*, June.

Olson, M. 1965. *The Logic of Collective Action: Public Goods and the Theory of Groups* (Cambridge, MA, Harvard University Press).

Orszag J. M.; Snower, D. J. 2002. *From Unemployment Benefits to Unemployment Accounts*, Discussion Paper 532 (Bonn, Institute for the Study of Labour).

Orszag, P.; Stiglitz, J. 2001. "Rethinking pension reform: Ten myths about social security systems", in Holzmann, R.; Stiglitz, J. (eds.): *New Ideas About Old Age Security: Towards Sustainable Pension Systems in the 21st Century* (Washington, DC, World Bank), pp. 17–62.

Owens, T.; Hoddinott, J.; Kinsey, B. 2003. "Ex-ante actions and ex-post public responses to drought shocks: Evidence and simulations from Zimbabwe", in *World Development*, Vol. 31, No. 7, pp. 1239–1256.

Pakistan Institute of Labour Education and Research (PILER). 2001. *Child Labour in Hazardous Industries: A Case Study of Urban Karachi* (Karachi).

Palacios, R.; Pallarès-Miralles, M. 2000. *International Patterns of Pension Provision* (Washington, DC, World Bank).

Palma, G. Forthcoming. *The Mexican Economy since Trade Liberalization and NAFTA*, SES Paper (Geneva, ILO).

Palme, J. 2002. *Foundations and guarantees of social security rights at the Beginning of the 21st Century*, paper presented at the ISSA Conference, Vancouver, Sep.

Parker, M.; Slaughter, J. 1994. *Working Smart: A Union Guide to Participation Programs and Reengineering* (Detroit, Labor Notes).

Patnaik, U.; Natrajan, S. 2000. "Output and employment in rural China: Some post-reform problems", in *Economic and Political Weekly*, pp. 3420–3427.

Pillai, M. S. 1996. "Social security for workers in unorganized sector: Experience in Kerala", in *Economic and Political Weekly*, Vol. 31, No. 3, pp. 2098–2107.

Pines, A.; Lemesch, C.; Grafstein, O. 1992. "Regression analysis of time trends in occupational accidents", in *Safety Science*, Vol. 15, pp. 77–95.

Pitt, M. M.; Khandker, S.R. 1998. "The impact of group-based credit programmes on poor households in Bangladesh: Does the gender of the participants matter?", in *Journal of Political Economy*, Vol. 106, No. 5, pp. 958–996.

Planning Commission of India. 2002. *Economic Survey of India 2000-2001* (New Delhi, Government of India).

Polanyi, K. 1957. *The Great Transformation* (Boston, MA, Beacon Press).

Pollack, E.; Keimig, D. E. 1987. *Counting Injuries and Illnesses in the Workplace: Proposals for a Better System* (Washington, DC, National Academy Press).

Price, M. E. 1994. "The market for loyalties: Electronic media and the global competition for allegiances", in *Yale Law Journal*, Vol. 104, No. 3, pp. 667–705.

Pritchett, L.; Wetterberg, A.; Alatas, V. 2001. *Voice Lessons: Evidence on Social Organisations, Government Mandated Organisations and Governance from Indonesia's Local Level Institutions Study*, Working Paper (Cambridge, MA, J. F. Kennedy School of Government, Harvard University).

Quinlan, M. 2003. *Regulating flexible work and organizational arrangements*, paper presented at the Conference on Australian Occupational Health and Safety Regulation for the 21st Century, Gold Coast, July.

Quisumbing, A. R. 2003. "Food aid and child nutrition in rural Ethiopia", in *World Development*, Vol. 31, No. 7, pp. 1309–1324.

Quisumbing, A. R.; Maluccio, J. A. 2003. "Resources at marriage and intrahousehold allocation: Evidence from Bangladesh, Ethiopia, Indonesia and South Africa", in *Oxford Bulletin of Economics and Statistics*, Vol. 65, No. 3, pp. 283–327.

Rabin, M. 1998. "Psychology and economics", in *Journal of Economic Literature*, Vol. 36, pp. 11–111.

Rahman, A. 1999. "Micro-credit initiatives for equitable and sustainable development: Who pays?", in *World Development*, Vol. 27, No. 1, pp. 67–82.

Rahmato, D.; Kidanu, A. 2003. *Vulnerable Livelihoods: People's Security Survey of Urban Households in Ethiopia*, paper presented at the ILO Workshop on Economic Security and Decent Work in Africa, Dar-es-Salaam, May.

Ramachandran, V.K.; Swaminathan, M. 2002. *Does Informal Credit Provide Security? Rural Banking Policy in India*, SES Paper No. 12 (Geneva, ILO).

Rawl, J. 1973. *Theory of Justice* (Cambridge, Cambridge University Press).

Reddy, S. G.; Pogge, T. W. 2003. *How not to count the poor* (New York, Columbia University), at: <http://www.socialanalysis.org> [27 Feb. 2004].

Rinehart, J.; Huxley, C.; Robertson, D. 1997. *Just Another Car Factory? Lean Production and Its Discontents* (Ithaca, NY, ILR Press).

Ritter, J.; Anker, R. 2002. "Good jobs, bad jobs: Workers' evaluations in five countries", in *International Labour Review*, Vol. 141, No . 4, pp. 331–384.

Rodrik, D. 1997. *Has Globalization Gone Too Far?* (Washington, DC, Institute of International Economics).

———. 1999. *The New Global Economy and Developing Countries: Making Openness Work*, Policy Essay No. 24 (Washington, DC, Overseas Development Council).

Rogoff, K.; Reinhart, C. 2002. *FDI to Africa: The Role of Price Stability and Currency Instability*, Working Paper (Washington, DC, IMF).

Rogoff, K., et. al. 2003. *The Effects of Financial Globalization on Developing Countries: Some Empirical Evidence*, Occasional Paper 220 (Washington, DC, IMF).

Rosenman, K. D., et al. 2000. "Why most workers with occupational repetitive trauma do not file for workers' compensation", in *Journal of Occupational and Environmental Medicine*, Vol. 42, No. 1, pp. 25–34.

Rosskam, E. 1996. *Your Health and Safety at Work* (Geneva, ILO).

———. 2003. *Working at the Check-In: Consequences for Worker Health and Management Practices* (Lausanne, University of Lausanne Press).

Sabates-Wheeler, R.; Kabeer, N. 2003. *Gender Equality and the Extension of Social Protection*, ESS Paper No.16 (Geneva, ILO, Extension of Social Security).

Samson, M., et al. 2003. "The social, economic and fiscal impact of a basic income grant for South Africa", in Standing, G.; Samson, M. (eds.): *The Basic Income Grant in South Africa* (Cape Town, University of Cape Town Press).

Samuel, P. 1998. *Making Voices Work: The Report Card on Bangalore's Public Service*, World Bank Policy Research Working Paper Series 1921 (Washington, DC, World Bank).

Sayeed, A.; Javed, S. Forthcoming. 2001. *Security Issues Among Urban Transport Workers in Pakistan*, SES Paper (Geneva, ILO).

Scherrer, C.; Yalcin, G. 2002. *The Globalization of Higher Education: The Trade Regime Dimension*, paper presented at the ILO Workshop on Globalization of Social Services, Dubrovnik, Sep.

Scheve, K. .; Slaughter, M. J. 2002. *Economic Insecurity and the Globalization of Production*, NBER Working Paper 9339 (Cambridge, MA, National Bureau of Economic Research).

Schone, P. 2001. "Analysing the effect of training on wages using combined survey-register data", in *International Journal of Manpower*, Vol. 22, No. 1/2, pp. 138–158.

Scott, J. 1976. *The Moral Economy of the Peasant* (New Haven, CT, Yale University Press).

Sender, J. 2003. "Rural poverty and gender: Analytical frameworks and policy proposals", in Chang, H.J. (ed.): *Rethinking Development Economics* (London, Anthem Press), pp. 407–423.

Sennett, R. 2004. *Respect: The Formation of Character in an Age of Inequality* (London, Penguin).

Singh, A. 2002. "Asian capitalism and the financial crisis", in Eatwell, J.; Taylor, L. (eds.): *International Capital Markets: Systems in Transition* (Oxford, Oxford University Press).

———. 2003. "Capital account liberalization, free long-term capital flows, financial crises and economic development", in *Eastern Economic Journal*, Vol. 29, No. 2, pp. 191–216.

Singh, A.; Zammit, A. 2000. "International capital flows: Identifying the gender dimension", in *World Development*, Vol. 28, No. 7, pp. 1249–1268.

Skordis, J.; Nattrass, N. 2002. "Paying to waste lives: The affordability of reducing mother to child transmission of HIV in South Africa", in *Journal of Health Economics*, Vol. 21, pp. 405-21.

Skoufias, E. 2003. "Economic crises and natural disasters: Coping strategies and policy implications", in *World Development*, Vol. 31, No. 7, pp. 1087–1102.

Skoufias, E.; Parker, S. W. 2002. *Labour Market Shocks and their Impacts on Work and Schooling: Evidence from Urban Mexico*, IFPRI-FCND Discussion Paper No. 129, (Washington, DC, International Food Policy Research Institute/Food Consumption and Nutrition Division).

Slaughter, M. J. 2001. "International trade and labour-demand elasticities", in *Journal of International Economics*, Vol. 54, No. 1, pp. 27–56.

Snook, S. 1993. "The practical application of ergonomics principles", in *Journal of Occupational Health and Safety: Australia and New Zealand*, Vol. 9, No. 6, pp.555–563.

Social Investment Forum. 2003. *Report on socially responsible investing trends in the United States*, at <http://www.socialinvest.org/areas/research/> [27 Feb. 2004].

Social Weather Stations Inc. 2000. *ISSP 1999 Module on Social Inequality III in the Philippines: Data and Documentation* (CD-ROM) (Manila, Social Weather Stations Inc.).

Somavia, J. 1999. *People's Security: Globalizing Social Progress* (New York, United Nations).

Soskice, D. 1990. "Wage determination: The changing role of institutions in advanced industrialized countries", in *Oxford Review of Economic Policy*, Vol. 6, pp. 36–61.

Souza, C. 2002. *Participatory Budgeting in Brazilian Cities: Limits and Possibilities in Building Democratic Institutions*, SES Evaluation Report, mimeo (Geneva, ILO).

Spurgeon, A. 2003. *Working Time. Its Impact on Safety and Health* (Geneva, ILO).

Standing, G. 1992. "Do trade unions impede or accelerate structural adjustment?", in *Cambridge Journal of Economics*, Vol. 16, No. 3, pp. 327–354.

———. 1996. *Russian Unemployment and Enterprise Restructuring: Reviving Dead Souls* (Basingstoke and New York, Macmillan).

———. 1999. *Global Labour Flexibility: Seeking Distributive Justice* (London and New York, Macmillan and St. Martin's Press).

———. 2000. *Modes of control: A Labour-status Approach to Decent Work*, SES Paper No. 4 (Geneva, ILO).

———. 2002. *Beyond the New Paternalism: Basic Security as Equality* (London, Verso).

———. 2002. "From people's security surveys to a decent work index", in *International Labour Review*, Vol. 141, No. 4, pp. 441–454.

———. 2002. *Globalization and Flexibility: Dancing around Pensions*, SES Paper No. 2 (Geneva, ILO).

———. 2002. "Ratcheting labour standards", in Fung, A.; O'Rourke, D.; Sabel, C. (eds.): *Can We Put an End to Sweatshops?* (Boston, MA, Beacon Press).

———. 2003. *The Decent Work Enterprise: Worker Security and Dynamic Efficiency*, SES Paper No. 37 (Geneva, ILO).

Standing, G. (ed.): 2003. *Minimum Income Schemes in Europe* (Geneva, ILO).

Standing, G.; Sender, J.; Weeks, J. 1996. *Restructuring the Labour Market: The South African Challenge* (Geneva, ILO).

Steinwachs L. 2002. *Extending Health Protection in Tanzania: Networking between Health Financing Mechanisms*, Extension of Social Security Paper No. 7 (Geneva, ILO).

Stewart, F.; Fitzgerald, V. 2001. *War and Underdevelopment* (Oxford, Oxford University Press).

Stewart, F.; Van der Geest, W. 1994. *Adjustment and Social Funds: Political Panacea or Effective Poverty Reduction?* (Oxford, International Development Centre, Queen Elizabeth House).

Stiglitz, J. E. 2000. "Capital market liberalization, economic growth, and instability", in *World Development*, Vol. 28, No. 6, pp.1075–1086.

— — —. 2002. *Globalization and its Discontents* (New York, W.W. Norton).

Stock, R. 2002. *Psychological Approaches to Work Security*, SES Paper No. 8 (Geneva, ILO).

Streeck, W. 1997. "German capitalism: Does it exist? Can it survive?" in Crouch, C.; W. Streeck (eds.): *Political Economy of Modern Capitalism* (London, Sage).

Sumarto, S.; Suryahadi, A.; Pritchett, L. 2000. *Safety Nets and Safety Ropes: Who Benefited from Two Indonesian Crisis Programmes – The "Poor" or the "Shocked"?* (Washington, DC, World Bank, East Asia and Pacific Region).

Suplicy, E. Forthcoming. "Legitimizing basic income in developing countries: Brazil", in Khan, A.; Standing, G. (eds.): *Income Security as a Development Right.*

Swank, D. 1998. "Funding the welfare state: Globalization and the taxation of business in advanced market economies", in *Political Studies*, Vol. 46, pp. 671–692.

Swift, A., et al. 1995. "Distributive justice: Does it matter what the people think?", in Kluegel, J. R. (eds.): *Social Justice and Political Change* (New York, Aldine de Gruyter), pp. 15–47.

Sykes, A. 2000. *Capitalism for Tomorrow: Reuniting Ownership and Control* (Oxford, Capstone).

Taswell, K.; Wingfield Digby, P. Forthcoming. *Accidents Can Happen. Collecting Occupational Injury Data Through Household and Establishment Surveys: An ILO Manual on Concepts and Methods* (Geneva, ILO).

Taylor, P. 1999. "The United Nations in the 1990s: Proactive cosmopolitanism and the issue of sovereignty", in *Political Studies*, No. 47, pp. 538–565.

Taylor-Gooby, P. 1987. "Citizenship and welfare", in Jowell, R.; Witherspoon, S.; Brook, L. (eds.): *British Social Attitudes: The 1987 Report* (Gower, Aldershot), pp.1–28.

— — —. 1991. "Attachment to the welfare state", in Jowell, R.; Brook, L.; Taylor, B. (eds.): British *Social Attitudes: The 8th Report* (Dartmouth, Aldershot), pp. 23–42.

Tornblom, K. Y.; Muhlhausen, S. M.; Jonsson, D. R. 1991. "The allocation of positive and negative outcomes: When is the equality principle fair for both?", in Vermunt, R.; Steensma, H. (eds.): *Social Justice in Human Relations, Vol. 1: Societal and Psychological Origins of Justice* (New York, Plenum), pp. 59–100.

Tulgan, B. 2001. *Winning the Talent Wars* (London, N. Brealy Publishing).

Tungaraza, F. S. K.; Mapunda, G. 2000. *The National Social Security Policy*, Government Policy Paper (Dar-es-Salaam).

Tversky, A.; Kahneman, D. 1991. "Rational choice and the framing of decisions", in *Journal of Business*, Vol. 59, No. 4, pp. 251–278.

United Nations Conference on Trade and Development (UNCTAD). 2000. *World Investment Report 2000: Cross-Border Mergersand Acquisitions and Development* (Geneva).

— — —. 2001. *World Investment Report 2001: Promoting Linkages* (Geneva).

— — —. 2003. *World Investment Report 2003 - FDI Policies for Development: National and International Perspectives* (Geneva).

United Nations Development Programme (UNDP). 2003. *Human Development Report for Latvia* (Oxford, Oxford University Press).

United Nations Educational, Scientific and Cultural Organization (UNESCO). 2002. *Education for All: Global Monitoring Report* (Paris).

United Nations Environment Programme (UNEP). 2001. *The Global Environment Outlook* (Nairobi).

United Nations Population Division, Department of Economic and Social Affairs. 2001. *World Population Prospects* (New York).

———. 2003. *The Impact of AIDS* (New York).

United Nations Programme on HIV/AIDS (UNAIDS). 2002. *Report of the Global HIV/AIDS Epidemic 2002* (New York).

Unni, J.; Charmes, J. 2002. *Measurement of Work*, paper presented at the Informal Consultation on Reconceptualizing Work, Geneva, ILO, Dec.

Unni, J.; Rani, U. 2002. *Insecurities of Informal Workers in Gujarat*, India, SES Paper No. 30 (Geneva, ILO).

Unni, J.; Rani, U. 2003. *Social Protection for Informal Workers: Insecurities, Instruments and Institutional Mechanisms*, SES Paper No. 18 (Geneva, ILO).

Urminsky, M. (ed.). 2001. *Self-regulation in the Workplace: Codes of Conduct, Social Labelling and Socially Responsible Investment*, Working Paper Series on Management Systems and Corporate Citizenship No.1 (Geneva, ILO).

Van Beers, C.; de Moor, A. 2001. *Public Subsidies and Policy Failures* (Northampton, Edward Elgar).

Van der Walt, L. 2000. "GEAR versus social security", in *South African Labour Bulletin*, Vol. 24, No. 5.

Velasquez Pinto, M. D. 2003. *The Bono Solidario in Ecuador: An Exercise in Targeting*, ESS Paper No.17 (Geneva, ILO, Extension of Social Security).

Verba, S., et al. 1987. *Elites and the Idea of Inequality: A Comparison of Japan, Sweden and the United States* (Cambridge, MA, Harvard University Press).

Vermeulen, H.; Govers, C. (eds.). 1994. *The Anthropology of Ethnicity: Beyond "Ethnic Groups and Boundaries"* (Amsterdam, Het Spinhuis).

Von Braun, J.; Vlek, P. L.; Wimmer, A. 2002. *Disasters, Conflicts and Natural Resource Degradations: Multidisciplinary Perspectives on Complex Emergencies – Annual Report 2001-02* (Bonn, ZEF, Centre for Development Research).

Wachtel, H. 2003. "Tax distortion in the global economy", in Beneria, L.; Bisneth, S. (eds.): *Global Tensions: Challenges and Opportunities in the World Economy* (New York and London, Routledge), pp. 27–43.

Wacquant, L. 1999. *Les Prisons de la Misère* (Paris, Éditions Raisons d'Agir).

Walsh, J. 2001. "Creating unions, creating employers: A Los-Angeles home care campaign", in Daly, M. (ed.): *Care Work: The Quest for Security* (Geneva, ILO), pp. 219–233.

Wangwe, S. M.; Tibandebage, P. 1999. *Towards Social Security Policy and Reform in Tanzania*, paper presented at the National Social Security Fund Symposium, Dar-es-Salaam.

Williamson, J. 2002. *Prospects for Curbing the Boom-bust Cycle in the Supply of Capital to Emerging Markets*, WIDER Discussion Paper No. 2002/3 (Helsinki, World Institute for Development Economics Research, United Nations University).

Wolfensohn, J. 2000. *Building an Equitable World*, Address to the Board of Governors of the World Bank, Prague, Sep.

Wood, G. 2003. "Staying secure, staying poor: The 'Faustian bargain'", in *World Development*, Vol. 31, No. 3, pp. 455–471.

Woolff, E. N.; Leone, R. C. 2002. *Top Heavy: The Increasing Inequality of Wealth in America and What Can Be Done About It* (New York, New Press).

World Bank.1993. *Investing in Health* (Washington, DC,).

———. 1994. *Averting the Old Age Crisis* (Washington, DC,).

———. 1994. *Higher Education: Lessons of Experience* (Washington, DC).

———. 2000. *The Quality of Growth* (New York, Oxford University Press).

———. 2001. *World Development Report 2000-2001: Attacking Poverty* (Washington, DC).

———. 2002. *Global Economic Prospects and the Developing Countries* (Washington, DC).

———. 2003. *Breaking the Conflict Trap: Civil War and Development Policy* (Washington, DC).

———. 2003. *World Development Report 2004: Making Services Work for Poor People* (Washington, DC).

World Commission on Dams (WCD). 2000. *Dams and Development: A New Framework for Decision-Making, Report of the World Commission on Dams* (London and Sterling, VA, Earthscan Publications).

World Commission on the Social Dimension of Globalization. 2004. *A Fair Globalization: Creating Opportunities for All* (Geneva, ILO).

World Health Organization (WHO). 2001. *Macroeconomics and Health: Investing in Health for Economic Development* (Geneva, Commission on Macroeconomics and Health).

———. 2003. *World Health Report 2003: Shaping the Future* (Geneva).

Yotopoulos, P. A. 1996. *Exchange Rate Parity for Trade and Development: Theory, Tests and Case Studies* (New York and London, Cambridge University Press).

Zoyem, J.-P. 2003. *Labour Market Security and Child Labour in Ghana*, paper presented at the ILO Workshop on Economic Security and Decent Work in Africa, Dar-es-Salaam, May.

Zsoldos, L.; Standing, G. 2002. *Coping with Insecurity: The Ukrainian People's Security Survey 2002*, SES Paper No. 17 (Geneva, ILO).